THE BEHAVIOR OF ANIMALS

## DATE DUE FOR RETURN

*To our wives Zsuzsi and Dominique, and our children, Nórika and Félix and Ophélie.*

# the behavior of animals

## Mechanisms, function, and evolution

EDITED BY JOHAN J. BOLHUIS AND LUC-ALAIN GIRALDEAU

Blackwell
Publishing

BLACKWELL PUBLISHING
350 Main Street, Malden, MA 02148-5020, USA
9600 Garsington Road, Oxford OX4 2DQ, UK
550 Swanston Street, Carlton, Victoria 3053, Australia

First published 2005 by Blackwell Publishing Ltd

3   2006

*Library of Congress Cataloging-in-Publication Data*

The behavior of animals : mechanisms, function, and evolution / edited by
Johan J. Bolhuis and Luc-Alain Giraldeau.
p. cm.
Includes bibliographical references and index.
ISBN 0-631-23125-0 (pbk : alk. paper)
1. Animal behavior.  I. Bolhuis, Johan J.  II. Giraldeau, Luc-Alain, 1955–
QL763.B39 2005
591.5 — dc22
2004008959

ISBN-13: 978-0-631-23125-7 (pbk : alk. paper)

A catalogue record for this title is available from the British Library.

Set in 10/121/2 Rotis Serif
by Graphicraft Ltd, Hong Kong
Printed and bound in Singapore
by Markono Print Media Pte Ltd

For further information on
Blackwell Publishing, visit our website:
www.blackwellpublishing.com

# contents

# contributors

Professor Johan J. Bolhuis
Behavioural Biology
Utrecht University
PO Box 80.086
Padualaan 14
3584 CH Utrecht
The Netherlands
email: j.j.bolhuis@bio.uu.nl

Professor Tim Caro
Department of Wildlife, Fish and Conservation Biology
University of California at Davis
Davis
CA 95616
USA
email: tmcaro@ucdavis.edu

Dr Nicola S. Clayton
Department of Experimental Psychology
University of Cambridge
Downing Street
Cambridge CB2 3EB
United Kingdom
email: nsc22@cam.ac.uk

Professor Martin Daly
Department of Psychology
McMaster University
Hamilton
Ontario
Canada L8S 4K1
email: daly@mcmaster.ca

Professor John Eadie
Department of Wildlife, Fish and Conservation Biology
University of California at Davis
Davis
CA 95616
USA
email: jmeadie@ucdavis.edu

Dr Mark A. Elgar
Department of Zoology
University of Melbourne
Victoria 3010
Australia
email: m.elgar@unimelb.edu.au

Dr Nathan J. Emery
Sub-department of Animal Behaviour
University of Cambridge
Madingley CB3 8AA
United Kingdom
email: nje23@cam.ac.uk

Professor Dr Jörg-Peter Ewert
Universität Kassel
Fachbereich Naturwissenschaften
Abteilung Zoologie/Physiologie, Neurobiologie
Heinrich-Plett-Str. 40
D-34132 Kassel
Germany
email: Ewert@uni-kassel.de

Professor David Fraser
NSERC Industrial Research Chair in Animal Welfare
Faculty of Agricultural Sciences and
   W. Maurice Young Centre for Applied Ethics
University of British Columbia
2357 Main Mall
Vancouver
British Columbia
Canada V6T 1Z4
email: fraserd@interchange.ubc.ca

Professor Luc-Alain Giraldeau
Département des sciences biologiques
Université du Québec à Montréal
Case postale 8888, succursale Centre-Ville
Montréal
Québec
Canada H4C 3P8
email: Giraldeau.Luc-Alain@uqam.ca

Professor Geoffrey Hall
Department of Psychology
University of York
York YO10 5DD
United Kingdom
email: gh1@york.ac.uk

Professor Robert A. Hinde, FRS
St. John's College
Cambridge CB2 1TP
United Kingdom
email: rah15@hermes.cam.ac.uk

Professor Jerry A. Hogan
University of Toronto
Department of Psychology
Toronto
Ontario
Canada M5S 3G3
email: hogan@psych.utoronto.ca

Dr Kimberly Kirkpatrick
Department of Psychology
University of York
York YO10 5DD
United Kingdom
email: k.kirkpatrick@psych.york.ac.uk

Professor Peter K. McGregor
Chair of Behavioural Biology
Animal Behaviour Group
Biological Institute
University of Copenhagen
Tagensvej 16
DK 220 Copenhagen N
Denmark
email: pkmcgregor@bi.ku.dk

Professor Ralph E. Mistlberger
Department of Psychology
Simon Fraser University
8888 University Drive
Burnaby
British Columbia
Canada V5A 1S6
email: mistlber@sfu.ca

Professor Anders Pape Møller
Laboratoire de Parasitologie Evolutive
CNRS UMR 7103
Université Pierre et Marie Curie
Bat. A, 7eme etage
7, quai St Bernard, Case 237
F-75252 Paris Cedex 5
France
email: amoller@snv.jussieu.fr

Professor Anne E. Pusey
Department of Ecology, Evolution and Behavior
University of Minnesota
1987 Upper Buford Circle
St Paul
MN 55108
USA
email: pusey001@umn.edu

Professor Benjamin Rusak
Director, Chronobiology and Sleep Program
Department of Psychiatry
Dalhousie University
5909 Veterans Memorial Lane
Halifax
Nova Scotia
Canada B3H 2E2
email: benjamin.rusak@dal.ca

Professor Michael J. Ryan
Section of Integrative Biology C0930
University of Texas
Austin
TX 78712
USA
email: mryan@mail.utexas.edu

Professor David F. Sherry
Department of Psychology and Program in Neuroscience
University of Western Ontario
London
Ontario
Canada N6A 5C2
email: sherry@uwo.ca

Professor Daniel M. Weary
NSERC Industrial Research Chair in Animal Welfare
Faculty of Agricultural Sciences
University of British Columbia
2357 Main Mall
Vancouver
British Columbia
Canada V6T 1Z4
email: danweary@interchange.ubc.ca

Dr Margo Wilson
Department of Psychology
McMaster University
Hamilton
Ontario
Canada L8S 4K1
email: wilson@mcmaster.ca

# foreword

ROBERT A. HINDE

Writing a foreword for such a stimulating series of chapters, which represent the state of animal behavior studies at this time, is a considerable responsibility. Perhaps I can do best by looking not forward, as might seem appropriate, but backward, and thus attempt to provide a context for the chapters that follow. Of course it cannot be a fully objective backward view, because I am looking from where I am now, and what I see is biased by my own experience. It is bound also to involve simplification. But I hope that it will provide a useful perspective.

In the early decades of the twentieth century, most studies of animal behavior fell into two groups. In one were the naturalists, mostly amateurs, without scientific pretensions but with a long tradition stretching back beyond the nineteenth century. In the other were the psychologists, producing an increasing body of data and theory mostly concerned with learning processes. Of course this dichotomy is already unjust and simplistic. Darwin himself could be called a naturalist; and an originator of learning theory (J.B. Watson) started from naturalistic observation. However the work of the learning theorists, impressive in its own right, was not to have much impact on the traditions that led to the chapters in this book until much later.

Those traditions can be said to stem from the emergence of ethology in the 1930s. This was due to Lorenz, an Austrian MD with a PhD in comparative anatomy, and Tinbergen, a Dutch zoologist who moved to England a few years after the end of World War 2. Both men had a passionate interest in animals, but this was expressed in very different ways. Lorenz kept a menagerie of diverse animals in his home, though also studying the local jackdaws and the semi-tame geese that he reared. Tinbergen, by contrast, was a dedicated field naturalist. Although he later worked with captive animals, it was always with problems that he had brought in from the field, and he liked best to be in the field himself. Tinbergen's first pupil, Baerends, suggested that the contrast lay in their attitudes to their subjects: Tinbergen saw himself as a nonparticipant hidden observer of animals, Lorenz as an adopted alien member and protector. Lorenz was a thinker who tried to relate or contrast his observations with current biological and philosophical views, while Tinbergen was much more empirical, an experimenter as well as an observer.

But both rejected the vitalist view that the phenomena of "instinct" were unanalyzable and the misuse of the Gestalt concept to imply that analysis is unnecessary because the whole is always more than the sum of its parts. They also rejected the focus of most learning theorists on the input/output relations of the whole organism, with neglect of the "physiological machinery," and the sterility of the artificial environments used to study animals in many psychological laboratories.

The term "ethology" has been applied primarily to the work of students who, though differing widely in the problems they tackled, the methods they used, the level of analysis at which they worked, and the theoretical interpretations (if any) that they adopted, shared certain orienting attitudes. They insisted that the proper description of behavior is a necessary preliminary to its analysis; and that the behavior of an animal must be studied in relation to the environment to which it has become adapted in evolution. In addition they held that full understanding of behavior required knowledge not only of its development and causation but also of its biological function and its evolution. The result was a vast amount of data on the behavior of animals and a certain amount of model-building to elucidate the mechanisms underlying behavior. In 1973 Lorenz and Tinbergen (together with von Frisch) were awarded the Nobel Prize in Physiology and Medicine.

Although ethology was primarily a European phenomenon in the early postwar years, two research workers in the USA were to have a considerable influence on its development, though in very different ways. Beach, a behavioral endocrinologist interested primarily in the hormonal control of sexual behavior, met Tinbergen in the USA and became a powerful supporter of ethology. Schneirla, a comparative psychologist working at the American Museum of Natural History, was intensely critical. One of his students, Lehrman, published a hard-hitting critique of ethology in 1953. There were three main issues. Lehrman and Schneirla took exception to Lorenz's distinction between "innate" and "acquired" behavior as neither empirically valid nor heuristically valuable. They objected to the energy model of motivation which Lorenz used, though this also came in for criticism from within ethology. And both were unhappy about the ethologists' tendency to apply concepts across a wide range of species differing in their levels of cognitive capacity. On their side, the ethologists felt that the adjective in "comparative psychology" was a sham, for contrasting distantly related species did not constitute comparison in a biological sense. They were also unhappy about the manner in which many comparative psychologists (though not so much those influenced by Schneirla) generalized on the basis of studies of a few mammalian species, predominantly the laboratory rat. For a while the differences between the two groups seemed irreconcilable. However, soon after his critique was published, Lehrman came to Europe and met a number of European ethologists. Tinbergen, Lorenz, and Lehrman were all bird-watchers, with a passionate enthusiasm for natural history. Lehrman had an infectious geniality, and friendships were soon made. This brought about a rapprochement between ethology and many of the members of Schneirla's group, a rapprochement which came not so much from academic discussion, but from the compatibility of personalities. On the issue of ontogeny, both sides changed their emphasis, the comparative psychologists withdrawing from their extreme emphasis on experience, and the differences in approach to the "comparative" issue were recognized.

It seems to happen not infrequently in the history of science that those regarded as originating a branch of science are subsequently seen to have been wrong in many of their generalizations. For instance, Freud (psychoanalysis) used a misleading model of motivation, Piaget (developmental psychology) based generalizations on a tiny sample of subjects, and Jeffreys (geophysics) refused to accept the evidence for continental drift. This was also the case with ethology. Many of the concepts that had been invaluable tools in the early days of ethology – the "innate releasing mechanism" and "fixed action pattern" for instance – were subsequently seen to involve oversimplification, and now seldom figure in the literature. But not surprisingly the change in outlook was not adopted simultaneously by all ethologists, and this led to some divisions within ethology. Lorenz, whose influence was particularly strong in Germany and the USA (through two research workers who had worked with him, Hess and Barlow), was slower to relinquish the innate/acquired dichotomy and energy model of motivation than Tinbergen and workers in the Netherlands and the UK.

An issue important for the nature/nurture debate became prominent in the 1960s. Both Tinbergen and Lorenz had long argued on the basis of empirical evidence that species were specially equipped for particular learning tasks that were biologically import-ant for them. Thorpe's book on birdsong, published in 1961, showed that the chaffinch was predisposed to learn the species-characteristic song pattern. A few years later, Rozin, Garcia, and others demonstrated a predisposition to avoid toxins in mammals. Such findings were directly contrary to the orientation of the learning theorists, who were searching for laws of learning valid for all species and all situations. It thus became apparent that, in many cases, what was "innate" was a predisposition to learn some things in particular contexts. This was to be of special importance for the study of human behavior.

Lorenz, originally a comparative anatomist, had used species differences and simil-arities as a taxonomic tool, and Tinbergen had always had an interest in the function of behavior. But, of the four problems of causation, development, function, and evolu-tion, the main (though by no means the only) emphasis in ethology had been on the first two. In the 1970s this changed with the publication of Wilson's *Sociobiology*. The orienting attitudes of ethology continued but the motivational models disappeared and many of the old concepts fell into disuse. Behavioral ecology came to the fore, and new theoretical approaches made possible the study of function in a quantitative fashion. Data on foraging behavior were compared with the behavior to be expected (on certain assumptions that were not always made fully explicit) from an organism foraging with maximal efficiency. Later, attention turned to such issues as sperm competition and the role of fluctuating asymmetry. Hamilton's work on kin selection, first published in 1964 but neglected for much of the next decade, made possible a new approach to social behavior. Game theory was recruited, and mathematical modeling came to be a much used tool in studies of behavior.

At the same time, the influence of ethology started to penetrate into a number of other disciplines. Lehrman and Rosenblatt, as well as Beach and his many students, adopted the orienting attitudes of ethology in their work on behavioral endocrinology. Von Holst had already studied the elicitation of fixed action patterns by brain stimulation through implanted electrodes, and the importance of using unconfined animals where possible was recognized by neurophysiologists. Bowlby, a psychoanalyst concerned with the effects of maternal deprivation in children, realized that what had been called the "irrational fears of childhood" (fear of falling, being alone, etc.) would have been highly adaptive in the environments in which early hominids lived, and an ethological element was incorporated in the "attachment theory" which he elaborated, an approach that was to become central in studies of child development. The study of human nonverbal communication profited from the input of ethologists, such as Eibl Eibesfeldt. The techniques of the behavioral ecologists were applied in studies of preindustrial human groups. An ethological influence is to be seen in studies of human personal relationships, and even in studies of religion and morality. Thus while ethology as a set of concepts or as a theory of animal behavior has been largely superseded, the influence of its orienting attitudes has increased and is potent in other disciplines.

While behavioral ecology took center-stage in the study of animal behavior, many felt it to be impoverished by the neglect of problems of development and causation. This book will go a long way toward setting the balance straight. Each of the four problems is covered, and the chapters introduce the growing points in the study of animal behavior at the start of the twenty-first century.

# preface

The idea for this book arose out of a need that we (and many of our colleagues) felt for a comprehensive textbook on animal behavior. There is no shortage of animal behavior textbooks, so why did we want to produce a new one? First, animal behavior is a dynamic field of research, and we believe that a modern textbook should incorporate all the contemporary subdisciplines of behavioral biology, such as animal welfare, conservation biology, evolutionary psychology, animal cognition, and behavioral neuroscience. In some way, the science of animal behavior has become a victim of its own success, as it covers a much wider field than it did initially. Gone are the days when one author could write a textbook both comprehensive and authoritative: Robert Hinde's classic *Animal Behaviour: A Synthesis of Ethology and Comparative Psychology* (1970) is an outstanding example of such a book, and it continues to inspire many of us. Given the breadth of contemporary animal behavior research, we felt that it was important to invite experts in the respective subdisciplines to write a chapter about their specialist topic.

Second, a large proportion of extant textbooks are single-author volumes that approach animal behavior from a particular perspective, for example from an evolutionary point of view or with the emphasis on mechanisms. We believe that a modern science of animal behavior should encompass both functional and causal approaches. For such a comprehensive approach, we found the classic formulation of the aims and methods of ethology (the study of animal behavior) by Niko Tinbergen, one of its founding fathers, most useful. Tinbergen suggested that there are four basic questions in animal behavior, namely about causation, development, function, and evolution. We agree with Tinbergen that all these four questions are equally important. Hence all of them are represented in this book. Like Tinbergen, we also find it important to distinguish between the four questions. In particular, it is important to realize which of the four questions is addressed, and to use a research approach appropriate for that question. Hence, in the first two sections of the book we make a distinction between problems that mainly concern mechanisms (including development) and those that concern function and evolution. The third section is concerned with problems in animal behavior that involve both function and mechanism and that perhaps have a more direct impact on our everyday lives.

    We are very pleased with the enthusiastic response we received from the authors invited
to contribute to this book. They are all leaders in their respective fields, and we feel
privileged that they participated in this project. We are very grateful to Robert Hinde,
one of the great names in animal behavior, for agreeing to write the Foreword to this
book. Thanks are due to Sarah Bird, William Maddox, Joanna Pyke, Rhonda Pearce,
and their colleagues at Blackwell Publishing for an outstanding job in producing this
volume. We thank David Sherry, Jerry Hogan, Louis Lefebvre, and three anonymous
reviewers for critically reading several draft chapters, and Gi-Mick Wu who so diligently
worked to prepare the final submission of the manuscript. Finally, we wish to thank
our wives, Zsuzsi and Dominique, for putting up with what may have seemed a nag-
ging evening and weekend obsession with *The Behavior of Animals*.

J.J.B., Utrecht
L.-A.G., Montréal
October 2004

# 1

# the study of animal behavior

JOHAN J. BOLHUIS AND LUC-ALAIN GIRALDEAU

## INTRODUCTION

The scientific study of animal behavior is also called **ethology**, a term used first by the nineteenth-century French zoologist Isidore Geoffroy Saint Hilaire but then used with its modern meaning by the American zoologist Wheeler (1902). Ethology is derived from the Greek *ethos*, meaning "character." There is some resemblance with the word "ethics," which is derived from the same Greek word. This makes sense, seeing that ethics is basically about how humans ought to behave. Unfortunately the word "ethology" is often confused with the word "ethnology" (the study of human peoples), with which it has nothing in common. In fact the very word processor with which we are writing this chapter keeps prompting us to replace "ethology" by "ethnology"! For whatever reason, the word "ethology" is not used as much as it used to be, although there is still an active animal behavior journal bearing this name. Instead of "ethology," nowadays many authors use the words "animal behavior" or "behavioral biology" when they refer to the scientific study of animal behavior.

## A Brief History of Behavioral Biology

### Early days

Scientists (and amateurs) studied animal behavior long before the word "ethology" was introduced. For instance, Aristotle had many interesting observations concerning animal behavior. The study of animal behavior was taken up more systematically mainly by German and British zoologists around the turn of the nineteenth century. The great British naturalist Charles Darwin (1809–82), pioneer of the theory of evolution by **natural selection** (1859), devoted a whole chapter of his classic book to what he called "instinct." As early as 1873, a British amateur investigator called Douglas Spalding recorded some very interesting observations on the behavior of young domestic chicks, a phenomenon that was later called **imprinting**, after the German *Prägung*, introduced by Konrad Lorenz (1935, 1937a,b; see Chapter 6). At the beginning of the twentieth century, the behavior of animals was also studied in the context of **learning** by the Russian physiologist Ivan P. Pavlov (1927) and the American psychologist Edward L. Thorndike (1911) (see Chapter 7).

## Lorenz and Tinbergen

In the middle of the twentieth century, the study of animal behavior became an independent scientific discipline, called ethology, mainly through the efforts of two biologists, the Austrian Konrad Lorenz (1903–89) and the Dutchman Niko Tinbergen (1907–88). It can be said that Lorenz was the more philosophical, theoretical of the two, whereas Tinbergen was very much an experimentalist, who together with his students and collaborators conducted an extensive series of field and laboratory experiments on the behavior of animals of many different species. Lorenz put forward a number of theoretical models on different aspects of animal behavior such as evolution and **motivation**. He was also the more outspoken of the two men, and some of his publications met with considerable controversy. In 1973 Lorenz and Tinbergen were awarded the Nobel Prize for Physiology and Medicine. They shared their prize with Karl von Frisch (1886–1982), an Austrian comparative physiologist and ethologist who had pioneered research into the "dance language" of bees (see Chapter 10).

## Ethology versus comparative psychology

During the early days of ethology there was a certain amount of scientific rivalry between mainly European ethologists and North American experimental psychologists, who also studied animal behavior in what was usually called **comparative psychology**. The European ethologists emphasized that animal behavior is a biological phenomenon, and as such a product of evolution. This is exemplified by the use of the word "instinct" (e.g., in the title of Tinbergen's 1951 classic book *The Study of Instinct*), which referred to the "**innate**" components of behavior that are subject to natural selection. A prominent critique of this way of thinking came from the American psychologist Daniel Lehrman, in his 1953 paper "A critique of Konrad Lorenz's theory of instinctive behavior." In this paper he argued against Lorenz's theory that behavior can be dissected into "innate" and "acquired" (or learned) components (see Chapter 6 for a more detailed discussion of these issues). In general, American psychologists emphasized the effects of learning on behavior. Pavlov had already demonstrated the importance of what we now call **Pavlovian (or classical) conditioning**. Later, Thorndike studied learning processes that are now known as instrumental or **operant conditioning** (see Chapter 7). Another difference between the ethologists and experimental psychologists was that the former often observed animals (of many different species) in their natural environment, whereas the latter (despite the name comparative psychology) often concentrated on one species (such as the rat or the pigeon) that was studied exclusively in the laboratory.

## Behaviorism

The emphasis of the North American psychologists on learning was epitomized by the rise of **behaviorism** in the 1930s. Behaviorism was a very influential school of thought initiated by the American psychologist John B. Watson (1878–1958), with his book *Behaviorism* (1924). Essentially, Watson considered psychological phenomena to be physical activity rather than some kind of mental event. Watson proposed that we cannot make any scientific statements about what might be going on in our minds, and that introspection was unreliable. Rather, psychologists can only investigate the physical manifestations that we can observe in the form of behavior. For behaviorists, psychology is the study of behavior and of the external physical factors that influence it. They find that it is not possible to make scientific statements about mental processes. This may sound odd to us, but at the time behaviorism was extremely influential in science and beyond. Within North American psychology it was the dominant school of thought for several decades. Behaviorist theory also affected education practice, particularly with Watson's book *Psychological Care of Infant and Child* (1928). Watson once made the famous statement:

> Give me a dozen healthy infants, well-formed, and my own specified world to bring them up in and I'll guarantee to take any one at random and train him to become any type of specialist I might select – doctor, lawyer, artist, merchant-chief, and, yes, even beggarman and thief, regardless of his talents, penchants, tendencies, abilities, vocations, and race of his ancestors.

This epitomizes behaviorist ideas about child rearing. Watson considered the upbringing of children to be an objective, almost scientific exercise, without the need for affection or sentimentality.

Watson's most famous student was Burrhus Frederic Skinner (1904–90), who applied behaviorist ideas to the study of learning. For Skinner and his behaviorist colleagues, learning had to do with changing relationships between visible entities, not with what might be going on inside the animal's head. In particular, behaviorist learning theorists suggest that learning involves the formation of associations between a stimulus and a response. Most of their experiments involve **instrumental conditioning** (see Chapter 7), where a certain response by the animal (e.g., pressing a lever) is rewarded ("**reinforced**") with food.

## Cognitive psychology

Within experimental psychology there came a reaction to behaviorism that took the form of what we now call **cognitive psychology**. In contrast to behaviorism, cognitive psychologists start with the assumption that individuals (humans and other animals) have a mental life that can be investigated (see Chapter 8). For instance, Skinner (1957) maintained that language development in children was a learning process, where responses (i.e., uttering certain sounds) were reinforced. The great American linguist Noam Chomsky (1959) wrote a lengthy and highly critical review of Skinner's book on language development, in which he suggested that language acquisition is not a case of instrumental conditioning but the development of certain cognitive mechanisms, the so-called universal grammar (see Chapter 8). Another important publication that signaled the beginning of the cognitive revolution is the book by the British psychologist Donald Broadbent (1958) who, in contrast to Skinner, analyzed learning and memory in terms of cognitive mechanisms rather than stimulus–response relations. Hogan (1988) has noted that what cognitive psychologists call "cognitive structures" are in fact the same as the causal mechanisms that were proposed by ethologists such as Lorenz and Tinbergen (see Chapter 3).

## Four Questions in the Study of Animal Behavior

Niko Tinbergen published a very important paper in 1963, in which he outlined the four major questions in the study of animal behavior, namely **causation, development, function** (Tinbergen called this **survival value**) and evolution. Tinbergen readily admitted that these questions were not very original, as three (causation, function, and evolution) had already been put forward by the British biologist Julian Huxley as the major questions in biology, and Tinbergen merely added a fourth, development. Tinbergen's four questions are sometimes collapsed into two categories: **proximate** and **ultimate** level questions, or "how" (causation and development) and "why" (function and evolution) questions respectively. No matter how these questions are broken up, it is crucially important that students of animal behavior be quite clear as to the type of question they are addressing when they study animal behavior. Tinbergen's analysis is so important that we would say that you cannot really understand animal behavior if you do not also understand the meaning of Tinbergen's four questions. Some of the more heated contemporary debates in the field of animal behavior can often be traced to misunderstandings about the meaning of the four questions (Hogan 1994; Bolhuis & Macphail 2001). It is essential, therefore, that any productive discussion about animal behavior involves participants capable of clearly stating which of the four questions they are addressing. This view of animal behavior has also served the organization of the present book, with Part I covering mostly causal and developmental topics and Part II dealing with functional and evolutionary questions.

Tinbergen's four questions are sometimes also called the "four whys," because they represent four ways of asking "Why does this animal behave in this way?" Let's consider a bird singing at dawn, say a male song sparrow (*Melospiza melodia*). The question is: why is this bird singing? This seems a perfectly straightforward question, but in fact it is not so easy, because it can take any of four different forms. These different forms – you've guessed it – have to do with Tinbergen's four whys. The first of the four questions concerns causation: what causes the bird to sing? Another way of asking this is: what are the mechanisms underlying the male's singing behavior? These mechanisms involve the "machinery" that operates within the animal and which is responsible for the production of behavioral output. Topics include the stimuli or triggers of behavior whether they be internal or external, the way in which behavioral output is guided, factors that stop behavior, and the like. These are questions concerning the generation of behavior. Sometimes this is called motivation, a subject discussed at length in Chapter 3. The second question is about development: how did the singing behavior of the bird come about in the lifetime of an animal? It turns out that a male song sparrow does not sing immediately after it has hatched from the egg – quite some time elapses before it has developed a song, a process that involves learning. Such questions that concern development of behavior, sometimes also called **ontogeny**, are discussed explicitly in Chapter 6. The third question has to do with function: what is the function of the bird singing and what is it singing for? This question has to do with the consequences of singing for the singer's **fitness**. Does singing help the bird keep intruding males away from his nest? Or does it simply serve to attract females? The topic of function, its methods of enquiry and main findings are discussed explicitly in Chapter 9 and provide the framework for all chapters in Part II. The fourth question concerns evolution: how did this behavior come about in the course of evolution? Behavior does not leave many fossils behind and so the study of its evolutionary history requires the development of special methods. These methods, based on taxonomy and comparisons among species, are discussed in detail in Chapter 13.

The previous paragraph illustrates that the question "Why does this bird sing?" is not very useful, as it can have four different meanings. It can be very confusing if a biologist studying birdsong does not make it clear which of the four "why" questions is being asked, and it could lead to futile arguments about whether the bird is singing to attract mates or because it learned its song. The same problem arises in all other areas of animal behavior and so it is very important to make it clear which of the four questions is to be addressed in any study. Of course, it is possible that a particular investigator wants to address more than one question at a time. This is perfectly legitimate, as long as it is made explicit which of the questions is addressed at what time. A famous example of this is an experimental paper by Tinbergen et al. (1962) on the behavior of black-headed gulls (*Larus ridibundus*). After the chicks have hatched, the adult birds remove the empty eggshells from the nest. Tinbergen et al. investigated both the causation and the function of this behavior using elegantly simple field experiments and reported results of both levels in the same paper. There is also considerable overlap between some of the four questions. For instance, the development of behavior is essentially a causal problem but may also involve functional aspects (see Chapter 6). The evolution of behavior often depends on mechanism. For instance, emergent properties of an animal's sensory and perceptual capabilities (mechanisms) may create opportunities for **sexual selection** to evolve extravagant traits (see Chapter 13). Finally, questions in one domain (e.g., function) can provide clues for questions in another domain (e.g., causation). For instance, a number of bird species cache food, some for a few hours, others for months (Vander Wall 1990). It is plausible that the ecological circumstances that have given rise to these different forms of food caching may have also influenced the animals' ability to memorize spatial locations. In fact, a large number of studies at a mechanistic level (e.g., learning, memory, cognition, **neuroethology**) are concerned with the spatial memory of food-caching versus nonfood-caching birds (see Chapters 5 & 8).

## Trends in the Study of Animal Behavior

## Behavioral ecology: from mechanism to function

Much of the early research and theorizing of early ethologists such as Lorenz and Tinbergen was concerned with the causation of behavior. When Tinbergen was invited to move from the Dutch University of Leiden to the University of Oxford, he established the Animal Behaviour Research Group while the famous ornithologist David Lack was taking over the newly founded Edward Grey Institute of Ornithology. The coincidence of having both these scientists and their followers in the same department in Oxford sowed the seeds of a discipline that was to blossom much later in the mid-1970s under the name of **behavioral ecology**.

Behavioral ecology arose out of the fusion of evolutionary ecology, population ecology, and ethology. A number of conditions were ripe in the mid-1970s for such an event. In 1975 the Harvard entomologist Edward O. Wilson published *Sociobiology: The New Synthesis*, the birth of what is known today as **sociobiology**. Wilson's book was firmly grounded in population genetics and evolutionary biology. Its clear presentation of William D. Hamilton's concept of **inclusive fitness**, **kin selection**, the evolution of both **altruism** and social groups among others provided the essential foundations for a successful evolutionary approach to social behavior. Not long after that, in 1978, John R. Krebs of Oxford University and Nicholas B. Davies at Cambridge coedited a book they called *Behavioural Ecology: An Evolutionary Approach*, which was to apply a similar evolutionary approach but this time to all, not just social, behavior. The publication of this book marks the official birth of behavioral ecology, which now includes sociobiology.

Behavioral ecology today is more of an approach than a body of accumulated fact. Its initial success grew out of a combination of **optimality theory** and evolutionary thinking that pictures the expression of behavioral traits as constrained tradeoffs between their evolutionary benefits and costs (see Chapter 9). The development of the concept of the **evolutionarily stable strategy** (ESS) by the British evolutionary biologist John Maynard Smith (1982) allowed this cost–benefit approach to be applied to a wide range of behavioral interactions. Evolutionary thinking and the cost–benefit approach cast a new light on behavioral systems such as foraging, fighting, and **habitat selection** (see Chapter 9). When applied to communication it raised an important number of questions concerning the design of **signals** and their functions (see Chapter 10). Whereas early ethologists tended to picture sexual reproduction as a cooperative venture between males and females, the evolutionary approach has somewhat subverted this idyllic view. **Mating systems** and mate choice (see Chapter 11) as well as conflicts of interests between mates (see Chapter 12) have become exciting and rapidly developing areas of the discipline. Darwin himself pictured behavior as a character that was modified over generations by selection. Hence behavior has a history that can be studied with contemporary organisms (see Chapter 13). When the evolutionary approach is applied to social groupings a number of interesting questions arise, especially in relation to apparently altruistic and **cooperative behaviors** that are often reported within groups (see Chapter 14).

## Neuroethology and cognitive neuroscience

The mechanisms underlying behavior are also somehow represented in the workings of the central nervous system, in particular the brain. In fact, Tinbergen often used neural analogies and metaphors in his models of behavior. We shall see in Chapter 2 how the central nervous system obtains and processes **information** about its external world. As knowledge about the brain, both its gross and fine-level morphology as well as the way **neurons** are connected, led to increased interface between brain and behavior, a new subdiscipline arose that became known as neuroethology (Ewert 1980; see Chapters 2 & 5). In the early days of this new discipline, researchers concentrated on the study of the neural mechanisms of perception and movement, often in insects or lower vertebrates. More recently the study of the brain mechanisms of behavior is also directed at higher cognitive processes such as learning and memory or spatial orientation. Often, the terms "**behavioral neuroscience**" or "**cognitive neuroscience**" are used to describe these disciplines (see Chapter 5). Now the combination of an extraordinary array of powerful techniques, from electrophysiological recording to molecular analyses of RNA sequences, allows researchers to delve deeper into the connection between behavior and its neural substrate.

## Cognitive ecology

Perhaps as a result of the success of behavioral ecology, the relationship between the brain and behavior has also been studied more recently from an evolutionary perspective. An animal's ability to collect and process information should be heavily influenced by its ecology. For instance, sexual selection operating within oscine birds has led to the development of diverse and complex songs that females are able to evaluate with great ability. How do the evolutionary pressures for complex birdsong affect the evolution of the underlying neural substrate? How does having a large **home range** affect the ability to navigate? Does having to store food place selective pressure on spatial memory? These questions, as well as those that explore the mental lives of animals and the way information is processed by brains, are treated extensively in Chapter 8.

## Animal welfare, conservation biology, and evolutionary psychology

Many people are interested in animal behavior out of mere curiosity, the need to know more about something. This is all very fine but there always comes a time where someone will ask "What is the purpose of studying animal behavior?" This question, whether from a research colleague, a friend, or a granting agency, requires an answer expressed in terms of benefits to society. We see three areas in which applications of animal behavior research can contribute to human society, **animal welfare**, conservation, and understanding human nature. These types of questions are addressed in the third and last section of the book.

Animals are important contributors to wealth and quality of life. They provide us with nourishment, the means to find cures and treatments for our illnesses, as well as invaluable companionship. Almost all the information contained in this book relies on experiments and research conducted with animals. However, there is a growing concern that animals used for human benefit be exposed to as little unpleasantness as necessary. Are housing cages too small, or densities of individuals too high? Is the knowledge acquired from experiments sufficiently important to authorize animal experimentation? The answer to such, often difficult, questions depends in many ways on knowing something about an animal's behavior (see Chapter 15).

Population growth and economic development have led to the increasing precariousness of a good number of species and as a result the intensity of research on conservation problems has increased exponentially in recent years. The way an animal responds to anthropogenic changes in its environment and its ability to cope with such modifications are likely dependent on its behavior, social organization, mating system, and ability to innovate. In that context we ask whether animal behavior can provide important, perhaps crucial, information on the conservation of the earth's biodiversity (see Chapter 16).

People are endlessly curious about people and the sheer number of disciplines devoted uniquely to the study of human beings is eloquent testimony to this fact (e.g., medicine, anthropology, psychology, sociology, criminology). Animal behavior can provide insight into human behavior in two ways. More conventionally, phenomena observed in animals can be generalized, although often in some modified way, to humans. For example, just as a new antibiotic drug that cures an infection in some nonhuman primate can also be used, perhaps in a slightly modified way, to cure infections in humans, so can knowledge about how an animal learns be extended and applied to human learning. The second way, however, involves generalizing an approach rather than a result. For instance, can we learn anything new about human behavior by applying an evolutionary cost–benefit analysis to the things we do? This is what a discipline known as **evolutionary psychology** does (see Chapter 17).

## SUMMARY AND CONCLUSIONS

Animal behavior has grown into a highly diverse set of approaches and disciplines. Its subject area ranges from molecules and neurons to individuals and populations. One of Tinbergen's major contributions to the study of animal behavior has been to make its goals explicit and clarify the four types of questions that can be asked of behavior: causation, development, function, and evolution. In this book we strongly advocate Tinbergen's position that behavior can only be understood through research on all four questions. In addition, we suggest that it is made clear which of Tinbergen's questions is addressed when a behavioral problem is investigated: a problem in one domain should not be investigated with concepts from another. That is why the chapters in the current book are organized explicitly into sections. The first is devoted to mechanisms and covers both cause and development. The next section is on function and covers both survival value and evolution. We end the book with a section on animal behavior and human society, dealing with animal welfare, conservation and human behavior in the hope of illustrating that answers to important questions will require addressing all four levels of questioning advocated by Tinbergen.

## FURTHER READING

Tinbergen's (1963) paper on the four whys is essential reading for any serious student of animal behavior. It was reprinted in Houck and Drickamer (1996), which is a collection of classic papers on all aspects of animal behavior. Tinbergen's (1951) classic book is still very much worthwhile. It was reprinted in 1992 and is still available. The great British ethologist William Thorpe (1979) has written a brief history of ethology, viewed from the inside, whereas Dewsbury (1989) provides a more recent account from the North American perspective. Boakes (1984) is an excellent review of the history of the study of animal behavior by psychologists, whereas Laland and Brown (2002) provide a very clear account of the different ways in which the behavior of animals (including humans) can be studied from an evolutionary perspective. Functional and evolutionary aspects of behavior are also discussed in the edited volume by Krebs and Davies (1978), of which there is already a fourth edition (Krebs & Davies 1997), with every edition containing new information.

## ACKNOWLEDGMENTS

We are grateful to Jerry Hogan and Euan Macphail for their comments on the manuscript.

part I

# mechanisms of behavior

# 2
# stimulus perception
### Jörg-Peter Ewert

## INTRODUCTION: SENSORY SYSTEMS CREATE SENSORY WORLDS

A person driving a car during rush-hour is exposed to a flood of **information** that bombards sensory systems along the various channels: vision, audition, **vibration**, somatosensory sensation, and olfaction. Although our sense organs and the **neurons** connected to them are responsive to many of these sensory modalities, if the central nervous system (CNS) were to respond **consciously** to all, tremendous chaos would emerge. This raises a problem: on the one hand, the brain must be ready to collect information from different channels and to process these concurrently and in parallel, while on the other it must be selective. In all cases we must be able to detect the right thing in the right place at the right time and respond to it appropriately. This implies filtering and analyzing, to draw attention to the essential features (e.g., a stop sign), and decision-making, which implies recognition of the sign, determination of its location, and selection of the adequate response (e.g., stopping the car).

In this chapter, I discuss the neurobiological principles of stimulus perception and the behavior that ensues. The chapter starts with a synopsis of the various sensory modalities and then shows that sense organs provide organisms with their own sensory worlds. The chapter goes on to analyze the causal relationships between stimulus and behavioral response, discussing Tinbergen's concept of **configurational sign-stimulus** and releasing mechanism in the light of current observations in different animal species and in humans. This leads to the question of the neurophysiological correlates of stimulus recognition. Finally, I discuss sensory processing structures with regard to rigidity and cross-modal plasticity.

One intention of this chapter is also to show that some concepts of classical **ethology** are still useful and should not be simply abandoned; rather, they should be regarded as evolving concepts and integrated into our current knowledge of perception in both animals and humans.

# Stimulus reception opens the sensory channels

Information to be processed comes from outside an organism's CNS and must first come in contact with the nervous system via its receptors. This information arises from four basic modalities.

1 Photoreception: response to radiant energy in the visible wavelength range of the electromagnetic spectrum (in the form of photons).
2 Thermoreception: response to radiant thermal energy in the non-visible wavelength range of the electromagnetic spectrum.
3 Mechanoreception: response to kinetic energy, including hearing, vibration, touch, balance, etc.
4 Chemoreception: response to chemical energy, including smell and taste.

Nociception, the reception of pain, involves responses to heat, mechanical and/or chemical energy. Special perceptual capabilities include electroreception (response to electrical energy) and magnetoreception (response to the energy of a magnetic field). The form of energy to which the receptor cells of a sense organ respond defines the organ's sensory modality. Within a sensory modality (e.g., vision), different stimulus qualities (e.g., color) and stimulus quantities (e.g., brightness) can be distinguished.

A stimulus is detected by a receptor cell which, depending on the cell type, translates it into nerve impulses. The information is transduced intracellularly by processes that lead to a change in the **cell membrane potential** (see also Chapter 5), the receptor potential. Some cells have their own amplifying system in order to respond to very weak stimuli. For example, in rod cell photoreceptors of the vertebrate retina the amplification of the visual signal is estimated to be in the order of $1 : 6 \times 10^6$. This means that one photon absorbed by one molecule of rhodopsin gives rise to a signaling cascade of intracellular biochemical events that affects $6 \times 10^6$ molecules of cyclic guanosine monophosphate (cGMP), leading to a change in the membrane potential of the photoreceptor. cGMP is an intracellular messenger that influences ion channels of the cell membrane.

Comparable signaling cascades occur in scent reception. In the olfactory mucosa of mammals, scent receptors are located on the dendritic appendages of the olfactory sensory cells. Here the estimated signal amplification ranges between $1 : 1000$ and $1 : 2000$. This means that one scent molecule gives rise to a cascade of events that activates up to 2000 molecules of cyclic adenosine monophosphate (cAMP). In this case, the intracellular messenger cAMP influences ion channels to change the membrane potential. In "scent experts" like the silkworm moth, *Bombyx mori*, one molecule of the sex attractant **pheromone** bombykol is sufficient to elicit a nerve impulse in the receptor cell specialized for bombykol (Kaissling 1987). In silkworm moths the behavioral olfactory threshold for bombykol is 1000 scent molecules/cm$^3$ in an airstream with a velocity of about 50 cm/s;

similarly in dogs the behavioral olfactory threshold for butyric acid is also 1000 scent molecules/cm$^3$.

## Receptors provide organisms with their own sensory worlds

Each organism is equipped with a set of sensory receptors that determine the world in which the organism lives. Von Uexküll (1921) pointed out that animal species live in, and communicate within, their own sensory worlds. Different animals perceive their environment (*Umwelt*) differently, and quite different from the way we perceive our environment. Knowledge about the capabilities of sense organs can suggest not only the kinds of stimuli perceived by an organism but eventually how their perceptual worlds may look.

Different organisms have evolved special perceptual talents that shape the world in which they live. Let us consider a few examples. In birds, visual spatial resolution is maximized by the enormous density of photo-receptors in the center of the retina: from high altitudes their eyes can detect the smallest features on the ground while at the same time monitor a wide field of vision. Bees and many birds and fish are sensitive to ultraviolet light and they may respond to the plane of polarization of light. Barn owls, hunting in complete darkness, are extremely sensitive to the weakest sounds from prey objects (see Chapter 5). Dogs and mice live mainly in a world of smell, spiders in a world of vibration. Rattlesnakes of the genus *Crotalus* have receptors sensitive to infrared radiation for object detection in the dark. Dolphins and **nocturnal** bats use biosonar and weakly electric fish produce electric fields for their orientation and communication (Heiligenberg & Rose 1985; Suga 1990; von der Emde & Schwarz 2001). Sharks use electroreceptors to locate their prey by detecting electric fields as small as 0.005 μV/cm, corresponding to the muscle potentials generated during breathing of a prey hidden in the sand. Hatchling loggerhead turtles, *Caretta caretta*, detect geomagnetic features that vary across the earth's surface and these provide navigational information for the animal's long-distance migration (Lohmann et al. 2001).

Whichever modality the receptor cell responds to, whether infrared light or sonar, the underlying sensory systems always have the same basic structure: sensory organs and nerve cells connected to them (see Chapter 5). Moreover, no matter what the modality, sensory systems always have two main perceptual tasks (Fig. 2.1a): the stimulus must be recognized and localized in space, i.e., the system must answer "what" and "where." Indeed, **signal** recognition requires that stimuli from the environment be classified into categories of functional (behavioral) significance. A category can be a class of behaviorally significant objects that share a set of defining features. How organisms sort objects in their environment into different

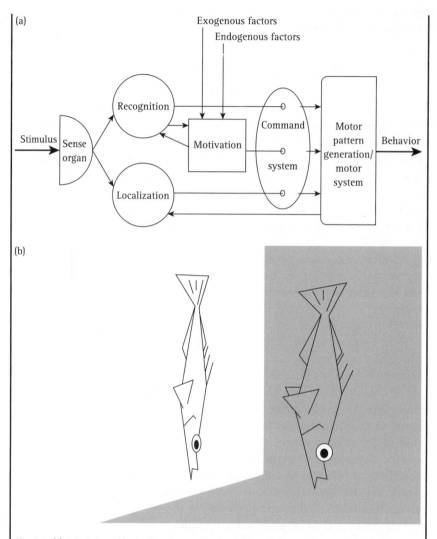

**Fig. 2.1** (a) Principles of brain function mediating between sensory input and adequate motor output. For details see text. (b) Male three-spined stickleback assuming a threat posture in front of a mirror. (Fig. 2.1(b) modified from Tinbergen 1951.)

categories according to features is one of the most basic questions in the behavioral and cognitive sciences: the problem is very general, as an "object" can be any recurring class of experience and "sorting" can be any differential response. **Categorization** hence plays a critical role in perception, thinking, and language (Harnad 1987).

The features by which animals discriminate and recognize objects was studied in detail by Niko Tinbergen and coworkers.

## Objects can be Abstracted in Terms of Sign-stimuli

### Tinbergen's sign-stimuli: stimulus perception in male sticklebacks

To understand how an animal interprets a stimulus means investigating how the animal responds to that stimulus. In his famous textbook *The Study of Instinct*, Tinbergen (1951) introduced the topic of stimulus perception with an experiment (Fig. 2.1b): a male three-spined stickleback, *Gasterosteus aculeatus*, sees its reflection in a mirror; it then assumes a vertically oriented body posture with the head pointing downward. Tinbergen listed a set of issues that must be addressed in order to answer why, at the level of **causation** (see Chapter 1), the animal does this. First, we must classify the motor pattern in a behavioral context (e.g., reproduction, male–male aggression) and investigate the features of the stimulus that releases the behavior. Then, we need to analyze the neuronal mechanisms that extract the features, i.e., explore the systems responsible for stimulus recognition and localization (Fig. 2.1a). Finally, we must identify the neural circuitry involved in generating the motor pattern response. The fact that only male sticklebacks in reproductive condition show the head-down response to a mirror image suggests the involvement of sex hormones (which require neurochemical investigations). What Tinbergen is suggesting is that the whole nervous system participates in what appears, initially at least, as a relatively simple stimulus–response.

A male stickleback encountering a conspecific male trespassing on its territory changes its longitudinal body axis into a vertical position, with the head pointing downward. Through a series of ingenious experiments Tinbergen and coworkers showed that the behavioral responses of territorial males in reproductive state depended on two types of stimuli from the intruder. Placing the male in a narrow transparent glass tube (Fig. 2.2a), they found that the response of territorial males was stronger when the tube was oriented vertically compared with when the tube was oriented horizontally (Ter Pelkwijk & Tinbergen 1937). They also showed that the red coloration of the male's belly contributes to response elicitation in territorial males. The strongest response was obtained when both features, vertical position and red color, occurred together. Tinbergen referred to such a stimulus (combination of vertical position and red color capable of eliciting the response) as a **sign-stimulus**. More generally, Tinbergen pointed out that a feature *A* combined with a feature *B* may provide a sign-stimulus but that feature *A* in combination with a feature *C* may provide a different sign-stimulus. For example, in male sticklebacks:

1  red belly and head-down posture release threat response in a conspecific male stickleback, not in a female;
2  red belly and **zigzag dance** (see below and Chapter 3) release courtship behavior in a female stickleback, not in a male.

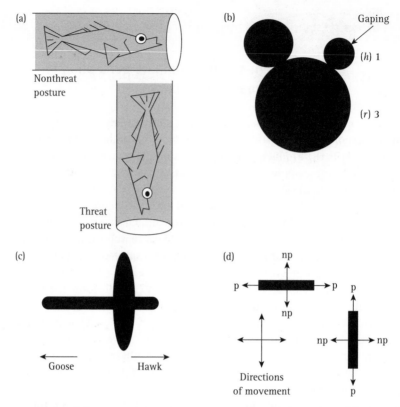

**Fig. 2.2** Configurational features in sign-stimuli. (a) Three-spined stickleback, in a glass tube, in threat posture and prevented from assuming a threat posture. (After Ter Pelkwijk & Tinbergen 1937.) (b) Parent thrushes can be abstracted by a head (h)/rump (r) model. The gaping response of nestlings is addressed toward the parent's head (arrow), preferably if the head-to-rump ratio is about 1 : 3, demonstrated by a "two-head" model that allows a choice. (After Tinbergen & Kuenen 1939.) (c) A bird model moving above turkeys elicits escape when flown like a hawk, with the short end and the wings leading; the same model is ignored when flown in the opposite direction, when it resembles a goose-like bird. (After Tinbergen 1951.) (d) Prey/nonprey phenomenon in common toads. A small bar signals prey if it is moved in the direction of its longer axis: p, prey configuration; np, nonprey configuration. (After Ewert 1980.)

# Principle of configurational sign-stimuli: picking out visual key features

## Static and dynamic configurations

Tinbergen showed that behaviorally meaningful objects can be abstracted in terms of sign-stimuli that are recognized easily and responded to rapidly. The effectiveness of sign-stimuli can be analyzed in experiments using dummies by changing, omitting, adding, or exaggerating certain features. The advantage of studying a sign-stimulus by successively changing its features is that the effects of these changes on perception can be evaluated. Sign-stimuli are often configurational. In this case the sign-stimulus consists of different feature components. Depending on the way the features are related to each other, we distinguish between a static configuration (involving spatial relationships) and a dynamic configuration (involving spatiotemporal relationships). In any case, the configuration is perceived as the whole. Furthermore, recognition is largely independent of stimulus changes as long as these do not affect the configuration. This phenomenon is called **invariance**.

An example of static configuration is the sign-stimulus for the gaping response of nestling thrushes, *Turdus merula*, when their eyes open at the age of 8 days (Fig. 2.2b). In experiments using dummies, the parent can be modeled by two adjacent solid disks of different diameters, the large one simulating the rump ($r$) and the smaller one, about one-third of $r$, the head ($h$) (Tinbergen & Kuenen 1939). Hence $h$ and $r$ are features; their spatial arrangement yields the configuration. A characteristic property of configuration is the nonalgebraic additive nature of the responses to its features. This means that the sum of the gaping responses to head or rump, when each feature is presented alone, is much less than the response to the whole configuration consisting of head and rump. The recognition of such a holistic configuration is largely invariant of a change in stimulus parameters, for example it is independent of size, within limits, provided the 1 : 3 ratio is maintained. Although movement of the head/rump configuration improves its efficacy, the spatial relationship between the head and rump features is independent of such movement.

An example of dynamic configuration concerns the goose/hawk discrimination (Tinbergen 1951). Turkeys, *Gallopavo meleagris*, avoid the silhouette of an airborne bird of prey, for example a bird model flown with the short end and the wings leading (Fig. 2.2c). However, the same bird model flown with the long end leading, thus resembling a harmless goose-like bird, is ignored. Subsequent research has shown that this configurational phenomenon results from stimulus-specific **habituation** (Schleidt 1961), as discussed in a later section of this chapter. Another example concerns prey/nonprey discrimination in amphibians (Ewert 1980). To distinguish prey from nonprey, common toads, *Bufo bufo*, evaluate the ratio of two features: object length to width in relation to the direction of movement. If length is greater than width, say a $3 \times 20$ mm bar moving in the direction of its longer axis, the bar is recognized as prey (Fig. 2.2d). However, the same bar is disregarded as prey if the longer axis is oriented across the direction of movement (width > length). This configurational discrimination is not learnt. It is present after metamorphosis from aquatic to terrestrial life.

Knowledge about sign-stimuli allows humans to communicate with animals. For instance, the zoologist Kent Clegg from the USA used his ultra-lightweight airplane as a sign-stimulus for young whooping cranes, *Grus americana*, that had lost their parents. He painted the tips of the plane's wings black, a signal present in parent birds, and succeeded in having the young follow the plane for 1200 km, from Idaho to their winter residence in New Mexico.

### Configurational stimuli in human perception

Configurational stimuli also play an important role in human perception. In social communication, gestures and faces contain important configurational (*Gestalt*) features that vary with expression.

Human neonates track a slowly moving face-like model markedly further than they will follow scrambled face components (Valenza et al. 1996). After 2 months of age, learned recognition of individual faces proceeds. By 3 months, infants seem to form different face prototypes. Studies in 6-month-old infants thus show discrimination even between individuals of different species, such as human and monkey faces. Interestingly, later, infants display a kind of "perceptual narrowing": the extensive experience with human faces strongly favors the human face prototype, so that 9-month-old infants (like adults) show a marked advantage for recognizing human faces (Pascalis et al. 2002). Presumably, individual human faces are encoded in terms of how they deviate from the human face prototype. Of course, this early tuning allows **learning** to discriminate other perceptual categories later. A comparable **ontogenetic** phenomenon of narrowing the perceptual window is known from speech perception.

The invariance phenomenon also plays a role in human *Gestalt* perception. For example, in email the symbols (:-)) and (:-((are correctly interpreted despite their sideways orientation because of what is referred to as invariance in terms of orientation. We recognize the letter B independently of its size (B) or font ($\mathcal{B}$). Invariances, however, are not unlimited: the configuration of the letter B is not orientation invariant and can thus, depending on context, be interpreted differently after a 90° rotation (ɯ). An example of invariance in the auditory domain concerns melodies. We recognize a melody independently of the key in which it is played or its instrumentation or whether it is whistled or sounded on a comb.

An advantage of configurational *Gestalt* perception is that a figure can be extracted easily from its background. A figure cannot be discriminated from its background if both figure and ground are composed of similar components: the figure is masked, like a needle in a haystack. However, if the components of the figure differ from the background in one aspect, say if they move coherently, the configuration isolates from the background and is recognized (Lee & Blake 1999). This happens, more or less consciously, if we look at a patterned stationary three-dimensional scene, a landscape for example. It is the way objects move relative to each other when the observer moves: nearby objects move across the visual field faster than those farther away. The objects isolate and can be quickly recognized as bushes, trees, hills, etc.

## Relational/combinatorial principle of stimuli in other sensory modalities

The reported observations that sign-stimuli often consist of characteristic combinations and relationships between different features accord with many examples of behaviorally significant stimuli from other sensory modalities. This is particularly true for signals used in animal communication (see Chapter 10).

Female moths use sex attractant pheromones to invite their males. In most moth species these pheromones consist of two components that are **displayed** by the female in a specific ratio (Priesner 1980; Kaissling 1987). Whereas the same two pheromone components can be emitted by **phylogenetically** related species, a species-specific signal can be produced by using a characteristic proportion of each of the two components. For example, in three species of North American leaf-roller moths the proportion of the two components $(Z)$-11-tetradecenyl acetate : $(E)$-11-tetradecenyl acetate in female pheromones is 90 : 10 in *Archips mortuanus*, 60 : 40 in *Archips argyrospilus* and 17 : 83 in *Archips cerasivoranus*. The recognition threshold depends on the proportion of the rarer of the two components, which can be as low as 10% or less. However, in cases where one of the two components is very rare, long-distance recognition is prevented.

Female leopard frogs, *Rana pipiens*, are attracted by conspecific males when certain low-**frequency** (300 Hz) and high-frequency (1700 Hz) components in the male's mating-call spectrum coincide. Maximum attractiveness occurs at a particular ratio of these frequencies (Capranica 1976). Similarly, the mating call of the green tree frog, *Hyla cinerea*, has a low-frequency peak around 900 Hz and a high-frequency peak at 3000 Hz. More specifically, Gerhardt (1981) showed that the combination of these tone components is maximally effective, particularly at low sound pressure levels (55 dB). Furthermore, each component may play a different role in attracting females: the 900-Hz low-frequency component serves to attract females from a distance, whereas the 3000-Hz high-frequency component is used for **species recognition**. Regarding the latter, in the North American cricket frog, *Acris crepitans*, the high-frequency tone component even varies with the geographic origin of the males (Capranica 1976): South Dakota males, 2500 Hz; Texas males, 3000 Hz; New Jersey males, 3500 Hz; Georgia males, 4100 Hz. This allows female cricket frogs to distinguish local dialects and to follow conspecific males only. In fact, it seems unlikely that, for example, females from Texas would have to distinguish males from Georgia, since the two populations are about 800 km apart. The distance between Texas and New Jersey is more than twice that. The idea behind this perceptual capability may be the geographic separation of species in the course of evolution.

Unlike *Rana* or *Hyla*, the advertisement call in male túngara frogs, *Physalaemus pustulosus*, consists of a sequence: a whine followed by several lower-pitched chucks (Ryan & Rand 1995). Whereas the whine serves species recognition, the chucks enhance the call's attractiveness to females. In fact, if given a choice, females of the related species *P. coloradorum*, whose males whine but do not chuck, choose *P. pustulosus* calls (see also Chapter 13).

Such enhancing effects may also result from combining feature components of different sensory channels. When prey is difficult to carry for *Aphenogaster* ants, they recruit help from workers by emitting a pheromone. If food competitors are in the vicinity and time is short, ants also deliver a vibrational stimulus. Vibration alone has no effect in this context, but combined with the pheromone it leads to a marked acceleration in both recruiting workers and retrieving the prey. Vibration here enhances pheromone detection by lowering the olfactory response threshold (Markl & Hölldobler 1978). Unlike *Aphenogaster* ants, workers of leaf-cutting ants, *Atta cephalotes*, respond to a pheromone or a vibratory stimulus with recruitment behavior, with the chemical stimulus being the stronger. However, when ants are given a choice between the chemical stimulus and the combined chemical/vibrational stimulus, they choose the combination, suggesting here a kind of summation effect (Hölldobler 1999).

## From heterogeneous summation to supernormal stimuli

As we have seen above, often more than one feature of a natural stimulus influences responding. There are cases in which separable stimulus features have a precisely additive effect, a phenomenon called **heterogeneous summation**. The attack rate of cichlid fish, *Haplochromis burtoni*, can be raised by a model fish having a black eye-bar (Heiligenberg 1974); a similar model with orange spots, but no eye-bar, reduced the attack rate. Interestingly, in a model composed of both stimulus features, these effects summed algebraically: a model with eye-bar and orange spots caused little change in the attack rate. This experiment shows that the effects of different (heterogeneous) stimulus features add together (summate) to influence behavior.

Such additive effects of stimuli introduce a curious phenomenon: in experiments using dummies to examine sign-stimuli, various cases show that exaggeration of a sign-stimulus leads to an extraordinary increase in its efficacy to elicit a response and is thus called a **supernormal stimulus**. For example, the courting behavior of a male stickle-back depends on the swollen abdomen of the pregnant female. When presented with two model females, one showing a normal swollen abdomen and the other a hyper-swollen abdomen, the male will choose the latter even when the size of the model's abdomen is far beyond the normal range (Rowland 1989).

Another example of supernormal stimuli concerns the egg-retrieval behavior of brood-ing greylag geese, *Anser anser*. These birds nest on the ground such that occasionally an egg may roll out of its nest. When this happens the goose sits on its nest, extends its neck toward the egg, applies its flat lower mandible to the far side of the egg, and slowly rolls it back toward the nest. If the goose is offered a choice of eggs of different sizes placed outside the nest, the largest one, even if it is twice the size of its own egg and hence difficult to handle, will be selected preferentially. Oystercatchers, *Haematopus ostralegus*, also show this amazing egg-retrieving size preference (Baerends 1982).

Humans use configurational sign-stimuli in cartoons, in which the expression of an object can be abstracted and emphasized. Messages can often be made appealing by the exaggeration of feature components. For example, certain features of the female face (the eyes or lips) can be strikingly accentuated cosmetically and thus turned into super-normal stimuli in order to make the face more attractive and also distinctive from others. Commercial products are often advertised with posters that use supernormal stimuli as "eye-catchers" to arouse attention and make the product inviting.

## Principles of stimulus selection

### *Stimulus-specific habituation generates stimulus discrimination*

Hinde (1954) showed that the responsiveness of animals to the same stimulus presented repeatedly increases gradually at first ("warming-up" effect), reaches a plateau, and then decreases until the stimulus is neglected (habituation) (see Chapter 7). There are many examples showing that habituation can be stimulus-specific, such that a small change in the stimulus to which an animal has become habituated can produce **dishabituation**, a sudden increase in response to prehabituation levels. Prey-catching activity in common toads habituates when the animal is repeatedly offered a small, orthogonal, triangular piece of cardboard moved with its small side leading and tip trailing; when the animal is offered the triangle's mirror image moved with its tip leading and small side trailing, the toad's prey-capture response is elicited immediately (Ewert et al. 2001).

When young gallinaceous birds are exposed to any shadow from a bird flying over them, they exhibit escape behavior. However, it has been observed that over time young turkeys, *Gallopavo meleagris*, become habituated to goose-like birds (long neck, short tail) flying overhead repeatedly in their environment, whereas the less frequently seen birds of prey (short neck, long tail) continue to be avoided, which explains the goose/hawk discrimination shown in Fig. 2.2c (Tinbergen 1951; Schleidt 1961).

The phenomenon of stimulus-specific habituation also occurs in human perception. During exercise in a fitness center we habituate rapidly to the smell of our own sweat, but will readily detect the smell of another person.

## *Search images facilitate stimulus recognition*

When birds discover a tasty cryptic prey in their environment, for example a type of insect difficult to detect because it is embedded in distractors, they use a **search(ing) image** of the preferred object (L. Tinbergen 1960). A predator with a search image takes one type of prey and neglects other types, even if both types are equally cryptic (Langley et al. 1996). The search image reproduces the original less from the complete image of the object being sought, but rather seems to focus attention on certain specific cues of the search object. The discrimination principle is in some ways opposite to stimulus-specific habituation, since the predator tends to see what it expects or "wants" to see: when the abundance of that prey type increases, an increase in predation follows. In contrast to the recognition mechanisms for sign-stimuli, the recognition with search images is short term.

Here, too, there are parallels in human perception. Suppose we want to pick blueberries in the forest; at first glance the bushes seem to be empty since the dark-green leaves distract from the berries. By concentrating on the dark-blue coloration of the berries, suddenly it seems quite easy to identify them. Similarly, when waiting for an expected visitor at an airport, we have a search image of what the visitor will look like, based upon previous experience or a photograph of the person.

## *Efficacy of sign-stimuli depends on motivation*

The response to a given sign-stimulus is not constant but depends on internal (e.g., hormonal) and external (e.g., photoperiod) factors (see Fig. 2.1a). For example, stimulus efficacy may be limited to a certain season in the year, depending on the organism's internal motivational state, i.e., its readiness to respond to a stimulus with adequate behavior (cf. Chapters 3 & 4). During spring, when mating **motivation** in toads is high, the male responds to a moving female with courtship clasping behavior. In summer, mating motivation is absent in toads and moving objects of the size of a female are ignored by the males or even avoided.

The sharpness of stimulus recognition may also depend on the level of motivation for the corresponding behavior (see Fig. 2.1a). During the mating season, if no female toad is available in the pond, the highly motivated male may clasp a piece of bark it encounters – somewhat reminiscent of Goethe's Mephisto who promises Faust "with this drink in your body, soon you'll greet a Helena in every girl you meet."

## The Concept of Releasing Mechanism

### Classical concept of innate releasing mechanism

What mechanism translates a sign-stimulus into an adequate motor pattern? The concept of **innate releasing mechanism** (IRM), introduced by Konrad Lorenz and Niko Tinbergen, concerns the observation that some organisms are apparently able to recognize behaviorally meaningful stimuli never before experienced in their environment and to respond to them adequately. The concept focuses on the close correspondence between sign-stimulus and the appropriate behavioral response (Tinbergen 1951). A sign-stimulus, also called "key-stimulus," is thought to activate the IRM much like a safe is unlocked by a key, such that the IRM then releases the corresponding motor pattern. The notion of the key–lock principle, however, should not be taken to imply that an IRM is responsive to a single highly specific stimulus because, as we have seen, it responds to configurational sign-stimuli. Moreover, much controversy surrounds the term "**innate**" (see Chapter 6). A revised concept of **releasing mechanism** (RM) considers that environmental and genetic factors contribute to all behavior (Baerends 1987; Ewert 1997; cf. Chapters 6–8).

### Neuronal correlates of RMs: the concept of command neurons/systems

The RM concept suggests a neural sensorimotor interface that translates perception into action (see Fig. 2.1a): at its afferent (input) side this interface has stimulus recognition and localization properties; its efferent (output) side activates ("commands") the corresponding motor systems. Theoretically, the simplest RM would consist of a command neuron (CN) that would operate in a chain of the type:

Sign-stimulus → sensory neuron[s] → CN → motor pattern generator (MPG) → behavior

The giant axons that control the escape tail flip in crayfish appear to express the CN principle in one of its simplest forms (Wiersma & Ikeda 1964; Edwards et al. 1999). The idea that a neuron might trigger a behavior pattern was challenging and thus sparked intense debate among neuroethologists. Kupfermann and Weiss (1978) pointed out that such a neuron must fulfill two conditions: its excitation should not only be necessary but also sufficient to activate the MPG, and this can be tested experimentally. If a CN works as hypothesized, electrically stimulating it should be sufficient to elicit the corresponding behavior; removing it must necessarily abolish the behavioral response to the sign-stimulus.

Testing these necessity and sufficiency conditions of CNs, the best candidate in vertebrates is the reticulospinal Mauthner cell of teleost fish that, in response to certain vibratory stimulation, triggers the fast-body-bend escape reaction (Eaton 2001). However, quantitative examination of Mauthner cells showed that the necessity criterion was not fulfilled clearly (therefore suggesting neuronal backup systems) and neither was the sufficiency criterion (therefore suggesting the participation of other reticulospinal neurons). Hence, the command neuron experiment shows that a revised command concept will have to consider a spectrum of possibilities by which command functions can be executed, also involving systems of command-like interneurons, so-called command elements (CEs) (Ewert 2002). Actually, the Mauthner cell may be such a CE operating in a command system.

In certain command systems CEs may activate the MPG cooperatively (like a logical *AND* gate), whereas in other command systems CEs may activate the MPG alternatively (like an *OR* gate). When the CEs of a command system are treated as a unit, the command system will indeed meet the necessity *and* sufficiency condition, both in *AND* and *OR* gates. In a **command releasing system** (CRS) (Ewert 1987, 1997), various types of CEs evaluate different aspects of a stimulus, such as features and locus in space, respectively; a CRS also considers input from motivational systems (see Fig. 2.7).

## Analyzing the Mechanisms Underlying Configurational Perception

Tinbergen (1951, p. 79) emphasized:

> The conclusion that a sign-stimulus is configurational is merely a provisional way of describing the complexity of the sensory stimulating process. It is thus a challenge rather than a solution, a challenge to analyse the complex system of processes denoted by the convenient collective name "stimulus."

Tinbergen noted that the analysis of these processes will require the application of a broad spectrum of experimental techniques and integration of sensory physiology, neurophysiology, neuroendocrinology, and neuroanatomy in which ontogenetic and phylogenetic aspects must be considered. He introduced this new direction of research as "ethophysiology," today known as **neuroethology** (for reviews see Ewert 1980, 1985; Delcomyn 1998; Carew 2000).

### Relational/combinatorial principles in scent coding by insects

Behaviorally relevant features can be analyzed in different sensory systems by a range of mechnisms, from receptor cells to differently tuned interneurons. This is demonstrated convincingly by olfactory perception in insects.

As mentioned previously, female moths attract their conspecific males with sex pheromones. In the silkworm moth, *Bombyx mori*, the scent hairs on the male's antennae are equipped with specialist odor receptor cells. These are tuned to a single key pheromone emitted by the female, the compound bombykol (Fig. 2.3a). Such a cell is somewhat responsive to chemically related compounds, but at much higher concentrations (Kaissling 1987). Other examples of such "narrow bands" are the meat receptor in *Necrophorus* beetles, the rotten-meat receptor in *Calliphora erythrocephala*, or the grass receptor in *Locusta migratoria*. For grass receptors on the scent hairs (sensillum coelonicum), compounds with six carbon atoms and certain chemically related functional groups are most effective, especially hexenic acid, hexenal, and hexenol as components of fresh grass; much less effective are hexanal and hexanol (Kafka 1970). Excitation of receptor cells specialized for an odorous substance would be sufficient to elicit the corresponding behavior (Fig. 2.3a).

In many other species, there are two types of specialized receptor cell each tuned to a different pheromone component, both emitted by the female in a characteristic proportion (Fig. 2.3d). The system of addressing conspecific males using characteristic proportions of two pheromone components may have evolved as a means of minimizing the risks of mating with males of the wrong species. In species of moth in which two (or more) pheromones are required, the excitation pattern from the receptor channels specialized for these compounds could be analyzed by concurrent inputs involving a logical *AND* gate (Fig. 2.3d).

Another way of reducing the risks of mating with males of the wrong species may be interspecific inhibitors. For example, females of the nun moth, *Lymantria monacha*, and the gypsy moth, *L. dispar*, both produce the male-attracting compound (+)-disparlure (Fig. 2.3b,c). However, the female nun moth also produces (–)-disparlure, which stimulates a specialist receptor cell in the male gypsy moth that inhibits its behavioral response to (+)-disparlure (Fig. 2.3c) (Hansen 1984).

The (–)-disparlure receptor in male gypsy moths raises some interesting evolutionary questions. Why do male gypsy moths have this receptor? Was it already present for some other **function**? If not, how did it evolve? It may prevent male gypsy moths from wasting time tracking female nun moths, hence separating different species. However, this would function in one "direction" only, since a male nun moth could be attracted by the (+)-disparlure signals of the female nun or gypsy moth. Maybe female gypsy moths are less attractive to male nun moths because of the relatively high emission concentrations of (+)-disparlure (cf. Fig. 2.3c and 2.3b).

The system of generalist odor receptor cells responds to a much larger number of odor compounds that need not be chemically related. The significance of a behavioral response to a biologically meaningful odor in these "broad bands" is unknown. Scent coding with generalist receptor cells requires complex pattern analyses and is not yet well understood.

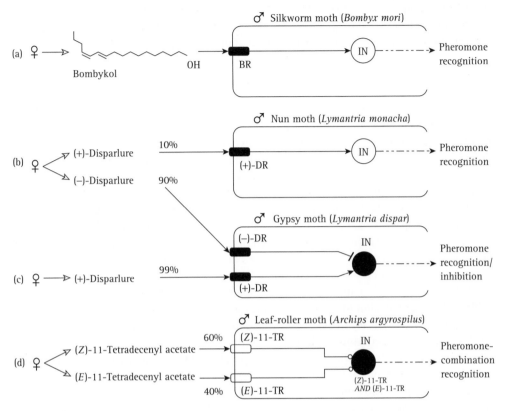

**Fig. 2.3** Principles of scent detection in insects by (a,b) specialist receptor cells, (c) specialist receptor cells and differentiating interneurons (IN), and (d) binding of features in coincidence circuits. Neurons with recognition properties are marked black; they exert their function as an assembly. (a) In male *Bombyx mori* the receptor channel (BR) is specialized for the sex pheromone bombykol; excitation of about 200 receptor cells by 200 bombykol molecules, emitted by the female, elicits a behavioral response. (b) In male *Lymantria monacha* the receptor channel (+)-DR is specialized for the sex pheromone (+)-disparlure. (c) In male *Lymantria dispar* two types of receptor channel, (+)-DR and (−)-DR, are specialized for the two pheromone compounds of disparlure; (+)-disparlure stimulates the male's behavior whereas (−)-disparlure inhibits the response to (+)-disparlure. (d) In male *Archips argyrospilus* the excitation of two receptor channels, (Z)-11-TR and (E)-11-TR, specialized for the two sex pheromone stereoisomers (Z)-11-tetradecenyl acetate and (E)-11-tetradecenyl acetate, requires across-fiber pattern analysis, e.g., by a coincidence circuit. (Compiled from data in Kaissling 1987.)

## Feature binding in prey selection by toads: a case study from behavior to neuron

In certain situations, toads and humans behave in a similar manner. A fly walking on our arm alerts us to its presence; we may turn our head toward it, fixate it, and try to catch it with the other hand. If a fly moves near a hungry toad, the toad responds by turning the head toward the prey, approaching it, binocularly fixating it, and catching it with its tongue. In the toad's prey-catching sequence each behavioral component is elicited by an RM that has recognition and localization functions. All RMs must answer the question "What is it?" but differ with regard to the question "Where is it?"

## What is prey for toads?

Toads respond best to moving objects whereby relatively small objects (e.g., woodlice, millipedes, bugs) elicit prey capture and relatively large objects (e.g., hedgehogs, birds of prey) elicit escape. Since prey-catching activity is measured easily, it is feasible to determine the relative effectiveness of rectangular, black, dummy prey objects moving against a white background (Fig. 2.4, top) when the object's dimensions are varied systematically: the edge length of the object parallel ($ep$) to the direction of movement, edge length across ($ea$) the direction of movement, or both. Hence, three configurations of stimuli are used: rectangular bars moving in the direction of their long axes (Fig. 2.4a); rectangular bars moving in the direction of their short axes (Fig. 2.4b); and square stimuli moving in the same direction as the bars (Fig. 2.4c). Other stimulus parameters (velocity, contrast, etc.) are held constant. Figure 2.4(a, panel P) shows that extending $ep$ (for constant $ea = 2.5$ mm) in successive experiments increases the prey value within limits, whereas extension of $ea$ (for constant $ep = 2.5$ mm) progressively reduces the prey value (Fig. 2.4b, panel P). In response to squares ($ep = ea$) of different sizes, the $ep$ and $ea$ influences interact, thus yielding an optimal prey object of 10 mm edge length (Fig. 2.4c, panel P). Interestingly, this size is preferred independently of the object's distance from the toad (up to 230 mm), a phenomenon called "size constancy." Large square objects of about 40–80 mm edge length elicit predator avoidance, such as ducking or turning away (Fig. 2.4c, panel A).

In fact, there is no unique prey sign-stimulus. Rather, by measuring the effects of changes of the object features $ep$ and $ea$ on prey-catching activity we learn something about the "key," namely the **algorithm** (calculation rule), that allows the toad's visual system to gain access to the category of prey in terms of configurational cues. Furthermore, we learn that small versus big does not sufficiently distinguish between prey and nonprey. For example, a $2.5 \times 20$ mm bar is actually quite small, but oriented parallel to the direction of movement it signals prey; however, oriented across the direction of movement its prey value is zero This configurational discrimination is invariant to changes of direction (cf. Fig. 2.2d) or speed of movement and even of size within limits.

We call the combinatorial algorithm that weights the features $ep$ and $ea$ for prey recognition (according to Fig. 2.4a–c, panel P) the $ep/ea$ features-relating algorithm. In common toads this algorithm is present immediately after metamorphosis with transition to terrestrial life. It is subject to maturation (**perceptual sharpening**) during early ontogeny without prey experience. It is common to members of the species *Bufo bufo*, shows variation among different species, and can be modified by learning.

For prey/nonprey discrimination, the feature $ea$ is most decisive. Toads faced with a bar oriented across its direction of movement are threatened, since they may respond with a stiff-legged avoidance/defense posture typical of behavior toward snakes,

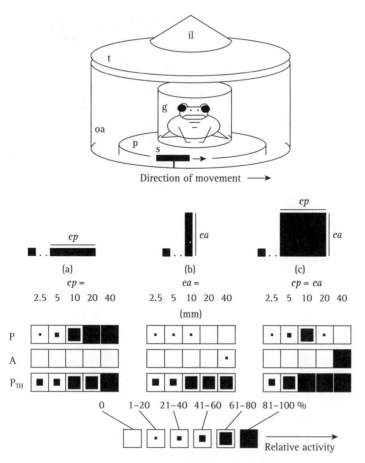

**Fig. 2.4** Example of stimulus feature analysis in toads. Three types of configurational moving stimuli are used: horizontal bars, vertical bars, and squares. Visual configurational features *ep* and *ea* determine the toad's prey or predator category. *Top*: experimental procedure for quantitative measurements of prey-catching orienting activity toward a black cardboard rectangle circling around the toad at constant velocity at a distance of 70 mm: oa, opaque arena; g, glass vessel with experimental animal; il, diffuse illumination; p, platform; s, motor-driven stimulus (cardboard); t, transparent screen. Starting with a small square object of $2.5 \times 2.5$ mm, various dimensions are changed in the three stimulus sets: (a) the edge *ep* parallel to the direction of movement; (b) the edge *ea* perpendicular to the direction of movement; (c) both *ep* and *ea*, for $ep = ea$ (1 mm corresponds to 0.8° visual angle). The behavioral activity (prey-catching orienting or escape avoiding responses per 30 s of $n = 20$ individuals) is expressed as a percent of the activity in response to the maximal releasing stimulus from the stimulus sets. Panel P, prey-catching activity; panel A, avoidance activity; panel $P_{TH}$, prey-catching activity after pretectal lesion. (Compiled from data in Ewert 1987.)

the toad's archenemies (Fig. 2.5). Certain snakes show such features in the movement pattern of their coils. Interestingly, when the much smaller caterpillar *Leucorampha ornata*, an insect larva, is threatened, it displays such an S-shaped configuration and is thus ignored as prey. Again this shows that configuration is more important than size in a

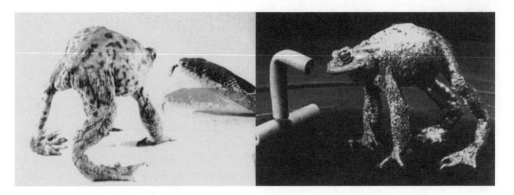

**Fig. 2.5** A common toad (*Bufo bufo*) responds to the head of a snake by assuming a stiff-legged avoidance/defense posture (left). The toad displays the same type of antipredator behavior toward a dummy (right) that stimulates characteristic threat features of the snake: elevated head/neck component oriented across its horizontal direction of movement. (After Ewert & Traud 1979.)

certain range. Other stimulus parameters (e.g., color, contrast, velocity, movement pattern) influence the efficacy of a prey object. Furthermore, learning and other modulatory influences affect prey selection (Ewert et al. 2001).

We now briefly discuss some behaviorally relevant brain structures (retina and retinal projection fields) and neurons in these structures that display sensitivities or selectivities in response to variation in the features *ep* and/or *ea* (Fig. 2.6).

## *What the frog's eye tells the frog's brain:*
### *Lettvin's concept of retinal detectors*

Barlow (1953) and Lettvin et al. (1959) recorded spikes of retinal ganglion cells from their fiber terminals in the optic tectum of leopard frogs (Fig. 2.6, top) in response to moving objects. In these experiments an object traversed the center of the visual **receptive field** of such a neuron. The receptive field of a retinal ganglion cell refers to a region in the visual field where a stimulus can excite or inhibit that cell. Morphologically, the receptive field corresponds to an area of photoreceptors that converge via interneurons (e.g., bipolar and amacrine cells) on the ganglion cell. Different classes of retinal (R) ganglion cells were distinguished, R1–R4. These have a circular excitatory receptive field (ERF) of different sizes: R1, 2–3° diameter; R2, 4–6° diameter; R3, 8–10° diameter; R4, 12–16° diameter. Each ERF surrounded by an inhibitory receptive field (IRF). As an object crosses the ERF, the projection of the object over the ERF activates the ganglion cell while the parts of the object that extend beyond the ERF activate the IRF, which attenuates the ganglion cell's activity. Consequently, R neurons prefer compact objects that fill their ERF without extending into the IRF. By working this way each R-type neuron in frogs or toads is optimally tuned to a different range of sizes (Fig. 2.6c, cf. R2–R4). Furthermore, these neurons display different sensitivities to the speed of a moving object, R1 and R2 neurons being sensitive to relatively low speed,

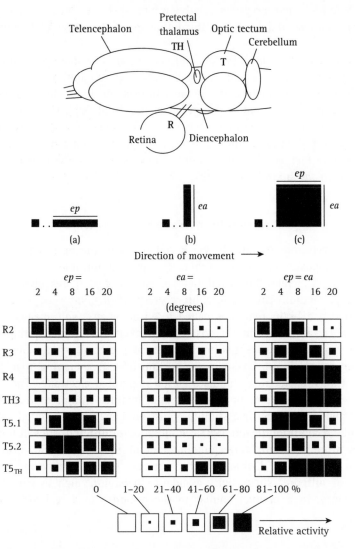

**Fig. 2.6** Stimulus features *ep* and *ea* of the three types of configurational moving object (a–c) are analyzed by ganglion cells in the retina (R), neurons in the optic tectum (T), and neurons in the pretectal thalamus (TH). *Top*: toad's brain in lateral view. (a–c) In response to changes of *ep*, *ea* and *ep = ea* in the stimulus sets, retinal ganglion cells (R2, R3, R4), pretectal thalamic neurons (TH3), and tectal neurons (T5.1, T5.2) display different patterns of discharge activity. Among these neurons the response activity of T5.2 neurons is best correlated with the toad's prey-catching activity. After pretectal lesions, configurational selectivity in tectal neurons (panel T5$_{TH}$) and prey-catching behavior (panel P$_{TH}$ in Fig. 2.4) are altered similarly. (Compiled from data in Ewert 1987, 1997.)

whereas R3 and R4 neurons prefer relatively high speed. R3 neurons are also sensitive to changing contrast and to color, and R4 neurons also respond to dimming of the visual field.

The pioneering work by both Barlow and Lettvin and coworkers opened a new chapter in neuroethology. Their work made us realize that retinal ganglion cells perform a first-stage stimulus analysis: neuron firing rates inform the brain about angular velocity, angular size, contrast, and color of objects in the visual field. However, prey-catching activity in response to changes of the object features *ep* and *ea* is not correlated with appropriate retinal ganglion cell responses (cf. Fig. 2.4a,b panel P and Fig. 2.6a,b panels R2–R4). In fact, configurational object recognition involves further processing of retinal output in the brain (Ewert 1987, 2004).

## Behaviorally relevant brain structures

The retina projects topographically via R-cell fibers in the optic nerve mainly to the **contralateral** (opposite) side of the brain: the optic tectum and the pretectal thalamus (cf. Fig. 2.6, top). Hence, the visual field of each eye is represented in the opposite tectum and pretectum. The topographic correspondence between loci in the visual field and loci in a brain region is called a "visual map." This means that an object moving at a certain locus in the visual field excites a corresponding locus in the tectal visual map and a corresponding locus in the pretectal visual map. What happens if, bypassing retinal input, a site in the tectum of a free-moving toad is excited by appropriate trains of electrical impulses via an implanted electrode? The toad responds with an orienting movement or snapping in a manner similar to that toward a real prey object and so the electrical stimulus must obviously have excited cells mediating output of prey recognition (Ewert 1987). Stimulation of different sites in the tectal visual map elicits turning toward corresponding loci of the visual field, also by exciting cells involved in prey localization. In the pretectal thalamus, however, focal electrical stimulation of different sites elicits avoidance behavior, such as ducking, jumping, or turning away, in a manner similar to the response to a real airborne or ground predator.

## Configurational perception involves parallel processing streams and their interaction

The results reported above suggest that both tectum and pretectum are involved in the perception of prey and predator. In fact, single-cell recordings from the pretectal thalamus reveal neurons of a type (TH3) that are sensitive to large areas of moving visual objects and that configurationally code for the feature *ea* (Fig. 2.6b, panel TH3). Recordings from the tectum reveal neurons of a type (T5.1) that configurationally code for *ep* (Fig. 2.6a, panel T5.1). Furthermore, there is another type of tectal neurons (T5.2) whose firing rates in response to variation of *ep* and *ea* resemble the toad's prey-catching activity (cf. Fig. 2.4 panel P and Fig. 2.6 panel T5.2) (Ewert 1997): increase of the firing rate to extension of a bar along *ep* (within limits) and decrease of the firing rate to extension of a bar along *ea*. We suggest that the feature *ep* is analyzed by a retino-tectal processing stream that originates in retinal R2 and R3 cells and terminates in tectal T5.1 cells, i.e., R2/R3 → T5.1. In parallel, feature *ea* is analyzed by a retinopretectal processing stream that originates in retinal R3 and R4 cells and terminates in pretectal thalamic TH3 cells, i.e., R3/R4 → TH3. The relation between *ep* and *ea* – the **binding** of these configurational features – may result from convergence of both processing streams on tectal T5.2 cells. These neurons differentiate between *ep* and *ea*. This suggests that T5.2 neurons weight the feature *ep* by excitatory input of T5.1 neurons and that they weight the feature *ea* by inhibitory input of TH3 neurons. Hence configuration perception would take the form:

R2/R3 → T5.1 → **T5.2** ⊢ TH3 ← R3/R4

where arrows refer to excitatory influences and the line with crossbar to inhibitory influence.

The differentiating property of T5.2 neurons can be tested by recording these cells in free-moving toads when a small bar oriented like a prey item is moved in front of them. Such recordings reveal a strong burst of spikes preceding the toad's prey-catching behavior. The same bar presented in a nonprey orientation by placing it across the direction of movement elicits very weak neuronal activity and no behavioral response. However, when a second electrode delivers an electrolytic lesion to the pretectum (Fig. 2.6, top) on the same side of the brain, burst firing of T5.2 neurons precedes the prey-catching response regardless of whether the moving bar is in the prey or nonprey configuration (Schürg-Pfeiffer et al. 1993). The pretectal lesion thus impairs the ability to distinguish between prey and nonprey both behaviorally and neuronally (cf. Fig. 2.4 panel $P_{TH}$ and Fig. 2.6 panel $T5_{TH}$).

## Command releasing systems as neuronal correlates of RMs

The CN concept cannot be applied to prey-catching in toads (Ewert 1980). Rather, the CRS concept suggests that different types of CEs cooperatively trigger the appropriate MPG (Fig. 2.7), whereby each type of CE evaluates a certain aspect of an object, such as configurational prey features by T5.2 neurons (Ewert 1997). The localization of an object in the *xyz* axis takes advantage of monocular neurons of visual maps, binocular tectal neurons, and tegmental neurons that compute visual map information with body segment orientation (Grobstein 1991; see Chapter 5). Together, the CEs of a CRS provide a **sensorimotor code**. The notion of coded commands stresses that firing of various types of CEs in certain combination (CRS) characterizes an object in space and selects the appropriate goal-directed MPG, for example

code {T4, T1.3, T3, T5.2} may say:

"a small object is moving in the visual field {T4}"

*and* "it moves in the frontal binocular field at a short distance {T1.3}"

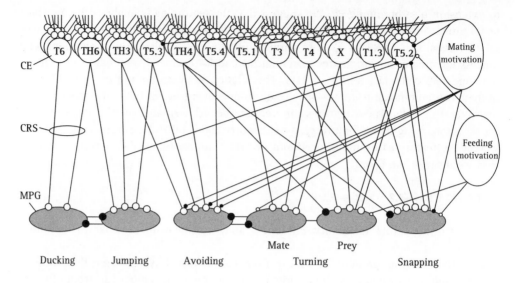

**Fig. 2.7** Command releasing systems as neuronal equivalents of releasing mechanisms in toads. Different neuron types in the toad's optic tectum, pretectal thalamus, and tegmentum are responsive to different aspects of moving visual stimuli: *ep* (T5.1), *ep/ea* (T5.2), *ea* (TH3, T5.3), *ep*ea* (T5.4), large object moving overhead (T6), small object moving in the binocular visual field at narrow distance (T1.3), small object moving anywhere in the visual field (T4), big object moving anywhere (TH4), small object approaching (T3), big object approaching (TH6), computation of object location and body segment orientation (hypothetical tegmental neurons X). CE, command element (set of neurons); CRS, command releasing system; MPG, motor pattern generator (neuronal circuit); open circles, excitatory influences; filled circles, inhibitory influences. (After Ewert 1997.)

*and* "it is approaching {T3}"

*and* "it has prey features {T5.2}" → *snap*

In such a multifunctional network CEs may be shared by different CRSs for different MPGs (Fig. 2.7). CRSs are connected to neural systems responsible for attention, learning, and motivation (Ewert et al. 2001).

## Perception in Primates: Dedicated, Modifiable, and Multifunctional Structures in Concert

As in other vertebrates, sensory information processing in primates proceeds in a parallel-distributed and partly interactive fashion. However, tremendous complexity also arises in cortical neuronal circuits with regard to plasticity, multisensory integration, and sensory substitution (Kaas 1991). Combining (e.g., binding of) features is a common task. As Singer (1995) put it, the cerebral cortex deals with the combinatorial problem of stimulus features in two basic ways: (i) analysis and representation of frequently occurring behaviorally relevant relations by groups of cells with fixed broadly tuned response properties and (ii) the dynamic association of these cells into functionally coherent assemblies involving coincidence circuits. There is no one single place for perception at the "top" of a sensory system. All processing levels contribute to the resulting picture. It appears that different neural systems are dedicated to the processing of certain features of entities and events, but that neural systems are not dedicated to the representation of certain perceptual categories (Damasio 1990).

In primate vision, Ungerleider and Mishkin (1982) showed that two neural processing streams are involved to answer the questions "what" and "where" respectively (see also Hubel & Livingstone 1987).

## Ventral visual processing stream answers the question "what"

The question "What kind of object?" is answered by the so-called ventral processing stream (Fig. 2.8). This stream originates in the small-celled system of the retina, is transmitted via the corresponding small-celled structures of the diencephalic lateral geniculate nucleus (LGN) to the related visual cortical areas V1, V2, V3v, and V4, and terminates in the inferior **temporal cortex** (ITC). In these brain structures, the visual features contrast, color, and shape are analyzed and combined differently. Layers II–IV of the striate visual cortical area V1 refine the retinal/geniculate feature analyses. For example, the orientation of contrast borders is analyzed in functional units of cell assemblies (Fig. 2.8, layers II and III), so-called orientation columns; adjacent columns detect different line orientations as a precondition for the analysis of letters and symbols in terms of orientations of lines (| / \ –) and the angles between combined lines (e.g., L V T K) (Hubel & Wiesel 1977).

Shape and color are analyzed separately in alternating layers of the extrastriate cortical area V2. Information on shape and color are combined in V4 thus allowing assignments, for example "yellow banana." Such associations depend on the connections of this area with the limbic system involved in experience. The ventral area V3v also feeds information on shape to V4, which in turn feeds to cortical association and integration fields of the ITC. In the ITC there are continuous maps for the analysis of different complex features. Some regions are involved in the analysis and recognition of gestures and postures suitable in social communication. Neurons of other ITC regions display various sensitivities for other *Gestalt* features such as faces or face components: eyes, or eyes–nose, or eyes–nose–mouth, etc. Furthermore, there are face-selective neurons (Perret & Rolls 1983; Rolls 1994; see also Chapter 5). Such neurons are also described in the temporal cortex of Dalesbred sheep (Kendrick 1994). Regarding the latter, different neuron types respond best to general face configurations, such as face outline and eyes; other types prefer the combination of any face with horns, others prefer the Dalesbred face configuration, and still others prefer faces of humans or dogs respectively. However, neither in monkeys nor in sheep is there evidence of a preference of a single neuron for the face of an individual. In other words, there is no evidence of a **grandmother**

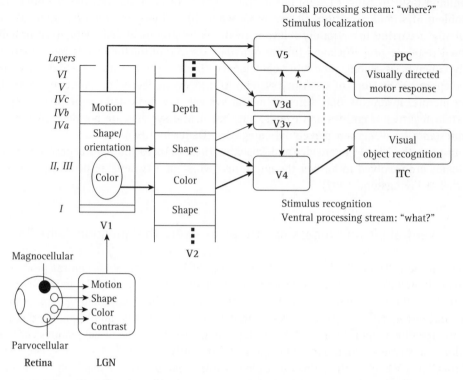

**Fig. 2.8** Neurophysiological steps in the visual analysis of objects in terms of shape, color, motion, and depth in the primate brain. The ventral and dorsal processing streams deal with stimulus recognition and localization respectively. Highly schematic diagram showing small-celled (parvocellular) and large-celled (magnocellular) systems of the retina and the lateral geniculate nucleus (LGN) respectively, and the corresponding cortical areas V1–V5. Layers I–VI refer to the striate visual cortex V1; in adjacent columns, for example, contrast borders of objects are detected whose orientations progressively deviate by about 10° visual angle. In extrastriate area V2 there is repetition of adjacent slices for the analysis of the object features color, shape, and depth. In V3, V4, and V5, features are combined such as shape and color and motion and depth. The inferior temporal cortex (ITC) and the posterior parietal cortex (PPC) are concerned with stimulus recognition and localization respectively. (Compiled from data in Ungerleider & Mishkin 1982; Hubel & Livingstone 1987; Jeannerod et al. 1995.)

neuron in humans or, of a comparable familiar individual, in monkeys or sheep (Barlow 1985). Therefore, an assembly of differently face-tuned neurons probably code for the recognition of an individual face (cf. also Cohen & Tong 2001).

## Dorsal visual processing stream answers the question "where"

The question "Where is the object?" is connected with the next question "How should it be responded to?" This requires analysis of object motion and depth. The analysis is performed by the so-called dorsal visual processing stream. This stream originates in the large-celled retina, is transmitted via the corresponding large-celled structures of the LGN to the related visual cortical areas V1, V2, V3d, and V5, and terminates in the posterior parietal cortex (PPC) (Fig. 2.8). Information on object motion and depth analyzed in V1 and V2 is combined in V5 with input from dorsal V3d, suitable for stereoscopic vision. The PPC contains neurons responsible for target-oriented reaching or grasping movements involving arm, hand, and fingers. Such neurons may fulfill integrating tasks and exert command-like functions regarding eye and grasping movements (Mountcastle et al. 1975). Motivation also plays an integral role in the activation of these neurons. If the monkey is satiated and a banana is placed in the field of visual fixation, there is no corresponding increase in the activity of visual fixation neurons; they just "ignore" the banana.

## Selective attention: what an individual does not like to see, it may not see

Animals and humans guide their conscious perception toward interesting parts of a scene and simultaneously suppress uninteresting parts (Motter 1994; Desimone & Duncan 1995; Barinaga 1997; Kastner et al. 1998). Let us pick an example: in a behavioral experiment monkeys were trained to guide their visual attention toward either a red or a green bar (cf. Barinaga 1997). In the neurophysiological experiment both stimuli, the red and the green bar, were located in the excitatory receptive field of a red-sensitive neuron in area V4. If the monkey was requested to focus on the red bar, the neuron fired. However, requested to focus on the green bar, the red-sensitive neuron was silent although nothing changed in the peripheral stimulus, i.e., the red bar was also present in the excitatory receptive field.

In humans, too, there are comparable ventral and dorsal neural processing streams for object recognition and localization, respectively. Studies applying brain imaging techniques such as **positron emission tomography** (PET), essentially a method for measuring regional blood flow in the brain, offer a look at the neural activity pattern in the entire visual areas. The cortical distributed activity depends on which feature the subject is attending to. If a person facing a colored moving object is asked to focus on the object's motion, an area corresponding to V5 is mainly activated. Paying attention to the color, an area corresponding to V4 is mainly activated. When shape is the focus, greatest activation is elsewhere along the "what" processing stream. In another task, photos of different human faces in frames were shown. When the person was asked whether the faces looked different, ITC was strongly activated; when this person was asked whether the faces were positioned symmetrically in the frame, activation shifted to PPC.

Whether the "what" and "where" visual processing streams are strictly segregated is disputed (Jeannerod et al. 1995). Critics suggest stepwise parallel distributed processing whereby at certain stages information from the parallel processing streams converges in order to be combined (e.g., connection from area V4 to V5; see Fig. 2.8). For example, patients with lesions in the "what" stream are still able to locate and grasp toward an object although it cannot be recognized. However, if the object has a particular shape that demands an adequate grasping pattern of the digits, the patient fails.

## Does visual imagination repeat processes involved in perception?

Looking for an object we have lost, we construct in our imagination an iconic **schema,** a search image. Evidence from PET in humans suggests that during the imagination of an object those visual cortical areas responsible for the previous analysis of that object are activated (Miyashita 1995; Kosslyn et al. 1999). During visual imagination of a particular object, the brain seems to reactivate the neural equivalent of the activity pattern protocol of the neurons that were active during visual perception of that object. Ishai and Sagi (1995) thus propose common mechanisms of visual perception and visual imagination. Therefore, humans with lesions in an area corresponding to V4 are unable to both identify and imagine colors. The ability to distinguish the neuronal activity pattern elicited during a sensory event from the "protocols" of previous sensory events is of critical importance. A lack of this differentiation may lead to hallucinations.

## Cortical maps of sensory space are plastic

Sensory space, like "motor space," is represented in the brain by topographic maps. Recall from the definition of "visual map" that the retina is mapped in different regions of the brain. From lesion experiments in fish and amphibians it is known that the map of the retina in the optic tectum can be either compressed or expanded depending on the available room in the tectum and on visual input provided by the retina. If half of the retina is destroyed, after cutting the optic nerve/tract, an enlarged map of the remaining retina will be established in the entire contralateral tectum, from the regenerating tract fibers. If half of the tectum is destroyed, after cutting the optic nerve/tract, a compressed map of the entire retina will be established in the rest of the tectum, from the regenerating tract fibers. This kind of plasticity is called **remodeling.**

The phenomenon that sensory maps may expand or shrink is consistent with functional remodeling in the cerebral cortex. Studies applying neuroimaging techniques to humans showed in the somatosensory cortex of string instrument players a significant expansion of the representation of the active digits of the left hand, except the less active thumb (Elbert et al. 1995). The expansion was stronger the earlier in life individuals started playing a string instrument. This shows that cutaneous representations of different parts of the body in the primary somatosensory cortex depend on tactual use by the individual. Obviously, sensory cortical regions expand or shrink depending on the available cortical space and the need for perceptual skills: underemployed regions are invaded by overemployed regions. In fact, functional neuroimaging studies of people blind from an early age showed that their visual cortex is activated by reading Braille or embossed Roman letters or by other tactile discrimination tasks. Evidence of this sensory substitution (cross-modal plasticity) was provided by a sophisticated experiment. Transient disruption of the function of visual cortical areas V1–V3 by means of the transcranial magnetic stimulation (TMS) technique induced errors in these tactual tasks and distorted tactile perception in blind subjects (Cohen et al. 1997). In control experiments, normal sighted subjects had no problems in comparable tactual tasks during TMS of their visual cortex which, of course, disrupted visual performance. Blindness from early age obviously causes the visual cortex to be recruited to a role in somatosensory processing, which may contribute to the superior tactile perceptual abilities of blind people.

Normal sighted subjects display cross-modal attention: a sudden touch on one hand can improve vision near that hand. In fact, it has been shown that tactile stimulation enhances activity in the human visual cortex (Macaluso et al. 2000).

## Same structure dealing with different perceptual tasks, same perceptual task implemented by different structures

How is cross-modal plasticity arranged? For example, sensory processing for touch and vision seems to be segregated up to their arrival in the primary somatosensory cortical area S1 and visual area V1, respectively. Early bimodal convergence occurs in cortical association areas. Cohen et al. (1997) suggest that connections between parietal cortical areas (cf. Fig. 2.8, PPC) and visual association cortical areas mediate the transfer of somatosensory information to the visual cortex in blind subjects.

Another question concerns the processing structure. Cortical structures have a "universal potential" in that they are capable of processing information from sensory modalities for which they were not originally designed. How can this be explained? First of all, wide regions of the cerebral cortex show a similar cytoarchitecture. Second, the number of connections between neurons is relatively high. Third, some connections mediate signal traffic, whereas other connections may be silent. The latter, if they are used, can probably be gated and rearranged functionally. This is called activity-dependent plasticity. Fourth, it is possible that neurons, depending on their activity, sprout new dendritic trees and axonal collaterals, thus providing new neuronal structures for processing of information and long-term storage (Kim et al. 2003; Pittenger & Kandel 2003). If the same structures deal with different perceptual tasks, one might expect that different structures may cope with the same or similar perceptual tasks. There are many examples showing that a perceptual principle can be applied by very different neural structures. For example, the principle of lateral inhibition, originally discovered by Hartiline and Ratliff (1957) in the compound eye of the horseshoe crab *Limulus polyphemus*, is also present in the vertebrate retina. Similarly, the *ep/ea* features-relating algorithm as the principle for prey selection in the common toad is also implemented in the different neuronal network of a predatory insect, the praying mantis *Sphodromantis lineola* (Prete 1992).

## SUMMARY AND CONCLUSIONS

The evidence I have reviewed shows that perceptual worlds in both animals and humans are related to the nature of their sensory systems. No matter what the world looks like, to orient oneself requires basic functions involving stimulus recognition and localization. Although humans at least can see their environment much like a photographic picture, during recognition or imagery of an object certain characteristic features and feature combinations play a decisive role. Animals abstract objects in terms of sign-stimuli and humans use sign-stimuli for various communicative purposes, such as advertisement. Interestingly, both animals and humans are sensitive to feature exaggerations. Both animals and humans apply principles of search image and stimulus-specific habituation for stimulus selection.

For most sensory modalities in both animals and humans there are sensory brain maps involving populations of neurons selectively tuned to different stimulus features or feature combinations. Certain assemblies of such neurons may yield a sensorimotor code suitable, for example, to select an appropriate motor pattern. Such common principles question the validity of the distinction between "lower" and "higher" organisms. Neuronal networks may be multipotent in that they display various degrees of plasticity. This is consistent with the idea that perceptions are dynamically determined by the characteristics of the sensory inputs in conjunction with the "openness" of the brain region receiving those inputs. The neurobiological phenomena of remodeling and cross-modal plasticity are consistent with, and justify, the artificial neuronal network approach. This shows that a similar structure (topology) of artificial neurons, depending on a training algorithm, can execute different functions. Artificial neuronal networks have broad applicability in neural engineering, ranging from face-detecting devices to perceptual robotics.

## FURTHER READING

*The Study of Instinct* by Tinbergen (1951) is a classic textbook of ethology, analyzing **releasing stimuli**, quantifying stimulus–response relationships, extracting principles, and providing concepts. It is especially impressive to read in view of developing (revised, redefined) concepts.

Manning and Dawkins (1998) offer the modern version of Tinbergen's book, covering aspects of behavior in terms of Tinbergen's four questions (see Chapter 1). Shettleworth (1998) provides an extensive quantitative description of the biology of behavior, emphasizing signaling and signal perception. Carew (2000) is among the best treatments of the neuronal fundamentals of animal behavior. Prete (2004) is a unique textbook because it tries to describe what the perceptual world of a given animal might be like within one or two integrated sensory domain(s). Such explanation entails integrated presentation of the behavioral, psychophysical, electrophysiological and neuroanatomical data collected on the animal in question.

# 3
# motivation

JERRY A. HOGAN

## INTRODUCTION: WHAT IS MOTIVATION?

The word "**motivate**" means "to cause to move," and I will use the concept of motivation to refer to the study of the immediate **causes** of behavior: those factors responsible for the initiation, maintenance, and termination of behavior. Thus, motivation is another word for Tinbergen's causal question (see Chapter 1). Causal factors for behavior include stimuli, hormones, and the intrinsic activity of the nervous system. How do these factors cause a female rat to behave maternally to her pups? Or a chicken to bathe in dust in the middle of the day? Or a male stickleback to stop responding sexually to receptive females? These are the types of questions asked in this chapter.

However, a major problem in the study of motivation has been, and remains, that different authors use the concept in different ways. Many of these differences can be more easily understood by noting some important conceptual distinctions (Hogan 1994). Distinctions between the causation and the structure of behavior are most relevant to the study of motivation.

Hogan (1988, 2001) has proposed perceptual, central, and motor mechanisms as the basic structural units of behavior. These entities are viewed as corresponding to structures within the central nervous system (CNS). They consist of an arrangement of **neurons** (not necessarily localized) that acts independently of other such mechanisms. Perceptual mechanisms analyze incoming sensory **information** and solve the problem of stimulus recognition. An example is the **releasing mechanism** discussed in Chapter 2. The motor mechanisms are responsible for coordinating the neural output to the muscles, which results in recognizable patterns of movement. The central mechanisms coordinate the perceptual and motor mechanisms, and provide the basis for an animal's mood or internal state. These units are called **behavior mechanisms** because their activation results in an event of behavioral interest: a particular perception, a specific motor pattern, or an identifiable internal state.

Behavior mechanisms can be connected with one another to form larger units called **behavior systems**, which correspond to the level of complexity indicated by feeding, sexual, and aggressive behavior (Baerends 1976; Hogan 1988, 2001). The organization of the connections among behavior mechanisms determines the nature of the behavior system. Thus, a behavior system can be considered a description of the structure of behavior. A pictorial representation of this concept is shown in Fig. 3.1. In this chapter I will examine the causal factors that activate a number of behavior systems, including hunger, sex, aggression, sleep, and exploration.

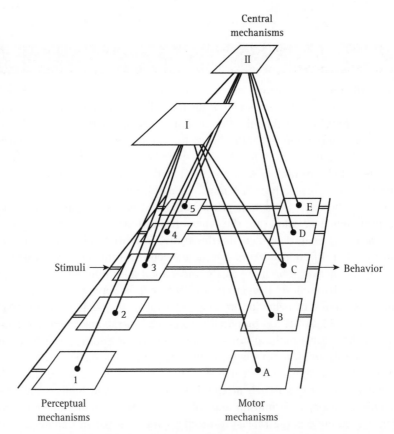

**Fig. 3.1** Conception of behavior systems. Stimuli from the external world are analyzed by perceptual mechanisms. Output from the perceptual mechanisms can be integrated by central mechanisms and/or channeled directly to motor mechanisms. The output of the motor mechanisms results in behavior. In this diagram, central mechanism I, perceptual mechanisms 1, 2, and 3, and motor mechanisms A, B, and C form one behavior system; central mechanism II, perceptual mechanisms 3, 4, and 5, and motor mechanisms C, D, and E form a second behavior system; 1-A, 2-B, and so on can also be considered less complex behavior systems. (From Hogan 1988.)

Causal factors not only motivate behavior but also change the structure of behavior; that is, they have developmental effects. The formation of associations and the effects of reinforcement (i.e., processes psychologists call learning) are developmental processes (see Chapters 6 & 7). Developmental processes have played an important role in many models of motivation, especially those proposed by psychologists (see Hogan 1998). These models are often concerned with the mechanisms mediating the rewarding and aversive properties of stimuli, and these models are mentioned briefly later in the chapter. With respect to the behavior system model shown in Fig. 3.1, motivation refers to the modulating effects causal factors have on the activation of the system, and development refers to the permanent effects causal factors have on the structure of the behavior mechanisms themselves and on the connections between the behavior mechanisms.

## Pervasive Problems in Motivation

In addition to problems concerning the definition of the concept of motivation, there have been three issues that have dominated discussions of motivation:

1 the relative role of internal versus external causal factors;
2 specific versus general effects of causal factors; and
3 central versus peripheral locus of action of causal factors.

I will consider each of these issues briefly.

### External versus internal causal factors

In general usage, the word "motivation" often refers to internal causes of behavior. We speak of an animal's search for food as motivated by hunger, but of chewing and swallowing as reflex actions to stimuli in the mouth. On close inspection, however, it turns out that a thoroughly sated animal will often spit out the same food it would have chewed if it were hungry; and hungry animals are clearly guided by environmental cues as they search for food. In fact, any behavior must be caused by some combination of both internal and external factors, and I will use the term "motivation" to refer to causal factors of both internal and external origin.

Many years ago, Lorenz (1950) proposed a motivational model of behavior that illustrates the interdependence of internal and external factors. This model is shown in Fig. 3.2. According to Lorenz, each behavior pattern is associated with a reservoir that can hold a certain amount of "energy." Whenever the behavior pattern occurs, energy is used up; but when the behavior pattern does not occur, energy can build up in the reservoir. The higher the level of energy, the more pressure it exerts on the valve. When the valve opens, as a result of external stimulation, energy is released and the behavior

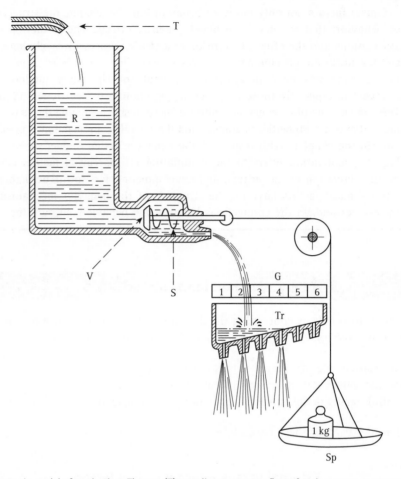

**Fig. 3.2** Lorenz's model of motivation. The tap (T) supplies a constant flow of endogenous energy to the reservoir (R). The value (V) represents the releasing mechanism, and the spring (S) the inhibitory functions of the higher coordinating mechanisms. The scale pan (Sp) represents the perceptual part of the releasing mechanism, and the weight applied corresponds to the impinging stimulation. When the valve is open, energy flows out into the trough (Tr), which coordinates the pattern of muscle contractions. The intensity of the response can be read on the gauge (G). (From Lorenz 1950.)

occurs. Thus, in this model, a particular behavior pattern cannot occur without at least some internal causal factors as well as some external ones. Further, the model makes it clear that internal and external factors can substitute for each other in determining the intensity of a behavior pattern: a strong stimulus can compensate for weak internal factors and vice versa. It should be noted that there have been many criticisms of Lorenz's concept of energy (Hinde 1960; see also Hogan 1997), and I will return to this issue.

The fact that both internal and external factors are essential for any behavior to occur does not imply, of course, that one cannot study the effects of internal and external factors separately. The effects of varying various internal factors can be determined if the external stimulus is kept relatively constant, as can the effects of various external factors be determined if the internal state of the animal is held constant. A classic example of such a study is the one by Baerends et al. (1955) on the courtship behavior of the male guppy (*Lebistes reticulatus*). Courtship by the male comprises a number of behavior patterns, including posturing in front of the female, a special sigmoid posture, and copulation attempts. These authors were able to derive a scale of internal motivation using the relation of marking patterns on the body of the male to the number of copulation attempts, and external stimulation was considered to be proportional to the size of a female. Figure 3.3 shows the results of an experiment in which females of different sizes were presented to males at different levels of internal motivation. The points plotted on the graph represent the relationship between the measures of internal and external stimulation at which particular patterns of behavior were observed. If it is assumed that the total motivation necessary for a specific behavior pattern to occur is always the same, the patterns "posturing," "sigmoid intention," and "sigmoid" can be seen to represent increasing values of courtship strength. The lines connecting these points of equal motivation have been called **motivational isoclines** by McFarland and Houston (1981).

## Specific versus general effects of causal factors

A second pervasive problem in motivation is whether causal factors have specific or general effects. Does a hungry dog merely eat its food more quickly and accept less preferred foods more readily, or does it also attack a stranger more fiercely and copulate more vigorously? This issue has been hotly debated, and there is much evidence to support either point of view. Common sense suggests that some causal factors are likely to have broad effects whereas others will have only limited effects. A man who is worried about difficulties at work may show exaggerated or even inappropriate responses in feeding, aggressive, and sexual situations. On the other hand, the same man will probably only drink an extra glass of water if he has lost more body fluid than usual on a warm dry day.

In general, any particular causal factor will most likely have both specific and general effects. Which effects are more important will depend on the question of interest. For example, specific effects of causal factors are implied in Lorenz's model of motivation. The model posits that the fluid in the reservoir is specific to the particular behavior pattern with which it is associated: Lorenz spoke about **action-specific energy**. On the other hand, the **circadian** clock will be seen to have an important influence on many behavior systems (see also Chapter 4). I will examine specific and general effects of causal factors in some detail in the section on displacement activities.

## Central versus peripheral locus of action

The third pervasive problem in motivation concerns the locus of action of causal factors. Do causal factors operate within the CNS or at a more peripheral level? Once again,

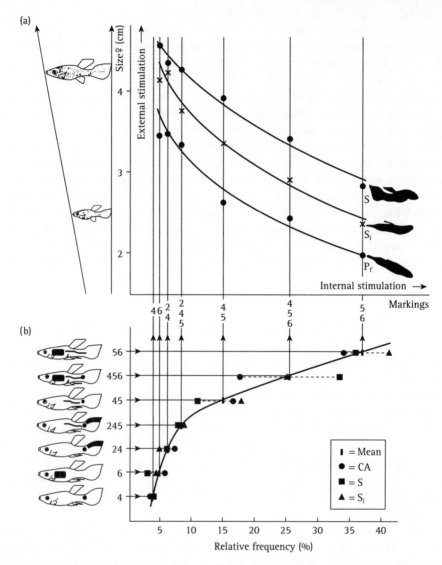

**Fig. 3.3** Results of an experiment on guppy courtship. (a) Relationship between the intensity of the external stimulation, the intensity of the internal stimulation, and the kind and degree of development of the resulting activity. (b) "Calibration curve" for determining the place of the different marking patterns on the abscissa of (a). CA, copulation attempt; S, sigmoid posture; $S_i$, sigmoid intention; $P_f$, posturing in front of the female. (From Baerends et al. 1955.)

common sense suggests that they must act in both places; nonetheless, this has also been a controversial issue.

Historically, the controversy arose as a reaction by the early behaviorist school in psychology (see Chapter 1) to the views of the introspectionists, who thought one could understand behavior by reflecting on one's own experiences. The behaviorists were skeptical of internal causes that could not be investigated directly, and they attempted to explain as much behavior as possible in terms of stimuli and responses that could be measured physically. However, as scientists have discovered more about how the brain works, it has become possible to measure and manipulate events that occur within the CNS, so one major objection to the postulation of central factors has been removed. Nonetheless, some researchers continue to emphasize central or peripheral factors, and some examples are presented in later sections.

## Motivational Factors

### Stimuli

Stimuli can control behavior in many ways: they can release, direct, inhibit, and prime behavior. Chapter 2 discussed many examples of stimuli that release and direct various behavior patterns. Some stimuli can have exactly the opposite effect: rather than facilitate behavior, they inhibit it. A good example is provided by the nest-building behavior of many species of birds. Birds typically build their nests using specific behavior patterns. The stimuli that release and direct their behavior have been studied in several cases, and conform to the general principles already discussed. However, at a certain point, the birds stop building and no longer react to the twigs, lichens, or feathers with which they construct their nest. There are numerous possible reasons why they stop, but one reason is that the stimuli provided by the completed nest inhibit further nest building. This can be seen when a bird takes over a complete nest from the previous season and shows very little nest-building behavior. Other birds, in the same internal state, that have not found an old nest show a great deal of nest-building behavior (Thorpe 1956).

Another example of the inhibitory effects of stimuli is seen in the courtship behavior of the stickleback (*Gasterosteus aculeatus*), a small fish (Fig. 3.4). Male sticklebacks set up territories in small streams early in the spring, build a nest of bits of plant material, and court any females that may pass through their territory. Courtship includes a **zigzag dance** by the male, appropriate posturing by the female, leading to and showing of the nest by the male, following and entering the nest by the female, and finally laying eggs and fertilization. The female swims away and the male then courts another female. The male could continue courting egg-laden females for many days, but usually he does not. Experiments in which eggs were removed from or added to the nest have shown that visual stimuli from the eggs inhibit sexual activity: if eggs are removed from the nest, the male will continue courting females, but if eggs are added he will cease courting, regardless of the number of eggs he has fertilized (Sevenster-Bol 1962).

Stimuli not only control behavior by their presence but in many cases continue to affect behavior even after they have physically disappeared. When a stimulus has arousing effects on behavior that outlast its presence, **priming** is said to occur. Aggressive behavior in the male Siamese fighting fish (*Betta splendens*) provides a good example (Hogan & Bols 1980). This fish shows vigorous aggressive **display** and fighting toward

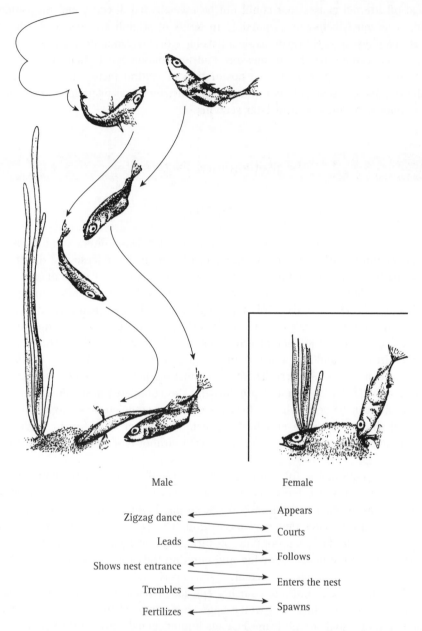

**Fig. 3.4** Courtship and mating behavior of the three-spined stickleback. The male is on the left and the female, with a swollen belly, is on the right. A typical courtship sequence is indicated below the diagram. (From Tinbergen 1951.)

other males of its species (including its own mirror image). If a fish is allowed to fight with its mirror image for a few seconds and the mirror is then removed, it is very likely to attack a thermometer introduced into the aquarium. If the thermometer had been introduced before the mirror was presented, the fish very likely would have ignored it. Thus, the sight of a conspecific not only releases aggressive behavior but must also change the internal state of the fish for some time after the conspecific disappears. We can say that the stimulus primes the mechanism that coordinates aggressive behavior or, more simply, that it primes aggression. Similar priming effects have been demonstrated with food and water in rats and hamsters, and with brain stimulation in several species (see Hogan & Roper 1978). A good host will prime a guest's hunger by offering a tasty "appetizer," though eating too many appetizers will have just the opposite effect!

These examples of priming all occur during the time span of a few minutes. Some stimuli prime behavior over a much longer period, and hormonal mechanisms are often involved. Stimuli from the eggs of the stickleback inhibit sexual behavior, as we have just seen, but they also prime parental behavior. Male sticklebacks fan the eggs in their nest by moving their fins in a characteristic manner, which directs a current of water into the nest and serves to remove debris and provide oxygen to the developing embryos. The amount of fanning increases over the 7 days it takes for the eggs to hatch. It has been shown that $CO_2$, which is produced by the eggs, is one of the stimuli releasing fanning, and the amount of $CO_2$ produced is greater from older eggs. Thus, one might expect that the increased fanning is a direct effect of $CO_2$ concentration. This supposition was tested in an experiment by van Iersel (1953). He replaced the old eggs on day 4 with newly laid eggs from another nest. There was a slight drop in fanning with the new eggs, but fanning remained much higher than the original day-1 level. Further, the peak of fanning activity was reached the day the original eggs would have hatched. This means that the stimuli from the eggs must prime a coordinating mechanism, and that the state of the coordinating mechanism is no longer completely dependent on stimulation from the eggs after 3 or 4 days.

A similar example is provided by the development of ovulation in doves. A female ring dove (*Streptopelia risoria*) will normally lay an egg if she is paired with an acceptable male for about 7 days. If the male is removed after 2 or 3 days, the developing egg regresses and is not laid. However, if the male is allowed to remain with the female for 5 days before he is removed, the majority of females will lay an egg 2 days later. Experiments by Lehrman (1965) and his colleagues demonstrated that it is the stimuli from the courting male that prime the mechanism responsible for ovulation.

## Hormones and other substances

Hormones are substances that are released into the bloodstream and have various effects on distant target organs in other parts of the body including the brain. In this chapter I will focus on effects that are more or less direct causal factors for behavior. As we shall see, the effect of hormones on behavior is one of the areas of motivation in which the problem of central versus peripheral locus of action has been prominent.

The effects of castration on male sexual behavior have been known since ancient times, but the discovery of the hormones that mediate these effects has been much more recent. Early experiments by Beach (1948) showed that castrated male rats (*Rattus norvegicus*), which had lost all signs of sexual responsiveness, could be returned to a state of sexual vigor by injection of the hormone testosterone. Similar experiments on female rats that had had their ovaries removed showed a somewhat more complicated relationship between female sexual receptivity and the hormones estrogen and progesterone. Since these early experiments, it has been shown that testosterone, estrogen, and progesterone (or chemically related compounds) have an important influence on sexual behavior in most species that have been investigated, from fish to birds and mammals (see Nelson 1999).

The mechanisms by which hormones influence behavior have turned out to be more complex and diverse than early investigators had hoped (Lashley 1938; Hinde 1970, chapter 10; Nelson 1999). One reason for this complexity is that a particular hormone can have indirect effects on behavior by affecting peripheral structures in the body as well as direct effects on the CNS. For example, testosterone affects the sensitivity of the penis in the male rat, which in turn affects the pattern of copulatory behavior. The effects of the hormone prolactin on the parental feeding behavior of the ring dove provide another example. Prolactin is responsible for the production of crop "milk," sloughed-off cells from the lining of the crop that are regurgitated to feed young squabs. Lehrman (1955) hypothesized that sensory stimuli from the enlarged crop might induce the parent dove to approach the squab and regurgitate. His experiments showed that local anesthesia of the crop region, which removes the sensory input, reduced the probability that the parents will feed their young. More recent experiments have confirmed that prolactin has both peripheral and central effects on the dove's parental behavior (Buntin 1996).

In addition to hormones, two other classes of chemicals are known to be important causal factors for behavior: **neurotransmitters**, which are released into the synapse, and psychoactive drugs, which are thought to exert their behavioral effects by altering neurotransmitter functioning in the brain (see Chapter 5). The neurotransmitter dopamine, for example, plays an important role in mediating the rewarding and aversive properties of stimuli (see Nader et al. 1997). In general, chemical factors influence all the behavior systems that have been studied, and particular chemicals often have analogous effects on behavior in different species. As we shall see, secretion of many of these chemicals is often under the control of external stimuli, and many of the priming effects, such as those discussed in the previous section, are mediated by biochemical factors.

## Intrinsic neural factors

Stimuli can cause neurons to fire and chemicals can modulate the rate at which neurons fire, but neurons can also fire spontaneously, i.e., without any apparent external cause. This does not mean that a neuron is behaving unlawfully or that some supernatural force must be invoked. Spontaneous activity of a neuron merely indicates that the causes of behavior are intrinsic or **endogenous**.

Behavior can also occur spontaneously, i.e., without any apparent external cause. This is not surprising because neural firing causes behavior, and neurons fire spontaneously. The spontaneous firing of an isolated neuron was demonstrated in 1930 by E.D. Adrian, but it is only much more recently that many students of animal behavior have felt comfortable with the idea of intrinsic causes of behavior. There is a long history of behavioral scientists fighting against mentalistic concepts such as **consciousness** or intentions as causes of behavior. However, it has gradually become clear that intrinsic causes can be studied scientifically, and that any explanation of behavior that only takes the effects of external stimuli into account will be incomplete.

One of the earliest attempts to incorporate intrinsic causes into the scientific study of behavior was made by Skinner (1938). His concept of the **operant** (see also Chapter 7) is a unit of behavior that occurs originally due to unspecified, intrinsic causes. It is only as a result of **conditioning** that the operant comes to be controlled by specific stimuli. The motivational model of Lorenz (1937b) was another attempt (see Fig. 3.2). Lorenz postulated that motivational energy builds up as a function of time. His model predicts that the probability that a particular behavior pattern will occur increases with the time since its last occurrence. One might imagine that as the pressure in the reservoir increases, it becomes more and more difficult to prevent the energy from escaping through the valve. In fact, behavior does sometimes occur in the absence of any apparent external stimulus. Such behavior has been called **vacuum activity**. Lorenz describes the behavior of a captive starling that performed vacuum insect hunting. This bird would repeatedly watch, catch, kill, and swallow an imaginary insect.

Lorenz's model implies a continuously active nervous system kept in check by various kinds of inhibition. The most systematic support for this aspect of the model is provided by the behavior of insects. A particularly striking example concerns the copulatory behavior of the male praying mantis *Mantis religiosa*. Mantids are solitary insects that sit motionless most of the time waiting in ambush for passing insects. Movement of an object at the correct distance and up to the mantis's own size releases a rapid strike. Any insect caught will be eaten, even if it is a member of the same species. This cannibalistic behavior might be expected to interfere with successful sex, because the male mantis must necessarily approach the female if copulation is to occur. Sometimes a female apparently fails to detect an approaching male and he is able to mount and copulate without mishap, but very often the male is caught and the female then begins to eat him. Now an amazing thing happens. While the female is devouring the male's head, the rest of his body manages to move round and mount the female, and successful copulation occurs.

In a series of behavioral and neurophysiological experiments, Roeder (1967) showed that surgical decapitation of a male, even before sexual maturity, releases intense sexual behavior patterns. He was then able to demonstrate that a particular part of the mantis's brain, the subesophageal ganglion, normally sends inhibitory impulses to the neurons responsible for sexual behavior. By surgically isolating these neurons from all neural input, he showed that the neural activity responsible for sexual activity is truly endogenous. These experiments, and many others, point out the importance of intrinsic factors in the motivation of behavior, and support the type of model proposed by Lorenz. Of course, these results do not mean that all behavior is primarily controlled by endogenous neural activity. We have already seen that external factors can prime internal motivational states, as can chemical factors. All these causal factors are integrated by the various behavior systems possessed by an animal. A general model of motivation incorporating these factors is discussed at the end of this chapter.

## Some Specific Behavior Systems

### Hunger

The hunger system comprises perceptual mechanisms for recognizing food, a central mechanism for integrating causal factors for eating (the hunger mechanism), and coordinating and motor mechanisms for locating and ingesting food. A diagram of the hunger system of a young chick is shown in Fig. 3.5.

The motor mechanisms used to locate, catch, and ingest food vary greatly among species, as do the causal factors controlling them. This is not the place to review all these differences, but it is an interesting fact about the hunger system of young chicks, and of many other young animals including rats and humans, that ingestion is not

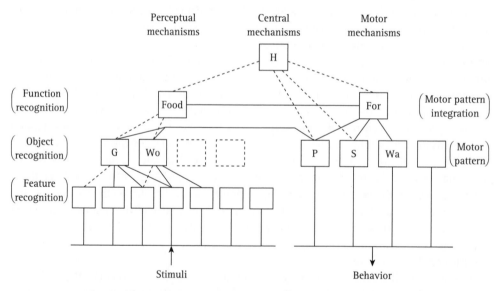

**Fig. 3.5** The hunger system of a young chick. Boxes represent putative cognitive (neural) mechanisms. Perceptual mechanisms include various feature recognition mechanisms (such as of color, shape, size, and movement), object recognition mechanisms (such as of grain-like objects G, worm-like objects Wo, and possibly others), and a function recognition mechanism (Food). Motor mechanisms include those underlying specific behavior patterns, such as pecking (P), ground scratching (S), walking (Wa) and possibly others, and an integrative motor mechanism that could be called foraging (For). There is also a central hunger mechanism (H). Solid lines indicate mechanisms and connections among them that develop prefunctionally; dashed lines indicate mechanisms and connections that develop as the result of specific functional experience (see Chapter 6). (From Hogan 1988.)

controlled by the hunger mechanism. Rather, the motor mechanisms (e.g., pecking or sucking) are relatively independent units, and their activation depends primarily on factors specific to each behavior pattern. For example, the factors that control pecking in young chicks during the first 2 days after hatching include the specific releasing characteristics of particular objects (see Chapter 2), the novelty of the objects (stimulus change), and by how much pecking the chick has recently engaged in (pecking drive). Nutritional state (hunger mechanism) does not affect pecking until day 3 of life, and then only when the chick has had certain kinds of experience (Hogan 1971, 1984; see also Chapter 6). A similar situation is seen in the control of suckling in rat pups, in which nipple search, nipple attachment, and amount of sucking are not affected by food deprivation until the pups are about 2 weeks of age (Hall & Williams 1983). It should be noted that even after nutritional state begins to control ingestion, factors specific to the motor mechanisms continue to have an important influence on their occurrence. This is especially true of the prey-catching motor patterns of many carnivore species (Polsky 1975; Baerends-van Roon & Baerends 1979).

The central hunger mechanism and its control have been studied in great detail in a number of species, especially the laboratory rat. In the rat, the central mechanism comprises several nuclei in the hypothalamus, including the ventromedial, lateral, and paraventricular. Cells in these nuclei are sensitive to a variety of chemicals in the blood, as well as to specific neurotransmitters. Activation of these nuclei can lead to increased or decreased food intake, as well as to intake of particular types of food. Nelson (1999) provides a good introduction to the complex workings of these chemicals on the feeding system. Signals from the circadian **pacemaker** (see Chapter 4) also influence activation of these nuclei, which is why rats and other **nocturnal** animals eat almost exclusively at night, whereas chicks and other **diurnal** animals eat primarily during the day.

A fundamental problem for young animals of most species is learning what foods they should eat. In other words, various kinds of experience are necessary for their food recognition mechanisms to develop. In many species, parental instruction of one kind or another provides the experience, though in most cases young animals are also able to fend for themselves (see Barker et al. 1977). Chapter 6 provides examples of how experience affects development of various perceptual mechanisms. Once the food recognition mechanisms have developed, stimuli from acceptable food items can release and prime feeding behavior, as we have seen above. Because developmental factors are so important in determining an animal's behavior with respect to food (and water), many psychologists have incorporated learning variables into their theories of motivation (see Hogan 1998).

## Parenting

Parental behavior refers to behavior patterns a parent uses to approach and care for its young, although the same behavior is sometimes shown to young that are not its own, or even to young of other species. In some species, parental behavior is shown exclusively by either the male or female parent, whereas in other species both parents share parental duties. Many species have no parental behavior at all. Parental behavior, of course, is controlled by both internal and external causal factors, and one important internal causal factor is often the hormone prolactin. A few examples illustrate some of these points.

We have already seen that, in sticklebacks, parental behavior is shown exclusively by the male. In other fish species, both parents care for the young. A well-studied example is the behavior of the cichlid fish *Symphysodon* spp. (discus fishes). In these species, eggs are laid and fertilized on an appropriate substrate, and both parents guard and fan the eggs. After the eggs hatch, the young feed on mucous cells that have developed on the bodies of the parents. Both the fanning behavior and the production of mucous cells are controlled by prolactin, which also inhibits aggressive behavior. The effect of prolactin on mucous cell production seems to be **homologous** with the production of crop milk in doves, as mentioned above, and with milk production in mammals (Blüm & Fiedler 1965).

Parental behavior in ring doves also illustrates the important role played by the circadian clock, as well as by other timing mechanisms. Both parents share in the building of the nest and in the incubation, brooding, and feeding of their young. However, doves partition their time on the nest, with the male incubating and brooding in the middle of the day, and the female caring for the young the rest of the time. Experiments have shown that the female's tendency to sit on the nest varies in a circadian manner, with the lowest level during the middle of the day. On the other hand, the male's tendency to sit on the nest seems to build up with the time he spends off the nest, and declines as a function of time sitting. The interaction of these two timing mechanisms results in the pattern of nest attendance typical of the species (Silver 1990).

In fowl, parental behavior is the exclusive task of the female. The hen sits on her eggs for more than 23 h a day for about 3 weeks until the chicks hatch. If the eggs are removed from the hen, she very soon stops sitting. On the other hand, as long as the eggs are present, her devotion to the nest is so strong that she will lose more than 15% of her body weight during the period of incubation even though plenty of food is at hand (Sherry et al. 1980). Once the chicks have hatched, the mother hen leads them to food and water, provides warmth by brooding them, and defends them from predators. A person who approaches a broody hen with chicks may be attacked vigorously, even though she would avoid the same person if she were not broody. In fact, a hen that is not broody may very well attack and kill the same young chick that she would just as strongly defend if she were broody. It has been known for some time that prolactin is an important determinant of incubation behavior in fowl. Recent experiments have shown that tactile stimuli from the newly hatched chicks cause a reduction in prolactin and an increase in luteinizing hormone, which is responsible for the change from incubation to parental behavior (Richard-Yris et al. 1998).

In rats, parental behavior is exclusively maternal behavior. Prior to the birth, the mother-to-be builds a nest. After the birth, the mother licks the pups, adopts a nursing or crouch posture over the pups that allows them to attach to her teats and suckle, and retrieves them if they stray out of the nest. A female that has gone through a normal pregnancy and is presented with a young pup will show this whole set of maternal behaviors whether the pup is her own or not. On the other hand, if the same pup is presented to a virgin female, the female will ignore, avoid, or possibly even attack and eat the pup. The difference between the two females is in their internal state: one is "maternal" and the other is not. The maternal state is determined in large part by particular levels of the hormones estrogen, progesterone, and prolactin. It is an interesting fact that a virgin female continuously exposed to a litter of young pups will usually become maternal after about 8 days. She will then show all the same behaviors – nest building, licking, crouching, and retrieving – as a mother rat (except for lactation). This is actually another example of priming. An important difference between virgin and mother rats is that mother rats find the odor of pups attractive, whereas virgin females do not. Exposure to young pups causes hormonal changes in the virgin female that result in changes in her odor preferences (Fleming & Blass 1994).

Hormonal state is also known to influence maternal responsiveness in human mothers, but experimental evidence is sparse because it is not permissible, ethically, to manipulate hormone levels in people for experimental purposes. Nonetheless, it is possible to measure hormone levels in pregnant women and new mothers and to ask women about their feelings toward babies. Several studies of this kind have been carried out. The results indicate that although hormones may facilitate a mother's responsiveness to her infant shortly after birth, hormones are neither necessary nor sufficient for maternal responsiveness. A mother's attitudes and prior experience with infants seem to be more important determinants (Fleming et al. 1997).

## Aggression

The word "aggressive" is often used to refer to any behavior that includes attack patterns, such as interactions between predator and prey, or defense of self or young. Here I will restrict its meaning to attack patterns of the sort directed to members of the same species (cf. Lorenz 1966). The aggression system is the behavior system responsible for producing these patterns. Most species possess an aggression system, and much research has been done investigating the causal factors that activate it. An important issue in many of these studies has been the relative role of external and internal causal factors: are animals lured or driven to fight? Experiments on Siamese fighting fish give some insight into this issue (Hogan & Bols 1980).

As we have already seen, a male fighting fish reacts to the visual stimulus of another male or its own reflection with vigorous aggressive behavior. In this case, an external causal factor can be said to lure the fish into fighting. However, a fighting fish will also learn to swim through a passageway at the end of which it finds a goal compartment with a mirror or another male. This fish will not swim through the passageway if the goal compartment is empty; it will choose a goal compartment with a mirror rather than one that is empty; and, under some conditions, it will even choose a goal compartment with a mirror rather than one with food. Further, a fish whose aggression has been primed just prior to testing will swim faster to the mirror than a fish that has not been primed. These results suggest that the fish is being driven to search for a fight in much the same way as a hungry animal is driven to search for food.

However, there is an important difference between the drives to fight and to eat. When an animal fights until it is exhausted, the tendency to fight will recover to a certain moderate level after a few days, but then it remains fairly constant or may even decline. When an animal eats until it is satiated, the tendency to eat also recovers after a few hours or days; however, if no food is eaten, hunger continues to increase to very high levels. The only way to increase aggression to very high levels is by priming; deprivation, by itself, is not sufficient. In terms of the Lorenzian motivational model, there is very little evidence that the reservoir can be filled endogenously.

Although Lorenz made the assumption that endogenous energy for each fixed action pattern is produced continuously, this assumption is not a necessary feature of an energy model. For example, Heiligenberg (1974) used the concept of "behavioral state of readiness" to model attack behavior in a cichlid fish. In Heiligenberg's model there is no endogenous production of energy at all; all the energy for attacking is produced by the perception of specific stimuli (in this case, a dummy of a conspecific male). Perception of these stimuli results in a short-term increase in energy (readiness) that lasts for a few seconds, but also a much smaller long-term increase in energy that lasts for several days. Continual presentation of appropriate stimuli results in a buildup of energy to high levels. In this example, the view of a conspecific is a stimulus that primes aggression. This model has many of the features of Lorenz's model, but it is external rather than internal factors that affect the level of aggressive motivation. It seems likely that similar considerations apply to the aggression system in most species.

## Sex

Sexual behavior is sometimes defined functionally as behavior leading to successful reproduction. The sex behavior system does include behavior patterns that are generally necessary for reproduction, but the organization of the system must be defined independently of reproduction. As with all other behavior systems, the sex system comprises a number of perceptual mechanisms that recognize a potential mate, a central mechanism that integrates information from the perceptual units and from other internal factors, and motor mechanisms that coordinate the performance of sexual activities. As we shall see later, behavior patterns belonging to nonsexual behavior systems are also necessary for successful reproduction in many species.

As with parenting, the sex system is almost always different in the male and the female of the species: different stimuli activate the system, different hormones are important internal causal factors, and different behavior patterns are expressed. A general review of the literature on sexual motivation is impossible here, and I will look at only one specific example.

Sexual behavior in a male rat consists of a number of ejaculatory series. In each series, the male approaches and mounts a receptive female. Mount bouts typically last a few seconds during which the male thrusts his penis rapidly and repeatedly, and may briefly insert his penis into the female's vagina. Mount bouts are followed by a period of about 1 min in which the male engages in genital grooming. After about eight mount bouts, the male ejaculates. A postejaculatory interval of about 5 min follows, in which the male makes a specific **ultrasonic** vocalization. A new series then begins. In later series, ejaculation generally occurs after fewer mount bouts. A normal male commonly has six to ten ejaculations before sexual behavior ceases; he is then unlikely to resume sexual behavior for several days. This pattern of copulation has been shown to coincide with the requirements of the female for maximizing the chance of pregnancy (see Sachs & Barfield 1976 for review).

Analysis of the causal factors responsible for this behavior led early investigators to propose that there are two major central mechanisms in the male sex system: a sexual arousal mechanism (SAM), and an intromission and ejaculatory mechanism (IEM). Beach (1956, p. 20) stated that:

> The main function of the SAM is to increase the male's sexual excitement to such a pitch that the copulatory threshold is attained. Crossing the copulatory threshold results in mounting and intromission.... The initial intromission and those that follow provide a new source of sensory impulses which serve to modify further the internal state of the animal and eventually to bring the male to the ejaculatory threshold.

The causal factors that activate the SAM are primarily external stimuli provided by a receptive female, while the factors that activate the IEM are stimuli arising from the performance of sexual behavior.

More recent studies have elaborated on this model, and Toates and O'Rourke have proposed a computer model that incorporates these findings and accounts quite well with observed behavior (see Toates 1983). An analysis of sexual behavior that includes both an SAM and an IEM can be applied to most male mammals, including humans. It should be noted that this analysis suggests that sex and aggression are very similar in that both systems are primarily aroused by external stimuli, and the highest levels of arousal can only be reached while the animal is engaged in the respective behaviors. Further, it is also true for both systems that the external stimuli are only arousing when the animal has an appropriate internal hormonal state (see Nelson 1999).

## Self-maintenance

Most animals possess behavior patterns that can be used for cleaning themselves or for keeping their muscles, skin, or feathers in good condition. These patterns range from simply stretching or rubbing up against some object to complex integrated sequences of behavior used for grooming in many species. One such sequence that has been studied in great detail is the dustbathing behavior of fowl, and these studies have found that this behavior illustrates a number of general motivational principles.

The dustbathing behavior of fowl consists of a sequence of coordinated movements of the wings, feet, head, and body of the bird that serve to spread dust through the feathers. The sequence of behaviors in a dustbathing bout begins with the bird pecking and raking the substrate with its bill and scratching with its feet. These movements continue as the bird squats down and comes into a sitting position. From time to time, the bird tosses the dusty substrate into its feathers with vertical movements of its wings and also rubs its head in the substrate. It then rolls on its side and rubs the dust thoroughly through its feathers. These sequences of movements may be repeated several

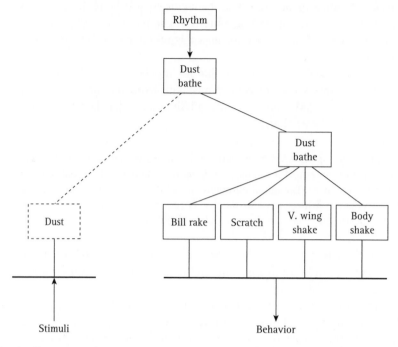

**Fig. 3.6** Dustbathing system of a young chick. See Fig. 3.5 caption for explanation. (Adapted from Vestergaard et al. 1990.)

times. Finally, the bird stands up, shakes its body vigorously, which releases the dust, and then switches to other behavior. In adult fowl, bouts of dustbathing last about half an hour. Dustbathing serves to remove excess lipids from the feathers and to maintain the feathers in good condition.

The dustbathing behavior system is shown in Fig. 3.6. A complete motivation analysis of dustbathing would investigate the properties of the stimuli that activate the dust recognition mechanism as well as the factors that control the central mechanism. Some progress has been made in analyzing the stimuli important for dust recognition, as well as the role played by light, heat, and the sight of other birds dustbathing (Petherick et al. 1995; Duncan et al. 1998), but I will concentrate here on factors intrinsic to the central mechanism and on the role of the circadian clock.

Vestergaard (1982) gave adult fowl limited access to dust and found that the latency to dustbathe was inversely related, and duration of bouts directly related, to the length of dust deprivation. Similar deprivation experiments on young chicks led to similar results. One way to explain these results is to postulate the buildup of endogenous motivation during the period of deprivation. Most authors, however, have tried to find an explanation in terms of changes in the external stimulus situation (see Hogan 1997). For example, the density or condition of lipids in the feathers could regulate the amount of dustbathing. It is also possible that there is a buildup of ectoparasites or other changes in skin condition during deprivation. These hypotheses were tested in experiments by several different investigators, none of which were able to provide convincing evidence supporting the view that increased dustbathing was primarily due to peripheral factors.

Perhaps the clearest evidence demonstrating the important role of endogenous motivation comes from some experiments using genetically featherless chicks (Vestergaard et al. 1999). These chicks dustbathe in the normal way and with normal **frequency** even though they have no feathers to clean. In the experiments, chicks were deprived of the opportunity to dustbathe for 1, 2, or 4 days, and then allowed access to dust for 1 h. Prior to access, the experimenters gently cleaned the chicks with potato flour to ensure that their skin condition was similar at all deprivation lengths. The results were essentially the same as the results from normal feathered chicks: the longer the period of deprivation, the more a chick dustbathed. Two-week-old chicks dustbathed for about 15 min after 1 day of deprivation, for about 20 min after 2 days of deprivation, and for about 30 min after 4 days of deprivation.

These results provide one of the best examples of a Lorenzian endogenous process governing behavior. Nonetheless, the occurrence of dustbathing is also influenced by many other factors. For example, Vestergaard (1982) found that most dustbathing occurred in the middle of the day, and he suggested an influence of circadian **rhythms**. More recent results demonstrate conclusively that a circadian clock is indeed a causal factor for dustbathing (J.A. Hogan, unpublished results). How circadian clocks work is discussed in detail in Chapter 4, and a behavioral model incorporating a circadian clock is presented in the next section.

## Sleep

Sleep is ubiquitous among species, but the form it takes varies widely. Some species have well-defined bouts of sleep at specific times during the day or night, whereas others sleep irregularly. Some species sleep for many hours a day, whereas others sleep only briefly. Still other species sleep with only one half of the brain at a time (see Webb 1998 for review). Much of the variation in sleep patterns can be correlated with variation in the ecological requirements of a species, but we are concerned here with the causes of sleep. We will also restrict our discussion to human sleep because most research has concentrated on this species.

Although sleep is a biological necessity, the actual bodily need state for sleep is not understood. Unlike hunger or thirst, there seems to be no specific depletion or accretion of any substance that underlies the drive. For example, Siamese twins who share a common blood circulation are quite capable of independent sleeping and waking states. Nonetheless, the occurrence of sleep is highly predictable if one considers the length of time a person has been awake or asleep, and the time of day.

Borbély (1982) originally proposed a two-factor model of the timing of sleep, and Daan et al. (1984) produced a quantitative version of this model. The first factor is considered to be a process that increases during wakefulness and decreases during sleep. Thus, the longer one goes without sleep, the more sleepy one becomes. The physiological basis for this factor is still unknown. The second factor is the sleep threshold. One puzzling aspect about sleep has always been that there are often occasions when one

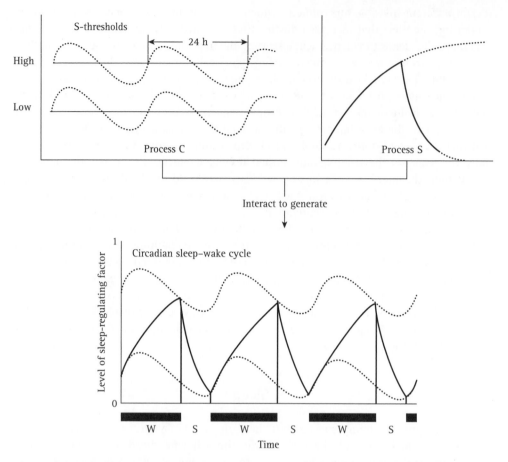

**Fig. 3.7** Model of human sleep. Process C is believed to be a circadian cycle determining thresholds for sleep and waking. Process S increases over time when there is no sleep and decreases when sleep occurs. Their interaction accounts for the sleep–wake cycle actually seen. (From Daan et al. 1984, with permission of the American Physiological Society.)

is very tired but cannot sleep. The two-factor theory can account for many of these occasions because going to sleep depends not only on how tired one is but also on a sleep threshold. When the sleep-regulating factor approaches the upper threshold, sleep is triggered; when it reaches the lower threshold, the person awakens. The thresholds vary during the day and are controlled by the circadian pacemaker. Figure 3.7 shows how these two factors are presumed to interact.

This theory predicts that one must be much more tired to fall asleep during the day than at night. It can account for the effects of **jet lag** on sleep because the circadian rhythm becomes disturbed when the time of light onset changes. It has also been successful in explaining a number of other sleep disorders found in human patients. Of course, as with all behavior systems, the occurrence of any particular behavior depends not only on internal endogenous mechanisms but also on the environmental context in which the animal finds itself. In the case of human sleep, this includes factors such as conscious **decisions** to set the alarm clock for a particular time. Much research has been carried out on these and other aspects of sleep and reviews of these studies can be found in Borbély et al. (2001) and Czeisler and Dijk (2001).

## Fear/exploration

The relation between fear and exploration has been discussed in a number of papers (Hogan 1965; Russell 1973; Inglis 2000). In this chapter I consider fear and exploration to be a unitary system that is expressed as approach at low levels, withdrawal at moderate levels, and immobility at high levels. The primary reason for considering this to be a unitary system is that both fear and exploration are aroused by novelty or un-familiarity, i.e., by a discrepancy between an actual situation and the animal's perceptual expectation of that situation (Hebb 1946). An example is provided by the behavior of a young chick toward a mealworm that it sees for the first time. Some chicks will approach, pick up and eat the mealworm, others will utter a fear trill and withdraw, whereas still others will stare at the mealworm and fall asleep (Hogan 1965).

Unlike the other behavior systems we have considered, the fear/exploration system appears to be activated almost exclusively by external stimuli. Nonetheless, intrinsic factors are also important in some cases. For example, monkeys will learn to press a lever that allows them to look out of their cage into an adjoining room (Butler & Harlow 1954), and also learn to solve a variety of mechanical puzzles with no extrinsic reward (Harlow 1950). A wide variety of studies with human subjects have also demonstrated that people seek out novel stimulation and find it rewarding (Berlyne 1960). Lorenz (1937b) even suggested that one reason zoo animals are so often skittish is that their threshold for withdrawal is lowered when they have not recently escaped from a threatening situation. All these cases implicate an important role for intrinsic factors even in a system that is normally activated only by external stimuli.

## Interactions Among Behavior Systems

Causal factors for many behavior systems are present at the same time, yet an animal can generally only do one thing at a time. This is a situation of motivational **conflict** (note that conflict in this sense does not refer to aggressive behavior). In this section we will consider the kinds of behavior that occur in conflict situations and some mechanisms that have been proposed for switching from one behavior to another. There have been two major ways of studying conflict, and we will consider both.

### Conflict: classification by consequence

One way to classify conflicts is in terms of the direction an organism takes from a goal object: either toward or away. Many psychologists have distinguished three basic kinds of motivational conflict, each designated according to the direction associated with the specific tendencies aroused: approach–approach, avoidance–avoidance, and approach–avoidance conflicts.

A classic study on the tendencies to approach or withdraw from a particular goal used rats as subjects and a narrow elevated runway with a goal box at the end as the test apparatus (Brown 1948). To examine the tendency to approach, a rat first learned to feed in the goal box. Then it was made hungry, placed at the far end of the runway, and allowed to run toward the goal. The rat wore a harness attached to a scale, and the experimenter measured the pulling force that the rat was exerting at 170 and 30 cm from the goal box. The strength of pull increased from about 40 g to about 60 g as the rat approached the goal. The function relating strength of pull to distance from the goal was called the **approach gradient**. To examine the tendency to avoid, a rat was first given a mild electric footshock in the goal box. Then, while wearing its harness, it was placed on the runway in front of the goal box. The strength of pull declined from about 200 g near the goal box in which it had been shocked to almost 0 g at 170 cm. This was called the **avoidance gradient**. When hunger was manipulated by varying the hours of food deprivation, and fear by varying the intensity of the shock, the overall strength of pull increased or decreased, but the slope of the gradients remained the same.

These results were explained by noting that fear is primarily aroused by the external cues associated with the goal box in its fixed location, whereas hunger is primarily aroused by internal cues that accompany the animal wherever it goes. Therefore, distance from the goal region will have a larger effect on fear-based avoidance than on hunger-based approach. The reason the approach gradient is not flat is that it is also based to some extent on the incentive value of the food in the goal box, which does decrease with distance. In general, the slope of the approach and avoidance gradients depends on the relative strengths of the internal and external factors activating the motivational systems.

These and similar results were used by Miller (1959) to deduce what will happen in the three types of conflict. When there are two relatively equal positive goals, there will be a point of equilibrium where the tendency to approach one goal is equal to the tendency to approach the other. If the animal is positioned exactly on this point, it will remain there indefinitely. Such a situation is inherently unstable, since the slightest movement in one direction or the other will cause the attractiveness of the two goals to become unequal, and lead the animal to approach the most attractive. However, the other two types of conflict are stable, and the animal should hover around the point of equilibrium. In an avoidance–avoidance conflict, the point of equilibrium is some-where between two negative goals; in an approach–avoidance conflict, the point of equilibrium is where the two gradients cross. A series of experiments by Miller and his associates, in which the goal box was associated with both food and shock, and hunger and fear were manipulated, confirmed these predictions.

## Conflict: classification by structure or form

An alternative way to classify conflict situations, used by **ethologists**, is to look at the specific behavior systems that are activated and analyze the behavior that is actually seen. At least four major types of outcome have been studied: inhibition, ambivalence, redirection, and displacement.

## Inhibition

The most common outcome in a conflict situation is that the behavior system with the highest level of causal factors will be expressed and all the other systems will be suppressed. A male stickleback that is foraging in its territory will stop foraging when a female enters and will begin courting. The male's hunger has not changed, nor has the availability of food. It follows that activation of the systems responsible for courtship must have inhibited the feeding system. In general, **inhibition** can be said to occur when causal factors are present that are normally sufficient to elicit a certain kind of behavior, but the behavior does not appear (or is at least reduced in strength) as a result of the presence of causal factors for another kind of behavior.

## Ambivalence

When a female stickleback enters the territory of a male, she is both an intruder and a potential sex partner. The appropriate response to an intruding conspecific is to attack it; the appropriate response to a sex partner is to lead it to the nest. The male essentially does both: he performs a zigzag dance. He makes a sideways leap followed by a jump in the direction of the female, and this sequence may be repeated many times. Sometimes the sideways leap continues into leading to the nest, and sometimes the jump toward the female ends in attack and biting. Thus, the zigzag dance can be considered a case of successive ambivalence. **Ambivalent behavior** is a behavior pattern that includes motor components belonging to two different behavior systems; in successive ambivalence, these components occur in rapid succession.

A somewhat similar case is provided by the "upright" posture of the herring gull (Fig. 3.8). This display often occurs during boundary disputes when two neighboring gulls meet at their mutual territory boundary. The bird's neck is stretched and its bill points down; the carpal joints (wrists) of the wings are raised out of the supporting feathers; the plumage is sleeked. The position of the bill and wings are characteristic of a bird that is about to attack (fighting in this species includes pecking and wing beating the opponent), and the stretched neck and sleeked plumage are characteristic of a frightened bird that is about to flee. Further, actual fighting or fleeing often follows the upright posture. Thus, the upright posture is a behavior pattern that includes motor components belonging to two different behavior systems. Unlike the zigzag dance of the stickleback, however, these components occur simultaneously. The upright posture can be considered a case of simultaneous ambivalence. Figure 3.8 also shows that the upright posture can occur in varying forms. In the "aggressive upright," components of attack predominate, whereas in the "anxiety upright," components of fleeing predominate.

The simultaneous occurrence of components belonging to different behavior systems greatly increases the number and variety of behavior patterns in a species' repertoire. A technique called **motivation analysis** can be used to explore such ambivalent behavior patterns, which include many of the bizarre displays exhibited by many species.

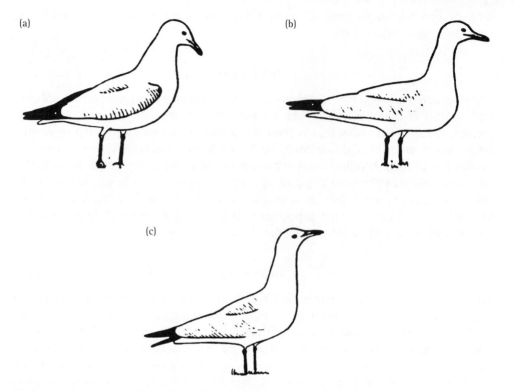

**Fig. 3.8** Upright postures of the herring gull: (a) "aggressive" upright; (b) "intimidated" upright; (c) "anxiety" or "escape" upright. (From Tinbergen 1959.)

In a motivation analysis, one looks at the form of the behavior, the situation in which it occurs, and other behaviors that occur in association with it (Tinbergen 1959). An example is provided by Kruijt's (1964, p. 61) analysis of "waltzing" by the male jungle-fowl (*Gallus gallus spadiceus*), the wild ancestor of the domestic chicken (Fig. 3.9).

> It is a lateral display: the waltzing bird walks sideways around or toward the opponent. Back and shoulders are held oblique, the inner side (the side nearest the opponent) lower than the outer side. Both wings are lifted out of the supporting feathers; the upper and lower arms are slightly lowered so that the rump becomes visible. Otherwise, the inner wing and upper and lower arm of the outer wing remain folded. The hand of the outer wing is lowered perpendicularly to the ground and pulled forward, its plane near the body. The primaries touch the ground and the outer foot makes scratching or stepping movements through the primaries. Head and neck are held at the level of the back and either in the medial plane or slightly turned toward the opponent. The tail spreads and is turned toward the opponent; breast and belly feathers are often ruffled, especially those of the other side.

Kruijt noted that the side of the bird's body nearer the hen expressed many components of escape behavior, whereas the side further from the hen expressed many components of attack behavior. It was "as if the part of the animal which is nearest to the opponent

**Fig. 3.9** "Waltzing" in a male junglefowl. (From Kruijt 1964.)

tries to withdraw, whereas the other half, which is further away, tries to approach" (Kruijt 1964, p. 65). He also noted that waltzing was always directed toward a conspecific. Somewhat surprisingly, young males directed waltzing equally to males and females, even though adult males almost always direct it toward females. In about two-thirds of the cases it was performed immediately before, during, or immediately after fighting, and in some of these cases behavior associated with escape was also seen. Thus, on the basis of form, situation, and associated behavior, Kruijt could conclude that waltzing is indeed an ambivalent behavior pattern expressing both attack and escape, with attack predominating. Sexual motivation appears to be unnecessary.

One aspect of this analysis that may seem absurd to some readers is the suggestion that part of the animal is approaching the opponent and at the same time another part of the animal is retreating. This interpretation may become more plausible by considering a similar human example. In a typical posture assumed by a boxer during a fight, the side of the body nearer the opponent is hunched with the arm drawn in (a defensive posture), while the side farther away is straight with the arm prepared to punch (an attack posture). Even the general inclination of the body toward the opponent and the movement of the feet are remarkably similar to those seen in the junglefowl. Different groups of muscles can be controlled by different behavior systems without implying any fragmentation of the animal.

Motivation analysis of many complex courtship displays in both birds and mammals has revealed that they are ambivalent activities very frequently involving primarily the attack and escape systems. Such activities are usually essential for successful courtship and reproduction. This means, as mentioned above, that the sex system by itself is often insufficient for achieving these ends, and illustrates clearly why causal and **functional** questions need to be kept separate.

### Redirection

When two herring gulls meet at their mutual boundary, causal factors for both attack and escape behavior are present. As we have just seen, the birds usually adopt the ambivalent upright posture in this situation. A common occurrence during this mutual display is that one of the birds viciously pecks a nearby clump of grass and then vigorously pulls at it. In form, "grass pulling" resembles the feather pulling seen during a heated fight between two gulls. This behavior can be considered a case of **redirected behavior** because the motor components all belong to one of the behavior systems for which causal factors are present (i.e., aggression), but it is directed toward an inappropriate object. The causal factors for the other behavior (in this case, escape or fear) must be responsible for the shift in object. Redirection of aggressive behavior seems to be especially common in many species including humans (Lorenz 1966).

### Displacement

Ambivalent behavior and redirected behavior are appropriate responses to causal factors that are obviously present in the situation in which the animal finds itself. Sometimes, however, an animal shows behavior that is not expected, in that appropriate causal factors are not apparent. A male stickleback meets its neighbor at the territory boundary and shows intention movements of attack and escape; then suddenly it swims to the bottom and takes a mouthful of sand (which is a component of nest-building behavior). A young chick encounters a wriggling mealworm and shows intention movements of approaching to eat the mealworm and retreating from the novel object; then, while watching the mealworm, the chick falls asleep. A pigeon, actively engaged in courtship, suddenly stops and preens itself. A student, studying hard for a difficult exam, puts down her book, walks to the kitchen, and makes herself a sandwich. These behaviors are all examples of **displacement activities** that are controlled by a behavior system different from the behavior systems one might expect to be activated in a particular situation.

In the case of the stickleback, it is reasonable to show components of attack and escape behavior at the boundary of its territory because the neighboring fish is an intruder when it crosses into our subject's territory, and our subject loses the security of home when it ventures into its neighbor's territory. But why should it engage in nest-building behavior? The stickleback has probably already built its nest elsewhere and, in any case, would not normally build it at the edge of its territory. What are the causal factors for nest building in this situation? Similar considerations apply to the other examples as well. In all cases, causal factors for the displacement activity appear to be missing. It is this apparent inexplicableness of displacement activities that has caused so much attention to be focused on them. Why does this unexpected behavior occur?

There have been two main theories put forward to account for displacement activities: the **overflow theory** and the **disinhibition theory**. The original theory was proposed independently by Kortlandt (1940) and by Tinbergen (1940), and is usually called the overflow theory. They proposed that when causal factors for a particular behavior system (e.g., aggression) were strong, but appropriate behavior was prevented from occurring, the energy from the activated system would "spark" or flow over to a behavior system that was not blocked (e.g., nest building) and a displacement activity would be seen. The appropriate behavior might be prevented from occurring because of interference from an antagonistic behavior system (e.g., fear or escape) or the absence of a suitable object or thwarting of any sort.

This theory was formulated in the framework of Lorenz's model of motivation, which accounts for the graphic metaphor of energy sparking over or overflowing. In more prosaic terms, this is actually a theory in which causal factors have general as well as specific effects. Many examples of displacement activities are described as being incomplete or frantic or hurried – the stickleback does not calmly proceed to build a nest during a boundary conflict – and such observations give support to a theory that posits general effects of causal factors. It can be noted that Freud's (1940/1949) theory of displacement and sublimation of sexual energy (libido) is basically the same as the overflow theory: sexual energy is expressed in nonsexual activities such as creating artistic works.

The alternative theory is called the disinhibition theory. In essence, this states that a strongly activated behavior system normally inhibits weakly activated systems. If, however, two behavior systems are strongly activated (e.g., sex and aggression) the inhibition they exert on each other will result in a release of inhibition on other behavior systems (e.g., parental) and a displacement activity will occur. The general idea was proposed by several scientists, but the most detailed exploration of the theory was made by Sevenster (1961). He studied displacement fanning in the male stickleback, which often occurs during courtship before there are any eggs in the nest. The sex and aggression behavior systems are known to be strongly activated during courtship. By careful measurements, it was possible to show that fanning occurred at a particular level of sex and aggression when their mutual inhibition was the strongest. Of special importance for the disinhibition theory, the amount of displacement fanning that occurred depended on the strength of causal factors for the parental behavior system. When extra $CO_2$ was introduced into the water, there was an increase in fanning.

The primary difference between the two theories is that according to the disinhibition theory the displacement activity is motivated by its own normal causal factors and the conflict between systems merely serves a permissive role, whereas according to the overflow theory the displacement activity is motivated by causal factors for one or both of the conflicting systems. In the disinhibition theory, causal factors always have specific effects; in the overflow theory, they have general effects. Which theory is correct? As is so often the case, neither theory, by itself, is able to account for all the phenomena associated with displacement activities. The disinhibition theory is in many ways more satisfying because it only requires that causal factors have their normal and expected effects on behavior. Nonetheless, more general effects of causal factors must be invoked to account for the frantic or excited aspects of displacement activities seen in many situations.

It is frequently true that the causation of a behavior pattern is even more complicated. For example, ground pecking occurs as a displacement activity during aggressive encounters between two male junglefowl. Arguments for considering this activity as a displaced feeding movement include the fact that it is often directed to food pieces on the ground and the fact that it occurs more frequently when the animals are hungry. This same activity can also be considered redirected aggression, and experimental evidence also supports this interpretation. Thus, one behavior pattern can be both a displacement activity and a redirected activity at the same time (Feekes 1972). Each contribution to the causation of a behavior pattern can be analyzed separately, but the list of causal factors affecting the behavior pattern can be very long. Indeed, multiple causation of behavior is the rule rather than the exception. The causation of behavior is a very complex question, and it is unreasonable to expect a simple answer.

## Mechanisms of behavioral change

What determines when a particular behavior will occur, how long it will continue, and what behavior will follow it? One can imagine that all an animal's behavior systems are competing with each other for expression, perhaps in a kind of free-for-all. For example, if the level of causal factors for eating is very high, the hunger system will inhibit other systems and the animal will eat. As it eats, the causal factors for eating will decline while the causal factors for other behaviors, say drinking, will be higher than those for eating and the animal will change its behavior. If a predator approaches, the escape system will be strongly activated, which will inhibit eating and drinking, and the animal will run away. And so on.

Unfortunately, as attractive as this account appears, it is clearly an oversimplification of reality. Perhaps its most serious shortcoming is that if there were a real free-for-all and only the most dominant behavior system could be expressed, many essential but generally low-priority activities might never occur. If a hungry animal never stopped to look around for danger before the predator was upon it, it would not long survive. Since most animals do survive, this must imply that the rules for behavioral change are more complex than the "winner take all" model. Lorenz (1966) has compared the interactions among behavior systems to the working of a parliament that, though generally democratic, has evolved special rules and procedures to produce at least tolerable and practicable compromises between different interests. The special rules that apply to interactions among behavior systems have only begun to be studied, but a few principles are beginning to emerge.

One important mechanism for behavioral change arises from the fact that most behavior systems are organized in such a way that "pauses" occur after the animal has engaged in a particular activity for a certain time. The level of causal factors for the activity may remain very high, but during the pause other activities can occur. For example, in many species, feeding occurs in discrete bouts; between bouts there is an opportunity for the animal to groom, look around, drink, and so on. It appears that the dominant behavior system (in this case, the hunger system) releases its inhibition on other systems for a certain length of time. During the period of disinhibition, other behavior systems may compete for dominance according to their level of causal factors or each system may, so to speak, be given a turn to express itself. McFarland (1974) has compared these kinds of interactions among behavior systems with the "time-sharing" that occurs when multiple users share the same computer system.

A striking example of this sort of behavioral organization is the incubation system of certain species of birds. Broody hens sit on their eggs for about 3 weeks. Once or twice a day, the hen gets off the eggs for about 10 min. During this interval she eats, drinks, grooms, and defecates. The proportion of the 10 min spent eating will vary depending on the state of the hunger system, but even 24 h of food deprivation does not change the pattern of leaving the eggs (Sherry et al. 1980).

Another type of mechanism for behavior change depends upon the reaction of an animal to discrepant feedback. A male Siamese fighting fish, for example, will not display as long to its mirror image as to another displaying male. This is because the behavior of the mirror image is always identical to the behavior of the subject, but identical responses are not part of the "species expectation" of responses to aggressive display. These mechanisms, and undoubtedly many others, all interact to produce the infinite variety of sequences of behavior characteristic of the animal in its natural environment.

## Models of Motivation

Toates (1983) has pointed out that the word "model" has various meanings with different authors. Here we will follow his emphasis that models are theories or formal statements of how systems are believed to work. Several kinds of variable have been used in models of motivational phenomena, including physiological variables, control theory variables from engineering, and behavioral variables. We have seen examples of some of these above and Toates and Jensen (1991) discuss these and other examples in more detail. In this section, we will consider one kind of behavioral model, a generalization of the two-factor model for sleep (see Fig. 3.7).

We can begin with the Lorenz model of motivation depicted in Fig. 3.2. In this model, the level of fluid in the reservoir represents the "energy" available, or the "behavioral state of readiness" for performing a specific behavior pattern. The reservoir itself together with the trough represents the structure of the motor mechanism, and the spring valve, which prevents the continuous outflow of energy, can be considered to represent the threshold. Lorenz originally proposed that the energy available increased as a function of time due to endogenous neural activity, and decreased when the behavior was actually performed. This formulation can account for some of the results for behaviors such as dustbathing, sleep, and feeding, but is not so successful with other behavior systems, such as sex and aggression. However, if one allows other factors such as the priming effects of stimuli and various chemicals to contribute to the level of energy, and factors such as performance of other behavior (displacement activities) and passage of time (a leaky reservoir) to dissipate the energy, then many more results can be accounted for.

The generality of the model can also be increased by expanding the factors contributing to the threshold. In the original model, the energy is held in check by the releasing mechanism, which is activated by appropriate external stimuli. One can imagine that the strength of the spring is also influenced by factors such as specific stimuli, the time of day (circadian clock), and inhibition from other behavior systems. For example, specific stimuli such as increased light intensity make behaviors such as dustbathing or sleep more or less likely, respectively. Further, the circadian clock has been shown to have a very strong influence on sleep and feeding in most species, as well as on dustbathing in fowl and parenting in female ring doves. Figure 3.7 shows how a wide range of other factors, such as conscious decisions, can also influence the threshold.

Hogan (1997) has discussed how a two-factor model of motivation (energy and threshold) can account for the wide variety of results that have been found for systems ranging from dustbathing in chickens, aggression in fish, and sex in rats to sleep in humans. Such a model can be used as a framework for studying motivation, in a way similar to the use of the behavior system model as a framework for studying structure.

## SUMMARY AND CONCLUSIONS

Motivation refers to the immediate causes of behavior. All behavior is caused by the action of a combination of internal and external causal factors, some of which have very specific effects on behavior and others more general effects. Stimuli can release, direct, inhibit, and prime behavior. These effects all depend on the internal state of the animal, which is controlled by hormones and other substances and by the intrinsic activity of the nervous system. Lorenz proposed a "psychohydraulic" model of behavior that provides a useful analogy for understanding how all these factors interact with each other. The hunger, parenting, aggression, sex, self-maintenance, sleep, and fear/exploration behavior systems are all described. They are seen to vary in the way they are organized and motivated across species and between male and female. In general, causal factors for more than one behavior system are present at the same time. Sometimes the system with the strongest causal factors inhibits all the other systems, but most of the time animals engage in some type of ambivalent, redirected, or displacement behavior. A two-factor model of motivation, derived from the Lorenz model, is described, which has an energy and a threshold variable, and which can be used as a general framework for studying motivation.

## FURTHER READING

*An Introduction to Behavioral Endocrinology* (Nelson 1999) provides an excellent source for details on the physiological control of most of the behavior systems discussed in this chapter. Toates's (1986) book *Motivational Systems* presents a review of behavior systems with an emphasis on control theory variables, while papers by Hogan and Roper (1978) and Hogan (2001) review behavior systems from a more psychological and historical perspective. Lorenz's (1966) controversial, but entertaining, book *On Aggression* gives his views on how ethological concepts can be applied to human behavior.

# 4
# biological rhythms and behavior
## Ralph E. Mistlberger and Benjamin Rusak

### A clockwork chipmunk

The eastern chipmunk *Tamias striatus* is a solitary terrestrial squirrel that inhabits the forests of eastern North America. It sleeps at night in complete darkness in an underground burrow. During the summer months, it emerges daily to collect food and eat. In the autumn it switches to hoarding prodigious amounts of acorns, beech nuts, and maple samaras, which it eats in its burrow during the winter months when the ground is under several meters of snow. If food runs short, the chipmunk becomes **torpid** to save energy. By early spring the chipmunk emerges from its den to seek a mate. The chipmunk's behavior thus varies predictably with time of day and season, expressing highly regular cycles in synchrony with its environment. How are these **rhythms** controlled? How does the chipmunk know the correct time to emerge from its den each day in the summer or at the end of the winter, given that it rests underground in constant dark and near constant temperature? These questions of timing are the topic of this chapter. As we shall see, biological organisms have evolved **endogenous** (internal) timing devices that can be used like clocks to enable them to do the right thing at the right time.

### Spectrum of biological rhythms

Life on earth evolved in environments characterized by regular and highly predictable changes in levels of light, temperature, humidity, tidal activity, and many secondary consequences of these cycles for environmental conditions. These changes are caused by the unique configuration and movements of earth, moon, and sun relative to each other. The spin of the earth on its own axis gives rise to the solar day (24 h), while the rotation of the moon around the earth creates the lunar day (24.8 h). The relative movements of earth and moon around the sun give rise to the lunar month (~ 29.5 days) and solar year (~ 365.25 days). The many changes in local conditions that result from these physical cycles have affected the course of biological evolution and provided a temporal framework for both the physiology and behavior of organisms.

Rhythmicity of form and **function** that mirrors the rhythmicity of the external world is evident in most organisms, from cyanobacteria to humans, and at all levels of biological organization, from the transcription of genes to the movements of animal populations. Daily (24 h) rhythms are especially prominent in virtually all eukaryotic organisms (those with nucleated cells), but cycles of behavior and physiology with periodicities of hours (**ultradian rhythms**, << 24 h), months or years (**infradian rhythms**, >> 24 h) are also evident in many species. In this chapter, discussion is limited primarily to a subset of periodicities known collectively as the "circa" rhythms. These rhythms share two characteristics: (i) under natural conditions, they are synchronized to major geophysical cycles in the environment; and (ii) under artificially constant conditions, they persist with a period that approximates that of the corresponding geophysical cycle.

Four circa rhythms are recognized.

1 **Circatidal**: approximately 12.4-h ultradian rhythm synchronized to the semidiurnal tidal rhythm.
2 **Circadian** (Latin *circa*, about; *dies*, a day): approximately 24-h rhythm synchronized to the solar day.
3 **Circalunar**: approximately 29.5-day infradian rhythm synchronized to the lunar month.
4 **Circannual**: approximately 365-day infradian rhythm synchronized to the solar year.

Circadian rhythms are by far the best known and most ubiquitous of the circa rhythms, and will therefore be the focus of most of this chapter, but the mechanisms and functions of some ultradian and infradian behavioral rhythms will also be discussed.

## Discovery of Circadian Rhythms

### Circadian rhythms persist in temporal isolation

The rest–activity cycle is among the most conspicuous of daily rhythms, and most animals can be classified as predominantly active during the day (**diurnal**), active during the night (**nocturnal**), or active at dawn and dusk (**crepuscular**). These

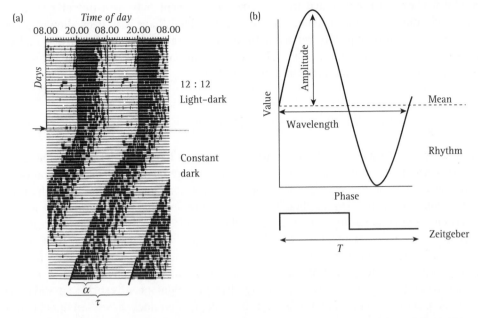

**Fig. 4.1** (a) An "actogram" illustrating the circadian wheel-running rhythm of a mouse housed first under an equatorial light–dark (LD) cycle (12-h days beginning at 08.00, and 12-h nights at 20.00) and then in constant dark (beginning on the day indicated by the arrow). Each line of this chart represents two consecutive days of recording, with time in 10-min bins plotted from left to right. Each 10-min bin is represented by a point (no wheel counts) or a bar (one or more wheel counts) on the line. Note that in the LD cycle running occurs primarily at night, whereas in constant dark running remains rhythmic but drifts earlier each "day" due to the "circadian" periodicity of the endogenous clock. (b) Circadian rhythms can be modeled mathematically by sine waves and other functions. These waves can be characterized by their duration ($\tau$) and amplitude relative to the mean level. The maximum defines the acrophase. Zeitgebers, such as the LD cycle, also have a cycle duration ($T$) and may have an amplitude.

temporal patterns could be the result of a direct effect on behavior of daily variations in light, temperature, humidity, or some other stimulus. Direct effects of light and dark on behavior are in fact well known; the activity of diurnal animals is typically inhibited by darkness whereas that of nocturnal animals is inhibited by light (Mrosovsky 1999). However, while such direct effects may reinforce daily rhythms, they are not necessary for their expression. Plants and animals maintained in carefully controlled conditions of constant light, temperature, and humidity (i.e., **temporal isolation**) continue to exhibit daily rhythms of biochemistry, physiology, and behavior. In many organisms these rhythms can persist (**free-run**) virtually indefinitely in the complete absence of environmental time cues, indicating that the rhythms are both endogenously generated and self-sustaining (Fig. 4.1). In such constant conditions, free-running rhythms express **periods** (denoted by the Greek letter $\tau$, the reciprocal of which is frequency, e.g., one cycle per day) that differ slightly from 24 h (which is why they are called circadian rather than daily rhythms). This deviation of $\tau$ from 24 h causes circadian rhythms in temporal isolation to gradually drift out of synchrony with local (external) time. Since free-running $\tau$ values vary both within and between individuals, the rhythms of organisms recorded in the same environment may drift out of synchrony with each other. Circadian rhythms in plants and animals have now been shown to persist even in orbit, completely removed from the natural cycles on the earth's surface. These observations constitute powerful evidence that daily rhythms are the product of an endogenous, self-sustaining, clock-like mechanism.

## Circadian rhythms are temperature compensated

Persistence in constant conditions with a $\tau$ near 24 h is one defining property of circadian rhythms; another is stability of $\tau$ despite large changes in the temperature of organisms. Homeothermic animals employ physiological and behavioral mechanisms to minimize the variability of their internal temperature, but the environment largely determines the temperature of plants and poikilothermic animals. Biochemical reactions normally vary with temperature, doubling or tripling in rate with every 10 °C increment. Early studies demonstrating the relative invariance of $\tau$ across a wide temperature range in poikilothermic organisms appeared to violate this physical "law," and led to considerable debate over whether daily rhythms might be driven by an unknown external physical factor rather than by an endogenous clock based on biochemical processes.

However, the exogenous hypothesis failed to account for the variation in $\tau$ among individuals, within individuals over time, or in different physiological conditions, and no mysterious "factor X" was ever identified. The exogenous hypothesis thus gradually fell from favor as the dominant explanation for persistent daily rhythms. There is now general agreement that an internal clock system drives these rhythms, and temperature compensation is viewed as a logical necessity for circadian timers. If the frequency of a mechanism that drives circadian rhythms varied with temperature, its output would reflect the organism's history of temperature changes rather than the passage of time. It would, in other words, make a fine thermometer but a poor clock. Recent advances in our understanding of the molecular basis of circadian timekeeping, discussed further below, suggest mechanisms by which temperature compensation is achieved physiologically.

## Rhythm Parameters and Terminology

Chronobiologists use a specialized terminology as convenient shorthand for communicating among themselves. However, the terms or their usage are often unfamiliar to nonspecialists, so it is worthwhile explicitly defining a few important terms in any introduction to this field. A **rhythm** may be formally defined as any process that repeats itself at regular intervals. A device that produces a rhythm is an **oscillator.** If more than one oscillator is involved in regulation of a rhythm, the one that ultimately sets the rhythm's long-term periodicity is the **pacemaker** for that rhythm. An oscillator can be used in several different ways. It can measure duration or elapsed time, for example by counting cycles or portions of a cycle and triggering events at certain specified intervals. It can also be synchronized to an external cycle (e.g., the solar day), and then consulted as a clock to recognize local time (e.g., any arbitrary time of day). The latter is a critical timekeeping function, since only a few times of day are sharply marked in the environment (e.g., dusk and dawn), but behavioral or physiological processes might be profitably linked to any number of other times.

Circadian rhythms of behavior and physiology, whether continuously variable (e.g., body temperature, blood pressure, heart rate) or discrete events (e.g., onset of locomotor activity, meal time, sleep onset), can be conceptualized as **hands** of the circadian clock. By monitoring these observable hands, we can identify the position (**phase**, or instantaneous state) of the clock within its cycle. These processes are distinct from the underlying clock mechanism (metaphorically, the "gears" of the clock), which may not be directly observable. The distinction is important because altering overt behavior or physiology (e.g., preventing sleep onset at its predicted phase) may have no effect on the underlying clock mechanism driving the observed rhythm, even if overt rhythmicity is altered temporarily. Failure to consider this distinction can lead to confusion in the interpretation of research results.

Under constant conditions, the period of an overt rhythm is an accurate reflection of the periodicity of the underlying pacemaker driving that rhythm. When a free-running pacemaker is exposed to a regularly recurring external cycle that affects its periodicity sufficiently, it becomes synchronized or **entrained** to that cycle, by adopting a stable phase relation to it and expressing the same periodicity as the external cycle. The latter is then referred to as a **Zeitgeber** (German "timegiver") for that pacemaker.

The timing of an entrained rhythm can be expressed relative to other rhythms by comparing particular phases of each cycle. For example, "wake-up" time, a phase of the daily sleep–wake cycle, can be expressed in minutes or in radian degrees of a full 360° cycle relative to a defined phase of the solar day, such as sunrise. For example, wake-up time may lead sunrise by 1 h or lag (follow) it by 2 h. Different overt rhythms have different phase relations to the solar day.

Some rhythms have proven to be particularly useful markers of circadian pacemaker phase. The most commonly used laboratory animals in circadian biology are hamsters, mice, and rats, in large part because they exhibit robust, easily measured daily rhythms of wheel-running activity. Wheel-running rhythms can be remarkably precise (e.g., Figs 4.1 & 4.3); the standard deviation of successive daily activity onsets by flying squirrels (*Glaucomys volans*) free-running for weeks in constant dark may be as low as 6 min, or 0.4% of a 24 h (1440 min) cycle. Thus, given the time of the last activity onset in a constant environment and with knowledge of the average $\tau$, the next activity onset can be predicted to within a few minutes. The underlying circadian pacemaker must be at least as stable as any of the measurable rhythms it drives, and its cycle-to-cycle precision has, in fact, been estimated to be twice that of the overt activity rhythm (Pittendrigh & Daan 1976).

The phase and period of circadian rhythms reflect the timing of the underlying circadian clock. Another feature of a rhythm is its **waveform**, which describes the variation in level (e.g., body temperature) across successive phases of the cycle (Fig. 4.1b). Circadian waveforms come in a variety of shapes (e.g., sinuosoidal, sawtooth), and may have one or more daily peaks. Sinusoidal rhythms can be described mathematically by a cosine function, the peak of which is designated the **acrophase**. The difference between acrophase and mean value can be used as a measure of rhythm **amplitude**. However, unlike the steady-state rhythm period, rhythm amplitude cannot be assumed to reflect a property of the underlying clock. A stopped clock has a zero amplitude oscillation, as will all the rhythms that it drives, but a stopped rhythm (e.g., if an animal is kept awake for 24 h, thereby eliminating the sleep–wake cycle) cannot be taken to imply a stopped clock. Many factors downstream from the clock can affect the expression, and therefore the waveform, of specific rhythmic variables.

## Evolution and Adaptive Uses of Circadian Clocks

### Circadian clocks are phylogenetically ancient

True circadian rhythms (i.e., those that persist in temporal isolation) are found in at least some prokaryotic organisms (those without nucleated cells, e.g., the cyano-bacterium *Synechococcus*) and in the simplest unicellular eukaryotes (e.g., the green alga *Chlamydomonas*). Circadian clocks must therefore have evolved very early in the history of life on earth, at least 3.5 billion years ago. Whether circadian timekeeping evolved once or several times in different evolutionary lines (convergent evolution) is unknown.

The early appearance of circadian clocks was likely driven by the need to shield certain biochemical processes from ionizing solar radiation ("escape from light" hypothesis; Pittendrigh 1993). Ultraviolet light damages DNA, which is particularly vulnerable during replication, the more so in essentially translucent unicellular organisms. Circadian clocks can minimize photooxidative damage by programming cell division to occur at night. In mobile organisms, the circadian clock can further contribute by stimulating movement away from sources of brighter light (e.g., the surface of the ocean) in anticipation of sunrise.

The evolution of circadian clocks may also have been favored by the need to separate incompatible biochemical processes. Cyanobacteria, for example, exhibit daily rhythms of nitrogen fixation and of photosynthesis that are in "antiphase": photosynthesis occurs in the day, nitrogen fixation at night. Photosynthesis releases oxygen, which inactiv-ates the nitrogen-fixing enzyme nitrogenase; thus these processes must be separated, either spatially or temporally. In simpler organisms lacking spatial barriers, circadian programming can achieve the necessary temporal segregation.

These two hypotheses about the origins of endogenous circadian timekeeping em-phasize two primary functions of circadian clocks: optimal coordination of the organism with the outside world, and optimal coordination of internal biochemical and physio-logical processes. There are numerous examples that illustrate the adaptive value of temporal coordination of behavior and physiology with the environment, but the importance of circadian timing for internal physiological coordination is far less well documented.

## Circadian clocks coordinate behavior with the external world

Complex multicellular organisms have evolved a variety of **adaptations**, such as pigmentation, to protect against solar radiation, and the circadian clock in these species is therefore no longer needed for "escape from light." However, the sensory and motor capacities of many species have become specialized for diurnal or nocturnal lifestyles. For these species, foraging, reproductive, and other behaviors are most efficient, and safest, if restricted to appropriate times of day. Diurnal animals have high-acuity, low-sensitivity visual systems optimal for daytime light levels. Foraging at night would be inefficient and potentially dangerous, if it were to increase exposure to daily extremes of local climate (e.g., cold) or to predators, particularly those advantaged by their own adaptations for nocturnal vision.

While circadian rhythmicity may be important for timing many daily activities, it is also very important for **developmental** events that occur only once in a lifetime. The prototypical example is the process of eclosion (emergence from the pupal case) in the fruit fly *Drosophila melanogaster*. Air that is too hot or dry may damage the wings of newly eclosed flies by drying them before they can flatten into an appropriate shape. Eclosion is therefore restricted to the early morning hours, when air temperature tends to be lowest and humidity highest. Although each fly emerges only once, there will be a detectable rhythm of eclosion measurable in a population of flies, with groups of new adults emerging only at a time corresponding to subjective morning, even under constant environmental conditions.

Circadian control of eclosion gains additional significance in insects that mate only for a brief time immediately after emergence; if members of the population do not emerge in synchrony, there will be fewer successful matings and fewer offspring. The necessity of synchronizing behavior to facilitate mating is likely to exert a significant selection pressure for accurate circadian timekeeping in many species.

In birds, fledging is a developmental event that may entail significant risk of predation. One solution to minimize mortality within a population is to restrict fledging to a particular time of day. If all fledglings leave the nest at the same time, this will reduce the total number lost to predation by overwhelming the maximum killing capacity of predators. Circadian control of fledging behavior, and its advantage for survival, have been documented in guillemots (*Uria lomvia*), cliff-breeding arctic sea birds that suffer heavy predation from glaucous gulls (*Larus hyperboreus*) (Daan 1981).

Circadian control of developmental events illustrates an advantage of circadian timing that may also be important at other life stages. At the time of a critical developmental event, the organism may lack the sensory capacity or access to **information** that would allow detection of optimal environmental conditions (e.g., detecting external humidity from inside a sealed pupal case). In the absence of access to the most relevant external cues, the circadian clock can program critical events to occur at the appropriate time by entraining to a correlated and more readily detectable cue (e.g., the lighting cycle). This same strategy is exploited by mature organisms in other situations, such as in the selection of nesting sites. Many species of bats roost in caves sufficiently deep to provide constant darkness and temperature. Many other animals, like the "clockwork" eastern chipmunk discussed at the beginning of this chapter, nest in burrows in the ground or hollows in trees, which also obscure daily variations in light and temperature. These habitats can be utilized because an appropriately synchronized circadian clock can function as an alarm clock to provide a precise wake-up signal that ensures emergence from the nest site at an appropriate time of day, without the need for continuous access to information about current external conditions.

The general rule that there is an optimal time of day for sleeping and waking extends to specific portions of the active phase. Different sources of food may be available at different times of day, so effective foraging strategies (see Chapter 9) may require attention to both spatial and temporal cues that define where and when food may be obtained. For example, flowers produce nectar and open their petals at particular times of day, thereby limiting the resources they must expend to attract potential pollinators. The same approach also enhances the probability that pollen will be transported within a species, and minimizes the spread of pollen to unrelated species. Honeybees can learn and remember both the time and the place at which a nectar source was available, and communicate this information to other foragers in the hive via the well-known **waggle dance** (see Chapter 10). Laboratory studies indicate that bees can remember as many as nine times of day, and that the time-of-day cues are provided by their circadian clock. This ability to "sense" time of day and organize behaviors appropriately for each phase (**Zeitgedächtnis**; German "time memory") demonstrates that the bee possesses a true clock, by which it can recognize local time, analogous to our use of a wristwatch to schedule activities precisely within our own time-ruled society. The circadian clock is thus more than an on–off switch for behavioral states; rather, it can be "continuously consulted" for use as a chronometer to permit a highly differentiated temporal program of daily foraging and other activities.

A similar ability to recognize time of day and generate phase-appropriate learned behaviors using internal circadian cues has now been demonstrated in several other species, including birds, rats, and insects. Rats can learn rapidly that food is available at one or two times of day, and exhibit so-called "anticipatory activity" prior to the daily mealtimes. However, if food availability is made contingent on both time of day and place, they acquire this information only very laboriously, at least under laboratory conditions, which may not be optimal for revealing their ability. Some bird species have been shown to be capable of **learning** at least four time–place associations for food access.

Anticipation of mealtimes highlights a primary adaptive feature of endogenous circadian timing, namely the ability to prepare in advance for the major environmental changes associated with the day–night cycle. In mammals and birds, body temperature is lowered during the daily rest period, which minimizes energy expenditure. To prepare for the active period, the circadian clock must initiate autonomic and hormonal events (e.g., cortisol secretion) to raise body temperature and mobilize stored energy reserves prior to dawn or dusk. Thus, when daylight brings the opportunity to forage, mate, or defend a territory, the organism is ready, rather than beginning its preparations only in response to the signal provided by dawn.

Organisms that forage over a wide area may have to begin the migration back to their resting sites well in advance of the onset of day or night. The need for anticipatory behavior may be particularly crucial for slow-moving organisms; for example worms vulnerable to desiccation during the day may need to migrate down in the soil before there are obvious changes in moisture or temperature, lest they be caught high and dry in the morning sun. Similarly, on a seasonal basis, organisms must prepare for and initiate long-distance migrations to favorable regions long before the cold and snow of winter (for example) make both feeding and migration impossible.

These examples illustrate how circadian timing can contribute to **homeostasis** (Latin "similar standing"), the regulation of vital physiological functions within certain optimal limits. It has traditionally been conceptualized as a reactive process, based on a negative feedback mechanism. Thus, changes in a regulated variable, such as body temperature, result in compensatory responses, such as shivering, sweating, or seeking sun or shade, until the variable is restored to the desired value. The circadian clock can minimize disruptions of homeostasis by initiating responses in anticipation of a predictable daily challenge. Vertical migration of a worm into the soil anticipates, and thereby prevents, a severe challenge to hydration. This adaptive feature of circadian timing has been referred to as "predictive" homeostasis (Moore-Ede 1986; see also Chapter 3).

Despite the many apparent advantages of circadian timekeeping for anticipating environmental change and coordinating behavior with daily cycles, few studies have attempted to test directly whether circadian organization of behavior is necessary for survival in natural habitats. One means of conducting such a test is to remove the circadian clock by a surgical or genetic procedure, and to evaluate survival and reproduction rates after release. This type of experiment has been attempted twice, using wild-caught diurnal rodents. In both cases the circadian clock was removed by a localized lesion of a part of the brain called the **suprachiasmatic nucleus** (SCN) (discussed later). In one study, SCN-ablated and intact white-tailed antelope ground squirrels, *Ammospermophilus leucurus*, were maintained in a large outdoor enclosure in their habitat of origin (DeCoursey et al. 1997). Squirrels with SCN ablations were active at food sites during both day and night, whereas control squirrels were almost exclusively day-active. The unplanned entry of a feral cat resulted in overnight loss of 60% of the squirrels with SCN ablations compared with 29% of the intact squirrels. In a second study, wild-caught eastern chipmunks (*Tamias striatus*) received SCN ablations and were returned to their **home range** after behavioral tests had confirmed that their circadian rhythms were either eliminated or severely disrupted (DeCoursey et al. 2000). Although telemetric recordings indicated that SCN-ablated and control animals remained in their burrows at night, the SCN-ablated group suffered significantly greater predation from nocturnally active weasels. It was hypothesized that nocturnal restlessness of SCN-ablated chipmunks in their burrows may have alerted weasels to their location. These results are consistent with the prediction that circadian rhythms of rest and activity states have adaptive significance, and suggest that any genetic mutation that greatly attenuates or alters the timing of circadian activity rhythms would be rapidly eliminated from the gene pool.

## The circadian clock is also a compass and a calendar

Circadian clocks have the capacity to be synchronized precisely to periodic environmental stimuli, such as daily light–dark (LD) cycles. A clock synchronized to the solar day provides not only knowledge of local time but also the basis for an internal compass (knowledge of direction) and a calendar (knowledge of season). Many species have exploited the circadian clock in one or both of these ways. The honeybee uses its circadian clock to recognize and remember the time at which good nectar sources are available, but it also uses the clock to navigate to and from the hive. The bee takes its heading relative to the sun's **azimuth** (the point on the horizon below the sun). The azimuth changes throughout the day as the earth rotates. The circadian clock is used to compensate for this continuous motion, so that the flight heading relative to the azimuth is continuously adjusted by reference to circadian clock phase. If the circadian clock is shifted artificially, the direction of flight also shifts in parallel. Circadian clock-compensated sun-compass orientation is also used by birds, mammals, reptiles, and fish that migrate over great distances, typically on a seasonal basis (Wallraff 1981).

Annual rhythms of activity, metabolism, reproduction, and other functions are widespread in animals and plants. In some cases, annual rhythms are controlled by an internal circannual clock which, in mammals, appears to be physically distinct from the circadian clock. More commonly, annual rhythms are timed in part by measuring seasonal changes in daylength (photoperiod) using a mechanism involving the circadian clock, sometimes in combination with endogenously timed components (see below for further discussion of seasonality).

## Environmental Synchronization of Circadian Rhythms

The circadian clock coordinates behavior and physiology with external cycles, and serves the ancillary functions of compass and calendar. All these adaptive functions depend on a stable synchronization of the circadian clock to the day–night cycle. In the absence of stable synchronization, behavior would not be timed appropriately to match the rhythmic constraints of the environment, and both compass and calendar functions would be compromised.

The most direct approach for achieving synchrony with a rhythmic environment might be to initiate a precise 24-h periodicity at some point during development and to maintain this rhythm indefinitely. This approach would have two major problems. First, it requires the evolution of a perfectly stable clock; any deviation of the length of even a single cycle from 24 h would permanently alter the phase relation between clock and environment. Second, it would not permit seasonal adjustments of the timing of the clock to preserve an optimal phase relation between behavior and a particular phase of the day–night cycle. Although the day–night cycle, measured from noon to noon, is 24 h, the lengths of the day and night phases comprising that cycle vary systematically with time of year in most places on earth because of the tilt of the earth on its polar axis. Away from the equator, daylength (photoperiod) grows shorter with each day after the summer solstice and longer with each day after the winter solstice. For many organisms, it is functionally important for daily wake-up or critical developmental events (e.g., eclosion) to track the seasonal movements of dawn and dusk, rather than to maintain a stable relation to midday or midnight.

To illustrate this point, if a diurnal bird living in the temperate zone were to become active at the same time daily (e.g., 6 h before noon), it would become active during total darkness in midwinter and several hours after light onset in midsummer. Both behaviors would be maladaptive. Since dawn and dusk shift earlier or later each day, the circadian clock must be capable of adjusting its phasing to track these biologically important phases. Thus a mechanism must be employed to permit stable synchronization to critical daily phases while maintaining an average period of 24 h throughout the year. The process of matching the phase and period of an endogenously rhythmic circadian clock to an environmental cycle is known as **entrainment**.

How is entrainment achieved? In temporal isolation, circadian rhythms typically deviate systematically from 24 h. For an LD cycle with a given periodicity $T$ (e.g., 24 h) to entrain a free-running rhythm with periodicity $\tau$ (e.g., 23.5 h), it must be capable of altering the motion of the circadian clock to correct for the difference $\tau - T$ (in this case 30 min). To maintain synchrony with the LD cycle, the clock must be either permanently slowed by 30 min/cycle (a "continuous" effect on its rate of oscillation) or reset (shifted) each day (a "discrete" effect on its phase, analogous to setting a fast wristwatch backward each day by 30 min).

The LD cycle appears to have both discrete and continuous effects on circadian timing. In constant light, $\tau$ lengthens (the clock runs slower) in proportion to light intensity in most nocturnal animals, and shortens (the clock runs faster) in most diurnal animals. (This is one of Aschoff's rules, named after one of the pioneers of circadian biology, the German scientist Jürgen Aschoff; some species do not conform to these generalizations.) In constant dark, a single "pulse" of light (from seconds to an hour or more in duration) can rapidly reset the phase of circadian rhythms in either direction, depending on when the light exposure occurs within the circadian cycle. Thus, continuous light can speed up or slow down the clock, whereas discrete pulses of light can acutely shift the clock phase. The "discrete" phase-shifting effect of light can account for both the "continuous" effect of light (modeled as an accumulation of discrete shifts) and the principal features of entrainment to natural lighting cycles.

Figure 4.2 illustrates a series of experiments that map out the phase-shifting effects of light exposure at different phases of the circadian cycle. **Phase shifts** can be readily quantified by comparing a standard phase of the circadian rhythm in the cycles before and after the light stimulus. For many organisms, the beginning of the daily active period is a convenient phase marker for measuring shifts. Regression lines can be fitted to successive daily activity onsets before and after the light stimulus. The temporal displacement of the two regression lines on the intercept day (e.g., the day after the light pulse) provides the magnitude and direction of phase shift. The data can then be summarized by plotting a **phase-response curve** (PRC) (see Fig. 4.2), which illustrates the relations between size and direction of phase shift and the circadian phase of stimulus presentation.

In an LD cycle, the nocturnal animal rests during the day and is active most of the night. In constant dark, the rest phase of the circadian cycle is designated the **subjective day**, and the active phase the **subjective night** (the opposite is true for diurnal animals). When light exposure occurs during the subjective day, there is little or no effect on the circadian clock. However, light exposure in the subjective night induces an abrupt phase shift. The direction and magnitude of the phase shift depend on the

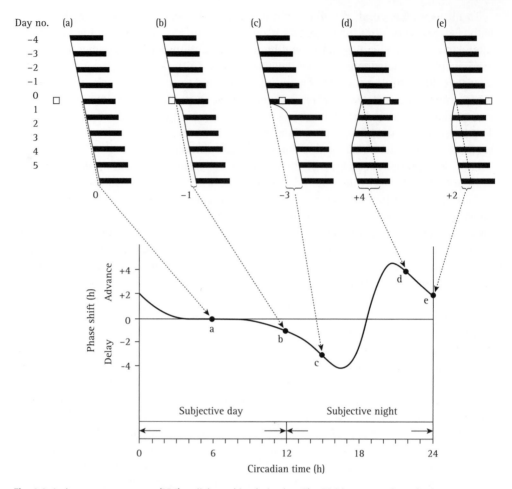

**Fig. 4.2** A phase-response curve (PRC) to light and its derivation. The PRC is a convenient plotting convention to summarize the empirical observation that light can phase shift circadian rhythms, and that the direction and magnitude of the shift depends on the circadian phase of the organism's clock. (a–e) Simulated free-running activity rhythms of nocturnal animals kept in constant dark, with the heavy bars denoting the active period of each circadian cycle. Free-running period is slightly greater than 24 h (the rhythms are drifting later each day). In each panel, the open square indicates the timing of a brief exposure to light (e.g., 15 min). In (a), light falls during the animal's rest period (in this case, the subjective day, when the sun would normally be up); no phase shift occurs. In (b–e), light falls early, mid, or late in the active period (the nocturnal animal's subjective night), and in each case this produces a rapid and permanent shift of the animal's rhythm. However, phase delays result only when light falls in the first half of the night (with larger delays the later the exposure), and phase advances only when light falls in the latter half of the night (with large advances the earlier in this half). The clock thus has a circadian rhythm of sensitivity to light that ensures entrainment. If the clock tends to drift later, "morning" light will advance it, whereas if it drifts earlier, "evening" light will delay it. (Modified from Moore-Ede et al. 1982.)

precise time of light exposure. Early in the subjective night, light induces a phase-delay shift, i.e., the next cycle occurs later than predicted based on the preceding cycles, and the rhythm resumes its free-run from this new phase. Later in the subjective night, light induces a phase-advance shift, i.e., the next cycle occurs earlier than predicted. The resulting PRC therefore has three regions: an unresponsive zone in the subjective day, a phase-delay zone in the early part of the subjective night, and a phase-advance zone late in the subjective night.

This basic PRC shape is characteristic of all organisms that can be entrained by light, regardless of whether they are nocturnal, diurnal, or crepuscular. It is a fundamental property of circadian clocks, and it explains why, within certain parameters, entrainment to LD cycles is inevitable. Consider a nocturnal animal with a fast-running circadian clock ($\tau < 24$ h). In constant dark, activity onset would occur earlier each day. However, in an LD cycle, an early onset of activity will mean exposure to light in the early subjective night, which is the phase-delay portion of the PRC. The clock will therefore undergo a phase-delay shift, which will counteract its progressive drift toward earlier wake-up times. The clock will stop drifting, and become stably entrained at that phase relative to the LD cycle when light produces a net daily shift that matches the difference between $\tau$ and 24 h. In cases where the circadian clock tends to run slow ($\tau > 24$ h), the clock will drift later relative to the LD cycle until light exposure occurs at a phase of the clock that produces a net phase advance precisely offsetting $\tau - 24$ h. Regardless of the direction of error, the bidirectional shape of the PRC ensures that at some phase relation between clock and LD cycle, stable entrainment will be achieved, even in cases where the LD cycle provides only a few minutes of light each day (nocturnal animals are particularly sensitive to light; diurnal animals may require longer or brighter periods of light exposure).

Although the procedure of exposing animals to brief light pulses may seem highly artificial from the perspective of diurnal animals (like humans) that are exposed to full natural photoperiods, there are likely many nocturnal animals that see very little light during most circadian cycles. In one study (DeCoursey 1986), wild-caught flying squirrels were housed in a seminatural environment with a light-proof nest box connected by a burrow to an open area with food, water, a wheel, and a standard LD cycle (Fig. 4.3). On most nights, the squirrels were observed to exit the nest box shortly after lights-off, and to return before lights-on. On these days, they saw no light. Over successive nights, wake-up occurred a few minutes earlier (i.e., the squirrels free-ran, with $\tau$ slightly less than 24 h) until eventually there was a night when the squirrels encountered light at the mouth of the burrow when they attempted to exit. This triggered an immediate return to the nest and a brief period of quiescence before a second attempt to exit ("light-sampling" behavior). On the night after this brief light exposure, wake-up was phase delayed by about 30 min, and no light was encountered at exit. This pattern was repeated every 4–5 days, such that total light exposure was limited to just a few minutes each week. Nonetheless, the small phase-delay shifts induced by these brief encounters with light were sufficient to maintain a relatively stable phase of entrainment, with wake-up closely synchronized to lights-off.

The PRC and $\tau$ together can account for individual and species differences in the precise phase relation between rhythm and LD cycle. For a given PRC shape, a shorter $\tau$

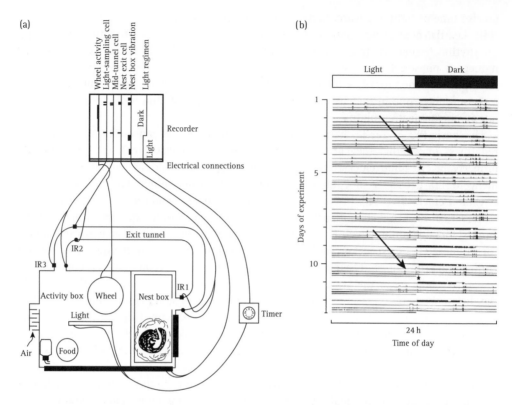

**Fig. 4.3** (a) Seminatural recording chamber housing a flying squirrel (*Glaucomys volans*). The squirrel slept in a nest box, which was completely shielded from light by a tunnel exiting to a small open field with a wheel, food, and water. Light exposure was monitored by photocells (IR1, IR2, IR3) strategically placed in the tunnel. (b) Event records illustrating the daily rhythm of wheel running, indicated by the heavy bars. Under each heavy bar are three thinner lines showing activity detected by the photocells. Note that running is exclusively nocturnal and that on most days there is little or no exposure to light. Despite this, the hamster remains stably entrained to the light–dark cycle. Entrainment is mediated by small phase delays induced by light sampling at the tunnel exit on days 5 and 10 (indicated by arrows and stars). (From DeCoursey 1986.)

will result in a more advanced phase of entrainment. In humans, this would result in early rising (the "early-bird" or "morning" type). A longer $\tau$ would result in late rising (the "night-owl" or "evening" type). This predicted relation between endogenous $\tau$ and phase of entrainment has been confirmed empirically in humans and other species. For a given $\tau$, differences in PRC shape will also have predictable consequences for entrainment. Thus, there are two circadian clock properties – its rate of cycling and its circadian rhythm of sensitivity to light – that can be modified to adjust or preserve the phase of entrainment as environmental conditions change seasonally or over generations.

There is also evidence that $\tau$, and therefore the phase of entrainment, changes over the lifetime of individuals. Some studies have demonstrated changes in $\tau$ associated with aging, although there is some controversy as to the direction of change in different species. In humans, the advanced phase of sleep onset and of awakening shown by many older people would be consistent with a shortened circadian $\tau$. Similarly, the delayed phase of both sleep onset and awakening preferred by adolescents would be predicted to reflect a lengthening of $\tau$ during and after puberty, for which there is some evidence (Carskadon et al. 1997). Such physiological changes would be potentiated by social factors promoting late-night activities in older adolescents, such that the phase of preferred awakening would be incompatible with societal demands for early morning attendance at school for example.

It should be noted that while we typically refer to sharply defined markers of the circadian cycle such as awakening or sleep onset, what is actually entrained is a complex circadian program that affects functions throughout the circadian cycle. Thus, most humans show a daily pattern of increasing alertness and improved performance throughout the day, until an evening hour when both alertness and performance begin to deteriorate. The timing of this pattern is predictably related to individuals' preferences for early or late awakening, with morning-type individuals showing earlier peaks and troughs of performance relative to external clock time.

The PRC and $\tau$ can also account for some empirically established constraints on LD entrainment. In some work settings, humans may lack exposure to natural time-of-day cues; examples include nuclear submarines that submerge for many days, and workstations in orbit or near the poles. In these settings, to meet requirements for continuous operation, it may seem desirable to employ work schedules that differ from 24 h. However, humans (and other animals) are unable to entrain to such schedules if they differ by more than 1 or 2 h from 24 h. This observation is predictable from the PRC to light: maximum phase shifts to single pulses of light are on the order of 1–3 h, suggesting a maximum range of entrainment of $24 \pm 3$ h.

The same phase-shifting constraints underlie the phenomena of jet lag and shift-work malaise. These conditions, characterized by transient sleep disturbances, daytime fatigue, and gastrointestinal complaints, are associated with rapid travel to new time zones or with rotations between day, evening, and night shifts. The cause is a temporary mismatch between circadian clock time and the new sleep–wake schedule. Travel between North America and Europe results in a rapid 4–9 h shift of the LD cycle (an advance if traveling east, a delay if traveling west). The circadian clock cannot shift by this amount in one cycle, but will reentrain to the new local time cues in jumps of about 1–2 h per day. The general rule is that the rate of reentrainment is equal to about one day per time zone. However, reentrainment is usually quicker after traveling west (in part because $\tau$ in humans is usually > 24 h, and thus its natural tendency to drift later is in the desired direction). Also, reentrainment can be greatly facilitated if travelers seek out light at the "right" circadian time (e.g., corresponding to the phase-advance zone of their PRC for trips east, and the phase-delay zone for trips west) and avoid light at the "wrong" circadian time (Fig. 4.4).

Complicating this analysis of the dynamics underlying jet lag and related phenomena is recent evidence that these observations apply only to the central neural pacemaker. Other parts of the body (muscles, liver, etc.) appear to have their own damped circadian oscillations (see Fig. 4.5), which may respond only sluggishly to the light-induced shifts of the pacemaker (Balsolabre 2002). Thus full physiological adaptation

(a)

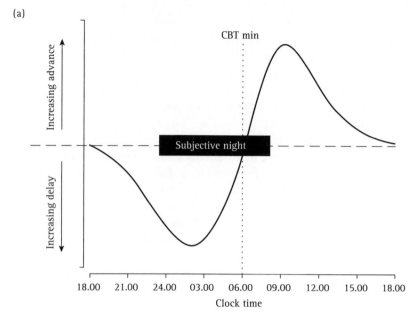

(b)

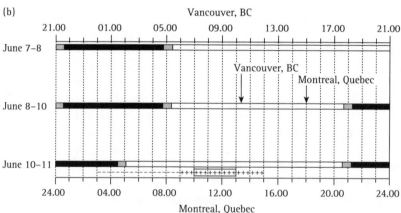

**Fig. 4.4** (a) Hypothetical phase-response curve to light in humans, aligned relative to local clock time (horizontal axis), subjective night (sleep time, indicated by black bar), and body temperature minimum (CBT min, vertical dotted line). Light exposure before CBT min causes phase delays, while light after CBT min causes advances. (b) Optimal light exposure schedule for adjusting the author's rhythms following a trip from Vancouver to Montreal, Canada. This requires a modest 3-h phase advance (three time zones), accomplished most rapidly by seeking out light exposure at times that will advance the circadian clock (indicated by +++) and, just as importantly, by avoiding light at times that will delay the circadian clock (indicated by ---). The optimal light exposure time is indicated by the boxed plus signs. Open bars, day; shaded bars, twilight; black bars, night.

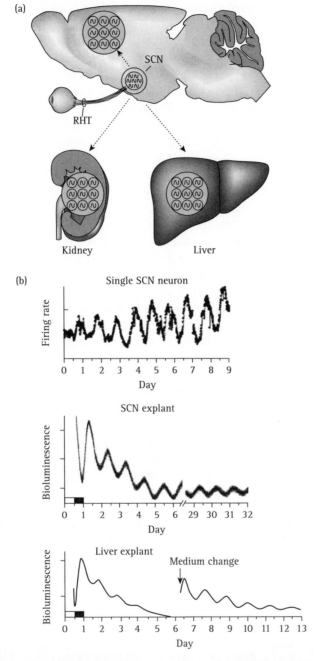

**Fig. 4.5** (a) Sagittal view of rat brain illustrating core structure of the "circadian system," i.e., input (eye) → clock (suprachiasmatic nucleus, SCN) → output. The SCN coordinates oscillators elsewhere in the brain and body, either directly or by its control over behaviors such as feeding. RHT, retinohypothalamic tract. (b) Circadian rhythms of a single SCN neuron, an SCN explant (isolated from the brain and genetically modified to express light when the neurons are active), and a liver explant (also modified to express light). These amazing experiments demonstrate that single SCN neurons oscillate, that the SCN ensemble oscillates for many days independently of the rest of the brain, and that circadian oscillators also exist in peripheral organs such as the liver. Peripheral oscillators tend to damp out, but the rhythm can be renewed by changing the medium sustaining the tissue. (From Reppert & Weaver 2002.)

to a major shift in local time cues may take many more days than suggested solely by analysis of the pacemaker itself or of rhythms closely regulated by it.

Shiftworkers face the same physiological challenges following rotations that require large shifts of the work day (Burgess et al. 2002). Two weeks or more may be required to reentrain fully following a change from day to night work. Because it is usually difficult to control light exposure, and because workers often revert to daytime activity on their days off during an extended night-work schedule, reentrainment is usually only partial, if it occurs at all. Therefore, modern shift schedules either employ rapid rotations (no more than 2–4 days on a shift), on the assumption that it is best to remain synchronized normally and minimize the consecutive number of night shifts, or they use very slow rotations (3 weeks or more between rotations), in order to minimize the number of shift rotations. The cost of the former approach is that workers may be doing very sensitive tasks (medical interventions, flight-traffic control, piloting) at circadian phases during which their physiology is dictating sleep. The latter approach attempts to avoid this cost, although the reality is that physiological adaptation to these shifted schedules is actually quite limited. The probability of industrial or automobile accidents peaks at times of day when the daily rhythm of alertness is at its circadian minimum (about 2–3 h before normal wake-up time, near the body temperature minimum, with a secondary peak at midday, the "siesta" time). Thus, an important aim of basic research on the circadian timekeeping system is to understand its properties and underlying neural and molecular mechanisms sufficiently to design effective strategies for rapid resetting of the circadian clock, for example by pharmacological and environmental interventions. Although LD cycles are the dominant Zeitgeber for most species, nonphotic stimuli can also phase shift or entrain circadian rhythms. Daily temperature cycles may be important Zeitgebers for some species (particularly plants and poikilothermic organisms), while daily cycles of food availability and social interactions can entrain behavioral and physiological rhythms in a variety of species (Mistlberger 1994). Entrainment by social cues may be mediated by their direct effects on behavioral state, because simply keeping an animal awake and active during its usual rest phase can induce large phase shifts, at least in some mammals (Mistlberger & Skene 2004). In humans, exercise very early in the morning (around the minimum of the daily cycle of body temperature, prior to usual wake-up time) can induce phase shifts. Much remains to be learned about how photic and nonphotic stimuli combine to regulate circadian timing of organisms in complex natural habitats.

## Neural Mechanisms of Circadian Rhythms

The physiological system responsible for circadian rhythmicity must include three parts: a self-sustaining circadian clock, one or more input pathways by which LD cycles (and other cues) can entrain the clock, and one or more output pathways by which the clock can control the timing of behavior and physiology. The available evidence suggests that in most, if not all, species there are multiple entraining inputs, clocks, and outputs. There appear to be many common themes across **phylogeny** in the organization of circadian systems, but there is also substantial species diversity in the details. The same is true at the molecular level of analysis.

## Mammals

### *Localization of a circadian pacemaker in mammals*

Localization of the circadian clock in mammals was guided by the reasonable assumption that it receives information about light and dark, possibly by a direct pathway from the retina. Cutting the optic nerves in mammals eliminates entrainment to LD cycles, but does not eliminate circadian rhythms of behavior and physiology; therefore, the eyes must contain the photoreceptors necessary for entrainment but not the circadian pacemaker itself. The axons of retinal ganglion cells form the optic nerves that communicate photic information to the brain. The two nerves cross, at least partially, forming the optic chiasm at the base of the brain just below the hypothalamus (Fig. 4.5). The nerves, now renamed the optic tracts, exit the chiasm and project to various areas of the brain responsible for vision, oculomotor reflexes, and other functions. If all optic tracts are cut posterior to the chiasm, the animal is rendered visually blind; however, it remains entrained to LD cycles. Therefore, the retinal pathway mediating photic entrainment must enter the brain at the level of the chiasm. Sensitive tract-tracing techniques revealed that some retinal fibers innervate the hypothalamus above the chiasm, particularly the SCN, which lies atop the chiasm. In 1972, two groups reported that surgical ablation of this small bilateral structure completely eliminated circadian rhythms of locomotor activity and corticosterone secretion in rats (Weaver 1998). In subsequent years, similar results were reported for other mammals and for other variables, permitting the generalization that under constant conditions, mammals without an SCN do not express spontaneous circadian rhythms of behavior or physiology.

Additional experiments were needed to clarify the role of the SCN. Is it the site of the clock or is it merely permissive for the expression of circadian rhythms, e.g., does it convey output from the clock to the rest of the brain? First, it was shown that stimulation of the SCN, electrically or with drugs, caused phase shifts of circadian rhythms that mimicked those produced by light or other stimuli. Then it was established, by measures of glucose uptake and electrical activity, that neural activity of the SCN expressed a circadian rhythm, both in vivo and when isolated from the rest of the brain in vitro (the SCN is dissected out and maintained in a special perfusion chamber providing oxygen and nutrients). Finally, it was demonstrated that transplanting an SCN from a donor animal to an animal in which the SCN was previously ablated surgically could restore free-running circadian rhythms of behavior. Notably, the restored rhythms displayed a $\tau$ characteristic of the donor animal not the host animal (Ralph & Lehman 1991). This remarkable series of lesion, stimulation, recording, and transplant experiments, conducted over approximately 20 years in numerous laboratories, established that the SCN is an autonomous circadian oscillator responsible for setting the phase and period of circadian rhythms (Klein et al. 1991). The SCN has thus been accorded the status of master oscillator, or pacemaker, within the mammalian circadian system.

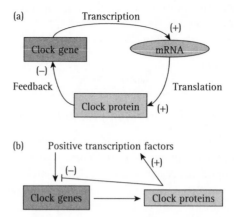

**Fig. 4.6** Molecular basis of circadian clocks. (a) Negative feedback loop by which the expression of a gene is controlled by its own protein product. The gene transcribes mRNA, which is translated into a protein, which then feeds back to turn off transcription. (b) More complex and realistic model summarizing the conceptual elements of the circadian clock that have so far been shown to generalize across eukaryotic species (e.g., bread mold, fruit flies, and mice). In this model, transcription of one or more clock genes is turned on by one or more "positive elements." Clock gene mRNA is translated into clock gene proteins, which then feed back to inhibit some positive elements and stimulate other positive elements. The positive elements and/or the clock proteins may also control other genes, thereby generating circadian rhythms in cellular functions controlled by these genes. The specific genes and proteins may differ somewhat across species, but the principle of positive and negative elements connected by feedback and feedforward loops appears to be general.

## Cellular and molecular clockworks

How does the SCN circadian pacemaker tick? One possibility is that SCN **neurons** are wired in such a way that signals passed from one neuron to the next take approximately 24 h to complete a single loop through the entire ensemble. An alternative to this "cell-assembly" model is that many or all neurons in the SCN are themselves circadian clocks, mutually coupled so as to produce a coherent circadian output signal. Electrical recordings from SCN neurons grown in culture support the latter hypothesis: single cells recorded from the same culture exhibited free-running circadian rhythms with different values of $\tau$ (Welsh et al. 1995; Fig. 4.5b). This result is consistent with evidence from unicellular organisms that circadian clocks are cell-autonomous, and confirms that the intracellular basis of circadian timekeeping has been conserved across phylogeny.

If the circadian clock is intracellular, there must be genes and proteins that cycle with a 24-h period, and these cycles must be self-perpetuating. The first putative **clock genes** were discovered in the 1970s in the bread mold *Neurospora* and the fruit fly *Drosophila*. These genes, *frequency* (*frq*) in *Neurospora* and *period* (*per*) in *Drosophila*, exhibit circadian rhythms of expression by virtue of autoregulatory negative feedback loops (Fig. 4.6; Panda et al. 2002; Reppert & Weaver 2002). Both genes code for proteins (FRQ and PER respectively) that accumulate in the cytoplasm, translocate back to the nucleus, and inhibit their own expression. This causes protein production to decline, and protein levels in the cytoplasm and nucleus to fall until the genes are no longer inhibited. An embedded molecular feedback loop drives a subsequent increase in expression, and the cycle is repeated. Mutations of these (and related) genes are associated with loss of circadian rhythmicity or changes in $\tau$, establishing their essential role for circadian cycling.

The principle of circadian cycling by autoregulatory feedback loops appears to have been widely conserved across phylogeny. Recent work indicates that there are at least two interacting loops at the core of the clock, one employing negative and one positive feedback. Species differences are apparent in the number of genes involved (e.g., mice have three *per* genes compared with only one in fruit flies) and in their specific roles. Stimuli that entrain the circadian clock may do so by acutely altering the level of clock gene proteins, either delaying their fall or advancing their rise, thereby resetting the timing cycle.

Surprisingly, mammalian clock genes are expressed in many brain regions outside the SCN, and in peripheral organs such as the heart, lungs, and liver. SCN ablation eliminates circadian behavioral rhythms in animals given free access to food, but if meals are restricted to one or two times a day, a food-anticipatory activity rhythm emerges that exhibits the formal properties of a true circadian rhythm (Mistlberger 1994). Presumably, clock genes in areas outside the SCN can be induced to oscillate in phase with feeding time, and these oscillators have access to behavioral effectors that drive foraging activity. A recent study has identified the liver as one of these areas, while confirming that SCN clock genes are not rephased by scheduled feeding in intact animals (Damiola et al. 2000; Fig. 4.6b). Thus, it may be that under certain conditions daily rhythms of hunger and food-seeking behavior are orchestrated by clocks in peripheral organs.

Another structure that contains circadian oscillators is the retina. Syrian hamster retinas maintained in culture exhibit circadian rhythms of melatonin secretion (Tosini & Menaker 1996). However, as noted above, optic enucleation does not eliminate circadian rhythms of behavior. The retina, like visceral organs, and possibly brain regions other than the SCN, contains a circadian oscillator that coordinates local processes but is itself normally coordinated by the master circadian pacemaker in the SCN. A recent study demonstrated that output from cultured SCN cells can entrain rhythms in other cell types, but rhythmic cells from the periphery lack this capacity. The special pacemaking role of SCN neurons may depend as much on their unique output signaling mechanisms as on their capacity for autonomous oscillation (Allen et al. 2001).

### Circadian output signals

The neural pathways by which the SCN is coupled to other circadian oscillators or to specific effectors regulating behavioral and physiological processes are only beginning to be identified. Most SCN neurons project only to other regions of the hypothalamus, and there is some evidence that they may employ both classical synaptic neurotransmission and diffusible factors to communicate timing information. One study has reported that a fetal SCN transplanted into an SCN-ablated animal within an implanted membrane that permits diffusion of small molecules, but not outgrowth of neural axonal connections, can still restore circadian activity rhythms (Silver et al. 1996).

Given that circadian rhythms of clock genes in peripheral tissues are rephased by restricted feeding schedules, it is possible that the SCN pacemaker in rats is not directly coupled to these organs. Rather, when food is freely available, the SCN may control the daily rhythm of food intake, the consequences of which synchronize peripheral oscillators. An externally imposed feeding schedule bypasses the output of the SCN, causing dissociation between its driven rhythms and those of food-regulated peripheral oscillators. This flexible coupling via a behavioral intermediate may ensure that, under unusual conditions of food availability, visceral organs vital for nutrient absorption and metabolism are appropriately synchronized with food intake. At the same time, other SCN functions that depend on its photic synchronization, such as timing of other daily rhythms, daylength measurement, and clock-based navigation, remain uncompromised. In other species, however, feeding-related signals may actually synchronize the SCN in some individuals.

## Nonmammalian vertebrates

The circadian systems of birds and reptiles (sauropsid vertebrates) are less centralized than those of mammals (Gwinner & Brandstatter 2001). In adult mammals, the photoreceptors for entrainment are found only in the retina. In sauropsid vertebrates, photoreceptors important for entrainment are found in the retina, pineal gland, and one or more parts of the brain (encephalic photoreceptors). In mammals, the SCN is a master pacemaker that coordinates secondary oscillators in the retina, periphery, and possibly other brain areas. In sauropsids, a homolog of the SCN is localized to one or more structures in the suprachiasmatic area, although ablation of this area in birds disrupts or eliminates circadian rhythms only in constant light or dark. In some avian species, circadian rhythms are eliminated or greatly disrupted by ablation of the pineal gland, whereas in others combined removal of the retina and the pineal is necessary to eliminate circadian rhythmicity. All rhythms may not be equally affected, at least in starlings (*Sturnus vulgaris*), leading to some ambiguity as to the interpretation of these lesion effects. In Japanese quail (*Coturnix coturnix japonica*), the circadian oscillator in the eyes is necessary for normal rhythmicity.

In most sauropsid species for which data are available, including the house sparrow (*Passer domesticus*), chicken (*Gallus gallus*), and anolis lizard (*Anolis carolinensis*), the isolated pineal maintains a circadian oscillation in vitro, whereas in mammals the pineal cannot oscillate without rhythmic input provided by the SCN. In the desert iguana (*Dipsosaurus dorsalisa*), as in mammals, only SCN ablations disrupt circadian rhythms, and the pineal does not oscillate in vitro. However, in another species, the green iguana (*Iguana iguana*), the pineal, retinas, and parietal eye all oscillate robustly in vitro, and an intact pineal is essential for circadian thermoregulatory rhythms but not for activity or electroretinogram rhythms (Tosini & Menaker 1996). The sauropsid circadian system is thus characterized by a more distributed circadian regulatory system, and marked species variability in the role of its oscillatory and photoreceptive elements. Mutual coupling of the primary oscillators in the retina, hypothalamus, and pineal, possibly by an endocrine factor such as melatonin, may serve to amplify and increase the precision of the aggregate circadian signal. The ecological significance of species variability in the details of sauropsid circadian organization remains to be explored.

Less is known about the neural and endocrine bases of circadian timekeeping in amphibians and fish, but the available evidence suggests an important role for the pineal as photoreceptor and pacemaker in the few species studied. In the clawed frog (*Xenopus*), retinal photoreceptors maintain circadian oscillations in vitro. In the hagfish (*Eptatretus stouti*), ablation of the hypothalamus eliminates circadian rhythms, but the site of the circadian clock within the hypothalamus is uncertain.

## Seasonal Rhythmicity

In many habitats, daylength, temperature, and precipitation change markedly with season, altering the availability of food, cover, and shelter, as well as the activity of resident predators, competitors, and parasites. These annual cycles present formidable challenges for survival and reproduction. One solution is seasonal migration to a more hospitable environment during the winter or dry season, and return migration at an appropriate time. Another solution is to remain in place but undergo seasonal changes in behavior (e.g., reproductive, ingestive, nesting), physiology (e.g., metabolism, reproductive), and morphology (e.g., fur or feather density and color) that facilitate survival and which restrict breeding to seasons optimal for survival of offspring. Both solutions require that behavioral and physiological adjustments begin well in advance of the target season. To anticipate the change of season, most animals measure daylength, and in some cases use daylength to entrain an endogenous circannual clock.

## Circannual clocks

Seasonal rhythms driven by a circannual clock are those that persist for one or more years in constant environments. Circannual clocks have been demonstrated in a variety of longer-lived species, including ground squirrels, marmots, deer, sheep, and some species of bats and primates. Although generated endogenously, circannual rhythms, like circadian rhythms, are entrained by environmental changes in light exposure. In all species studied, annual changes in daylength are the primary, if not exclusive, circannual Zeitgeber. In some species, entrainment may require a gradual change in photoperiod, as occurs in the natural habitat.

The location of the circannual clock is not known for any species (Zucker 2001). Ablation studies have ruled out a necessary role for the SCN circadian clock in most species, although in experiments with ground squirrels a minority of animals with SCN ablations failed to exhibit circannual rhythms in body mass. Under some conditions, the circannual cycle of hibernation is also disrupted by SCN damage.

Although the pineal gland is also not necessary for the generation of circannual rhythms, it is necessary for their entrainment by photoperiod. The pineal gland secretes the hormone melatonin at night, under the control of the SCN circadian pacemaker. Neural activity in the SCN increases during the daytime (in both diurnal and nocturnal animals) and the duration of this increased activity is proportional to daylength. Also, pineal melatonin synthesis is directly inhibited by light. The duration of melatonin secretion each night thus varies with daylength, and serves as an endogenous signal of season when combined with information about the direction of change in duration. Surgical removal of the pineal abolishes entrainment of circannual rhythms.

## Photoperiodism and interval timers

Annual rhythms in most species do not involve a fully autonomous circannual clock, but depend on seasonal changes in photoperiod for one of more of the annual physiological transitions (Gorman et al. 2001). Decreasing daylength in the fall induces behavioral and physiological responses appropriate to autumn and winter, whereas increasing daylength induces responses appropriate to spring and summer. However, the critical daylength for eliciting a seasonal physiological change varies with the species, the particular variable being measured, and the animal's recent photoperiod history. History dependence is important because, apart from the annual extremes, most daylengths are ambiguous as to season, given that they occur twice a year, once before and once after the summer solstice. Consequently, the response to an intermediate photoperiod often depends on whether it is longer or shorter than the prior photoperiod. In rare cases, winter responses may occur only within a narrow range of photoperiods, with summer responses stimulated by longer or shorter days.

In some species, the winter state reverses spontaneously after several months of continuous exposure to short days. In a well-studied model system, the Syrian hamster, the gonads regress and reproductive behavior ceases in response to decreased daylength, but within 20–25 weeks the gonads spontaneously recrudesce (regrow) even if the animals are maintained in short days or continuous darkness, presumably in preparation for the end of winter and the onset of the breeding season. For several months after recrudescence, hamsters are unresponsive to short days. Photosensitivity is only restored by several weeks of exposure to long days. The annual cycle therefore appears to be regulated by an endogenous interval timer that is triggered by short days and reset by long days. The circadian clock plays an essential role in photoperiodic time measurement, due to its intrinsic circadian rhythm of sensitivity to light. The daily pattern of light exposure differs in summer and winter, stimulating different phases of the circadian clock. Even very brief pulses of light, timed to occur at certain circadian phases, can trigger long-day physiological responses. Thus season is sensed by the timing of light relative to a circadian template, although there are alternative hypotheses about the exact mechanisms involved in daylength measurement. A consensus view is that daylength affects circadian cycling of the clock and that changes in clock output signals affect neuroendocrine regulators of seasonal responses, such as the duration of nocturnal melatonin secretion.

The issue of human photoperiodic responses has attracted considerable attention, partly because of the psychiatric syndrome **seasonal affective disorder** (SAD), a regularly recurring seasonal (usually winter) depression (Lam 1998). The fact that in many patients this condition can be treated successfully with timed brief light exposure that effectively extends the light phase of a short winter day has prompted an exploration of whether it is based on photoperiod. There is evidence that supports the idea that the circadian profile of melatonin secretion differs between SAD patients and normal controls in the winter but not when patients are asymptomatic in the summer. This evidence reinforces the conclusion from a review of many years of birth records that humans express at least a rudimentary seasonal rhythmicity (Roenneberg & Aschoff 1990). The degree to which this rhythmicity has been modified in industrial societies by artificial regulation of light and temperature, and the proximal cues that regulate seasonality, remain open questions.

## Ultradian Rhythmicity

Ultradian rhythms can be defined as those that complete two or more cycles per circadian day. The definition is broad and the cutoffs arbitrary because, unlike circadian and circannual rhythms, ultradian rhythms do not correspond to any geophysical cycle in the environment. Ultradian rhythms can be further classified as those controlled by **interval timers** and those controlled by self-sustaining oscillators.

Interval timers can express a rhythm only if they are reset periodically. An example is the hourglass timer. The duration of a single cycle is set by the length of time it takes for sand to run out, and the cycle will not be repeated unless the hourglass is reset. Ultradian rhythms in feeding and locomotor activity evident in many organisms likely reflect the rate at which ingested nutrients are absorbed and metabolized, an hourglass process reset by each major feeding.

In some rodent species, ultradian cycles of activity have been shown to persist even if food is withheld, indicating that these rhythms are generated by a true ultradian oscillator (Gerkema et al. 1993). The physical location and cellular mechanisms of such ultradian oscillators remain to be established.

From a functional perspective, it has been hypothesized that synchrony of ultradian rhythms of foraging within a local population of animals vulnerable to predation may reduce both the probability of being killed (safety in numbers) and the total number of kills (swamping the predator's capacity; see also Chapter 14; Daan 1981).

Ultradian rhythms are also evident in sleeping organisms. In normal adult humans, sleep progresses through four nonrapid eye movement (NREM) sleep stages, followed by a rapid eye movement (REM) sleep episode. This cycle is repeated at intervals of approximately 90–120 min through a typical 7–8 h sleep period. The cycle is modulated by circadian phase, such that the duration of the REM sleep episode is greatest near the nocturnal body temperature minimum (late in a typical night's sleep). The latency to the first REM bout is also shorter when sleep is initiated closer to the temperature minimum, but sleep-onset REM episodes in adults are rare and are normally symptomatic of a sleep disorder. Thus, the NREM–REM cycle reflects an ultradian process that is reset by sleep onset but modulated by circadian phase.

Discovery of the 90-min sleep cycle stimulated the search for a comparable periodicity in waking activities. Numerous behavioral and physiological variables have since been shown to exhibit rhythmicity in the 90-min range during waking, leading to the hypothesis of a "basic rest–activity cycle" manifest in neurobehavioral functions during waking and in the NREM–REM cycle during sleep (Kleitman 1963, 1993). However, the evidence for continuity between waking 90-min cycles and the sleep cycle is weak, possibly because the sleep-stage cycle is clearly reset at sleep onset. The mechanism for ultradian cycles in waking functions, and whether these cycles reflect multiple independent processes or a single common process, is unknown.

## SUMMARY AND CONCLUSIONS

Under usual environmental conditions, a large proportion of the variance in animal behavior can be accounted for by a stable behavioral program regulated by ultradian, circadian, and circannual oscillators and timers. The precision of circadian timekeeping is such that the activities of bees and flying squirrels can be predicted to within minutes from knowledge of the timing of their rhythms during the previous circadian cycle. Human behavior is similarly predictable: the probability of sleep or wake onset is closely related to circadian phase, as is appetite and cognitive and physical performance. Neurobehavioral analysis of endogenous rhythmicity is central to understanding the temporal dimension of animal behavior and the human condition.

## FURTHER READING

Chronobiology as a modern identifiable field of scientific inquiry can arguably be traced to the landmark Cold Spring Harbor Symposium on Quantitative Biology held in 1960, which summarized empirical findings and general principles of biological rhythms to that date (Chovnick 1960). Comprehensive updates of note include two volumes of the *Handbook of Behavioral Neurobiology* (Aschoff 1981; Takahashi et al. 2002), the Proceedings of the Ringberg Conference on Vertebrate Circadian Systems (Aschoff et al. 1982), and the Proceedings of the Ciba Foundation Symposium on Circadian Clocks (Chadwick & Ackrill 1995). Textbooks of note include those by Moore-Ede et al. (1982), Refinetti (2000), and Dunlap et al. (2004). An entire volume devoted to the suprachiasmatic nucleus is also available (Klein et al. 1991). References to classic empirical publications and to other reviews and books can be found in these volumes. As of July 2003, the US National Library of Medicine search engine identified 44,900 scholarly publications related to circadian rhythms alone.

# 5

# brain and behavior

### DAVID F. SHERRY

## INTRODUCTION

The brains of animals do many things. For the purposes of this chapter the things brains do are organized into three broad categories. Brains obtain **information** from the environment, they carry out cognitive operations, and they control movement: input, central processing, and output. These categories are broad because although they are certainly the conventional way of thinking about the brain and behavior, from the beginning of systematic work on the topic (Lashley 1929) to present-day research (Gazzaniga 2000), it is often not possible to find a clear demarcation between, say, receiving sensory input from the environment and performing cognitive operations on that input. The "cognitive" category itself is a very broad one, including everything from memory to spatial orientation, timing, **decision**-making, and social interactions. These categories are therefore more an organizational convenience that corresponds to how we think about the things a brain has to do than how the nervous system actually divides up the tasks it performs. With this in mind, let us proceed to the first category, how animals obtain information about their environment.

## Sensing and Perceiving the Environment

## The auditory world of the barn owl (*Tyto alba*)

Just below the eaves of an abandoned farmhouse, a barn owl pokes its full-moon face through a gap in weathered grey boards. It hunches forward and launches itself into the darkness. It will spend the night flying in and out of a nearby orchard, tracing long loops over meadows and pastures in search of prey. Its flight is almost silent. It can hunt successfully on the darkest nights because it finds its prey, mostly mice, voles, and shrews, by sound. The sounds the barn owl detects are faint, quiet as a mouse in fact, but its sensitive hearing pinpoints sound sources with such accuracy that it can swoop even in complete darkness and fly off with prey in its talons. How the barn owl brain constructs auditory scenes from environmental sounds provides our first illustration of neural processing of the sensory world.

## The barn owl's auditory map of space

All sound, like the rustling of a mouse in dry grass, comes from a location in space. The question is: how does the auditory system determine where the sound is coming from? The key to answering this question is that the two ears, whether owl ears or human ears, placed on opposite sides of the head, hear the same sound slightly differently. The auditory system combines the signals received by the two ears to produce the perception of a single sound source at a fixed location, a process called **binaural fusion**. Stereo recordings exploit binaural fusion to create the illusion of different instruments and voices occupying different places in the space between two stereo speakers.

When sound from a single source in the environment reaches the ears of the barn owl, the sounds received by the two ears are not the same. There is a difference in the timing of the sound at the two ears, and there is a difference in the intensity of the sound. The time difference is a consequence of the spacing between the ears: an expanding wave of sound will reach one side of the head before it reaches the other. The intensity difference occurs because **diffraction** of sound by the head reduces the intensity at one ear compared with the other. The structure of barn owl ears also exaggerates intensity differences because the ears are asymmetric. The right ear is located below eye level and is directed upward, whereas the left ear is located above eye level and is directed downward. A sound coming from above eye level, for example, will be perceived as louder in the right ear than in the left. Timing differences and intensity differences between the two ears are handled by two separate processing streams in the barn owl auditory system. Input from each ear is processed first as separate time and intensity signals, then combined to detect timing and intensity differences between the two ears, before being finally assembled into an auditory map of space.

### *Two auditory processing streams*

In the abstract, the problem of locating a sound in space is the problem of specifying the coordinates of a point on an imaginary sphere centered on the head of the listener. One of these coordinates is the **azimuth**, the horizontal position on the sphere, and the other is the **elevation**, the vertical position. In the barn owl, one processing stream is dedicated to each coordinate. Interaural time differences are almost perfectly correlated with the azimuth of a sound source, whereas interaural intensity differences are correlated with its elevation. Konishi and his colleagues confirmed this by recording sound from tiny microphones placed in the ears of barn owls (Moiseff & Konishi 1981). As they moved a speaker in a predetermined pattern around the barn owl's head, interaural time differences varied systematically with the azimuth of the speaker, whereas interaural intensity differences varied systematically with its vertical position. By attaching two coils of copper wire to the barn owl's head at right angles, and placing the barn owl in a larger array of coils carrying an electrical current that produced a magnetic field, they were able to record the orientation of the barn owl's head as the location of the speaker was changed (Moiseff 1989). This technique showed that barn owls turned their heads very accurately to face the speaker when it produced a sound. Furthermore, an owl will do the same to a phantom sound source created by delivering sounds to tiny earphones placed in the owl's ears (Moiseff & Konishi 1981). Varying interaural time and intensity differences between these earphones caused the owl to turn and face the location in space that would correspond to a sound that produced the same time and intensity differences between the ears.

Sounds are converted to neural signals by auditory receptors in the basilar membrane of the **cochlea**, a small spiral chamber inside the ear. The site of stimulation on the basilar membrane of the cochlea corresponds to the **frequency** of the sound, high-frequency sounds stimulating receptors at the proximal end, nearest the tympanum or

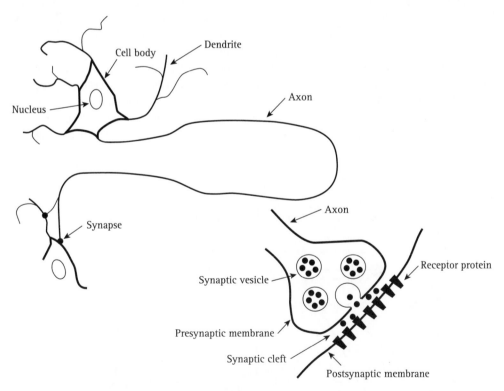

**Fig. 5.1** Schematic diagram of a neuron, showing the cell body and nucleus, dendrites, and axon. Electrical signals, in the form of depolarization of the cell membrane, travel along the axon to the axon terminal. This signal is relayed chemically across the synapse to the next neuron by release of neurotransmitter from vesicles at the presynaptic membrane. Neurotransmitter binds to receptors in the postsynaptic membrane and, depending on the state of the postsynaptic neuron and the amount of neurotransmitter released, initiates an electrical signal in the next neuron.

eardrum, and low-frequency sounds stimulating receptors at the distal end. Movement of the basilar membrane causes **neurotransmitter** release in hair cells, which causes excitation of the primary auditory **neurons**. Figure 5.1 illustrates the general features of the transmission of neural signals. The firing patterns of primary auditory fibers in response to movement of the basilar membrane encode both sound intensity and frequency. Sound is a waveform and auditory neurons convey frequency information by firing at a particular **phase** of the sound wave (Fig. 5.2). Such cells are said to be **phase-locked**. Auditory neurons responsive to the same frequency are locked to the same phase angle of the sound wave (see Fig. 5.2a). The frequencies of most sounds are much higher than the frequency at which neurons can fire. A 10-kHz pure tone oscillates 10,000 times per second whereas few neurons can fire faster than several hundred times per second. So not all phase-locked neurons fire at every cycle of the sound, but when they do fire, they fire at the same phase of the waveform.

The primary auditory fibers travel along a branch of the eighth cranial nerve to the first sound-processing station in the barn owl brain, the cochlear nucleus magnocellularis, located in the **brainstem**. It is in this nucleus that the temporal properties of the monaural signal from each ear are extracted. Recordings from single neurons in this nucleus show that these cells fire with the same phase-locked pattern found in the auditory fibers, but do not respond differentially to the intensity of the auditory signal.

Signals from the **ipsilateral** and **contralateral** nucleus magnocellularis converge at the next step in the time-processing pathway, the nucleus laminaris, also located in the brainstem. Neurons in this nucleus are maximally responsive to phase-locked signals from the two ears that arrive in synchrony. That is, these neurons act as coincidence detectors, firing when stimulated simultaneously by signals from the left and right nucleus magnocellularis that are in phase with each other. Because the signals from the two

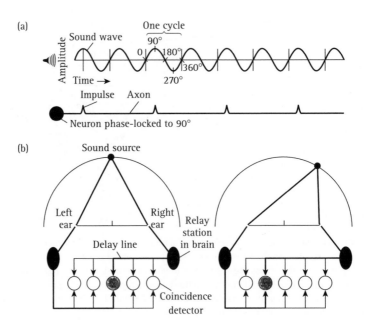

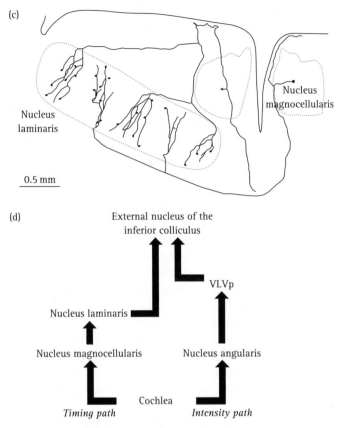

(c)

Nucleus
laminaris

Nucleus
magnocellularis

0.5 mm

(d)

External nucleus of the
inferior colliculus

VLVp

Nucleus laminaris

Nucleus magnocellularis

Nucleus angularis

Cochlea

*Timing path*        *Intensity path*

**Fig. 5.2** (a) Auditory neurons and neurons in the nucleus magnocellularis of the barn owl brain code sound frequency by firing only at a particular phase angle of a sound wave. The phase angle of a periodic wave is described by an angular value ranging from 0 to 360°. This illustration shows a neuron that fires only at the 90° phase angle of the sound wave. Because of the neuron's refractory period, it does not fire at every 90° phase angle. Such a neuron is phase-locked and neurons sensitive to the same frequency are locked to the same phase angle. (b) A sound that travels different distances to the two ears will cause phase-locked cells in the brain relay station, the nucleus magnocellularis, to fire out of phase with each other. How much out of phase the two signals are is determined by the horizontal location of the sound and can be estimated by a coincidence detector that uses a delay line to bring the signals from the two ears into register. Different coincidence detectors are fired by different characteristic delays between signals from the two ears. (c) A coronal section through the dorsal brainstem shows axonal projections from the contralateral and ipsilateral nucleus magnocellularis converging on the nucleus laminaris. The long indirect path from the ipsilateral nucleus magnocellularis acts as a delay line and neurons in the nucleus laminaris act as coincidence detectors. (d) Timing and intensity differences between the ears are relayed by different neuroanatomical paths to the inferior colliculus. This schematic drawing omits reciprocal connections between the two sides of the brain as well as other nuclei involved in auditory processing. VLVp, nucleus ventralis lemnisci lateralis, pars posterior. (From Konishi 1993, 1995.)

ears are out of phase unless the sound is directly in front of or behind the head (Fig. 5.2b), some mechanism is required to bring these two phase-locked signals into register (Jeffress 1948). This is accomplished in the barn owl brain by a remarkably simple arrangement: the axonal paths from the contralateral and ipsilateral nucleus magnocellularis are different lengths (Fig. 5.2c). The contralateral path crosses the midline between the hemispheres and goes directly to the ventral portion of the nucleus laminaris. The ipsilateral path follows a more circuitous route before terminating in the dorsal portion of the nucleus laminaris. This roundabout path from the ipsilateral nucleus magnocellularis acts as a delay line, slowing the time of arrival of its phase-locked signal. The contralateral and ipsilateral axons travel through the nucleus laminaris, intermingling and terminating on large laminaris cells as they do. At some laminaris cells, the phase-locked signals from the two ears will arrive in register, and the identity of the cells that fire indicates the timing difference between the auditory signals received by the left and right ears. Because of the delay in projections from the ear on the same side of the brain, laminaris cells triggered by left and right ear signals that are in phase are in fact responding to a particular time difference between the left and right ear signals, a time difference called their characteristic delay. The nucleus laminaris is organized **tonotopically** (i.e., different parts of this nucleus receive input encoding different frequencies of sound) and axonal conduction delays vary along the dorsal to ventral dimension of the nucleus. Thus the neuroanatomical address of laminaris cells stimulated by signals arriving from the two ears in phase encodes the interaural timing difference at the two ears over the range of frequencies that make up the sound (Peña et al. 2001). The magnitude of the interaural timing difference is used by the owl auditory system to determine the azimuth of the sound impinging on the two ears (Moiseff & Konishi 1983; Carr & Konishi 1990).

Intensity differences between the two ears are handled by a different processing stream in the owl brain that determines the elevation of the sound source. Another brainstem nucleus, the cochlear nucleus angularis, contains neurons sensitive to intensity signals carried by the auditory fibers (see Fig. 5.2d). A nucleus in the **pons**, the nucleus ventralis lemnisci lateralis pars posterior (VLVp), receives excitatory input from the contralateral nucleus angularis and inhibitory input from its own counterpart on the opposite side of the brain, the contralateral VLVp. VLVp neurons thus receive an excitatory signal conveying loudness from the opposite ear, and an inhibitory signal conveying loudness from the ear on the same side of the brain, relayed through VLVp on the opposite side of the brain. VLVp cells respond selectively to particular loudness differences in the two ears, with a topographical representation of loudness differences in the VLVp similar to the topographical representation of time differences in the nucleus laminaris. Neurons in the ventral part of the VLVp respond more strongly when the sound is louder in the ear on the same side of the brain. Neurons in the dorsal part respond more strongly when the sound is loudest in the opposite ear (Konishi 1995).

### The auditory map

The time- and intensity-processing streams eventually converge in the **midbrain** in the external nucleus of the inferior colliculus (see Fig. 5.2d). Cells in this nucleus are selectively sensitive to different combinations of interaural time differences and inter-aural intensity differences that specify both the azimuth and elevation of the sound source. As described earlier, barn owls will turn their head toward a sound in their environment, and will also turn their head toward phantom sound sources created by presenting combinations of time and intensity differences to the two ears using tiny earphones. In this way, Konishi and his colleagues tested hypotheses about how time and intensity differences between the two ears are interpreted by the owl. Using the same technique for sound presentation, but with anesthetized owls, they were able to find neurons in the inferior colliculus sensitive to particular combinations of time and intensity differences. These cells had as their **receptive fields** specific combinations of azimuth and elevation on the imaginary sphere surrounding the owl's head. These were neurons that fired only when a sound came from a particular point in space. Selective inactivation of time and intensity inputs to the external nucleus of the inferior colliculus, by injection of minute amounts of local anesthetic into the nucleus magnocellularis and nucleus angularis respectively, confirmed that these two cochlear nuclei were the origin of azimuth and elevation inputs (Takahashi et al. 1984). The space-specific neurons of the inferior colliculus in turn project to motor areas controlling the owl's head-turning and to the optic tectum, where a further auditory and visual representation of space is assembled.

To summarize, barn owls localize sounds in space by first decomposing sounds into a phase-locked time component and a loudness component for each ear. Time differences between the two ears are computed by coincidence detectors in the nucleus laminaris that respond maximally when signals from the two ears arrive in phase (corresponding to a characteristic delay between the signals from the two ears). Intensity differences between the two ears are computed by neurons in VLVp that receive an excitatory signal from one ear and an inhibitory signal from the other. These two variables, time difference and intensity difference, are relayed to the inferior colliculus where a map of space is assembled using time difference to specify azimuth and intensity difference to specify elevation of the sound source.

There are many additional questions about sound localization in barn owls that we have not discussed. The barn owl map of auditory space that has been described is two-dimensional; it localizes sounds on an imaginary sphere surrounding the owl's head. Barn owls are also sensitive to the third dimension, depth, but it is not clear how this is computed by the auditory system. Furthermore, Konishi has shown that the barn owl brain can detect interaural time differences as short as 10 μs, even though a single neural impulse is a hundred times longer than this. Some additional mechanism must exist which is able to extract these tiny timing differences from neural signals that are much less precise in their temporal firing properties (Konishi 1995).

Research on sound localization by barn owls illustrates two general principles about the brain and behavior. The first is that the brain interprets environmental events like sounds by **parsing** them into their component parts in parallel processing streams and then reassembling the components into a neural representation of the external world. Vision in vertebrates and invertebrates, bat sonar, electroreception by fish, and most other sensory systems operate in this way. The second general principle shown by this research is that understanding the **function** of a complex system such as auditory localization in the barn owl makes it easier to search for and analyze its causal structure. As Konishi (1995, p. 270) puts it, "had the researchers not known the perceptual problems the animals must solve, they would not have looked for neurons selective for these natural stimuli."

## Perception of action

The barn owl auditory system analyzes sound pressure waves to determine where these sounds originate. The nervous system can also analyze visual input to extract astonishingly specific information about another category of environmental events, the behavior of other animals. In the **temporal cortex** of the rhesus macaque (*Macaca mulatta*), specifically the anterior region of the superior temporal sulcus (STSa), are populations of cells that respond selectively to faces, to the direction of gaze of the eyes in these faces, and to the relation between gaze and limb movements of another animal (Jellema et al. 2000).

The superior temporal sulcus is, like all other sulci, a deep furrow of cortical tissue (Fig. 5.3a). In the cortex that makes up the banks of this sulcus, Perrett and his colleagues have recorded the electrical activity of a remarkable population of neurons. The basic procedure is to record the activity of candidate cells while the monkey watches human experimenters adopt a series of head and body postures, change their direction of gaze, or move their arms and legs. In some experiments photographic slides of humans or monkeys adopting different head and body postures are also used as stimuli. Simultaneous recordings of the head and body postures of the human or monkey demonstrator, the eye movements of the subject monkey, and the electrical activity of neurons make it possible to determine the range of stimuli to which cells in the STSa respond.

The first group of cells identified in this way responded to faces and the direction of gaze (Jellema et al. 2000). Some cells fired maximally to faces in which gaze was directed toward the macaque, others fired most to faces when the gaze was directed anywhere except at the macaque (Fig. 5.3b). Such cells continued to exhibit this selectivity for direction of gaze even when the human demonstrator appeared in the visual periphery, 45° off center rather than directly in front of the subject monkey. Although it had previously been proposed that such face-sensitive cells play a role in individual recognition in primates, many cells show the same response to different monkey and humans faces. The interpretation favored by Perrett and colleagues is that such cells are actually sensitive to the direction of attention of other animals.

Other cells in the STSa are insensitive to face or gaze but respond selectively to the limb movements of other individuals. Some respond to arm movements not leg movements, some to leg movements not arm movements, and some to movement of either arms or legs. Static views of limbs do not stimulate such cells, and for most cells the direction of movement is important. A cell might, for example, be most sensitive to movement of an arm toward the macaque or to the macaque's right, but not to movement in other directions and not to the same movement by a leg or a stick, even a stick articulated to move like an arm.

(a)

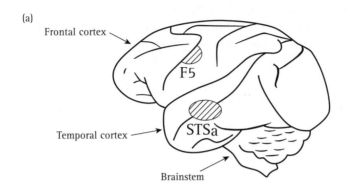

(b)

(i)

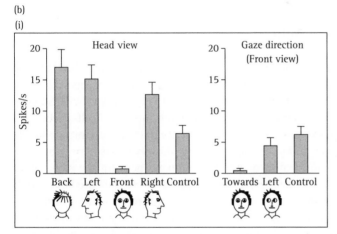

(ii)

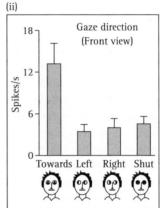

(iii)

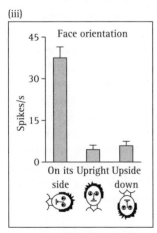

**Fig. 5.3** (a) Macaque brain (*Macaca* spp.) showing the anterior superior temporal sulcus (STSa), site of face-, gaze-, and action-sensitive neurons, and F5, site of mirror neurons. (b) The cell shown in (i) decreases firing below control levels when gaze is directed at the monkey. The cell resumes firing when gaze is directed away, either by turning the head or averting the eyes. The cell shown in (ii) responds most to gaze directed at the subject. The cell shown in (iii) exhibits a peculiar response to sideways face and gaze directed at the subject. Stimuli for (i) and (ii) were live human demonstrators and for (iii) were slide images. (Fig. 5.3(b) from Jellema et al. 2000.)

Finally, and perhaps most interestingly, cells have been described that are responsive to arm movements but achieve maximal firing rates only when the gaze of the demonstrator is also directed at the target of the reaching movement of the arm (Jellema et al. 2000). These cells, in effect, respond selectively to the limb movements of an animal whose attention is focused on the apparent target of its movement. These findings are interpreted as showing that single cells in the STSa are sensitive to visual input that characterizes the goal-directed or intentional action of others. Such cells must integrate signals from many pools of cells in many different visual processing areas, and achieve their selectivity by filtering the visual input that characterizes objects and direction of movement. The final outcome, however, is neurons that are remarkably selective in their response to the behavior of others.

## Mirror neurons

Even more unusual in their functional specificity is another population of cells, found in region F5 of the premotor area of the **frontal cortex** of the pig-tailed macaque (*Macaca nemestrina*) (Fig. 5.3a; Gallese et al. 1996; Rizzolatti et al. 1996). Unlike the STSa cells described above, these cells are electrically active when the monkey itself executes a particular hand movement, grasping a piece of food for example, or rotating its hands to break or tear a piece of food. Some of these neurons, however, also fire when the monkey observes a human demonstrator, or another monkey, perform the same hand movements. These cells have been called "**mirror neurons**" because they are active both when the animal makes a hand movement and when the same movement is "mirrored" by another animal. A mirror neuron that is active when the monkey picks up a piece of food using a precision grip of the thumb and index finger is also active when a human experimenter picks up a piece of food in the same way, but not when the experimenter picks up the piece of food with pliers or forceps. Such cells do not respond when the experimenter pantomimes the hand action with no piece of food present. Like STSa neurons, some mirror neurons respond in an inhibitory fashion, with a cessation of firing during a particular motor action, and, as their mirror property would predict, are also inhibited by observing the performance of the same action by another animal. Some mirror neurons become active when grasping movements are made not with the hand but with the mouth, either by the macaque or by a human demonstrator. Some mirror neurons that respond to hand movements exhibit a handedness preference. Mirror neurons with a handedness preference behave in a true mirror-like fashion: if the neuron fires most when an action is performed with the monkey's own right hand, it will fire most when the same action is performed by the left hand of a human facing the monkey (Gallese et al. 1996).

Rizzolatti and his colleagues have carried out various control experiments testing alternative explanations for the unusual properties of mirror neurons. One such explanation is that mirror neurons become active in preparation for the performance of a motor action and observation of another animal performing this action initiates the same preparatory routine. However, results show that mirror neurons do not become active in the period preceding execution of behavior by the monkey, but instead during its execution and during execution of the same action by another animal. Mirror neurons do not become more active as performance of a motor action like grasping becomes imminent, for instance as a piece of food on a tray is moved within reach. Experiments in which electromyograms were recorded from muscles in the macaque's hands also showed that muscle activity in the hands did not accompany observation of hand movements that were made by the experimenter or another monkey.

Another possible alternative explanation for mirror neurons is that they actually respond to viewing selected motor actions. They therefore fire when the macaque sees its own hand make an action like a precision grip or a twisting motion, and also fire when the hand of another animal does the same thing. This explanation has been tested by recording from neurons while the monkey executes hand movements with its own hand out of view, or when movements are performed in the dark. Mirror neurons continue to fire under these conditions, indicating that they do not simply respond to visual input from motor actions.

It is not surprising that mirror neurons participate in the execution of highly specific motor actions, because many cells in the premotor cortex have similarly narrow patterns of activation. What is surprising is that they also respond to highly processed visual input depicting not just the movement of an object, or movement of a limb like STSa cells, but the movement of a limb performing the same motor action in which the cell participates (Williams et al. 2001). In contrast to cells in the inferior colliculus of the barn owl that process the spatial location of sound, mirror neurons process complex events with a social component. Mirror neurons are apparently part of an "observation/ execution matching system" (Rizzolatti et al. 1996) with functions that may include communication and anticipation of the actions of others.

## Cognition

We turn next to the cognitive functions of the brain. "Cognition" in animals means many things to many people (see also Chapter 8). For some it implies that animals think, possess **consciousness**, and experience the world as we do (Griffin 2001). In this chapter we will not be using the term "cognition" in this sense. Apart from the obvious problem of independently verifying what another organism, even another human, thinks or experiences, using our own thoughts or conscious experience to understand cognition can be misleading. Neuropsychological research with humans shows that what we experience is rarely a reliable guide to how our cognitive processes actually work (Schacter 1996). In addition, using human experience as a model for cognition in animals seems likely to seriously underestimate the diversity and variety of animal experience, whatever it might be.

The term "cognition" is used by many researchers, and in this chapter, in quite a different way, to refer to information processing in a general sense. The term is broad enough to embrace widespread forms of **learning**, like **Pavlovian conditioning** (see below), as well as kinds of learning that seem to follow rules of their own, like song learning, **imprinting**, and some learned components of navigation. So at the cost of fuzziness about exactly what cognition is and what it is not, our working definition of cognition will be the processing of information about the animal's environment.

## Honeybee learning

Honeybees (*Apis mellifera*) have a characteristic response to sugars that does not require learning. When sensory cells on their legs, antennae, or mouthparts detect sucrose, usually in the nectar of a flower, bees extend their **proboscis** and siphon up the nectar (Fig. 5.4). However, honeybees do not respond to the colors, shapes, or odors of flowers in this way. They have preferences for approaching certain colors, shapes, and odors more than others, but identifying which flowers within flying distance of the hive are producing nectar and which are not requires learning the visual and olfactory characteristics of flowers and associating them with the presence of nectar.

The neural pathways involved in learning the olfactory traits of flowers and associating them with the presence of nectar have been investigated extensively by Menzel

**Fig. 5.4** Electron micrograph of the head of a honeybee showing the antennae and proboscis. (From the Centre for Electron Optical Studies, University of Bath, Bath, UK; www.bath.ac.uk/ceos/)

and his colleagues (Menzel & Müller 1996). The neuroanatomical circuitry, especially the intracellular processes involved in the formation of memory, are the topics of the next section. Learning in the honeybee provides an illustration of the neural basis of what is, conceptually at least, a relatively simple cognitive event: forming a Pavlovian association between two stimuli (see Chapter 7).

Pavlovian conditioning involves an **unconditioned stimulus** (US) that elicits an unlearned response. For the honeybee, the US is sucrose and the response is extension of the proboscis. The second stimulus is the **conditioned stimulus** (CS), in this case floral odor, to which the bee does not initially respond with proboscis extension. As a result of experiencing a contingent relation between detecting the odor and encountering sucrose, the odor eventually comes to elicit the **conditioned response** of proboscis extension. In the terminology of contemporary Pavlovian learning theory, an association is formed between odor and sucrose because the odor is a good predictor of the presence of sucrose. Conditioning of the proboscis extension response (PER) in the honeybee provides an opportunity for examining the cellular and molecular processes that take place in the honeybee brain during the formation of this learned association.

The idea that a record of experience – whether we call it an association, a memory trace, or an engram – involves a structural change at the cellular level was most clearly articulated by Donald Hebb in 1949, and this idea has come to be called Hebb's rule:

> When an axon of cell A is near enough to excite a cell B and repeatedly or persistently takes part in firing it, some growth process or metabolic change takes place in one or both cells such that A's efficiency, as one of the cells firing B, is increased. (Hebb 1949, p. 62)

A "Hebb synapse" is thus a connection between neurons that becomes more effective at stimulating its target neuron as a consequence of correlated activity in the two cells. A great deal of contemporary research in the neurosciences has been directed at finding cells and synapses that conform to Hebb's rule. Neurons in the **mushroom bodies** of the honeybee brain responsible for Pavlovian conditioning are one example of a system that has been discovered to follow Hebb's rule.

### Mushroom bodies

The mushroom bodies are a paired structure, one on the left and one on the right, in the most anterior part of the honeybee brain, the protocerebral lobe. The mushroom bodies vary enormously among insects and can be identified in many other arthropods, including spiders, scorpions, horseshoe crabs, and the pycnogonids or sea spiders (Strausfeld et al. 1998). The honeybee mushroom body consists of two cup-shaped structures, the calyces, joined by a stem called the peduncle to two further structures, the $\alpha$ and $\beta$ lobes, that form the lower part of the mushroom body (Fig. 5.5a). Surrounding the calyces are the cell bodies of Kenyon cells, which receive converging input from olfactory receptors in the proboscis and antennae and sucrose receptors in the **tarsae**. Much of the structure of the mushroom body consists of densely packed fiber projections of the Kenyon cells and axons conveying input from, or sending output to, other parts of the brain.

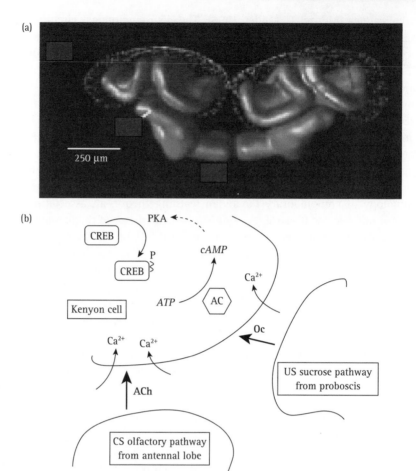

**Fig. 5.5** (a) Paired bilateral mushroom bodies of the honeybee (*Apis mellifera*). In the honeybee two cup-shaped calyces are found on each mushroom body. The halo of small white points surrounding the calyces represents the cell bodies of Kenyon cells. The structures below the calyces, i.e., the peduncle and the $\alpha$ and $\beta$ lobes, consist largely of fiber projections. (b) Acetylcholine (ACh) released at the conditioned stimulus (CS) synapse causes an influx of calcium ions ($Ca^{2+}$) in the Kenyon cell. Octopamine (Oc) released at the unconditioned stimulus (US) synapse causes an influx of $Ca^{2+}$ and activation of adenylate cyclase (AC). Adenylate cyclase converts ATP to cyclic AMP (cAMP), which activates protein kinase A (PKA). PKA phosphorylates the cAMP-binding protein (CREB).
(Fig. 5.5(a) from www.evolbrain.neurobio.arizona.edu)

Signals from olfactory receptors in the honeybee antennae, the pathway conveying information about the odor CS, are relayed first to the antennal lobes and then to the mushroom body calyces. Input from receptors in the proboscis, the pathway conveying the information about the sucrose US, is relayed first to the suboesophageal ganglion and then along a branch of the ventral unpaired median neuron (VUM) to the mushroom body calyces. Electrical stimulation of this branch of the VUM or injection of octopamine, the neurotransmitter used by this neuron, can substitute for the sucrose US and produce conditioning of the PER to an odor.

### Converging input

Encountering a floral odor followed by detection of sucrose should thus cause firing of Kenyon cells by input from the antennae and, immediately following or concurrently, further firing caused by input from the proboscis. If Pavlovian conditioning of the PER follows Hebb's rule we would expect to find mushroom-body Kenyon cells which, as a result of this concurrent neural activity, are more easily fired by odor input alone. Such change in the ability of an odor to activate a Kenyon cell would be the fundamental basis of the conditioned PER to odor. A great deal of progress has been made identifying the molecular events within Kenyon cells that follow CS and US stimulation. Interestingly, these molecular events are broadly similar to the intracellular events that underlie conditioning in the sea slug *Aplysia* and are also involved in the phenomenon of **long-term potentiation** (LTP) in vertebrates (Bliss & Lømo 1973). LTP is an experimental procedure that follows the Hebb rule par excellence. Repeated stimulation of neurons in the rat hippocampus, for example, results in a greater response by these cells to subsequent stimulation. This increased responsiveness can persist for days or weeks (hence "long-term" potentiation) and is thought to resemble processes involved in neural plasticity and learning. Induction of LTP depends on one of several different receptors for the neurotransmitter glutamate, the *N*-methyl-D-aspartate (NMDA) receptor. These receptors only function when there is both **depolarization** of the postsynaptic neuron and activation of the NMDA receptor by glutamate released from the axon terminals of the presynaptic neuron (see Fig. 5.1). Induction of LTP thus depends on simultaneous activation of the presynaptic and postsynaptic neuron, virtually the same mechanism that Hebb proposed almost 25 year earlier.

Activation of mushroom-body Kenyon cells by a CS signal from the antennae and a US signal from the proboscis initiates a cascade of molecular events inside the cell that leads ultimately to **gene transcription**, protein synthesis, and the permanent structural or metabolic changes in neurons that Hebb envisioned. The discussion that follows describes only a few of these molecular events, but enough to give an impression of the molecular processes known to characterize learning and the formation of memory across a wide variety of animals.

Release of acetylcholine, the neurotransmitter in the CS pathway from the antennal lobe to the mushroom bodies, causes an increase in the concentration of calcium ions ($Ca^{2+}$) inside the Kenyon cell (Fig. 5.5b). Release of octopamine, the neurotransmitter in the US pathway from the proboscis, increases activity of the enzyme adenylate cyclase as well as increasing the intracellular concentration of $Ca^{2+}$. Adenylate cyclase converts adenosine 5′-triphosphate (ATP) to cyclic adenosine monophosphate (cAMP). cAMP is one of the best known and the first discovered second messengers, agents that respond to signals originating outside the cell and which relay these signals inside cells. One of the effects of cAMP is to activate protein kinase A (PKA). The protein kinases are a family of catalysts that facilitate phosphorylation, the transfer of phosphate from ATP to a wide variety of proteins, regulating the activity of these proteins.

If the two events of CS activation and US activation occur successively, their effects not only summate but interact. This is because one consequence of elevated $Ca^{2+}$ concentration inside the cell is greater adenylate cyclase activity, the signal that ultimately leads to elevated levels of PKA. Thus if $Ca^{2+}$ levels produced by the CS odor signal are still high when the US sucrose signal arrives, there will be greater PKA activity than produced by the sucrose signal alone.

PKA activity, and the effect it has on phosphorylation of proteins inside the Kenyon cell, is known to be a necessary step in conditioning of the PER in the honeybee. Interfering with PKA synthesis impairs memory measured 1 day after training (Fiala et al. 1999). Similar memory impairments occur in the fruit fly *Drosophila* with mutations affecting PKA activity.

How does phosphorylation of a protein by PKA result in memory formation? The activity of some genes is regulated by a region of DNA called the cAMP-response element (CRE). Activation of the CRE sequence is in turn controlled by a protein, the CRE-binding protein (CREB). CREB is one of the proteins under the control of phosphorylation mediated by PKA.

This series of interacting switches and controls, initiated by CS and US stimulation, leads finally to gene transcription and the synthesis of proteins inside the Kenyon cell. In the honeybee, disruption of protein synthesis has little effect on learning in the first 24 h after odor conditioning, but 3 days later there are significant impairments (Wüstenberg et al. 1998). The activity of genes coding for many proteins are regulated by CREB. One such gene codes for synapsin I, a protein that releases vesicles containing neurotransmitter and which allows them to move to the axon terminal (see Fig. 5.1) where they can be released into the synapse (Montminy & Bilezikjian 1987). Another gene regulated by CREB codes for ubiquitin, a protein that forms part of a feedback loop that causes successive bouts of PKA activity to be increasingly long-lasting, producing long-term changes in cell chemistry, gene transcription, and protein synthesis (Chain et al. 2000).

The second messenger system and its target, gene expression, are tightly regulated to produce functional behavioral consequences. Molecular signals of the kind involved in Pavlovian conditioning of proboscis extension in the honeybee are known to underlie learning and memory, as well as other forms of neural plasticity, in a wide variety of animals and appear to be relatively conserved in evolution despite enormous change in behavior. Molecular signaling systems and the regulation of gene expression are essential cell functions throughout the body, not just in the nervous system, and even in the nervous system serve many functions beside forming permanent records of experience. These cell signaling systems have been recruited to produce the neural plasticity involved in the formation of associations and give us a glimpse of the events inside neurons that make cognitive processes possible.

## Control of Behavior

We come finally to the output side of the brain's control of behavior. There are many illustrations of the neural control of behavior that we could examine: the control of flight in insects, the sequencing of complex behavior in rodents, eye movements, loco-motion, reaching, grasping, orientation, and many others. However, one of the classic models for research on the control of behavior is the neural control of birdsong, a topic of fascination for students of animal behavior for many years and one that continues to yield new insights about the brain and behavior.

## Song control nuclei

There are many vocalizations produced by both male and female songbirds year round, but the term "song" is usually reserved for "long complex vocalizations produced by males in the breeding season" (Catchpole & Slater 1995, p. 10; see also Chapter 6). Although song is sometimes heard outside the breeding season and is sometimes produced by females, this broad definition applies for most species of songbirds (or oscines). Song has a variety of functions. It can announce territory occupancy, resolve contests over territory ownership, and provide cues used by females to choose mates.

Song production is controlled by a series of nuclei in the avian forebrain (Fig. 5.6). One of these nuclei, the **high vocal center** (HVC), sends projections to another, the robust nucleus of the archistriatum (RA), which in turn sends projections to the tracheosy-ringeal component of the hypoglossal nucleus controlling motor output to the **syrinx**. Song is learned in every species of oscine that has been studied. There are other fore-brain nuclei involved in song learning and song perception. HVC is also part of the neural circuits involved in song learning and auditory feedback during song produc-tion, but the focus in this section is on the motor side of song production (see Chapter 6 and Nottebohm 1999 for discussion of song development and learning).

Song can be produced at very high rates during the breeding season and is heard less often at other times of year. There is variation among species in the exact seasonal timing of song production, but in general song is produced only when it can serve the functions of territory defense and mate attraction. Nottebohm (1981) discovered that in male canaries (*Serinus canarius*) not only does singing behavior wax and wane seasonally, but so does the size of two brain nuclei responsible for song production, HVC and RA. The seasonal change in size of the song control nuclei can be substan-tial. In the wild, HVC and RA can be 50–100% larger during breeding in sparrows of the family Emberizidae (Tramontin & Brenowitz 2000).

Increase in the size of HVC and RA occurs in different ways. In RA, the size of neurons and the spacing between them both increase (Tramontin 1998). In contrast, in HVC the number of neurons increases (Goldman & Nottebohm 1983). Like the increase in total size of HVC, the increase in neuron number can be dramatic. In song sparrows (*Melospiza melodia*), the number of neurons in HVC increases from about 100,000 outside the breeding season to over 200,000 in early spring (Tramontin & Brenowitz 1999). Although there had been previous reports of neurogenesis in the adult brain (Altman 1962), the discovery that new neurons were formed in the canary song control nuclei, and in such large numbers (Goldman & Nottebohm 1983), over-turned the prevailing view in neurobiology that neurons can only be lost from, not added to, the adult brain.

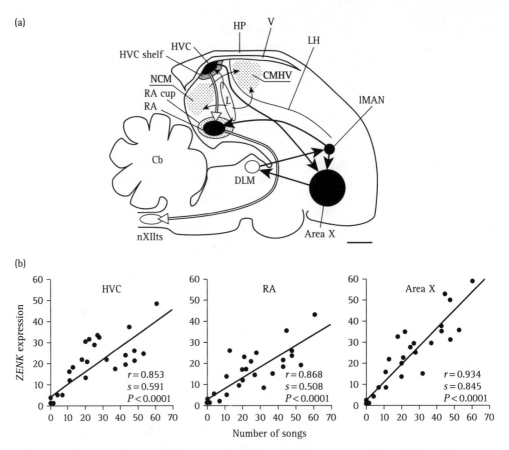

**Fig. 5.6** (a) Schematic sagittal view of the songbird brain showing the motor and auditory feedback pathways for song with approximate positions of nuclei and brain regions. The motor pathway (open white arrows) descends from the high vocal center (HVC) to the robust nucleus of the archistriatum (RA), then to the tracheosyringeal area of the hypoglossal nucleus (nXIIts), and then on to the syrinx. Other areas comprise the auditory feedback pathway and circuits involved in song learning (thick black arrows), some of which also include HVC and RA. Thin black arrows indicate known connections between Field L (L), an auditory projection region, and other forebrain regions. In male canaries, motor production of song causes *ZENK* expression in HVC, RA, lateral magnocellular nucleus of the anterior neostriatum (IMAN), and Area X (black areas), whereas hearing song without singing leads to increased *ZENK* expression in a number of brain regions including caudomedial hyperstriatum ventrale (CMHV) and caudomedial neostriatum (NCM) (stippled areas). In male zebra finches, *ZENK* expression in NCM is related to the strength of song learning (see Chapter 6). Cb, cerebellum; DLM, dorsolateral nucleus of the medial thalamus; HP, hippocampus; LH, lamina hyperstriatica; V, ventricle. Scale bar = 1 mm. (Adapted from Bolhuis & Eda-Fujiwara 2003, with permission.) (b) *ZENK* expression in male canaries, shown as a multiple of the control level, in HVC, RA, and Area X as a function of the number of songs sung in the 30-min period preceding sacrifice of the bird. Each dot represents one bird. Values describe the linear correlations between the number of songs sung and the amount of *ZENK* expression. (From Jarvis & Nottebohm 1997, with permission.)

New neurons in the avian brain originate along the ventricle and migrate into the brain from these proliferation zones following the long radial processes of **glial cells**. New neurons can be identified by injecting cell division markers, such as [³H]thymidine or bromodeoxyuridine (BrdU). Both are incorporated into the DNA of dividing cells during the S-phase, the DNA synthesis phase, of mitotic cell division. Because [³H]thymidine is radioactive, cells that have divided and incorporated it can be identified in brain sections autoradiographically. BrdU can be identified immunocytochemically with antibodies to BrdU that attach a fluorescent chemical or other visible marker to cells that have incorporated BrdU into DNA in their nucleus. Not all cells labeled by these methods are necessarily neurons, so additional tests must be used to confirm the neural identity of these newborn cells, such as a neuronal phenotype seen in a light or electron microscope, or the presence of neuron-specific proteins.

Newly divided cells identified in this way are found mostly along the ventricle in the first few days following injection, concentrated in proliferation "hotspots" (Alvarez-Buylla et al. 1990). At this early stage, the new cells do not have a neuronal phenotype. In the following days and weeks these cells move into the forebrain, **differentiating** into neurons as they travel and eventually taking up positions in HVC, the hippocampus, and elsewhere. They establish functional connections with other neurons in the brain, confirmed by injecting an anterograde chemical tracer into the cells that travels along the axon to target cells, or by injecting a retrograde tracer that travels backward along the axon from projection areas to the new neuron.

Only a small proportion of the large number of new neurons born along the ventricles survive for long in the avian brain. Most die within a few weeks. Those that do survive and establish connections with other neurons can survive for months or longer. Neurogenesis in the avian brain therefore seems to involve populations of cells that are regularly replaced.

Why are new neurons incorporated annually into the song control nuclei of birds? There have been many proposals. Because some species learn new songs each year, or modify their existing songs, new neurons may be required in the areas that control song output to store instructions for producing new songs. Memory for new motor instructions to be sent to the syrinx may require new neurons. Like adult neurogenesis, this idea overturns some conventional beliefs about the brain. Neural plasticity was widely believed to involve changes in the effectiveness with which one neuron activates another, as in our earlier discussion of Hebb's rule. This can be achieved through changes at the level of the synapse or by growth of new synaptic connections, but was not believed to involve the replacement of neurons. However, since neurons can be replaced in adulthood, neurogenesis may play a role in neural plasticity and the formation of memory. The difficulty with this idea as a general account of the function of neurogenesis is that some species of songbirds that do not modify their songs from year to year still incorporate new cells into HVC (Tramontin & Brenowitz 1999).

An alternative possibility is that neurogenesis in the song control nuclei is not directly involved in storing new motor programs for song but rather is involved in seasonal stereotypy of song (Tramontin & Brenowitz 2000). When song is produced during the breeding season, the acoustic characteristics of song are highly stereotyped. The same identifiable song syllables (in some species very large numbers of different syllables) are produced over and over with almost exactly the same frequency and time properties. On those occasions when song is produced outside the breeding season, it is much less stereotyped. Perhaps new cells in the song control nuclei play a part in song stereotypy, ensuring that songs do not deviate from a narrowly prescribed structure, analogous to recruiting additional workers to ensure quality control in a difficult manufacturing process.

Whether the function of new neurons involves memory or not, other questions remain about adult neurogenesis. New neurons obviously have the useful property that they can form new synaptic connections, and the processes that guide neuronal migration may be able to influence where new cells take up residence and send their projections. New neurons also differ physiologically and neurochemically from mature neurons (Gould et al. 1999). New neurons can have very large action potentials compared with mature cells, have longer-lasting LTP, and respond differently to some neurotransmitters. It is possible that some brain functions exploit the properties of immature neurons and that adult neurogenesis serves to maintain a pool of new neurons with these properties.

## Gene expression and song production

In the earlier discussion of honeybee learning we saw that structural change in neurons of the kind Hebb envisioned ultimately involves the transcription of genes coding for proteins that alter the properties of neurons. The control of song production by HVC, RA, and other song nuclei provides an opportunity to see gene transcription in action. **Immediate early genes** are genes that are transcribed very rapidly, usually within minutes after stimulation of a cell, for example by depolarization of a neuron. Most immediate early genes code for transcription factors, proteins that influence the expression of other genes. Jarvis and Nottebohm (1997) determined the amount of expression of the immediate early gene *ZENK* in the song nuclei of male canaries that either sang or heard canary song, or both. The amount of *ZENK* activity was determined with a radioactive riboprobe, a segment of RNA complementary to the mRNA produced during *ZENK* transcription.

The birds were exposed to different conditions and experimental treatments in order to create groups of birds that differed in singing behavior and what they heard. Some birds heard playback of taped canary song, which induced them to sing themselves. These birds showed striking increases in *ZENK* expression, up to 60 times greater than control levels in the song control nuclei HVC and RA. Other birds could sing but not hear song. *ZENK* expression in this group was found in the song control nuclei HVC and RA but not in auditory areas. This result shows that singing alone does not activate auditory nuclei. Unexpectedly, high levels of *ZENK* expression were also found in a forebrain nucleus called Area X that was not thought to be part of the circuit controlling song motor output. Area X can be removed in adults without affecting song production in the short term and electrophysiological recording from cells in Area X indicates no increased activation during song. Nevertheless, strikingly elevated *ZENK* expression also occurred in this area (see Fig. 5.6b), for reasons that remain to be determined. A final group of birds was made unable to sing by sectioning the hypo-glossal nerve that innervates the syrinx. These birds adopted a singing posture and opened their bill but produced no song. *ZENK* expression in these birds was like that of canaries that sang but did not hear the song of other birds. This last result is import-ant because it shows that it is the execution of motor routines for singing, whether or not song is produced as a result, that causes immediate early gene activity in the song control nuclei.

What does *ZENK* expression reveal about how the brain organizes motor output? Because immediate early genes are the first step in transcription of other genes that code for proteins, it may reveal a number of things. It may be that proteins are rapidly depleted in neurons involved in song production and so must be synthesized and replenished. *ZENK* activation is also thought to indicate long-term changes in neurons. If this is the case, these results may indicate that motor performance, like singing, can lead to further **consolidation** of the motor routine each time it is performed (Jarvis & Nottebohm 1997).

## SUMMARY AND CONCLUSIONS

We began by looking at neural mechanisms for sensing and perceiving the environment and found that there can be remarkable specialization in the processing of information by the brain. Complex auditory signals are decomposed by the barn owl auditory system, then reassembled to construct a map of auditory space. Neurons in the primate cortex respond selectively to the actions of other animals and can detect a correspondence between the execution of behavior and performance of the same beha-vior by another animal. We looked next at the formation of associations by the honeybee brain. Cognitive processes in animal behavior can, of course, be more complex than the formation of Pavlovian associations by honeybees and can involve more complex neural processes than the ones we looked at in the honeybee brain. Cognitive processes of all kinds, however, ultimately depend on relatively permanent changes that take place inside neurons in response to the signals they receive from other parts of the brain. Finally, we saw that what may seem to be the rather straightforward matter of motor output can involve phenomena such as the incorporation of new neurons into the adult brain and the rapid transcription of genes.

This survey of a few areas in current research on the neural basis of animal behavior has also given a glimpse of the many methods available for answering questions about the brain and behavior, from electrical recording of single neurons to molecular methods for identifying intracellular signals that initiate gene transcription. Techniques are techniques, however, not ideas, and powerful techniques offer no substitute for careful observation of behavior and curiosity about its cause, function, development, and evolution. There has been explosive recent growth in the neurosciences and rapid progress in many areas. It is important to remember as research probes deeper into the brain and nervous system that there is only one reason to care about the brain at all – discovering more about the brain will help us understand the causes of behavior.

## FURTHER READING

Recent research on the neural basis of hearing in barn owls and songbirds is described in Köppl et al. (2000). Ideas about the function, evolution, and neurobiology of gaze-sensitive neurons are discussed in Emery (2000). A special issue of the journal *Learning and Memory* (vol. 5, nos. 1–2, May–June 1998) is devoted to the mushroom bodies of the insect brain, and recent research on cognition in honeybees is reviewed by Menzel et al. (2001). The seasonally variable brain of songbirds is discussed in Tramontin and Brenowitz (2000) and contrasting views on adult neurogenesis are presented in a collection of papers in the *Journal of Neuroscience* (vol. 22, no. 3, February 2002). Chapters on the neural basis of animal communication can be found in Hauser and Konishi (1999), and Gazzaniga (2000) contains many chapters by researchers in the neurosciences on sensory and motor systems, development, neuroplasticity, cognition, and evolution.

## ACKNOWLEDGMENTS

I would to thank Scott MacDougall-Shackleton and Peter Cain for their many helpful comments and suggestions on this chapter.

# 6
# development of behavior

JOHAN J. BOLHUIS

## INTRODUCTION

### The importance of behavioral development

What is behavioral **development**? Roughly, it is about the changes in behavior and particularly its underlying mechanisms in individuals from conception to death. This definition includes the behavior of individuals before they are born, which may come as a surprise. In fact, the embryo has a rich behavioral repertoire, with which it communicates with its parents or siblings. Also, embryos can learn and remember. Later in this chapter we shall discuss some examples of behaviors studied in what is known as behavioral embryology. Is behavioral development important? Classical ethological theory had surprisingly little to say about the development of behavior, in spite of the fact that early in the last century Konrad Lorenz (1935) had published a landmark paper on the phenomenon of **imprinting**, a key concept in behavioral development that is discussed in detail later in this chapter. For instance, Niko Tinbergen's (1951) famous book, *The Study of Instinct*, has only one short chapter on development, and only one paragraph on imprinting. Lehrman (1953), in his influential critique of ethological theory, pointed out this neglect of developmental questions, which subsequently led many behavioral biologists to consider problems of development (Kruijt 1964; Bateson 1966). It also led Tinbergen (1963), some 10 years later, to reformulate his views on the aims of ethology. In the first chapter of this book, we described how in this seminal paper Tinbergen considered development to be so important that he added it to Huxley's three questions in biology and made it one of the four main problems in the study of animal behavior. So it is important, then. It is certainly the case that some of the major scientific discussions in animal behavior involve different concepts of development and we will discuss these debates. In addition, we shall see that many concepts and findings concerning behavioral development in animals have had important consequences for the study of human development.

## Learning and development

**Learning** is often interpreted as being part of behavioral development; this is because learning, like other developmental processes, involves changes in the mechanisms underlying behavior over time. For example, during associative learning (see Chapter 7), **representations** are formed of the stimuli or events that are associated, and these representations are somehow linked to each other. Representations are cognitive structures in which the external or internal environment of an individual is somehow coded or represented. Thus, after successful learning there will be behavior patterns and psychological and neural structures in the individual that were not there before the learning episode, which according to our broad definition above is a form of development. Many developmental processes, such as filial and sexual imprinting and birdsong learning, explicitly involve learning, but they also involve other mechanisms. This raises the difficult question of the difference between learning and other forms of development. The difference is gradual, and has to do with the specificity of the representations. In learning, representations are formed (of the stimuli or events and the relationship between them) that are specific to those external events. That is, the representation of the sound of the bell in Pavlov's dogs (see Chapter 7) is only addressed when the dog hears the bell (or perhaps something that sounds very much like it, in the case of **generalization**). In other forms of development the influence of external experience may be nonspecific, or internal **causal factors** may be involved. For instance, an increase in sex hormones around the time of birth may lead to the development of sexual behavior in a certain direction; one would not call this learning. These differences are not substantial, however. One could say that learning is a subset of behavioral development in general. Learning as such is discussed in Chapter 7, while imprinting and song learning are dealt with separately later in this chapter.

## Embryology and behavioral development

The Dutch ethologist Jaap Kruijt (1964) argued that the study of behavioral development could benefit greatly from concepts developed in embryology. Indeed, many concepts in the contemporary study of behavioral development originated in embryology, particularly the work of the Scottish embryologist Conrad Waddington. Waddington was far ahead of his time, and wrote very clearly about the basic concepts in embryology, which are still important and which have proved to be crucial also for the understanding of the development of behavior after birth. Waddington pointed out that a major dichotomy in developmental thinking ever since Aristotle has been the distinction between **preformation** and **epigenesis**. Preformation refers to the idea that at the time of fertilization, the egg or the sperm already contains the basic features of the adult individual. Shortly after the invention of the microscope, some eighteenth-century anatomists believed they could see the shape of an adult individual in an egg, or even a little man coiled up in a sperm! This is of course, as Waddington put it, "mere imagination, dependent on the inadequacy of their instruments." However, later versions of preformationism held that certain aspects of the adult are somehow represented in the embryo. Epigenesis, in contrast, believes that none of the adult features of individuals are represented in the embryo but rather that they develop. As Waddington suggests, embryological development is in fact a combination of preformation (such as the expression of genes) and epigenesis, and the same can be said for the development of behavior.

An important concept introduced by Waddington is that of **canalization**. This basically means that under certain circumstances a particular developmental process will follow a fairly fixed and predictable path. This is reflected in the fact that many developmental processes are quite consistently similar between individuals of the same species. This is certainly the case in embryonic development. However, certain events can disturb this stereotyped ("canalized") developmental process, and development can proceed in a different direction. We will later see examples where in the absence of normal conditions, perceptual preferences in chicks or ducklings may develop in quite a different way. To illustrate the principle of canalization and its possible disturbance, Waddington introduced the concept of the **epigenetic landscape** (Fig. 6.1). This is a metaphor for developmental processes, with balls rolling down a hill representing the

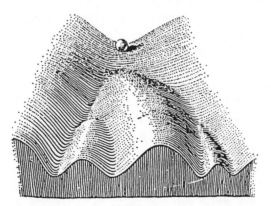

**Fig. 6.1** "Epigenetic landscape" suggested by Waddington (1966). See text for further explanation

development of different morphological traits. A similar metaphor could be used to illustrate the development of different behaviors. Waddington stressed the correcting effect of the walls of the valley on the path of the rolling ball. When a ball moves to the left, the slope of the wall pushes it back on to the right course. Such regulatory mechanisms lead to balanced development overall. A particular ball can follow a fixed path down the slope in one of the valleys, but it can hit a ridge and be diverted in another direction and follow quite a different path. A major question in embryology is that of **differentiation**: how is it that various parts of the embryo develop into different organs, or, using the metaphor of the epigenetic landscape, how do different balls end up in different valleys? Essentially, differentiation comes about through the "switching on" or expression of different genes in different cells of the embryo or at different times during development.

A related concept in embryology is that of **induction**. Waddington defines **embryonic induction** as the process by which one part of an embryo influences a neighboring part, thereby making that part develop into an organ when it would not otherwise have done. For example, cells taken from an egg of a newt (a small amphibious animal) that would normally develop into skin cells can be induced to develop into **neurons** when placed in a salt solution together with cells taken from a different part of the embryo known as the crescent region (because it is shaped like a crescent in many species; this region normally develops into the structures of the backbone). Alternatively, one can transplant crescent region cells into another embryo, such that these cells are positioned next to a part of the host embryo that would normally develop into the skin. In this case also the presence of the crescent region cells leads to induction, such that the host cells now develop into the brain. Gottlieb (1980, 2002a) later adopted the term "induction" to denote the effects of nonspecific external experience on perceptual development, as we shall discuss later. Related to induction is a phenomenon called **competence**. This refers to the fact that certain parts of the embryo can cause induction of different other parts at different times. Waddington (1966) gives the example of a piece of tissue of a newt embryo called ectoderm. When this ectoderm tissue is removed and immediately wrapped around the brain–eye region taken from an older embryo, the host tissue will develop into a brain and eye. However, when the ectoderm is kept in a saline solution for 36 h before it is wrapped around the host tissue, the latter will develop into a lens rather than brain and eye. This is known as competence: the host tissue is first competent to develop into a brain and eye, but at a later stage is competent to develop into a lens. In terms of gene expression this means that certain genes can only be switched on at particular times during development. This is an example of **sensitive periods**, which can also occur in behavioral development and which we will discuss in detail later in this chapter.

## Beyond the "Nature/Nurture" Debate

### Genes and behavior

Especially in the popular literature one often comes across the word "**innate**" to characterize certain behaviors. For instance, it is sometimes suggested that aggression is "innate." This is unfortunate, because it is not clear what is meant by "innate," which does not make it a very useful term. In addition, we shall see that "innate" is actually meaningless as a developmental process. Bateson (1999) listed seven possible different meanings of the word "innate": (i) present at birth; (ii) a behavioral difference caused by a genetic difference; (iii) adapted over the course of evolution; (iv) unchanging throughout development; (v) shared by all members of a species; (vi) present before the behavior serves any **function**; and (vii) not learned. Discussions of the concept of "innate" are not made any easier by the fact that authors rarely state which of these possible meanings they are using. In popular discussions, "innate" usually implies that a behavior is somehow "genetically determined" or "in our genes." One should keep in mind that there is no direct, one-to-one effect of genes on behavior. Genes are sections of DNA that code for proteins, not for behavior patterns. (In fact, only a small proportion of DNA has genes that code for proteins: more than 90% of DNA is known as "junk DNA," consisting of so-called pseudogenes that appear to have no function at all.) This is not to say that behavior has nothing to do with the expression of genes, but the relationship between the two is far more complex than the naive idea that there are genes for certain behaviors, as one often reads in the popular press. For a start, it is likely that several genes are somehow involved in a certain behavior, and that they interact with each other as well as with the animal's internal and external environment. Also, as we have seen already in the previous section, during embryology gene expression is very much dependent on where in the embryo the cells are, and on the particular time during development. This is likely to be the case in behavioral development as well.

What one can say is that differences in behavior may vary with genetic differences. For instance, it is possible to select animals artificially on certain behavioral traits, such as aggression. Lagerspetz (1964) selected mice on certain characteristics of aggressive behavior, in particular the time it took for an individual to attack another individual in a standard situation. Fast attackers were mated with each other, and so were slow attackers. After selecting in this way over a number of generations, two subpopulations developed, with one subpopulation showing a high aggression score and the other showing a much lower aggression score. Clearly, the differences between the two behavioral extremes are related to genetic differences. However, we do not know much about the relationship between genes and behavior in this case, which is likely to be complex. For instance, it is not clear which aspect of aggressive behavior, or its underlying mechanisms, was actually selected for. Work by van Oortmerssen and collaborators (Benus et al. 1990) shows that the two extremes of mice selected for attack latency also differ in a number of behavioral and physiological measures other than aggressive behavior. For instance, mice that have a high "aggression" score also show more exploratory activity when confronted with a novel environment. Thus it is not clear what was actually selected for: a whole complex of genes, or some factor that varies with genetic differences and which is somehow involved in a host of different behaviors. Also, we do not know the exact nature of the genetic difference between the two extremes. Suppose the difference is in only one gene (or one allele), we do not know for which protein (or proteins) this gene codes (and it may do so in collaboration with other genes). This protein (or proteins) could have all kinds of functions, for example it could be a receptor for testosterone, or an enzyme or receptor in the cell membrane. These cellular effects need not have an effect on aggressive behaviors, but could also somehow affect any of a whole host of other behavioral factors involved in aggression or, alternatively, in various other behaviors. All these considerations make it very difficult to say anything meaningful about a direct role of genes in behavior. Importantly, they show that statements about behavior being "genetically determined" or "innate" are not particularly helpful. For this reason, whenever the word "innate" is used in this chapter (because it is still widely used in the literature) it will be placed in quotation marks.

## The "nature/nurture" debate

The early days of ethology saw a battle of ideas between those who thought that behavioral development could be analyzed in terms of "innate" and acquired components (Lorenz 1935, 1937b) and those who thought that development was more complex (Lehrman 1953, 1970). Other terms used in this dichotomy are "innate" versus "learned," "genes" or "genetically determined" versus "environment," and "instinct" versus "learning." A general expression for this dichotomy is "nature versus nurture." Konrad Lorenz (1935, 1937b) postulated that behavior could be considered a mixture of "innate" and acquired elements (*Instinkt-Dressur-Verschränkung*, intercalation of fixed pattern and learning), and that analysis of the development of the "innate" elements (fixed patterns) was a matter for embryologists. Lorenz suggested that the influence of the environment could be controlled for by rearing animals in isolation. This is known as a Kaspar Hauser experiment, after the boy who was found abandoned at the market in Nürnberg (Germany) in 1828. No one seemed to know the boy, who was very confused and could not tell where he came from. Kaspar Hauser died at the age of 20. Up to this day his story is shrouded in mystery, with numerous conflicting publications and an extensive folklore as to who he was and where he came from. The myth arose that he was reared in social isolation; hence the use of his name for experiments involving isolated animals. Lehrman (1953), in an important critique of ethological theory, argued that it is impossible to rear an individual in complete isolation from the environment: it simply would not survive, because "structures and activity patterns" (Lehrman 1953) at any time during development need to interact with the internal and external environment of the organism. Lehrman argued that terms such as "innate" or "genetically fixed" obscure the importance of investigating processes in order to understand mechanisms of behavioral development. He suggested a much more complex process of continual interaction between the organism and its internal and external environment at every stage of development. Lehrman stressed that the interaction during development is not

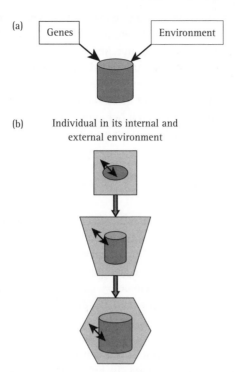

**Fig. 6.2** Schematic illustration of two different views of behavioral development. (a) Simple view that the individual and its behavior are influenced by both genes and environment. (b) More complex view of development such as suggested by Lehrman (1953, 1970). In this view the individual organism (represented by the dark forms) continually interacts (represented by bidirectional black arrows) with its internal and external environment (represented by lighter, larger two-dimensional shapes). The individual (and its environment) are different at different times during development

between what he called "heredity" and environment, but between the organism and its (internal and external) environment. Furthermore, he noted that an organism is different at each different stage of development. Lehrman's view evokes a much more complex and dynamic picture of behavioral development than Lorenz's suggestions (Fig. 6.2).

In reaction to Lehrman's (1953) critique, Lorenz (1965) changed his formulation somewhat. He argued that the **information** necessary for a behavior element to be adapted to its species' environment can only come from two sources: from information stored in the genes or from an interaction between the individual and its environment. Lorenz insisted that it is possible to isolate an individual from relevant environmental information; one could then determine whether the behavior element still developed in its normal adaptive form. He also argued that learning itself is a mechanism that adapted in the course of evolution. He used the expression "innate schoolmarm" to indicate that the organism in some sense "knows what is good for it." The "schoolmarm" was thought to determine what an animal does or does not learn.

Lehrman (1970) published a reaction to Lorenz's book, his last major paper before his untimely death. In this important paper, Lehrman notes that both he and Lorenz agree

on the facts, which means that their disagreements must depend on their differing interpretations of those facts and on the different meanings they give to the same words.
That is, Lehrman thought that Lorenz and he were really interested in two different
problems. Lehrman was interested in studying the effects of all types of experience on
all types of behavior at all stages of development, very much from a causal perspective, whereas Lorenz was interested only in studying the effects of experience on behavior at the stage of development at which behavior patterns begin to function as modes
of **adaptation** to the environment (see Hogan 1988, 2001 for further discussion).

## Beyond nature/nurture

It is important to realize that the debates between the Lorenz and the Lehrman camps
were not about nature *versus* nurture, although it is the case that European ethologists
tended to emphasize "instinct" whereas North American comparative psychologists focused
on learning (see Chapter 1). Rather, the debates were about viewing development as
having both "nature" and "nurture" elements as against regarding development as a
much more complex and dynamic process. Despite these long-standing debates, and
modern developments in behavioral biology, Lorenz's view corresponds to the way many
people, laymen as well as scientists, still think about development. In the popular press
one can still regularly read stories about how a certain behavior is thought to be "innate,"
thereby completely ignoring development. In behavioral biology, on the whole authors
are much more sophisticated when it comes to these issues, but many of them still find
it difficult to abandon Lorenzian terminology (and thus presumably Lorenzian concepts),
even when they want to be "interactionists." One often finds that the old Lorenzian
dichotomy is merely rephrased in interactionist terms, for instance when development
is seen as a continuous interaction between "innate predispositions" and "environmental factors." We have already seen that use of the term "innate" is problematic.
Furthermore, Lehrman (1953) has shown that during development the "interaction" is
much more complex than that. The problem is that Lehrman's views are not easily expressed
in a catchy sound bite, so this issue is likely to remain contentious.

## Developmental Discontinuities and Ontogenetic Adaptations

Is behavioral development a continuous process, with different phases following each
other in a predictable fashion, and behaviors at a certain stage emerging out of preceding behaviors? In this view, behaviors at one stage of development are a kind of
preparation for a subsequent stage, the former being essential for the emergence of the
latter. Alternatively, are there discontinuities in the development of behavior, with abrupt
changes, where there is no causal relationship between two subsequent behaviors (and
between their underlying mechanisms)? Both these views have been proposed, and it is
likely that behavioral development is a mixture of both. Hinde and Bateson (1984) have
discussed this issue in some detail. They suggest that overt changes in behavior during

development do not necessarily imply changes in the underlying mechanisms. This makes the investigation of developmental (dis)continuities not as straightforward as it may seem at first sight.

In the first chapter of this book, we argued that Tinbergen's four main questions in the study of animal behavior are all important, but that they should also be separated conceptually. It has been argued that behavioral development is essentially a causal problem, i.e. it has to do with mechanisms, not with function or evolution (Hogan 1988, 1994). Nevertheless, it is important to realize that different phenotypes at different developmental stages can be subject to different selection pressures. Consequently, behavior at a particular developmental stage may have a different adaptive value compared with earlier or later stages. This was recognized by the embryologist Oppenheim (1981), who discussed in great detail what he called **ontogenetic adaptations**. Oppenheim suggested that stages in development are often not merely a kind of immature preparation for the adult state, although they certainly can be, but that each developmental phase may involve unique adaptations to the environment of the developing animal, i.e., ontogenetic adaptations. As a consequence, certain early behavior patterns may disappear in the course of development, a phenomenon that Oppenheim termed a **"retrogressive process."** A clear example of ontogenetic adaptation is metamorphosis such as occurs in insects and amphibians. For instance, a butterfly emerges from a pupa, which is itself preceded by the caterpillar stage. In each of these stages the animal looks completely different and also behaves in a completely different way. For instance, a butterfly flies but a caterpillar clearly does not, whereas a pupa does not seem to show much behavior at all. It is unlikely that the movements of the caterpillar are a necessary prerequisite for the flight of the butterfly. Rather, their respective behavior patterns are adaptations for those particular stages in development. However straightforward the example of metamorphosis may seem, Hinde and Bateson (1984) cite examples of underlying continuities even here, where experience in the larval phase affects adult behavior. For instance, adult female moths of certain species lay their eggs on substrates on which they were reared as larvae. Oppenheim (1981) also suggested that imprinting and birdsong learning (both discussed later in this chapter) may be other examples of ontogenetic adaptations because they occur only early during ontogeny.

## Suckling is not feeding

A good example of ontogenetic adaptation is provided by Hall and Williams' (1983) review demonstrating that in rat pups "suckling isn't feeding." Suckling behavior is qualitatively different from later feeding behavior and is the sole means of food intake until weaning, which according to Oppenheim (1981) qualifies it as an ontogenetic adaptation. Hall and Williams (1983) discuss two possible developmental scenarios for suckling and feeding in rats. One possibility is that suckling merges into feeding at weaning, and the two behaviors share internal and external causal factors. Alternatively, the two behaviors are relatively separate and they share only some internal and external causal factors. Hall and coworkers found that adult ingestion is not a continuation of suckling, as the two behaviors have different internal and external causal factors.

Furthermore, if pups were deprived of suckling by feeding them with a cannula, later feeding behavior emerged normally, suggesting that suckling is not a necessary antecedent for adult feeding (Hall 1979).

## Imprinting

Imprinting has often been regarded as a showcase for behavioral development in general. The phenomenon of **filial imprinting** has been known for a long time and was described as early as 1518 by Sir Thomas More in *Utopia*. However, imprinting was investigated experimentally much later by the British amateur biologist Douglas Spalding in 1873 and by the German naturalist Oskar Heinroth in 1911. Konrad Lorenz, who gave the phenomenon its name, subsequently provided a detailed description of imprinting in a number of bird species in an influential work published in 1935; a shorter, English version was published in 1937 (Lorenz 1937a). Contemporary researchers define imprinting as the learning process through which the social preferences of young animals become restricted to a particular stimulus or class of stimuli (Bateson 1966; Bolhuis 1991). Images of Konrad Lorenz being followed around by a group of goslings are well known. These images illustrate some of the characteristics of imprinting, but they have also led to some confusion. Most of the research into imprinting has indeed been conducted with young individuals of precocial bird species, such as geese, ducks, or chickens. These are species where the young can move around and are relatively independent soon after hatching. The example of Lorenz also shows that, apparently, young birds can form a social bond with something that does not resemble their natural mother at all. However, these images also suggest that the goslings have acquired an irreversible social bond with Lorenz, that they treat him as their mother or even as a potential mating partner, and that they ignore members of their own species. Indeed, Lorenz thought that imprinting was a unique process, for at least three reasons. First, he thought that imprinting was unlike any other form of learning, such as **classical conditioning** (see Chapter 7), as it did not require any kind of reward or **reinforcement**. Second, imprinting was thought to occur only during a particular period in development, what Lorenz called a **critical period**. Third, Lorenz thought that the process of imprinting was **irreversible**: once the animal had formed a social bond with a particular individual, it could not form a bond with another individual. Lorenz also thought that the main outcome of imprinting was that the animal learned the characteristics of its future mating partner. Nowadays a distinction is made between filial imprinting, where a social bond is formed between the young animal and its parent, and **sexual imprinting**, which involves the formation of sexual preferences that are expressed later in life.

## Filial imprinting

Although filial imprinting may occur in mammals (Sluckin 1972), it has been studied mostly in precocial birds. Soon after hatching, these birds will approach and follow an object to which they are exposed. In a natural situation the first object the young bird encounters is usually its mother. In the absence of the mother, other animals or even Lorenz can be adequate mother-surrogates. Amazingly, inanimate mother-surrogates such as colored balls or illuminated boxes are also effective in eliciting approach and following behavior and the animals will readily form a social preference for these unnatural stimuli (Bateson 1966; Sluckin 1972; Horn 1985; Bolhuis 1991). When the chick or duckling is close to an appropriate object (see below), it will attempt to snuggle up to it, frequently emitting soft twitters. Initially the young bird approaches a wide range of objects. After the bird has been exposed to one object long enough, it remains close to this object and may run away from novel ones. If the familiar object is removed, the bird becomes restless and emits shrill calls. When given a choice between the familiar stimulus and a novel one, the bird preferentially approaches the familiar stimulus. It is important to realize that filial imprinting refers to the acquisition of a social preference and not just an increase in following (Sluckin 1972).

## Conditions for imprinting

To study visual imprinting in the laboratory, chicks or ducklings may be hatched in darkness, and exposed for a period of 1–2 h to a conspicuous object when they are about 24-h old. The animals are then returned to a dark incubator and kept there until their preferences are tested by exposing them to the familiar object and a novel object. A widely used measure of filial preference is approach to the familiar object relative to approach to a novel object. The effectiveness of imprinting stimuli varies. For example, young ducklings approach and follow objects larger than a matchbox, but peck at smaller objects. For chicks, red and blue objects are more effective imprinting stimuli than yellow and green objects. Movement, brightness, contrast, and sound all enhance the attractiveness of an imprinting stimulus.

## Imprinting and learning

Lorenz (1935) thought that imprinting had "nothing to do with learning." Indeed, filial imprinting proceeds without any obvious reinforcement (see Chapter 7) such as food or warmth (see Bolhuis et al. 1990 for discussion). However, an imprinting object may itself be a **reinforcer**, i.e., a stimulus which an animal finds rewarding. Just as a rat can learn to press a lever to receive a food reward, so a visually naive chick is able to learn to press a pedal to see an imprinting object. As we will see in Chapter 7, this is a case of instrumental or **operant conditioning**, and in the case of the chick the mere sight of an imprinting object is reinforcing the response. Similarly, when chicks are exposed to two imprinting stimuli (e.g., a visual object and a sound) simultaneously, they learn more about the individual stimuli than when they are exposed to the stimuli sequentially or to only one stimulus. This so-called **within-event learning** has also been found in conditioning paradigms in rats and humans (Bolhuis & Honey 1998). So although imprinting looks quite different from classical or operant conditioning, nevertheless it shares many characteristics with these forms of associative learning. Thus it may be that only the characteristics and the circumstances in which imprinting occurs differ from other forms of learning, but that the underlying mechanisms are similar if not the same.

## Sexual imprinting

Lorenz suggested that the main consequence of imprinting is the determination of adult sexual preferences. Recent research suggests that filial imprinting and sexual imprinting are two separate (although perhaps partially overlapping) processes. First, the time of expression of the preference differs, with filial preferences being expressed in very young birds, whereas sexual preferences are expressed during courtship, when the animals are sexually mature. Second, the period of time during which experience affects preferences also differs between filial and sexual imprinting. Sexual preferences continue to be affected by experience up to the time of mating. Furthermore, filial preferences may be formed after a relatively short period of exposure to an object. In contrast, sexual preferences develop as the result of a long period of exposure to, and social interaction with, the parents as well as the siblings. Normally, sexual imprinting ensures that the bird will mate with a member of its own strain or species. However, when the young bird is **cross-fostered** (i.e., reared with adults of a different species) it may develop a sexual preference for the foster species. For instance, when young zebra finch (*Taeniopygia guttata*) males are reared with Bengalese finch (*Lonchura striata*, also known as the society finch) parents (Fig. 6.3), they will later show courtship behavior mostly to Bengalese finch females. Interestingly, when young zebra finch males are reared with mixed parents (one Bengalese finch and one zebra finch), they will later show a sexual preference for a female of the species with which they had interacted most. More specifically, in Japanese quail (*Coturnix coturnix japonica*) and domestic chickens, mating preferences are for individual members of the opposite sex that are different, but not too different, from individuals with which the young bird was reared (Bateson 1978).

**Fig. 6.3** Zebra finch (left) and Bengalese finch (right). (Photograph courtesy of C. ten Cate.)

## Is imprinting really irreversible?

Lorenz's assertion, often cited in animal behavior textbooks, that imprinting is irreversible has strengthened the myth that the main developmental processes cannot be reversed. It is important to realize that there are two ways in which Lorenz's claim of irreversibility of imprinting can be interpreted. On the one hand, it could mean that once the young bird has formed an **attachment** with a particular object, it will never direct its social behavior toward a different, novel object. A weaker form of the claim is that although the animal may show social behavior toward novel objects, it will not forget what it has learned about the object to which it was exposed originally. The latter form of the claim of irreversibility is in fact more in line with Lorenz's (1937a) account, for instance when he says that "the recognition response cannot be 'forgotten'!"

The strong form of the claim of irreversibility has been refuted, both for filial imprinting (Salzen & Meyer 1967; see Bolhuis 1991) and for sexual imprinting (Kruijt & Meeuwissen 1991; see Bolhuis 1991). For instance, Salzen and Meyer (1967) reared chicks with a colored ball that was suspended in their home cage for 3 days. When given a simultaneous preference test, the animals preferred the familiar stimulus to a novel stimulus of a different color. When the familiar stimulus was then removed and replaced with the alternative colored ball for a further 3 days, the chicks had reversed their preference to a preference for the novel stimulus.

More recent research has addressed the weak version of the claim of irreversibility, i.e., that information about the first stimulus is not forgotten. Specifically, it was found that although filial preferences are reversible, under certain circumstances the original preference may return (Bolhuis & Bateson 1990). Bateson (1987) suggested a simple **competitive exclusion model** to explain these findings. He distinguished between a large-capacity recognition system and a limited-capacity executive system that is responsible for the animal's behavioral output. During exposure to an imprinting stimulus, links are made between the recognition system and the executive system, with limited access to the latter. Once part of the executive system is "captured" by links from the recognition system, that part cannot be captured by inputs from another store in the recognition system. Connections between the two systems can wane with disuse, but can be reestablished if used again. The model predicts that when the animal is exposed to an attractive stimulus for a certain length of time, it will be difficult to change its preference by exposing it to a novel stimulus. Furthermore, under certain circumstances the original preference may "resurface" (see Bateson 1987 for further discussion).

In sexual imprinting, as in filial imprinting, it has been found that the strong claim of irreversibility cannot be maintained, whereas there is evidence that supports the weak version of the claim (Bischof 1994). When zebra finch males were reared with Bengalese finch foster parents for the first 40 days of life they showed a strong courtship preference for Bengalese finch females in preference tests when adult. When such males were exposed to a zebra finch female for several months they would show courtship behavior toward that female, but after separation from the zebra finch female the males once again preferred a female of the foster species in preference tests. However, if the males did not receive a preference test before exposure to the zebra finch female, most of them altered the direction of their courtship behavior toward a stable preference for zebra finch females. Direct physical interaction with the females was not necessary, either during the brief preference tests or during the longer exposure periods when the animals were sexually mature. Thus, sexual preferences could be altered by later exposure to a female of the other species and, furthermore, brief exposure to a female of the rearing species was sufficient to "consolidate" or "stabilize" the animal's sexual preference. When zebra finch males reared by Bengalese finch parents were exposed to a Bengalese female first they subsequently courted Bengalese finch females; however, when they were exposed to a zebra finch female first, a large proportion of the males changed their preference toward a zebra finch female. On the basis of these and other results, Bischof (1994) suggested that sexual imprinting is a two-stage process, with an acquisition phase during which the animal learns the characteristics of its parents and siblings, and a **consolidation** phase during which the sexual preference is stabilized or modified according to the species of the individual to which the male is exposed.

## Development of Attachments in Humans and Other Primates

Theories and methods employed in animal behavior research have played an important role in the formulation and development of British psychiatrist John Bowlby's (1969) theory of attachment in humans. This theory was originally developed to explain the behavior of children who had been separated from their mothers and raised in a wartime nursery during the Second World War, and was greatly influenced by Lorenz's ideas about imprinting. In many ways, the attachment system postulated by Bowlby is analogous to the systems involved in filial behavior in young birds. In both cases, the newborn infant or chick possesses a number of behavior patterns that keep it in contact with the parent (or other caregiver) and which attract the attention of the parent in the parent's absence. Further, both infant and chick must learn the characteristics of the parent, which is important for the formation of a social bond between the two. Factors influencing the formation of the bond are also similar, including all the factors discussed above such as length of exposure, sensitive periods, and predispositions. Studying the importance of these factors in the human situation has resulted in a large body of literature, some of which has supported the theory and some of which has not (see Rutter 2002). The theory itself has been modified to take these results into account, and has also been expanded to include development of attachments throughout life.

Ironically, the study of attachment behavior involved experiments with monkeys that nowadays would be considered too cruel to be allowed. To study the effects of maternal separation on infant behavior, Harlow (1958), for example, raised infant rhesus monkeys in complete social isolation, which had severe effects on the infant's subsequent behavior. Less intrusive methods, such as raising infants with other infants (Harlow & Harlow 1962) or separating infants from their mothers for brief periods of time (Hinde 1977), led to less dramatic results, although these methods are still unacceptable for human research. Harlow and his collaborators conducted an extensive series of experiments that involved rearing young rhesus monkeys with surrogate mothers. In many of these experiments the infant monkey could choose between a cloth mother surrogate and a wire mother surrogate, with only the latter providing food to the infant. Whenever there was some stressful situation, the infant invariably preferred to stay close to the cloth mother. Again, these experiments appear to us nowadays as cruel. However, they must be seen in the light of prevailing ideas at the time concerning child rearing. These were strongly influenced by behaviorist ideas (see Chapter 1) suggesting that reinforcement (e.g., food) was the main factor in the development of children as well as animals. Harlow's work has been extremely important in showing rather poignantly that, unlike behaviorist dogma, infants need the type of contact and assurance provided by parents in order to develop as normal social beings.

Bowlby felt that the best method for studying human development was to observe infants in real-life situations, in much the same way as many ethologists study the behavior of other animals in natural or seminatural settings. Much of his theorizing about human attachment was based upon such research carried out by his colleague Mary Ainsworth. She and her colleagues (1978) developed a standardized **strange situation test** in which a stranger approaches an infant with and without the parent being present, and various aspects of the infant's behavior are measured. This method is now widely used, and has allowed researchers to characterize specific patterns of attachment and their determinants.

## Birdsong Learning

Approximately half of all bird species belong to the order Passeriformes, the songbirds. A subgroup of this order known as the oscines (real songbirds) need to learn their song from a "tutor," usually an adult male of their own species, often the bird's father. The developmental time at which this learning takes place varies widely between species: in some species learning occurs early in development, whereas in others learning takes place when the birds have dispersed to an area other than where they were reared, usually when they are in their first breeding season (see Snowdon & Hausberger 1997 for review). In addition, a distinction is made between "open-ended learners" (e.g., the canary *Serinus canarius*) that can learn new songs throughout life, and species (e.g., the zebra finch) where one song is learned early in life and remains unaltered (Marler 1987). We will discuss only these "age-limited learners" (Marler & Peters 1987; for reviews see DeVoogd 1994; Marler 1976). Pioneering work on birdsong was done by William Thorpe at the University of Cambridge. The classic work of one of Thorpe's students British-born ethologist Peter Marler and his coworkers has led to the distinction of two main phases in the song copying process: a memorization phase and a sensorimotor phase (Fig. 6.4). During the memorization phase (when the bird does not yet sing itself) the young male is thought to form a "template" or memory of the tutor song. Later, during the sensorimotor phase, the young will start to vocalize, gradually matching its own vocalizations with the information stored in the template. Song learning in age-limited learners thus goes through various stages, called subsong, plastic song, and crystallized or full song, respectively (Fig. 6.4). During subsong, the animal produces

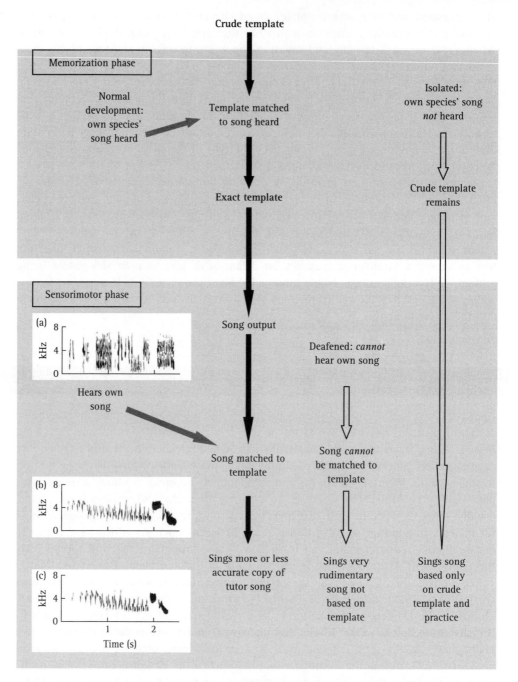

**Fig. 6.4** Stages in song development in some songbird species and their presumed underlying mechanisms. On the left are sonograms (frequency over time) of the song of a chaffinch (*Fringilla coelebs*) at different stages of development: (a) early subsong; (b) plastic song; (c) crystallized song. See text for further explanation. (Adapted from Slater 1983 with permission.)

highly variable and unstructured song patterns. During the period of plastic song, the male produces song patterns that it has learned earlier, but there is still a degree of plasticity in song output. This is the phase when the animal is thought to "match" its own song output with the stored template. Eventually, there is crystallization of vocal output into full song, which is fixed for life (Marler 1976, 1987).

## Birdsong and the development of speech in human infants

There are some interesting parallels between birdsong learning and the development of speech in human infants. As in songbirds, human infants go through a phase in development where they do not yet vocalize themselves but during which they hear others vocalize, the characteristics of which they may learn. Later, the infant starts to vocalize itself; this cannot yet be termed proper speech but is called "babbling." The infant produces sounds that resemble real words but which are not intelligible as such. This is very much like subsong in songbirds, as described above (Snowdon & Hausberger 1997; Doupe & Kuhl 1999). In both cases it looks like the young individual is "practicing" its vocalizations, comparing them to information stored in memory. In humans, speech is a vehicle for language. However, it would seem far-fetched to compare birdsong with language. It is not clear, for instance, whether birdsong has a form of syntax or grammar in the way that human language has. Certain bird species do have a certain structure in the order of elements in a song, and the sequence of these elements is not random, but it is not clear whether this "syntax" has meaning in the way that our syntax has.

## Predispositions

As we have discussed, the difference between learning and other forms of behavioral development is gradual, and has to do with the specificity of external experience. There are many examples of perceptual preferences that may develop without any experience with the particular stimuli involved. In this case, researchers often use the term "predispositions" to denote the behavioral tendency or indeed the underlying mechanism. Predispositions have been found to play a role in birdsong learning (Marler 1991) and auditory preferences in ducklings (Gottlieb 1980). Further, there is an important influence of predispositions in the perception of faces in neonatal human infants (Johnson & Morton 1991) and in the development of filial preferences in chicks (Johnson et al. 1985; Bolhuis 1996). In the study of the development of filial preferences in chicks, the term "filial predispositions" has been used (Bolhuis 1996). These were defined as perceptual preferences that develop in young animals without experience of the particular stimuli involved (Bolhuis & Honey 1998).

A predisposition for species-specific sounds has been demonstrated in song learning in certain avian species (Marler 1987, 1991). Under certain circumstances, young males of some songbird species can learn their songs, or at least part of their songs, from tape recordings of tutor songs. When fledgling male song sparrows (*Melospiza melodia*) and swamp sparrows (*Melospiza georgiana*) were exposed to taped songs that consisted of equal numbers of songs of both species, they preferentially learnt the songs of their own species. Males of both species are able to sing the songs of the other species, and it appears therefore that perceptual predispositions are involved in what Marler (1991, p. 200) called the "sensitization of young sparrows to conspecific song."

In an extensive series of elegant experiments, the American biologist Gilbert Gottlieb (1976, 1980) investigated the mechanisms underlying the preferences that young ducklings of a number of species show for the maternal call of their own species over that of other species. This might suggest that these preferences are "innate," in the sense of "present at birth." However, it turns out that reality is much more complex. Gottlieb (1980, 2002a) found that differential behavior toward the species-specific call could already be observed at an early embryonic stage, before the animal started to vocalize itself. However, a posthatching preference for the conspecific maternal call was only found when the animals received exposure to embryonic contact-contentment calls, played back at the right speed (Gottlieb 1980) and with a natural variation, within a certain period in development. Thus, the expression of the species-specific predisposition in ducklings is dependent on particular experience earlier in development. In fact, Gottlieb found that these preferences can be **induced**, **maintained**, and **facilitated** by external experience. An illustration of these principles of perceptual development is shown in Fig. 6.5.

The development of filial behavior in the chick involves two systems that are neurally and behaviorally dissociable (Horn 1985, 1998; Johnson et al. 1985; Bolhuis 1996; Bolhuis & Honey 1998). Behavioral evidence for the existence of a predisposition was provided by a study in which day-old dark-reared chicks received imprinting training by exposing them to either a rotating red box or a rotating stuffed junglefowl hen (Johnson et al. 1985). Chicks in a control group were exposed to white overhead light for the same amount of time. The approach preferences of the chicks were measured in a subsequent test where the two training stimuli were presented simultaneously. Preferences were tested at either 2 h (Test 1) or 24 h (Test 2) after the end of training (Fig. 6.6). At Test 1 the chicks preferred the object to which they had been exposed previously. At Test 2 there was a significantly greater preference for the fowl in both experimental groups as well as in the light-exposed control group. Thus, the preference for the junglefowl increased from the 2-h to the 24-h test, and did so regardless of the stimulus with which the chicks had been trained.

These results suggest that the preferences of trained chicks are influenced by at least two different systems. On the one hand, there is an effect of experience with particular stimuli (reflected in the differences K1–K4 in Fig. 6.6), i.e., filial imprinting. On the other hand, there is an emerging predisposition to approach stimuli resembling conspecifics (reflected as $\Delta_Y$ for the control group in Fig. 6.6). Training with a particular stimulus is not necessary for the predisposition to emerge. In fact, visual experience is not necessary to "trigger" or induce the predisposition (Gottlieb 1976; Bolhuis 1996). The predisposition can emerge in dark-reared chicks, provided that they receive a certain amount of nonspecific stimulation within a certain period in development (Johnson et al. 1989).

Stimulus characteristics that are important for the filial predisposition to be expressed were investigated in chicks that had developed the predisposition. The tests involved an intact stuffed junglefowl versus a series of increasingly degraded versions of a stuffed

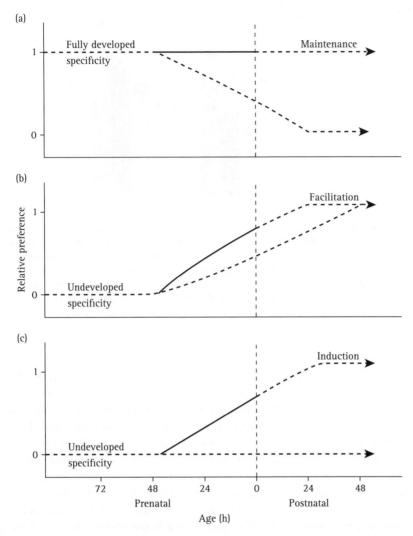

**Fig. 6.5** Three ways in which experience can influence the development of perceptual preferences: (a) maintenance, (b) facilitation, and (c) induction. The behavior of interest is shown on the y-axis as a measure of preference, e.g., for the maternal call of the bird's own species in ducklings (Gottlieb 1980) or for a stimulus with a head and neck in domestic chicks (Bolhuis 1996). The time of onset of divergence of the two lines can be before hatching, as in the case of auditory predisposition in ducklings (Gottlieb 1980), or shortly after hatching, as in the case of visual predisposition in chicks (Bolhuis 1996). Maintenance and facilitation were demonstrated in some of Gottlieb's own work on the development of auditory preferences in ducklings (see Gottlieb 1980) and in other paradigms (see text). Induction was demonstrated, for example, in the development of filial predisposition in domestic chicks (Bolhuis 1996). Solid line, experience; dashed line, no experience. (After Gottlieb 1980, with permission.)

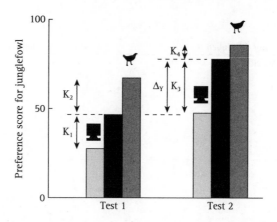

**Fig. 6.6** Mean preference scores (expressed as a preference for the stuffed fowl) of chicks previously trained by exposure to a rotating stuffed junglefowl, a rotating red box, or white light. Preference scores are defined as activity when attempting to approach the stuffed junglefowl divided by total approach activity during the test. Preferences were measured in a simultaneous test either 2 h (Test 1) or 24 h (Test 2) after the end of training. K1–K4, differences between the preferences of the trained chicks and the controls; $\Delta_Y$, difference in preference between the control chicks at Test 2 and at Test 1. See text for further explanation. (Adapted from Horn 1985, by permission of the Oxford University Press, after Johnson et al. 1985.)

junglefowl (Johnson & Horn 1988). The degraded versions ranged from one where different parts of the model (wings, head, torso, legs) were reassembled in an unnatural way to one in which the pelt of a junglefowl had been cut into small pieces and stuck onto a rotating box. The intact model was preferred only when the degraded object possessed no distinguishable junglefowl features. In addition, chicks did not prefer an intact junglefowl model over an alternative object that contained only the head and neck of a stuffed fowl. Thus, the head and neck region contains stimuli that are relevant for the predisposition. In subsequent experiments it was found that the chicks did not prefer a stuffed junglefowl hen over a stuffed Gadwall duck (*Anas strepera*) or even a stuffed polecat (*Mustela putorius*). Thus, the predisposition is not species or even class specific. Subsequent studies showed that eyes are an important stimulus, but that other aspects of the stimulus are also sufficient for the expression of a predisposition (Bolhuis 1996).

## Predispositions in chicks and human infants

There are interesting similarities between the development of filial preferences in chicks and the development of face recognition in human infants (Johnson & Morton 1991). British psychologist Mark Johnson and his colleagues tested visual preferences in human babies as young as 30 min old. The newborn babies were shown various slowly moving objects that resembled table tennis rackets. On these rackets were painted either four dots in the configuration of two eyes, a nose, and a mouth, or the dots were jumbled up; the control was a racket with no dots. Newborn infants followed a moving face-like stimulus with their eyes significantly more than the other two stimuli (Johnson & Morton 1991). It is not known whether the development of face preferences in infants is dependent on previous experience, but the parallel with the emergence of perceptual predispositions in birds is striking. Similarly, in both human infants and young precocial birds, the features of individual stimuli need to be learned.

## Sensitive Periods

Sensitive periods are an important characteristic of developing behavior. At the same time, the concept of "sensitive period" is often misunderstood. It needs to be separated from the idea of "critical period," which implies a much stricter separation of sensitivity and insensitivity to external influences. The idea of a critical period simply does not correspond with biological reality, and within the study of animal behavior the term is hardly used. However, there is considerable evidence to suggest that during development there are periods of increased sensitivity to external experience, preceded and followed by periods of less sensitivity. The transition between these developmental states may be gradual.

Bateson (1979) likened some of the different interpretations of sensitive periods to a train traveling through a landscape. The train is a metaphor for the developmental process. At the beginning of the journey all the windows of the train, which are opaque, are closed so that passengers cannot see the landscape outside the train. In the simplest interpretation, the windows open at some stage and close at a later stage. This is very much like the old idea of a critical period. Another interpretation is that some windows open at some stage and others open at other stages, i.e., different onset of sensitivity at various stages. The different windows may or may not close again. The most realistic interpretation, inspired by studies of filial imprinting, is that windows may open at different stages and not close again. The passengers can obtain information from outside the train and may decide on the basis of that information that they need to get off the train at the next station. In other words, the end of an apparent sensitive period is not a result of an end to external experience influencing the organism (i.e., windows being closed again) but the result of the effect that external experience has on the organism. In the case of imprinting, when the young bird has been exposed to an imprinting stimulus and learned its characteristics, it will form a social preference for this stimulus. As long as that stimulus is present, the animal will follow it around and spend most of its time close to it, so the animal will not have much opportunity to imprint on other stimuli. As we saw earlier, if the original imprinting stimulus is removed and replaced with a novel stimulus, the animal can imprint on the novel stimulus, suggesting that sensitivity for experience relevant for imprinting has not waned.

Various models have been put forward to explain sensitive periods, ranging from **endogenous** factors (e.g., "clock models") to self-terminating mechanisms, where an apparent sensitive period comes to an end solely as a result of external experience (Bateson 1979; ten Cate 1989). It has become clear that sensitive periods should not be seen as rigid mechanisms where a window to the external environment opens briefly, never to be opened again. Rather, sensitive periods are regarded as flexible mechanisms, the timing of which can be modified, and that depend for a large part on external influences on the organism (Bolhuis 1999).

## Brain, Hormones, and Development

## Hormones and development

Hormones constitute an important internal causal factor that can affect behavior in many ways (see Chapter 3). An important distinction must be made between the effects of hormones on adult behavior, so-called **activating effects** (see Chapter 3), and the effects of hormones on differentiation during development, known as **organizing effects**. The most prominent organizing effects of hormones are on **sexual differentiation**. In humans and most other animals, males and females differ enormously in both morphology and behavior. For instance, the primary and secondary sexual organs of males are different from those of females, and the same can be said of the brains and behavior of the two sexes. How do these differences come about? To begin with, there are genetic differences between males and females. In mammals, there are sex differences in chromosome pair 23: females have two X chromosomes whereas males have one X and one Y chromosome.

Genetic sex is only part of the story, however, as the levels of sex steroid hormones around birth determine whether the morphological sex of the young animal will be the same as its genetic sex. In other words, in mammals female is the default phenotypic sex; whether a genetic male develops as a male depends on the effects of a surge in the male sex hormone testosterone around birth. This is known as **masculinization**. To make matters even more complicated, in birds the situation is exactly the reverse. Female birds have two different sex chomosomes, whereas male birds have two identical sex chromosomes. Another difference between mammals and birds is that female birds need a surge of the female sex hormone estrogen around hatching to confirm their genetic sex, a process know as **feminization**.

Apart from the effects of sex steroids produced by the animal's own sex glands, in both mammals and birds there are also effects of external steroids. For instance, the adult behavior of female rats is affected by who their neighbors were while they were still in the uterus (Vom Saal & Bronson 1980). Birds still in the egg can be exposed to sizable quantities of testosterone deposited in the egg yolk by the mother. It is thought that the mother can actively regulate the amount of testosterone in the egg yolk, which in turn affects the behavior of the young after they hatch (Schwabl 1993).

## Development of brain and behavior

Many developmental processes (including behavioral processes) are constrained by the developing nervous system. An illustrative example is the development of face recognition in human infants, as discussed above (Johnson & Morton 1991). For some time there were conflicting reports about whether newborn infants showed a preference for stimuli that look like faces over stimuli that do not. Some researchers claimed that it was not until infants were 2–3 months old that they could recognize faces, whereas others reported face recognition in 10-min-old babies. Johnson and his collaborators discovered that these conflicting findings have something to do with the method of testing. When newborn infants are tested by showing them static figures, they do not prefer to look at faces compared with nonfaces. However, when the stimuli are moved around, the infants follow faces with their eyes and head significantly more than nonfaces. How can we explain this?

Johnson and his colleagues suggested that it has something to do with the differential development of the human neocortex and subcortical structures. Certain subcortical visual structures such as the superior colliculus are fully developed at birth, whereas the development of the cortex continues for a considerable time after birth. The subcortical structures, which are sufficient for face recognition, receive projections particularly from the peripheral part of the retina. When the infant has to follow a moving stimulus with its eyes, there is a greater chance of light reflected by this stimulus falling on the periphery of the retina, and thus of the subcortical structures being activated. Thus, as the subcortical structures are fully developed at birth, and the visual cortex is not, only when stimuli are moving are the fully developed neural structures involved and faces recognized.

Experience during development can also affect the structure of the nervous system. Rats reared in "enriched" environments (with a running wheel and toys, and sometimes with other rats) have a different cortex from control rats reared in standard laboratory cages (Greenough et al. 1987). In particular, the overall weight of the cortex is greater in the "enriched" rats and they have more elaborate dendritic branching (see Chapter 5). Arguably more interesting are direct relations between cognitive experience and brain structure, as in the case of learning. Filial imprinting has become a prominent model for the study of the neural mechanisms of learning and memory (Horn 1985, 1998). A big advantage of imprinting is that domestic chicks do not actually eat food until they are about 3 days old. Thus they can be kept in the dark until the start of an imprinting experiment (just like in the natural situation where they spend most of their first days in darkness, under the mother hen). Exposure to an imprinting stimulus will then be their first visual experience and, as we have seen, relatively limited experience can have a big impact on the animal's behavior. Cambridge neurobiologist Gabriel Horn and his collaborators have studied the neural mechanisms of filial imprinting in great detail. They have found that there are a number of plastic changes in a restricted region of the chick forebrain, the intermediate and medial hyperstriatum ventrale (IMHV) (Fig. 6.7) during imprinting. For instance, there is increased protein synthesis in the IMHV and also increased expression of **immediate early genes** (see Chapter 5), suggesting increased neuronal activation. The level of this neuronal activation correlates with the strength of imprinting, as measured in preference tests. In other words, the more the animals have learned, the more neuronal activity in the IMHV and not in other parts of the brain. Thus there appears to be localization of function, as only a very restricted part of the brain seems to be involved in memory storage. Analysis of the brain at the

(a)

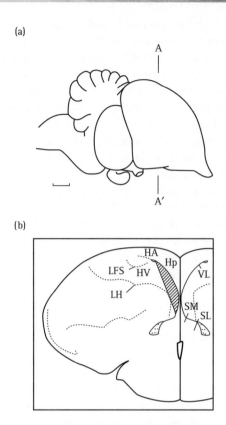

(b)

**Fig. 6.7** Schematic drawings of the brain of the domestic chick. (a) Lateral aspect of the brain. Line A—A′ indicates the approximate plane of the coronal section of the brain in (b). Scale bar, 2 mm. (b) Simplified diagram of a coronal section of the chick brain at the level of the intermediate and medial hyperstriatum ventrale (IMHV). The extent in the coronal plane of the left IMHV, as removed in biochemical studies (see Horn 1985), is indicated by the hatched area. HA, hyperstriatum accessorium; Hp, hippocampus; HV, hyperstriatum ventrale; LFS, lamina frontalis superior; LH, lamina hyperstriatica; SL, nucleus septalis lateralis; SM, nucleus septalis medialis; VL, ventriculus lateralis. (From Bolhuis 1996, with permission.)

subcellular level, using an electron microscope, revealed that imprinting led to a significant increase in synaptic contact area between neurons. This suggests that learning may lead to increased synaptic efficiency, which is consistent with proposals put forward by the Canadian psychologist Donald Hebb as long ago as 1949 (see Chapter 5).

In Chapter 5, the neural correlates of birdsong were discussed (see also DeVoogd 1994; Nottebohm 2000). Despite the enormous research effort in this field, we still do not know where in the songbird brain information about the tutor song is stored. Recently it was found that hearing a song led to neuronal activation (again measured as expression of immediate early genes) in brain regions outside the conventional song pathways, i.e., caudomedial hyperstriatum ventrale (CMHV) and caudomedial neostriatum (NCM) (see

Fig. 5.5). Interestingly, the level of neuronal activation in one of these regions (NCM) is correlated with the strength of song learning, measured as the number of song elements that a bird has copied from its tutor (Bolhuis et al. 2000). Thus, analogous to the imprinting case, there may be learning-related neuronal activation in a restricted brain region. Further research is needed to test the hypothesis that the NCM is (part of) the neural substrate for song memory. It is interesting that both imprinting and song learning, two prominent models for the neural mechanisms of learning and memory, are occurring during development. It could be that such developmental events are so prominent in the life of an individual that it is easier to detect neural correlates of learning in such behaviors.

## Development of Motivational Systems

Kruijt (1964) was one of the first to describe the development of **behavior systems** in detail. He provided a detailed description of the development of behavior in the Burmese junglefowl (*Gallus gallus spadiceus*), the ancestor of the domestic chicken. He suggested that, initially, many of the motor components of behavior appear as independent units prior to any opportunity for practice, and that only later, often after specific experience, do these motor components become integrated into more complex systems such as hunger, aggression, or sex. An example is aggressive behavior in young male junglefowl chicks: behavioral components such as hopping, pecking, and kicking occur quite independently at first, but later become integrated into behavioral sequences seen during agonistic encounters with other males.

Hogan (1988) has generalized these proposals and suggested a general framework for the analysis of behavioral development using the concept of behavior systems, as described in Chapter 3. A behavior system consists of various elements: a central mechanism, perceptual mechanisms, and motor mechanisms. These mechanisms correspond to structures in the brain, and one could also call them cognitive structures. The structural definition of a behavior system is "any organization of perceptual, central and motor mechanisms that acts as a unit in some situations" (see Chapter 3 and Fig. 3.1). According to Hogan (1988), behavioral development is essentially the development of these mechanisms and the changes in the connections among them. As we shall see, many of these mechanisms and their connections only develop after functional experience, i.e., experience with the particular stimuli involved, or with the consequences of performing specific motor patterns.

## Hunger

An example of a developing behavior system is the hunger system in the junglefowl chick (Hogan 1988). This system involves perceptual mechanisms for the recognition of features (color, shape, etc.), objects (grain, worms, etc.), and functions (food versus nonfood). Then there are motor mechanisms underlying behavior patterns such as ground scratching and pecking, and there is a central hunger mechanism. Importantly, several of these mechanisms and the connections between them (dashed lines in Fig. 3.5) develop as a result of specific functional experience. For instance, only after a substantial meal will the chick differentiate between food items and nonfood items to eat.

On the motor side of the system, the mechanisms underlying pecking, scratching, and walking are present as soon as the chick hatches, as is the effective coordination of these behaviors into foraging sequences. On the other hand, for at least 3 days, feeding-related behavior (in this case pecking) is not dependent on the level of food deprivation. Thus, the central hunger mechanism and the pecking motor mechanism are not initially connected. Only after the experience of pecking and swallowing (and not necessarily of food: pecking and swallowing sand is equally effective) do the two mechanisms become connected, and only then is the level of pecking dependent on the level of food deprivation (Hogan 1984). A similar phenomenon occurs in the case of suckling in rat pups, as described earlier (Hall & Williams 1983). Suckling decreases as weaning approaches but, importantly, suckling behavior does not become deprivation dependent until about 2 weeks after birth. Unfortunately, we still do not know whether functional experience is required, and if so what type of experience is needed, to connect the suckling motor mechanism with the central hunger mechanism in the rat pup.

## Dustbathing

The development of behavioral structure is not uniform but may proceed along different pathways for different behavior systems. An example of this is the development of dustbathing in junglefowl chicks, as studied by the Danish ethologist Klaus Vestergaard and coworkers (Vestergaard et al. 1993; see also Chapter 3). Dustbathing is a behavior that adult birds of many species frequently engage in. It consists of a sequence of coordinated movements of the wings, feet, head, and body that serve to spread dust through the feathers (see Fig. 3.6). The function of this behavior is to remove excess lipids from the feathers and to maintain good feather condition. Unlike the development of feeding behavior in rats or chicks, dustbathing is deprivation dependent as soon as it appears in the animal's behavioral repertoire (Hogan 2001). Thus, in this case chicks do not require functional experience to connect the motor mechanisms with the central dustbathing mechanism.

On the perceptual side, other experiments have shown that initially the chick will perform dustbathing on virtually any kind of surface, including wire mesh, suggesting that the perceptual mechanism and the central mechanism are not yet connected. The perceptual mechanism itself develops more quickly with some substrates than with others, which is similar to the development of perceptual mechanisms in song learning and filial predispositions discussed earlier. Furthermore, it turns out that preferences for functionally unlikely surfaces (e.g., a skin of junglefowl feathers) can be acquired as a result of experience with them. This is another example of the development of a perceptual mechanism, and one that is not dissimilar to filial imprinting.

## SUMMARY AND CONCLUSIONS

The study of the development of animal behavior has been hampered by misrepresentation, mainly in the popular literature, of early theoretical proposals. In particular, interpretations of Lorenz's early suggestions concerning development have led to a stubborn belief in the existence of "innate" behaviors, and the mistaken idea that genes "determine" behavior. Also, some of Lorenz's intuitions about imprinting have led to a rather rigid view on behavioral development, where events occurring during "critical periods" early in life are crucial for the development of behavior, an idea that could be expressed metaphorically as once one has missed the developmental bus there is no way back. It turns out that there is considerable plasticity in development, extending into adulthood. However, particularly in social behavior, even brief separation from the mother can have profound effects on the development of attachment. Events during development have a great influence on adult behavior, but the way in which these events affect development is often different from what had been thought previously: there is considerable plasticity and flexibility in the development of behavior.

## FURTHER READING

A number of classic papers on behavioral development, supplemented with some important recent ones, have been collected in the book by Bolhuis and Hogan (1999), which has crucial publications on all aspects of development. A collection of contemporary essays on the development of behavior can be found in Hogan and Bolhuis (1994). Gottlieb (2002b) provides a monograph on the relation between development and evolution. Classic and contemporary papers on the development of brain and cognition have been collected in a comprehensive reader (Johnson et al. 2002), while a concise introduction to the field of developmental cognitive neuroscience is provided by Johnson (1997). Recent review papers on behavioral development include Bolhuis (1999) and Hogan (2001).

## ACKNOWLEDGMENTS

I would like to thank Luc-Alain Giraldeau, Gabriel Horn, and Jerry Hogan for their comments on an earlier version of this chapter.

# 7
# learning and memory

KIMBERLY KIRKPATRICK AND GEOFFREY HALL

## INTRODUCTION

One of the most striking features of the behavior of animals is the way in which it can be modified by experience. When first faced with a particular set of circumstances, an animal will behave in a certain way; but when these same circumstances occur again, its behavior may be quite different. The animal, having interacted with its environment, is changed by the experience and thus becomes capable of behaving differently in the future. The process of interaction that produces the change in the animal is called **learning**, and the mechanisms involved in this process form the subject of the first two main sections of this chapter; the change itself is often referred to as the formation of a memory, and the properties of animal memory will be considered in the third and fourth sections of the chapter.

Most of this chapter discusses not the **functional** implications of learning but the mechanisms by which it is achieved. And although field studies have supplied some important information, our knowledge of these mechanisms comes mainly from experimental work conducted in contrived and artificial situations with laboratory animals; discussion of such experiments forms the bulk of the chapter. Those who have done this work (often experimental psychologists rather than ethologists) claim to have detected learning mechanisms of general relevance, mechanisms that form the basis of a whole range of seemingly different types of learning and that operate in most or all species. Others have doubted this claim, suggesting that the narrow focus of laboratory studies of learning has led researchers to overlook a range of specialized mechanisms of learning and memory that have evolved. This issue will be discussed in the final section of the chapter.

## Procedures for the Study of Learning and their Results

### Exposure to a single event

Given the definition of learning offered above, the most obvious way to study the phenomenon is to present the animal with a well-defined stimulus, observe the behavior that results, and then determine how behavior changes with repeated presentations of the stimulus. The usual outcome is that the likelihood or vigor of the response declines. For example, in a classic early experiment, Humphrey (1933) demonstrated that if a sharp tap is applied to the substrate on which a snail (*Helix*) is moving, the animal will respond by retracting it horns. The same may happen the second time this stimulus is applied, but after a series of applications of the stimulus the animal will continue on its way with horns extended. This phenomenon, the waning of a response with repeated presentation of its eliciting stimulus, is known as **habituation**. Examples are found throughout the animal kingdom.

Consideration of habituation allows us to refine our definition of learning. Although all learning involves a change in behavior as a result of experience, it is possible that such a change may sometimes occur because of the operation of processes that do not deserve this label: the change in the snail's behavior might be a consequence simply of fatigue in the muscular system responsible for the response or of a loss of sensitivity in the sensory system that detects the stimulus. In other cases a change in responsiveness may be attributed to **motivational** variables (see Chapter 3), as when an animal initially responds with vigor when offered food (by eating it) but responds less eagerly on subsequent presentations (as its hunger is satisfied). Learning, it is usually supposed, involves longer-term changes than these; in order to be sure that learning has occurred it is necessary to demonstrate that the change observed is not a consequence of these other, short-term, processes. In the case of habituation the relevant evidence comes from an effect called **dishabituation**. If a habituated snail is subjected to a novel and intense stimulus (Humphrey dropped a weight onto the board on which the snail was moving), it is found that the response to the original stimulus is restored, at least for a short time. It remains to explain why this dishabituating stimulus should have the effect it does (one possibility is that it temporarily boosts the animal's general level of arousal), but the fact that the response reappears shows that its previous nonoccurrence cannot have been a consequence just of muscular fatigue or its sensory equivalent.

In some cases, exposure to a stimulus produces not merely a waning of the original response but establishes a new one. A classic example is **imprinting** (see Chapter 6). The initial response of a newly hatched domestic chick to a salient object (e.g., a brightly colored moving box) may be to show signs of fear, but this will soon be replaced by a characteristic set of filial responses that include approaching the object and following it when it moves. Although imprinting involves some special and interesting features, one of the learning processes involved may be quite general. In order to show the behavior it does, the chick needs to learn the characteristics of the object to which it is exposed and discriminate these from those possessed by other similar objects. Examples of this **perceptual learning** effect (an enhanced ability to discriminate after mere exposure to stimuli) may be found in other species and are not confined to immature animals. For example, Hall (1979) found that adult laboratory rats, exposed in their home cages to simple geometrical shapes, subsequently showed an enhanced ability to learn a discrimination task in which they had to choose one shape over the other in order to obtain a food reward.

# Pairing of events

## *Classical conditioning*

Although the phenomenon of imprinting had been demonstrated some years earlier, the experimental study of animal learning began in earnest only about 1900 when the Russian physiologist I.P. Pavlov turned his attention to the topic. Pavlov's experimental procedure involved not simple exposure to a stimulus but the explicit pairing of stimuli. From his earlier work on the processes controlling digestive secretions, Pavlov knew that a dog (his chosen experimental subject) would salivate in response to a wide range of stimuli: not just the presentation of food but, for instance, the appearance of the laboratory attendant who supplied the food. This latter response clearly depended on experience, and by taking a version of it into the laboratory Pavlov hoped that he would be able to use it to elucidate the brain mechanisms responsible for learning.

In his standard experimental situation (Pavlov 1927), a lightly restrained dog (isolated in a quiet room) was subjected to a series of training trials in which presentations of food were paired with (usually slightly preceded by) presentations of a neutral event, such as the flashing of a light or the clicking of a metronome. From the outset, the presentation of food evoked salivation; this response did not require special training and was therefore described as an **unconditional** (or **unconditioned**) **response** (UR). The event that elicited it was called an **unconditioned stimulus** (US). Over the course of training, the light, which had originally been ineffective in this respect, acquired the power to evoke salivation; this response, since it was conditional on the animal having received training, was called a **conditioned response** (CR) and the light itself a **conditioned stimulus** (CS). The whole procedure thus became known as conditioning; since this term has also been applied to other examples of learning, Pavlov's original version is distinguished by the qualifier "classical."

The central feature of the **classical conditioning** procedure is that the animal is subjected to the paired presentation of two stimuli. The result is a change in behavior (the dog salivates to a stimulus that did not originally elicit this response), but it should be noted that there is nothing in the procedure that requires the animal to do anything, since pairings of the stimuli are scheduled irrespective of what the animal does. Although Pavlov's salivary conditioning procedure has been little used in recent years, its essence is to be found in other widely used training paradigms. In all of them the animal receives paired presentations of a CS and a US and a change in its response to the CS is observed. Some examples are described below.

- The **autoshaping** procedure, used with pigeons, is similar to Pavlov's original in that the bird is given trials in which the presentation of a light (the CS), projected onto a movement-sensitive response key, precedes the delivery of food (the US). With training, the bird's behavior changes in that it comes to peck at the lit key prior to the arrival of food.
- In the **conditioned emotional response** procedure as used with rats, the CS is the presentation, for a period of a minute or so, of an initially neutral stimulus (a light or the sounding of a tone). A brief electric shock (the US) follows the CS. After just a few trials the rat's behavior changes: it starts to show signs of fear (e.g., freezing) when the CS occurs.
- In **flavor aversion** (also called **conditioned taste aversion**) **learning** the paired events are a distinctive taste as the CS (e.g., saccharin in a rat's drinking water) and a state of gastric distress as the US (e.g., produced by injection of a mild toxin). After just one such trial the rat's behavior changes so that it now refuses the sweet solution that it consumed readily when first presented.

In their details, the procedures used in these examples move progressively further away from that used by Pavlov for salivary conditioning. However, all share the following features: what the experimenter does is to arrange paired presentations of CS and US; and what happens is that the CS comes to evoke behavior that it did not evoke originally.

### Instrumental (operant) conditioning

As a physiologist, Pavlov took to the study of learning as a way to discover about the workings of the brain. In the West a different perspective prevailed. During the latter half of the nineteenth century, biologists had become interested in the nature and extent of animal intelligence. Darwinian theory required "continuity" among species and thus it might be expected that intelligence, of the sort shown by humans, should also be detectable in nonhuman species (see also Chapter 8). Experimental attempts to demonstrate this involved setting animals puzzles of various sorts and showing that they could learn to solve them. Perhaps the best-known example comes from the work of Thorndike, a psychologist from the USA. He confined cats in an apparatus (appropriately called a puzzle box) from which they could escape, and gain access to a food reward, by manipulating an arrangement of latches and levers. Initially the cat took a long time to escape but, with repeated trials in the apparatus, performance improved to the extent that the cat became able to open the box in just a few seconds with a deft flick of the paw. Whether this behavior is evidence of real intelligence is open to debate (Thorndike's own interpretation, that reward simply "stamps in" or reinforces the pattern of behavior that happens to precede it, implies that it is not). Nevertheless, a version of this basic procedure has been extensively used in subsequent laboratory studies of animal learning.

The apparatus most commonly used has not been Thorndike's puzzle box but that devised by another psychologist from the USA, B.F. Skinner (and thus known as the Skinner box). The experimental subject (usually a rat) remains within the box for the duration of a training session, and presses on a lever to operate a mechanism that delivers a reward (also referred to as a **reinforcer**) to an adjacent food cup (see Skinner 1938). The measure taken is rate of responding, which is low initially but increases with successive reinforced lever-presses. This is an example of **appetitive conditioning** (so called because the procedure is one in which the animal comes to satisfy an appetite, in this case for food). The apparatus can also be used to study the **aversive conditioning** paradigm known as **punishment** by arranging that the response produces an aversive event, such as an electric shock to the rat's feet. With this procedure the rate of a pretrained response is observed to decline.

Much research has been done, particularly for the appetitive case, on the effects of scheduling **reinforcement** for only some lever presses. Response rate shows great sensitivity to such schedules. For example, the rat will show bursts of rapid responding when it is arranged that reward will be delivered only after a certain number of responses have been made (the fixed ratio schedule, so called because a fixed number of responses is required to earn each reward). In contrast, on the variable interval schedule only one response is required but the experimenter arranges that reward will be made available only when a certain length of time has passed since the last rewarded response. The interval between consecutive rewards varies around some mean value (e.g., from a few seconds to several minutes, around a mean of 1 min). In these circumstances the rat comes to respond at a fairly steady rate. Other commonly used schedules include the variable ratio schedule, in which the number of responses required to earn the reward changes unpredictably, and the fixed interval schedule, in which reward is presented for the first response that occurs after a fixed amount of time since the previous reward was earned.

At the time of its introduction, the distinction between the instrumental training procedure and that used by Pavlov was not fully appreciated, and the term "conditioning" was applied to both. As Skinner himself was at pains to make clear, there is an important difference. Both involve the presentation of a biologically important event (such as food), but in the Pavlovian procedure this is independent of what the animal does whereas in **instrumental conditioning** it is a consequence of the animal's response (the response is instrumental in producing the outcome). Skinner preferred to use the term "**operant conditioning**" to emphasize the fact that in this form of learning the animal operates upon its environment.

## Complex conditioning procedures

In the simple conditioning procedures just described, the experimenter arranges a contingency between two events, the CS being followed by the US in the classical procedure, the response by the reinforcer in the instrumental case. More recent research has continued to use these basic procedures but has introduced a variety of elaborations. Two require notice.

## Conditional control

The experimenter can arrange, for a rat lever-pressing in the Skinner box, that the response will produce food only when certain other conditions are met (e.g., only when a tone is sounding). The response-reinforcer contingency holds therefore only when the tone is on. The rat will come to respond only in the presence of the tone and will withhold responding in its absence. This phenomenon, known as **stimulus control**, reveals an ability to learn about higher-order conditionalities (food will be presented only if a response is made, and even then only when the tone is present). Such conditional learning is not confined to the instrumental procedure. In the Pavlovian analog the animal receives trials in which CS A is followed by the US only if it is accompanied or preceded by some other stimulus B; no US occurs when A is presented on its own. The animal shows its sensitivity to this conditional relationship as it comes to produce the CR to A only on the B-A trials.

## Discrimination learning

In the procedure just described the animal must discriminate between two sets of circumstances in which a given CS occurs. The standard **discrimination training** procedure is similar in principle, but two different stimuli are used and they are given different consequences. For example, a pigeon may be given autoshaping training consisting of trials in which presentations of a red light (the positive stimulus) are followed by food, intermixed with trials where a green light (the negative stimulus) is presented but no food follows. Not only will the bird come to respond to the red light, as might be expected, but it may also, at least initially, show some responding to green. This phenomenon is known as **generalization** (the CR established to the CS generalizes to another, similar stimulus). With extended training, however, the tendency to respond to green will decline and a discrimination between red and green will be established.

The instrumental version of discrimination training often involves a choice procedure. For example, a rat at the choice point of a maze can be confronted with two arms, one black and one white. If a move into the white arm gives access to food whereas choice of the black does not, the rats will, after a few training trials, come to choose the white arm on each occasion even when the left–right position of the arms is switched at random from trial to trial. This same apparatus can be used to study **spatial discrimination**. In this case no visual cues are presented and reward is available after choice of, say, the left arm and never after choice of the right. Rats learn spatial discriminations readily, even when the task cannot be solved by learning to perform a specific response. In one widely used procedure (Morris 1981), the rat is placed in a pool of water from which it can escape by climbing onto an invisible platform, the top of which lies just below the surface. After a few trials the rat learns to swim directly to the platform from whatever point it is placed in the pool. In order to do this, the rat must have learned something about the spatial relationships between the platform and the various cues present in the room in which the pool is located.

## Mechanisms of Learning

## Associative analysis of conditioning

### *Classical conditioning*

In classical conditioning the experimenter arranges that two events, the CS and the US, occur together. What could be more natural, then, than to assume that what the animal learns directly reflects this. Pavlov's own interpretation was that activation of the brain center responsible for perception of the CS, at the same time as the center responsive to the US was also activated, resulted in the strengthening of a link or association between them. The existence of this stimulus–stimulus (S–S) association means that presentation of the CS will be able to activate the US center (via the link shown by arrow 1 in Fig. 7.1a) and thus produce the behavior normally evoked by the US

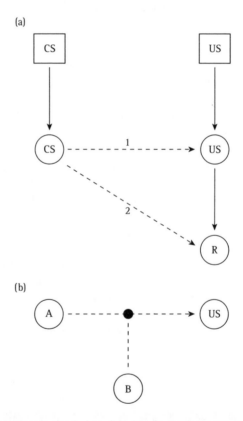

**Fig. 7.1** (a) Associative connections in classical conditioning. Rectangles represent events in the environment and circles the brain centers activated by these events. Solid lines represent inbuilt links and dotted lines links that might form as a result of conditioning: (1) S–S link; (2) S–R link. CS, conditioned stimulus; US, unconditioned stimulus; R, response. (b) An associative mechanism for conditional control. CS A has a connection to the US, but this will only operate fully when CS B has been presented.

Table 7.1 Experimental designs in classical conditioning.

|  | Phase 1 | Phase 2 | Test |
|---|---|---|---|
| Sensory preconditioning | A → B | B → US | A |
| Blocking | A → US | AB → US | B |

A and B, conditioned stimuli; US, unconditioned stimulus. In each phase of training several presentations of each set of events will occur.

itself (i.e., produce a CR). This analysis implies that classical conditioning should be possible even when the event used as the US elicits no response. **Sensory preconditioning** supplies an example of such an effect. In this procedure (Table 7.1), the animal receives initial conditioning trials in which the two stimuli are both neutral and elicit no obvious response, for example a light is paired with a tone. After a second stage of training, in which the tone is paired with an orthodox US, it is found that the light is now able to elicit the CR that has been conditioned to the tone. This result seems to indicate that the light has acquired the power to activate the representation of the (subsequently conditioned) tone, i.e., the initial stage of training has established an (S–S) association between the light and the tone.

It has often been suggested that another type of association is important in classical conditioning. Although the experimenter arranges a pairing of stimuli, the animal will necessarily experience (in the standard procedure in which the US evokes a UR) a pairing of a stimulus (the CS) and a response (the UR). A stimulus–response (S–R) association could thus form between the center activated by the CS and the center responsible for organizing and emitting a response (via the link shown by arrow 2 in Fig. 7.1a). Indeed, for many years around the middle of the last century, this S–R account was the dominant interpretation of classical conditioning, being championed by adherents of a version of **behaviorism** that tried to explain all behavior in terms of the S–R formula. However, experimental analysis has failed to support this doctrine. In one study, for example, Holland and Straub (1979) gave rats pairings of a noise (CS) and a food pellet (US) so that the rats acquired the CR of approaching the site of food delivery, the food cup, when the noise came on. In a second stage of training the rats were given free access to food pellets followed by a nausea-inducing injection: flavor aversion learning occurred (see above) and the rats were now unwilling to eat pellets of this type. A final test in the original conditioning apparatus revealed that the noise was now much less effective in evoking the CR. This result is not predicted by S–R analysis: there is no reason why the link between CS and response (arrow 2 in Fig. 7.1a), once formed, should be affected by a subsequent change in the value of the US; however, if the S–S theory is correct and the CR depends on the ability of the CS center to activate the US center, then sensitivity to change in the value of the US is just what would be expected.

Although it is now widely accepted that S–S associations play a dominant role in classical conditioning, it would be wrong to jump to the conclusion that animals cannot form S–R associations; indeed, the experiment just described provides some evidence indicating that they can. In addition to measuring food-cup approach, Holland and Straub (1979) measured another CR: the increase in general activity that occurs in the presence of an auditory CS signaling food. They found that the vigor of this CR was not influenced by devaluation of the US, suggesting that in this case the behavior depends on the rats having formed an S–R link. This observation points to a more general conclusion. For some psychologists the debate about S–R and S–S mechanisms for classical conditioning has been seen as a battle over rival approaches to the discipline as a whole, some equating behaviorism with the S–R account whereas others, persuaded of what is sometimes referred to as a "cognitive" perspective, argue in favor of the S–S account (see also Chapter 1). As the results just described show, the choice between these alternative approaches cannot be made in terms of the nature of the association in conditioning. Animals will form both types of association, according to the details of the training procedure employed; to that extent, at least, everyone is right (some of the time).

## Instrumental conditioning

The associative analysis has also been applied to instrumental conditioning, and the debate over the nature of the association involved has much in common with that described for classical conditioning. Again, the S–R account, which dominated for many years, has been challenged by recent research showing the importance of another association (in this case between the response and its outcome); once more, the resolution turns out to be that both forms of association may be established, given the appropriate conditions.

Thorndike's own interpretation of instrumental learning was that the relevant association was between S and R. This was couched in terms of his **law of effect**. In its most general form, this law simply states that the effect produced by an action will change the likelihood of that action for the future (e.g., the **frequency** of lever-pressing will increase when that behavior produces a food pellet). In the specific form proposed by Thorndike it was suggested that the mechanism responsible for the increase in response frequency was the strengthening (reinforcement) of a connection between the current stimulus situation (the sight of the lever in this example) and the response (depressing the lever).

Experiments investigating this interpretation have made use of a reinforcer-devaluation procedure, analogous to the US-devaluation experiment of Holland and Straub (1979) described earlier. In one of these, Adams and Dickinson (1981) trained rats to press the lever in a Skinner box for food, training that should, according to the theory, simply establish a link between the S of the lever and the R of pressing. In a further stage of training the rats were allowed to eat food pellets of the type they had previously earned by lever-pressing and this was followed by an injection known to induce nausea. The fact that the rats now showed an aversion to this form of food should, according to the S–R theory, be irrelevant to the behavior shown in the Skinner box: the reward would have done its job of reinforcing the S–R connection in the first stage of training and subsequent changes in its value to the animal should be of no consequence. It was found, however, that when the rats were returned to the Skinner box, those that had been subjected to the reinforcer-devaluation procedure showed a reduced willingness to press the lever. We may conclude that the role of the reinforcer in this procedure is not simply to stamp in some connection between a stimulus and a response; rather, the animal clearly knows something about what the outcome of its response will be. Put in associative terms, this means that the critical link is between R (in this case the lever-press) and S (the outcome of the response). When the outcome is of value, the R–S connection results in a high rate of response; when it is not, the rate of response will be low.

What remains is to point out that some conditions of instrumental training will generate responding that is independent of the current value of the reinforcer; in these cases the rat will continue to perform a response that was initially established using a reinforcer that is no longer of value. There are several possible reasons why this result might arise, but among them is the possibility that what the animal has learned in initial training is an S–R rather than an R–S association. Particularly intriguing in this context is the observation that animals given extensive initial training can become insensitive to the value of the reinforcer, an outcome consistent with everyday experience that an act acquired initially with reference to the effect it produced can, if repeated often enough, turn into an automatic habit.

## Principles of association formation

The notion that learning might depend on the formation of associations had a long history in philosophy before being taken up by experimental scientists. For several centuries, philosophers speculated about the nature of the "laws of association" (i.e., the conditions that determine when an association will form or undergo a change in strength); the study of conditioning in animals (particularly classical conditioning) provided a way in which this issue could be investigated empirically.

Experimental study has confirmed that **contiguity** is important for association formation: conditioning occurs best when the CS and the US are presented close together in time. If a delay is imposed between the offset of the CS and the presentation of the US, conditioning is impaired. This is not to say that conditioning is impossible in these conditions (in the case of flavor aversion learning some effect is found even when several hours separate CS and US), but the observation may simply indicate that the central activity induced by the CS may persist for a time and thus still be present when the US occurs. A more fundamental issue is raised by experiments showing that sometimes conditioning can fail to occur even when the animal receives contiguous presentations of a CS and US.

The clearest demonstration that contiguity does not necessarily generate conditioning is supplied by the phenomenon known as **blocking**. This was discovered by Kamin (1968) in experiments using the conditioned emotional response. The procedure involved two stages of training and two CSs (see Table 7.1). In the first stage, rats received trials in which one of the CSs (say a light) was followed by shock US so that a CR was established. CS–US pairings continued in the second stage but now another CS (say a noise) was presented along with the light. The animal thus experienced a series of contiguous presentations of the noise and the shock; nonetheless, in a final test phase in which the noise was presented on its own, no CR was observed. Pretraining with the light had blocked learning about the noise that was added in the second stage (control subjects that received just the stage of training with the noise–light compound showed perfectly adequate conditioning to the noise).

What this result seems to show is that contiguous presentation of the CS and US is not enough to establish a link between them; rather the CS must supply **information** about the upcoming US. In this blocking experiment the first stage of training ensures that the occurrence of the US is fully predicted by the light, whereas the noise is redundant (supplies no new information) and is thus not learned about. To some extent, this interpretation is just a redescription of the result obtained and the task of the learning theorist remains that of determining the mechanism by which it occurs. This was addressed in the influential theory first proposed by Rescorla and Wagner (1972) (Box 7.1) and subsequently developed by Wagner (1981). These theorists took as their starting point the notion that a CS–US link would not form if the US was already expected. To say

---

## Box 7.1 Rescorla–Wagner model

The account of conditioning proposed by Rescorla and Wagner (1972) was expressed in terms of a simple equation that specifies by how much the strength of the associative connection between a CS and US will change as the result of a conditioning trial. A simplified version is given below. The change in the associative strength ($\Delta V$) that occurs on a conditioning trial is determined by:

$$\Delta V = \alpha(\lambda - \Sigma V)$$

where $\alpha$ represents a parameter that varies with the salience of the CS, $\lambda$ the maximum associative strength that the US can support, and $\Sigma V$ the summed associative strength of all CSs present on the trial. It will be noted that when $\Sigma V$ equals $\lambda$ there can be no further change in associative strength, as the value inside the parentheses will be zero. Conditioning with A as the CS (as in the first stage of the blocking experiment; see Table 7.1) will thus proceed until the associative strength of A ($V_A$) has risen to the value of $\lambda$. Further trials in the second stage, in which A is presented in compound with B will produce no further increase in $V_A$. What is more, they will not produce any increase in the associative strength of the newly introduced B, as the value of ($\lambda - \Sigma V$) will be zero by virtue of the associative strength of A. This outcome is the result obtained experimentally (the blocking effect).

This simple equation neatly captures the notion that an expected US (one preceded by a CS that has a high level of associative strength) will be poor at supporting further learning. It has proved to have wide explanatory power and has been very influential not only in the study of conditioning but also in the psychology of cognition more generally.

that a US is expected means, in terms of the associative account, that the US center is already activated, via a CS–US link, before the US actually arrives. If we assume that a US center that is already activated in this way cannot react normally when the US is presented, then the experimental results may be explained. Although the experimenter, in the blocking experiment, arranges contiguous presentations of a noise CS and the US, this is not what the animal experiences: the CS will activate its center but (given that the relevant center is already activated by the light) the US will not. In a sense, therefore, the central role of contiguity is maintained in this account. What matters, however, is not the contiguous occurrence of events in the animal's environment, but the concurrent presence of appropriate activity in the relevant brain centers.

## General applicability of associative theory

The associative theory of conditioning is important not simply because it can explain (most of) the effects observed in conditioning experiments. Its wider importance comes from the suggestion (put forward originally by Pavlov but taken up enthusiastically in recent years by adherents to the theory known as **connectionism**) that associative mechanisms may underlie all forms of learning. To establish this point it would be a useful first step to show that the associative analysis can apply satisfactorily to the various forms of learning described earlier in this chapter. For the case of discrimination learning and generalization, this is a fairly simple matter. Generalization will occur because two similar stimuli hold features in common; pairing one of these stimuli with a US will thus mean that features of the other will also be associated with the US, and thus this untrained stimulus will tend to evoke the CR to some extent. However, presentation of a CS in the absence of the US will reduce the effective strength of any association that may exist between them (a phenomenon referred to as **extinction**). What follows is that the discrimination training procedure will reduce the strength of these common features. As a result the animal will cease to respond to the negative stimulus but will continue to respond to the positive stimulus, the unique features of which will still be strongly associated with the US. These principles also successfully predict the behavior shown when the animal is required to choose between the two stimuli.

The explanation of conditional control is still a matter for debate. One possibility is that it reflects the formation of an association between a stimulus and another association. When an animal comes to respond to CS A only when B has been presented, this may be because a link has been formed between B and the A–US association that allows B to activate the association (see Fig. 7.1b). (Stimulus control is explained in much the same way by the suggestion that the stimulus is able to activate the R–outcome association.) An alternative possibility is that the animal is able to put A and B together as a **configural cue** and that conditioning occurs to this configuration rather than to any of the separable elements. An advantage of this interpretation is that it suggests a possible explanation of the spatial learning phenomena described above. The ability of the rat to find its way to the platform in a swimming pool is not easily explained in terms of conditioning to any single event, but it can be analyzed in terms of the acquisition of behavior guided by a configuration of cues.

More problematic for the associative analysis are the seemingly simple learning effects produced by exposure to a single stimulus. By their very nature (since only one stimulus is presented) it is difficult to explain these effects in terms of the formation of an association between two events. Rather it seems that mere exposure to a stimulus can engage a learning process that changes the way in which that event is perceived. One popular account of habituation is that repeated exposure to a stimulus allows the animal to build up a "model" or central representation of that event. Habituation occurs because the incoming stimulus is found to match an existing central representation; a novel stimulus, one that finds no match, evokes a response. And animals that possess well-formed representations of stimuli might be expected to be good at discrimination between them, i.e., they should show the perceptual learning effect. It remains to be seen whether associative mechanisms are involved in the learning process by which such representations are formed.

## Procedures for the Study of Memory and their Results

The preceding sections considered the means by which behavior can be modified by experience. In order for this process to occur, there must be some representation of past experience. In simple conditioning, for example, a CR could not emerge during the CS unless there was some memory of the previous pairings with the US. Thus, memory can be thought of as the effect of past experience on behavior in the present.

There may be many kinds of memory, but the two major divisions are between shorter-term **working memory** and longer-term **reference memory**. The memory of previous pairings in a conditioning task would be an example of reference memory. The reference memory formed is the content of learning. Thus reference memory would not exist without learning and vice versa. Working memory, on the other hand, is a more short-term form of storage. The ability to remember where you parked your car while you are in the market is an example of working memory. You may well forget the information as soon as its purpose has passed.

### Working or short-term memory

The study of working memory was first undertaken by W.S. Hunter (1913) when he developed the delayed-response paradigm. An animal would be placed in an apparatus that contained several boxes, one of which was baited with food. The baited box would be signaled by the presentation of a light stimulus. Then, after a delay (with the light off) the animal would be allowed to select the box marked earlier. If the animal chose the correct site, then it received the food. A correct choice indicates that the animal remembered the baited location over the delay period. One of the problems with Hunter's procedure was that some animals would learn to orient themselves toward the baited box during the delay period, thereby avoiding having to retain any memory of which box was baited.

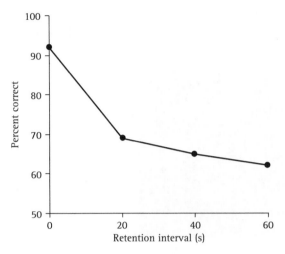

**Fig. 7.2** Effect of increasing retention interval on performance in a choice delayed matching-to-sample task with pigeons. As the time between the sample and choice is increased, performance progressively deteriorates, demonstrating the time-limited nature of working memory. (Adapted from Grant 1976.)

The next major procedural development for studying working memory was not to occur for nearly 50 years until Blough (1959) introduced the **delayed matching-to-sample** (DMTS) paradigm for studying memory in pigeons. A trial typically involves the presentation of a sample stimulus (e.g., a red keylight) followed by two choice stimuli (e.g., red and green keylights). The pigeon has to choose the same color as the sample in order to receive a reward. By inserting a delay or **retention interval** between the sample and choice, it is possible to determine how well the pigeon can remember the sample over time. Figure 7.2 displays some data from a DMTS task (Grant 1976). Accuracy was nearly perfect with zero retention interval, but fell systematically as the interval between sample and choice was increased, providing evidence that the sample is forgotten over time. Thus it can be seen that a key feature of working memory is its time-limited nature. Additional aspects of forgetting will be considered in the following section.

A final method for studying working memory is list learning, which has been popularly used with humans and more recently adapted for study with animals. There are a number of different methods for teaching lists to animals (although many of these methods often yield similar results). In one experiment, Harper et al. (1993) demonstrated list learning in a 12-arm **radial maze**. The rats were taught a list of seven items by allowing them access to only one baited arm at a time. The rat would be placed in the center of the radial maze and one arm would be opened. The rat would travel down the arm and retrieve the reward and then return to the center. The first arm would then close and a second arm would open, and so on until seven arms had been visited. After a 5-s delay, the rats were then given tests with pairs of arms. One arm would have been a member of the previous list, whereas the second arm would be novel. The rat was required to remember which arm was familiar and visit the novel arm in order to

(a)

(b)

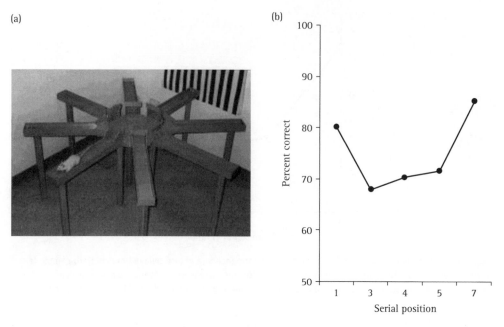

**Fig. 7.3** (a) Radial-arm maze. (b) Serial position curve obtained from rats in a radial-arm maze. Memory is superior for items at the beginning (primacy effect) and end (recency effect) of the list, but poorer for items in the middle of the list. (Fig. 7.3(a): photograph by Cedric Williams; (b) adapted from Harper et al. 1993.)

receive food. By testing different pairs of arms, Harper et al. were able to determine how well the rats remembered the individual items in the list. Figure 7.3 demonstrates that (like humans) the rats best remembered the first and last items in the list and performed more poorly on intermediate items. This U-shaped curve is the **serial position function** or **serial position curve**. The superior memory for early items in a list is a **primacy effect,** whereas the superior memory for items near the end of a list is a **recency effect.** Recency effects are much easier to demonstrate in animals than primacy effects. The possible source of primacy and recency effects will be discussed in the following section on forgetting.

## Forgetting of items in working memory

As noted earlier, working memory is typically quite short in duration. This section will consider factors involved in the loss of information from working memory. One source of forgetting is passive decay (the results in Fig. 7.2 provide an example of this phenomenon). Roberts and Grant (1976) proposed that stimulus items in working memory consist of traces that decay over time. The strength and durability of the trace are determined by factors such as the intensity and duration of the stimulus. In a DMTS task, there may be multiple items in memory (current sample, previous samples, previous choices). The item with the strongest trace value will determine the choice on the current trial.

Errors occur when the traces of items become so weak that there is no clear winner, as is the case when the delay interval is long. This account correctly predicts two common effects in DMTS: increasing either sample duration or the time between trials increases performance (Roberts & Grant 1976; Nelson & Wasserman 1978). Increasing sample duration would enhance the strength of the trace of the current sample, whereas increasing the time between trials would allow previous items from earlier trials to decay further and thereby produce less interference with the current trace.

A second source of forgetting is thought to be due to the limited capacity of working memory. The classic $7 \pm 2$ rule in humans exemplifies the capacity issues of working memory (Miller 1956). It has been consistently reported that humans can only maintain about seven items (give or take a couple) in short-term memory before interference effects begin to occur. The same also appears true in other animals. Wagner (1976) proposed that there is a limit on the number of traces that can be maintained at once. The introduction of a new item in working memory will weaken or displace previous traces, and previous items in working memory can interfere with new information.

One factor that can alleviate the problem of limited capacity is the ability to "chunk" items together into meaningful clusters. An example of **chunking** was provided by Terrace (1991) in a list-learning experiment with pigeons. Pigeons learned lists of five items, which were composed of colors and/or shapes (Fig. 7.4b). The pigeon had to peck five lighted keys in a specified order to receive a reward. The five lit keys appeared at random positions in an array of eight possible keys (Fig. 7.4a). Different groups received different lists. The list for group II contained a natural chunk, with three colors followed by two shapes. Group IV received a larger initial chunk of four colors followed by one shape. The remaining groups experienced sequences that did not contain meaningful chunks of items. It was discovered that the pigeons in groups II and IV learned more quickly and were faster at completing their sequences at the end of training. The results indicate that the presence of chunks in a list aids learning, perhaps by decreasing the load on working memory.

One facet of limited capacity is that interference effects may occur. There are two main types of interference: proactive and retroactive. **Proactive interference** is the effect of past information on current retention ability. The interfering effect of short intertrial intervals in the DMTS task is one example. **Retroactive interference** is the effect of information that intervenes between exposure to an item and later recall of the item. This can be produced in DMTS by adding a distractor cue between the sample and choice. One situation where proactive and retroactive interference may operate together is the serial position curve (see Fig. 7.3). It is thought that performance in the middle of the list may be impaired because both proactive interference (earlier items) and retroactive interference (later items) operate together (Baddeley 1976). Items near the start of the list would be remembered more easily because they suffer solely from retroactive interference, and items at the end of the list would be remembered more easily because they suffer solely from proactive interference.

A final feature of working memory is that **rehearsal** aids the maintenance of items for longer periods of time. One way that rehearsal has been studied in animals is with the **directed-forgetting paradigm** (Maki & Hegvik 1980). The paradigm is an extension of the DMTS procedure in which a cue is added after the sample to indicate whether

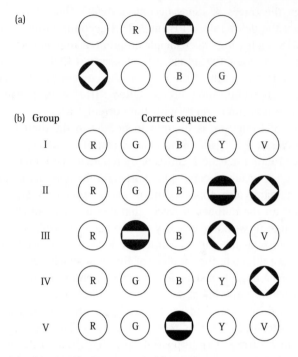

**Fig. 7.4** Experiment on chunking in a list-learning task. (a) Pigeons were given an array of eight keys, of which a random five were lit with different colors or shapes. The pigeons had to peck the lit keys in a previously specified order. (b) Different groups were trained with different sequences of keylights that contained either two chunks (groups II and IV) or no chunks (groups I, III, and V). The lists that contained chunks were learned faster than lists that did not contain chunks. (Adapted from Terrace 1991.)

the animal will be tested for sample memory or not. Occasionally, the animal receives a forget cue, but is given the choice memory test anyhow. On these special forget-cue trials, performance is usually impaired relative to remember-cue trials. The fact that a forget cue results in poorer memory than a remember cue indicates that animals engage in some sort of maintenance rehearsal when they have to remember the sample.

## Reference or long-term memory

All learning involves the formation of reference memory and vice versa, so in many ways the concept of reference memory is difficult to distinguish from the concept of learning. Any distinction to be made between learning and reference memory comes from the prevalent questions that are asked. Most studies of learning assess the formation of reference memories, whereas most studies of reference memory assess the capacity and durability of information that is learned. Reference memory can be assessed in the context of almost any experiment in which new information is learned.

Reference memory, unlike working memory, appears to have an unlimited capacity and long duration. One of the most striking examples in animals is found in the New World corvid, Clark's nutcracker (*Nucifraga columbiana*), which stores about 30,000 seeds in around 3000 different locations. The nutcrackers store the seeds in the fall and retrieve them throughout the winter and spring, with a high success rate. Laboratory studies have indicated that this ability is due to memory, rather than other factors such as storing or retrieving strategies (see Chapter 8 for fuller description of cache recovery behavior). Thus, reference memory can contain a large number of distinctive items over a period of at least months.

This ability has been demonstrated in other species as well. For example, pigeons have been observed to remember a large number of different snapshots over a long period of time. Vaughan and Greene (1984) trained pigeons to discriminate between pairs of photographs. For each pair, one of the photos was designated consistently as the reinforced stimulus and the other photo as the nonreinforced stimulus. The pigeon would be shown a particular pair together on a viewing screen. If the pigeon correctly pecked the reinforced stimulus, then it would receive food. On the other hand, if it erroneously responded to the nonreinforced stimulus, then food would be withheld on that trial. Initially, the birds were trained to discriminate 40 pairs of photographs. Once they had successfully learned these, they were given a further set of 40 photos, and so on until they had successfully learned to discriminate 160 different pairs of slides, with very high accuracy. At the end of training, the pigeons were given a test with all 320 individual slides to see whether they had learned (and remembered) the individual slides from each of the pairs. During this test, the pigeons successfully discriminated both the reinforced and nonreinforced slides, indicating that they had learned about all the photos. Although learning of 320 slides over a period of hundreds of training sessions may not be as impressive as the cache-recovery behavior of Clark's nutcracker, the study by Vaughan and Green nonetheless indicates that pigeons can maintain a large number of items in reference memory.

Vaughan and Greene (1984) went on to test the durability of the pigeons' memory for the photos that they had received over the course of the study. The pigeons were tested for memory of the 320 photos after either 237 or 629 days and were found to have retained the discrimination well above chance. These results and other studies indicate that animals can retain information over periods of weeks to years much like humans. However, long-term retention is not perfect; there is some degree of forgetting.

## Forgetting of items in reference memory

Information in reference memory may simply be lost over time due to passive decay. Experimentally, passive decay is difficult to disentangle from other sources of forgetting. In working memory, passive decay occurs quite rapidly so it is easy to observe in the absence of other factors that may cause forgetting. However, in reference memory, passive decay may occur over the course of months to years.

There are two main factors that have been demonstrated to affect storage and/or recall of information in reference memory: **consolidation** and **retrieval**. Consolidation is a hypothetical process that has been proposed to occur when new memories are formed. In the minutes to hours following a learning experience, it is believed that there is an ongoing process in the nervous system that results in new memory formation. If this process is disrupted, then memory formation may be incomplete, resulting in poor recall of information. For example, **retrograde amnesia** is commonly observed in people following head trauma. Patients suffer a loss of memory for recent events that occurred prior to the injury. Retrograde amnesia has been studied more systematically in psychiatric patients undergoing electroconvulsive shock (ECS) treatment for severe depression (Squire & Slater 1975; Squire & Fox 1980). ECS treatment may alleviate depression considerably. The patients showed deficits in recall of information that had been learned up to 3 years prior to ECS treatment, but information acquired earlier was not affected. Retrograde amnesia is usually temporally graded, i.e., the severity of disruption in memory is greatest for most recent events and becomes progressively less severe as a function of time prior to the onset of amnesia.

Evidence of memory consolidation has also been obtained in a variety of other species. For example, Duncan (1949) examined the effect of ECS on reference memory in rats. The rats were trained with a light that was followed by a shock to the feet. To prevent the shock from occurring, the rat had to move to the other side of the box before the light went off. Following each training trial, the rats received ECS, with the time of ECS administration varying from 20 s to 14 h between different groups. Figure 7.5 shows that when ECS occurred soon after the trial, avoidance learning was greatly disrupted, but delayed ECS had no effect on avoidance behavior. These results indicate that trial

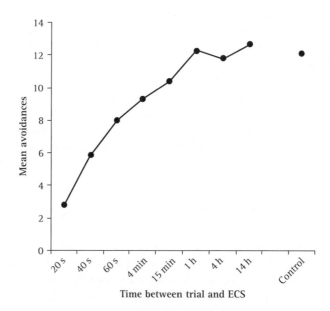

**Fig. 7.5** Effect of electroconvulsive shock (ECS) treatment on reference memory. When ECS was given soon after avoidance training, performance suffered suggesting that ECS had disrupted memory consolidation. (Adapted from Duncan 1949.)

information was still being consolidated during the first few minutes after a trial and was vulnerable during this time.

Although interruptions in consolidation may result in poor memory formation, once a memory is formed then any memory failures appear to be due primarily to failures in retrieving information. Retrieval accounts (Spear 1973; Lewis 1979) maintain that memories are not lost, but rather forgetting occurs because of a failure to retrieve information from reference memory. Retrieval theories propose that reference memories exist in two categories: active and inactive. An item in active memory is highly likely to be retrieved, whereas an item in inactive memory is much less likely to be retrieved.

The primary evidence in support of retrieval theories comes from studies that have used **reactivation** treatments. Deweer et al. (1980) trained rats on a six-arm radial maze. One group of rats was tested immediately after training (Immediate group), a second group was tested in the maze after 25 days (Delay group), and a third group was tested after 25 days but with a brief reactivation treatment prior to testing (Reactivate group). The reactivation treatment involved placing the rat in a wire cage next to the maze for 90 s. The Immediate group performed at a high level of accuracy, but the Delay group demonstrated decrements in performance indicating that they had forgotten the task. However, the Reactivate group performed at similar levels of accuracy as the Immediate group. Thus, despite the 25-day delay, the reactivation treatment resulted in recovery of performance on the task. These results suggest that the Delay group had not lost information from reference memory but rather were failing to retrieve the relevant memories for the task. By reactivating those memories, retrieval was boosted to normal levels.

## Working versus reference memory

There are a number of differences between working and reference memory that have been described thus far. For example, working memory operates over a much shorter time span, has a much more limited capacity, and is more prone to interference than reference memory. However, we have not yet described the relationship between working and reference memory. This relationship is perhaps best explained by the following example.

Suppose that you decide to order a take-out from a local Chinese restaurant that has just been recommended by a friend. You look up the telephone number in the phone book and then dial the number. If you rehearse the number, you are more likely to remember it. If you are delayed or interrupted before dialing, you are more likely to forget the number. Between the time when you look up and dial, the phone number must be maintained in working memory and thus would be susceptible to the sources of forgetting described above. Now suppose that a few days later you decide to order from the restaurant again. You will probably not remember the number and will repeat the previous process of looking it up and dialing. However, if you use the number repeatedly over the course of weeks, the likelihood of remembering without looking in the phone book increases until you know the number by heart. At this point, the telephone number has been stored in long-term memory and can be recalled readily. If you stop ordering Chinese food for a few months, then you may forget the phone number, perhaps because of passive decay or retrieval failure.

This familiar example demonstrates that information must pass through working memory (perhaps with rehearsal and/or repeated use) before that information will be stored in reference memory. Moreover, when an item is recalled from reference memory, it is held in working memory during the time that the item is in use. Items that are recalled more frequently are also recalled more easily, through the facilitation of retrieval processes.

## General and Special Processes

The experimental studies of learning and memory described in previous sections of this chapter were conducted for the most part on species (rats, dogs, pigeons, etc.) chosen largely for the readiness with which they accommodate to the special conditions of the laboratory. The events manipulated in the experiments (those used as stimuli and reinforcers) and the patterns of behavior chosen for observation were selected as much for the convenience of the experimenter (tones are easy to generate, lever presses easy to record) as for any other reason. The experimenters who conducted this work were sustained by the hope that these factors might be irrelevant – that their laboratory studies might reveal principles of learning and memory that apply to most or all species and to most or all stimuli and responses. To some extent this hope appears not to be without foundation. For example, Pavlov's original results were obtained from studies of the salivary reflex in dogs but, as we have seen, the basic associative principles he discovered have been applied successfully to a range of other procedures and species. Studies of the mechanisms of memory have also revealed a high degree of similarity across a range of species. In the DMTS, task performance deteriorates as a function of retention interval, regardless of the species of animal being tested; serial position curves of a similar shape have been obtained with rats, monkeys, and pigeons; and there is considerable evidence for a capacious and durable long-term memory in rats, chimpanzees, honeybees, and a variety of bird species. An exhaustive survey of the relevant evidence conducted by Macphail (1982) led him to conclude that the same basic learning mechanisms operate in all nonhuman vertebrate species. (Humans were excepted by Macphail on the grounds of their unique ability to use language to organize and encode information.)

This "general-process" view of learning was never widely accepted by those who studied the behavior of wild species in their natural environments, but its dominance was challenged most effectively by the results of a variety of experimental studies carried out with domesticated species in the later decades of the twentieth century. These were of two types: cases in which learning failed to happen when the general-process account would expect it to occur; and cases in which learning occurred with extraordinary ease. An example of the former was provided by Shettleworth (1975) who found that operant conditioning in hamsters was quite ineffective when applied to some patterns of behavior: food reinforcement will increase the frequency of some behavior patterns (e.g., scrabbling at the wall of the cage) but has little effect on others (e.g., when the delivery of a food pellet is made contingent on face-washing). The most striking example of very rapid learning has already been mentioned. A single pairing of a novel taste with nausea will establish an aversion to that taste in the rat. This effect can be obtained even when a period of several hours intervenes between the taste and the nausea, and is not what would be expected on the basis of an interpretation that emphasizes the importance of contiguity in producing conditioning.

One reaction to results of this sort was to reject general-process theory entirely. According to one influential learning theorist, such results show that "our principles of learning no longer have a claim to universality . . . that learning depends in very important ways on the kind of animal being considered, the kind of behavior that is required of it, and the kind of situation in which the behavior occurs" (Bolles 1979, p. 165). Pursuing this view leads to the suggestion that general-process learning theory has quite overlooked the significance of the phenomenon, namely that the mechanisms responsible for learning have evolved like all the other attributes an animal possesses, and that they should be viewed as specializations that help the individual to survive in the particular habitat in which its ancestors have evolved. Rather than looking for general processes, the investigator should accept that each species may possess a niche-specific learning mechanism, different from that possessed by other species. The remarkable cache-recovering abilities of food-storing birds are often cited in this context. Birds that are heavily dependent on food storing have been shown to have a larger hippocampus (a brain structure known to be involved in spatial memory) than related species that engage in very little storing behavior (see Chapter 5 for a detailed discussion of these issues and Bolhuis & Macphail 2001 for a critical review). The implication is that the special selection pressures operating on food-storers might have induced structural **adaptations** that allow them to exhibit learning processes substantially different from those found in other species.

Having sketched out the rival theoretical positions, it is time now to attempt an assessment. The first thing to say is that, on closer examination, much of the evidence cited against the general-process position is not as damaging as it may seem. It consists largely of showing that there are quantitative differences between the learning that occurs in different training situations, not that the mechanisms involved are different in principle. Most species can be trained to acquire spatial discriminations (and in these the hippocampus has often been found to play an important role); food-storing birds may be better at it, but may not be doing anything radically different from the rat that learns to find the platform in a water tank. Flavor aversion learning may occur very rapidly, but the laws governing this form of learning turn out to be identical to those that govern more orthodox forms of classical conditioning. It is possible that such quantitative differences reflect not so much differences in the basic learning mechanisms involved as differences between animals in their sensory and perceptual systems (see Macphail 1982).

Simple demonstrations of exceedingly rapid (or rather slow) learning do not, in themselves, constitute good evidence against the general-process view. However, more problematic for this view are experiments that make use of a design that allows both effects to be observed in the same procedure. The classic example comes from a study of flavor aversion learning in rats by Garcia and Koelling (1966), which not only made use of a taste as the CS and nausea as the US (as is usual) but also employed exteroceptive cues as a CS and footshock as a US. During training, the rats drank a saccharin-flavored solution and at the same time a compound exteroceptive cue (a flash of light and a burst of noise) was presented. Half the animals then experienced a nausea-inducing treatment as the US; the others were given electric shock. In a subsequent test, rats in the first condition showed an aversion to saccharin but were willing to drink plain water even when this was accompanied by the light and noise. Rats in the other condition drank saccharin readily but refused the "bright noisy water." The important feature of this pattern of results is that it contains evidence that all the events used as CSs and USs were effective and fully perceived by the rats. Clearly the taste was effective as a CS since it readily became associated with nausea; equally clearly, the shock was effective as a US because it supported conditioning perfectly well with the noise–light CS. Standard learning theory thus has no reason to expect that an association would fail to form between the taste CS and the shock US (the failure of the exteroceptive cues to become associated with nausea is equally troublesome for this theory).

What the Garcia and Koelling results seem to show is that association formation can occur selectively: gastric upset is especially readily associated with taste, whereas an event that impinges on the body surface becomes associated more readily with exteroceptive cues. It is not hard to see this as being a specialization generated by the evolutionary history of the species. Given that an attack on the body surface is likely to be preceded by exteroceptive cues (as when a predator strikes) and that gastric illness is likely to be preceded by the characteristic taste of a particular food, an animal that was good at forming the relevant associations would be at an advantage. To acknowledge this point does not absolve us from trying to determine the mechanism by which such selective association formation might come about. There is, as yet, no general agreement about this, but one possibility (see Hall 1994) is that the phenomenon arises from the operation of a more general principle of association, the notion (long held by associationist philosophers but hitherto neglected by experimentalists) that associations form particularly readily between similar events. To adopt this interpretation might allow standard associative theory to incorporate the findings on selective association; rather than causing us to abandon general-process theory, these findings could lead to its extension and refinement.

The dispute between theorists who emphasize the generality of learning mechanisms and those who are impressed by the special abilities shown by certain species (Shettleworth 1998; Macphail & Bolhuis, 2001) will not be easy to resolve. A perspective may be obtained by considering learning as a biological process like many others, for example respiration. At one level of analysis, all animals that respire aerobically share certain common processes – the demands of a biochemical system that depends on oxidation for the generation of energy require that this be so. However, the precise nature of the environment in which these processes operate in a given species may require specializations (gills are good for gas exchange when the oxygen is dissolved in water; lungs are more effective for air-breathers). Learning and memory can be viewed in the same light. At one level all animals must live a world in which events have consequences and accordingly it would be no surprise to find that all are equipped with mechanisms that allow them to internalize such relationships. Nevertheless, the special features of the niche occupied by any given species make it possible that special mechanisms may evolve to supplement the general processes shared by all.

## SUMMARY AND CONCLUSIONS

Learning has been studied in the laboratory using procedures such as classical and instrumental conditioning. In classical conditioning, pairings of a previously neutral CS followed by a US result in the emergence of conditioned responding during the CS. In instrumental conditioning, a particular target behavior such as pressing a lever is reinforced through the presentation of an appetitive event such as food or punished through the presentation of an aversive event such as shock. Over trials, the target behavior will increase (with food delivery) or decrease (with shock delivery) in probability of occurrence. These changes in behavior can be explained by presuming that a link or association occurs between the events that the experimenter arranges. Memory may be closely related to learning; it is operationally defined as a delayed effect of an experience on behavior. Working memory is studied with a delayed-response paradigm and is usually time-limited, capacity-limited, and susceptible to interference. Reference memory is the source of storage of learned information and has no clear capacity or duration limits, but interference can occur in the form of consolidation and/or retrieval failures. Although the basic mechanisms of learning and memory vary somewhat across species, a general-process view can incorporate most instances of learning and memory across the animal kingdom.

## FURTHER READING

Spear et al. (1990) cover animal memory and learning. In addition to the topics dealt with in the present chapter, that by Spear et al. includes information on the **development** of learning and memory in young animals. The book edited by Mackintosh (1994) is an advanced text that will make considerable demands on the reader but which provides state-of-the-art expositions by specialist contributors on most of the topics covered in the present chapter. The contributors to this book are mainly experimental psychologists. For a different perspective, the book by Shettleworth (1998) offers an emphasis on the evolutionary approach to the understanding of learning and memory.

# 8
# animal cognition
## Nathan J. Emery and Nicola S. Clayton

## Introduction: What is Animal Cognition?

Animal cognition is the scientific study of the mental lives of animals and thus encompasses **learning**, memory, and thought. It also involves the ability to think about how another individual might think, and to project one's own experiences onto the intentions of another. Our perception of how an animal behaves may be based on their use of "intelligent" strategies that require complex cognitive processes such as rational decision-making, insight, and forethought. Until quite recently, however, animals were described as "mindless" automatons driven by instinct, genes, or subtle changes in the environment, not by internal mental representations. It is the aim of this chapter to describe some of these examples and to discuss whether the evidence at present supports the case for or against animal cognition.

## Problems and Pitfalls of Studying Animal Cognition

There are three pitfalls one must avoid when studying animal cognition: **anthropomorphism** (the tendency to view animals as people), **anthropocentrism** (the tendency to observe animals from a human perspective), and the use of anecdotes as "evidence." Consider the case of nest provisioning by hunting wasps (*Ammophila* spp.). These wasps perform a complex sequence of actions that lead them to provision their nests with prey items. An anthropomorphic account of the behavior might be couched in terms of the wasp's ability to anticipate the needs of its offspring. However, hunting wasps perform a fixed invariant routine that is insensitive to any consequences of their actions. Similarly, a bird might avoid eating a pleasant-tasting moth because it mimics an unpleasant tasting one but that does not mean that the moth was deliberately lying to the bird.

When attempting to study animal cognition it is also essential that we design experiments to test our hypotheses. Consider the famous case of a horse known as Clever Hans and his trainer, Mr von Osten, who purportedly taught the horse to count. Clever Hans would clop with its hoof the correct number of times when asked to solve a question in arithmetic such as "How much is $7 \times 7$?" Subsequent analysis by Oscar Pfungst showed that the horse could only perform correctly if he could see the experimenter, and if the experimenter knew the answer to the question. Pfungst (1965, quoted in Roberts 1998) reported that:

> As soon as the experimenter had given a problem to the horse, he involuntarily bent his head and trunk slightly forward and the horse would then put the right foot forward and begin to tap, without, however, returning it each time to its original position. As soon as the desired number of taps was given, the questioner would make a slight upward jerk of the head. Thereupon the horse would immediately swing his foot in a wide circle, bringing it back to its original position.

It is important to note that none of the experimenters were aware of these involuntary movements. Indeed, the horse was detecting very slight movements of the head that the experimenters were not aware they were making. Pfungst concluded that the horse could not count, but was in fact responding to involuntary movements of the experimenter's head. The work is usually cited in support of the need to design carefully controlled experiments in which a double-blind technique is used when testing the animal's responses so that the subject does not have the opportunity to pick up any signals that the experimenter emits, intentionally or unintentionally.

A good example of how an experimental approach can aid our understanding of cognition comes from a set of studies by Cristol et al. (1997) who studied the walnut-dropping behavior of crows (*Corvus corone*). Individual crows perch on lamp posts and drop walnuts on to the streets to crack them open. It has long been speculated that these crows deliberately drop the walnuts in front of cars, wait for the cars to drive over the nuts, and then fly down to collect them. Cristol devised a set of experiments to test whether crows intentionally drop the walnuts in front of cars, but found no evidence to support this. Thus, although the birds were selective in their choice of substrate on which to drop the nuts, preferring hard surfaces over soft grassy ones, and were also selective about the height at which they dropped the nuts, they were not selective about when they dropped the nuts. Sometimes birds dropped walnuts as cars were approaching, but they were equally likely to drop the nut in front of a car that was reversing or when no vehicle was approaching at all. So there is no evidence that crows deliberately use cars as nutcracking devices.

This example serves to illustrate that there is a fourth pitfall that we must avoid, namely unnecessarily complicated explanations of why an animal behaves in a certain way. Any careful scientist knows the importance of finding the most parsimonious (simple) explanation. Given how easy it is for us, as humans, to place a human perspective on a problem, it may be an especially important caution when studying the mental lives of animals. This point was first raised by Colwyn Lloyd Morgan in response to Romanes' exotic explanations of intriguing anecdotes and has become known as Lloyd

Morgan's canon (Morgan 1894, p. 53): "In no case may we interpret an action as the outcome of the exercise of a higher psychical faculty, if it can be interpreted as the outcome of the exercise of one which stands lower in the psychological scale." Of course the canon is not without its own problems. What exactly is a "higher psychical faculty"? And the notion of a psychological scale is also outdated. Nonetheless, we should heed the main message, namely that one should test the simplest hypothesis first, and only if it is found wanting should we move on to more complex ones that are less easy to disprove.

Finally, it is also important to test the hypothesis in question, and not just assume the simplest explanation is necessarily the best one. In other words, one needs to use an experimental method so that one can make predictions and evaluate these experimentally. Consider a simple associative learning experiment in which a bell repeatedly signals the presentation of food to a hungry dog, as in Pavlov's original experiment (see Chapter 7). Initially the dog will not salivate when hearing the bell. However, after several presentations of the bell and food the dog begins to salivate whenever it hears the sound of the bell. Perhaps the sound of the bell arouses a memory of food, thus triggering the salivation response, but an alternative explanation is that training results in the dog reflexively salivating when it hears the bell, without any knowledge of the food that will be presented shortly thereafter. Although the second explanation is simpler because it does not assert that animals possess memory processes, we now know from subsequent **conditioning** experiments that the first explanation is the correct one (see Chapter 7).

With these problems and pitfalls in mind, we will now discuss some specific abilities of animals that are thought to depend critically on cognitive mechanisms.

## Spatial Representations

The ability to learn and remember spatial **information** about places in the environment, and the objects that occupy them, is essential for survival in many animals because resources such as food, nests, and mates are often separated from refuge spots. The animal must be able to find these resources and then return home to safety. In order to do this, the animal must form a representation of the location of the goal, and how to reach it. Some organisms create such a representation in the external world using a chemical trail, e.g., the Mediterranean high-shore limpet (*Patella rustica*) foraging for food over the rockface at high tide, and male silkworm moths (*Bombyx mori*) following a scent trail to find a mate. However, many animals acquire an internal representation of the goal's location through spatial learning.

### Spatial learning using landmarks

The classic example comes from a study on digger wasps (*Philanthus triangulum*) by Niko Tinbergen. Each female "learns, with astonishing rapidity and precision, the locality of each new nest it builds" (Tinbergen 1951, p. 147). The female lays her eggs in a hole she has dug in the ground, and then flies off in search of a suitable prey item, which she buries with the eggs to provision the young when they hatch. Before flying off to capture the prey item, she makes a series of loops. How does the wasp identify the location of her nest, and find her way back to it, given that the prey is often found tens of meters away from the nest hole? While the wasp was in her hole, Tinbergen placed a circle of 20 pinecones around the entrance. After the wasp had departed, he moved the circle about 30 cm away, but kept its shape. When the wasp returned 90 min later, she flew to the center of the pinecone circle, even though the disturbed sand indicating the nest entrance hole was still visible. This result suggests that the female wasp used the pinecones as landmarks to identify her nest hole.

To discover which nearby landmarks are used, the wasps were tested with two types of landmark circles, both circles being placed equidistant from the nest. The wasps showed a clear preference for using landmark objects that were nearby, and ones that were large and three-dimensional. Large, three-dimensional objects are more easily visible from a distance, and the nearer the object is to the goal the more accurate the localization. Similar preferences have been found in other animals. For example, European jays (*Garrulus glandarius*) prefer to rely on large, vertical, nearby landmarks when searching for previously hidden food caches, and honeybees also rely on landmarks nearest to a goal.

## How are landmarks used to navigate?

Experimental work on bees (*Apis mellifera*) and gerbils (*Meriones unguiculatus*) has provided much insight into the mechanisms by which animals use landmarks to navigate (Cartwright & Collett 1983; Collett et al. 1986). Animals were trained to find food located at a given distance and compass bearing from a landmark. Once trained, both bees and gerbils would search in that location even when no food was present in the test arena, demonstrating that they had learned about the spatial location of the food in the absence of any cues emanating directly from the food. Note that in these studies the position of the landmark was moved from trial to trial and the animals were released from different points on the edge of the testing arena so that they could not use **dead reckoning** (i.e., they could not solve the task by moving a fixed distance and at a fixed orientation from the release point).

Collett and colleagues have suggested that when bees are trained with a single landmark they remember the size of its retinal image at the goal by making a **retinal snapshot** of the landmark. On subsequent visits to the goal they can compare their current view of the landmark with the snapshot in their memory. When there is a close correspondence between the size of the image of the landmark they see and the size in the retinal snapshot, the bee will begin searching for the goal. To test this hypothesis, they first tested bees with a single landmark that varied in size. When the landmark was halved in size, the bees searched twice as close; when the landmark size was doubled, the bees searched twice as far away.

They then trained the bees with three landmarks located at different compass bearings from the goal. Although the location of the array was moved from trial to trial, the orientation of the array always remained the same. Once the bees were trained to use this configuration, they were given two types of test: on some trials the distance from the goal was altered but the landmarks remained the same size; for other trials the distance from the goal was held constant but the size of the landmarks was altered. Neither manipulation had any effect on where the bees searched. Irrespective of the size of the landmarks, the bees continued to search in a location that was defined simply by its compass bearing from three landmarks (Fig. 8.1a). So when multiple landmarks are used, what seems to be important is their compass bearing from the goal, not their

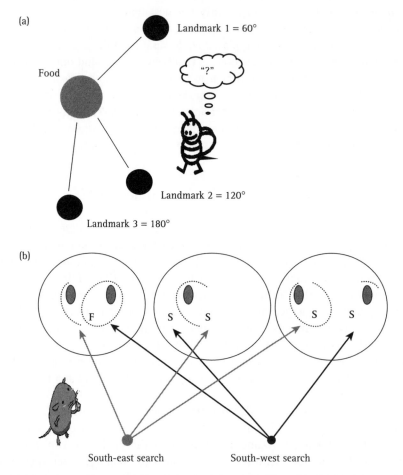

**Fig. 8.1** (a) Landmark learning experiment in honeybees by Cartwright and Collett (1983). Three landmarks are located around a food source at different geometric positions in relation to the landmark: landmark 1 is 60° from the food, landmark 2 is 120° from the food and landmark 3 is 180° from the food. The bee is required to locate the hidden food by computing its position relative to the spatial configuration of the landmarks. (b) Representation of landmark learning experiment in gerbils by Collett et al. (1986). Two landmarks (gray ellipses) are located next to a food source (F) either north-east or north-west from the food. If one of the landmarks is removed, the gerbils should search (S) either south-west or south-east of the landmark. If both landmarks remain but the distance between them is increased, the gerbils should search south-west by the left landmark and south-east by the right landmark.

size. Note that when the landmark array was rotated so that the angle between the top landmark and north was no longer 60°, the animals failed the task. This result suggests that the bees were unable to use information about the relative position of the landmarks to identify the location of the food.

Parallel studies were conducted to establish whether gerbils use landmarks in the same way as bees. When gerbils were tested with a single landmark, changing its size had no effect on where the animals searched. Unlike bees, gerbils appear to know how far they have to travel when they set their course on the basis of a landmark. In contrast to the very simple method the bees used when presented with three landmarks, gerbils can use information about the relative position of a number of landmarks (Fig. 8.1b).

## Multiple bearings hypothesis

Attending to multiple landmarks may increase the precision of searching at the target location, particularly when the goal and landmark are far apart. Kamil and Cheng (2001) proposed the **multiple-bearing hypothesis**, namely that food-caching birds such as Clark's nutcrackers (*Nucifraga columbiana*) may use multiple landmarks to work out their position and thus help them to relocate their caches of hidden food. The birds could do this by taking compass bearings to individual landmarks or by using the relative geometric positions of the landmarks. Kamil and Cheng ran a computer-simulated model and found that as the distance between the goal (in this case a cache site) and the landmark increases, the virtual birds estimate distance more inaccurately than direction. However, the accuracy of finding the goal increases with the number of landmarks used. Elegant though this theory may be, clearly the next step is to conduct experimental studies to test various predictions of the model. An important first step will be to determine whether these birds rely on multiple compass bearings or on the geometric relationships between landmarks.

## Food caching and spatial memory

The ability to encode, and later recall, information about the position of numerous landmarks might pose a considerable load on memory, as might the ability to remember the spatial location of thousands of cache sites over periods of up to 9 months. An individual nutcracker may cache as many as 33,000 seeds in 6000 different places, and a typical nutcracker must recover at least 2500 pine seeds in order to survive the winter. Indeed, laboratory studies have shown that Clark's nutcrackers do have accurate, long-lasting, spatial memories.

However, there are good reasons to believe that at least some food-caching birds would need to encode more complex representations of the caching event. It is known, for example, that a number of food-caching species do not return to sites from which they have retrieved all the food, which suggests that they can remember whether they have emptied a cache site as well as where they cached the food. Some of these species, including western scrub jays (*Aphelocoma californica*), cache insects and other perishable items as well as seeds. It may be useful, therefore, for them to encode and recall information about what has been cached when, as well as where. Indeed, Clayton and Dickinson (1998) have shown that scrub jays can remember when and where they cached perishable and nonperishable food on the basis of a single caching episode. These results suggest that the jays remember specific past experiences about what happened where and when, an ability that in humans is known as **episodic recall**.

## Representations of Number

The ability to understand numerical concepts, such as the number of a group of objects or that two groups have the same or different numbers of items, would seem important for many animals. For example, a foraging animal may need to keep track of the number of items it has recovered and how many still remain, so that it does not expend energy revisiting sites already depleted. Foraging parties may need to estimate quantity in order to focus the most appropriate number of group members to different-sized foraging **patches**. Lions (*Panthera leo*) may form representations of the number of lions in a rival pride by their roars, and use this information to determine whether they should approach or retreat. These examples may not necessarily require human-like concepts of number, but in this section we will describe the aspects of number that some animals may understand.

When evaluating the relationships between different groups of objects, it may be important to determine which is the largest or smallest. Two food patches, for example, may provide different amounts of food, one that could sustain an entire group foraging, the second only a couple of individuals. If these patches are costly to reach and a **decision** has to be made about which one to forage in, an understanding that they differ in size will be of primary importance. These discriminations are called **relative number judgments** (more or less than). In the 1950s, Otto Koehler presented a number of different bird species with two containers with a different number of grains attached to the lids. Subjects were rewarded if they chose either the container with the larger or smaller number of grains. All species performed this discrimination, even when the difference between the numbers was small (i.e., the birds were almost as proficient at discriminating four vs. five as three vs. eight). However, the birds may have been attending to the quantity of grain or area of coverage, rather than the number of grains per se. This argument has been disputed by a recent experiment where color, pattern, grouping, and area were controlled, and pigeons could discriminate successfully between slides with six to seven dots ("many") and those with one to two dots ("few") and could transfer to three, four, or five dots (Emmerton 1998).

These judgments do not necessarily require that an animal has a concept of a specific number independent of the actual **stimuli** that it perceives or is trained on (e.g., the number 7, which can be used to describe seven cars, seven apples, seven infants, etc.). Understanding this is called **absolute number judgment**. A raccoon (*Procyon lotor*) named Rocky was tested for his ability to understand absolute number, using clear plastic cubes containing different numbers of objects (one to five). The cube containing three objects

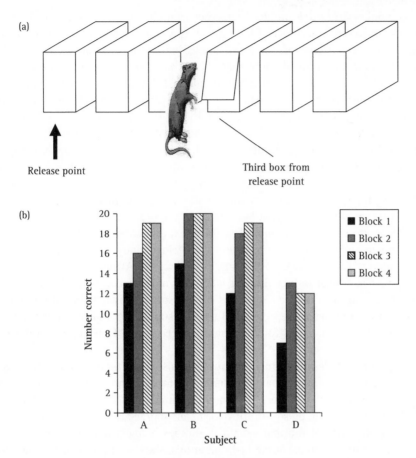

**Fig. 8.2** Counting experiment by Davis and Bradford (1986). (a) The rat is placed into an arena containing six boxes. All of the boxes contain food, but only one of the doors to the boxes can be opened. The rat is released randomly into the arena by one of the boxes and has to count a specific number to locate the open box. For example, if a rat that has been trained to count "three" is released by the first box, it must move along to the fourth box in the series to locate the food. (b) Correct number of trials per block for subjects A–D trained on the number "three." Each block is 20 trials and at least three subjects achieved a high success rate by the third block.

was rewarded, and Rocky learned to discriminate this cube from the other cubes containing different numbers of objects.

Rats (*Rattus* sp.) have also been tested for their understanding that numbers differ using a paradigm based on locating food. Davis and Bradford (1986) trained rats to choose the third of six tunnels, all containing food, but only the door to the third tunnel was open (Fig. 8.2a). All potential positional cues were removed by changing the location of the open tunnel (although it was always the third tunnel from where the rat was released). After initial training, the rats went directly to the third tunnel (Fig. 8.2b). This representation of number has been termed "**ordinality**."

Rhesus monkeys (*Macaca mulatta*) have been taught to touch groups of objects presented on a touch screen in order of their numerosity, for example two oranges, then three cars, then four trees. However, the most impressive feat of ordinality has been demonstrated in the language-trained chimpanzee (*Pan troglodytes*), Ai. She was taught by Biro and Matsuzawa (1999) to respond to the numbers 1–5 (out of a possible range of 0–9) randomly presented on a touch-sensitive screen. Ai learned to touch the lowest numeral first and then the rest in ascending order until the last. Matsuzawa also found that Ai had an incredible memory for the location of series of numbers presented on the screen. All 10 numerals (0–9) were presented at random locations on the screen. Once Ai had touched the lowest numeral, each of the others was covered by a white square occluding the numeral. Ai then had to use her memory to touch the sequence of numbers even though they were no longer present on screen. She learned to do this very quickly.

In humans, we commonly use a "symbol" or "tag" for a number, such as the arabic numeral "5" representing the number five. If an experimenter points toward a fruit bowl with five apples in it and the subject is asked "How many apples?" she can respond with the answer "five." This is called **tagging**. Alex, the African gray parrot (*Psittacus erithacus*) that has been taught English labels for objects, colors, and arabic numerals by Pepperberg, can also answer questions of this sort and is accurate 80% of the time (see later section and Pepperberg 1999). If the types and colors of the objects are mixed, such as six purple cubes and four red balls, when asked "How many purple cubes?" Alex would again answer "six."

Alex's abilities suggest not only tagging but also **cardinality**, where the last item in a sequence is given a tag that represents the total number of items. For example, in the sequence "one, two, three," the cardinal number is three, as the total number of objects is three. Both these abilities form an appreciation of counting. This may represent the endpoint of the mathematical abilities of most animals, whereas humans perform many more complex numerical operations, such as trigonometry, calculus, and algebra. However, some animals may possess a rudimentary form of arithmetic (summation and subtraction that forms the basis of all human mathematics).

Not surprisingly, studies on arithmetic have only been performed on nonhuman primates. Semi-free-ranging rhesus monkeys were presented with addition problems, typically hiding an eggplant behind a screen, removing the screen, and recording the monkey's looking time. The monkeys looked longer if two eggplants were revealed compared with the expected one eggplant. An example that may be less subject to alternative explanations was demonstrated by Boysen and Berntson (1989) with their language-trained chimp, Sheba. Sheba was trained to select cards with arabic numerals that corresponded to the number of items presented in a tray. She was then placed in a room in which oranges were located in three places, each containing a different amount of oranges and she had to visit each location and pick an arabic numeral that corresponded to the total number of oranges (from the three locations). Not all locations contained oranges, and the total was never greater than four. Therefore the possible number of potential correct combinations may have been learned. Also, three oranges are a larger quantity than one orange, so the problem may have been solved using quantity. Most interestingly, when the oranges were substituted with cards with arabic numerals printed on them, Sheba performed as proficiently as she did with the oranges.

Probably of most importance to nonhuman animals is an understanding that objects differ in quantity, e.g., food patch A is larger than food patch B. The ability to discriminate quantity works in the same manner as relative number judgments described earlier. For example, squirrel monkeys (*Saimiri sciureus*) were trained successfully to respond to one food well if two sets of stimuli had the same volume and a second food well if the volumes were different.

# Reasoning

## Insight

**Insight** is the mechanism by which a novel problem encountered for the first time is solved immediately without recourse to trial-and-error learning. The classic studies on animal insight were performed with chimpanzees by the German psychologist Wolfgang Köhler on the island of Tenerife during the First World War (Kohler 1925). The chimpanzees were presented with different food acquisition problems, and a number of objects that could be used to solve those problems. A famous example is a banana hanging out of reach on a string and a collection of boxes located underneath. A chimpanzee eventually hit upon the idea of stacking the boxes one on top of the other, climbing up and hitting the banana with a stick, thereby knocking the banana from its string and allowing it to fall to the ground to be retrieved, thus demonstrating insight. For this to be evidence of insight, however, we would need to show that the animals could not have solved the task by conventional **instrumental conditioning** (trial-and-error learning; see Chapter 7). The fact that the chimps did not solve the task immediately, but required extensive experience with sticks and boxes, suggests that it arose as a consequence of many trial-and-error responses.

A more controlled experiment was performed by Heinrich (1996), with a group of hand-reared ravens (*Corvus corax*). Heinrich presented his ravens with a novel opportunity to gain food, by attaching pieces of meat to string suspended from a branch. To obtain the meat, a raven would have to pull the string up with its feet, and trap each piece of pulled-up string at least five times before it could grab the meat in its bill. At first, the ravens attempted to grab the food from underneath or pecked at the string on the branch. Three birds pulled up the string and grabbed the meat at their first attempt. The ravens did not attempt to fly off with the food when chased away (i.e., they understood that the meat was attached to the string). When presented with two strings, one attached to the meat and a second attached to a similar-sized rock, the ravens tended to pull on the string attached to the meat (or immediately moved onto the correct string if they attempted to pull up the string with the rock attached). When the birds were presented with a novel string (dark-green shoelaces rather than twine), the birds almost exclusively pulled on the shoelaces attached to the food. This suggests that the birds did not just form an association between a particular string and food, but had **generalized** to all string-like substrates connected to food. This is perhaps a more convincing example of insight than Kohler's chimpanzees as the ravens were hand-reared and therefore Heinrich could be certain that the birds were experiencing the problems and materials for the first time.

# Making and using tools

The propensity to manufacture, transport, and use tools was previously thought to be exclusive to humans, but in the 1960s Jane Goodall reported the use of tools by chimpanzees at Gombe, Tanzania. Chimpanzees strip the leaves off tree stems and poke them into termite mounds, thereby extracting the termites. The last 30 years have provided numerous examples of tool use in primates in the wild and the laboratory, with different populations of chimpanzees using different tools for different uses, e.g., a wooden anvil and stone hammer to crack open palm nuts, or chewing leaves into a sponge so that it can be used to collect liquids. It has been claimed by some that these variations in tool use are cultural. However, neither the occurrence of **social learning** nor the mechanisms underlying it can be inferred from observation alone. With field studies one never knows precisely what previous experiences the individuals have had, and whether they have learned by trial and error. The common assumption is that if a particular behavior is common in one population of a particular species and not in another, then that behavior must have depended upon social learning. This is not necessarily the case.

Tool use has also been demonstrated in monkeys and apes to some degree in the laboratory. Visalberghi and her colleagues presented capuchin monkeys (*Cebus paella*) with a problem that required knowledge of the relationship between objects and tools. The monkeys were given a "trap-tube" problem in which a clear tube contained a hole and a well in the middle (Visalberghi & Limongelli 1994). A piece of food was placed next to the well and the monkey was provided with a stick of the correct length to push the food out of the tube. The monkey should have pushed from the side furthest away from the food to avoid pushing it into the well (Fig. 8.3a). In fact, only one of four capuchins succeeded in the majority of trials. When the trap was inverted (so that it was no longer a barrier to gaining the food), the monkey that was originally successful used the same technique as previously (Fig. 8.3b). This suggests that this particular monkey was using the rule "always push from the side furthest from the food" rather than possessing a conceptualization of how the problem should be solved. Finally, the monkeys were provided with a series of problems associated with the functionality of the sticks: sticks were either tied together or smaller sticks were pushed through them, or the monkeys were presented with a series of smaller sticks (Fig. 8.3c). The capuchins readily learned to solve these additional problems. When the "trap-tube" experiment was repeated with chimpanzees, only two of five performed correctly, thereby suggesting that there are few appreciable differences between capuchins and chimpanzees in their understanding of tool use in this task.

Tool use in animals is not restricted to primates. For example, Asian elephants (*Elephas maximus*) and African elephants (*Loxodonta africana*) manufacture tools to swat away flies, and the Galapagos woodpecker finch (*Camarhynchus pallidus*) uses sticks to probe for insects in ordinarily inaccessible holes in trees. Perhaps the most spectacular use and manufacture of tools is demonstrated by the New Caledonian crow (*Corvus moneduloides*).

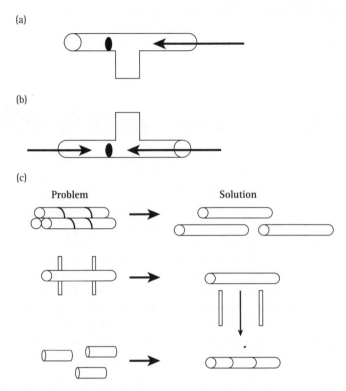

**Fig. 8.3** (a) "Trap-tube" problem used in capuchin monkeys (Visalberghi & Limongelli 1994), chimpanzees, and more recently New Caledonian crows. The plastic tube is transparent so that the food (black ellipse) can be seen by the subject, and an enclosed trap is located in the center of the tube. To successfully remove the food, the subject must push a stick in the direction of the arrow, i.e., over the trap. (b) In the control condition, the trap is inverted so that it is no longer functional, i.e., it no longer makes a difference from which side the stick is pushed. The subjects are said to not understand the function of the trap if they persistently push the stick from the previously successful side. (c). Additional problems based on changing the physical properties of the sticks: a bundle of sticks tied together (problem) that need to be separated (solution); a stick with small sticks pushed through the center (problem) that need to be removed (solution); and three small sticks too small to be functional (problem) that need to be stuck together (solution).

Hunt (1996) observed four crows manufacture two types of tools and 68 crows carry or use tools in three forests in New Caledonia in order to catch insects in trees or under detritus leaves. Hunt categorized the tools into two main types: hooked-twig and stepped-cut tools. The hooked-twig tools were made from living secondary twigs that were stripped of their leaves and bark, with a hook at their wider end. The stepped-cut tools, in contrast, were fashioned from *Pandanus* leaves by tapering the ends into points. Different techniques were employed in using the tools depending on the location of the prey. If the prey was located under detritus, the tool was used with rapid back-and-forth movements, whereas if the prey was located at the base of holes and leaves, slow deliberate movements were used. New Caledonian crows studied by Kacelnik and colleagues were presented with a tube containing food and a "toolbox" containing twigs of differing lengths; the crows consistently chose the appropriate length of twig to push the food out the other end of the tube. A single crow also fashioned a straight piece of wire into a hook so that it could pull up a small bucket containing food (Weir et al. 2002). This may demonstrate a case of insight as the crows had previous experience of wire that was bent into hooks but not of straight pieces of wire.

## Social Representations

So far we have discussed the ability of animals to form mental representations of objects; how they can be located, how many there are, and what they can be used for. However, can animals form mental representations of other individuals, and mental representations of other individuals' mental representations (**metarepresentation** or "**theory of mind**")?

**Social intelligence** is the ability to deceive, manipulate, and predict the intentions of others in the social group and has been suggested to be one of the primary causes of the dramatic expansion of the brain during primate evolution. The "social intelligence" hypothesis developed by Humphrey (1976) states that all long-lived, large-brained social animals should possess the cognitive abilities required to perform these complex social functions. Dunbar (1992) has gone on to suggest that the evolution of such cognitive abilities in primates was constrained by a significant increase in the relative size of the neocortex, and this in turn provided the impetus for larger social groups.

### Social perception (species and individual recognition)

Before social animals can begin to understand the behavior and intentions of other group members (social cognition), they must form representations of other individuals as (i) belonging to the same species (conspecifics vs. heterospecifics; same–different judgment) and (ii) being an individual, with individual physical, vocal, and behavioral characteristics (**social perception**). This information is essential for the formation of more complex social representations based on an individual's previous and current relationships, such as understanding that each individual has a particular kin and social network, essential in the formation of coalitions and alliances. Understanding others as individuals at the perceptual level is also important for understanding others at the psychological level (mental state attribution or theory of mind).

A number of investigators have examined animals' preferences for different species' faces and their ability to discriminate between them. For example, rhesus monkeys (*Macaca mulatta*) can discriminate between images that include rhesus monkeys and images that contain other animals. Japanese macaques (*Macaca fuscata*) can discriminate between closely related species of macaques. The ability to distinguish members of your own species from other closely related species is an essential first step in the performance of successful social interactions.

Although recognizing familiar individuals by their visual features, such as faces, would appear to be an essential component in forming alliances and coalitions and maintaining friendships in primates, laboratory studies of individual recognition in the visual domain are few. Macaques rapidly habituate to the repeated presentation of one individual (measured with bar-presses or touches to a screen), but when the identity of the stimulus monkey is changed, the subjects dishabituate quickly (i.e., they increase their rate of responding; see also Chapter 7). Thus the animals demonstrate an understanding that the stimulus monkey's identity has changed. Dasser (1988) trained long-tailed macaques (*Macaca fascicularis*) to discriminate between slides of different individual monkeys all with a frontal orientation (i.e., of the face). During testing, the monkeys rapidly learned to discriminate slides of novel views of the familiar monkeys (i.e., profiles) from those of unfamiliar monkeys.

Animals that rely on other forms of communication, such as olfaction, have been tested on these types of problem. For example, female mice (*Mus musculus*) encode the olfactory identity of a particular male with whom they have mated via specific chemicals in the male's urine. If an intruder male takes over the nest and/or kills the resident male, the pregnant female will abort her fetus before full term. This has been termed the **Bruce effect**, after Hilda Bruce who discovered the phenomenon. One possible **function** for the formation of this olfactory memory (individual recognition) may be to alert the female to the presence of an intruder male who will kill the offspring of her previous mate. Therefore, terminating the pregnancy before full term will prevent the female from investing in an infant that will not survive and will allow the new male to mate as rapidly as possible with the female.

## Understanding social relationships

Once an individual has been recognized, an animal needs to ascertain which relationships it possesses, who these relationships are with, and their current status. To do this, social animals must be able to match related individuals. The ability of primates to understand the relationships between individuals has been observed in the wild, quantified by the **frequency** of grooming and the formation of alliances within certain pairs of individuals (dyads). Kummer and colleagues, for example, found that male hamadryas baboons (*Papio cynocephalus hamadryas*) controlling a harem of females could associate certain females with their male mate. The males observed the interactions between a male and an unknown female, and 15-min observation was sufficient for the observing male to ignore the female in subsequent tests when placed in an arena with the observed pair. When both males observed an unfamiliar female on her own, they both courted her in subsequent tests and occasionally fought each other over possession (Bachmann & Kummer 1980).

Dasser (1988) also examined long-tailed macaques' understanding of relationships between others (third-party relationships) by training them on sets of slides that consisted of known mother and offspring pairs. Dasser found that the monkeys could transfer their knowledge of the learned pairs to match unknown mother and offspring pairs. Similarly, Parr and de Waal (1999) found that chimpanzees could match the facial images of unknown mother and son dyads, but not mother and daughter dyads, compared with unrelated control pairs. They suggest that this is because male chimpanzees remain within the group and their dominance status is largely related to their mother's status.

## Understanding another individual's visual perspective

Gaze is an important component of social interaction that provides information about an individual's knowledge of the external environment and their emotional state. Social gaze is especially important for nonhuman primates and other social animals with a particular reliance on visual communication. Gaze cues may also function in complex forms of social cognition, such as visual perspective-taking, deception, empathy, and theory of mind.

Povinelli and Eddy (1996a) examined the ability of a group of chimpanzees to follow human gaze cues. The chimpanzees were trained to produce a natural begging gesture toward an experimenter in order to receive food at the end of a trial. Once the chimpanzees were trained to do this, the experimenters produced specific attention cues for the subjects: (i) eyes and head, where experimenters shifted their head and eye gaze to behind and to the left or right of the subject; (ii) eyes only, where experimenters only shifted the direction of their eyes; and (iii) no change in attention. In the eyes and head condition, 50% of trials elicited a gaze-following response to the correct side; in the eyes-only condition, 30% of trials elicited a correct response, each significantly greater than in the control condition.

Rhesus macaques can follow the gaze cues of conspecifics, looking more toward the direction in space and the specific object a conspecific was looking at than elsewhere. Domestic dogs (*Canis familiaris*) also use conspecific cues to locate food. Hare and Tomasello (1999) studied the responses of dogs to either local enhancement cues (i.e., proximity to food as a cue) or gaze, body orientation, and pointing cues simultaneously, provided by humans or conspecifics. The dogs used both human and dog local enhancement cues and human and dog gaze and pointing cues. The ability of dogs to use conspecific cues may have evolved as their wild ancestors were traditionally pack hunters. Hunting as part of a group requires a degree of coordination, which may rely on gaze or body orientation monitoring. Domestic dogs, but not hand-raised wolves (*Canis lupus*), also follow human cues; therefore domestication may have provided dogs with the additional ability to use human attention cues.

## Theory of mind

The term "theory of mind" first appeared in a paper by Premack and Woodruff (1978). They examined whether a language-trained chimpanzee, Sarah, could appreciate the correct solution to a problem presented to a human demonstrator. Sarah was presented with short video sequences containing images of an actor locked in a cage, shivering next to an unlighted heater, unable to clean a dirty floor, or unable to listen to music on a stereo that was unplugged. After each sequence, Sarah was presented with a number of alternative answers to the problems as photographs, for example a key, a lighted paper wick, a connected hose, and a cord that was plugged into a socket; she had to match the correct image with the appropriate video. Sarah could match all the photographs to the appropriate video, and it was argued that she therefore understood the actor's intentions ("they wanted to get out of the cage," "they intended to listen to music," etc.). Needless to say, this interpretation has been criticized. Perhaps Sarah had merely associated the objects (e.g., lock and key) from her previous life in captivity. However, the fact that some of the solutions were novel suggests that this explanation cannot account for all the abilities displayed by this particular chimpanzee.

For almost 30 years, positive evidence of theory of mind in nonhuman animals has remained elusive. Premack has proposed three levels of understanding in theory of mind: perceptual (seeing, attention), motivational (desire, goal, intention), and informational (belief, knowledge). These may help in designing experiments to test for theory of mind in animals. We describe some of these experiments here.

## Visual perspective-taking

Distinguishing another individual's visual perspective from one's own is thought to be an important step in interpreting intentions and thoughts about the world. Long-tailed macaques, for example, do not appear to appreciate a human's visual perspective, as they do not discriminate between a hidden bottle containing juice and a bottle in full view of a threatening human experimenter.

Povinelli and Eddy (1996b) also tested the ability of chimpanzees to choose between an experimenter who could see them and another who could not. The chimpanzees were presented with a choice of two experimenters: one whose eyes were open or free from occlusion, and a second whose eyes were covered with different barriers, such as blindfolds, buckets, or tinted goggles. The animals were rewarded for begging toward the experimenter that could see them. The chimpanzees did not differentiate between the two experimenters. The only discrimination they made successfully was between an experimenter facing toward them compared with another whose back was turned. Povinelli and Eddy suggested that chimpanzees use a sophisticated level of gaze following but that they do not possess an understanding of another individual's mental states from gaze cues.

A more realistic test for visual perspective-taking in chimpanzees based on competition rather than cooperation for food has recently been designed by Hare et al. (2001). A subordinate and a dominant chimpanzee were allowed access to an arena where food had been hidden previously. The subordinate chimp could see both pieces of food, whereas the dominant chimp could only see one of them. Would the subordinate chimp make a decision on which food to approach based on the knowledge state of the dominant animal (i.e., go for the food the dominant did not know about)? The subordinate chimp did exactly this. Hare and colleagues suggested that they had found a positive result because the paradigm was competitive rather than cooperative, a more natural situation for chimpanzees, whereas Povinelli's experiments required the chimps to make a begging response for which they had to be trained. The use of a conspecific as a protagonist rather than a human experimenter could also be an important reason for the positive results.

## Knowledge attribution

Povinelli et al. (1990) have also examined the ability of chimpanzees to attribute different knowledge states to human experimenters. They asked the question: "Do chimpanzees understand that seeing leads to knowing?" A chimp was present while one of four containers was baited with food, although it could not see which container was

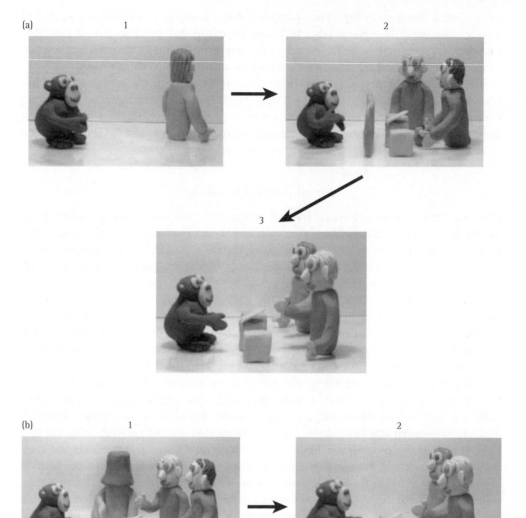

**Fig. 8.4** The "Guesser–Knower" paradigm of Povinelli et al. (1990). (a) A chimpanzee first observes a human experimenter (the Guesser) leave the experimental room (1); then a second human experimenter baits one of three boxes with food behind a screen so that the chimpanzee cannot observe which box is baited. A third human experimenter (the Knower) observes which box is baited (2). The Guesser then returns and both the Knower and the Guesser point to one of the boxes, the Knower to the correct box, the Guesser to one of the other wrong boxes (3). The chimpanzee then has to point to one of the boxes. (b) In a transfer phase, used to eliminate the possibility that the chimpanzee was using presence or absence as a cue, the Guesser remained in the room during baiting but was prevented from observing by a bucket or a bag placed over the head.

baited (Fig. 8.4a, panel 2). One experimenter baited the container, a second left the room before baiting (the Guesser; Fig. 8.4a, panel 1), and a third observed the baiting (the Knower; Fig. 8.4a, panel 2). Once the container had been baited, the Guesser reentered the room and both the Knower and Guesser pointed to a container (Fig. 8.4a, panel 3). The chimp had to point to the container that the Knower pointed to in order to get the food reward. The chimps pointed toward the Knower in the majority of the trials; however, they only achieved this greater than 70% accuracy after 200–300 trials, suggesting that they had learned to associate the Knower with the location of the food. In an additional experiment, the Guesser did not leave the room as previously but was prevented from observing by a bucket or a bag placed over the head (Fig. 8.4b, panel 1). In this case, the chimps pointed significantly more toward the Knower (Fig. 8.4b, panel 2). However, a reanalysis of the data found that the chimps only consistently did this after five trials, whereas if they had understood the nature of the experiment they should have transferred their knowledge from the previous experiment and responded correctly at the first trial. Therefore, it is unclear whether this study enables us to form any firm conclusions about chimpanzees' understanding of others' mental states that are independent from associative learning.

### Experience projection

A final component of theory of mind, **experience projection**, has only been tested once in animals, and in a bird not a great ape. Experience projection is the ability to use your own experience to predict other individuals' intentions and understand their state of mind ("putting yourself in someone else's shoes"). Many corvids hide food for later consumption, and often steal other individual's caches. They also display a number of complex caching strategies in order to protect their caches from potential thieves. Emery and Clayton (2001) examined these strategies in western scrub jays, in particular what the jays did when recovering their caches depending on whether they had been watched during caching. When the birds had been observed by another bird during caching, they recovered and rehid their caches in new places unbeknown to the observer. In contrast, they did little recaching when they had previously cached in private and certainly did not discriminate where they recached, by recaching in both old and new sites.

Of particular relevance here to an understanding of mental attribution is the fact that birds only recached when they themselves had previous experience of pilfering another bird's caches. Birds without this experience recached very little, irrespective of whether they had cached in private. This result is exciting because it suggests that birds with pilfering experience might be projecting their own experience of being a thief onto the observing bird, and so act to counter what they would predict a thief would do in relation to their hidden food.

## Tactical deception

The intentional manipulation of others' beliefs that leads them to believe something contrary to the truth, known as **tactical deception**, has been proposed as another important component of understanding others' mental states. Unfortunately most of the data is based on anecdotes, derived from field studies on monkeys and apes. It is extremely difficult to design and implement well-controlled experiments on tactical deception. Byrne and Whiten accumulated anecdotes sent to them by field primatologists, and sorted them into certain categories that represented different forms of tactical deception. One classic case of potential tactical deception involving baboons (*Papio anubis*) is as follows:

> Subadult male ME attacks one of the young juveniles who screams. Adult male HL and several other adults run over the hill into view, giving aggressive pan grunt calls; ME seeing them coming, stands on hindlegs and stares into the distance across the valley. HL and the other newcomers stop and look in this direction; they do not threaten or attack ME. (Whiten & Byrne 1988, p. 237)

Whiten and Byrne suggest that ME stares into the distance with the "intention" of forming a "false belief" into the "minds" of the other baboons that there is a predator located close to them. Of course, this actual scenario could have happened previously in which there *was* a predator present, or ME may actually have heard something in the bushes to divert his attention. Although Byrne stated that he could not see anything, he may not have been in a position to. While anecdotes are important for formulating testable hypotheses, direct evidence requires an experimental approach.

Menzel (1974) provided tantalizing evidence for tactical deception. He led one chimpanzee (Belle) to a hidden food source located in a naturalistic enclosure, out of view of the other members of the social group. Belle was then placed back in her group and all the animals were released into the enclosure. Belle immediately headed toward the hidden food, the group following her to the food source, which she revealed and allowed everyone to share. However, the dominant male chimpanzee (Rock) increasingly monopolized the food bonanza, not sharing with any group members. Over time Belle became less likely to move toward, or indicate, the location of the food if Rock was present. Rock countered this by moving her off a patch if she was down for too long, and examined the locations where she had been previously or had used her body orientation to determine where the food might be located. Finally, Belle led the group off in completely the wrong direction, and quickly returned to retrieve the food when the others' attention was elsewhere.

This study has been replicated in sooty mangabeys (*Cercocebus t. torquatus*) and more recently pigs (*Sus scrofa*). It appears that tactical deception may not be restricted to mammals, as Bugnyar and Kotrschal (2002) recently found that ravens would interrupt caching or change cache sites when competitors were in the vicinity.

## Social learning

Social learning is the ability to learn from other individuals in the social group. Although in many cases, trial-and-error learning is sufficient to learn about the world, when it comes to predators and certain food choices, it may be easier, safer, and quicker to profit directly from the experience of other individuals. For example, Norway rats (*Rattus norvegicus*) are largely influenced in their food choices by others. The foods that a rat mother eats during pregnancy have a massive effect on what foods the offspring chooses when it begins to eat solid food after weaning. Jeff Galef and colleagues have shown that flavor preferences are also transferred between individuals housed together. Individuals from a pair of rats were isolated, deprived of food for 24 h, and then given a novel food, either cinnamon or cocoa. When it was returned to its partner, the rat that had remained in the cage ate more of the novel food its partner had eaten than an alternative food (i.e., cinnamon if the partner had eaten cinnamon, or cocoa if the partner had eaten cocoa). Galef suggested that the rats could use information about what type of novel foods to eat by sensing the breath of conspecifics, in order to make choices without the possibility of subsequent illness (Galef 1996).

Social learning is not one process but is categorized into a number of cognitively distinct mechanisms (Fig. 8.5a–e). We describe the different types of social learning below.

1 **Local enhancement** is a related phenomenon. Individual A is located in a particular area. Individual B's attention is drawn to the same area, because of individual A's location in that area (Fig. 8.5a). For example, A is standing next to a tree with an abundant source of fruit (X). B becomes initially attracted to the tree (not observing the fruit) because A is located next to it.

2 **Stimulus enhancement** is where an individual (A) interacts with an object (X), and the attention of an observing animal (B) is drawn to the object because of the interaction (Fig. 8.5b).

3 **Observational conditioning** is a form of **Pavlovian conditioning** (see Chapter 7) in which the response of the demonstrator acts as an **unconditioned stimulus** that elicits a matching response on the part of the observer (Fig. 8.5c). Mineka and Cook (1988) provided an example of this in laboratory-raised rhesus monkeys. Monkeys are not naturally fearful of snakes, but can be conditioned to be fearful of real, fake, and toy snakes when in the presence of naturally fearful wild-born parents, directing fearful expressions toward the snakes. However, there is also a predisposition (see Chapter 6): thus fear is not so readily conditioned to biologically irrelevant objects such as flowers as to snakes and other long wiggly snake-like stimuli such as garden hoses.

4 **Goal emulation** refers to situations in which the observer attempts to reproduce the results (goal) of the demonstrator's action rather than precisely copying the form of his or her action (Fig. 8.5d). Tomasello and colleagues studied the responses of chimpanzees watching actors using a rake to collect food that was out of reach. The method demonstrated involved turning the rake over onto the straight-edged side and pulling in the food, rather than using the rake with the prongs downward and hoping that the food did not pass through the spaces between the prongs (Fig. 8.5d, panel 1). The chimpanzees did not copy the specific actions of the demonstrator (i.e., using the straight-edged side and pulling), but tended to achieve the goal randomly using the serrated edge of the rake (Nagell et al. 1993; Fig. 8.5d, panel 2).

5 **Imitation** literally involves the observer copying the actions of the demonstrator in order to achieve the desired goal (Fig. 8.5e). The "artificial fruit" study by Whiten

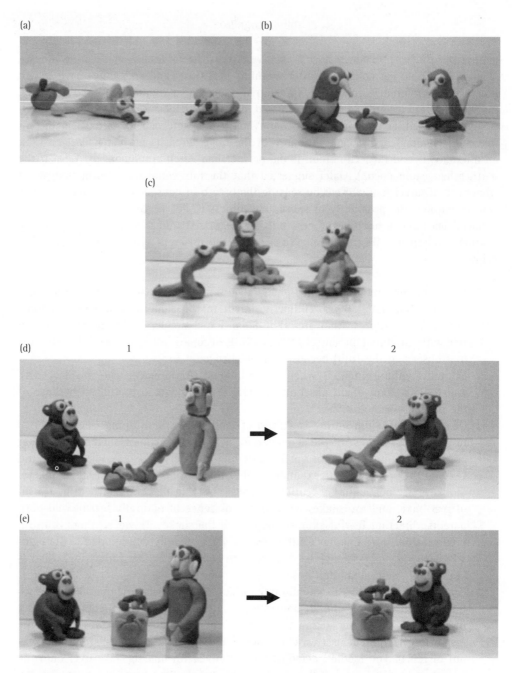

**Fig. 8.5** Different types of social learning. (a) Local enhancement: the observer is drawn to an area by the demonstrator and so becomes attracted to objects in the same location. (b) Stimulus enhancement: the observer is drawn to the object based on the interaction between the demonstrator and the object. (c) Observational conditioning: an observer is conditioned to an object because of the demonstrator's reactions to the object, e.g., conditioning of snake fear (Mineka & Cook 1988). (d) Goal emulation: a specific action is performed by a demonstrator, such as using a rake (prongs up) to pull in food (1), whereas the observer uses a different action to achieve the same goal, such as using a rake with the prongs down (2) (Nagell et al. 1993). (e) Imitation: a demonstrator performs a sequence of novel actions in a particular order to achieve a goal, e.g., poke, twist, and pull to open an artificial "fruit" (Whiten et al. 1996).

et al. (1996) illustrates the difference between true imitation and goal emulation. The "fruit" was a clear plastic box that could be opened by performing two actions in sequence, such as twisting the barrel while pulling it out (Fig. 8.5e, panel 1). Thus opening the "fruit" required not only goal emulation but also copying the exact actions required to open the fruit. Both children and chimpanzees were more likely to copy the human experimenter's method of extracting the fruit than perform the alternative action (Fig. 8.5e, panel 2). The tendency to imitate was greatest in 3- and 4-year-old children, and least in chimpanzees. However, the chimpanzees did direct their behavior toward the correct part of the box even when they did not use the same actions as the human experimenters. It does not seem surprising that observers learn rapidly that performing a particular action achieves a certain goal; however, precise copying or true imitation is not the only social learning mechanism that can be used. In the majority of cases there is no need to pay close attention to precisely how the demonstrator obtains the reward. So precise copying of actions might be more likely to be seen in the absence of a **reinforcer** (although a lack of reinforcement might result in a lack of motivation to imitate in the first place). Perhaps the best case of imitation of actions, uncontaminated by social reinforcement, comes from Bruce Moore's parrot, Okichoro, who lived alone in a room and was visited by the human experimenter several times a day. The human would perform various **stereotypic behaviors**, such as waving while saying "ciao" or poking out his tongue and saying "look at my tongue." Gradually the bird began to imitate both the actions and the words. Because each vocalization in effect labeled a specific movement, it was possible to separate imitation from nonimitative gestures. Eventually many cases of imitative behavior were recorded. Note that the behavior was observed over closed-circuit TV when the parrot was alone to avoid the Clever Hans effect, and Moore stopped data collection on any imitative pattern once it had occurred in the presence of the experimenter to ensure that the imitative action was novel. For gestures and vocalizations then, the best example of imitation in nonhuman animals comes from birds, in this case an African gray parrot.

What is clear is that the ability to determine the focus or object of another individual's attention is vitally important for social learning. Actions may be directed onto objects (e.g., tools, food, conspecifics, or parts of the body). The capacity to learn about objects by observing others' interactions with them requires that the observing individual's attention is drawn to the object in question. Nothing can be learned about an object if attention is directed elsewhere, such as another unrelated object.

## Mirror self-recognition

The ability to understand another's mental states may be dependent on an appreciation that they are different from one's own mental states. Mirror self-recognition emerges in human infants before the **development** of an understanding of others as intentional agents (2 years old). As yet, the only evidence that an animal can recognize its reflection in a mirror and therefore that it might have an appreciation of "self" versus others has been provided for chimpanzees, orangutans, and dolphins (*Tursiops truncates*). Individuals of these species, when initially presented with a mirror, behave as though the reflection in the mirror is a conspecific. They act either aggressively or affiliatively, depending on the species examined. This is also what normally occurs in those species that do not demonstrate self-recognition, such as macaques, elephants, and African gray parrots. However, these species are able to use mirrors to guide their actions.

In contrast, after some exposure to the mirror, chimpanzees, orangutans, and dolphins begin to use the mirror to investigate areas of their own body to which they normally do not have visual access, such as their backs or inside their mouths. It has been suggested that these animals develop an appreciation that the image in the mirror is themselves rather than another member of their own species. Nevertheless, a number of alternative explanations are possible, and the challenge is to devise further rigorous experimental tests.

Gallup (1970) devised the "mark test" to provide an objective method of examining whether nonhuman animals do indeed recognize themselves in mirrors. Chimpanzees were anesthetized and a nontoxic, nonperfumed red dye was applied to different areas of the chimpanzee's face, which could only be seen in a mirror. When the subjects had recovered from the anesthetic, they were observed for 30 min and were then placed in front of a mirror. Face-touching was recorded before and after the anesthesia. Gallup found that the chimpanzees touched the marks made on their faces more than touches to comparable areas before anesthesia.

Is this evidence of self-recognition? Many behavioral scientists, such as Heyes (1994), have criticized the mark test, suggesting that increased face-touching in front of the mirror may have been a consequence of recovering from the anesthetic. The fact that the chimpanzees did not show an increase in face-touching during the 30-min period before the mirror was presented to the subjects makes this explanation less likely. Perhaps the animals were simply intrigued by the novel paint marks and automatically touched the equivalent places on their own bodies in much the same way as any other sort of contagious behavior, such as laughing, scratching, or yawning. This issue has been examined in more detail by Povinelli et al. (1997) who recorded face-touching behavior toward two marks on the face (right eyebrow and top of left ear) and compared the number of touches to two compatible control locations without marks on the opposite side of the face (left eyebrow and top of the right ear). These researchers found that the majority of subjects touched the marks compared with the nonmarked control regions, suggesting that the effects were not due to random face-touching.

Perception in dolphins is less visually based than that in primates and this, plus the fact that dolphins do not have hands that could respond by touching marks placed on the skin, suggest that the mark test may not be appropriate for this species. However, Reiss and Marino (2001) examined the reactivity of two dolphins to marks placed on their bodies. The dolphins had extensive previous experience with reflective surfaces present on the walls of their aquarium, and they were marked, sham marked (using waterproof dye as a control for lack of anesthesia), or received no mark directly after hand-feeding (so the tactile sensation of marking was presented but without leaving a mark). The dolphins were marked on three areas of the body that were visually inaccessible without the use of a mirror. Their behavior in front of the mirror or when the mirror was absent was recorded 30 min before and after the marking procedure. Reiss and Marino found that the dolphins spent more time in front of the mirror when marked than when either sham marked or not marked, and that they investigated marks, by positioning the marked part of the body toward the mirror, more in the marked condition than in the sham-mark and no-mark conditions.

Although chimpanzees, orangutans, and dolphins produce self-directed behavior in relation to their reflection in the mirror, does this mean that these species understand that the reflection in the mirror is their own? Does passing the mark test present an appropriate indication of a "self" concept? The mark test is good for determining whether an individual can use a mirror to guide its inspection of inaccessible body parts. Passing the mark test only requires the possession of a simple proprioceptive sense to match the perception of the reflection with perception of self-touching. No concept of self is required, and so the importance of this ability for theory of mind seems negligible. Other nonverbal methods that are not dependent on the mark test will be required before this issue can be addressed further.

## Teaching Human Language to Animals

Why attempt to teach nonhuman animals human language? The capacity for language has been suggested to be the ability that separates *Homo sapiens* from the rest of the animal kingdom. What is it that prevents animals communicating using a verbal or symbolic language system that obeys the rules of grammar and syntax? Do they possess the means to utilize any of these core components of human language? Early studies attempted to teach chimpanzees to speak, raising them with human babies; however, nonhuman animals do not have an appropriate vocal tract to form the speech sounds used in human language (Fitch 2000).

Later studies utilized the fact that apes perform hand gestures in their natural communication, and therefore researchers concentrated on the animals' use of American Sign Language (ASL) that was acquired from observing human trainers who signed but never spoke. For example, Washoe, a chimpanzee, was taught over 100 signs by Allen and Beatrix Gardner and could combine these signs into new combinations, such as "water bird" to represent "swan." However, Herb Terrace and colleagues, using the same method of teaching ASL, found that another chimpanzee, Nim Chimpsky (named after the famous linguist Noam Chomsky), learned 125 signs and produced four sign combinations but had no understanding of syntactical structure, as the signs were often repeated and most used personal pronouns such as "me." Terrace later reanalyzed the videotapes recorded during signing sessions and found that Nim tended to sign exactly the same as the experimenter, and was therefore demonstrating imitation of signs rather than spontaneous formation of signs in response to questions. Terrace's scathing article based on this later reanalysis had the effect of halting research funding on many animal language projects based on signing (Terrace et al. 1979).

Other studies in chimpanzees examined the understanding of symbols as representations of objects. Premack taught the chimpanzee Sarah (described earlier) to associate plastic tokens of various colors and shapes with the objects they represented. Similarly, Rumbaugh taught the chimpanzee Lana that geometric designs on a keyboard represented different words, so-called "Yerkish" (named after Robert Yerkes, the pioneer of cognition research in primates in the early twentieth century). Most impressively, a bonobo named Kanzi learned a version of Yerkish after observing his foster mother being taught to use the lexigrams by Savage-Rumbaugh, and eventually learned to respond to human speech (equivalent to that of a 2-year-old human child; Savage-Rumbaugh & Lewin 1994).

Whether you agree or disagree that these studies have demonstrated human language abilities in apes, for the purpose of this chapter the important point is that similar abilities have been reported in great detail for an African gray parrot named Alex (see earlier). Parrots are excellent vocal mimics and can therefore communicate by mimicking human speech. In the language studies, Alex was provided with live interactive human trainers who supplied referential and contextual use of each word that was associated with each object it represented, and the rewards were either social (such as praise) or nonfood objects (such as toys) rather than food (Pepperberg 1999).

Pepperberg used the model/rival technique developed by Todt (1975), in which the parrot is trained in the presence of two humans: a model trainer who shows an object to the second human (model and rival). The trainer asks the model/rival questions about the object (e.g., "What's here?") and gives praise and the object as a reward. The trainer also displays disapproval if the answer is incorrect. Therefore, the parrot can learn which is the correct label for each object. Alex has demonstrated object identification by requesting specific objects, can categorize objects based on their color and shape, can form abstract concepts such as same/different or absent, and appears to have a concept of number of objects.

Human words and phrases in the form of gestures have also been taught to dolphins and sea lions. Herman et al. (1984) taught the dolphins Akeakamai and Phoenix over 50 signs that represented objects (surfboard, Frisbee, etc.), places (water, left, right, etc.), or actions (fetch, spit, tail-touch) that could be formed into grammatically correct sentences. The dolphins were then given a command (gesture sentence) by a trainer wearing goggles (supposedly to prevent inadvertent signals, although other cues such as head direction were not controlled). The dolphin then correctly performed the task in the sentence "Fetch + Frisbee + Right" by collecting the Frisbee and moving it to the right of the pool. The dolphins appeared to be focusing not only on the words but also on their order. Two California sea lions (*Zalophus californianus*), Rocky and Bucky, were also trained to comprehend 20 and 16 signs respectively by Schusterman and Krieger (1984) using a similar gestural language to that taught to the dolphins.

Studies of both Alex the parrot and the two California sea lions suggest that the potential for learning aspects of human language may occur in a variety of species, particularly those that have very different neural systems than present in apes and dolphins. Fitch (2000) has suggested that songbirds and sea lions are better than primates when studying the evolution of speech, because they are more proficient at vocal imitation than primates.

# SUMMARY AND CONCLUSIONS

In many of the cases, particularly those related to human-like abilities, such as theory of mind and language, the evidence is equivocal. Specifically, many of these abilities may be explained by relatively simple associative processes that underlie conditioning rather than by complex cognitive processes that underlie some aspects of physical and social intelligence. The relative absence of evidence for complex cognition in nonhuman animals may be due more to human limitations in developing appropriate tests than an absence of these processes altogether. For example, Macintosh has suggested that we need to design our experiments with the different perceptual worlds of the species under study in mind. Rats, for example, are nocturnal and have notoriously poor visual acuity when compared with many diurnal primates. Yet many of the spatial memory tasks on which rats are tested depend on visual processing of spatial information during daylight. Perhaps experiments on vision may not be as revealing about rat cognition as those based on olfaction.

We should not be surprised if we find positive evidence for complex mental attributes in animals. Charles Darwin was the first to suggest that mental characteristics are subject to natural selection in much the same way as morphological traits, and that human mental capabilities therefore share many features in common with those of other animals. The question is what, if any, evolutionary precursors of human cognition can be observed in animals and whether such precursors are more likely to be found in our close relatives, the great apes. The fact that a parrot and several species of corvid provide some of the most convincing evidence for complex cognition, from cardinality and tagging to tool use and aspects of theory of mind, suggests that the latter is not necessarily the case. Moreover, it should not be assumed that higher cognitive abilities have evolved only once. It is possible that elements of some of the abilities that were thought to be uniquely human, such as episodic memory and mental attribution, have evolved more than once because of the selective pressures imposed by the environments in which animals live, e.g., the corvids and parrots within the Aves, and the primates and possibly bats and dolphins within the Mammalia. This in turn raises the question of convergent evolution in cognitive processes, namely how analogous brain structures (such as the neocortex of mammals and hyperstriatum and Wulst of birds) achieve the same function.

In this chapter, we have presented a brief overview of cognitive abilities in a wide variety of animals from insects to fish, birds to mammals, stressing the importance of examining cognition in a greater number of species than the traditional rat, pigeon, rhesus monkey, or chimpanzee. We have described the different mechanisms that animals use to find their way around, such as path integration, retinal snapshots of the environment, and cognitive maps. We have discussed how some animals appear to understand numbers and human language, and how they may utilize this information to reason and solve novel problems. We have also argued that an animal's behavioral ecology may help predict which cognitive skills an animal possesses, such as superior spatial memory in food-caching animals or the ability to learn through observation in highly social species. Perhaps most exciting is the fact that some large-brained animals, such as corvids, parrots, dolphins, and apes, possess some of the cognitive skills that have been suggested to be exclusively human: tool use, mental time travel, theory of mind, and self-recognition. As such, the intellectual distance between humans and animals may be smaller than we believed previously.

## FURTHER READING

Pearce (1997) is an excellent introduction to many of the issues raised in this and the previous chapter, whereas a useful more recent introduction to the entire field of animal cognition is presented in Wynne (2001). A good source of information on representations of number and language is Roberts (1998). Many experiments in animal cognition are performed on nonhuman primates, and Tomasello and Call (1997) provide an encyclopedia of primate cognition. Perhaps the most comprehensive overview of the field of animal cognition in relation to ecology and evolution is Shettleworth (1998). This book is specifically for higher-level courses for final-year undergraduates and graduates.

# function and evolution
# of behavior

# 9

# the function of behavior

### Luc-Alain Giraldeau

## INTRODUCTION

Avian migration, the seasonal displacement of millions of birds from one hemisphere to another is, as all mass migrations, an astonishing phenomenon: tons of biomass moving from one continent to another, spending enormous amounts of energy in the process and all to what end? This remarkable sequence of events can be approached from a purely mechanistic point of view. Birds, for instance, respond to changing photoperiod which, added to signals from an internal clock, trigger a hormonal cascade that leads to accumulation of fat reserves and makes the bird inclined to fly off at night with a strong directional preference based on stellar position. However, as we pointed out in Chapter 1, no matter how hard you study this chain of events and learn how birds migrate, no matter how detailed your knowledge of the physiological processes involved in hormone production or the way the bird uses the stars as a compass, you will be no closer to knowing why birds migrate in the first place. Why is it that the internal machinery of some bird species, but not others, reacts to changing photoperiod in a long chain of events that lead to long-distance migration? To answer this type of question we must first leave the realm of **cause** and mechanism and enter the sphere of **function** and **adaptation**. Function is not a question that is usually addressed in science because function implies a design, and the design a designer. Ever since Charles Darwin and Alfred Russel Wallace suggested that design follows from the operation of a material force called **natural selection** that leads to evolutionary adaptation, function has become a legitimate scientific question in biology. The designing agent, natural selection, removes among the existing design variants the ones that provide their bearer with a lower ability to gain representation in the next generation: **fitness**. The consequence of this process is evolution toward adaptation; designs that confer relatively greater fitness become more common as each generation replaces another. **Selection**, therefore, is a physical, material, and natural force just as much as gravity and electromagnetism (Barrette 1999). This chapter reviews some of the approaches and methods used to study the adaptive function of behavior (see also Chapter 13). It first looks at how adaptation can be studied by formulating quantitative hypotheses about function using **reverse engineering** and simple **optimality models**. The approach will be illustrated with two now classic examples taken from foraging theory: prey choice and patch residence times. The next section introduces another version of the optimality approach, evolutionary **game theory** and its solution the **evolutionarily stable strategy** using three examples: the Hawk–Dove and **producer–scrounger** games, and the **ideal free distribution**.

## Introducing Simple Optimality

That natural selection causes evolution toward enhanced design of organs and behavior can be inferred through examples of convergent evolution. Compare, for instance, the shapes of appendages in a number of different aquatic organisms such as fish, sea turtles, dolphins, and penguins. Despite the diverse evolutionary origins of these fin-like appendages (some were wings, others legs or arms), their forms now resemble each other. This resemblance no doubt follows because they serve a similar purpose: a means to power movement through a dense medium. The similarity in shape can be an adaptation if we can ascribe it to the action of natural selection that favored certain design variants from originally quite different-looking appendages to make them more efficient at accomplishing their function of propelling individuals through water. The argument seems reasonable. However, in order to go beyond such apparently sensible comments about adaptation and turn them into science, we need to be a bit more quantitative and explicit about what we expect natural selection to have produced.

### Reverse engineering

Engineers are asked to design machines that will accomplish some function with maximal efficiency. They build the machine knowing its purpose. However, biologists have the complete machine before them and puzzle about its purpose. They do this by following the reverse route, postulating a function and then asking whether the details of the machine are consistent with maximal efficiency of this function. That, in essence, is what we mean by reverse engineering. The method of reverse engineering assumes that selection has shaped traits, organs, limbs, behaviors, etc. so that after many generations of being submitted to the same selective pressures they offer the greatest possible efficiency in the accomplishment of their purpose. We say "greatest possible" because evolution (much like the engineer) is often constrained. The design is assumed to be maximally efficient given physical, genetic, morphological, historical, and other constraints. So if a trait is thought to be adaptive, we hypothesize its function and ask: what would be the characteristics of a trait that is optimally designed to accomplish this hypothetical function? We use mathematical, economic, and engineering techniques to predict these characteristics of optimal design and compare them with observations. If we find a quantitative fit between some feature of an organ, say its length or width, and the precise length or width expected of an organ optimally designed to accomplish that same function, then we would feel more confident that selection honed the trait we are dealing with to accomplish that purpose and can with more certainty conclude that it is an adaptation.

## Optimal flight speeds: an example of the logic of reverse engineering

Each bird species flies at some typical speed when engaged in its everyday activities. Is this speed chosen randomly or is it an adaptation? Has selection designed it to accomplish some specific adaptive function? One possibility is that selection favored birds that minimize energy use per unit time spent flying: the minimum power speed. Alternatively, selection might have favored birds that maximize the distance covered per unit energy used: the maximum range speed. These are two hypotheses about the adaptive function of flight speed, hypotheses concerning the selective pressures that have given rise to the flight speeds we observe in birds today. Let's see how a behavioral ecologist would set out to test these hypotheses.

The physics of flight is well known and so we can use reverse engineering to construct an optimality model that generates quantitative expected flight speeds for each hypothetical adaptive function. From the shape of a bird's wing and its body mass it is possible to construct a power function that describes the relationship between the power required to sustain level flight and flight speed for that wing shape. This power function is generally a parabola, which first declines as speed increases, reaches a minimum, and then increases again (Fig. 9.1). The minimum point of the function gives the minimum power speed. That is the speed that requires the least power and hence provides the greatest energetic savings. The maximum range speed can be obtained by drawing a line from the origin tangential to the power curve. The point of tangency gives the maximum range speed, i.e., the speed that allows the animal to cover the greatest distance per unit power used. If flight speed is an adaptation to minimize power, then birds should fly at precisely the minimum power speed. Alternatively, if flight speed is designed to maximize the range, the birds should fly at the maximum range speed. We can test these hypotheses by comparing the predicted flight speeds with the observed flight speeds.

If we found that dark-eyed juncos flew at the minimum power speed calculated from its mass and wing shape, we could legitimately conclude that the junco's flight speed is an adaptation to reduce its flight costs. However, it is more important to agree about what it means if the bird does not fly at either of the predicted optimal flight speeds or, more formally, when the hypothesis is rejected.

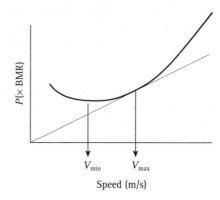

**Fig. 9.1** Power (*P*) expressed as multiples of basal metabolic rate (BMR) required to sustain level flight of different speeds by a bird. Very slow and very fast flight speeds are extremely costly. $V_{min}$, speed that requires the least power; $V_{max}$, speed that covers the greatest range per unit energy spent. Both are potential optimal flight speeds that are subject to empirical testing.

## What does it mean when a hypothesis about adaptation is rejected?

Some may argue that the negative result should be taken as evidence that flight speed simply has no function; it is not an adaptation so we should give up the quest and move on to something else. The problem with this view is that not only does it simply end the enquiry but it is difficult to be certain that the speed does not serve any function after only one or two rejected hypotheses. After all, flight speed could serve some other adaptive function that remains to be investigated. Because of this, the absence of adaptation can only be invoked as a last resort, once most reasonable alternatives have been found to be wrong. When a model's predictions are wrong we must first be certain that the assumptions upon which the predictions were based are correct. Only if all the assumptions happen to be correct can we clearly reject the hypothetical adaptive function we were testing. If we do reject it, then the next step is to come up with an alternative functional hypothesis that will also be subject to testing. This position of constantly hypothesizing adaptation for traits has given evolutionary and behavioral ecologists a bad name (Gould & Lewontin 1979). Because of it, behavioral ecologists are often depicted as naive optimists, arguing that everything must and does have a purpose. However, it is important to understand that to study adaptation, and hence function, it is necessary to hypothesize adaptation as a starting proposition. This is not decreeing that adaptation exists but rather stating that it is a hypothesis open to scientific scrutiny. Behavioral ecologists do not believe that all traits are adaptive; in fact it is likely that many traits are neutral or have no current function. However, we all agree that any claim for adaptation must be subjected to empirical testing (Williams

1966). Concluding that a trait has no adaptive value is simply an absolute last resort because it ends any further functional investigation.

## Optimality Models in Foraging: Prey Choice

One of the most successful applications of **optimality theory** to the study of behavior is known as **optimal foraging theory** (Stephens & Krebs 1986; Giraldeau & Caraco 2000). Indeed the very birth of this theory can be traced to the pioneering work of a few ecologists such as Robert MacArthur and Eric Pianka (1966) who realized that the answers to a number of questions in population ecology required some knowledge of animal behavior. That thought was a radical departure from the way ecologists then considered foraging behavior: they assumed that animals eat what they find and stop when they are sated or when the food is gone. But is it reasonable to expect that natural selection would have optimized the shape of wings and flight speed, a bumblebee's tongue length, the architecture of a spider's orb web, and the morphology of a fish's mouth while leaving untouched the very behavior that allows the collection of the energy required to live and reproduce? MacArthur and Pianka thought it was not and proposed an optimality analysis of diet choice for predators that encounter their prey sequentially. Since then the optimality approach they pioneered has been applied to the diet selection of large herbivores that must deal with toxins and predators that encounter prey simultaneously or even that ambush prey rather than search for them. Reviewing all these different optimal diet models would require a book in itself and goes beyond the objective of introducing the optimality approach (but see Sih & Christensen 2001). We deal here only with the simplest sequential prey encounter optimal diet model to illustrate the approach.

### To choose or not to choose: that is the diet question

A black-capped chickadee (*Poecile atricapillus*), a territorial small passerine bird that inhabits the forests of North America, is busy collecting insects to feed itself and its noisy and growing nestlings during the late spring. Let's imagine that there are only two species of insects at the moment in the forest: large, rare, and nutritious insects and small, common, but less nutritious ones. An animal that takes what it finds will eat each type of insect in proportion to their relative abundances in the environment. The less nutritious one being more common, it should be more common in the parents' and nestlings' diets. Could the chickadee do better by being more selective? Could it nourish itself and its young more effectively by exercising some choice over the items it eats and brings back to the nest? If it could do better by choosing, then should we not expect that selection would have favored choosy individuals over those that were not? And if this were the case, then how should the frequency of prey captured by a forager be affected by the preys' relative abundances? To answer these questions we must use reverse engineering and build an optimality model.

## Three steps to building the optimal prey model

### *Step 1*

The first thing we need to do is make explicit the alternative courses of action that we wish to analyze. In the case of sequential prey choice it is: given an encounter with prey item X, should the predator attack, capture, and eat prey X *or* should it ignore the prey and continue searching?

### *Step 2*

Next we need to devise a way to compare the fitness consequences of the two alternative courses of action. To do this we formulate a hypothesis concerning the adaptive function or **survival value** that we can assign to each alternative. One possibility is that the faster the rate at which a bird harvests food, the greater its fitness. This makes sense given that greater harvest rates would allow nestlings to grow faster, fledge sooner, and be healthier when they fledge. Let's hypothesize that the function of prey choice is to maximize the rate of prey harvesting. Surely fitness is not just correlated with the number of prey harvested but must also be affected by their quality. Assigning units to prey quality is not simple. Nutritive value may be important but it is difficult to quantify in a single axis as it involves proteins and lipids, carbohydrates, minerals, and a number of other nutrients. However, nutrition above all fuels the animal's metabolism and the offsprings' growth. So let's assume that energy is a good approximation of nutritive value and hypothesize a function: prey choice has been designed to maximize the rate of energy intake ($E/T$) with joules per time spent foraging as units. In the behavioral ecologist's jargon, rate of energy intake is the **currency of fitness** or adaptive function that is under experimental scrutiny. This is the currency with which we will be able to compare the adaptive value of alternative courses of action, such as being choosy or not.

### *Step 3*

Finally, we need to specify the assumptions and constraints under which we assume the animal makes its **decision**. These constraints often take the form of assumptions required to keep the model realistic, simple, and general. The sequential prey encounter model makes a number of assumptions about the world in which the animal lives. It assumes that energy ($E$) can only be acquired by consuming a prey item and that consuming an item requires some **handling time** ($H$). The profitability of a prey type is set by the ratio $E/H$ and all individuals of a prey type offer the same exact profitability. $E$ and $H$ are characteristics of the prey and the forager cannot do anything to change these prey characteristics (e.g., handle them faster or get more energy from one by eating it differently). The model assumes that each prey type is encountered randomly during search ($S$) at some rate $\lambda$ that depends on its abundance in the environment. The model also makes assumptions about the foraging predator. It assumes that it knows what encounter rates to expect from each prey type, that it is capable of recognizing each prey type instantly without error upon encounter, that it cannot search while it is eating a prey item, and its search efficiency and speed remain constant and unalterable.

These assumptions may seem peculiar, possibly even unrealistic. However, it is impossible to capture all the elements of the real world in a single quantitative model. It would make the mathematics very complicated such that it would require a model to study the model! Modelers secretly hope that not every element present while the animal is behaving is important. In trying to capture the essential features of the problem, they discard some elements, simplify others, and ignore many. To do this successfully, however, it is essential to have a good idea of the biology behind the problem being addressed. Not too surprisingly, models often oversimplify and this is why, when a model fails, instead of flatly rejecting the adaptive hypothesis behavioral ecologists first turn to scrutinizing the validity of the assumptions.

## Two steps to testing the optimal prey model

### Step 1: formulating the predictions

Now that the decision, the currency, and the main constraints are known we can formulate the predictions that will be subjected to testing. We predict that if $E/T$ is the real currency of fitness, then the animal should adopt the diet that provides the highest value of $E/T$. So we need to calculate the $E/T$ outcomes of all possible diets. For simplicity we assume that only two prey types exist (the same argument and conclusions would apply to any number of prey types). In such a two-prey system there are just two reasonable outcomes: take all prey as encountered (no choice), or always attack the most profitable item (prey type 1) and never attack the less profitable item (prey type 2). An animal that does not choose behaves as a **generalist** and the one that chooses only the best item is a dietary **specialist**.

To compare the value of each option we must calculate their respective adaptive value or function using the currency of fitness. We calculate the $E/T$ that corresponds to a generalist diet by calculating first the numerator $E$. After $S$ time spent in search, a predator will have encountered $S\lambda_1 E_1$ prey of type 1, and $S\lambda_2 E_2$ prey of type 2. Its overall energy harvest will be:

$$E = S(\lambda_1 E_1 + \lambda_2 E_2)$$

To estimate $T$, the denominator, we must account for the time spent in each activity during foraging. Each time the predator eats prey type 1 it spends $H_1$ time handling it (we assume attack time is zero). So in total it will have spent $S\lambda_1 H_1$ time handling prey type 1 and $S\lambda_2 H_2$ handling prey type 2. To this handling time we must add the time spent searching, such that the total amount of time spent is:

$$S + S(\lambda_1 H_1 + \lambda_2 H_2)$$

Placing numerator over denominator we get:

$$\frac{E}{T} = \frac{S(\lambda_1 E_1 + \lambda_2 E_2)}{S + S(\lambda_1 H_1 + \lambda_2 H_2)}$$

which corresponds to the adaptive value of a generalist diet. Now we can do the same for the specialist diet, which gives:

$$\frac{E}{T} = \frac{S\lambda_1 E_1}{S + S\lambda_1 H_1}$$

When does being a specialist provide a higher currency of fitness than being a generalist? When:

$$\frac{S\lambda_1 E_1}{S + S(\lambda_1 H_1)} > \frac{S + (\lambda_1 E_1 + \lambda_2 E_2)}{S + S(\lambda_1 H_1 + \lambda_2 H_2)}$$

which, after some algebra, simplifies to:

$$\frac{1}{\lambda_1} > \frac{E_1 H_2}{E_2} - H_1$$

When this inequality holds, the forager should be a generalist and accept the less profitable prey when it encounters it. When it does not hold, the forager should exclude the less profitable prey and specialize only on the most profitable. This inequality makes a number of rather interesting predictions that follow from the hypothesis that choice is designed to maximize $E/T$.

1 The relative abundances of each prey type should not affect the choice. Only the encounter rate with the most profitable prey (prey type 1) remains in the final equation. That means that whether prey type 2 gets included in the diet does not depend on its own abundance but on the abundance of the other, more profitable item. The more prey type 1 is abundant, the more likely prey type 2 will drop out of the diet.

2 The optimal diet policy does not depend on the duration of the search time, because the variable $S$ falls out during simplification. That means the same policy holds whether an animal searches just briefly or for long foraging periods.

3 The optimal diet does not allow **partial preferences**; a prey type is either always accepted or always rejected.

### Step 2: experimental testing

The main difficulty with testing this model is obtaining an accurate estimate of the forager's encounter rates with prey types. John Krebs and his colleagues at Oxford University devised an ingenious experimental apparatus to overcome this difficulty

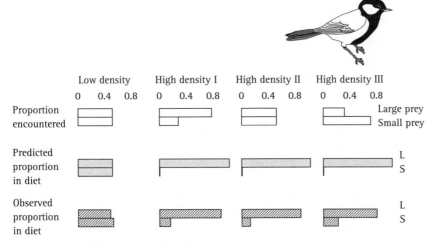

**Fig. 9.2** Conveyor belt experiment of Krebs et al. (1977). Great tits (*Parus major*) could pick pieces of mealworms from a moving conveyor belt. The pieces were either long or short, corresponding to the most and least profitable items respectively. The birds were exposed to four prey densities, corresponding to the four columns of the histograms. At low prey densities they encountered both prey types equally. The diet model predicts unselective foraging and that is what the birds did. When the density of the profitable mealworms was increased, the model predicts that the birds should now specialize on only the longest, more profitable ones. The results show that they almost always chose to ignore the least profitable items. When the density of long items was kept constant but the density of less profitable short items was increased and made equal to the density of good items, the model still predicts specialization and the birds continued to take almost exclusively only the most profitable longest items. Finally, keeping the density of good items constant but making the density of the least profitable items double the density of good items still predicts that animals should specialize. The birds again conform closely to this prediction. (From Krebs 1978.)

(Krebs et al. 1977). They placed small captive wild birds (great tits, *Parus major*) in an experimental apparatus where they could obtain mealworms by perching above a small window giving access to a conveyor belt upon which prey of each type appeared at experimentally set rates. Hence, the experimenters could set the encounter rates for each prey type in this microcosm. Once a prey item was attacked and held in the bill, the bird had to fly away from the window to a perch in the rear of the apparatus in order to eat it. In this way the bird could not handle and search at the same time. The birds encountered two types of prey sequentially (only one prey type appeared in the window at a time) on the conveyor belt: short four-segment and long eight-segment mealworms. The handling times were similar for both types of prey and so the short mealworms were less profitable than the long ones.

The results of the conveyor belt experiment were remarkable (Fig. 9.2). They provided the first experimental evidence that relative prey abundances were irrelevant to the animal's choice; choice was independent of the abundance of the least profitable prey type. No matter how many short mealworms were available, if the long mealworms were sufficiently common, the shorter ones would simply be rejected (almost always). Although the birds followed the qualitative predictions of the model, they nonetheless exhibited partial preference rather than the all-or-nothing choice predicted by the model.

This deviation from expectations is not really surprising and several hypotheses, based on reappraisal of the initial constraint assumptions, have since been formulated to account for the result. For instance, it may not be correct to expect that foragers instantaneously and without error always recognize each prey type upon encounter. Also, maybe predators expect prey types to change in quality over time and so sample them once in a while to update their **information** (Getty & Krebs 1985).

Sih and Christensen (2001) provide a recent review and appraisal of the optimal diet approach. Their analysis includes 134 published studies that were either experimental or observational, conducted in the laboratory or the field. They conclude that optimality models have worked well for systems in which predators exploit immobile prey. However, the models do poorly when prey are mobile because the current models do not take into account the effectiveness of prey evasion strategies on the value of pursuing alternative prey. The current trend at the moment is to include these factors in optimal prey models. For instance, we will see in Chapter 10 that prey that have detected their predator may be more difficult to capture. It pays these prey to communicate to predators that they have been detected, indicating that their profitability as prey has just declined compared with other prey that have not yet detected the predator (see Getty 2002).

## Foraging Theory: Patch Residence

Organisms are rarely uniformly distributed in space. As a consequence, an animal's food often occurs in **patches**: clumps of eggs, fruit in a bush, flowers on a plant, etc. When resources are in clumps, what should the optimal patch exploitation strategy be? Should foragers consistently deplete clumps or exploit them only partially? What is the function of patch exploitation decisions? What ecological factors affect this decision? Consider the following example: a bumblebee takes nectar from a flower. Each time its tongue is inserted in the nectary (the structure that holds nectar) it draws a bit less nectar: the nectary is depleting. At some point the bumblebee must give up the current flower and search for another, hopefully fuller one. At what point during flower exploitation should this occur or, in terms of the currency of fitness we used for prey choice, at what point during the exploitation of a patch would giving it up maximize long-term rate of energy intake? Let's use reverse engineering once again and construct an optimality model to analyze the decision and predict the optimal patch departure time. This model is known as the patch model and like all optimality models it has three parts.

## Three steps to building an optimal patch residence model

### Step 1: the decision

The decision in this model is whether to continue searching for prey in the current patch *or* cease exploitation and begin searching for the next patch. What is being traded off here is current intake rate against a potential intake rate achieved by foraging at a better fuller patch, taking the time required to travel to this patch into account.

### Step 2: the currency of fitness

As for the optimal diet model above, we must choose a currency of fitness with which to compare the adaptive values of all possible patch exploitation times. For the same reasons as in the diet model let's adopt $E/T$ as a reasonable currency of fitness.

### Step 3: the constraints

The model assumes that all prey items are randomly distributed within identifiable patches; no food can be found between patches. The time required to uncover patches is set by patch density in the habitat, so that as patch density declines the time required to find a patch ($T$) increases. A forager can only gain energy while spending time ($P$) in a patch. The density of items in the patch sets the forager's encounter rate with prey and, because the density declines as exploitation progresses, so does the forager's encounter rate with prey.

The model also makes assumptions about the forager. It assumes that the forager has no say in the way its rate of encounter with patches and its encounter rate with prey within a patch progresses. The model assumes that a forager does not know beforehand the precise time it will take to reach the next patch nor does it know whether the patch it finds will be rich or poor. The decision must therefore be based on the average time to reach a patch in a given environment and the average patch quality expected in that environment. The model also assumes that a forager cannot estimate the actual quality of the patch it is currently exploiting and behaves toward it as if it was a patch of average quality for that habitat.

## Two steps to testing the optimal patch residence model

### Step 1: drawing the predictions

The patch problem consists of looking for an optimal patch residence time that corresponds to the maximum rate of energy intake for a habitat characterized by a given density of patches of known average quality. The predictions, therefore, will concern how a change in patch density or a change in average patch quality in a habitat will affect the extent to which resource clumps of that habitat will be depleted by foragers. These predictions, descibed below, are best obtained graphically and the method is illustrated in Box 9.1.

1  When the patch density declines and hence the average travel time between patches increases, animals should spend longer foraging within patches and deplete them to a greater extent.
2  When average patch quality in a habitat increases, foragers should spend less time exploiting each patch and deplete each to a lesser extent.

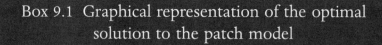

# Box 9.1  Graphical representation of the optimal solution to the patch model

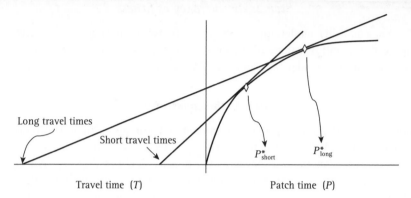

In this graph the $x$-axis runs in two directions from the $y$-axis. To the right, patch time increases. To the left, travel time increases. The curve gives the cumulative increase in energy intake as the animal spends time in the average patch. Note that as the animal spends longer and longer in the patch its instantaneous rate declines. This is the result of patch depletion. There are two habitats represented here, one with short travel times and the other with long travel times, each one represented on the $x$-axis.

When the animal forages in the habitat with the short travel time it can leave at any point on the exploitation curve. The problem consists in finding the point that provides the maximal long-term intake rate. The intake rate will have units $E$ divided by the sum of travel time and the chosen patch time. The slope of the line starting at the short travel time and touching the exploitation function will have a slope that gives the rate of intake. The slope of any line linking a travel time to a point on the exploitation function will give the rate of intake achieved by that patch time. We are looking for the patch time that corresponds to a line with the maximum slope. That line has to be the point of tangency to the curve. Note that the point of tangency for short travel time corresponds to a short optimal patch time, whereas the longer travel time leads to a point of tangency at a longer optimal patch time. This means that the optimal patch times are predicted to increase when the average travel time between patches in an environment increases.

### Step 2: experimental test of the prediction

Like the diet model presented above, there have been numerous tests of the patch model's predictions (see Stephens & Krebs 1986). In most cases experimenters have found a qualitative fit for both predictions listed above (Nonacs 2001). A typical example of such studies involves the collecting of seed loads by eastern chipmunks (*Tamias striatus*), a ground-living squirrel indigenous to the east coast of the northern USA and Canada. Chipmunks are central-place foragers because rather than eating food where they find it they collect seeds (maple samaras, acorns, beech nuts, etc.) in extensible cheek pouches and carry them back to their underground burrow to be eaten later, often during winter. Seed loading by chipmunks while in a clump occurs at a decelerated rate as the cheek pouches fill and adding prey becomes more difficult. If the chipmunk's patch exploitation decision is an evolutionary adaptation to maximize its rate of seed delivery to the burrow, then as the distance between burrow and patch increases the chipmunk should spend more time in the patch to collect larger seed loads (Box 9.1). In a field experiment, chipmunks were given the opportunity to collect loads of sunflower seeds from artificial patches placed at known distances from their burrow. They were observed to collect larger loads when the distance to the food patch increased (Fig. 9.3; Giraldeau & Kramer 1982; Giraldeau et al. 1994) as predicted by the patch model. However, the model was also somewhat of a quantitative disaster given that the load sizes observed to be collected by the chipmunks were much smaller than those predicted by the model: a clear case of qualitative support and quantitative mismatch that requires closer scrutiny of the constraint assumptions of the model.

This type of qualitative fit but quantitative failure seems to be a common result in optimal foraging tests. In a recent survey of the literature on tests of the marginal value theorem, Nonacs (2001) notes that of the 26 studies he examined most met the model's qualitative predictions, but quantitatively they almost always predicted longer patch residence times than those exhibited by the foragers. Nonacs suggests that this systematic departure indicates an important omission of the model rather than simply imprecision. He proposes a reformulation of the model that takes the forager's energetic state into consideration as a means to correct this systematic bias. Another factor invoked to account for the model's quantitative shortcomings is whether foragers really ignore information about the quality of the patch they are currently exploiting. Another possibility is that prey or patches may not be randomly distributed so that predators may learn tricks to find them more effectively as they exploit them. There are many other possibilities, including the potential effects of competitors on optimal exploitation times.

## Game Theory and Evolutionarily Stable Strategies

The optimality models presented up to now are simple in the sense that it is possible to compute the outcome of all strategies available to the animal (the various diets in the prey model, or all possible patch residence times for the patch model) without reference to the behavior of other individuals. Sometimes, however, the benefits derived from a given course of action cannot be specified without also specifying the frequency with which the other animals use that alternative. This section considers three **cases** in which the payoffs are characterized by this sort of frequency dependence: (i) fighting **displays**, (ii) resource-harvesting strategies, and (iii) where to settle.

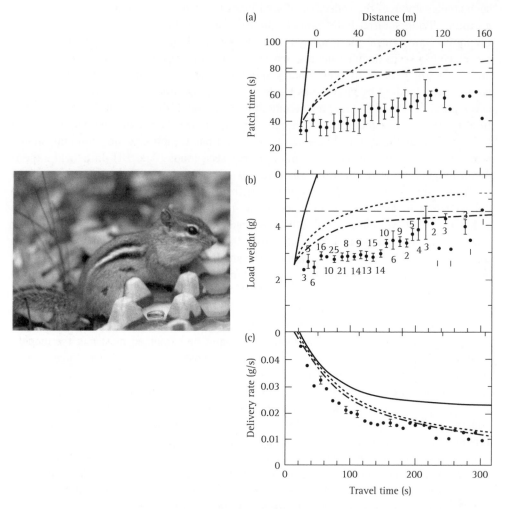

**Fig. 9.3** Central place foraging experiment of Giraldeau and Kramer (1982) using the eastern chipmunk (*Tamias striatus*). Chipmunks were offered trays of sunflower seeds at various distances from their burrow. They made repeated trips to the same tray collecting seeds in their cheek pouches and carrying them to their burrow, where they were stored. (a) Mean observed time spent in the patch collecting seeds, (b) weight of sunflower seeds collected, and (c) rate of food delivery achieved at various distances and hence travel times between tray and burrow. The lines on the graphs are the quantitative predictions of changes in patch time, load size, and corresponding rates of food delivery from the optimal patch model presented in Box 9.1 using three different estimated exploitation functions. The chipmunks did collect larger loads and spend more time doing this as distance and hence travel time to the burrow increased. The rates of food delivery achieved were generally lower than those they would have achieved had they taken the larger loads. (From Giraldeau & Kramer 1982.)

# Function of fighting displays

In a contest over resources individuals often engage in aggressive encounters. Bald eagles fight over access to the carcasses of dead salmon; male dragonflies chase male intruders from their territory in order to maintain a monopoly over females that come to lay their eggs there. What is the function of behavior expressed during fighting? Is the behavior meant to inflict injury upon opponents or does it serve some other purpose? Except for some of the fighting scenes in Walt Disney's classic *Bambi*, male deer rarely use their antlers to inflict injury by ramming each other by surprise, or in any other place but the other male's antlers. Male deer (and other ungulates) that fight with their antlers use them in rather **stereotyped** fighting displays: they slowly and purposefully interlock them before they engage in an all-out pushing match at the end of which one male leaves promptly as the other chases it away. Similarly, when cichlid fish are engaged in a conflict over a territory or access to a female, two highly valuable resources, they interlock jaws and push and pull until one gives up, conceding victory to the other without inflicting any injury despite their razor-sharp teeth. When early **ethologists** such as Konrad Lorenz and Niko Tinbergen described fighting displays they were struck by the fact that very little blood if any was drawn during fights, a stark contrast with the outcome of aggression among people. They assumed, as many did in those days, that noninjurious fighting displays evolved by **group selection** and that their adaptive function was to avoid the useless waste of individuals during animal fights. We now know that it is unlikely that group selection could have been strong enough to favor such widespread occurrence of noninjurious fighting displays (Williams 1966). The challenge for behavioral ecologists therefore is to determine the adaptive function of noninjurious displays given that they must have arisen by selection acting at the level of individuals.

John Maynard Smith and G.R. Price (1973) met this challenge by applying a mathematical technique known as game theory to the evolutionary problem of aggression. Game theory existed in economics and was used to analyze problems in trade, auctions, and even war. However, to apply this mathematical tool to evolutionary problems, it was important to realize that solutions to the game depend on the evolutionary process: these solutions need to be the most likely evolutionary outcome of the game. The stage was set for one of the first formal analyses of an evolutionary game.

Can noninjurious fighting displays exist as the most plausible evolutionary outcome when selection acts to maximize the fitness of individuals and not species? Should not an individual designed to maximize its fitness go all out and risk injury by attempting to injure its opponent? To answer the question we must first specify the payoff derived from using either strategy. The payoff provided by each strategy depends on whether the opponent is likely to use injurious or noninjurious levels of fighting itself. Hence simple optimality modeling is of little utility here and we must use game theory to analyze the problem and predict the most likely evolutionary outcome.

# Three steps to analyzing the fighting game

## *Step 1: specifying the alternative strategies*

To analyze a game we must first specify the alternatives open to the players. We can simplify the options and place them in two discrete categories: a noninjurious option called **Dove** and an all-out escalating option called **Hawk**. Dove displays until it or the opponent gives up or until the opponent escalates to injurious levels of fighting. Hawk always uses escalated fighting and leaves only if injured.

## *Step 2: specifying the payoffs to each alternative*

We will not specify whether the animals are fighting for food, mates, shelter, or whatever. Let's keep our analysis general, and so instead of a currency of fitness we will use fitness directly to measure the payoffs of both strategies. To calculate the payoffs of each alternative we must first specify the value ($V$) of the resource that is sought in terms of its replacement cost expressed in fitness units. If the animals were fighting over food, then the same food resource would have greater value for a starving individual compared with a well-fed individual because the starving individual would incur a greater risk of death by having to replace the lost food than the well-fed individual. Individuals that get injured in a fight suffer a cost ($C$), also in fitness units. To keep the analysis simple, we assume that the players are of equal strength and each value the resource equally. Technically, this means the players are "symmetric" so that we can represent the payoffs of individuals strictly by what they and their opponent play.

No matter what strategy one plays, the payoffs from fighting against Dove will be different from the payoffs of fighting against Hawk. There are four possible combinations of strategies. The payoffs for a Dove that encounters a Hawk are written as E(D,H), so that the other three remaining combinations are E(D,D), E(H,D), and E(H,H). We can analyze what happens in each one of these encounters.

*When Dove meets Dove.* When two Dove individuals meet they both use a noninjurious display. Because the players are symmetric, let's assume that they each win encounters half of the time. Thus E(D,D) = $0.5V$.

*When Dove meets Hawk.* Dove always runs away when Hawk escalates. Dove avoids injury but never obtains the resource. Thus E(D,H) = 0.

*When Hawk meets Dove.* Hawk always wins against Dove because Dove always avoids escalated fighting by running away when the opponent escalates to injurious levels. Thus E(H,D) = $V$.

*When Hawk meets Hawk.* When two Hawks meet we assume that one wins half the time and the other wins half the time because the players are symmetric. Because Hawk only leaves if it gets injured, the loser suffers a fitness costs $C$ and the winner gets the resource $V$. Thus E(H,H) = $0.5V + 0.5C = (V + C)/2$. The four potential payoffs can be expressed in a matrix (Table 9.1).

**Table 9.1** Payoffs to the row player engaged in a Hawk–Dove game.

|        | Hawk              | Dove           |
|--------|-------------------|----------------|
| Hawk   | $E(H,H) = (V + C)/2$ | $E(H,D) = V$   |
| Dove   | $E(D,H) = 0$      | $E(D,D) = V/2$ |

### Step 3: finding the expected evolutionary solution

The solution to an evolutionary game is known as the evolutionarily stable strategy (ESS) (Maynard Smith & Price 1973; Maynard Smith 1982). An ESS is a strategy such that, when all members of a population adopt it, no mutant strategy can invade. An evolutionary thought experiment comes in handy to find the ESS in the Hawk–Dove game. Imagine an ancestral population of individuals that all play Dove. Can a rare mutant that plays Hawk invade this population? Because the population is all Dove, the Hawk mutant meets only Dove players and so will do well because $E(H,D) > E(D,D)$ (or $V > V/2$ from the payoff matrix). Hawk therefore can invade a population of Dove. But the argument does not stop there. It is not enough to know that Hawk can invade a population of Dove; we also need to know whether a population of Hawk can resist invasion from rare Dove mutants or, more formally, $E(H,H) > E(D,H)$. Using the values in the payoff matrix, Dove will be unable to invade Hawk when $(V - C)/2 > 0$. As long as $C < V$, the costs of injury are smaller than the replacement value of the resource, and Hawk will remain the ESS to the game. So we conclude from the analysis that a population of individuals engaged in noninjurious fighting is simply not an evolutionarily stable solution.

### What happens when $C > V$?

When $C > V$, Hawk is no longer the ESS. Under this condition rare Dove mutants do better in a population of Hawk than do Hawk individuals, i.e., $E(D,H) > E(H,H)$. This happens because Hawk individuals are inflicting costly injuries to each other whereas Dove never gets injured (even though it never gets the resource). Even though rare Dove mutants do well, they cannot form an ESS because, as we saw above, there is no condition under which Dove can ever be an ESS, i.e., $E(H,D) > E(D,D)$. In this case neither Hawk nor Dove can be evolutionary solutions to the game. Each time the population evolves toward all of one strategy, the **alternative strategy** can invade. In this case there must be a combination of Hawk and Dove that is an ESS. Going back to our evolutionary thought experiment, we start once again with a population of all Dove in which a mutant Hawk arises. This mutant does much better than Dove and so it spreads. However, as it spreads in the population, it starts encountering more and more of its own kind and so suffers an increasingly important injury cost. At some point the average payoff of Hawk declines until it reaches the payoff to Dove. When the payoff to Hawk and Dove are the same, selection can no longer favor one over the other and no further change in the frequency of alternative fighting strategies is possible: evolution is stuck. This happens whenever the population reaches an ESS mixture of the two strategies. We can use the fact that at the ESS the fitness payoffs to both strategies must be equal to calculate the ESS frequency of Hawk ($p^*$). The proportion of Hawk strategists in a population is $p$ and that of Dove $1 - p$. At ESS:

$$(p)(E(H,H)) + (1 - p)(E(H,D)) = (p)(E(D,H)) + (1 - p)(E(D,D))$$

Placing the payoffs from the matrix in their appropriate places gives:

$$p\left(\frac{V - C}{2}\right) + (1 - p)V = p \times 0 + (1 - p)\frac{V}{2}$$

which after some algebra and simplification gives $p^* = V/C$. This means that the ESS proportion of Hawk in the population depends on the ratio of the value of the resource to the costs of injury; the greater the ratio, the more Hawk individuals are expected at equilibrium.

## Lessons from the Hawk–Dove game

The results of the analysis are a little disappointing. The Hawk–Dove game predicts that Dove, the noninjurious display we are trying to account for, is never an ESS. Moreover, the Hawk strategy of injurious fighting is the ESS when the costs of injury are less than the value of the resource. If Dove exists at all, it can only be in a mixed ESS where the frequency of Hawk is set by the ratio of the value of the resource to the cost of injury. Noninjurious displays are much more common than this and so there must be some important element here ignored by the Hawk–Dove model.

In the real world, players are unlikely to be as equal in fighting ability as those imagined in the simple Hawk–Dove game. It turns out that when players are asymmetric, the predicted ESS is quite different. In Box 9.2 we have modified the Hawk–Dove game to allow for a third strategy called **Assessor** that assesses the fighting ability of its opponent relative to itself. Assessor plays Hawk when it assesses to be stronger and Dove when it assesses to be weaker. The payoff matrix of the Hawk–Dove–Assessor game in Box 9.2 shows that so long as there is a cost to being injured ($C > 0$) Assessor is the only ESS. When asymmetries occur, the ESS fighting strategy is to assess asymmetries *reliably*. Now it so happens that a population composed of Assessor would almost never use injurious fighting. All the individuals would be engaged in assessing each other's strength until one contestant, having realized it was the weakest and hence most likely to be injured, played Dove and abandoned the contest. Injurious fighting would occur only in those unlikely cases where opponents were so closely matched in fighting ability that they would be incapable of assessing which is the weaker individual.

This means that noninjurious fighting can be the most likely evolutionary outcome of fighting games so long as injuries impose a fitness cost. When deer interlock antlers and push as hard as they can, they are likely assessing their relative strengths. The information obtained by using this display is highly reliable because individuals cannot pretend

## Box 9.2 Hawk–Dove–Assessor game: when players are different

Say a contest involves asymmetric players, either because the resource represents a different value for the players or because players differ in fighting ability. A strategy called Assessor compares the values of the resource for both contestants or their fighting abilities and plays according to the asymmetry: it plays Hawk if it values the resource more or has higher fighting ability and Dove if the opponent values the resource more or has higher fighting ability.

### Defining Payoffs

Since we have already gone through the explanations of the payoffs to the Hawk–Dove game we only consider here the interactions that involve the Assessor strategy.

### When Hawk meets Assessor, E(H,A)

For simplicity let's assume that half the time the individual playing Hawk has greater fighting ability (or values the resource more) than the individual playing Assessor. When the individual playing Hawk is stronger, its Assessor opponent assesses this and plays Dove. The individual playing Hawk then gets all the resource. When the individual playing Hawk is weaker, however, the Assessor knows this and now plays Hawk. Because the Assessor individual is stronger, it always wins and inflicts an injury on Hawk. The average payoff of Hawk against Assessor is therefore $^1/_2V + ^1/_2C = (V + C)/2$.

### When Dove meets Assessor, E(D,A)

Let's assume that half the time Dove has greater fighting ability (or values the resource more) than Assessor. When this is the case Assessor plays Dove but, unlike with Hawk strategies, because there is no actual fighting, the asymmetry has no consequence on the outcome. So, half the time Dove wins and half the time the Dove-playing Assessor wins, so the payoff to Dove when it is the stronger of the two is $^1/_2(^1/_2V)$.

In the other situation Dove has less fighting ability (or values the resource less) than Assessor. Assessor then plays Hawk and Dove loses the contest and gets 0. So the average payoff is $^1/_2(^1/_2V) + ^1/_20 = V/4$.

### When Assessor meets Assessor, E(A,A)

In this case half the time one individual, call it *ego*, has greater fighting ability (or values the resource more) than the other, call it *alter*. *Ego* plays Hawk, *alter* plays

Dove so that *ego* gets *V*. The other half of the time, *ego* has lower fighting ability (or values the resource less) than *alter* so that *ego* plays Dove and *alter* plays Hawk. In this case *ego* gets 0 (and hence avoids the costs of injury). The average payoff in this case is $^1/_2V + ^1/_20 = V/2$.

## When Assessor meets Hawk, E(A,H)

When Assessor has greater fighting ability (or *V*) than Hawk, both play Hawk but Assessor always wins. When Assessor has lower fighting ability than Hawk, Assessor plays Dove and gets 0. The average payoff is then $^1/_2V + ^1/_20 = V/2$.

## When Assessor meets Dove, E(A,D)

When Assessor is the stronger of the two, it plays Hawk and gets *V* against Dove. When Dove is the strongest, Assessor then also plays Dove but because they do not really fight the outcome is independent of the asymmetry. So each wins the resource half the time. The average payoff to Assessor against Dove is then $^1/_2V + ^1/_2{}^1/_2V = ^3/_4V$.

The payoff matrix of a game between Hawk, Dove, and Assessor, in a situation where Assessor has perfect information about any asymmetry, is shown below.

| Payoff to | Hawk | Dove | Assessor |
|---|---|---|---|
| Hawk | $E(H,H) = ^1/_2(V - C)$ | $E(H,D) = V$ | $E(H,A) = ^1/_2(V - C)$ |
| Dove | $E(D,H) = 0$ | $E(D,D) = ^1/_2V$ | $E(D,A) = ^1/_4V$ |
| Assessor | $E(A,H) = ^1/_2V$ | $E(A,D) = ^3/_4V$ | $E(A,A) = ^1/_2V$ |

## Analysis of the Game

We know from the Hawk–Dove game that Dove can never be an ESS. The question that needs to be answered is whether Hawk can still be an ESS against Assessor, i.e., is E(A,H) > E(H,H)? Using entries in the payoff matrix we see that $V/2 > (V - C)/2$ and so Assessor can invade Hawk. Clearly, Hawk is not an ESS in an asymmetric game so long as the cost of injury is nonzero. So yes, Assessor can invade Hawk.

We know that Hawk is not a pure ESS against Assessor but this does not mean that Assessor is an ESS. Can Assessor resist invasion from Hawk or is E(H,A) > E(A,A)? Using entries from the payoff matrix we find that this requires that $^1/_4(V - C) > ^1/_2V$. Clearly this can never be true given that $C > 0$, and thus Assessor cannot be invaded by Hawk.

Can it be invaded by Dove? For this to happen E(D,A) > E(A,A) or, using entries from the matrix $^1/_4V > ^1/_2V$, which clearly can never be true. Hence we can conclude that so long as $C > 0$, i.e., there is a cost of being injured, Assessor is the pure ESS.

to be stronger than they really are in a pushing contest. The same holds for many other displays, such as mouth wrestling in fish. The displays are forceful but noninjurious.

## Alternative resource-harvesting strategies

There are often many alternative ways to harvest resources and the game-theory frame-work described for fighting can help us understand how polymorphisms and alternative strategies can be maintained within populations. For instance, when male natterjack toads *Bufo calamita* sing (if we can call it that) to attract females it is possible for some individuals to acquire females without singing at all, intercepting them as they travel toward the singing individuals (Arak 1988a). These satellite males (so called because they remain on the periphery of singing male territories) obtain females at little cost compared with the energy invested in calling by the males they exploit. The same has been noted for singing crickets (*Gryllus integer*; Cade 1978). To reproduce, female golden digger wasps *Sphex ichneumoneus* dig a burrow, provision it with katydids, and then lay an egg (Brockmann et al. 1979). Sometimes, instead of digging her own burrow, she enters and provisions a burrow that has already been dug by another female. Sometimes she digs, other times she enters. Coho salmon males *Oncorhynchus kisutch* that spawn in streams on the west coast of North America come in two forms: large hooknose males that mature after many months at sea, and jacks that mature more quickly but reach a smaller adult size. Large males use their hook noses to fight among each other for opportunities to spawn with females. Small jacks are not likely to win a fight with a hook-nose. Nonetheless, they get to spawn by exploiting the hooknoses' courtship behavior. Once a hooknose male has courted a female that is just about to shed her eggs, a jack that has been hiding in the neighboring rocks sneaks into position between the male and female and sheds his own sperm, some of which will fertilize the female's eggs (Gross 1985). The list of examples of such cases of alternative resource-harvesting strategies can be quite long (see Barnard 1984). What is common with all these instances is that one of the alternatives (silent male toads, female enterers, jacks) exploits the behavioral investment of the other strategy (calling males, digger females, hooknose males). The exploiting strategy could not exist without the presence of the investing strategy. It was Christopher Barnard and Richard Sibly (1981) who first recognized the generality of this phenomenon and proposed a general game they called the producer –scrounger game to help analyze the conditions in which to expect the co-occurrence of alternative resource-harvesting strategies.

## Producer–scrounger game

The producer–scrounger game assumes that resources can be harvested in two mutu-ally exclusive ways: producer, which consists of investing effort in making the resource available (calling mates, finding food, building nests, provisioning young, etc.); and scrounger, which consists of seeking opportunities to exploit the resources that have become available as a result of the producer's efforts. The game is characterized by strong

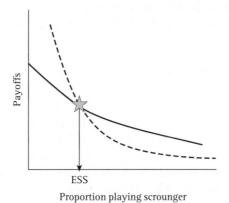

**Fig. 9.4** Payoff functions of the producer–scrounger game expressed as a function of the frequency of the scrounger strategists in the group. When there are no scroungers in the group, the payoff of producers (solid line) is maximal. The payoff to the scrounger (dashed line) indicates that the first few scroungers do much better than the producers. The evolutionary consequence of this is that scroungers will increase in frequency and replace producers in the population. As the scrounger frequency increases, the payoff to scroungers declines. At some point the payoffs to scrounger and producer are equal and the combination of the two strategies qualifies as an evolutionarily stable strategy (ESS).

negative frequency-dependent payoffs: scroungers do very well when they are rare (and hence producers common) but very poorly when they are common (and hence producers rare) (Fig. 9.4). Scroungers do well when they are rare because they have the opportunity of exploiting a large number of producers while suffering little competition from other animals. However, when they become common the numerous scroungers must compete for the resources made available by a dwindling number of producers. Given this negative frequency dependence, what is the ESS solution to the producer–scrounger game? Scrounger cannot be the ESS because it cannot gain any resource on its own and would thus go extinct. Producer is not an ESS because scroungers who take advantage of the many opportunities for exploitation can invade it. Once again, as seen earlier in the Hawk–Dove game, the solution to the game is a mixture of strategies that occur at a frequency for which the payoffs to each strategy are equal.

## Lessons from the producer–scrounger game

The producer–scrounger game is a general game. To make predictions for specific cases of alternative resource-harvesting behavior it would be necessary to go through the three steps of building optimality models: stating the decision to be analyzed, formulating a hypothetical currency of fitness, and listing the constraint assumptions. The game has rarely been taken to this level of detail, except perhaps for its application to the study of alternative foraging tactics within flocks of seed-eating birds (Giraldeau & Beauchamp 1999). The producer–scrounger game has been qualitatively successful at predicting the change in the stable frequency of the scrounger tactic within bird flocks

(Giraldeau & Caraco 2000). However, beyond its specific applications the game provides a general lesson for all those interested in the study of evolution and adaptation. Whatever the system explored, scroungers often impose a cost on group living; they take resources away from producers and do not contribute to the group's corporate effort at uncovering resources. The producer–scrounger game helps us understand that scroungers exist, despite the cost they impose upon other group members, because that is the only stable evolutionary outcome. A group of all producers would no doubt do much better; however, scroungers inevitably invade because a mixture that includes scroungers is the ESS.

Earlier we saw that one of the critiques aimed at behavioral ecologists is that they live in a rosy world where every trait seems to exist for the benefit of individuals. Our analysis of the producer–scrounger game makes a serious dent in this shiny view of selection by showing that evolutionary stability is not always synonymous with maximization of benefits. The solution is expected because it is evolutionarily stable, not because it is better. Scroungers exist despite making it worse for all, including themselves, because that is the only outcome that can be expected from natural selection. So much for the rosy world of adaptationists.

## Predictions for games with behavioral adjustment

The producer–scrounger game, as with most evolutionary games, is formulated in terms of evolutionary stability. This means that the alternative strategies equilibrate over evolutionary time as selection adjusts the frequency toward the equilibrium. In many situations animals have the behavioral plasticity to adjust rapidly to local conditions, perhaps using **learning** (see Chapter 7; Beauchamp 2000). **Behavioral adjustment** is expected to lead to the same solution to a game as would evolution. In fact the birds tested in the foraging producer–scrounger game can adjust to a new equilibrium scrounger frequency within a few hours (Giraldeau & Livoreil 1998). When animals can adjust so rapidly, the stability of the frequency is not really evolutionary. This is why the **stable equilibrium frequency** may be a more appropriate expression for solutions to evolutionary games solved by behavioral assessment (Mottley & Giraldeau 2000).

The simple optimality diet and patch models we presented earlier predict the behavior expected of each individual in a population. If they all forage under the same conditions, all the chickadees should exhibit the same prey choice. This is no longer the case for predictions that follow from a game-theory analysis. The game can predict the coexistence of two strategies within a population but it does not predict the behavior of a given individual in the population. For example, a game analysis of producing and scrounging could predict that the stable frequency of scrounger is 75%. This level of scrounging can be achieved by (i) having 75% of the population always playing scrounger and 25% always playing producer (i.e., a polymorphism); (ii) having all individuals playing scrounger 75% of the time and producer 25% of the time; or (iii) having a range of individuals each playing different combinations of producer and scrounger that happen to average out over the population to 75% scrounger and 25% producer. All these solutions are equally stable but only one of them (can you figure out which it is?) actually predicts the behavior expected of each group member; all others merely specify the group mean.

## Choosing where to live: the ideal free game

In the section on patch models we mentioned that organisms were rarely uniformly distributed. They occur in aggregations. Sometimes these aggregations result from the benefits derived from being with others (see Chapter 13). Sometimes, however, there are no advantages and perhaps even competitive costs of being close to others, a situation known as a dispersion economy. We can ask in these conditions what selective pressures have led animals to adopt the distribution they currently have. The answer requires some evolutionary game-theory analysis because if all animals go to the best place, then competition can become so intense for resources that it is better to go elsewhere, somewhere less suitable but with less competition. This distribution decision has been analyzed by a game known as the ideal free distribution (IFD), by far the most successful theory produced by **behavioral ecology**.

## The IFD game

Stephen Fretwell (1972) proposed a simple model that allows us to analyze an animal's decision to establish in one habitat or another. Inspired by the theory of perfect gases he simply assumed that animals (i) know the value of all alternative habitats (i.e., they are ideal) and (ii) are free to go in the best habitats (i.e., they are free). If animals are ideal and free they will always go instantaneously to the habitat with the highest current value. If all animals do this, then all movement will cease once the experienced value in each habitat becomes equal; no improvement is possible when this happens. Knowing this, in a world of $k$ individuals having to colonize two habitats, one that is initially of greater value than the other (Fig. 9.5), Fretwell predicts the following.

1  A stable distribution will be attained when the value experienced in each habitat is equal.
2  If habitat 1 had higher initial value ($B_1$) than habitat 2 ($B_2$), the density of animals at stability will be greater in habitat 1 than in habitat 2 ($d_1 > d_2$, $d_1 + d_2 = k$).
3  At stability, the ratio of the populations in each habitat will be the same as the ratio of resources available in the habitats, i.e., $d_1/d_2 = B_1/B_2$. This form of the IFD has been called "**habitat matching**" (Pulliam & Caraco 1984). Another way to express this prediction is to say that the proportion of individuals in a habitat should match the proportion of resources provided by that habitat:

$$\frac{d_1}{(d_1 + d_2)} = \frac{B_1}{B_1 + B_2}$$

The general empirical success of the model is impressive, but a number of tests of the predicted distribution indicate consistent deviations from proportional habitat matching (Kennedy & Gray 1993; Tregenza 1995).

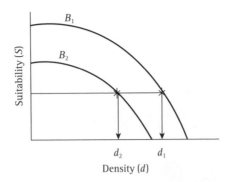

**Fig. 9.5** Value of two habitats ($B_1$ and $B_2$) declines as the density of competitors in them increases. Habitat $B_1$ has a higher initial value than habitat $B_2$. The first ideal free individuals should go to habitat $B_1$. As the density of individuals in habitat $B_1$ increases, its value declines until the value in $B_1$ becomes equal to the value in $B_2$. When this happens, all new arrivals should distribute equally to habitats $B_1$ and $B_2$ until the population has been completed distributed. The stable distribution will have individuals that experience equal values in both habitats but there will be a higher density of competitors in habitat $B_1$ than in $B_2$ ($d_1 > d_2$).

### Testing the IFD

Testing the IFD requires that we apply it to the specific decision of interest. For instance, in a foraging problem we must replace the "value" of a habitat by a more specific state- ment or currency of fitness. We can then use the IFD to generate a prediction based on the hypothesis that animals distribute over concurrently available foraging patches in a way that is consistent with maximizing their rate of energy intake. This is exactly what Harper (1982) did when he and his undergraduate students measured how a population of 33 adult, free-living mallard ducks (*Anas platyrhynchos*), resident in a pond in the University Botanical Gardens of Cambridge University (England), distributed themselves at two feeding stations located 20 m apart on the edge of the pond. The resources available in the habitats consisted of precut, preweighed pieces of white bread that were thrown at constant rates into the water by two student observers. The initial value of the two habitats could be changed in two ways: (i) by changing the rate at which the bread was thrown, and (ii) by changing the size of the pieces of bread thrown into the pond. During the experiments, there was a student observer at each habitat who counted the number of mallards in that habitat at regular intervals. Harper tested two predictions based on maximization of food intake: that the proportion of birds at a site would match the proportion of resources there, and that at stability all indi- viduals in the habitats would obtain similar feeding rates (Fig. 9.6).

He found that when the two sites provided equal food input rates, the birds divided themselves equally between the two sites. When he doubled the food input rate of one of the two sites, the birds reassorted themselves 2 : 1, as predicted by an IFD based on food intake maximization (Fig. 9.6a). He then kept the throwing rates constant at both sites but doubled the size of the pieces of bread at one site, thus doubling its suitability over the other. The birds were tricked at first by the throwing rates and distributed equally between both sites. However, after a few seconds the birds

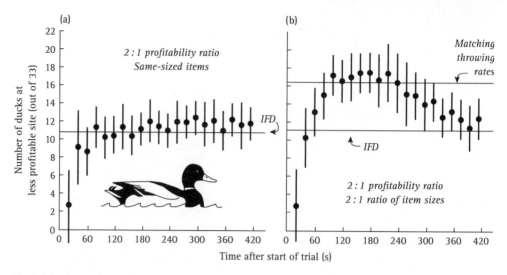

**Fig. 9.6** Duck experiment where students threw bread at two stations on a pond in University Parks, Cambridge (Harper 1982). (a) Students in one station threw bread at twice the rate as in the other. The points show the number of ducks present at the poor patch from the time the experiment began. The horizontal line gives the predicted number using the ideal free distribution (IFD) game, assuming the ducks are designed to maximize their food intake. (b) Students threw bread at the same rate, but in one station the size of bread was double that in the other. The ducks initially used the rate of throwing to distribute but then slowly approached the number predicted by the IFD based on the quantity of food offered. (Modified from Shettleworth 1998.)

redistributed according to the amount of bread being thrown (Fig. 9.6b). However, even though the individuals assorted themselves in an ideal free way, a more detailed analysis revealed that not all ducks were deriving similar feeding rates from their foraging, a clear violation of the second prediction of the game. His results would turn out to be typical of most other studies of the IFD (Kennedy & Gray 1993). Harper's experiment is one you could easily replicate yourselves using a flock of city pigeons.

The IFD has been documented in an extraordinary diverse set of taxa and circumstances (Tregenza 1995; see also Giraldeau & Caraco 2000). In most cases, animals adopt near ideal free distributions despite important deviations from the game's assumptions. The most important and consistent violation of IFD assumptions has been the existence of unequal competitive abilities among animals. Some individuals are simply capable of outexploiting others or of keeping them away from good resource patches (Milinski & Parker 1991). Even when many of these changes in assumptions (unequal competitors, perceptual limitations, costs of moving among habitats, etc.) are dealt with, the outcome has always been similar: a predicted deficit of individuals in the best habitats and slight overcrowding in the poorer ones. Plots of the log ratio of animals in each habitat against the log ratio of resources in those habitats should produce a slope of 1.0 when animals follow the IFD. In their reanalysis of 24 experimental studies of IFD in a range of organisms, Kennedy and Gray (1993) report that in most cases the density of animals in good habitats increases more slowly than the quantity of resources in that habitat. Nonetheless, given the general robustness of this theory to violations of its assumptions, it is no surprise that it has become one of the first important contributions of behavioral ecology to applied issues such as conservation ecology (Goss-Custard & Sutherland 1997; see Chapter 16).

## SUMMARY AND CONCLUSIONS

The existence of natural selection makes it possible to study the adaptive function of an organism's traits. Adaptations are characters that exist as a result of the action of natural selection because they accomplish a function that contributes to an individual's fitness. To study function it is important that the adaptive hypothesis be submitted to scientific testing. This requires generating predictions by using reverse engineering to build an optimality model. Simple optimality and reverse engineering have been used with some success to predict prey selection behavior as well as optimal patch exploitation decisions.

When the payoff associated with a behavioral option cannot be defined without reference to the behavior adopted by other members of the population, simple optimality must be replaced by game theory and the ESS. We used a game-theory analysis of the Hawk–Dove game to show that selection operating at the level of individuals could lead to evolutionarily stable noninjurious fighting strategies. However, we pointed out using the producer–scrounger game that selection does not always lead to maximization of individual fitness. Scroungers occur despite the costs they impose because the only probable evolutionary outcome is a mixture of producers and scroungers. Finally, we considered choice of habitats and the IFD, which predicts that animals should settle in the most profitable habitats. The outcome is that at equilibrium individuals in all occupied habitats should experience the same fitness.

## FURTHER READING

Krebs and Davies (1993) provide an excellent and easy-to-read introduction to behavioral ecology. More about foraging theory can be obtained by reading Dave Stephens and John Krebs' (1986) now classic book. Those who wish to know more about games of foraging should read Giraldeau and Caraco's (2000) book on social foraging. For those interested in more general game theory, Geoff Parker's (1984) excellent chapter as well as John Maynard Smith's (1982) book are two important sources, while Lee Dugatkin and Kern Reeve (1998) provide an up-to-date view of the many applications of game theory in animal behavior. For exploring the interaction between functional and mechanistic approaches students should consider Sara Shettleworth's (1998) excellent book and Reuven Dukas' (1998) multiauthored book on cognitive ecology.

## ACKNOWLEDGMENTS

I thank Johan Bolhuis and Louis Lefebvre for having read and commented on an earlier version of this chapter, and Jerry Hogan for having so convincingly taught me the profitable distinction between cause, mechanism, and function.

# 10
## communication

### PETER K. MCGREGOR

## INTRODUCTION

Communication is an important and often conspicuous part of the behavioral repertoire of animals. It is a topic that links areas of study within behavior and, more widely, it can be a window into the cognitive worlds of animals and also has practical applications of value to us. These are all compelling reasons to study animal communication.

Communication behavior can contribute to esthetic aspects of our lives. It is often spectacular: think of the deafening choruses of cicadas and the pulsating light shows of flashing fireflies. It can also be beautiful: think of birdsong during the dawn chorus and the haunting singing of humpback whales, recordings of which became a best-selling album. Understanding the biological basis for these displays enhances our appreciation of such natural spectacles.

In this section we will look first at the ways communication matters, both to animals and to us, then introduce the terms used when discussing the topic and briefly consider the difficulties of defining communication, before outlining the content of the rest of this chapter.

## Communication matters

### Underlies survival and reproduction

Communication matters to animals because it mediates fundamental aspects of their lives. It is intrinsically part of much social behavior and therefore most aspects of reproduction and survival.

Communication is important at many stages of reproduction. Initially, it brings together individuals of the right gender and species for mating; it also mediates choice for several aspects of mate quality. Communication coordinates the behavior of mates to achieve successful mating, including physiological coordination by stimulating the secretion of sex hormones. If there is parental care, communication is the basis for parent–offspring and parent–parent cooperation.

Communication can also mean life or death. For example, potential prey can be alerted to the presence of predators by warning calls produced by other, possibly related, individuals. Prey communicate with predators too. Species with chemical or physical defenses usually advertise the fact to avoid attacks from predators and the associated risk of damage. Similarly, prey that have detected a stealthily approaching predator may communicate their awareness to the predator. Some predators hijack the communication system of their prey, for example by mimicking the prey's mate-attraction behavior. Communication can be used to indicate the location of food sources and therefore it can prevent individual and colony starvation (e.g., dance language used by foraging honeybees; see below). Defending food resources (e.g., a feeding territory) usually involves communication at each stage of the defense. The ability to defend particular resources (e.g., a nest site) can be a prerequisite for successful breeding, showing how communication links aspects of survival and reproduction.

## Links and interfaces with other disciplines

Communication matters to science in the sense that it links and interfaces with other fields of study. In the study of behavior, Niko Tinbergen identified four types of question that could be asked: **function**, mechanism, **development**, and evolution (see Chapter 1). Communication is probably the area of behavior that best illustrates how answers to all four questions come together to provide more complete explanations.

There are interfaces between communication and many areas of biology, including evolution, ecology, population genetics, neurobiology, and physiology. These can give important new insights; the discovery of seasonal variation in brain volume of birdsong control centers overturned accepted notions of brain neuroanatomy (see Chapters 5 & 7).

There are also interfaces with other sciences. For example, ideas and techniques from psychology are used to understand how communication is perceived, and information from physics and chemistry can help explain how communication is achieved.

## Applications and implications

Communication matters in the sense that it can have applications, for example in pest control, conservation, and **animal welfare**. Studies of communication can also have implications for human behavior. For example, communication can be used to study the cognitive world of animals and the results can influence how we think of, and treat, other species. We will return to these points at the end of the chapter.

# Terms used in communication

## Communication components

There are three major components in communication. The **signal** is the information carrier; examples are a bird's song and the waving of an enlarged claw by a male fiddler crab (*Uca*). The signaler is the animal producing a signal; examples are a singing bird and a waving crab. Such individuals are also referred to as senders, generators, or actors. The receiver is the animal picking up a signal; examples are another bird or crab. Such individuals are also referred to as detectors or reactors. They do not have to be the same species as the signaler.

## Interrelationship between components

Most general explanations of communication show the relationship between these three components as "signaler → signal → receiver" using either words or diagrams. Although this represents the simplest possible communication behavior at one instant in time, it gives a poor indication of the way communication occurs naturally because it omits two features of natural communication systems. First, several individuals can be involved in communication behavior simultaneously, i.e., communication occurs in a network rather than a dyad of one signaler and one receiver (McGregor 2004). Second, the same individual can be both signaler and receiver, either simultaneously or sequentially. Figure 10.1 incorporates both these aspects of natural communication systems and also tries to indicate the dynamic nature of communication.

## Information

This is a fundamental concept of communication because all communication involves **information** (although, as we shall see in the later sections, not everything involving information is communication). The word "information" is used in two senses in the communication literature. In the everyday sense it means knowledge, and this use is sometimes referred to as **semantic information**. Information also has a technical meaning, derived from information theory, a branch of applied mathematics. Sometimes referred to as **statistical information**, the term means the reduction in a receiver's uncertainty following reception of a signal, where uncertainty ($H$) is calculated by the Shannon–Weaver (or Shannon–Weiner) function: $H = -\sum p_i \log_2 p_i$ (where there are $i$ possible behavior patterns and $p_i$ is the probability that the $i$th will occur). The problem with using statistical information lies in determining the reduction in the receiver's uncertainty. Partly for this reason, the term "information" is most commonly used in the everyday sense (i.e., semantic information) and this is how it will be used in this chapter.

(a)

(b)

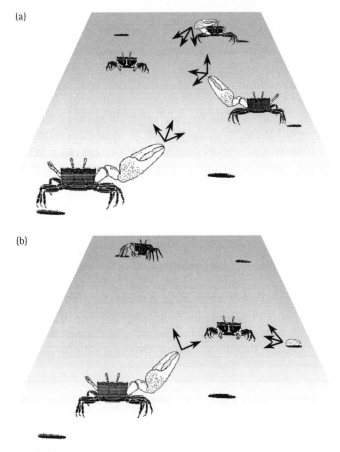

**Fig. 10.1** Representation of a natural animal communication system based on fiddler crabs (*Uca*). The male crabs have one greatly enlarged claw, the major chela, and are associated with a burrow (shown as a dark ellipse). Note that several males are present; most are signaling by waving (indicated by the arrows) and are probably simultaneously receiving. One female receiver (equal-sized chelae) is also shown. The communication network is probably more extensive than indicated because waving males may be received by crabs outside the area shown and signals from this surrounding area could be received by the crabs shown in the diagram. The dynamic nature of natural communication is indicated by the difference between (a) and the situation a few seconds later at the same site (b): one signaler/receiver (top right) has retreated into his burrow; the male middle right is entering his burrow followed by the female; the male bottom left is still waving and has approached the female; and another male (top left, b) has entered the area and is exploring a burrow entrance (i.e., he is receiving but not waving).

### *Transmission medium*

This is what the signal is conveyed by; air, water, or solids depending on the signal in question. For example, the **transmission medium** for birdsong and firefly flashes is air and for humpback whale song it is water. For the **vibrational signals** produced by a rabbit stamping its foot, the transmission medium is the ground.

## Signal modality or channel

This refers to the sense used to detect the signal. The most common **signal modalities** are hearing, vision, and smell/taste. Three less common modalities use the vibration detection sense, the sense of touch, and the electrical sense. Signals may have several features that require different senses to receive. Such signals are referred to as **multimodal**.

We will briefly look at the main features of modalities here. A synoptic treatment of modalities, including the structure and function of signal detectors of the various senses, can be found in Bradbury and Vehrencamp (1998).

- *Visual signals* usually use reflected light but a few animal groups, such as fireflies (actually beetles) and deep-sea fish, can generate light. Many visual signals involve transitory movement, such as the waving of a fiddler crab's enlarged claw or the head-bobbing of a lizard. In contrast, some visual signals can be permanent, such as the colors of reef fish. However, color patterns can also be transitory, by being hidden and exposed (e.g., eyespots on butterfly wings) or by changing the reflectance of the surface – in chameleons (*Chamaeleo*) and cuttlefish (*Sepia*) this is done by changing the shape of the chromatophores, the cells that contain pigment.
- *Acoustic signals* and the closely related vibrational or **seismic signals** are always transitory (cf. permanence of some visual signals). The type of receptor needed to detect sound in air depends on proximity to the source: very close to the signaler (the "near field," defined as within a few wavelengths of the signal's source), sensors need to detect the actual displacement of air caused by the sound; further from the animal than this (the "far field"), sensors need to detect the pressure change caused by the sound. This means that small animals communicating with high-**frequency** sounds at close range will be doing so in the near field and therefore need displacement detectors (e.g., the courtship sounds of the fruit fly *Drosophila* have wavelengths of about 1 cm and the flies court within millimeters of each other).
- *Chemical signals* can be broadcast by diffusion (this is slow because it is limited by the speed of movement of molecules) or by movement of air or water currents (somewhat faster but still limited by the speed of movement of the currents). Alternatively, chemical signals can be deposited on the substratum (e.g., ground or vegetation) and receivers make contact with the chemical signal directly. An example is scent marking by territorial mammals such as hyena (*Crocuta*).
- *Tactile signals* rely on contact between the signaler and receiver and therefore can only operate at very close range. (e.g., beetles touching antennae).

- *Electrical signals* are characteristic of two groups of freshwater fish (African mormyrids and South American gymnotids) that have an electric sense and can generate electrical signals. The electrical impulses are generated by modified muscle or nervous tissue.
- *Multimodal signals* are directed at several senses. For example, the warning signals of some moths use three modalities to communicate with predators: bright colors stimulate the visual sense of birds, sounds stimulate the hearing sense of bats, and chemicals stimulate the smell/taste sense of predators that have caught the moth.

## Defining communication

A common feature of definitions of communication is that they exclude (explicitly or implicitly) an animal achieving an effect on another through direct action; yelling "Go jump in the lake!" is communication, whereas pushing someone into the lake is direct action. Despite the fact that communication is an important and often conspicuous behavior, there has been considerable debate about its definition. There is not space here to go into the details of the debate (for that, see chapter 5 in Dawkins 1995), but it is worth having a brief look at the main issues.

Almost all definitions of biological terms have exceptions, but the diversity of communication virtually guarantees that any definition of communication will have many exceptions. It is these exceptions that lie at the heart of the definition debates. For example, communication is commonly defined as mutually advantageous information exchange. In many cases this definition holds true, but excludes several types of communication such as some **mimicry**. **Batesian mimicry** (in which edible species mimic inedible species) and predators that attract their food by mimicry of prey communication are cases where there is no mutually advantageous information exchange; the mimic (signaler) benefits at the cost of the duped receiver.

Information, used in the everyday sense (see previous section), is a common part of definitions of communication. For example, communication has been defined as the transmission of information. The problem with this definition is that communication (as understood by most people) is only a subset of information transmission. A tree bending in the breeze transmits information about wind direction and strength but we would not call this communication. In the same way, a small mammal moving across the forest floor will generate noise containing information on location that can be used by a predatory owl. Once again, we would not call this communication. Narrowing the definition to "intended information transmission" is an attempt to exclude waving trees and rustling rats as communication. However, this definition raises the practical difficulty of determining what an animal intends.

One definition of communication that works reasonably well in most circumstances is "behavior involving signals." This obviously requires a definition of "signal." If a signal is defined as something evolved (by **natural selection** as described in Chapter 9) to transmit information, the problem of establishing whether information transfer is intentional is avoided. By analogy, we identify a wind vane or wind sock as something that was designed to transmit information on wind direction, whereas the bending of a tree contains such information incidentally. As described in Chapter 9, identifying **adaptations** is not without difficulty, but as much of modern biology involves studying adaptations there are several approaches that can be used (see Chapters 9 & 13). A benefit of the "behavior involving signals" definition is that it draws attention to all three components of communication: the signals, the signalers, and the receivers.

## Outline of rest of chapter

The emphasis in the rest of the chapter is on signals, the transmitters of information unique to communication. After a quick look at signal diversity, we concentrate on the factors that affect signal form, signal origin, and when and where it is best to communicate. The chapter concludes with a brief look at the broader relevance of communication, i.e., its applications and implications.

## Signal Diversity

One of the most striking features of animal communication is its diversity. We have already seen that several signal modalities are used for communication, but within each modality the range of signals is astonishing. To get an impression of this aspect of diversity, think of the varied colors and patterns of tropical reef fish, or the different birdsongs heard during the dawn chorus. Diversity is also generated by graded signals, in which the form of the signal varies with factors such as **motivation** (see Chapter 3). An example of a graded signal is the song used by male European blackbirds (*Turdus merula*) in territorial encounters: the song changes in form as motivation changes (Dabelsteen 1992). Even signals thought to be discrete (i.e., have a fixed form, or are perceived as discrete categories and therefore the opposite of graded signals) can vary somewhat in form between and within individuals and in their rate of performance. Such diversity has been well studied in birdsong (e.g., several chapters in Kroodsma & Miller 1996) and may be ubiquitous in animal signals.

Much of this chapter will examine features that contribute to signal diversity. However, to emphasize that our unaided human senses can only detect some animal signals, we will begin by looking at human perception of signals.

# Human perception of signals

Although signals are known that can be detected by each of the senses of animals, we tend to think of visual and acoustic signals as the most common because these are modalities that humans readily perceive. However, given that chemical communication is particularly common in insects and that this group of animals has large numbers of both species and individuals, chemical signals are probably the most common signal produced by animals.

We may think that we readily perceive acoustic and visual stimuli, but it is important to remember that human perception does not cover the whole range of these modalities used by animal signals (Fig. 10.2). Outside our range of perception our senses need technical help to detect animal signals. Using such aids, we know that animals use acoustic signals with frequencies inaudible to humans, either because they are below the lower frequency hearing threshold of humans (infrasound, e.g., the rumbles of elephants) or because they exceed the upper frequency hearing threshold of humans (ultrasound, used by some insects and rodents) (Fig. 10.2a). Similarly, animal visual signals use wavelengths of light on either side of the spectrum visible to human eyes; examples are the ultraviolet colors of some birds and butterflies and the infrared light generated by some deep-sea fish (Fig. 10.2b).

In many ways it is easier to study signals that we can only detect with the help of technology, such as the electrical signals of fish, because then we go some way toward avoiding the problem of **anthropocentrism** in animal communication.

## Signal Form

One way of making sense of the bewildering diversity of signals is to look for common influences on their form. In this section we look at what influences the form of a signal, i.e., the modality used to transmit information and the signal's information content. Signals are adaptations that carry information and, as with any adaptation, natural selection has to work within constraints that are inherent in the original material. In terms of signals this means constraints (properties) of the signal modality. Two other major influences on signal information content are environmental effects and conflicts of interest between signalers and receivers.

## Properties of signal modalities

Each signal modality has inherent properties, such as speed and pattern of spreading, that create opportunities for natural selection to fashion signals but which also limit its scope. Four of these properties are particularly relevant to animal signals: **speed of propagation, persistence, directionality**, and effect of obstacles.

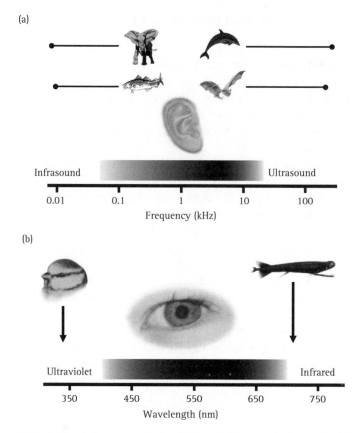

**Fig. 10.2** Human perception in relation to animal signals (compiled from several sources). (a) Hearing: humans are most sensitive to frequencies from 1 to 4 kHz (densely shaded part of bar; note log scale) but can hear loud sounds above and below these frequencies (lightly shaded part of bar). Examples of animals that produce sounds outside the normal human hearing range are elephants and cod, which produce lower frequencies than humans can hear (infrasound), and bats and dolphins, which produce higher frequencies than humans can hear (ultrasound). (b) Vision: humans are most sensitive to wavelengths of light between red and violet (densely shaded part of bar) as a consequence of the three types of cone found in the retina (red, sensitivity peak at 575 nm; green, 535 nm; blue, 435 nm). Many parts of animals reflect wavelengths of light shorter than humans can see (ultraviolet, < 400 nm), including the head of blue tits (*Parus caeruleus*). Some animals, such as the deep-sea dragon fish (*Malacosteus*), generate wavelengths of light longer than humans can see (infrared, > 700 nm).

## Speed of propagation

Visual signals travel at the speed of light ($\sim 300 \times 10^6$ m/s in air) and are therefore propagated almost instantaneously over the range of distances that animals communicate. Although the speed of light in water is 75% of that in air, the speed is so high ($225 \times 10^6$ m/s) that signal propagation is still essentially instantaneous. Chemical signals are the slowest traveling signals because they rely for propagation on diffusion or the speed of movement of air or water currents (of the order of a few meters per second) and propagation can take anything from a few seconds to some days. Acoustic signals achieve intermediate speeds of propagation that depend on the medium in which the signal is generated. Sound travels at about 340 m/s in air and about five times faster in water. Vibrational signals could be considered to be sound transmitted in solids and travel at about 5000 m/s. Tactile signals propagate instantaneously as the signaler and receiver are in physical contact. Electrical signals are also propagated instantaneously.

The speed of propagation of signals of all modalities is affected by the transmission medium's physical state (e.g., temperature). The effects are appreciable for acoustic signals in air. The speed of sound (sound velocity) in air varies from 331 m/s at 0 °C to 349 m/s at 30 °C. The relative humidity of air has a smaller effect on sound velocity (about an order of magnitude smaller than temperature effects), for example sound velocity in air at 20 °C and 0% relative humidity is 343 m/s, whereas at the same temperature at 100% relative humidity it is 345 m/s.

One effect of the speed of propagation on communication concerns signal timing. The relatively slow speed of sound in air means that the relative timing of signals produced by animals separated by a few hundred meters can be perceived quite differently by the individuals concerned and by other receivers (conspecifics, predators, or humans) depending on their positions in relation to each other (Dabelsteen 1992). Such effects are negligible for visual and electrical signals because of their high speed of propagation.

### Persistence

An important feature of chemical signals is that they can persist, a feature related to their slow speed of propagation. A chemical signal such as a rodent scent mark can persist for several days, even weeks, in the absence of the signaler. This means that in contrast to most other signal modalities, receivers can come to the signal rather than letting it come to them. It also means that the signal can transmit information after the signaler has died. This feature is used to good effect in the alarm **pheromones** generated by social insects such as ants defending their nests: the defenders may have died but their chemical signal will continue to recruit other colony members to the defense of the nest.

As mentioned above, there is also a sense in which some visual signals persist. Permanent visual patterns, such as the warning black and yellow stripes of stinging wasps, persist in that they can be detected whenever the individual is present and conditions allow, for example the individual is in the line of sight of the receiver and illuminated (e.g., by daylight).

However, the rate at which a signal can vary in time is inversely related to the signal's persistence. Chemical signals rapidly lose temporal patterning in the release of chemical, whereas signals of other modalities do not. Very rapid changes of light, sound, and electricity are generally maintained during propagation (e.g., the frequency and **amplitude** changes of a bird's song and the intensity, duration, and interval between each flash of light emitted by fireflies). In modalities that allow rapid patterning of signals, the extent of such patterning is determined by the production apparatus and perceptual mechanism rather than anything intrinsic to the modality.

## *Directionality*

Signals of all modalities tend to spread out from their source. The extent to which a signal can be made directional depends on the signal modality and specific features of the signal.

Visual signals are sometimes claimed to be inherently directional on the basis that signalers and receivers have to be in line of sight for communication to occur. Although it is usually true that obstacles can block visual signal propagation, this does not mean that a visual signal is inherently directional. However, some visual signalers have behaviors that act to make their signals more directional. An example is the cuttlefish, which can restrict changes in body surface coloration to the side of the body closest to a particular receiver.

The directionality of acoustic signals depends on the wavelength of the sound in relation to the size of the signaler, with higher frequency (i.e., shorter wavelength) sounds being easier to direct. As a consequence of the frequencies they sing and their size, many songbirds are reasonably directional (about as directional as a hi-fi tweeter). Their commonly observed behavior of turning in several directions during bouts of singing may be a way of broadcasting their signal more widely. Dolphins use a kind of acoustic lens on their head (the "melon organ") to produce a highly directional beam of sound.

Chemical signals are spread in the direction of movement of the medium, carried on currents of water or air. This might seem to indicate that the direction of spread is outside the control of the signaler. Although this assumption is generally correct, some animals create currents to direct their chemical signals. One example is the crayfish *Astacus*, which fans urine (known to contain chemical signals) toward opponents in aggressive interactions.

## *Effect of obstacles*

The visual modality is usually singled out as being particularly vulnerable to obstacles in the propagation path, but obstacles also affect propagation of signals of other modalities. The effect of an obstacle on an acoustic signal depends on the obstacle's size relative to the wavelength of the sound. Sound with a wavelength longer than the obstacle's size will pass around it, sound with a much smaller wavelength will be reflected, and sound with about the same wavelength as the obstacle will be refracted (bent) to a greater or lesser extent around it. Some species, such as bowerbirds, remove items that are potential obstacles to visual signals from display sites. However, in most cases the easiest way to overcome the effects of obstacles is for the signaler or the receiver to move so that signals are no longer blocked.

## Environmental effects on signals

Although not obstacles as such, the particular propagation conditions can have import-ant consequences for the broadcasting of a signal. Such conditions can be the result of the habitat, particularly vegetation in a terrestrial habitat, or the activities of signalers of the same or different species. Signals and signaling behavior can also be affected by the presence in the environment of "unwanted" receivers, called **eavesdroppers**.

## Habitat effects on signal propagation

Signals change during propagation, sometimes to the extent that although a receiver can detect them, they cannot be discriminated. An example we are all familiar with is attempting to hold a conversation over a distance (or in conditions) where we can detect that another person has shouted something but we cannot discriminate the words. This change results from **signal distortion (degradation)** by the transmission medium and habitat during propagation. It is accompanied by an overall loss of energy contained in the signal (attenuation) caused by the signal spreading out. The effect of **signal attenuation** can be considerable; usually the amount of energy contained in a signal falls exponentially with distance from the transmitter.

The acoustic and visual propagation conditions of a forest that has lost all its leaves in winter and the same forest in summer are very different. Transmission conditions also differ greatly between an open field or grassland and a forest. Habitat differences such as these affect the propagation of signals of all modalities to some extent and have consequences for both the form of signals and where signalers produce them (Endler 2000). Such effects have been best documented for birdsong (Fig. 10.3) and bird and fish coloration (see Endler 1993; Marshall 2000).

## Interference from other signalers

As we all know from our experience of trying to talk when several others are talking, an important environmental "obstacle" to communication is the signaling activity of others, particularly of the same species. Such interference from other signalers can be severe in communication networks with a high density of signalers, for example an adult penguin returning to feed its chick has to make its call heard and also hear its chick in the cacophony of the breeding colony. Receivers have a number of perceptual adaptations that increase their ability to detect signals in noise (Langemann & Klump 2004). Signalers also adapt their communication behavior. For example, male frogs calling in a chorus are usually less successful in attracting a female and in subsequent mating if another calling male is close by – there is competition between the males' signals for "airtime" and thus female attention and also actual physical competition to mate with the female. This can lead to males varying the timing of their calls in relation to close neighbors and chorus synchrony (Grafe 2004). It can also have a more physical manifestation: males may fight to displace others that are calling from close by and small males may move away when a large male begins calling near them.

Over evolutionary time, it is the characteristics of the signal that are displaced rather than close neighbors. Traditionally, it has been assumed that the important selection pressure is the attraction of the right species. This is often reported as a lack of overlap between the signal characteristics of two species living in the same area (sympatric species) compared with the same two species living alone (allopatry) and is a type of character displacement (see Chapter 13). This difference is usually interpreted as divergence of

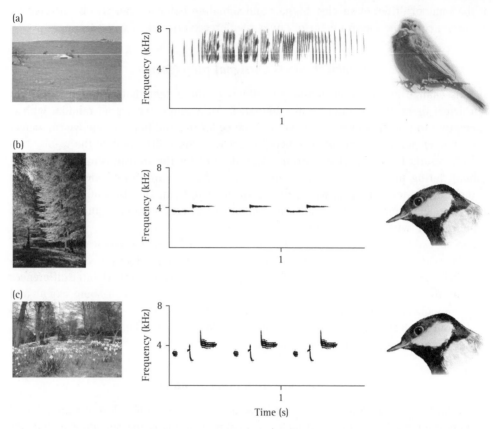

**Fig. 10.3** Habitat effects and propagation of birdsong. Habitat-related variation in song structure between species can be seen by comparing (a) and (b). The same effects can be seen within a species by comparing (b) and (c). Songs are shown graphically as spectrograms, i.e., frequency vs. time plots of amplitude. Representative habitats are shown on the left and the songbird species on the right. (a) Species found in open habitats such as cereal fields and grasslands (e.g., corn bunting *Miliaria calandra*) sing songs with rapid temporal patterning (trills rather than whistles) that cover a wide frequency range. Degradation in open habitats is mainly caused by irregular changes in air temperature and wind speed. (b) Species found in deciduous woodland (e.g., great tit *Parus major*) sing songs with rather little rapid temporal patterning and rather low mean frequencies. These features minimize the effect of signal degradation by reverberation (echoes) caused by the many reflecting and refracting surfaces (e.g., leaves and tree trunks). (c) Great tits in parkland sing songs with more notes per second and a wider frequency range than great tits singing in woodland (cf. b). Parkland has a lower density of smaller trees and shrubs than woodland and degradation conditions in parkland resemble open habitat more than woodland.

calls in sympatry over evolutionary time so that species characteristics do not overlap and therefore mistakes in species identity are not made. Such a difference is found in two species of south-eastern Australian frogs: in allopatry both species produce pulsed calls at 70–85 pulses/s, but in sympatry one calls at less than 70 pulses/s and the other at more than 130 pulses/s.

## Eavesdropping

In the previous section we saw that signals could be affected by one aspect of the social environment, namely the activity of other signalers. Another aspect of the social environment that affects signals is the presence of receivers that are not the primary target of the signaler but which nevertheless use information in the signal. Such receivers have been called eavesdroppers and are of two sorts (Peake 2004). The first sort intercepts signals directed to other receivers, usually at the cost of the signaler. Good examples of such **interceptive eavesdropping** are predators that use the mate-attraction signals of other species to prey upon them (e.g., bats that prey upon calling male frogs). In many instances the response of signalers to the presence of eavesdropping predators is to stop signaling. However, signals warning of the presence of a predator must necessarily be produced in its presence and therefore could be intercepted. In such circumstances the form of the signal has evolved to reduce the opportunity for interceptive eavesdropping. For example, great tits (*Parus major*) give a characteristic "seet" warning call in response to aerial predators. Great tits have an auditory system that is particularly sensitive to frequencies of 8 kHz, closely matching the frequency of the "seet" call. However, their commonest aerial predator, the sparrowhawk (*Accipiter nisus*), is not so sensitive to this frequency (Klump et al. 1986). As a result, the predator can less easily eavesdrop on its prey.

The second sort of eavesdropper obtains information from a signaling interaction between others, an interaction in which the eavesdropper does not take part. Such **social eavesdropping** is expected to be common because interactions are a rich source of information on relative aspects of the animals involved. Laboratory experiments on fish using visual signals and experiments in the field with territorial songbirds have shown social eavesdropping by both sexes: males eavesdropped on aggressive signaling interactions between other males and females eavesdropped on male–female courtship interactions (Peake 2004). The presence of social eavesdroppers can change signaling behavior and the form of signal used in interactions. For example, many songbirds use "quiet" song (a form of song that travels only short distances) in circumstances when they wish to restrict social eavesdropping (Dabelsteen 2004).

In many, but not all, circumstances eavesdropping shows the conflict of interest that characterizes much of communication. We will explore such conflicts in more detail in the following section.

# Conflicts of interest between signalers and receivers

Although early ideas about communication assumed that information transmission was to the mutual benefit of signaler and receiver, it is now clear that there are usually conflicts of interest between them (sometimes referred to as payoff asymmetries; see Chapter 9). This realization has led to several ideas that can explain features of signals that were puzzling, such as the difference in conspicuousness of signals used in different contexts. It has also identified the sources of the conflicts of interest between signalers and receivers. These ideas are important for understanding the information content of signals and how signals may have evolved.

## Coevolution, arms races, and honesty

The conditions for **coevolution** exist when two groups of organisms exert a selection pressure on each. Signalers and receivers coevolve in the same way as other well-known examples of coevolution: predators and their prey, flowers and their pollinators, hosts and their parasites. (However, interesting differences can result when signaler and receiver are the same species, and when the same individual can, in quick succession, play signaler and receiver roles.) When the interests of signaler and receiver largely coincide, signals tend to be rather inconspicuous. Such signals have been called "conspiratorial whispers." An example are the sounds uttered by crop-raiding monkeys when the farmer appears; these sounds are too quiet to be heard by the farmer but loud enough to sound the alarm for other monkeys raiding the crop, with the result that the monkeys leave without attracting the attention of the farmer. When the interests of signaler and receiver differ, the conditions for an **evolutionary arms race** are established (see Chapter 13). We can think of such arms races as analogous to the advertising we are all familiar with: as receivers (potential buyers) experience more and more adverts (signals) we are less likely to be influenced by them (we develop "sales resistance"); in response the advertisers (signalers) have to increase their "salesmanship," working harder to make us buy, for example by introducing humor, vivid graphics, or louder sounds into adverts. So the sales resistance of receivers drives signalers to increasing levels of salesmanship. The result of a difference in the interests of animal signalers and receivers is that signals can become elaborate, exaggerated, and conspicuous (Dawkins & Krebs 1978). The dramatic train of male peacocks (*Pavo*) and complex birdsongs are likely results of such coevolutionary arms races. (Of course this communication-based explanation is a part of, and consistent with, the workings of **sexual selection** and mate choice discussed in Chapter 11.)

One aspect of sales resistance in receivers is that signals might be expected to contain honest information. **Honest signaling** has received considerable attention in three contexts: mate choice, resource defense, and predator–prey interactions. There has been considerable debate about how honest signals can be ensured in mate choice and resource defense. If honest signals are difficult or costly to produce, the signal's honesty is ensured because only individuals with the necessary ability or resources can produce the signal. For example, imagine that an individual's body size is related to its ability to defend a resource such as a breeding territory; imagine also that the size of the individual determines the frequency of its call. In such circumstances (which may occur in some frogs and toads) the call would contain honest information on territory defense ability because the frequency of the call would be determined by the individual's size, which in turn determines its territory-defending abilities. The idea that signal cost ensures honesty lies at the heart of the considerable debate about the role of **handicaps** in communication (Zahavi 1993; Getty 1998). Handicap in this context refers to the conspicuous cost of the signal, a cost that diverts resources away from other aspects that might otherwise increase the **fitness** of the signaler (in our hypothetical example above this would mean that the energy used to call could otherwise have been used to grow a larger body). However, the debate is complex and various types of handicap are now recognized; I strongly recommend those interested in handicaps to read chapter 5 in Dawkins (1995). Other conflicts of interest between signalers and receivers in mate choice and resource defense contexts are well covered by Chapters 11 and 13 as well as by other authors (Maynard Smith 1994; Bradbury & Vehrencamp 1998), so here I briefly look at the predator–prey context.

Prey sometimes signal their ability to escape if attacked, and these signals are often called **pursuit-deterrent signals**. Such predator-directed signals might be expected to be honest, otherwise predators would not be deterred from pursuing the signaling prey. Honesty in this sense means that only prey capable of escaping the predator would be capable of producing the signal (for a formal treatment see Getty 2002). Examples that seem to fit these requirements are the jumping displays (stotting) performed by gazelles (*Gazella*) in the presence of wild dogs (*Lycon*) and the singing of skylarks (*Alauda*) when chased by merlins (*Falco*).

Signals used by mimics in a predator–prey context are clearly not honest. (As we might expect there are exceptions to this general statement. The biggest class of such exceptions is the striking resemblance between different species that are all dangerous as prey. This is termed **Mullerian mimicry** in order to distinguish it from Batesian mimicry, in which harmless prey gain protection by mimicking dangerous prey (see below). Most species of sea snake are poisonous and therefore dangerous prey and they have a very similar pattern of warning coloration. They are considered an example of Mullerian mimicry and their convergence on a single warning pattern is thought to result in more rapid avoidance **learning** by predators.) A clear example of dishonest signaling by predators involves two species of firefly. Females of one species (*Photuris*) mimic the pattern of flashes used by females of a different species (*Photinus*). As a result, the *Photuris* "femme fatale" attract and prey upon male *Photinus*. This example, and others like it, have made it apparent that two further selection pressures act on the nature of information contained in signals: rare enemies and **relatedness**. We will look at these factors in the next section.

### Rare enemies and relatedness

Two factors that can result in the persistence of communication even when signalers have very different benefits from receivers (i.e., large payoff asymmetries) are the frequency of occurrence of the signal and the degree of relatedness between signaler and receiver. The most extreme payoff asymmetries are found when the signal is a rare occurrence (rare enemy effect) and involves communication between different species. Examples in which the interests of signaler and receiver differ greatly are predatory firefly mimics and their prey (see above) and Batesian mimics (e.g., edible hoverflies Syrphidae that gain protection from bird predators by mimicking the black and yellow abdominal stripes of stinging social wasps Vespidae).

The most striking examples of cooperative signaling occur in circumstances where (i) relatedness favors cooperation in general (see Chapter 14), namely when individuals within a species are closely related (e.g., social Hymenoptera, see honeybee dance language discussed at the end of this chapter), or (ii) communication takes place between species. Striking images of cooperation between species often feature in television natural history programs. One example is a small African bird, the honey guide (*Indicator*) that feeds on the developing brood found in nests of bees. The nests are usually inaccessible to the bird (e.g., in a tree trunk); when it locates a nest it will call and display to humans, leading them to the nest so that they can break into it. The humans eat the honey and the bird eats the brood. Another striking case of cooperation involves species that remove external parasites from other species. The best known is the cleaner fish (*Labroides*), a small wrasse that cleans "clients" many times its size, clients that would be quite capable of eating it. To minimize this risk, the cleaner performs a visual display toward a potential client and the client usually adopts a posture to indicate willingness to be cleaned. Although this may be the usual pattern of communication between cleaner and client, there are several interesting complications that result in variations in signaling by the cleaner and illustrate the effect on communication of changing payoff asymmetries (Bshary & D'Souza 2004).

## Signal Origins and Information

How signals originate, i.e., how they evolved to become specialized to carry information, is an important question in the study of communication. The question focuses attention on the information that signals contain and in this section we will also look at two rather tricky issues: inferring the function of a signal and incidental information content.

### Signal origin

Two ways in which signals originate have been suggested: **ritualization** and **sensory exploitation**. Each of these ways differs in who benefits from the information in the signal. The first, ritualization, follows from the assumption that both signaler and receiver benefit from the information transfer (see also Chapter 13). Ritualization assumes that signals originate as a consequence of selection for increasing efficiency of information transfer. In ritualization, a behavior that initially contains some information evolves into a signal, i.e., a behavior selected to contain such information. Ritualization generates a signal by the simplification, exaggeration, repetition, and increased **stereotypy** of the behavior that predated the signal (sometimes termed the signal precursor). Three types of behaviors commonly become ritualized.

1 Intention movements: these occur immediately before a behavior (because they prepare the body for the behavior that follows). An example is a dog baring its teeth before attacking.
2 Displacement activities: these are behaviors that seem to be out of context and may be related to motivational conflicts (see Chapter 3). An example is a bird preening itself in the middle of an aggressive interaction.

3  Autonomic responses: these are usually involuntary changes that control the body's state (e.g., temperature, oxygen levels). An example is the way many mammals raise their body hair before physical activity in anticipation of the need to lose heat.

Sensory exploitation (see also Chapter 13) follows from the view (Dawkins & Krebs 1978) that communication is the manipulation of receivers' behavior by signalers. In sensory exploitation, signals exploit "preexisting **sensory biases**" built into receivers (Chapter 13). For example, male spiders use signals for mate attraction that stimulate females' prey-detection receptors.

Signal origin is an aspect of the evolutionary history of an adaptation and can employ techniques used to infer historical aspects of adaptation more generally (see Chapter 13). Bradbury and Vehrencamp (1998) give examples of plausible evolutionary histories and signal precursors for signals of several modalities.

## Inferring signal function

The discussions in much of this chapter assume that we can identify signals. Although this may be true, in many cases it is much more difficult to determine the information content that a signal has been selected to contain, i.e., the function of the signal. These difficulties are apparent when considering two common ways of deducing the function of a signal.

### Deducing the function of a signal from context

In some instances, the function of a signal would seem to be obvious from the context in which the signal is given. For example, male songbirds in temperate regions sing during the period of the year in which they breed, and therefore it seems reasonable to conclude that song has something to do with reproduction. More specific contextual information (including more singing during male–male encounters and before males acquire a mate) suggests a dual function of territory defense and mate attraction. (However, it has been suggested by Searcy and Nowicki (2000) that the evidence for this conclusion needs to be reexamined.) A case in which it is now accepted that the original function was misidentified is the "food calling" of plunge-diving feeders such as terns (*Sterna*). These species often feed on dense shoals of fish and call when doing so. Initially, calling was interpreted as a signal to attract conspecifics to the food source. However, careful observations revealed that birds only called immediately before diving and that there were collisions between diving birds and others preparing to dive (the collisions were usually fatal to both birds). It now seems reasonable to interpret these calls as warning calls evolved to clear the diver's path (much as an outfielder yells "My ball!" when rushing in to make a catch). This example shows how contextual evidence for signal function needs to be used with care: it was the dangerous diving aspect of the feeding context that was important rather than the food availability with which it was correlated.

### *Deducing the function of a signal from matches between characteristics of signal and receptor*

Another way of identifying the function of a signal is the match between the characteristics of the signal and the receptors of the presumed receiver. It would seem obvious that receivers should have sense organs that have sensitivities matching the characteristics of the signal if the function of the signal has been correctly identified. An example is the match between the sensitivity of great tits to frequencies of 8 kHz and the frequency of their "seet" alarm call warning other great tits of the presence of an aerial predator (see above). Similarly, the ultraviolet (UV) wavelengths of light reflected from some bird plumage are similar to the maximum sensitivity of the UV-sensitive cones in their retina (Cuthill et al. 2000).

However, a match between signal and receptor organ is not universal. For example, many reef fish reflect in the UV but are probably unable to detect such wavelengths as adults (Marshall 2000), raising the possibility that the signal may be directed at juvenile conspecifics or possibly UV-sensitive predators. A more obvious mismatch is found in deep-sea fish that emit infrared light. The dragon fish *Malacosteus* (Fig. 10.2b) emits light with a wavelength of 705 nm, but has no receptors sensitive to this wavelength. It overcomes this limitation with a fluorescent molecule that, when stimulated by infrared light, emits light that stimulates its green–blue receptors (Douglas et al. 1998). The message of this finding is that correspondence between signal and receptor can be complicated and likely to be overlooked, with the consequence that the match between signal and receptor properties may not give a simple indication of the function of a signal.

## Incidental information

An issue related to the previous section is whether the information contained in the signal has been selected to be present or whether it is present for other reasons. For example, the nature of sound production in many animals means that there is a relationship between the size of the caller and the frequency of its call (bigger individuals have lower frequency calls). Although it is possible that this aspect of the signal was selected for, it is also possible that it is a byproduct of the way that sound is generated. It is difficult to decide between these possibilities. If receivers can extract information on the caller's size from the frequency of the call, this shows selection for that ability of receivers. However, it does not mean that the call was selected to contain such information. This is an important point because information on aspects of the signaler (e.g., quality) is of great interest in studies of sexual selection (see Chapter 11) and yet may be present in signals incidentally.

A related question is whether the components of apparently multimodal signals are the product of selection for a multimodal signal or whether they are byproducts of production of one modality. For example, fiddler crabs strike the ground with their enlarged claw, producing substratum-borne (seismic) vibrations and airborne sound. These crabs have sensitive seismic detectors but they cannot detect airborne sounds. In this case it would seem probable that the signal is present in one modality (vibration) and the sound is an incidental consequence of signal production.

## When and Where to Communicate

The **decision** or motivation to communicate rather than perform any other type of behavior (including achieving an effect on another individual through direct action) is influenced by many factors that may change rapidly from moment to moment (see Chapter 3). However, given that the decision to communicate has been made, we would expect animals to do so in the most effective way. Two factors that affect efficiency are the choice of when to communicate and from where. The efficiency of signaling and receiving behavior should be affected by similar factors, although receiving is a less obvious behavior than signaling and therefore considerably less is known about it in natural contexts. Most of what is known about receiving behavior comes from studies of the abilities of animals to perceive information of all kinds in their environment (see Chapter 2), of which signals are a subset.

### When to communicate

The best time to signal varies from second to second and also over much longer time scales. Spring in temperate zones of the world is characterized by long-range mate attraction and territory defense signals, such as birdsong and the choruses of frogs and insects. Seasonal triggers of breeding, such as rainfall in equatorial areas, occur throughout the world and are usually accompanied by the signals of breeding animals. There are noticeable annual cycles in signaling behavior. Indeed, since much animal behavior occurs in cycles (see Chapter 4) it is not surprising to find cycles in signaling behavior. Such cycles include the **circalunar** and **circatidal** cycles shown by aquatic or intertidal animals, such as the waving of fiddler crabs, and the marked **circadian** cycles of birds (e.g., dawn chorus) and fireflies (e.g., **nocturnal** activity).

Similar considerations apply to receiving behavior, but there has been little study of these factors. It might be expected that conditions for receiving would vary cyclically because propagation conditions are known to vary on various time scales (see above). A social context in which receiving would be favored is signaling interactions between others because this is when information on relative aspects of the signalers would be easiest for the receivers to extract (see social eavesdropping above).

### Where to signal

As explained above, various environmental factors affect signal propagation. As these effects vary with location, careful choice of a signaling location can have important consequences for the effectiveness of signaling. Studies of the propagation of birdsong in forests have shown that the perch height that favors best song propagation is lower than that which favors best sound reception. Another well-described effect is the influence of incident light regimes in terrestrial and aquatic environments. Chemical signals propagated by wind or water currents will be most effective if produced at locations that best exploit these currents.

An interesting finding in frogs is that the water temperature of the calling site can alter the frequency of the call; therefore, the nature of the signal has been altered by the choice of signaling site. This is taken a stage further by those animals that modify the acoustic properties of the calling site. Mole crickets (*Gryllus*) call from a burrow they dig in the shape of an exponential horn, a shape that amplifies the call in the same way as the horn attached to early gramophone players. Similarly, some tree crickets (e.g., *Oecanthus*) limit the spread of their calls by chewing a hole in the leaf from which they are calling, very like the way that the housing of a loudspeaker limits the spread of sound in a hi-fi system (by acting as an acoustic baffle).

Another aspect of where to communicate relates to the use of space. One of the many considerations here is how to ensure that the signal covers the area of interest. One solution is to produce (or deposit in the case of scent marks) signals around the perimeter of the defended area. Given such a pattern of signaling, it might be expected that receiving would often take place on perimeters, always assuming that such perimeters can be detected.

## The Broader Picture: Applications and Implications

In the introduction to this chapter, it was pointed out that communication is fundamental to the lives of animals: to quote the first sentence of a book on the evolution of communication "Nothing would work in the absence of communication" (Hauser 1996, p. 1). This importance of communication opens up opportunities for using animal communication in pest control, conservation, and welfare.

## Pest control, conservation, and welfare

### Pheromones and insect pests

Many ways of reducing the numbers of pests do so by disrupting their breeding behavior. For example, the chemical signals used in mate attraction (sex pheromones) can be used to control insect pests like the tsetse fly (*Glossina*). The insects are attracted by the sex pheromones emitted from a box and when they enter the box they are killed, usually electrocuted by the high-voltage grid in the box. A major advantage of such a system is that it only attracts the pest species because sex pheromones are so species-specific. Another advantage is that the type of selection pressure that pheromone traps exert on the flies is very different from that exerted by an insecticide. Exposure to insecticides selects for individuals resistant to the insecticidal chemical and therefore pest control becomes less effective until new insecticides are developed. In contrast, pheromone traps favor flies that respond weakly to the pheromone (because they are not attracted to the traps and therefore are not killed). However, such unresponsive individuals are unlikely to detect the sex pheromones of a potential mate, and therefore they fail to find a mate and breed. Pest control is still effective but is just achieved by another route. The subtlety of such a system and the lack of "collateral damage" are in stark contrast to the widespread application of broad-spectrum insecticides. Many applications that use an understanding of animal communication are characterized by this subtlety.

### Conservation and bird vocalizations

At the heart of any conservation effort is the need to identify species and to count (census) the number of individuals in a population (see also Chapter 16). Long-range advertising signals in most signal modalities are species-specific. We can readily identify bird species from their long-range vocalizations and also use vocal activity to estimate population sizes. Vocalizations allow species to be identified and counted when they cannot be seen because of dense vegetation or a nocturnal pattern of activity. In consequence, vocalizations form the basis of many bird census techniques. More detailed information, such as survival, habitat use, and immigration rates, can be obtained from individually identifiable birds. Such identification is often achieved by adding marks such as leg bands; however, there are circumstances when such marks are undesirable (disturbance of catching, modification of behavior) or ineffective (they cannot be seen). Techniques that allow individuals to be identified from distinctive aspects of their vocalizations can be useful in such cases. As these techniques use naturally occurring variation they can be used to assess the biases inherent in catching, marking, and resighting processes (further details in McGregor et al. 2000).

### Welfare, husbandry, and communication

It has been argued that animals can communicate their need honestly in some circumstances and therefore we can use such communication to assess their welfare. The squealing of piglets during weaning and procedures such as castration are circumstances where the signals are likely to be honest (see Chapter 15).

A failure to consider the communication behavior of captive animals can adversely affect their welfare. An example that illustrates this point comes from the best of motives: cleaning rodent cages to prevent disease. Many rodents use urine and feces as scent marks, with the result that their cages rapidly become extensively soiled. However, frequent cleaning removes these marks and the disturbance caused by scent-mark removal can distress the animals to the point that females cannibalize their litters. Partial cleaning of cages so that some scent marks remain minimizes disturbance while maintaining adequate hygiene.

A case where communication has been overlooked, rather than being in conflict with husbandry, involves ultrasound in rodents. Rat pups and other infant rodents emit ultrasonic calls when distressed (e.g., when they have fallen out of the nest). These calls are similar to ultrasound emission by equipment such as video monitors that may be close to their holding cages in a laboratory. The noise from such equipment could adversely affect the welfare of captive adults and infants. In a domestic setting, the same considerations apply to pet rodents and computer monitors or television screens. The potential importance of scent marks and ultrasound noise is recognized by their inclusion in the Code of Practice issued by the UK Home Office (www.homeoffice.gov.uk/animalact/hcadb4.htm), arguably the world's most stringent requirements for the housing and care of animals.

## Language and cognition

Historically, communication has played a central role in discussions of animal cognition (Griffin 2001; see also Chapter 8); this in turn influences the way we think of, and treat, other species. The question of whether any nonhuman animal communication can be considered to be a language is of perennial interest to the general public and the media, as well as to many scientists. Often language is defined in such a way that the only possible answer to the question is no. This is obviously the case if the definition is a description of features of human language. However, as most people consider (rightly or wrongly) that language use indicates high cognitive ability, identifying language-like features in animals can have important consequences for how we consider them and therefore their welfare and perhaps conservation.

Do other animals show features of human-like language? Two approaches have been used to answer this question. The first relies on identifying key features of any language and looking for evidence of similar abilities in animal communication. The second approach looks for evidence that animals can acquire human or artificial languages. This approach seeks to discover whether nonhuman animals have the cognitive abilities to use language, regardless of whether they do so naturally, and therefore links the issues of communication and cognition. Both approaches have generated considerable discussion and controversy (see Hauser 1996 for details).

### *Language-like features*

Two features commonly thought to be properties of any language are ability to communicate information on objects or events that are remote (in time and space) and use of signals that are referential (symbolic). Unlikely as it may seem, honeybees (*Apis mellifera*) clearly show the first of these features in their **waggle dance**, often referred to as a dance language in consequence. Karl von Frisch was awarded a Nobel prize for the early work establishing that worker bees returning to the hive from a newly discovered source of food can recruit other workers to exploit this resource; more importantly, the returning workers communicate its location to the new recruits. The way information on location is transferred has been established by various experiments, usually using von Frisch's technique of creating new food sources by setting out saucers of sugared water. The waggle dance is now sufficiently well understood that a dancing robot bee can direct new recruits to locations at the whim of the robot operator. The dance follows a figure-of-eight pattern. It is performed by returning worker bees on the vertical face of the honeycomb in the darkness inside the hive. When moving in a relatively straight section of the dance (i.e., going toward the top of the figure of eight), the dancing bee makes a number of rapid side-to-side movements of the abdomen (the waggles) and the number of waggles encodes the distance to the food source. The angle, relative to the vertical, of the straight section in which the bee waggles (the waggle run) encodes the direction of the source relative to the sun. Two pieces of extra detail show that the bees are transmitting information about food that is remote in space and remote in time. First, the waggle dance is only performed if the source is further than 100 m from the hive (i.e., remote in space). Second, the dance can be performed some time after the food was found, meaning that direction in relation to the sun will have changed. The dancing bees adjust the angle of the waggle run to compensate for movement of the sun (i.e., the information is remote in time).

Some animal alarm calls may be examples of the use of signals that are referential. Several species of primates and birds have different alarm calls for different predators. The call's specific reference to the type of predator appears similar to the use of a specific word in human speech. For example, vervet monkeys (*Cercopithecus aethiops*) have alarm calls for leopards, eagles, and snakes. In response to such calls from other vervets and to playback of recordings of the calls they will, respectively, run up a tree, dive into thick cover, or stand up on their hind legs (Cheney & Seyfarth 1990). As such alarm calls elicit a response that is specific to the predator, this would seem to be similar to a human yelling the warning "Leopard!" and eliciting a response different from that produced by the more general warning "Look out!" There is debate about how similar the use of such alarm calls by animals is to the use of a specific word in human speech and therefore whether animal alarm calls can be considered symbolic (also termed "referential") communication and therefore language-like.

### Acquisition of human language: talking parrots and signing apes

Some primates, marine mammals, and birds have been taught to use languages (for details see Chapter 8). The aim of these studies was to show that some nonhuman animals have the ability to use language. The results are contested, but the fact that there is room for discussion at all suggests that nonhuman animals perform similarly enough to humans to challenge the view that our use of language sets us apart from other animals.

Perhaps a more interesting aspect of these studies is that language can be used to explore the cognitive abilities of animals in much the same way that questioning humans can. So Alex the parrot, who famously communicates with human speech (Pepperberg 2000), can be asked directly about features of objects such as color, shape, and number, and his answers can be interpreted as cognitive **insights**. Such insights must be inferred indirectly from animals that cannot be directly questioned in this way.

## SUMMARY AND CONCLUSIONS

Communication is behavior involving signals (where signals are adaptations for transmitting information) and often occurs in a communication network of several signalers and signal receivers. Many aspects
of survival and reproduction are mediated by communication and therefore it is an important and often
conspicuous part of animal behavior. Signals are diverse, with several signal modalities (e.g., vision,
hearing, smell) used for communication, and it is worth remembering that humans cannot detect many
animal signals unaided (e.g., UV color patterns of butterflies and the ultrasonic calls of bats). Some
signal diversity can be explained by inherent properties of the modality (e.g., light signals travel faster
than chemical signals) and the effects of the propagation environment (e.g., low-frequency sounds
generally suffer less distortion in dense vegetation than high-frequency sounds). Signal diversity also
results from conflicts of interest between signalers and receivers, often characterized as a coevolutionary
arms race. Large differences in interest can persist when signalers are rare (e.g., "femme fatale" fireflies).
Signals originate by ritualization (of behaviors that incidentally contained some information such as
intention movements) or by sensory exploitation (i.e., signals use the preexisting sensory biases of
receivers). Animals are adept at communicating at appropriate times (on time scales from seasonal to
second by second) and from suitable locations, sometimes even creating such sites (e.g., amplifying
burrows of mole crickets). In a wider context, communication has applications in pest control, conservation, and welfare (as a consequence of the importance of communication to animals), and aspects
such as language-like features are prominent in considerations of cognitive abilities.

## FURTHER READING

The chapter on communication by Dawkins (1995) clearly explains the most problematic aspects of the topic and is an essential foundation for a deeper understanding. Read
alongside a recent review (Johnstone 1997), it also explains much of the interest of the
research reported by current papers in scientific journals (e.g., *Animal Behaviour*). There
are several sorts of book that deal solely with animal communication. Popular accounts
(Uhlenbroek 2002) are the easiest to read and are often beautifully illustrated. Their disadvantage is that references to the source of the information rarely appear in the text,
making it difficult and time-consuming to delve deeper into topics. Specialist texts do
reference their sources, but they are usually harder to read. Some cover the whole topic
of animal communication (Hauser 1996; Bradbury & Vehrencamp 1998) and therefore
run to several hundred pages. Others are selective and concentrate on particular signal
modalities such as pheromones (Wyatt 2003) or on a group of animals such as arthropods
(Greenfield 2002). Many do both, for example dealing with acoustic communication
in insects (Gerhardt & Huber 2002) or birdsong (Catchpole & Slater 1996; Kroodsma &
Miller 1996). Books on one particular aspect of communication, such as communication
networks (McGregor 2004), usually encompass several modalities and taxonomic groups.

# 11
# mate choice, mating systems, and sexual selection

ANDERS PAPE MØLLER

INTRODUCTION

Male crickets *Gryllus integer* sing to attract females but thereby run the risk of being parasitized by tachinid flies that are also attracted to the calls (Cade 1975). Similarly, foxes *Vulpes vulpes* prey on peacocks *Pavo cristatus* that are likely to be easier to catch because of their cumbersome ornamentation, with exaggerated feathers that weigh more than 1 kg and when wet after a shower more than 3 kg (Petrie 1992). How can such apparently maladaptive traits that reduce the probability of survival evolve? Charles Darwin developed the theory of **sexual selection** to account specifically for the evolution and maintenance of exaggerated traits that do not benefit the individual in terms of survival prospects. Many characters, such as the antlers of deer, the train of the peacock, the calls of frogs and crickets, and the exaggerated body size of one sex but not the other in the gorilla *Gorilla gorilla*, can be attributed to the effects of sexual selection. Sexual selection is a result of nonrandom variance in **mating success** in one or both sexes. It is important to note that males (or females) may vary in mating success for simple stochastic reasons: for example, because of random rates of encounter with individuals of the other sex, and because of a finite number of individuals in the local neighborhood. Nonrandom variation in mating success (hereafter called variation in mating success) may result in the evolution of exaggerated traits when there is a **quantitative genetic** basis (several genes with additive effects on the expression of a trait) for such traits and when individuals with more extreme **phenotypes** enjoy increased mating success.

Sexual selection differs from **natural selection** in terms of the kinds of characters that can be attributed to the two processes of sexual selection (**intrasexual selection**, usually male–male competition, and **intersexual** selection, usually female mate choice) and, therefore, in terms of the effects of the two kinds of processes on the relative importance of survival and mate selection. While natural selection results in the evolution of traits that are beneficial in terms of survival, sexual selection is generally detrimental to the survival of individuals. The reason for this effect is that traits that become exaggerated by sexual selection may progress beyond the optimum under natural selection, because of the mating advantages that they confer. However, phenotypic traits can become immensely exaggerated and cumbersome to the extent that males suffer dramatic reductions in survival prospects; this process of exaggeration will continue as long as some males are more than compensated for the costs by advantages in terms of mating success.

Why is sexual selection important? Sexual selection accounts for most differences in phenotype between males and females, and an understanding of any phenomenon that can be attributed to differences between the sexes among reproducing adults can only be achieved by considering sexual selection (see Chapter 12). Since sexual selection usually affects males and females differentially, ecological questions such as the distribution of males and females can also only be understood by considering sexual selection. Sexual selection also has profound effects on the mortality rates of the two sexes, the stochastic component of population fluctuations in the numbers of individuals of the two sexes, the probability of and variance in successful reproduction, and hence the likelihood of survival of a population. An understanding of basic problems of conservation biology (see Chapter 16) will generally require that differences between males and females are taken into consideration when attempting to calculate population viability or components of risk of extinction of small populations. Finally, most aspects of life among adult humans differ between men and women, and we can only understand such differences and the social, psychological, and medical problems that they cause by considering sexual selection (see Chapter 17). Thus, we cannot understand ecology, life-history theory, conservation problems, or human existence without considering sex and sexual selection.

This chapter starts with a definition of **mating systems** and their determinants. Next, I describe male–male competition and its consquences. In the third part, I analyze female choice and the adaptive and non-adaptive bases for mate choice. In the fourth part, evolutionary conflicts between the sexes and their consequences are discussed briefly (this phenomenon is treated more extensively in Chapter 12). Fifth, I investigate the cost of **secondary sexual characters** and its ecological and evolutionary consequences. In the sixth part, the reasons for the presence of multiple secondary sexual characters and their significance are discussed. In the final part, I analyze **sex ratio** theory and how it relates to sexual selection.

## Mating Systems

Mating system is the label used for describing the way in which males and females are distributed in reproductive units, and the consequences of this distribution for reproductive behavior and parental care. Why are some species **polygynous** (one male, several females), whereas others are **polyandrous** (one female, several males)? Why do females in most mating systems provide parental care whereas males less frequently do so? Before answering these questions we have to remember that a mating system is more than meets the eye. Although a **monogamous** mating system is described as a reproductive relationship between a single male and a single female, sexual relationships between a "monogamous" female and other males may render the term "monogamy" redundant. Great advances during the last 15 years in the study of parentage as a result of the introduction of molecular genetic analyses have clearly demonstrated that social and **genetic mating systems** are sometimes not at all congruent. This superimposition of social and genetic mating systems can most readily be resolved by considering that sexual selection is a sequence of selection events starting from the acquisition of a social mate, time required for acquiring and processing these mates, followed by copulation, fertilization, abortion, infanticide, parental care, and differential parental investment (Fig. 11.1). Intraspecific variation in each of the variables in Fig. 11.1 may be associated with the expression of male secondary sexual characters. For example, attractive peacocks with extravagant trains have shorter search time, take shorter time to handle a female, and thus have a shorter mate processing time. This results in such males having more copulation partners and hence higher fecundity. Such attractive males cause females to invest differentially in offspring, which increases fecundity per mate, again increasing total fecundity. Since attractive peacocks also have

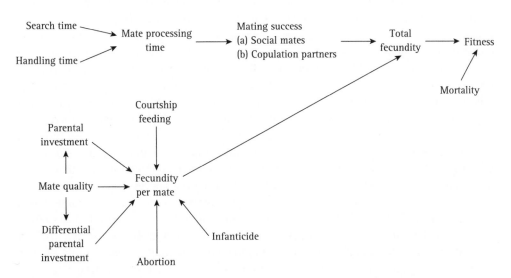

**Fig. 11.1** Mating system described as a sequence of sexual selection events. (Adapted from Møller 1994.)

lower mortality, total **fitness** is presumably greater for the most attractive males. Thus a thorough description of the mating system requires quantification of components of sexual selection at these different sequential stages and their interactions.

Behavioral biologists have described a wide variety of mating systems in different taxa. How do mating systems arise? What determines whether males, females, or both are the choosy sex? Originally, Bateman (1948) showed that although female fecundity in *Drosophila* fruit flies did not increase after mating with a couple of males, male fecundity continued to increase with number of mates. Thus, the two sexes should differ in their willingness to mate since only males would benefit from continued mating with additional females. Hence male fruit flies should seek additional females, whereas females should be reluctant to mate and therefore become choosy. Later Emlen and Oring (1977) suggested that the **operational sex ratio**, defined as the ratio of fertilizable females to sexually active males at any given time, is the main determinant of the opportunity for sexual selection. For instance, when many females are available per male we expect that the mating system is biased toward polyandry (many males, one female), whereas a male-biased operational sex ratio should result in a polygynous or **lekking** mating system. However, several studies have indicated that there is no clear relationship between operational sex ratio and stronger sexual selection for male traits favored in competition over mates and thereby mating systems. For example, female water striders *Gerris odontogaster* are generally reluctant to mate, but this reluctance decreases when the sex ratio becomes male biased (Arnqvist 1989, 1992). Males of this species use an abdominal grasping organ for holding on to reluctant females, and the success of males with large abdominal organs decreases with increasing male-biased sex ratios. Hence, female behavior may clearly influence the strength of sexual selection. Clutton-Brock and Vincent (1991) suggested that relative reproductive rates, measured as the potential rate of offspring production of the two sexes, should reflect their relative level of sexual competition. In an extensive review of animal species with exclusively male parental care, they revealed that almost all cases could be predicted from the rate of offspring production of males relative to females. For example, in some species of pipefishes in which males carry embryos in a placenta-like structure, males take longer to produce a brood than do females. Males therefore have slower reproductive rates than females, and they are predicted to be less intensely sexually selected than females. Indeed, females are larger and more colorful than males in these species, in accordance with the prediction (Berglund et al. 1989). Such male limitation of female reproductive success is rare, and polyandry is therefore much less prevalent in the animal kingdom than is polygyny.

Although mating systems may be explained by a number of ecological or evolutionary factors, as described above, we should not forget that particular mating associations may arise for entirely random reasons. For example, Sutherland (1985) showed that chance alone can generate a sex difference in variance in mating success, and he was able to explain Bateman's famous result in fruit flies simply on the basis of randomness. Surprisingly, a simple null model based on chance alone has only recently been developed to predict variation in mating systems. Bessa-Gomes et al. (2003) created artificial populations of males and females in a computer program, and by using finite populations of males and females randomly skewed sex ratios were demonstrated to cause clear patterns in mating systems. This was the case even without any variation in parental

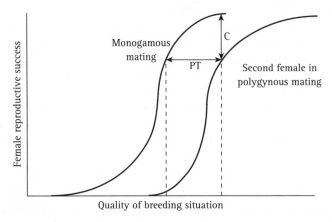

**Fig. 11.2** Polygyny threshold model with curves showing the fitness of females in terms of reproductive success of monogamously mated and secondary polygynously mated females. C, cost in terms of fitness for a female mated to an already-mated male; PT, polygyny threshold, i.e., gain in breeding situation necessary for a female settling on the territory of an already-mated male compared with an unmated male. (Adapted from Orians 1969.)

care or the strength of mate preferences by individuals of the two sexes, implying that the operational sex ratio was not the important factor resulting in a particular mating system. For example, lek breeding systems may arise due to randomly skewed sex ratios biased toward females, whereas polyandry may arise when the reverse sex ratio is found. Thus, random factors in small populations may cause a skew in sex ratio, giving rise to particular mating systems, even without any effects of operational sex ratio.

Modeling of mating systems may thus provide important information concerning evolution. A good example of a heuristic model is the **polygyny threshold model**, first proposed by Verner (1964) and Orians (1969). If females and males are distributed according to the distribution of resources, and if individuals of the choosy sex behave as if individuals of the chosen sex are yet another resource, we can predict the distribution of females and hence the mating success of males. The polygyny threshold model suggests that sometimes a female may be better off by becoming a secondary female of a polygynously mated male rather than the mate of a monogamous male on a poor-quality territory (Fig. 11.2). The polygyny threshold is thus the difference in quality of the breeding situation for a monogamous and a secondary female, whereas the cost incurred by a female for settling with an already-mated male is described by the difference in reproductive success between a simultaneously mated monogamous and secondary female. Recently, Pribil and Searcy (2001) have provided experimental evidence for red-winged blackbirds *Agelaius phoeniceus* consistent with these predictions.

## Intrasexual Selection

Intrasexual selection is a very important force resulting in the evolution of armament and greater body size in one sex compared with the other. This component of sexual selection is usually male–male competition because males gain higher reproductive success by acquisition of additional mates, although female–female competition is intense in the relatively few cases when polyandry has evolved. Therefore, males will typically compete with each other for access to more or higher quality females, and the outcome of such competition is decided by differences in brute force or armament between the contestants. Males and females often differ in body size, and such differences may be consequences of natural or sexual selection. Either sex may enjoy an advantage of small or large body size, and sex differences in such advantages may account for the evolution of **sexual size dimorphism**. For example, in some species females with larger body size may have higher fecundity and therefore enjoy an advantage over smaller conspecifics of the same sex. In other species small females may enjoy a selective advantage because they mature earlier and have shorter generation times. Similarly, in males large body size may be advantageous because larger size provides an advantage in competition over females or resources. However, in other species, such as some spiders, small body size may be advantageous because small males are more maneuverable, mature earlier, and have higher success in certain kinds of competition.

Interspecific patterns of sexual size dimorphism have received considerable attention. For example, Arak (1988b) investigated sexual size dimorphism in nine species of anurans in relation to the difference in selection gradients between individuals of the two sexes. The selection gradient is estimated as the partial regression coefficient of relative fitness on the trait (in this case, body size). A positive difference in selection gradient implies that males benefit more from large size than do females, whereas a negative difference implies the reverse situation. Indeed, species of anurans with relatively large males had a greater selective advantage of large body size for males than for females. Similarly, Alexander et al. (1979) investigated sexual size dimorphism in pinnipeds, ungulates, and primates including humans and found consistent evidence across taxa of greater dimorphism in species in which reproducing males were able to monopolize a larger number of females. Perhaps surprisingly, Alexander et al. (1979) even found evidence of greater sexual size dimorphism in human societies with a higher frequency of polygyny, suggesting that sex differences in body size within species evolve readily in response to differences in selection pressures on the two sexes. Arak (1988) found evidence of a similar intraspecific phenomenon among populations of anurans.

Extravagant weaponry such as spurs, horns, antlers, and exaggerated canines in males are commonly found across many taxa. The evolutionarily stable level of weaponry is predicted to reflect the size of contested groups of females. Males have been shown to use their weapons in fights with other males, providing a direct link between morphological structure and context of use. Although large morphological characters may appear to have a **function** as weapons, alternative explanations should also be considered. Male characters may also play a role in defense against predators, although this hypothesis has received little support. Packer (1983) in his analysis of horns in African antelopes showed convincingly that males have evolved large horns that are thicker at the base compared with horns in females. Female horns are mainly present in antelopes with large body size, and their straight and thin structure make them eminent stabbing devices when encountering or defending offspring against a predator. The greater thickness of male horns seems to have evolved directly in response to selection for greater strength,

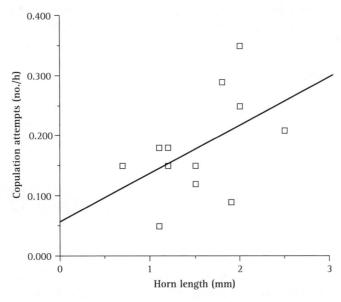

**Fig. 11.3** Male mating success in relation to horn length in the forked fungus beetle *Bolitotherus cornutus*. (Adapted from Conner 1989.)

since males have a higher frequency of broken horns compared with females. Male characters have also been suggested to function as **signals** of strength to other males or as indicators of sexual vigor to choosy females. There is very little evidence for these alternative explanations, although the few and generally small experimental tests may caution against any general conclusions.

Several studies have suggested that males with large degrees of weaponry indeed enjoy a mating success through male–male competition. The forked fungus beetle *Bolitotherus cornutus* is a small beetle that lives on or near fungi growing on the bark of deciduous trees in North America. Conner (1988) has extensively analyzed the relationship between length of male horns and sexual selection, after controlling statistically for potentially confounding factors such as body size. Selection analyses revealed a positive association between horn length and male success (Fig. 11.3), supporting the prediction that males benefit in terms of sexual selection by having long horns. In this species females do not appear to choose mates based on horn length.

The role of male–male competition in the evolution and maintenance of weaponry is further supported by the evolution of defensive properties in males of the same species. Any male able to sustain a blow from the weapon of a competitor would potentially enjoy an advantage. Hence, Jarman (1989) argued that there should be selection for thick skin in males of species that have evolved weaponry. Not only is the skin of males thicker than that of females in large herbivores, it is also relatively thicker in the particular parts of the body that commonly receive blows during fights. Kangaroos use feet for fighting and therefore the skin has become thicker on upper parts of the body that are subject to scratching. In antelopes that use horns for fighting, the skin has become thicker on flanks and other places susceptible to injury by horns. Such differences in skin thickness between the sexes and among species would be difficult to explain except when viewed in the light of sexual selection and the evolutionary **arms race** of armament and counterarmament.

Males differ considerably in the architecture of their weaponry, from pointed stabbing devices in some antelopes, through broad shovel-like structures in some deer, to intricate branched structures in beetles and deer and elaborate lifting or grasping devices in beetles. The variety of use of weapons fully matches the variety of morphological structures that have evolved. Hence, interpretations of function of weapons will rely on observation of the actual behavior during male–male interactions in fights.

## Intersexual Selection

### Female preferences

Intersexual selection occurs because individuals of the two sexes differ in their reproductive rates and hence in their willingness to mate. Usually females do not benefit from mating with additional males because it does not increase their fecundity, whereas males benefit from mating with additional females. Females are therefore choosy in most mating systems, whereas male choosiness occurs in polyandrous and monogamous mating systems. Females often show considerable concordance in mate preferences, with most females agreeing upon which potential partner is most attractive. This is epitomized in lekking species where one or a few males may account for most matings, and the remaining males have few or no matings at all. This is all the more surprising given that any genetic benefit should long have been depleted due to persistent directional selection. Why females show great consistency in mate preferences despite the genetic benefits being small constitutes the so-called lek paradox.

Quantitative genetic studies (which compare the phenotype of offspring with that of their parents) or selection experiments (in which individuals with extreme phenotypes are selected each generation and used as breeders to produce the subsequent generation) of more than 25 species have shown that mate preferences have a significant **heritability** (Bakker & Pomiankowski 1995). This implies that mate preferences can readily evolve and that any changes in the costs and benefits of such preferences may result in microevolutionary change. The environmental determinants of mate preferences are linked to previous or current experience, own phenotype, and own attractiveness. For example, studies of the stickleback *Gasterosteus aculeatus* have shown that females in prime condition show stronger preferences for males with sexual coloration than do females in poor condition (Bakker et al. 1999). Similarly, studies of preferences for facial characteristics in terms of asymmetry in humans show that women who themselves are attractive also have a strong preference for more attractive men (Little et al. 2001). Such a preference can be beneficial if women mated to a relatively attractive partner invest relatively more in reproduction (see Differential investment below). Differential investment in reproduction will be costly, and the ability of women to make such an investment may depend on their own condition.

Mate preferences can be considered to have two components: the preference curve and the behavioral **decision** rule that a female uses to choose a mate. Female mate preferences can be described by the mathematical function that accounts for the relationship between intensity of preference and expression of the male trait. Several theoretical models have assumed that preference functions have an intermediate maximum, reach an asymptote, or are "open-ended," i.e., "more is better." Empirical studies of a few invertebrates have suggested that the shape of preference curves may often be open-ended. Decision rules have been hypothesized to be based on random choice, sequential assessment, or a best-of-$n$-males rule (Janetos 1980). Empirical studies of individual females and their mate-searching behavior under field conditions suggest that females often visit a number of males, albeit a relatively small number (usually less than 10), before making a mate choice. Females will often return to a previously visited male and mate with that particular individual. For example, a study of great reed warblers *Acrocephalus arundinaceus* using females provided with transmitters that allowed radio-tracking showed that each female on average only visited six males (range 3–11 males) before making a choice, and that females followed a best-of-$n$-males rule of mate choice (Bensch & Hasselquist 1992). Thus, there is much evidence that females do not choose the first best male they encounter but spend considerable amounts of time and energy searching for mates, thereby running risks of being eaten by a predator, infected by parasites, or being too late to find an appropriate mate and hence lose the possibility of any reproduction at all.

The evolutionary origin of female mate preferences has received considerable attention. Some theories suggest that preferences evolved in conjunction with male traits, whereas other theories propose that the female preference in fact predates the evolution of the mate preferences. For example, Ryan et al. (1990) suggested that **sensory exploitation** is the basis for evolution of male traits. Female mate preferences for particular traits in frogs and fish appear to be present in a group of species that evolved earlier than the group with the male trait. Such analyses are inherently only as reliable as the **phylogenetic** hypothesis on which they are based (see Chapter 13). They also make assumptions about the origin of male traits, and the absence of as yet undescribed or extinct species renders this hypothesis difficult to test.

## Benefits of mate choice

Why should females go to great lengths in finding a particular partner rather than mating with any randomly chosen individual? Given that females spend considerable lengths of time and amounts of energy on mate-searching behavior, we can infer that there are considerable benefits accruing to choosy females, otherwise natural selection would have eliminated choosy females from the population. Female mate preferences have long been suggested to arise and be maintained in order to allow mating with individuals of the right species. There is very little empirical evidence supporting this hypothesis, and it is only presented here as a matter of completeness. Fitness benefits accruing to choosy females are traditionally categorized as direct or indirect benefits. **Direct benefits** are material benefits that females obtain in the current generation, whereas

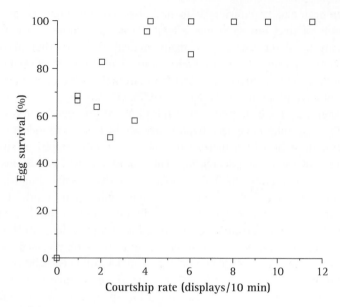

**Fig. 11.4** Egg survival (%) in relation to male courtship rate in the bicolor damselfish *Stegastes partitus*. (Adapted from Knapp & Kovach 1991.)

**indirect benefits** are genetic benefits that females gain through their offspring in the subsequent generation. Given this time delay in acquisition of indirect benefits, we can predict that direct benefits will be more important than indirect ones. Theoretical models have generally not considered direct material benefits because the mechanism and the advantages are so intuitively simple that no underlying formal genetic model is needed and no problem of maintenance of genetic variation arises. **Direct fitness benefits** accrue to a choosy female if the expression of a secondary sexual character directly reflects the quality of a territory, the quality or the quantity of male parental care, the quality of sperm provided by a male, or simply the absence of any directly transmitted disease from a male to his partner (and then on to the offspring). An example of a direct fitness benefit is the study of parental care in the bicolor damselfish *Stegastes partitus* (Knapp & Kovach 1991). Males of this fish court females vigorously, but males differ considerably in the intensity of their courtship **display**. Females prefer males that court more intensely. Males that courted females more intensely were also more efficient at providing paternal care, measured as the survival rate of eggs (Fig. 11.4), and females therefore benefit directly from their mate choice.

Surprisingly, many species show exactly the opposite pattern, with attractive males providing *less* care than unattractive males (see Differential allocation below), and general patterns of sexual selection for direct fitness benefits therefore need to be considered carefully. Numerous studies have investigated how the expression of male traits reflects the magnitude of direct fitness benefits. Møller and Jennions (2001) quantitatively assessed the literature and found that male traits or attractiveness on average accounted for 6.3% of the variance in direct benefits in terms of fertility of eggs, for

2.3% of the variance in fecundity in females through courtship, food, or ejaculate components, for 1.3% of the variance in male parental care in terms of feeding of offspring, and for 23.6% of male parental care in terms of hatching rate in male-guarding ectotherms. Thus although some systems, such as egg-guarding fish, provide considerable amounts of direct fitness benefits that far exceed the genetic benefits in terms of "**good genes**" (see below), the direct benefits for species of birds with male provisioning of offspring are on average of a magnitude similar to the indirect benefits of "good genes." Why there are such large differences among ectotherms and endotherms remains to be determined.

Indirect fitness benefits are genetic benefits that accrue to choosy females through offspring, i.e., through delayed effects in the subsequent generation. The initial hypothesis for such indirect fitness benefits is due to Ronald Fisher (1930), who suggested that mate preferences and male secondary sexual characters would **coevolve** to ever more exaggerated versions, provided that both were partly genetically determined. Imagine that initially males differed slightly in morphology and females in their ability to perceive such differences. Females that were better able to discriminate among potential partners would tend to mate with males that were first detected. Such pairs would produce sons that had slightly enlarged characters which could more readily be detected and daughters that also had a strong preference for such males. Genes for male trait and female preference would tend to co-occur in the same individuals and hence become linked. During subsequent generations both male trait and female preference would coevolve in a **runaway** fashion to ever more extreme versions, until one or both traits had gone to fixation (i.e., no more genetic variability present because all individuals only had the dominant alleles since these alleles would confer the greater selective advantage) or until the benefits for males in terms of mating success were balancing the costs in terms of reduced viability due to the presence of the exaggerated male trait. A pure **Fisherian character** will not show any signs of condition dependence but entirely rely on attractiveness to females for its maintenance. This is the reason why pure Fisherian traits can be distinguished from **condition-dependent traits** (e.g., those associated with the "good genes" hypothesis; see below) by differences in the relationship between character size and viability; males with the most exaggerated traits are likely to survive better if the traits are condition-dependent (Jennions et al. 2001). In practice, it is difficult to distinguish between this hypothesis and the hypothesis of "good genes" (see below) because sample sizes need to be sufficiently large to conclude that the generally small effects of "good genes" are absent in purely Fisherian traits. However, the Fisher hypothesis will always be at work if the assumptions of the model are met. Many traits in species with little or no direct fitness benefits of sexual selection are therefore likely to show a component of Fisherian attractiveness.

"Good genes" provide genetic benefits that accrue to choosy females as a consequence of mating with an attractive partner. If the secondary sexual character reflects the genetic constitution of a male, a female mating with an attractive male may produce offspring that inherit the genetic qualities of the father. For example, the expression of a secondary sexual character may directly reflect the ability of an individual to resist parasites (Hamilton & Zuk 1982), and attractive males will thus tend to sire resistant offspring. Alternatively, attractive males may sire offspring that have general high viability independent of disease resistance. An example of the effect of "good genes" is offspring viability in the gray tree frog *Hyla versicolor*. "Good genes" effects are difficult to estimate because breeding designs must take maternal and common environment effects into account. Welch et al. (1998) used a clever breeding design controlling for such effects by randomly allocating males to groups of females. This allowed estimation of the offspring viability effect to 10.4% of the variance in viability among sires. Although this breeding design forcefully controlled for any obvious effects of maternal or common environment, it did not control for differential investment effects by females due to differences in perceived quality among sires.

How large are the so-called "good genes" benefits in general? Møller and Alatalo (1999) quantified "good genes" benefits in terms of increased viability of offspring sired by attractive males, and found that viability increased by about 1.5% due to "good genes" effects across 22 species. There were significant differences in the magnitude of the viability effect, with studies of birds showing stronger effects than studies of other kinds of organisms. In addition, species with a stronger skew in mating success among males indeed had greater "good genes" benefits, as predicted if the basis for the generally strong consistency in mate preferences among females in lekking species is offspring viability benefits. Although this effect may seem extremely small, a viability difference of this magnitude is very large on an evolutionary time scale, and costly female mate preferences can readily be maintained by the presence of such a "good genes" effect.

Hamilton and Zuk (1982) suggested that male sexual displays may reliably reveal the health status of a **signaler** because only high-quality individuals would be able to sustain attacks from parasites. Choosy individuals could thus obtain reliable but indirect **information** on the level of resistance of a male to parasites by simply inspecting costly secondary sexual characters. Numerous studies have investigated this hypothesis and found general evidence for males with larger degrees of ornamentation indeed having fewer parasites than the average male in the population (review in Møller et al. 1999). The original hypothesis of Hamilton and Zuk was based on an argument about resistance. Hence, this hypothesis makes predictions about the level of resistance rather than the level of parasitism (the latter might reflect exposure as well as resistance). A quantitative analysis of the literature revealed that measures of immune response were better predicted by the size of secondary sexual characters than were parasite loads (Møller et al. 1999). Hence, females seem to be better able to obtain reliable information on immune responses than on parasite loads by assessing male secondary sexual characters. Saino et al. (1997) showed that male barn swallows *Hirundo rustica* with long outermost tail feathers, which are the subject of a directional female mate preference, have better immune responses than short-tailed males, and that an experimental elongation of tail length causes a reduction in antibody production to challenge with a novel antigen. Antibody titers of males were a very good predictor of male survival during the annual migration to sub-Saharan Africa and back, independent of tail manipulation, with naturally long-tailed males surviving the best. This suggests that the male secondary sexual character subject to a female preference provides direct information about the ability of males to produce an immune response, and that both male trait and its information on immune status are reliable predictors of survival prospects.

The immune system is a very costly physiological defense system that is closely integrated with the endocrine system, sexual selection, and life history. The link between sexual display, immune function, and endocrinology was formalized by the **immunocompetence handicap hypothesis**. Folstad and Karter (1992) suggested that the level of reliability of sexual signals may come about because the ontogeny of such displays is under the influence of the endocrine system, which in turn may have detrimental effects on the immune system. Hence, individual signalers might be forced to adjust their level of signaling to their body condition because otherwise they would risk sacrificing their own survival. The original hypothesis was based on the enhancing effects of testosterone on the level of sexual display but antagonistic effects on immunity; effects of other hormones or indirect effects of hormones on sexual display are also possible. Yet another twist to this story was raised by von Schantz et al. (1999), who proposed that the currency of extravagant sexual display and efficient immune defense is free radical scavengers such as carotenoids and vitamins A and E. Since many sexual displays are based on carotenoids and since carotenoids cannot be synthesized but only obtained through ingestion, individual signalers would have to allocate limiting amounts of carotenoids to sexual signals and competing physiological functions such as immunity and free radical scavenging (Møller et al. 2000). In this scenario, individuals may have to balance the use of such antioxidants to sexual signals and to physiological functions such as immunity and detoxification.

Recently, more than 100 studies have investigated the relationship between bilateral asymmetry and sexual selection. The basis for this interest is that small differences in morphology between the two sides of the body may reveal **developmental instability**, which is defined as the inability of individuals to develop a stable phenotype under given environmental conditions. Small asymmetries are generally randomly directed, with most individuals in the population being symmetrical. Choosy individuals may benefit from having a symmetric partner because such a partner is better at providing parental care, since an asymmetric phenotype interferes with efficient locomotion. However, since the same patterns are found across taxa independent of parental care, it is possible that the advantage accruing to choosy individuals is in terms of the ability to produce offspring with a symmetric and regular phenotype. Many experimental studies and observations have shown that the degree of **fluctuating asymmetry** of an individual is negatively associated with mating success or attractiveness (reviews in Møller & Thornhill 1998; Møller & Cuervo 2003). This holds for visual, auditory, and olfactory signals and for as diverse organisms as insects, fish, birds, and mammals including humans. These patterns are independent of publication bias and other sources of error (Møller & Cuervo 2003), and the relationships are as strong as for character size in the species where both relationships have been investigated (Thornhill & Møller 1998).

A third genetic hypothesis concerning mate choice is based on **genetic complementarity**. Individuals that differ in alleles at particular loci may enjoy an advantage in terms of fecundity. For example, individuals with different alleles at loci of the major histocompatibility complex (MHC, an assemblage of loci involved in production of immune defenses) are able to produce more diverse defenses against parasites than individuals with similar alleles. Hence, a female able to recognize the genotype of a potential mate through its phenotypic characters and preferentially mate disassortatively with males with a complementary genotype would produce more viable offspring. This mechanism has been suggested to account for mate preferences for males that differ in body odor in mice and humans, since MHC genotype can be directly assessed from odor (Wedekind et al. 1995). The generality of preferences for genetic complementarity in animals remains to be determined.

The distinction between genetic and nongenetic components of sexual selection is far from trivial, and empirical tests addressing these issues have been marred by the difficulties of partitioning the variance into its various component parts without confounding genetic effects with **maternal effects** or **common environment effects**. A particularly interesting phenomenon that seems to bridge the "good genes" effects and maternal effects is differential parental investment. Females of several species have been shown to invest differentially in reproduction when mated to an attractive partner. For example, Nancy Burley (1986) showed for the zebra finch *Taeniopygia guttata* that females mated to males with attractive red leg rings worked harder, laid more eggs, and reproduced more frequently than females mated to males with unattractive green rings. This maternal effect of differential investment is costly to females since the increased parental activity and the elevated rate of reproduction are costly in terms of time and energy use and in other respects. In a field experiment de Lope and Møller (1993) manipulated the length of the outermost tail feathers of male barn swallows after males had acquired a mate. Subsequently, females mated to males with elongated tails worked harder in terms of feeding of offspring than did females mated to males with shortened tails. This feat was repeated in the second brood, since females mated to tail-elongated males more often laid a second brood and also worked harder than their mates when feeding the offspring. Females mated to presumably attractive, long-tailed males suffered a reduction in survival of 20% as a consequence of these kinds of maternal effects. Subsequent studies have shown similar effects of differential parental investment in many other species, including differential allocation of testosterone, antibodies, and antioxidants by females to their eggs depending on the phenotype of the male partner (Gil et al. 1999; Petrie et al. 2001). Costly maternal effects can only be maintained in the population if females benefit in terms of increased viability of offspring and/or increased mating success of their sons. Thus, the mere presence of maternal effects underlying differential parental investment suggests strong indirect fitness benefits of mate choice.

## Sexual Conflict

Male and female evolutionary interests are rarely if ever congruent, and sexual conflicts of interest are a direct consequence of sexual reproduction and differences in selection pressures on individuals of the two sexes. This subject will be dealt with in greater depth in Chapter 12, but it is important to make a few general points here that link conflict and mating systems. Such conflict can be a great force in evolutionary divergence. For example, Eberhard (1996) suggested that female control of fertilization has resulted in very strong selection pressures on males, leading to divergent evolution in reproductively related phenotypic traits. A case in point is the evolution of genitalia, which generally show dramatic divergence compared with other morphological traits, the one and only other exception being secondary sexual characters. This divergence in genital morphology is so dramatic that species identification in invertebrates is often based primarily on such characters. Arnqvist (1998) demonstrated in a comparative analysis of genital morphology in insects that divergence among species is indeed much greater than for ordinary morphological characters. This finding suggests that ongoing sexual selection is likely to exert intense pressure on any male trait associated with reproduction and traits associated with control of reproduction in females.

Sexual conflict may in fact be running sexual selection. The **chase-away** model of sexual selection suggests that females evolve resistance to male traits that increase male fitness at the expense of female fitness (Holland & Rice 1998). For example, seminal fluid proteins of male *Drosophila* fruit flies that reduce the remating propensity of females are deleterious to female fitness. In an elegant experiment, female evolution was arrested to investigate the effects of continued male evolution on female fitness. As predicted, there was a significant reduction in female fitness caused by ongoing male–male competition resulting in male evolution (Rice 1996). Conversely, when male evolution was arrested, the reverse effect was found (Holland & Rice 1999). Although these effects were demonstrated for seminal fluid proteins, similar mechanisms based on other phenotypic traits are certainly imaginable.

## Costs of Sexual Ornamentation

Costs of exaggerated phenotypes are an inherent aspect of evolutionary models of sexual selection. Such costs arise because characters become exaggerated beyond the optimum under natural selection. Even in the case of condition-dependent expression of secondary sexual characters, a cost is an inevitable consequence of sexual selection. Condition-dependent characters are more exaggerated among individuals in prime condition, and a positive phenotypic correlation between ornamentation and condition should therefore arise. What this means is that those individuals with the most exaggerated secondary sexual characters tend to be in better condition both before and after development of the character. Therefore, such individuals have higher survival prospects than the average individual in the population. For example, a study of the wolf spider *Hygrolycosa rubrofasciata* demonstrates this point. In early spring (April–May) males of this spider use old leaves on the ground to produce a drumming sound, and females are attracted to this acoustic display. Males with higher drumming rates are more successful in terms of mating success, but are also of superior viability under both laboratory and field conditions compared with less vigorously drumming males (Kotiaho et al. 1999). Male drumming explains 6.8% of the variance in survival rate among males.

This relationship between male sexual display and viability is a general one since males with the most exaggerated secondary sexual characters also tend to be those that survive the best (Jennions et al. 2001). On average, male ornamentation or attractiveness accounted for 1.4% of the variance in male survival rate across studies.

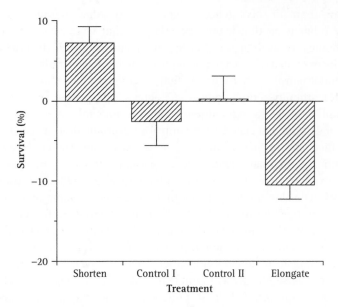

**Fig. 11.5** Survival rate of male barn swallows *Hirundo rustica* in relation to the length of their tails. Males had the length of their tails experimentally reduced, increased, or kept as controls (I, treated control group; II, untreated control group). Values are mean (SE) deviations for each of four experiments from the mean survival rate in the populations, which was set at zero. (Adapted from Møller 1994 and Møller & de Lope 1994.)

Surprisingly, the amount of variance explained was of very similar magnitude to that in studies of viability effects in "good genes" sexual selection (Møller & Alatalo 1999). The positive relationship between ornamentation and survival prospects does not imply that secondary sexual characters are cheap, only that the tradeoff between survival and mating success as determined by sexual display is masked by individual differences in condition. Genetic and environmental determinants of male differences in viability are possible, and studies of "good genes" effects suggest that part of this difference in viability is caused by genetic effects. Only an experiment can reveal the underlying costs of ornamentation by displacing individuals randomly from their once chosen optimum. An experiment manipulating the length of the outermost tail feathers of male barn swallows reversed the positive relationship between survival and ornamentation among unmanipulated males to the predicted negative association after experimentally increasing or decreasing the tail length of males (Fig. 11.5). This study demonstrates that the underlying costs of ornamentation may be revealed by phenotypic manipulations.

The two sexes often differ markedly in mortality rate, and these differences appear to be related to sexual selection. Larger male mortality rates are associated with more intense competition among males for access to females. In comparative studies of sex-specific patterns of mortality in birds, Promislow et al. (1992, 1994) have shown that males have greater mortality in species where males have a greater degree of exaggeration of plumage color than females, and that the difference increases proportionally with the increase in sexual dichromatism. Likewise, sex differences in longevity are common in all human societies, with men living 5–10 years less than women in

Western societies. This difference is caused by dramatic differential mortality between ages 16 and 28 years, when men suffer a nearly 200% higher mortality than women (reviews in Trivers 1985; Wilson & Daly 1985). Causes of death that partly account for this difference include a threefold greater risk of being murdered, and higher risks of mortality from accidents, including car accidents, even when taking the number of kilometers driven into account. Men generally take much greater risks than women and seek medical treatment much more rarely than women, even for the same ailments (see also Chapter 17). Men also suffer from a number of different diseases to a greater extent than women; some of these effects are caused by recessive alleles on the male's unguarded X chromosome being expressed in men but not women (Trivers 1985). The overall sex difference in mortality can best be understood as arising from intense male–male competition and sexual differences in sexual psychology of men and women.

The actual mechanisms giving rise to sex differences in mortality in animals arises from predation and/or parasitism. Many studies have investigated predation risk in relation to sexual display or the expression of secondary sexual characters. There is ample evidence that predators use sexual signals to target males, and that predation can be considered a general cause of sex differences in mortality (review in Zuk & Kolluru 1998). However, several studies have shown that males with the most extravagant secondary sexual characters in fact run lower risks of predation than the average male. In such cases, male condition seems to be a confounding factor because males with large secondary sex traits not only pay the costs of sexual display, but do so based on an initially superior condition. Hence, we can only expect to reveal the tradeoff between display and predation risk when males are displaced experimentally from the chosen level of sexual signaling.

Males often show a greater prevalence of parasites than females, and many diseases also predominate in males. Parasitism can be considered the second major cause of sex differences in mortality (Alexander & Stimson 1989; Zuk 1990). Such sex differences in level of parasitism may be partly mediated by endocrine effects on susceptibility and parasite resistance, as suggested by Alexander and Stimson (1989) and Folstad and Karter (1992). A comparative study of birds showed that males generally had smaller immune defense organs (bursa of Fabricius and spleen, a primary and a secondary lymphoid organ) than females (Møller et al. 1998). Furthermore, the sex difference in the size of immune defense organs was negatively related to the frequency of extrapair paternity, which is a measure of the intensity of sexual selection. Thus, in species with frequent extrapair paternity and hence intense competition among males for access to fertile females, males had a much larger reduction in spleen size compared with females than in species with little or no extrapair paternity.

Reductions in the viability of individuals of an intensely sexually selected population may result in a population decrease in viability, particularly during periods of adverse environmental conditions. Similarly, a high variance in reproductive success, the associated strong mate preferences for individuals with particular phenotypes, and differential investment by females into reproduction with attractive males may all be detrimental to the survival prospects of small populations of threatened species. There are numerous examples of small populations of threatened species in nature reserves or in captivity with little or no reproductive success, and where numbers remain small or decrease because of little or no reproduction. For example, newspapers and magazines often feature stories of giant pandas *Ailuropoda melanoleuca* or other enigmatic animals being transported from one zoo to another to make yet another attempt at successful reproduction.

A hypothesis that accounts for such problems is that sexual selection causes a reduction in population viability (Møller & Legendre 2001). Costs of sexual selection may reduce viability of small populations because there is a biased number of individuals of the two sexes for completely stochastic reasons. This effect may become exaggerated by strong female mate preferences for particular males, since all such males may be absent for random reasons. Similarly, females may in such situations reduce investment in reproduction or not reproduce at all when mated to unattractive males. Thus, small populations or populations in captivity, such as those of species threatened by extinction, may run increased risks of extinction simply because they have an evolutionary history of intense sexual selection.

A common objection to the idea of costs of sexual selection is that it may be balanced or even exceeded by benefits in terms of the positive effects of "good genes." This is not necessarily so. Depending on the nature of the "good genes," there may be little or no positive effect on individuals in the population. For example, differences in genetic constitution among males in the population may arise as a consequence of more individuals of poor genetic quality being present in a highly sexually selected species.

## Multiple Ornaments

The previous sections have generally dealt with sexual signaling for a single phenotypic character. However, in real cases of signaling individuals often simultaneously exhibit many different kinds of secondary sexual characters, such as exaggerated morphological traits, colors, and vocalizations. The evolution and maintenance of such multiple signals need to be explained. The evolution of multiple characters can derive from the following.

1 Each character provides information about different aspects of the phenotype of a signaler.
2 Each secondary sexual character provides redundant information about the overall condition of an individual. A single signal may not reveal complete information about a particular quality of an individual, and multiple signals may provide independent information that in combination reflect its overall quality.
3 Some characters do not currently reflect properties of the signaler but did so in the past. If the traits are not particularly costly, they may be maintained for a long time after they cease providing information on signalers (Møller & Pomiankowski 1993).

The junglefowl (*Gallus gallus spadiceus*) provides a well-known example of multiple signals. Cockerels have elongated tail and hackle feathers, bright coloration of different parts of the body, a red wattle and comb, and a crowing call. Studies of sexual selection in this species have revealed that only a single trait, the size of the comb, provides reliable information about infection status with a nematode parasite. During mate-choice sessions, females only paid attention to this single trait revealing parasite status (Zuk et al. 1990), suggesting that the other traits were not currently reflecting information about the condition of males. Other studies of other organisms have revealed evidence for the first and second hypotheses of multiple ornaments. A general understanding of the function and importance of multiple signals is still far from being achieved.

## Sex Ratios

Why are equally many males and females born in most species? Ronald Fisher (1930) suggested that an equal sex ratio would be advantageous to an individual because any deviation from this ratio on average would result in the production of fewer grand-parental offspring. This view of Fisher's sex ratio theory is based on the premise that sons and daughters cost the same, whereas the sex ratio in fact should be based on the combined cost of sons versus daughters. Deviations from these predicted patterns of equal sex ratios occur when siblings mate with each other, in which case sex ratios are generally biased strongly toward daughters.

Adaptive variation in sex ratio has attracted considerable attention recently, particularly because of its relationship with sexual selection. If males are especially sexually attractive for genetic reasons, male offspring of such sires should enjoy a disproportionate mating success compared with the average male in the population. Females mated to such attractive males should therefore produce relatively more sons than daughters. Indeed, attractive males of several species seem to have mates that produce more sons than daughters. Nancy Burley (1981) in a classic study of the zebra finch showed that when males became more attractive by simple experimental manipulation of the color of their plastic leg rings, this affected the sex ratio of their offspring. Female zebra finches preferred males with red rings and avoided males with green rings. Females mated to red-ringed males produced significantly more sons than did females mated to green-ringed males, as predicted by theory (Fig. 11.6). Subsequent studies of several other species have provided similar evidence for adaptive adjustment of sex ratio in response to the phenotype of the sire, although experimental studies testing this prediction are still the exception.

Numerous studies have demonstrated evidence of female condition being related to sex ratio of their offspring. If sons are more costly to produce than daughters and if female condition changes consistently with age, we should expect sex ratios to change similarly. Many studies have shown a preponderance of sons being produced by dominant females or by females in prime condition. Likewise, senescence seems to be associated with a sex ratio bias toward daughters.

Studies of sex ratios in humans provide equally striking effects of environmental conditions. For example, studies at the US West Point military academy of the sex ratio

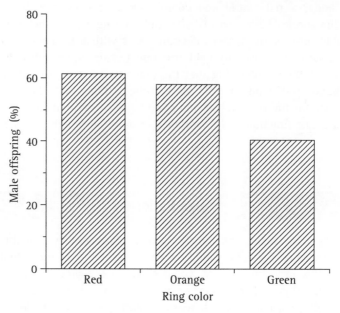

**Fig. 11.6** Sex ratio of zebra finches *Taeniopygia guttata* in relation to the color of plastic leg rings of their mates, where red rings are attractive and green rings are unattractive. (Adapted from Burley 1981.)

of cadets in relation to military rank show a preponderance of sons produced by women married to high-ranking officers. A similar result has been reported for the sex ratio of the offspring of US presidents, vice-presidents, and cabinet secretaries. Among the US executive branch, a staggering 70% of sons have been recorded during the first 20 presidents, falling to 53% during the following 20 presidents, compared with the null expectation of 50% recorded in human populations in general (Betzig & Weber 1995). Similarly, many different studies have recorded changes in sex ratios associated with resource abundance and other indicators of environmental conditions. For example, in rural Portugal during the period 1671–1720 the sex ratio was 112.1 sons per 100 daughters in good harvest years but only 90.7 sons per 100 daughters in poor harvest years (Trivers 1985). Twins are more costly to produce than two singletons, and we should thus expect the sex ratio of twins to be biased toward daughters. In fact, the sex ratio of human twins is 3% lower than that of singletons (Trivers 1985). If this deviation from an equal sex ratio is adaptive, we should expect that male twins have disproportionately lower reproductive success than female twins. Indeed, both male and female twins have lower reproductive success than singletons, based on data from eighteenth- and nineteenth-century Mormons in the USA. However, the reduction in reproductive success among male twins is twice as large as that for female twins, consistent with the prediction (Trivers 1985). More recently, sex ratio theory has been invoked to explain variation in sex ratios in societies with enforced family planning such as China. Families generally favor sons over daughters when a one-child policy is enforced, and this happens as a consequence of selective abortion, infanticide, and other mechanisms. Surprisingly, in families with more than a single child there are dramatic changes in sex ratios of the second and later children, depending on the sex ratio of the first child (Low 2000). If the first child is a son, the sex ratio of any subsequent children is biased toward daughters; the reverse situation occurs when the first child is a daughter. These studies, and many others reviewed by Trivers (1985), suggest that human sex ratios are closely linked to sexual selection and the advantages that accrue to women in terms of future reproductive potential through the sex of their offspring.

## SUMMARY AND CONCLUSIONS

The pervasive effects of reproduction on parents in sexually reproducing species have caused sexual selection to affect most aspects of the lives of individuals. Sexual selection and mate choice does not only affect the appearance of individuals and how they behave toward each other during the breeding season. The effects of sexual selection appear before this, when parents make decisions about the sex ratio of their offspring and how these offspring are to be provisioned. This is followed by decisions about developmental rates for secondary sexual characters, when these first appear, and the degree to which these characters are exaggerated. Individuals of the choosy sex are equally affected by sexual selection, namely their sales resistance when approached by potential mates, their choice of partner, and their subsequent reproductive decisions. Sexual selection also affects the way in which individuals are spatially distributed and therefore has important consequences for social organization. The costs of secondary sexual characters can be dramatic and may affect populations to the extent that they may constitute an important risk of extinction for some species. These effects of sexual selection on most aspects of the life of different organisms are equally prominent in humans, where everything from sex ratio, sex differences in mortality, and sex differences in sexual behavior and risk-taking can be considered to have arisen as a consequence of this evolutionary force.

## FURTHER READING

Andersson (1994) provides a general overview of sexual selection theory and summarizes the empirical evidence. Monographs on sexual selection in particular species include Houde (1997) on the guppy, Møller (1994) on the barn swallow, and Ryan (1985) on the túngara frog. Sex ratio theory is reviewed extensively by Trivers (1985). Low (2000) provides an extensive treatise on the consequences of sexual selection for humans. The consequences of sexual selection for conservation are described by Møller (2000) and Wilson et al. (1998).

# 12

# polyandry, sperm competition, and sexual conflict

MARK A. ELGAR

## INTRODUCTION

A remarkable range of selective processes may determine the fate of individual sperm in fertilizing an egg. The previous chapter described how **sexual selection** influences mate acquisition, but mate acquisition is only one stage in a continuous selective process that may persist after insemination or spawning has occurred. The potential for sexual selection to persist after mating arises if females mate with more than one male, and the sperm of these males subsequently coexist in proximity to the female's unfertilized ova. The result is that the sperm from these different males compete for fertilization success. **Multiple mating** by females, and the subsequent opportunity for **sperm competition**, is thought to be responsible for an extraordinary diversity of male behavioral, morphological, and physiological **adaptations** that have evolved apparently in response to the **risk of sperm competition**.

Geoff Parker of the University of Liverpool first argued that sperm competition represents an extension of sexual selection through male–male competition (Parker 1970). Indeed, most instances of physical contests between males over access to females involve one male attempting to prevent his rival from copulating with his intended or actual mating partner. Nevertheless, it is now evident that females are not passive in this process and have the potential to bias paternity in favor of particular males by exploiting the various processes of sperm transfer, storage, and utilization. For example, females might adjust the **frequency** and/or timing of copulations with favored males in order to ensure that these males are the primary sires of their offspring. In this case, it is not sperm competition per se that influences a male's **fitness** but rather the behavior of the females that allows the male of her choice to be in the right place at the right time.

The importance of processes influencing fertilization success after insemination has become widely recognized only relatively recently, despite Parker's important paper being published over 30 years ago. Historically, there have also been interesting taxonomic biases in the nature of empirical research. Studies of vertebrates have tended to focus on the role of **secondary sexual traits** on **mating success**, albeit with increasing sophistication as molecular markers have facilitated accurate assignment of paternity. In contrast, the most elegant work on sperm competition has, with a few exceptions, been carried out on invertebrates, and these studies have contributed the most significant advances to our understanding of postinsemination processes.

The potential for competition between the ejaculate of different males arises because females mate with more than one male. Although the consequences of **polyandry** (i.e. multiple mating by females) have been examined extensively, the reasons why females mate with more than one male have, surprisingly, been largely ignored. Nevertheless, several lines of evidence reveal a number of benefits to polyandry that are likely to apply to a broad range of taxa. On the one hand, selection favors females that copulate with several different males but, on the other, selection also favors males that reduce or eliminate the possibility of rivals fertilizing the eggs of their mates. Thus, there is likely to be an evolutionary conflict of interest between the sexes over the paternity of the female's offspring. This sexual conflict of interest can generate a process of **antagonistic coevolution**, in which male adaptations to ensure exclusive fertilization success act as a selective pressure on female counteradaptations to secure their choice of who sires their offspring. These female counteradaptations then act as a selection pressure on male adaptations, and so on.

This chapter describes the circumstances under which sexual selection persists even after the male has secured a mating opportunity. In particular, it describes how selection for polyandry on the one hand and for protecting paternity on the other can create a fascinating conflict of interest between the sexes.

## Benefits of Polyandry: Why Females Mate with Several Males

Sexual selection through sperm competition can only occur in polyandrous species, in which females mate with more than one male during a single reproductive cycle. It is therefore surprising that so few studies have attempted to identify the selective pressures favoring the evolution of polyandry. There may be both sociological and intellectual reasons for this oversight, but the prevailing view of **monogamous** females is likely to have been important (see Birkhead 2000). Robert Trivers (1972) of Rutgers University emphasized in an influential paper that males improve their reproductive success by mating with many females, whereas the reproductive success of females depends upon their efficient conversion of food into either eggs or nutrients for offspring. This difference in reproductive strategy could be conveniently described as either indiscriminate **promiscuous** multiple mating males or choosy monogamous females. There was also little evidence that females attempted to copulate with several partners. Most birds were regarded as monogamous and Bateman's (1948) experimental study of the fruit fly *Drosophila melanogaster* (see Chapter 11) suggested that well-fed females did not improve their reproductive success by mating with several males.

However, the advent and subsequent use of modern molecular genetic techniques made it possible to identify the sire, or father, of the female's offspring. These techniques revealed that females of what appeared to be monogamous species based on their social behavior routinely copulated with males that were not their social partners, often at spectacularly high rates. For example, between 60 and 70% of the brood of female fairy wrens *Malurus cyaneus* are fathered by males that are not the social partner (Mulder et al. 1994). More fundamentally, it is now widely recognized that the risk of sperm competition arises precisely because females mate with several males. Since mate searching and copulation can be energetically costly or increase the risk of predation or infection by pathogens, there must be some benefit to polyandry or the behavior would be uncommon.

It is convenient to distinguish between genetic and nongenetic benefits (**direct benefits**) of polyandry (see Chapter 11). Nongenetic or material benefits are essentially those that improve female fecundity, whereas **indirect genetic benefits** derive from the paternal contribution to the genotype of the offspring (Table 12.1). Indirect benefits can potentially apply to females of all sexually reproducing species. However, direct benefits may be taxonomically restricted, for example to species in which the male makes some material contribution. The taxonomically widespread distribution of polyandry suggests that genetic benefits are the most typical selective pressures favoring the maintenance of polyandry.

Table 12.1 Benefits to females of mating with more than one partner during a single reproductive cycle.

---

*Direct, nongenetic benefits*
    Fertility assurance
    More paternal care
    Nutrients derived from courtship feeding, including seminal fluids and prey items
    Protection from and avoidance of male harassment, including infanticide

*Genetic benefits*
    Genetic diversity
    Genetic complementarity
    Viability genes
    Attractiveness genes

---

# Direct material benefits

The nongenetic or material benefits associated with polyandry are well known (see Chapter 11). Polyandrous females may obtain more parental care and thus increase their reproductive output if paternal care depends upon the degree of brood paternity (Burke et al. 1989; Davies 1992). Similarly, males of certain insects transfer nutrients during mating, sometimes referred to as **nuptial gifts**, which their mates can then utilize for improving egg production (Vahed 1998). Although a single gift does not necessarily improve fecundity in some species, two or more gifts may well do so. In some mammals, multiple mating may stimulate ovulation and the likelihood of conception (Hoogland 1998) or decrease the possibility of infanticide of her offspring by males that did not mate with her (Smuts & Smuts 1993). Females may mate again in order to reduce male harassment, which may have a negative impact on, for example, her foraging success (Rowe et al. 1994; Watson et al. 1998).

Polyandry may also ensure that females have sufficient sperm to fertilize their eggs, a problem that may be common in external fertilizing animals. The argument that females mate repeatedly in order to obtain enough sperm may seem surprising, since it is not unreasonable to expect that there is strong selection on males to produce at least sufficient sperm in a single mating to fertilize all the female's eggs. Indeed, there is considerable variation in the quantity of sperm delivered per mating across different species that is partly explained by mating frequency, and sperm has impressive longevity in some social insects such as honeybees (Page 1986). Nonetheless there are also reasons to expect that females will not obtain all the sperm required to fertilize their eggs. Some males may be sterile or partition their limited sperm among several females; or, when fertilization is internal, females must replenish stored sperm that has died or been lost from the sperm-storage organs (Barnett et al. 1995). Recent evidence suggests that males do not have an unlimited supply of sperm, at least in the short term. For example, males of the **lekking** (see Chapter 11) sand fly *Lutzomyia longipalpis* mate multiply but become sperm-depleted after their fifth copulation. Females are unable to discern the mating history of males, and thus face a potential cost of obtaining insufficient sperm as a result of mating only with the most successful male at the lek (Jones 2001). Thus, polyandry may provide females with a fertilization "assurance" against mating with males that have a highly successful mating history and, as a consequence, relatively few sperm.

# Indirect genetic benefits

Some of the direct benefits that females may gain from mating more than once within a reproductive cycle are similar whether she mates with a previous or novel partner. For example, the fecundity advantage of additional nuptial gifts will be roughly similar whether the female mates with several males or repeatedly with the same male. However, females can obtain indirect genetic benefits only by mating with different males. Accordingly, if selection has favored multiple mating as a result of indirect genetic benefits, then females should prefer to mate with novel males rather than previous mating partners.

Two lines of evidence suggest that polyandrous females do seek novel mating partners. First, extrapair mating is widespread among birds (Birkhead & Møller 1992), including those species in which the extrapair mates do not provide any obvious material benefits. The second, and more compelling, line of evidence comes from two experimental studies demonstrating that females prefer to mate again with a novel rather than the same male (Zeh et al. 1998; Archer & Elgar 1999).

The genetic benefits of multiple mating essentially fall into two categories: reducing the risk of producing genotypes with low fitness, and increasing the proportion of genotypes with higher fitness (see Jennions and Petrie 2000 for an insightful review). Females may obtain these benefits passively, by increasing the genetic diversity of their offspring, or actively, by biasing the paternity of her offspring according to some feature of the male. For example, the reproductive success of colonies of social insects in which the queen mates with several males is greater than that of colonies in which the female mates with only one male. One reason for this is that the colonies with greater genetic variability suffer lower parasite loads (Baer & Schmid-Hempel 1999). Interestingly, there appears to be a relationship between multiple mating and colony foundation in social insects that result in broods of mixed parentage. Singly mated queens are common in species in which the colony is founded by several queens, whereas multiply mated queens are more common in species in which the colony is founded by a single queen (Keller & Reeve 1994a). Studies of several other nonsocial species reveal greater offspring viability in polyandrous than monandrous females (Jennions & Petrie 2000). The intriguing issue is whether these differences in offspring viability arise because females actively select the sperm of particular higher quality males.

There is extensive evidence that females can improve their reproductive success as a result of choosing to mate with particular males (see Chapter 11). In this way, females can bias paternity to favor absolutely a particular male by mating exclusively with him. However, it may not always be possible for a female to select the most preferred male as her initial mating partner, particularly if she is likely to encounter a superior male at some other time or place. Multiple mating therefore provides a female with the opportunity to "trade up" by mating with males that have potentially superior genotypes than her previous partner (Jennions & Petrie 2000). Although there is widespread evidence that females are selective about their mates (see Chapter 11), extrapair mating in socially monogamous birds allows the females to mate with a male of higher quality than their social partner (Kempenaers et al. 1992). Thus, multiple mating can be viewed as essentially a consequence of sequential premating female choice.

Females may not be able to obtain reliable **information** about the relative quality of males before mating, and instead rely on postcopulation or in-copula mechanisms to assess male quality. In this case, multiple mating allows females to make choices about the sire of their offspring after mating has commenced. Randy Thornhill of the University of New Mexico initially suggested that females could "choose" the sire of their offspring after mating has commenced, and coined the term **cryptic female choice** (Thornhill 1983). The choice is cryptic because any bias in fertilization success would not be detected in studies that focused primarily on mating success. The significance of cryptic female choice was largely neglected until William Eberhard at the University of Costa Rica assembled extensive **comparative** data on the mating biology of animals, which he used to make a case for female control of the paternity of offspring (Eberhard 1996).

The extent to which females can exercise cryptic choice remains controversial. Females could bias fertilization success in a variety of ways, such as influencing the quantity of sperm delivered by controlling the duration of copulation, ejecting unwanted sperm, or influencing the passage of sperm to the fertilization duct. However, there is some doubt about the effectiveness of these influences beyond avoiding fertilizations between genetically incompatible gametes. Female reproductive success can be reduced as a result of inbreeding or genetic incompatibility, and multiple mating may provide females with the opportunity to minimize this possibility.

Swedish sand lizards *Lacerta agilis* are long-lived and highly promiscuous. Females show little discrimination between males, sometimes mating with close relatives and thereby producing offspring with relatively lower viability. Mats Olsson, now at the University of Wollongong in Australia, and his colleagues monitored the mating partners of females in the field, using genetic markers to determine their genetic similarity with their partner and the proportion of brood they sired. Impressively, males with a relatively higher genetic similarity to their partner sired a relatively lower proportion of her offspring. The underlying mechanism of this pattern remains to be discovered, but the data suggest that polyandry allows females to avoid the costs of inbreeding that may arise through indiscriminate mating.

Do females have the ability to choose the sire of their offspring cryptically, after insemination has taken place? The existence of multiple sperm-storage sites within the tracts of many insects may well provide females with the opportunity to bias paternity by influencing sperm transport, survival, and access to ova (Eberhard 1996; Ward 2000). However, the problem is one of distinguishing whether the outcome arises through active female choice or whether the sperms of different males differ in their ability to fertilize the female's eggs.

Tim Birkhead of the University of Sheffield highlights several difficulties in demonstrating cryptic female choice, particularly with attributing the variation in paternity to female rather than male effects (Birkhead 1998a). For example, it may be easy to demonstrate that a male's share of paternity is determined by the duration of copulation, but more difficult to determine whether copulation is terminated by the male or female (Andrés & Cordero Rivera 2000). This ambiguity is less evident in the orb-web spider *Argiope keyserlingi* because the sexually cannibalistic females terminate copulation when they attack the male. When female *A. keyserlingi* mated with two males, and the second mating was terminated by **sexual cannibalism**, the females delayed attacking relatively smaller males thereby allowing them to copulate for longer and thus sire relatively more offspring (Elgar et al. 2000). Female feral fowl similarly bias paternity against less favored males by ejecting their ejaculates and retaining the sperm of dominant males (Pizzari & Birkhead 2000). Of course females can only benefit from this cryptic choice if the variation in paternity is correlated with some characteristic or attribute of the male. In the case of *Argiope*, smaller males sired more offspring, although why small males are preferred is unclear.

## Evolution and maintenance of polyandry

Most discussions of the benefits of polyandry, or multiple mating by females, infer that understanding the costs and benefits of multiple mating will provide insights into the evolutionary origins and maintenance of this behavior. An underlying assumption is that multiple mating evolved from a monogamous ancestral state. There is no obvious reason for expecting this transition, and many of the identified benefits can only explain the maintenance rather than evolutionary origin of multiple mating. For example, the benefits of polyandry that derive from the competition between sperm of different males within the female reproductive tract cannot explain the evolution of polyandry, since this benefit arises only after polyandry has become established. A more parsimonious assumption is that multiple mating was the ancestral state, and that there has been strong selection to maintain the opportunity for multiple mating, despite male adaptations to counter this behavior. In other words, the identified benefits of multiple mating are responsible for the maintenance of this behavior but not necessarily its evolutionary origin.

## Male Adaptations to Counter Polyandry

Polyandry creates two opposing selective pressures on males (Parker 1970). On the one hand, selection will favor traits that allow males to maximize their fertilization success, typically by protecting their paternity at the expense of other males. On the other hand, selection will favor traits that allow males to overcome precisely those paternity protection traits. In other words, sexual selection favors adaptations that allow males simultaneously to avoid and engage in sperm competition. In short, the "ideal" male is one that can ensure exclusive fertilization of the progeny of both virgin and previously mated females. The situation may be further complicated if these male adaptations are opposed by female traits that favor female control of paternity. The resulting complex of selection pressures is responsible for the myriad male adaptations for maximizing fertilization success.

It is helpful to distinguish between the risk of sperm competition and the **intensity of sperm competition**. The former refers to the probability that females mate multiply, and thus refers to the probability that males engage in sperm competition. For species in which males have adaptations for avoiding sperm competition, multiple mating by females can result in complete loss of paternity rather than an increase in the risk of sperm competition. The intensity of sperm competition refers to the absolute number of males whose sperm compete for the ova of a single female, and will increase with the number of mating partners. The intensity of sperm competition will depend upon the degree of overlap of sperm from different males, and will decrease if the sperm from rivals is displaced prior to or during insemination.

The next two sections describe various male adaptations for maximizing fertilization success when there is a risk of sperm competition (Table 12.2). We can identify two general groups of male traits: those that **function** to prevent sperm competition and those that maximize paternity when engaging in sperm competition. Of course, the

**Table 12.2** Mechanisms used by males to maximize their fertilization success under the risk of sperm competition.

*Preventing sperm competition*
  Mate guarding
  Reducing or inhibiting female receptivity
  Creating physical barriers to insemination
  Sexual interference
  Sperm removal

*Engaging in sperm competition*
  Ejaculating greater quantities of sperm
  Repeated mating
  Male mate choice and strategic allocation of ejaculate

distinction between these two categories can become blurred, and they more properly describe two ends of a continuum rather than two discrete categories.

## Preventing direct competition between sperm

### *Mate guarding*

Physically guarding a female is perhaps the most taxonomically widespread mechanism used by males to avoid sperm competition. It is extremely common in birds, where the pair may become almost inseparable in the period leading up to the formation of the clutch of eggs. In mammals, the copulating male may vigorously attack any male that approaches his consort. Indeed, preventing rivals from gaining access to females, i.e., **mate guarding**, is likely to have been a powerful selective agent favoring the evolution of the secondary sexual armaments characteristic of many mammals (see Chapter 11).

Mate guarding in birds typically involves the male remaining near his partner, closely following her when she moves. This behavior may deter other males from approaching his mate and/or prevent her from courting and mating with rivals. The close association between male and female birds was once thought to reinforce the pair bond. While this certainly may be true, the evidence is more consistent with a mate-guarding interpretation. The intensity of mate guarding varies between species of birds, ranging from the relatively casual red-winged blackbird to the highly assiduous male feral pigeon that is, on average, 60 cm from his mate during the days of her fertile period (Birkhead 1998b). Mate guarding in birds also seems to vary according to the likelihood that females can obtain extrapair copulations. For example, female barn swallows nesting in colonies tend to be guarded more intensely than are those nesting solitarily (Møller 1987). Poor-quality males paired to good-quality females also invest relatively more time in mate guarding, primarily because these females seek extrapair matings from higher quality males.

The idea that the close association between members of the pair bond represents mate guarding has been tested experimentally in several species of birds by removing males when their partners are fertile. In all cases, the females without males increased their attempts to solicit extrapair copulations (Birkhead 1998b). Of course, this may simply reflect female attempts to seek copulations from any male in order to ensure her eggs are fertilized, rather than seeking extrapair copulations, which highlights the problems of testing the paternity protection explanation of mate guarding in birds. Nevertheless, there is little evidence for other explanations of the close associations between males and females and on balance the data support a mate-guarding explanation of this behavior.

Mate guarding is common in insects and mostly occurs after copulation has taken place, with the male remaining in close proximity to or in direct contact with the female. The latter is quite dramatic in certain species of dragonflies and damselflies, in which the male grasps the female with his terminal claspers, forming the characteristic tandem-wheel position while the female lays her eggs. Males of other dragonfly species guard their mates by hovering and perching near where the female **oviposits** (lays her eggs), and in some species males guard their mate using both methods, with and without contact. In the latter species, males may switch between the two forms of mate-guarding behavior according to the risk of sperm competition. In fact, studies of insects have clearly demonstrated that the intensity of postcopulatory associations can be increased by experimentally increasing the number of males in the population.

In some insects, males guard their mates against rivals by copulating for much longer than is necessary just to transfer sperm. For example, the monarch butterfly *Danaus plexippus* may remain copulated for up to 14 h, depending upon when copulation was initiated. Sperm is not transferred until near the end of copulation, typically around nightfall, and females oviposit the day after copulation. Extending copulation until nightfall, after which mate searching ceases, reduces the opportunity for females to remate with rivals before they commence ovipositing. Similarly, certain damselflies remain in copulation until the end of the mate-searching period, thereby reducing the risk that the female will copulate with a rival.

### Reducing or inhibiting female receptivity

Mate guarding has a number of potential costs, including a greater risk of predation from being more conspicuous or a reduction in the time available for foraging to replenish resources. Perhaps more significantly, males guarding their mate may have fewer opportunities to search for and mate with other females. Thus, there are likely to be substantial advantages to guarding a female without remaining in close proximity, because this allows the male to seek other mating opportunities while simultaneously ensuring that his sperm do not compete with those of his rivals. Males of certain web-building spiders have a simple but effective way of reducing the likelihood of sperm competition. Virgin females of these spiders incorporate a sex-attracting **pheromone** into their web. The pheromone is slowly released into the air and alerts males to the location of these receptive females. Males that arrive at the web of a virgin female typically reduce the size of her web by excising the silk and gathering it into a dense ball or rope. However, this behavior does not take place when a male arrives at the web of a mated female.

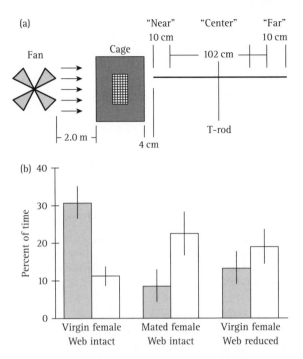

**Fig. 12.1** Experimental apparatus used to investigate how web reduction reduces the transmission of sex pheromones in the sierra dome spider. Air is blown across a cage containing either a virgin female and intact web, virgin female and reduced web, or mated female and intact web. A male is released at the base of the T-rod and he then moves to either end of the rod. Males were more attracted to the intact webs of virgin females than to the intact webs of mated females or the reduced webs of virgin females. Shaded columns, near cage; open columns, far from cage. (After Watson 1986.)

Experiments by Paul Watson of the University of New Mexico revealed that virgin females with reduced webs attracted fewer males than those with intact webs, whereas mated females failed to attract males (Fig. 12.1). Destroying the web before rather than after mating allows the male to court and mate without interference from rivals (Watson 1986).

Insects provide a rich source of examples of the ways males effectively mate guard in absentia. Females of many insects become sexually unreceptive after mating, entering a so-called **refractory period**, and this change is typically attributed to certain substances in the semen transferred during copulation. For example, male moths in the genus *Cecropia* transfer chemicals in the **spermatophore** (a membranous sac that contains the sperm and other substances) that inhibit the production of sex pheromones and thus the arrival of rival males. Copulating male houseflies *Musca domestica* also transfer chemicals, probably manufactured by the accessory glands, that result in the female failing to respond positively to the courtship of other males. Studies of fruit flies provide the most detailed analysis of the role of seminal fluids in controlling female receptivity. For example, the seminal fluid of *D. melanogaster* not only induces a refractory period but also increases the oviposition rate of the female.

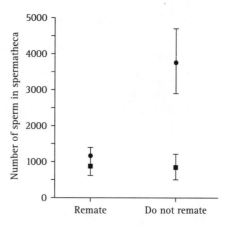

**Fig. 12.2** Likelihood that female green-veined white butterflies remate with another male depends on the amount of apyrene sperm delivered in her last mating; females that do not remate have more apyrene sperm in storage (circles) than females that do remate, but there is no difference in the quantity of eupyrene sperm (squares). (After Cook & Wedell 1999.)

In some insects, females are more likely to remate when the quantity of sperm remaining in their sperm-storage organ declines to a particular level, so males can ensure non-receptivity by completely filling this organ. Male moths and butterflies have exploited this mechanism of regulating female receptivity by producing two distinct types of sperm: normal, fully functional, fertile (**eupyrene**) sperm, and nonfertile (**apyrene**) sperm that lack nuclear material and therefore cannot fertilize eggs. Penny Cook and Nina Wedell, now at the University of Leeds, discovered that in female cabbage white butterflies *Pieris rapae* the quantity of apyrene but not eupyrene sperm transferred during mating influences whether the female is likely to remate with another male. They also found that remated females had fewer apyrene sperm than did those that did not remate, but there was no difference in the number of eupyrene sperm (Cook & Wedell 1999) (Fig. 12.2). Presumably, the cost of producing nonfertile apyrene sperm is less than that of eupyrene sperm and hence provides a cheaper way of prolonging the refractory period.

The ejaculate of male orthopterans (grasshoppers and crickets) is transferred from a spermatophore that is externally attached to the female genitalia. The spermatophore comprises a sperm-free mass (**spermatophylax**) and the sperm-containing **ampulla**. The female may detach and consume the spermatophylax, often before there is complete insemination of the sperm from the sperm-containing ampulla. It is possible to manipulate experimentally the length of time the spermatophore is attached to the female, and thus the volume of sperm transferred. Such experimental manipulations demonstrate that the length of the female's refractory period depends upon the dose or quantity of ejaculate in the ampulla (Simmons & Gwynne 1991). More generally, there is a positive correlation across species of bush crickets (tettigonids) between the duration of the refractory period and the mass of the ampulla, suggesting that larger ejaculates contain a greater quantity of seminal products that, in turn, inhibit female receptivity for a longer time.

## Physical barriers to insemination

Rather than reduce female receptivity, many insects prevent sperm competition by placing physical barriers in or over the female genital opening. These barriers, or **mating plugs**, typically consist of a solid mass of material that may persist in the female's reproductive tract for some time. Mating plugs are particularly prevalent among insects, and have also been reported in several species of marsupials (although their function in marsupials is unclear).

Mating plugs are likely to incur some cost to the male and, depending on their size, may constrain male mating frequency. Mating plugs may also consist of part of the male's reproductive anatomy, thereby preventing him from mating more than once. In many species of predaceous ceratopogonid biting midges, the female pierces the male cuticle while they mate and dissolves and sucks out his bodily fluids (Fig. 12.3). The female then disengages from the desiccated male by breaking the terminal part of his abdomen (containing his genital organs), which then remains attached to the female genitalia. Although it is not known how long the remnant of the male remains attached to the female, it presumably prevents subsequent mating by other males at least until she commences oviposition. Competition for mating is likely to be intense in these species that form mating swarms and perhaps males are **monogynous** in order to prevent sperm competition.

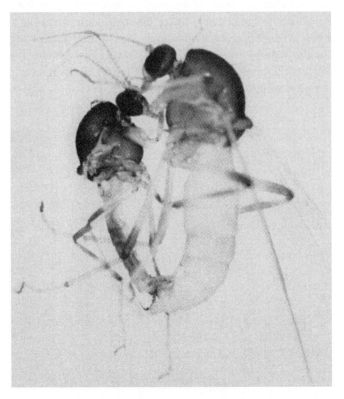

**Fig. 12.3** Biting midges in copulation: the larger female (right) pierces the head of the smaller male, extracting his haemolymph, while the male transfers sperm. (After Downes 1978.)

More conventional mating plugs have been recorded for several groups of insects but are particularly common in the butterflies. For example, the big greasy butterfly *Cressida cressida* prevents mating by rivals by placing a large structure, called a sphragis, over the female's genitalia. The mating plugs created by males of other butterflies are less elaborate and may be simple cap-like structures or an amorphous mass that exudes from the female genital opening. The efficacy of these mating plugs varies across butterflies, but experiments clearly indicate that they are effective at both preventing males from copulating and, in the case of the sphragis, providing a visual deterrent to mating. Moreover, interspecific comparisons across species of butterflies reveal that the mating frequency of females is reduced in species that have larger or more elaborate mating plugs (Simmons 2001).

### Sexual interference

The transfer of sperm in some species, including salamanders and springtails (Collembola), involves the male depositing a spermatophore on the substrate that is picked up by the female a few moments later. Male salamanders often congregate at a breeding site and males attempt to prevent females from picking up the spermatophores of rivals by so-called sexual interference. For example, a rival male may **mimic** female receptive behavior so that the male is induced to deposit a spermatophore. The rival may then lead the female away and initiate spermatophore transfer elsewhere. Male spotted salamanders *Ambystoma maculatum* may deposit their spermatophore above that of the original male, thereby making it inaccessible to the female. The original male may then deposit another spermatophore above that of his rival, resulting in a tower of spermatophores, of which the sperm from the last male only are used (Fig. 12.4).

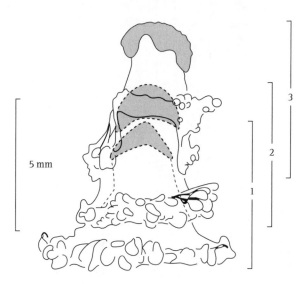

**Fig. 12.4** Stack of spermatophores deposited by several male salamanders. Only the sperm from the highest spermatophore will be picked up by the female and fertilize her eggs. (After Arnold 1976.)

Male springtails similarly deposit a spermatophore on the substrate. In the springtail *Dicyrtomina minuta*, the male constructs a "fence" of spermatophores around the female, which apparently prevents his rivals from replacing his spermatophore before the female has picked up one of his.

### Sperm removal

The final mechanism by which males may ensure that their sperm do not compete with those of their rivals is to physically remove the sperm, or manipulate them into a space within the female's reproductive tract that makes it unlikely they will fertilize her eggs. Nicholas Davies of the University of Cambridge made a surprising discovery when he studied the reproductive behavior of dunnocks (*Prunella modularis*), small passerine birds common to Europe. The birds engage in a curious precopulation **display** that involves the female quivering her wings and raising her tail to expose her cloaca to the male that hops around her (Davies 1983). The male then pecks her cloaca and Davies discovered that a small droplet of sperm is subsequently ejected. It seemed likely that this display allowed males to reduce both the risk and intensity of sperm competition by removing the sperm of rivals. However, there was no evidence that the behavior varied according to any measures of the risk of sperm competition (Davies 1992) and its significance is still uncertain.

The best-known examples of sperm removal and manipulation come from studies of dragonflies and damselflies (Odonata). In these species, the end of the male intromittent organ enters the female's sperm-storage organ during copulation. This allows males to displace the sperm from the exit of the female's sperm-storage organ, and there are essentially two ways in which this can be achieved. First, the copulating male removes some or all of the stored rival sperm before inseminating the female. Second, the male may reposition the sperm, moving them away from the exit of the female's sperm-storage organ to a region where they are unlikely to fertilize her eggs. Removing or displacing all the rival's sperm ensures that there is no direct competition between sperm for fertilization success, at least initially, because the sperm do not overlap spatially. However, sperm may eventually compete as the extent of spatial overlap breaks down.

## Sperm in competition

### Fair raffles

Males of many species are unable to prevent sperm competition, and thus their primary option for maximizing fertilization success is limited to their investment in ejaculate volume relative to other reproductive expenditure. Put another way, how many sperm should a male invest in each ejaculate? The answer depends in part on the investment strategies of other males in the population, which suggested to Geoff Parker and his colleagues that the problem can be best solved using **game theory** (see Chapter 9) and their models are neatly summarized in Parker (1998). In their most simple form, these games assume that the sperm in competition is analogous to a "**fair raffle**" or lottery.

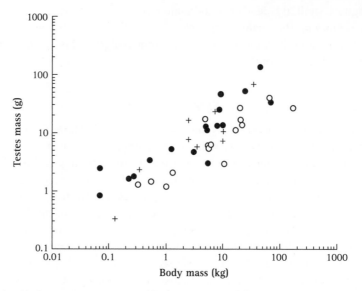

**Fig. 12.5** Relationship between testes mass and body mass across different species of primates. Closed circles represent species in which females may mate with several males and thus there is a risk of sperm competition; open circles represent species in which females typically mate with a single male and thus there is little risk of sperm competition. Species for which the risk of sperm competition is uncertain are indicated by crosses. (After Harcourt et al. 1996.)

Thus, a male's fertilization success can be increased by inseminating more sperm, just as the chance of winning a raffle is increased by purchasing more tickets.

This approach reveals the intuitively obvious prediction that, across species, investment in sperm will increase with greater risk and intensity of sperm competition. There is now widespread evidence for this prediction: species in which there is a high risk of sperm competition typically have relatively larger testes for their body weight than species in which the risk of sperm competition is low. For example, a male gorilla can weigh up to 170 kg and he uses his considerable size and strength to prevent rival males from mating with his mates. In contrast, female chimpanzees may mate with several males, thereby increasing the risk of sperm competition. Athough male chimpanzees are about one-quarter of the weight of male gorillas, the testes weight of chimpanzees (118 g) is very considerably heavier than that of the gorilla (30 g). More generally, although body and testes mass are positively correlated among primates, the testes mass of species in which there is a high potential for sperm competition are relatively heavier than that of species in which sperm competition is typically absent (Fig. 12.5). Patterns of this sort have emerged for a broad range of taxa, including mammals, birds, butterflies, externally fertilizing fish, and Australian frogs. These patterns are consistent with the idea that testis size is subject to selection through sperm competition but only if evidence shows that species with relatively larger testes have higher rates of sperm production, which seems to be the case for birds and mammals. Males within species may also differ in sperm production. Males of blue-headed wrass *Thalassoma bifasciatum* are either large and territorial or small and highly gregarious. The small males can only

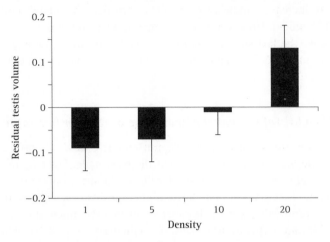

**Fig. 12.6** Testis volume, relative to body size, of male Indian meal moths *Plodia interpunctella* reared as larvae in high densities is much greater than that of males reared in low densities. (After Gage 1995.)

mate in swarms with a single female, and these males produce vast quantities of sperm and their testes are very enlarged. Selection experiments over several generations with yellow dungfly *Scathophaga stercoraria* revealed that males in polyandrous treatments evolved larger testes than males that were prevented from mating more than once.

More remarkably, Matthew Gage, now at the University of East Anglia, discovered that males of the Indian meal moth *Plodia interpunctella* adjust their investment in sperm production according to a predicted risk of sperm competition. Adult populations of this moth can vary from less than five to many thousands of individuals, depending upon the initial number of immature larvae. When larvae are raised in high densities on artificial media, the adult males have relatively large testes for their body size and ejaculate large volumes of sperm. In contrast, when larvae are reared in low densities, adult males had relatively small testes (Fig. 12.6).

Increases in the size of the ejaculate when there is an increased risk of sperm competition has been documented in a number of insects (see Simmons 2001). This pattern seems to depend upon whether the female is likely to remate shortly after she has copulated. For example, in such species, like crickets, fruit flies and beetles, males produce larger ejaculates when rival males are present. However, in species where remating occurs much later, as in bushcrickets and some butterflies, the presence of rivals does not result in an increase in the number of sperm transferred during mating.

Males of the golden orb-web spider *Nephila edulis* also increase the quantity of ejaculate per female when in the presence of rivals, but do so by copulating more frequently rather than producing a larger ejaculate. Such a strategy is only possible for males of species in which the female is relatively sedentary and thus the male can remain in close association with her. Frequent pair copulation is common in many species of birds, particularly birds of prey and polyandrous species. For example, goshawk (*Accipiter gentilis*) pairs will copulate between 500 and 600 times per clutch. Frequent copulations may increase a male's likelihood of fertilizing his mate's eggs, as suggested by the fair raffle model. However, sperm competition in birds does not appear to be a fair raffle, because the last sperm inseminated usually fertilizes the eggs. Thus, frequent copulations may increase the chance that the male is the last to mate and thus fertilize the eggs.

### Loaded raffles and the knowledge of roles in fair raffles

There are many instances where sperm do not compete in a fair raffle, but rather the sperm of one male are favored over those of the rival male. For example, the last male to mate in birds and some insects typically fertilizes a higher proportion of sperm, whereas in some spiders the first male to mate has a higher fertilization success. In such "**loaded**" **raffles**, if males randomly take on favored or disfavored roles, then all males should have similar ejaculate expenditures. This is predicted in species in which there is an effect of mating order on fertilization success but males are unable to control their mating order, so that each male is sometimes the first and sometimes the last to mate. However, if males always have the same role throughout a significant portion of their lives, the individuals in the disfavored role should invest more in the production of ejaculate than the ones in the favored role.

A male that mates with a virgin female has less information about the risk or intensity of sperm competition than a male that mates with a mated female. The former male has no information about sperm competition with that particular female, so he must adjust the size of his ejaculate according to the mean risk for the population. In contrast, the latter male has information that when he mates his sperm will be in competition. In a fair raffle, the model predicts greater ejaculate size when mating with a mated female than with a virgin female. The outcome for a loaded raffle is more complicated, and depends upon the nature of any mating-order effects. For example, Leigh Simmons and his colleagues at the University of Western Australia found that the first male to mate has the favored role in the bushcricket *Requena verticalis*. Although males should prefer to mate with virgin females, the number of virgin females declines over the course of the mating season, so males are increasingly likely to be in the disfavored role. As predicted by the loaded raffle model, males transfer about twice as much sperm when mating with older compared with younger females, the age of the females being closely correlated with their mating status (Simmons *et al.* 1994). Clearly, there are substantial advantages for males to be able to distinguish between virgin and mated females, and there is compelling evidence that males of some species have this ability.

## Sexual Conflict

Reproduction in **dioecious** species clearly requires a degree of **cooperation** between males and females, otherwise the gametes most likely would not come together. However, as revealed in Chapter 11, the "evolutionary" interests of males and females frequently differ over a broad range of issues, resulting in sexual conflict. Sexual conflicts may give rise to an antagonistic coevolutionary process, in which an adaptation in one sex acts as a selection pressure favoring a counteradaptation in the other. These antagonistic coevolutionary processes are especially evident in conflicts over the paternity of offspring, where selection favoring multiple mating in females clearly opposes selection favoring **exclusive paternity** in males.

## Identifying traits associated with sexual conflict

### *Sexual cannibalism*

Sexual cannibalism, in which the female kills and cannibalizes a courting or mating male, might seem to represent a particularly graphic form of conflict between the sexes. The female effectively controls whether mating takes place and the male may, depending upon the timing of sexual cannibalism, never reproduce. Selection might therefore favor traits in males that reduce the risk of sexual cannibalism, and traits in females that improve their ability to capture and cannibalize males. However, studies of web-building spiders suggest that the sexual conflict in sexual cannibalism may be more imagined than real. Early theoretical analyses of sexual cannibalism suggested that there may not be a conflict because males could improve their reproductive success by allowing females to convert their cannibalized bodies into eggs that the victims fertilize. This explanation assumes that males are unlikely to find subsequent mates and that females are typically monogamous, otherwise the additional number of eggs fertilized by the male's body would be less than the expected number of eggs fertilized by future matings. However, multiple mating is common among web-building spiders, and there is little evidence that consuming a single male has a significant impact on female fecundity.

Males of the sexually cannibalistic redback spider *Latrodectus hasselti* are small and females will mate with more than one male, suggesting that males are unlikely to increase female fecundity and may not have exclusive paternity. Maydianne Andrade of the University of Toronto showed that the victim of sexual cannibalism copulates for longer as the female imbibes the contents of his abdomen. Longer copulation improves his relative fertilization success in competition with rival males, and apparently reduces female receptivity to further mating (Andrade 1996). Thus, male redbacks improve their reproductive success through sexual cannibalism not by increasing female fecundity but by increasing their share of paternity. There may not be a sexual conflict in this instance because the females initiate sexual cannibalism.

In contrast, sexual cannibalism in the golden orb-web spider *Nephila plumipes* does not provide a simple benefit to males in terms of sperm competition (Schneider & Elgar 2001). A sexually cannibalistic female will attempt to pull the male away from the copulatory position in order to wrap him in silk. Although this terminates copulation in the orb-weaver *Argiope keyserlingi* (Elgar et al. 2000), the conductor (part of the intromittent organ) of males of *N. plumipes* is apparently difficult to dislodge and it sometimes breaks from the male's body. The presence of the conductor does not reduce the fertilization success of rival males, but males that lose their conductor typically copulate for longer, perhaps against the interests of the female (Schneider & Elgar 2001).

A small process on the conductor may allow males to lock it into the female's genital tract, thereby preventing the sexually cannibalistic female from terminating copulation.

### Genital damage

Bean weevils *Callosobruchus maculatus* provide a striking, but not immediately obvious, illustration of sexual conflict. Male bean weevils have tough spines on the tip of their intromittent organ, which only become obvious under electron microscopy. Observations by Helen Crudgington and Mike Siva-Jothy of the University of Sheffield indicated that the spines are unlikely to be used to remove the sperm of rival males, and instead they penetrate the cuticular lining of the genital tract of the female. Genital wounding of the female may benefit the male by reducing the risk of sperm competition if wounded females are less likely to remate and/or are stimulated to oviposit sooner. Females can repair the punctures, but multiply mated females die younger than singly mated females, perhaps as a result of genital damage incurred during copulation. Although there is no clear evidence that genital wounding reduces female fitness, it does appear to be an antagonistic male trait because females repeatedly kick males toward the end of copulation, a behavior that reduces the duration of copulation and the extent of genital damage (Crudgington & Siva-Jothy 2000).

## Conflict over copulation frequency

Conflicts of interest over paternity can arise by females attempting to mate multiply against the interests of her various mates, or by males attempting to mate with a female against her interest. Both can result in antagonistic coevolutionary processes, as illustrated by studies of fruit flies *D. melanogaster* and water striders (Gerridae) respectively.

### Males opposing female copulation attempts

During mating, males of *D. melanogaster* transfer chemicals in the seminal fluid that reduce female receptivity and stimulate oviposition, thereby increasing male fertilization success. However, these chemicals not only reduce female control over paternity but also have a toxic side effect, with increasing quantities resulting in decreasing female survival. An antagonistic coevolutionary model would predict an increase in female resistance to the toxic effects of male seminal fluids. William Rice of the University of California, Santa Cruz conducted a set of ingenious experiments using *D. melanogaster* that was the first test of this coevolutionary idea. In his first experiment, Rice (1996) showed that traits, such as seminal fluid products, that improve male fertilization success at the expense of females can rapidly evolve in the absence of evolving female counter-adaptations. In a second experiment, Rice and colleagues investigated whether male *D. melanogaster* that were prevented, over many generations, from mating more than once evolved to be less harmful to females and whether selection favored lower female resistance to male-induced harm when this harm is reduced. They found that after 47 generations, males in the enforced single-mating populations evolved to be less harmful to their mates, and females in these populations evolved to be less resistant to male-induced harm, precisely as predicted by an antagonistic coevolutionary model. More generally, these results suggest that there is a potentially widespread cost of sexual selection caused by sexual conflict arising through multiple mating (Holland & Rice 1999).

## Females opposing male copulation attempts

Goran Arnqvist from the University of Uppsala and Locke Rowe from the University of Toronto have investigated how sexual conflict influences male and female morphology in water striders (Gerridae). Males of most of these species engage in little, if any, courtship, preferring instead to grasp the female with their forelegs and immediately attempt to insert their genitalia. The male rides on the back of the female during this time, which likely imposes some costs on the female. Females respond invariably with some degree of resistance, using a variety of behaviors that assist in dislodging the male. The duration of this precopulatory struggle varies from a few seconds to many minutes. Both males and females mate repeatedly, and double-mating experiments indicate that the last male to mate fertilizes most of the female's eggs. Thus, the male remains on top of the female after mating, attempting to prevent rivals from mating with her before she has had time to oviposit (Arnqvist & Rowe 2002). Although any benefits of multiple mating for females have not yet been identified, there may be substantial costs because the risk of predation increases substantially as a result of mating activities. Thus, there is a sexual conflict of interest over the **decision** to mate and, in some instances, over the duration of mating behavior.

Male and female water striders have a number of morphological traits that assist males to prolong and females to reduce the duration of their mating associations. The male uses his specialized grasping structures, located on his genitalia, to gain a greater purchase on the female and thus allow him to endure her attempts to dislodge him. Although it is possible that these structures are used in male–male competition, it seems unlikely because males rarely encroach on mating pairs. Females have a variety of morphological structures that apparently allow them to resist mating attempts by males. These include extended abdominal spines and the ability to tilt the abdominal tip downward, both of which reduce the duration of the mating association. Measures of male persistence and female resistance are highly correlated across species, indicating that in species with high measures of male persistence there are also high measures of female resistance and, conversely, in species with low levels of female resistance there are low levels of male persistence (Fig. 12.7).

## Conflicts not always ubiquitous

The conflicts of interest illustrated by studies of water striders and fruit flies represent instances in which the interests of all males are essentially similar and conflict with those of all females. However, in some instances there may be a congruence of interest between females and certain males that may conflict with rival males. This is nicely

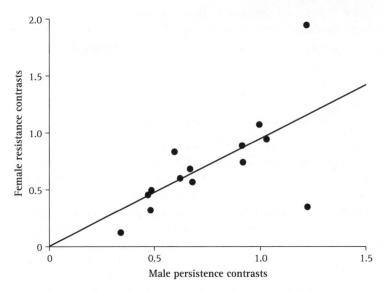

**Fig. 12.7** Relationship between composite measures of male persistence and female resistance traits associated with premating struggles across different species of water striders. The correlated evolution between male persistence and female resistance involves different traits in the two sexes, and is not correlated with a common trait such as body size. (After Arnqvist and Rowe 2002.)

illustrated in research by Jutta Schneider, now at the University of Hamburg, on male infanticide in the spider *Stegodyphus lineatus*. Female *S. lineatus* care for their offspring by feeding them with regurgitated food for about 2 weeks, after which the spiderlings consume her (matricide). Unusually, late-maturing *S. lineatus* males may encounter females that have already oviposited and are guarding their eggs. These females do not remate and lay another clutch unless the original egg sac is removed. So, if a late-maturing male encounters a guarding female, his only chance to mate will be to overpower her and practice infanticide by cutting open her egg case, and depositing the damaged egg case away from the nest, where the eggs will perish.

The benefit to the infanticidal male is straightforward since he cannot sire offspring with a female that is guarding her egg sac. However, both the female and her original mate sustain substantial costs: the clutch size of the second brood is significantly smaller and he is likely to fertilize only half of it; the additional time required to form a new clutch substantially decreases her expected survivorship; and her smaller body mass means that her matriphagous offspring may have less to consume and thus a lower expected survival. Females resist infanticidal males, and roughly half of the male attempts are unsuccessful. Nevertheless, selection has favored another counteradaptation that reduces the probability that a male will encounter females with a clutch of eggs. Females that mature earlier in the season, and which are thus more likely to encounter late-maturing males, delay oviposition and thus reduce the cost of losing a clutch of eggs (Schneider 1999).

## SUMMARY AND CONCLUSIONS

There is a potential for sexual selection to persist after mating if females mate with more than one male, and the sperm of these males subsequently coexist in proximity to the female's unfertilized ova. This arises because the sperm from these different males compete to fertilize the female's eggs. Although several benefits of multiple mating for females have been identified, this behavior may be costly for males because it could result in a loss of fertilization success. An extraordinary diversity of male traits have evolved apparently in response to the risk of sperm competition. These traits may prevent sperm competition from taking place or may increase a male's fertilization success when engaging in sperm competition. The study of sperm competition provides considerable scope for an interdisciplinary approach, since an understanding of the evolutionary processes responsible for the mating behavior of males and females requires knowledge of the physiology and anatomy of their reproductive organs, as well as their behavior and ecology. Although much has been discovered, there is still much scope for future research in this field. For example, little is known of the significance of sperm competition in simultaneous hermaphrodites. Many of these species are especially intriguing because individuals must receive sperm in order to "donate" sperm: an individual might not be choosy about a recipient of its sperm, but it may be particular about the donor.

## FURTHER READING

Essentially, this chapter outlines the causes and consequences of multiple mating, which is the subject of Birkhead's (2000) highly readable book. The costs and benefits of multiple mating by females are reviewed more formally by Jennions and Petrie (2000) and Arnqvist and Nilsson (2000), while Smith (1984) and Birkhead and Møller (1998) provide comprehensive accounts of the role of sperm competition in sexual selection. The monograph by Leigh Simmons (2001) is not only an excellent review of the insect literature but also essential reading for anyone interested in sperm competition. Eberhard (1996) documents compelling evidence that females exert considerable control over the paternity of their offspring, and Chapman et al. (2003) have written a very thorough review of sexual conflict and antagonistic coevolution. Finally, the study of sperm competition owes much to Geoff Parker, and his personal insights (Parker 2001) are inspirational.

# 13
# evolution of behavior
### Michael J. Ryan

## INTRODUCTION: WHAT IS THE EVOLUTION OF BEHAVIOR?

As we have seen in Chapter 1, Tinbergen (1963) summarized the four main "questions" of **ethology** as **causation**, ontogeny, **survival value** (or **function**), and evolution. It is the last question we will explore here – evolution. In much of animal behavior, and especially **behavioral ecology**, the term "evolution" encompasses two subjects. One is the process of selection that gives rise to the evolution of **adaptations**. The other is the historical pattern by which biological diversity has come about. Such an approach to evolution encompasses two of Tinbergen's questions, survival value and past evolutionary history. The functional aspects of behavior have been addressed in Chapter 9. This chapter will focus on its historical patterns, what Tinbergen meant by "evolution."

Evolutionary thinking has been applied to behavior for several reasons. Humans are obsessed with historical roots, whether it be their own genealogies, the derivation of Roman mythology from that of the Greeks, or the possibility that the American game of baseball might be a descendant of the English sport of cricket. It is this same interest that motivates some behavioral biologists' pursuit of evolution. Charles Darwin (1872), the first evolutionary biologist, analyzed the evolution of emotions in animals, including humans. There are striking similarities in the facial expression of humans and some of their closest relatives. Did such expressions come about in each species separately or can their similarities be best explained by being inherited from a common ancestor of humans and other primates? Thus behavioral biologists have always been interested in explaining the history by which behavior evolved.

Some of the early behavioral biologists were trained in the traditions of **comparative** morphology and taxonomy. Characters that are shared through common descent give some indication of how species are related to one another. During the development of ethology, morphology provided the primary data used to derive **phylogenetic** relationships, much as genetic methods today provide the bulk of data used in phylogenetics. Konrad Lorenz (1967, 1971) thought that the analysis of differences and similarities in behavior might also provide useful information for taxonomy and phylogeny, as well as being used to understand the historical patterns of behavioral evolution. In fact, Lorenz's emphasis on comparing **homologous behaviors** among species to understand patterns of behavioral evolution presages the current trend in studies of behavioral evolution.

Besides describing historical patterns and using behavior for taxonomy, behavioral biologists have more recently been using historical information to test hypotheses about the adaptive function of behavior (reviewed in Brooks & McLennan 1991; Harvey & Pagel 1991; Martins 1996). For example, consider how variation in a species' **mating system** might drive the evolution of a species' morphology (as discussed in Chapter 12). One might hypothesize that large testis size is an adaptation for **sperm competition** in **promiscuous** mating systems, as opposed to having small testis size in **monogamous** mating systems. This hypothesis can be tested by reconstructing the evolution of these two traits, testes size and mating system, and determining how often the predicted correlation between the traits evolves (see Fig. 12.5).

When we ask questions about history we are asking about the past. Unlike the three other areas of Tinbergen's ethology, experimentation and observations in the wild are usually not sufficient tools for glimpsing what has already happened. In this chapter we will be exposed to a different logic and a different set of tools for exploring behavior, those of historical analysis.

## Behavior, Taxonomy, and Phylogenetics

In biology, one uses the phenomenon of descent with modification to reconstruct the phylogenetic relationships among organisms. Many behavioral biologists have asked whether behavioral characters, like morphological and genetic characters, can be used for taxonomic assignment of individuals to species. Others have used these same data to gain insights into the historical relationships among species.

The premise underlying the first question is that there are species-specific behaviors that can act as diagnostic characters in assigning species status. This is true for an obvious reason. Species are often operationally defined as a group of potentially interbreeding individuals. Individuals will only interbreed if they recognize each other as mates. Most sexually reproducing species have evolved species-specific behavior, such as courtship **displays**, calls, songs, and **pheromones**, that one sex (usually females) uses to judge the appropriateness of other individuals as mates (usually males). There is strong selection to mate only with conspecifics since mating outside the species rarely produces viable and vigorous offspring. This is why species-specific courtship is usually dimorphic, with the males being the more elaborate. More specifically, this is why the plumage of birds and the songs of insects, frogs, and birds often allow one to correctly identify species (see Chapter 11). In fact, in many cases researchers first note differences in courtship **signals** that then lead them to describe populations as new species.

The second question, whether behavior provides insights into the historical relationships among species, is more complicated. The logic underlying this question is that similarities in traits among species result from either inheritance from a common ancestor or independent evolution under similar selection regimes. Traits that are similar among species because they were present in the common ancestor are called homologous. Traits that are similar but which evolved independently are called **homoplasious**, and the particular pattern of similarity is called convergence. The pattern of shared homologous traits is the footprint of evolution; if this pattern can be distinguished correctly from convergence, then we should be able to reconstruct the branching pattern or **phylogenetic tree** by which species diverged from one another. The challenge is distinguishing between homologous and homoplasious traits. Under the assumption that evolution is a conservative process, many scientists rely on the **principle of parsimony**, which is that the simplest explanation is more likely to be correct than a more complicated one. For an example of the logic of parsimony, consider that there are approximately 5000 species of mammals and they all have four-chambered hearts. We can ask, did this trait evolve 5000 times independently or is it present in all mammals because it is shared through a common ancestor? Parsimony favors the latter explanation. This exercise in logic is applied only to the evolutionary origin of the trait. It does not make any judgment as to whether the trait has current survival value, i.e., whether it is maintained by selection.

When phylogeneticists assess species relationships, they analyze the similarities of traits among species and present the results as species arranged on a phylogenetic tree. This tree is a representation of the way the species have diverged from one another over time. For any given number of species there are many possible trees. Phylogeneticists usually attempt to find the tree that explains the distribution of data by invoking the fewest number of evolutionary changes under the principle of parsimony. In principle, any traits can be analyzed but those subject to strong selection are more likely to evolve similarities through convergence than are traits that are selectively neutral. One way to avoid the effects of misleading data is to analyze a variety of types of characters, especially traits that are somewhat different from those of immediate interest. This is one reason why current phylogenetic studies often use DNA sequences in addition to morphological and behavioral traits. Although there are noteworthy exceptions, many studies have shown that phylogenetic analyses of behavioral traits yield hypotheses about relationships that are similar to analyses based on molecular characters (Wimberger & de Queiroz 1996).

## Patterns of Behavioral Evolution

### Deduced from strong inference

In some cases a detailed understanding of an animal's behavior in the wild combined with a basic understanding of evolution is sufficient to allow one to propose likely scenarios for how behaviors have evolved. A simple and stunning example concerns the star orchid of Madagascar. In his book on how orchids are fertilized, Darwin (1862) described this flower as having its nectar in the bottom of a flower spur almost a third of a meter in depth. Such nectar could only be accessed by a very special pollinator, one with a tongue at least as long. No such beast was known from Madagascar at the time, but Darwin predicted one would be found. And it was, a hawkmoth with the longest known tongue in the Old World (*Xanthopan morganni praedicta*; Fig. 13.1). In this case, a simple observation about a plant yielded a specific and testable prediction about a behavioral adaptation of an animal that was not even known to exist at the time.

Understanding the evolution of behavior is usually not as simple as in the case of the hawkmoth. Darwin's theory of natural selection suggests that complex traits arise by small incremental changes from more simple traits. The evolution of complex traits can thus present a challenge (Dawkins 1996). One could argue that behavioral traits are among the most complex of phenotypic traits. They did not arise out of whole cloth. So we can ask: what is their evolutionary history and how do we go about studying it?

As mentioned at the outset of this chapter, closely related species often share similar behaviors, and it seems likely that these behaviors are shared through a common ancestor. Consider the following quote from Darwin's book *The Expression of the Emotions in Man and the Animals* (1872, p. 91):

> When male animals utter sounds in order to please the females, they would naturally employ those which are sweet to the ears of the species; and it appears that the same sounds are often pleasing to widely different animals, owing to the similarity of their nervous systems, as we ourselves perceive in the singing of birds and even in the chirping of certain treefrogs giving us pleasure.

In this passage Darwin is suggesting that similar behaviors, in this case acoustic signals used by males to court females, result from a variety of species sharing the same properties of the nervous system that deem such sounds attractive. He even suggests, quite boldly, that female animals and humans might share the same esthetic preferences for animal song due to such evolutionarily shared properties. Thus ever since Darwin it was thought that some of the similarities in behavior among species might be due to descent with modification.

Sometimes there can be striking similarities between behaviors associated with different activities within the same species. Julian Huxley (1914) pondered the complicated courtship patterns of the grebe *Porpodiceps cristatus*. In one part of the grebe's courtship, the penguin dance, the birds exhibit **stereotyped behavior** patterns that bear a striking resemblance to other behaviors associated with nest building. It seemed to

**Fig. 13.1** Darwin predicted that the Madagascar star orchid *Angraecum sesquipedale* would require pollination by an insect with an exceptionally long tongue. Later, the hawkmoth *Xanthopan morganni praedicta* was discovered. (From *Trends in Ecology and Evolution* 1998, 13, 259.)

Huxley unlikely that such complex motor patterns, so gracefully coordinated between mates, arose de novo and just happened to resemble behaviors used in other contexts. Instead, Huxley thought such display behaviors were derived or **"ritualized"** from more simple motor patterns that served other functions. How does ritualization take place?

Here is a simple example. When a dog is about to attack an opponent it must open its mouth; thus the open mouth becomes a cue of an impending attack. The open mouth may then evolve into an exaggerated and stereotyped behavior that evolves into a threat signal. Tinbergen (1952) summarized the ways in which an original behavior can become ritualized into a display behavior: the original behavior becomes more intense, is performed more slowly, is repeated **rhythmically**, is combined with other behaviors, and is no longer directed toward the stimulus that originally elicited it. A bird squatting and pointing its beak skyward prior to flight evolved from behaviors associated with preparation for flight and is one example of a ritualized behavior. Another example is the rhythmic courtship drumming that woodpeckers evolved from their behavior of hunting insects. Thus similarities in behavior within as well as among species can give us clues as to how they evolved.

One sort of behavioral evolution that is a little more complicated is when the behavior of one species influences the behavior of another and vice versa. Fireflies have species-specific patterns of flashing that are used in conspecific mate choice (summarized in Lloyd 1984). Male fireflies search for a mate by signaling with a flash, the female responds with her own flash, and the male approaches the female and mates with her. Or at least that is usually how it happens. Fireflies in the genus *Photuris* prey on other fireflies, including those in the genus *Photinus*. Female *Photuris* sometimes **mimic** the flashing signal of female *Photinus*. When the male *Photinus* approaches he is not mated by a female of his own species but eaten by the female *Photuris*. This game of deceit is continued by the male *Photuris*. Male *Photuris* will sometimes mimic the flash of the male *Photinus* as a way to locate their conspecific female *Photuris*. The female *Photuris* mimics her prey, female *Photinus*, in replying to the flashes of what appears to her to be a male *Photinus*, but instead when the male approaches she finds it is a potential mate rather than a potential meal.

How did all this come about? By what pattern did this sequence of deceitful behaviors evolve? Strong logic suggests what seems to be the most likely hypothesis. First, each species has its own species-specific flash pattern; then female *Photuris* evolves to exploit male *Photinus*; then male *Photuris* evolve to exploit female *Photuris*. Although we cannot prove that this scenario is the correct one, none of the alternatives seems to be as feasible. If there were no species-specific signals, there would be nothing for the female *Photuris* to exploit; if female *Photuris* did not try to lure their prey by mimicking the flashes of *Photinus* females, they could not be exploited by *Photuris* males. The logic seems tight, the scenario seems right. Of course, the scenario is just a hypothesis which could be wrong.

This type of logic has also been applied to a more complicated pattern of evolution, the widely cited courtship behavior of a group of empidid flies known as balloonflies, described by Kessel (1955). In some species males form **leks**, areas where males aggregate solely for the purpose of displaying to females (see Chapter 11), and present females with large empty balloons of silk. Females choose mates as if they are evaluating the size of the balloons. Can we possibly understand how something like this might evolve? Kessel studied other species of empidids and found an interesting range of courtship behaviors. Some species hunt small insects which they use as **nuptial gifts**, and some but not all of these species with nuptial gifts gather in leks. Furthermore, the presentation of these gifts to females varies among species: some partially wrap the nuptial gifts in a single strand of silk, others totally wrap the gift in silk, whereas the males of other species suck the juices out of the gift before wrapping it. Even empidids that feed on nectar instead of insects buy into this gift-giving scheme, but instead of hunting down a prey item they wrap the balloon around dead insects they find. And finally, back to where we started, some species present the female with a large empty balloon.

Given the behavior of the various species of empidids, there is a very logical series of behavioral transitions. Among insect-hunting empidids there is first the evolution of nuptial gift giving, and then the adornment or "packaging" of the gift. Once packaged, males cheat either by sucking the juices out of the prey or by not even putting a gift in the package. An alternative explanation is that females, for some reason, evolve to be more impressed by the package itself than what it contains. Thus, males are free to devalue the gift (sucking out the juices) or just give an empty package. In addition, it also appears that when at least some of these flies shift from an insect to a nectar diet they are still "stuck" with the ancestral gift-giving tradition. Again, the logic seems tight, the scenario seems right. As Cumming (1994) points out, however, these scenarios are drawn from a few species of balloonflies in different genera of the subfamily Empidinae and range from seemingly simple to more complicated behaviors. The subfamily contains more than 1500 species and this popular scenario still needs to be verified using some of the more rigorous phylogenetic tools we discuss below.

## Deduced from phylogenetic comparisons

In the above examples, variation in behavior among species was examined and a logical scenario of how such behaviors might have evolved was proposed. A more rigorous approach is to propose such logical scenarios in a phylogenetic context, in the knowledge that phylogeny could eliminate certain explanations of patterns of evolution as being unlikely.

Such an approach was taken in a study of song evolution in fruit flies of the *Drosophila repleta* group of species (Ewing & Miyan 1986). Fruit flies produce low-**frequency** love songs by flapping their wings. The researchers analyzed the courtship songs of 22 species. All the songs had either one of two components, labeled A and B, or both components (Fig. 13.2a). The authors surmised that component A was important in **species recognition** whereas component B evolved under **sexual selection** (see Chapter 11). They used a phylogenetic tree of the species relationships that was derived from an analysis of chromosome variation. They then mapped the songs onto the phylogenetic tree (Fig. 13.2b). The challenge is to derive major patterns of evolutionary changes in the song from this combined dataset of behavior and phylogeny.

Ewing and Miyan proposed that the ancestral call type contained both A and B components. Figure 13.2(c) shows how the substantial variation in song can be explained by a relatively small number of evolutionary changes, including loss of A song in one group, loss of B song in another, and elaboration of the B song in a third. This analysis is similar to those above in that it is based on strong inference, but it does so in a phylogenetic context. Without having an independent hypothesis of phylogenetic relationships, one might have assumed, for example, that the three species with only A-song components (*D. martensis*, *D. repleta*, and *D. limensis*) must be each others' closest relatives. This might have resulted in a quite different interpretation of the pattern of song evolution. Thus unlike some of the previous examples that were based

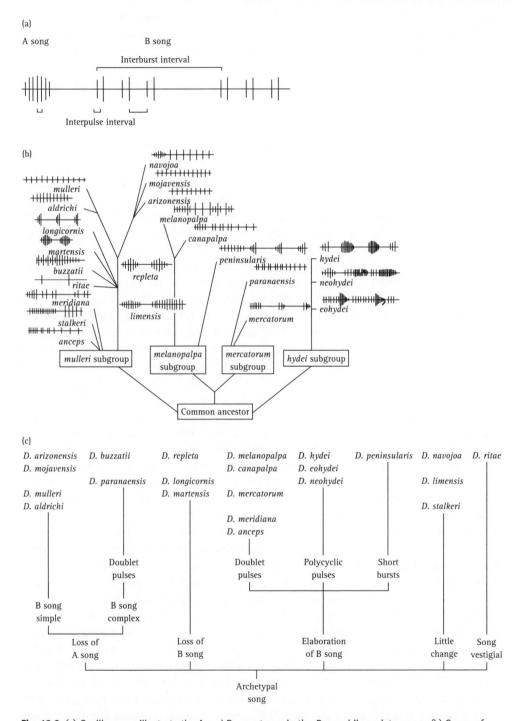

**Fig. 13.2** (a) Oscillograms illustrate the A and B song types in the *Drosophila repleta* group. (b) Songs of the different species on a phylogeny of the species group. The phylogenetic relationships were determined from cytological data and not data from songs. (c) Interpretation of song evolution by the researchers. (Redrawn from Ewing & Miyan 1986.)

only on a strong inference about how behavior evolves (e.g., simple to complex), the phylogenetic tree of the group constrains the likely explanations of *Drosophila* song evolution by viewing them in the context of phylogeny. This example should suggest caution in accepting evolutionary scenarios in which behavior is postulated to evolve from simple to more complex in the absence of any independent phylogenetic information.

## Deduced from phylogenetic analysis

In the example of fruit fly song evolution, phylogenetics is explicitly used to determine which scenarios might be more likely. A more formal application of this approach is called **character mapping**. Before delving into an example of this approach, we need to understand how phylogeneticists attempt to reconstruct the historical relationships among taxa.

**Phylogenetic reconstruction**, as it is called, involves comparing homologous traits among species in order to derive a hypothesis of the most likely pattern of relation-ships among species. There are many possible patterns of relationship and the challenge is to decide which one is most likely given a set of data. To do so, phylogeneticists are often guided by the operating principle of parsimony, mentioned above. Parsimony assumes that the pattern of relationships most likely to be true is the one that requires the fewest number of evolutionary changes in the characters being studied. (Maximum likelihood is another **optimality** criterion often used. Parsimony and maximum likelihood analyses of the same data often lead to similar results.)

To illustrate the approach consider Fig. 13.3. There are four taxa for which we would like to predict the phylogenetic relationships, labeled A–D. For each of these taxa we measure four traits, labeled 1–4. Each of these traits has two simple types of variation or character states: they are either absent (0) or present (1). In this example we will assume that all these traits are absent in other closely related species. For four taxa the number of possible patterns of relationship would be 15. Three such patterns are represented in Fig. 13.3. Of these three, which is most likely to be true? If we rely on the principle of parsimony we will accept the phylogenetic tree that requires the fewest number of evolutionary changes. Since these traits are absent in close relatives, there needs to be at least one evolutionary change to explain the presence of a trait. If the relationships depicted in Fig. 13.3(a) are correct, there will have been four evolutionary changes. Trait 4 was acquired (changed from character state 0 to 1) after taxa B, C, and D diverged from taxon A, explaining why trait 4 is lacking in taxon A (character state 0) but is present in the other three taxa (character state 1). Traits 1 and 3 were acquired after taxa C and D diverged from taxon B, and thus are absent in taxa A and B but present in taxa C and D. Finally, this phylogenetic hypothesis suggests that trait 2 was acquired (character state 0 → 1) after taxon D diverged from all the others, which is why this trait is present in only a single taxon. If the phylogenetic hypothesis rep-resented by the tree in Fig. 13.3(a) were true, then parsimony predicts that there would have been four evolutionary changes in the characters under study. The phylogenetic hypothesis in Fig. 13.3(b) posits five changes, as character 4 is gained at the root of the

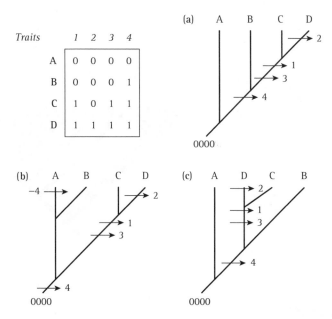

Fig. 13.3 Hypothetical relationships among species. Table shows traits 1–4 for taxa A–D, where 0 indicates the trait is absent and 1 indicates it is present. The branching diagrams (a–c) represent three hypotheses for the phylogenetic relations of taxa A–D; arrows indicate the pattern of evolution of each character state that these various sets of relationships would predict. A negative integer on the left of the arrow represents loss of that trait (−1 → 0) and a positive integer on the right of the arrow the gain of that trait (0 → 1).

tree and again lost in taxon A. (There is another pattern of character evolution for Fig. 13.3b that requires five changes. What is it?) Thus parsimony would favor the hypothesis in Fig. 13.3(a) over that in Fig. 13.3(b). We see that the relationships depicted among taxa in Fig. 13.3(c) are quite different from those shown in Fig. 13.3(a). However, like Fig. 13.3(a), this pattern also requires only four changes. Thus parsimony cannot discriminate between the two hypotheses represented in Fig. 13.3(a, c).

Character mapping involves the same logic used in phylogenetic reconstruction but instead one starts with a single phylogenetic hypothesis and asks what is the most parsimonious explanation for how a set of particular traits evolved if the phylogenetic hypothesis is true. An example of this more explicit approach to a phylogenetic analysis of behavior was used to study display behavior in ducks, a problem that had been addressed by one of the founders of ethology, Konrad Lorenz (1971). The sexual displays in ducks were divided into one of two categories, initial postcopulatory or additional postcopulatory displays (Johnson et al. 2000). The researchers analyzed these behaviors in 48 species for which there was a hypothesis of phylogenetic relationships from analysis of mitochondrial DNA. The behavioral data were "mapped" onto the phylogeny. What this means is that the character states of the displays (present/absent in this study) were assigned to the species. Given that information, the researchers mapped onto the phylogeny when evolutionary changes for each character took place.

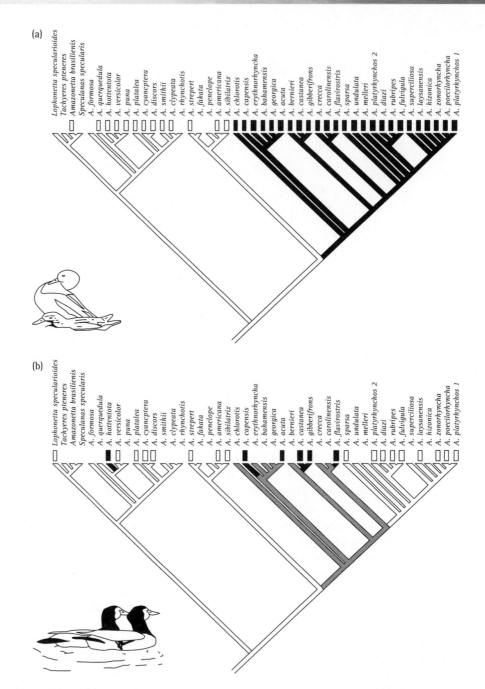

**Fig. 13.4** Duck displays. (a) Bridle display of the mallard *Anas platyrhynchos* and depiction of a hypothesis of its evolution. (b) Erect broadside display of the Chiloe wigeon *Anas sibilatrix* and depiction of a hypothesis of its evolution. Open branches indicate the display is absent, closed branches that it is present, and gray branches that assigning the state is equivocal. (Modified from Johnson et al. 2000.)

A general finding of the study is that the four initial postcopulatory displays analyzed are quite conservative, i.e., there are few evolutionary changes, whereas the four additional postcopulatory displays are less conservative, i.e., they exhibit more changes. This is illustrated in Fig. 13.4, which compares the pattern by which one initial post-copulatory display (Bridle) has changed over time with the pattern deduced for the evolution of one additional postcopulatory behavior (Erect Broadside).

# Testing Process with Patterns

## Coevolution

The studies discussed above were designed primarily to uncover patterns of behavioral evolution, and not specifically to test hypotheses. In many cases, however, the patterns by which characters evolve can be used to test specific hypotheses about evolutionary processes. One such hypothesis is **coevolution**. In the narrow sense, such studies address how multiple species influence the evolution of one another. As an analogy, consider the "coevolutionary" cycles of pesticide resistance by insects and the use of new pesticides in agriculture, and the evolution of drug resistance by bacteria and the development of new antibiotics by pharmaceutical companies (Bull & Wichman 2001). These examples are not true cases of coevolution in the Darwinian sense, as new pesticides and anti-biotics do not evolve but are produced by humans. Furthermore, in these cases, the coevolutionary cycle is sometimes easy to document as there are human records of the new innovations in pesticides and antibiotics. So how does one test the hypothesis of coevolution between species in the wild?

A particular type of coevolution that has seen widespread interest is that of **cospeciation**. This phenomenon has often been suggested as an explanation of the patterns of herbivore diet specialization and plant defense one sees in the wild. Ehrlich and Raven (1964) postulated the following scenario:

1  the diet of an insect is determined by chemical plant defenses known as secondary compounds;
2  selection generated by an insect feeding on a plant will cause the species of plant to evolve new defenses;
3  the evolution of an especially effective innovation in defense will allow the plant lineage to diversify in the newly found herbivore-free "adaptive zone";
4  insect species specializing on other plants will eventually adapt to the defenses of the newly radiating plant species, which will result in the diversification of the insect taxa.

Futuyma and Mitter (1996) compared the phylogenetic relationships of several species of leaf beetles (*Ophraella*) to that of its host plants to test the hypothesis of cospeciation. As Fig. 13.5 shows, there is little evidence in this system for cospeciation. Instead, it is argued that when insects change the plant species on which they feed they are

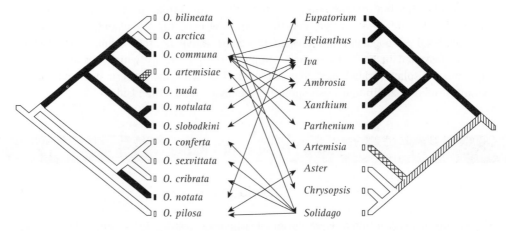

**Fig. 13.5** Phylogenies of the leaf beetle genus *Ophraella* (left) and its host plants (right). The lines indicate the host plants used by each species. The shading on the beetle phylogeny illustrates when host shifts took place.

likely to change to a closely related species, as opposed to the scenario of cospeciation proposed by Ehrlich and Raven.

A convincing case of cospeciation is provided by studies of figs and the wasps that pollinate them. In general, each species of fig is pollinated by a single species of wasp, and each fig-pollinating wasp will pollinate only that species of fig. This is one of the most extreme cases of obligate pollination known. A female wasp will enter a fig, which has its flowers enclosed within the fruit. The female will pollinate some of the flowers, lay eggs in others, and then die inside the fig. After her offspring hatch, the male and female offspring mate, the females gather pollen from some of the flowers and then leave to find another fig in which they can oviposit, die, and thus continue the life cycle (Machacado et al. 2001). A detailed phylogenetic analysis of the relationships of figs and wasps shows that there are 20 genera of fig-pollinating wasps and, with a few exceptions, each wasp genus is restricted to pollinating the same fig subgenus, as predicted by the hypothesis of cospeciation.

## Sexual selection and sensory exploitation

In a broader sense, coevolution can also encompass patterns of character evolution within a species lineage. This is expected to be important when the function of one aspect of the phenotype depends on other aspects of the phenotype. Since much of the phenotype appears to be a larger integrated unit rather than a series of unrelated modules, we might expect coevolution within lineages to be critical. A prominent example might occur in communication systems associated with reproduction.

In many sexually reproducing species, males produce advertisement signals specific to the species; females are attracted preferentially to males producing the conspecific signal in contrast to males producing signals of other species. The evolution of such mate-recognition systems is a critical part of the **speciation** process. In one simple scenario of how speciation comes about, it is supposed that the range of an ancestral species becomes split by a geographic barrier, resulting in two isolated populations. Reproductive interactions are constrained to individuals on either side of the barrier. These populations become different in various aspects of their phenotype, including the mate-recognition system, due to random genetic drift or local adaptation. Eventually the populations differ to a degree that they no longer recognize their former conspecifics as appropriate mates. Speciation has occurred (Mayr 1942).

During the process of speciation there is often evolution of a new communication system that recognizes mates. For this to happen, it is thought, there must be a change not only in the signal used by males but also in females' perception of that signal. Many studies have shown that various aspects of the **receivers'** neural systems are tuned or biased to properties of the species-specific signal, whether it be in the auditory, visual, chemosensory, or electrical modality (see also Chapter 2).

Sexual selection is responsible for the evolution of exaggerated male, and sometimes female, traits that enhance an individual's ability to acquire mates even if the exaggerated traits reduce survivorship. Sometimes the exaggerated traits give the bearer tools that are used in combat, but in many cases the elaboration involves signals that males use to attract females (see Chapter 11). Although sexual selection can be important in driving evolution of traits used in species recognition (Lande 1982; West Eberhard 1983), much of the interest in sexual selection is in trying to explain the evolution of exaggerated traits within a lineage.

A central focus in the study of sexual selection is understanding why females would prefer males with traits that reduce survivorship, especially in mating systems in which males offer no resources to females but their sperm. Two hypotheses have received most of the attention: the "**good genes**" theory and Fisher's theory of **runaway sexual selection** (see Chapter 11). Both hypotheses posit that the variation in the genes underlying the male trait and the female preference become correlated, and that evolution of the male trait in response to female preference generates correlated evolution of the preference itself. Thus tight coevolution of the trait and preference should be apparent. A third hypothesis is **sensory exploitation**. This hypothesis states that females will have general sensory or perceptual biases, as detailed by the more general theory of sensory drive, and that males who evolve traits that exploit these biases will be favored by sexual selection.

The two hypotheses of coevolution can be distinguished from that of sensory exploitation if one can reconstruct the evolution of sexually selected traits and female preferences for those traits. If the trait is restricted to one lineage but the preference for that trait encompasses not only the lineage with the trait but others without it, then the most logical interpretation is that the preference existed prior to the trait. However, if the preference is restricted to the lineage in which the trait is present, then the coevolution hypotheses are more tenable.

This approach to sexual selection was initially taken in two groups of animals, swordtail fishes (*Xiphophorus helleri*; Basolo 1990) and túngara frogs (*Physalaemus pustulosus*; Ryan et al. 1990; Ryan & Rand 1993). Female swordtails prefer males with longer swords, an elaboration of the bottom rays of the caudal fin. At the time of the

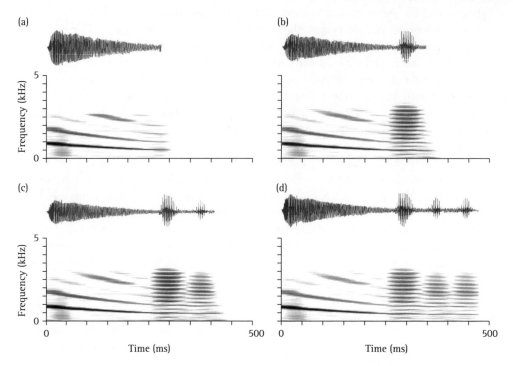

**Fig. 13.6** Example of the call complexity series of the túngara frog *Physalaemus pustulosus*. Each diagram shows a waveform (top) and a spectrogram (bottom). (a) Whine with no chucks; (b) whine with one chuck; (c) whine with two chucks; (d) whine with three chucks.

experiments, swordtails were thought to be a **monophyletic** group consisting of two smaller groups, northern swordtails and southern swordtails. A third group, the platy-fish, is a monophyletic group belonging to the same genus. Male platyfish lack swords, but Basolo showed that if she appended a plastic sword to a male platyfish his own females found him more attractive. Later, there was some debate as to the origin of the sword within *Xiphophorus*, and whether southern swordtails and platyfish were indeed separate groups (Meyer et al. 1994). Although the phylogeny of these fish is not fully resolved, Basolo's interpretation of sensory exploitation seems to hold, as she repeated the experiments with another fish, *Priapella olmacae*. This fish is in a genus closely related to *Xiphophorus* but which, like platyfish, has swordless males. And like platy-fish, they have females that prefer swords (Basolo 1995).

A similar result was found in a very different mating system that relies on acoustic rather than visual cues. Male túngara frogs produce a call consisting of a whine and a number of chucks (zero to six) (Fig. 13.6). Females prefer males with chucks, and particularly the larger males that make lower frequency chucks. Except for its sister species *P. petersi*, all other known *Physalaemus* species (> 30) lack chucks, so the chuck seems to have been derived from the ancestor of these two species. Females of a closely related species, *P. coloradorum*, prefer the whines of their own species; however, when a túngara-frog chuck is appended to the normal call of a *P. coloradorum* male, females prefer this more than the normal chuckless whines. Thus it appears that among some *Physalaemus* species there is a preexisting bias for chucks and male túngara frogs evolved chucks to exploit that bias (Ryan & Rand 1993). There is also a more subtle exploitation occurring. The relationship between the tuning of one of the frog's two inner-ear organs and the frequencies in the chuck results in female túngara frogs preferring the lower frequency chucks of larger males. However, other species of *Physalaemus* in the same species group all have similar tuning properties (Ryan et al. 1990; Wilczynski et al. 2001). Thus it seems that the properties of the chuck evolved to match what is a very conservative feature of this animal's neurobiology.

## Correlations of variables with independent contrasts

Hypotheses about how behavior evolves are often tested using a comparative approach by determining if two variables are correlated as would be predicted by independent convergent evolution of traits. For example, as we saw in Chapter 12 and especially Fig. 12.5, males should have larger testes in more promiscuous mating systems, primates that eat fruit should have larger brains than those that eat leaves, and birds that are more susceptible to parasites should have brighter plumage than birds that reside in parasite-free zones. The two variables for a number of species are compared to determine if these variables exhibit the predicted correlation. If so, the hypothesis is supported; if not, it is rejected.

Using the species as the unit of comparison implies that the relationship between the variables in question evolved independently in each species, as if the species had no evolutionary connection to each other. But this may not be the case. Consider one of the predictions just mentioned: males should have larger testes in more promiscuous mating systems, a prediction from sperm competition theory (see Chapter 12 and Fig. 12.5). For example, assume that we have data on testis size and mating system of a group of primates. The variation in the mating system is quantified as the number of males per group. The more males in a group, the greater the possibility of sperm competition due to females mating multiple times. Assume that when we examine these two variables there is a strong correlation: males of species with more promiscuous mating systems have larger testes. These data would seem to support the sperm competition hypothesis. However, such an interpretation depends not on the number of species that have the predicted relationship between testis size and mating system, but the number of times this relationship evolved.

Assume that the mating system of the common ancestor was monogamous (one male per group) and that the males had small testes. This common ancestor then gave rise to a large number of descendant species, and in each species independently there was an increase in both testis size and the number of males per group. This pattern would support the sperm competition hypothesis because the two variables have changed in concert a large number of times. Alternatively, assume that the same common ancestor, monogamous with small testes, gave rise to two descendants, one with testes and a mating system like itself and the other with larger testes and a more promiscuous mating system. Each of these two species then gave rise to many descendant species

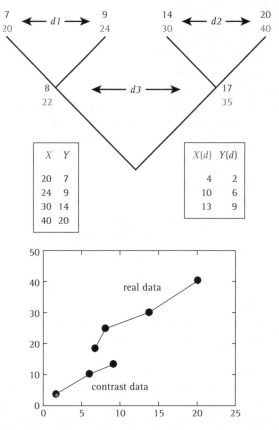

**Fig. 13.7** Example of independent contrasts. The distribution of two variables, *X* (blue) and *Y* (red), are shown for four extant taxa (tips of the branches). The relationship between these two variables is shown on the graph (real data). The estimates for *X* and *Y* for the two ancestors of the four extant species is shown at the two nodes. The three independent contrasts are shown indicated on the tree as *d1–d3* and the values listed in the table on the left and the relationships of the contrasts of *X* to the contrasts of *Y* are plotted on the graph (contrast data).

but there was no further evolution of testes size or mating system. Although in this scenario there are many species with the predicted relationship between testes size and mating system, there is only one independent evolutionary event, the initial evolution of larger testes and more promiscuous mating system. All the other species exhibit their values of these two variables because they inherited them from a common ancestor rather than by independent evolution.

How can we estimate the degree to which associations between traits within species have evolved independently? A popular method is called **independent contrasts** (Felsenstein 1985), and this approach is illustrated in Fig. 13.7. Again, one must begin with a hypothesis of phylogenetic relationships. Here one is not interested in the actual values of the variables of interest for each species, but in how much these variables have changed between species since they have diverged from a common ancestor. Thus the first step is to estimate the variables of interest for the ancestors or the nodes on the phylogenetic tree. The second step is to determine the degree to which the two variables differ between sister taxa, be they on the tips or the nodes of the tree. It is these differences or independent contrasts that are tested for the predicted relationships. As Fig. 13.7 indicates, the relationships between the variables of the extant species and their contrasts can be quite different.

There is somewhat of a consensus among behavioral biologists that the comparative approach needs to control for history. Many studies that predated this consensus have been reevaluated. For example, the data first presented by Harcourt et al. (1981) showing the predicted relationship in primates between testis size and mating system did not control for phylogenetic relationship. When this hypothesis was tested with a larger taxonomic range of species with appropriate phylogenetic controls, the data still supported the sperm competition hypothesis (Harvey & May 1989). Alternatively, Hamilton and Zuk (1982) predicted that species of birds that were more exposed to parasites would have brighter plumage, and a comparison of species without considering phylogeny supported this hypothesis. This support, however, withered when the data were reanalyzed with the appropriate phylogenetic corrections (Read & Harvey 1989).

## Brain, Behavior, and Evolution

When selection favors the evolution of traits needed to face environmental challenges, such as survival in harsh temperatures, there could be the evolution of an optimal solution that would be stable over time. For example, animals in arctic climes might evolve an optimal degree of fat and fur given the various tradeoffs of such an adaptation. As long as the temperature and other aspects of the environment are stable, we would not expect to see further evolution of these traits. In many social situations, however, evolution is best characterized as an **arms race** in which the traits of organisms drive the evolution one another. A predator evolving more efficient hunting tactics and a prey evolving greater ability to evade those tactics is one example. An arms race can also take place within a species. A **signaler** might evolve the ability to be deceptive and a receiver the ability to detect such **deceptions**, even though a single individual can act as both signaler and receiver depending on the social situation (Dawkins & Krebs 1978; see also Chapter 10).

It has long been known that the neural and cognitive mechanisms by which signals are processed by a receiver can lead to the evolution of elaborate or exaggerated signals without concomitant change in the receiver. This is amply illustrated by Tinbergen's notion of the **supernormal stimulus**, where a stimulus with certain properties exaggerated relative to the normal stimulus elicits a greater response (see Chapter 2). Two examples from the early ethological literature include male sticklebacks in their bright-red nuptial coloration rushing toward a large red postal van driving past their aquarium (Tinbergen 1952), and oystercatchers preferentially retrieving a large model of an egg in preference to the smaller real egg that has been removed from their nests (Tinbergen 1951). There are other types of stimulus–response patterns that suggest that internal biases of animals can drive evolution in certain directions.

In a more artificial setting, pigeons exhibit a well-known psychological phenomenon called **peak shift displacement**. In such an experiment a bird receives positive **reinforcement** to one wavelength of light, say 550 nm, and negative reinforcement to another, say 555 nm: if it pecks the keys in its box in the presence of one wavelength, it is rewarded with food; if it does so in response to the other wavelength, the lights in the box are turned off. After **conditioning**, the strength of the pigeons' responses are measured across a variety of wavelengths. One might predict that the most vigorous key-pecking would be to 550 nm, the wavelength at which the bird was rewarded. But no, the peak of responsiveness is shifted away from that wavelength to one more different than the wavelength associated with the negative reward, i.e., to wavelengths less than 550 nm (Staddon 1975).

Humans show similar directional biases in how they recognize faces. Enquist and Arak (1998) reviewed experiments by Brennan (1985) in which subjects were given several line drawings of faces. One was a "prototypical" face derived from an average of a large number of faces. One was a realistic drawing of the face of former US president Ronald Reagan, and another a caricature of Reagan. The caricature, almost by definition, exaggerated the traits of Reagan that made it distinctive from the face of others in general and from the prototypical face specifically. When asked to choose the true rendition of Reagan, most subjects chose the caricature rather than the more accurate rendition of Reagan.

Enquist and Arak (1993) showed how these perceptual biases can even be instantiated in some artificial intelligence systems known as artificial neural networks. These networks are arrays of computational units that respond to digital inputs of stimuli, such as visual patterns. These networks can be trained with an evolutionary **algorithm** to recognize patterns. To do so, a large number of networks are constructed, they are all given the same target stimuli, there is selection in which the networks that respond best to some criterion are chosen to be represented in the next generation, and some of these networks are mutated by changing details of the algorithms that govern their response. This procedure is conducted until the networks achieve the specified recognition criterion. In their experiments Enquist and Arak selected networks to respond positively to a cross in which one of the arms was longer than all the others, and to respond negatively to a cross in which all of the arms were of equal length. Once the networks evolved the ability to make such a discrimination, they were tested with novel stimuli. Although most novel stimuli elicited a smaller response than the positive-training stimulus, some novel stimuli elicited an even greater response. In the language of ethology, these seemed to be supernormal stimuli. In the language of some animal communication workers, these were stimuli that exploited the response biases of the receivers.

In all the above examples (sticklebacks, oystercatchers, pigeons, humans, and artificial intelligence), recognition decisions have directional biases. We assume that those biases would generate selection for certain signal traits if they were to evolve. This might be the explanation for some, although certainly not all, of the examples of sensory exploitation that have been offered.

In the above examples, the animal's brain influences the evolution of signals it needs to process. But the alternative could be true. It could be that the problems a brain needed to solve in the past might influence how it solves current problems. A good analogy is

Luchin's (1942) water jug problem. Subjects were given a large jug of water and measuring cups of three sizes: 3, 23, and 49 ounces (1 ounce is equivalent to ~ 29 mL). They were asked to remove a given volume. One group was trained on a simple problem that could be solved in two steps. They were told to measure 20 ounces of water. Most subjects filled the 23-ounce cup to the brim and then used the other cup to remove 3 ounces. A second group was given a problem that could be solved with a minimum of three steps. They were given cups of 3, 21, and 127 ounces and asked to measure out 100 ounces. They filled the 127-ounce cup and emptied it once with the 21-ounce cup and twice with the 3-ounce cup. This second group was then asked to solve the two-step 20-ounce problem. Instead of solving it in two steps (see above), they solved it in three steps: they filled the 49-ounce cup and emptied it once with the 23-ounce cup and twice with the 3-ounce cup. Their solution was no less correct than that of the group initially trained with the simpler problem, but it was different and it was more complex. And, more importantly, their previous experience influenced their solution.

There appears to be an evolutionary analog to the water jug experiment in that the evolutionary history of the brain influences which solutions the brain will use to achieve various functions. Or at least that is what is suggested by some studies of túngara frogs. We mentioned above that these frogs produce whines for species recognition and that some species add chucks to make the call more attractive. The female preference for chucks did not coevolve with the chucks, but appears to be a preexisting bias that was exploited by males that evolved chucks. On the other hand, it appears that the details of the whines that needed to be recognized by ancestors influenced how túngara frogs decode this species-specific character.

Ryan and Rand (1995, 1999) used the independent contrast approach to estimate calls at ancestral nodes of the phylogenetic tree of the *Physalaemus pustulosus* species group. They determined the probability that females would approach a speaker broadcasting a heterospecific call, but these calls could be of extant species or the estimated calls of ancestors. They then asked if the phylogenetic relatedness between the túngara frog and the heterospecific/ancestor would predict any of the variation in the female's behavior independent of the overall acoustic similarity between the túngara frog call and the target call. The answer was yes; phylogenetic relatedness, or more generally, history, explains a substantial proportion of variation in female responses. It seems that indeed "evolution leaves a footprint on the frog's brain." This conclusion was critically borne out by Phelps and Ryan (2000) using artificial neural network simulations. These networks were used to simulate brain evolution. A population of networks was trained to recognize calls at the root of the phylogenetic tree using an evolutionary algorithm somewhat similar to the one described by Enquist and Arak. Once the networks recognized this call, they were trained to recognize the immediate ancestor of this call on the direct path of descent to the túngara frog. This continued until the networks reached the end of the path, the túngara frog itself, and were selected to recognize the túngara frog call. The same procedure was conducted in which the history of the neural networks was randomized. In these cases, the networks were trained with three calls chosen at random before finally being trained to recognize the túngara frog call. After the networks evolved to recognize the túngara frog call, their ability to predict the behavior of real females was measured. This was done by testing real frogs and the networks with all the heterospecific and ancestral calls and computing the correlation between the response strength of females and networks. Only the networks with the real histories significantly predicted the response of the real frogs. Even though past history does not constrain the ability to evolve the adaptation of species recognition, it does influence how the artificial networks, and presumably the frogs, go about doing it.

## SUMMARY AND CONCLUSIONS

Tinbergen considered understanding the past evolutionary history of behavior as one of the four major aims of ethology. We have seen that in some cases sufficient knowledge of the animal's natural history can suggest how behavioral adaptations have come about. However, arguments based only on strong logical inference, especially when making a priori assumptions about how behaviors should evolve (e.g., from simple to complex), might be more prone to error than arguments that are framed in the context of the animal's phylogenetic relationships. Furthermore, it is becoming clear that knowledge of the mechanisms underlying behavior, what Tinbergen called causation, is also critical since such mechanisms can bias the direction of evolution. Although we have concentrated on the evolution of behavior, a deep understanding of behavior must involve all Tinbergen's four questions.

## FURTHER READING

Lorenz (1967) provides some instructive examples of how the early ethologist explored patterns of evolution of homologous behavior, whereas Greene (1994) offers a more recent as well as insightful synopsis of the general issue of establishing behavioral homology. Felsenstein's (1985) independent contrast method was critical for promoting the use of phylogenetic data to test hypotheses of adaptation. Thornton et al. (2003) use phylogenetic information to reconstruct ancestral characters of hormone receptors and test the functionality of the ancestral receptor. Finally, Autumn et al. (2002) argue that incorporating information about phylogenetics is critical to understanding the evolution of complex phenotypes.

## ACKNOWLEDGMENTS

I thank D. Cannatella, M. Cummings, and H. Farris for their detailed comments on the chapter.

# 14
## social systems
### ANNE E. PUSEY

# INTRODUCTION

Many, even most, animals live almost wholly solitary lives, feeding and hiding from predators alone, and only coming together briefly with a member of the opposite sex to mate. Even this is not necessary in some marine organisms that spend their adult lives attached to the ocean floor and simply extrude their gametes into the sea, to be taken in the ocean currents to meet gametes from other individuals, or in some animals that reproduce parthenogenetically.

In contrast, some animals form groups for at least part of their lives. Groups can involve any collection of animals, ranging from temporary aggregations such as fish schools, insect swarms, and bird flocks in which individuals may be anonymous with no lasting social bonds with other members, to permanent groups with considerable social structure and distinct patterns of interaction between the individuals. Florida scrub jays (*Aphelocoma coerulescens*), meerkats (*Suricata suricata*), and Princess of Burundi cichlid fish (*Lamprolous brichardi*) are examples of **cooperative breeders**. They live in permanent social groups consisting of a breeding pair and several other individuals ranked in a **dominance hierarchy** that all help to defend the territory and feed the young. Many primates such as baboons (*Papio anubis*) live in groups of several breeding females with one or more adult males, with strict dominance hierarchies. Lions (*Panthera leo*) live in permanent social groups, prides, consisting of several equally ranked breeding females that cooperate in hunting and guarding their young and a coalition of males that cooperate to defend the territory. The social insects (ants, bees, wasps, and termites) show the most structured societies. Colonies usually contain just one or a few breeding females and some contain thousands (even millions) of sterile workers that build and guard the nest, forage, and tend the young. In many ant and termite species, sterile workers exist in morphologically distinct castes, specialized to perform different tasks in the colony. Such species are so successful that in many parts of the world the biomass of social insects exceeds that of all vertebrates in the area.

Closely related species often show very different levels of social structure. Unlike lions, most other cat species are solitary. Some wasps are solitary. Primates and antelope exhibit a very wide variety of social structures. Some species are solitary; others live in **monogamous** pairs, small groups of females with a single male, or large groups containing several adults of both sexes.

Sociality raises many fascinating questions for students of animal behavior. What are the advantages of group living and how does ecology influence grouping patterns? How can we explain the cooperative and **altruistic behavior** often observed between group-living animals in terms of modern evolutionary theory? Does conflict occur between group members? How do ecological factors and forces leading to cooperation and conflict interact to determine how group resources get divided between individual group members?

## Why Live in Groups?

Numerous advantages of grouping have been identified in various species, but some stand out because of their general importance, especially those concerning avoidance of predators or increased efficiency of resource harvesting.

## Evading predators

Living in groups can protect individuals from the danger of being eaten by a predator in a number of different ways.

### Dilution

Perhaps most simply, an individual may benefit from the **dilution effect** (Hamilton 1971; Cresswell 1994) if it reduces its chances of being selected by a predator by joining a group. This will be effective as long as the conspicuousness of the group to predators does not increase linearly with group size, and the predator only kills one or a few individuals when it detects the group. For example, whirligig beetles (*Gyrinus* spp.) are a common sight on rivers and ponds, circling in groups on top of the water. Although the number of strikes by predatory fish increases with group size, the number of strikes per individual decreases (Watt & Chapman 1998).

## Selfish herd

An individual might also reduce its chances of being selected if it hides behind others in the herd. Hamilton (1971) modeled this idea and showed that animals that bunch together reduce their individual chances of being eaten. He named this effect the "selfish herd" to emphasize that the apparently highly coordinated group movements of fish shoals and bird flocks can result from the selfish cover-seeking movements of each individual (Kitchen & Packer 1999). Guppies (*Poecilia reticulata*), small fish that inhabit streams in Trinidad, associate in shoals. The cohesion (tightness of the school) is greatest in streams that have the most predators (Seghers 1974).

## Confusion effect

Grouping individuals might also benefit from the **confusion effect**, where predators have difficulty picking out one prey from the crowd. In a laboratory study, Carsten Schradin (2000) found that leopard geckos (*Eublepharis macularius*) presented with one or 20 mealworms and marmosets (*Callithrix jacchus*) presented with one or 10 beetles took longer to fixate or capture an individual prey from the group than when presented with just one.

## Vigilance

If animals are able to take avoiding action when they detect a predator or the escape responses of group members, they are likely to benefit from the increased **vigilance** provided by the group's many eyes and ears. Several studies have shown that groups of individuals detect predators at a greater distance than single individuals. Because of the effects of increased vigilance of groups, individual group members are often able to reduce their scanning rate and feed more efficiently than they would alone. Although in many species vigilance behavior is performed randomly by all group members, in a few such as meerkats and Arabian babblers (*Turdoides squamiceps*), individuals post themselves as sentinels on high vantage points and give alarm calls that warn their group-mates feeding on the ground of the presence of a predator. Different individuals switch places as sentinels so that there is usually at least one watching (Clutton-Brock et al. 1999a).

## Group defense

Group defense against predators can be very effective in cases where a lone individual would not be able to repel or chase off a predator. The larvae of some insects that have noxious defenses group together thus producing a much greater deterrent effect on the predator than a single individual (Wilson 1975). Some birds gather together to mob predators such as raptors, rapidly flying around and darting at the predator. Colonially nesting gulls are very effective in chasing aerial predators away with mass attacks. Dwarf mongooses (*Helogale undulata*) gather around snakes and together drive them away from the den. Musk oxen (*Ovibos moschatus*) form defensive circles around their young, facing out and fending off wolves with their horns. Finally, group defense by the specialized soldier castes of social insects are highly effective against large predators.

In many cases several of these antipredator advantages act together to influence grouping. For example, redshanks (*Tringa tetanus*), wading birds that feed on mudflats, are very susceptible to attack by raptors. Will Cresswell (1994) made detailed observations with a telescope of individuals feeding in different-sized flocks, and the behavior of three species of raptor. The dilution effect was clearly very important. Although larger flocks were attacked more often, individual birds were much less likely to be attacked as flock size increased (Fig. 14.1a). Vigilance was also greater in groups. Birds in larger flocks scanned less (Fig. 14.1b), but larger flocks were better able to detect raptors hunting by surprise. When raptors used nonsurprise hunting tactics, flying in plain view

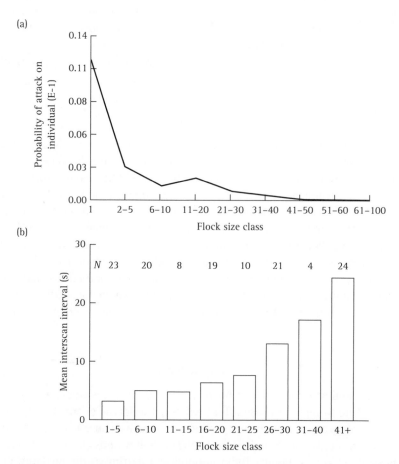

**Fig. 14.1** (a) Probability that an individual redshank in a particular flock size class will be attacked by a sparrowhawk or peregrine relative to the occurrence of that flock size class on the saltmarsh. The probability of attack × proportion of total flocks × 1/midpoint for each flock size class is plotted. (b) Distribution of mean interscan intervals for individual redshank within increasing flock size classes. (From Cresswell 1994.)

before selecting a prey, they were more likely to take solitary birds than those in groups, probably because of the confusion effect.

# Finding food

Food distribution has a profound effect on animal spacing patterns. It is easy to see that if food is sparsely distributed animals may be forced to feed solitarily, whereas if it occurs in superabundant **patches** animals are likely to be attracted to the same patches and can feed together without suffering competition and depletion. Besides being a permissive factor in animal grouping, can food distribution provide positive advantages to grouping?

## *Local enhancement*

Studies of several species have shown that animals are attracted to others that are feeding, or search for food more actively if their neighbors are feeding alone. Under some specific set of conditions this type of response to others' foraging activities can result in more efficient feeding by individuals in groups than when alone. Using others as indicators of food location can be profitable if, once found, the food is so abundant that all group members can gain a meal, so there is no cost of sharing. An alternative way to reduce this cost of competition is if the food clump is so ephemeral that the amount each group member can obtain from another individual's discovery is independent of the number of competitors but depends only on the time since the clump has been discovered. This would apply, for instance, when the food clump is composed of organisms that escape quickly once a predator discovers them.

## *Information centers*

About 13% of bird species breed in colonies (Lack 1968), and others form communal roosts even when not breeding (Barta & Giraldeau 2001). An influential idea is that a major advantage for such grouping is that the colony or roost serves as an **information center** about large but ephemeral patches of food (Ward & Zahavi 1973). Once some members of the colony have located rich patches of food (e.g., schooling fish or swarming insects), others can follow them to the patch and thus feed more efficiently. This theory has spawned a great deal of research and debate. Empirical studies on the whole do not support the idea: few species have been identified in which individuals clearly follow successful foragers. Also, theoretical objections have been raised, including the fact that the idea is implicitly **group selectionist** (see below). Why should an individual go out and search, rather than wait and then exploit the knowledge of others? This objection arises from the misuse of simple optimality analysis when in fact the payoffs in this situation are frequency-dependent and call for a **game-theory** approach (see Chapter 9). When such an approach is used, the problem becomes one of **producer** and **scrounger** in which a stable mixture of searchers and followers can persist in the population. Empirical evidence in favor of this model has yet to be collected and will

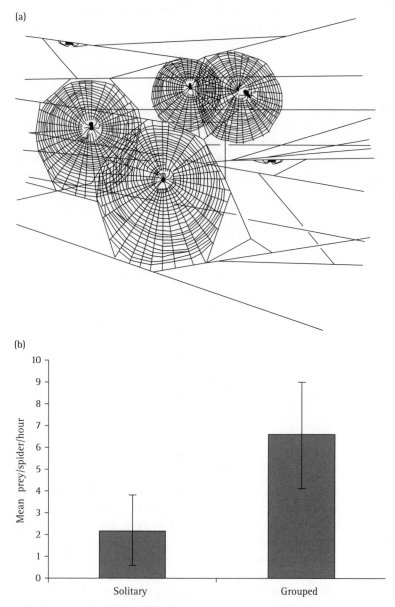

**Fig. 14.2** Cooperative hunting in social spiders (*Metepeira incrassata*). (a) Portion of a colony from Fortin de las Flores, Veracruz, Mexico, showing several individuals with orb webs. (Drawn by George Uetz from his own photograph.) (b) Spiders whose webs were not near any others of the same species caught fewer prey than those in groups. (Drawn using data in Uetz 2001.)

be difficult because it predicts that only a low number of successful follows needs to take place to maintain the advantage (Barta & Giraldeau 2001).

## Capturing difficult prey

In a few species, individuals gain obvious advantages from grouping to catch prey. Carnivorous fish called jack (*Caranx ignobilis*) capture more anchovies when hunting in groups. Orb-weaving spiders (*Metepeira incrassata*) in the tropical montane rainforests of Mexico catch more insects when they build their webs in colonies because an insect that bounces off one web ricochets into another web and is caught (Fig. 14.2). Often, however, animals that capture single large prey only do better hunting in groups than when they are alone if the chances of capturing the prey by themselves is very low, as is the case with lions hunting springbok (*Antidorcas marsupialis*) in the Kalahari (Stander 1992). This is because there is a cost to hunting, and cheats that refrain from hunting but still feed on the prey can invade the system if a single hunter can bring a prey animal down by itself but not defend the carcass from others. In a general review of **cooperative hunting** in animals, Packer and Ruttan (1988) concluded that in most cases the evidence does not support the idea that advantages of group hunting are sufficient to have led to the evolution of grouping.

# Other factors

Several other factors, while not so generally applicable as predator evasion and food searching, are important for group living in at least some species.

## Scarce refuges

Mexican freetailed bats (*Tadarida brasiliensis*) roost in large caves in millions (Davis et al. 1962). Although there may be advantages from grouping in terms of thermoregulation, it is likely that these large groups are also due to the scarcity of suitable caves. The same may also be true of elephant seals (*Mirounga angustirostris*). Females haul up in large numbers on beaches, especially on islands that give some protection from ground predators, to give birth and mate, even though they suffer the risk of their young being trampled by the much larger males (LeBoeuf & Briggs 1977).

## Modification of the environment

Even at a simple level, the presence of several individuals may make the environment more hospitable. Allee (1926) showed that woodlice that huddled together were better able to resist desiccation. The most complex cases are shown by social insects. Termites of the subfamily Macrotermes build huge nests of mud that take intricate forms. Those in rainy areas have roofs. The nest is cooled by an air-conditioning system in which warm air from the colony rises through mud vents (which can be taller than a person) while cool air is drawn in through holes around the base of the nest. On hot days workers spread water on the internal surfaces of the nest so that it is cooled by evaporation. In this way the nest remains at a remarkably constant temperature and humidity despite large daily and seasonal environmental fluctuations.

## Resource defense

Many animals defend territories, food resources, or mates for at least some periods of their life. Although this is usually done alone, individuals sometimes show joint defense. Pied wagtails (*Motacilla alba*), small black and white birds, defend individual feeding territories along river banks in the winter. When food is plentiful and intruder pressure becomes high, the territory holder will accept another bird that helps defend the territory (Davies & Houston 1981). The advantage of joint defense of territory by female lions is thought to be an important reason for the evolution of group living in this species (see below), and some social insects are highly territorial with larger colonies being able to exclude new colonies from the area (Wilson 1975).

## Mate defense and defense against infanticide

Because of competition with other males for mates (see Chapters 11 & 12), males may sometimes benefit by staying with a female to guard her from other males and ensure paternity of her infants. Females may also benefit by associating permanently with a male that can protect her from sexual harassment and sometimes infanticide by other males. In a number of species, males kill infants of other males, thereby ending the mother's investment in her young and speeding up her availability as a mate for the infanticidal male (van Schaik & Janson 2000). Van Schaik and Kappeler (1997) suggest that permanent association between females and adult males is particularly common in primates because, unlike most mammals, females carry their young and a male constantly in attendance can protect her infant from infanticidal males. In support of this idea, they show that male–female associations do not occur in primate species that hide their young rather than carrying them. Females may also group together with other females to protect young from infanticide (e.g., lions, see below).

# Costs of group living

It should be remembered that the benefits of group living are inevitably offset by a variety of costs. Animals in close proximity are more susceptible to disease, competition for resources, disruption of mating, infanticide, and so on. Whether animals form groups and, if so, the size of groups they live in will depend on tradeoffs between costs and benefits. For example, in a classic comparative study of African antelope, Jarman (1974) explained the different group sizes of each species in terms of a tradeoff between benefits of predator evasion, which are highest in large groups, and costs of feeding competition, which depend on the abundance and distribution of food. Small-bodied antelope such as dikdik (*Madoqua kirkii*) need to eat high-quality food such as flowers and shoots that are often sparsely distributed, so that foraging in a group is impossible even though they may benefit from grouping to evade predators. Instead, they live in monogamous pairs and hide from predators. Large antelope such as buffalo can subsist on lower quality forage such as coarse grass that occurs in large swathes, and so can afford to live in large groups.

## Grouping and Evolutionary History

For some animal societies, selective pressures that were important for the evolution of grouping in that species may be the same ones that are currently maintaining group-ing behavior. For example, long-tailed macaques (*Macaca fascicularis*) that live with both aerial and feline predators on the mainland live in larger groups than those on islands where feline predators are absent (van Schaik & van Noordwijk 1985). In other cases, especially societies with specialized **helpers**, the selective pressures may have changed over their evolutionary history. Examination of the solitary relatives of the social Hymenoptera suggest that a major selective pressure that originally led to group nest-ing by females is the risk that eggs are attacked by parasitoids. Groups of females can share in defense of the eggs. Current advantages of group living in social insects include specialized nests, efficiency in food gathering, and the potential to produce hundreds of closely related reproductive individuals (see below).

## Social Behavior: Cooperation and Conflict

Once animals live in groups, there is the opportunity for social behavior in which the behavior of one individual has effects on others in the group. These effects may be positive or negative. The nature of such behavior influences, and is influenced by, the structure of the group and the social relationships within it.

### Cooperation: selfish benefit or altruism?

Animals in groups often appear to help each other. They may attract other group members to a food source with food calls, give alarm calls when they detect predators, defend each other from predators or aggressive members of their own species, and even feed and care for each other's young. Until the 1960s, this kind of behavior was not considered surprising. By helping each other, they helped their group to survive better. This idea was made explicit in the 1960s in a book by V.C. Wynne Edwards (1962). He argued that if animals behaved selfishly, for example by breeding as fast as they could, this would lead to a population explosion in which the group would outstrip its food supply and go extinct. Since this does not happen he proposed that animals have evolved social mechanisms of self-restraint and altruistic behavior, for example responding to a high number of individuals in their group by acquiescing to a low dominance rank and refraining from breeding, or by limiting their reproductive rate below that of which they were physiologically capable. He felt that such mechanisms could not evolve by classical Darwinian selection that acts on individuals and favors individuals that leave the greatest number of offspring. So he proposed that social behavior that limited group size evolved by a special process of group selection. Here, groups containing individuals that practiced self-restraint survived better than groups of **selfish individuals**, and so the behavior would spread in the population by a process of group selection and group extinction. Although this idea seems plausible, it was criticized on theoretical grounds by a number of scientists (Williams 1966; Maynard Smith 1976). They argued that unless groups are completely isolated from each other such that there is no migration between them, individual selection would generally be a much stronger evolutionary force than group selection and that selfish individuals would eventually predominate in the population. This is because a selfish mutant in a group would likely outreproduce others in the group before the group went extinct, and a selfish migrant to a self-restraining group would do the same. David Lack (1968) also criticized the theory on the grounds that several species of birds he studied showed no evidence of self-restraint, but actually reproduced as fast as they could.

Since this debate over the relative importance of group and individual selection in the evolution of social behavior, biologists have shown intense interest in the evolutionary basis of **cooperative behavior**. Classical Darwinian theory predicts that individuals should behave in ways that maximize their own **fitness** (their genetic representation in future generations) through the production of surviving offspring. So how can we explain altruistic behavior where an individual performs an action, such as chasing a predator or feeding the young of another individual, that is helpful to the recipient and costly to itself? The social insects provide some of the most extreme cases of altruism. For example, colony guards frequently die in defense of the colony. The barb on the sting of the honeybee (*Apis mellifera*) ensures that it remains buried in the intruder, inevitably detaching from the worker and causing its death. Most workers in social insect colonies never breed, but spend their whole lives helping others breed.

Other behavior, such as cooperative hunting or group mobbing of predators, also confers advantages on other members of the group, but such behavior is not necessarily so clearly altruistic because each actor may also benefit from the kill or from deterring the predator. However, there would often seem to be a selfish temptation to cheat and allow others to do the work, and yet this does not necessarily occur in many social animals, so this kind of behavior seems to demand special explanation as well.

## Kin selection

Hamilton (1964) published an enormously important and influential theory to explain the evolution of altruistic behavior. He pointed out that individuals can improve their fitness not only by their efforts in the production and care of their own offspring but also by helping other relatives pass on shared copies of genes. He specified the conditions under which individuals could pass on more copies of their genes by helping, or refraining from harming, their relatives rather than by selfishly reproducing themselves. Using a population genetic model he derived an equation now known

(a)

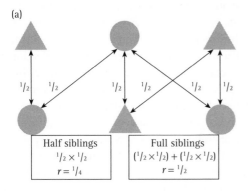

| Class of relatives | Relatedness |
|---|---|
| Parent–offspring | $^1/_2$ |
| Full siblings | $^1/_2$ |
| Half siblings | $^1/_4$ |
| Grandparent–grandchild | $^1/_4$ |
| Uncle/aunt–nephew/niece | $^1/_4$ |
| First cousins | $^1/_8$ |
| Second cousins | $^1/_{32}$ |

(b)

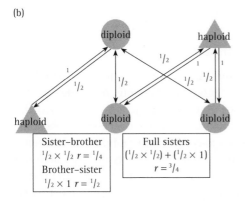

| Class of relatives | Relatedness |
|---|---|
| Mother–daughter | $^1/_2$ |
| Mother–son | $^1/_2$ |
| Father–daughter | 1 |
| Father–son | 0 |
| Daughter–mother | $^1/_2$ |
| Son–mother | 1 |
| Brother–sister | $^1/_2$ |
| Sister–sister | $^3/_4$ |
| Sister–brother | $^1/_4$ |

**Fig. 14.3** (a) Coefficients of relatedness in (a) diploid and (b) haplodiploid organisms. Circles, females; triangles, males.

as **Hamilton's rule**: $Br - C > 0$. This states that a gene **causing** an altruistic behavior will spread as long as the cost ($C$) to the individual performing the altruistic act is less than the benefit ($B$) to the recipients multiplied by the probability ($r$) that the recipients share the gene with the actor. The **coefficient of relatedness** ($r$) is the probability that an individual shares a gene with another by common descent. Most sexually reproducing individuals are **diploid**, i.e., they contain two sets of chromosomes. The gametes that they produce by the process of meiosis contain just one set of chromosomes (and are thus **haploid**). The probability that any particular gene is passed on by a parent to an offspring is therefore one-half. Figure 14.3 shows how to calculate $r$ between different kinds of relatives.

A vivid understanding of Hamilton's rule can be gained by considering the fate of a gene that causes an animal to give an alarm call. This gene will spread, even if the caller is eaten by the predator (thus removing one copy of the gene), provided that the caller thereby saves more than two offspring or full siblings (each of which have a one-half chance of containing the gene by common descent, Fig. 14.3), more than four half siblings, and or more than eight cousins (Trivers 1985).

Hamilton (1964) suggested that animals should behave in ways that maximize a quantity that he called their inclusive fitness. This is the sum of **direct fitness** gained by the individual's production of offspring and **indirect fitness** gained by its effects on the reproduction of nondescendant relatives (Brown 1980). Direct selection is selection for traits that improve direct fitness, indirect selection for traits that improve indirect fitness. **Kin selection** (Maynard Smith 1964) is selection for traits that improve the survival of shared genes whether they are in the bodies of offspring or nondescendant kin.

At first glance, kin selection would seem to explain much of the apparent paradox of altruistic behavior we observe. The first question scientists now ask when they observe such behavior is whether the altruist is related to the recipient of its behavior. In the majority of cases, individuals that perform obviously costly behavior such as feeding others' young or risking their lives in chasing predators away from others' young are aiding close relatives.

## Kin selection in vertebrates

In cooperatively breeding birds, mammals, and fish in which a breeding pair is helped by nonbreeding adults, the helpers are very often the previous offspring of the pair. Most are thus helping full siblings that are as closely related to them as their own offspring would be, although if one or the other breeder has died they are helping half siblings (Brown 1987). In some cases, animals make fine discriminations between relatives of different degrees of relatedness. White-fronted bee-eaters (*Merops bullockoides*) live in colonies where pairs of birds nest in holes close to their relatives, and these have been studied for 10 years by Steve Emlen and his colleagues. Although most pairs start to breed each year, many give up the attempt. This often results in nonbreeding adults being present in the colony. Such birds often help at others' nests. They usually have a choice of individuals of various degrees of relatedness that they could help, and the researchers found that they were most likely to help their closest relatives, even discriminating between half siblings and first cousins (Emlen & Wrege 1988).

Female rhesus monkeys (*Macaca mulatta*) spend much time grooming each other, removing ectoparasites. Time spent grooming is time that could be spent feeding, and females groom their closest relatives more than others (Fig. 14.4a). Female lions of the same pride often give birth at the same time and then raise their cubs together (see below). Often the females are sleeping while they are with their cubs, and cubs try to nurse from females other than their own mother. Females try to resist nursing attempts from foreign cubs, but are more tolerant of the cubs of their closest relatives (Fig. 14.4b).

## Kin selection in social insects

Social insects provide some of the most compelling support for the importance of kin selection (Bourke 1997; Queller & Strassmann 1998) **Eusociality** (true sociality) is defined as involving the following three characteristics:

1 cooperation by individuals other than parents in caring for the young;
2 overlap of at least two generations capable of contributing to colony labor;

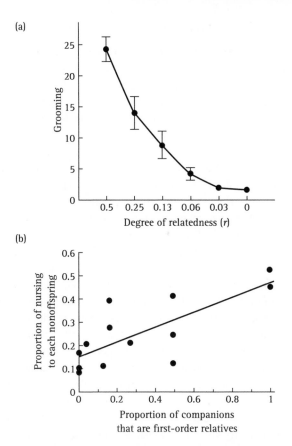

(a)

(b)

**Fig. 14.4** Mean percentage of time spent grooming females of different degrees of relatedness by adult female rhesus macaques on Cayo Santiago. (From Kapsalis & Berman 1996.) (b) Mean proportion of nursing that went to cubs that did not belong to the mother in 13 different communal litters of lions in which the average degree of relatedness between mothers differed. Relatedness varied from 0 when none of the females participating in the crèche were related as closely as mother and daughter or sisters (first-order relatives) to 1 where all the females were either mother and daughter or sisters. If females nursed only their own young, the value on the y-axis = 0. If they nursed their own young and others equally, the value on the y-axis = 0.5. (From Pusey & Packer 1994.)

3 reproductive division of labor, with a mostly or wholly sterile worker caste working on behalf of individuals engaged in reproduction.

The social insects include all of the more than 10,000 ant species, over 1000 species of social wasps, the several thousand species of social bees, all the 2200 species of termites, and 43 species of aphids. In these species, one or a few breeding females (queens) in the colony produce the young, and more or less sterile workers help raise these young. In the majority of cases, queens only mate with one male. Therefore, workers are helping to raise their full siblings. In aphids, females usually reproduce asexually, so here the workers are helping individuals that are genetically identical to themselves.

## Haplodiploidy hypothesis

Eusociality has evolved more often in the Hymenoptera (ants, bees, and wasps) than in other groups of animals. It is estimated that eusociality evolved 11 or 12 separate times in the Hymenoptera, at least five times in the Hemiptera (aphids), but only once in the Isoptera (termites) (Bourke 1997). Hamilton (1964) suggested that eusociality may have evolved so often in the Hymenoptera because of a special genetic predisposition that results in workers being more closely related to their mother's daughters than to their own daughters. The Hymenoptera have an unusual form of sex determination called **haplodiploidy**. The females, like most other animals, are diploid. Their eggs, produced by meiosis, are haploid. Diploid queens lay unfertilized eggs that develop into haploid males, and fertilized eggs that develop into diploid females. This leads to an asymmetric pattern of relatedness between a female's young. Each female inherits half of her genes from her mother and half from her father. If the queen mated just once, female siblings share identical genes from their father and one-quarter of their mother's genes, on average. Therefore $r$ is $3/4$ between sisters but only $1/4$ between sisters and brothers (see Fig. 14.3). So females are more closely related to their sisters than they are to their daughters ($r = 1/2$). Thus they can pass on more of their genes by helping their mother raise sisters than by producing their own daughters. Termites show the more usual diploid pattern. Both sexes are diploid and $r = 1/2$ between full siblings of both sexes. In line with Hamilton's hypothesis, all sterile helpers are female among the eusocial Hymenoptera, but among the termites both sexes help their parents produce offspring. Although not all haplodiploid species are eusocial, this genetic system would make eusociality easier to evolve provided that other conditions are also suitable.

**Sex ratio** patterns in the social insects are particularly intriguing examples of the power of kin selection theory. Because of the asymmetry in relatedness in haplodiploid social insects, queens and workers should have a conflict of interest over the sex ratio of reproductive individuals produced. Using Fisher's theory of stable sex ratios (see Chapter 11) and kin selection theory, Trivers and Hare (1976) showed that if a queen were in control of the reproduction in her colony she should produce males and females in a 1 : 1 ratio because she is equally related to her sons and her daughters. Now consider the sex ratio that would produce the greatest payoff to a worker in a social hymenopteran colony. If her mother has mated only once, the female will be related to her sisters by $3/4$ and her brothers by $1/4$. She will therefore do best by helping rear reproductive females and males in the ratio 3 : 1.

As Trivers and Hare pointed out, there will be a conflict between mother and workers in the sex ratio of the reproductives produced. Who wins and are the sex ratios as predicted? Trivers and Hare produced initial evidence that the ratio of investment in female and male reproductives in many species is 3 : 1. Thus workers win (presumably by manipulating the rearing of the brood), and follow the predictions from kin selection. Sex ratios in species in which slaves captured from other colonies or species rear the young, and which therefore have no genetic interest in either sex, show a 1 : 1 ratio. This is also true in termites, which are diploid and thus have no disagreement over sex ratio between breeders and workers, and in solitary Hymenoptera where the laying female will have control over the rearing of the young.

## Kin recognition

When Hamilton pointed out the inclusive fitness advantages of modifying social behavior toward kin, he raised the question of how individuals might recognize their relatives. This has been the subject of a great deal of research in the last three decades (Sherman et al. 1997). If populations are structured, or viscous, such that individuals remain close to their relatives at their place of birth, a simple rule of thumb such as "treat those near you as kin" could suffice. However, when individuals move around more, further discrimination mechanisms will be advantageous. Social bees and wasps have been shown to use nest odor to discriminate between nest-mates and foreigners. Many species of birds and mammals learn the identity of individuals with whom they had close contact when they were young, and later treat them as kin. This is probably the mechanism of discrimination in the bee-eaters, monkeys, and lions described above. This process has been demonstrated by cross-fostering experiments in a number of species.

Beldings ground squirrels (*Spermophilus beldingi*) provide a classic example. They live in colonies in which females nest in individual burrows and feed on vegetation in territories outside the burrow. They were the subject of an extensive study by Paul Sherman and a large group of students and assistants. By marking individuals over many years, Sherman found that daughters usually settled near their mothers and that close female relatives were less likely to fight over burrows or territory than unrelated females. Indeed, unrelated females sometimes tried to usurp burrows or kill the young, and were fiercely chased away. To examine mechanisms of kin discrimination, Holmes and Sherman (1982) brought squirrels to the laboratory and raised their pups in various kinds of litters: those with just their siblings and their mother, and those reared with nonsiblings. They then tested them in an arena to determine the levels of aggression they showed toward different classes of individuals (Fig. 14.5). It was found that both true siblings reared together and nonsiblings reared together showed low levels of aggression when they met, whereas siblings reared apart and nonsiblings reared apart showed significantly higher levels of aggression. This suggests that they learn who their kin are early in life. A further exciting finding, however, was that siblings reared apart were not as aggressive as nonsiblings reared apart. Therefore, the squirrels seemed to be able to discriminate between unfamiliar siblings and nonsiblings. In addition, individuals with the same mother discriminated between full siblings and half siblings (which occurred in the same litter because the mother mated more than once), being significantly less aggressive to full siblings (Fig. 14.5). This discrimination ability is known as **phenotype matching**: the individual compares phenotypic cues such as odor or appearance of other individuals with either the individual's own cues or the cues that they have learned from their close relatives such as parents or siblings. Evidence for this ability has since been found in a large number of species and is often based on odor-producing molecules that are the products of the genes of the major histocompatibility locus (MHC) of the immune system (Brown & Eklund 1994). For example, inbred mice are able to distinguish the urine of individuals that differ only in the MHC genes.

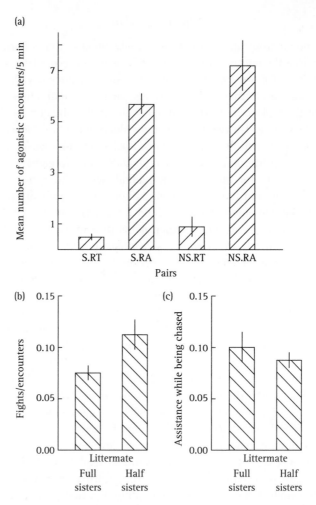

**Fig. 14.5** Kin recognition in Belding's ground squirrel (Holmes & Sherman 1982). (a) Laboratory experiments: mean number (±1SE) of agonistic encounters between pairs of yearling squirrels in arena tests. Nonsiblings reared together (NS.RT) are no more aggressive than siblings reared together (S.RT). However, nonsiblings reared apart (NS.RA) are more aggressive than siblings reared apart (S.RA). (b, c) Field observations: aggression and cooperation among yearling females that were full or half sisters. (From Krebs & Davies 1993.)

## Nonkin cooperation

Kin selection is not enough to explain all cooperative behavior. Cooperation sometimes occurs between unrelated individuals, and in many cooperatively breeding species the helping behavior of helpers does not seem to result in sufficient indirect fitness to explain the costs incurred on the basis of kin selection alone. A classic way of thinking about cooperation has been to use game theory (see Chapter 9) to model the payoffs of

(a)

| | Player B | |
|---|---|---|
| | Cooperate | Defect |
| **Player A** Cooperate | R Reward for mutual cooperation | S Sucker's payoff |
| **Player A** Defect | T Temptation to defect | P Punishment for mutual defection |

(b)

| | Player B | |
|---|---|---|
| | Cooperate | Defect |
| **Player A** Cooperate | R 3 | S 1 |
| **Player A** Defect | T 0 | P 0 |

(c)

| | Player B | |
|---|---|---|
| | Cooperate | Defect |
| **Player A** Cooperate | R 3 | S 0 |
| **Player A** Defect | T 5 | P 1 |

**Fig. 14.6** (a) Payoffs to the row player in the prisoner's dilemma game. (From Axelrod & Hamilton 1981.) (b) Illustrative numerical values for payoffs in a game of mutualism. (c) Illustrative numerical values for payoffs in the prisoner's dilemma.

cooperating for two players (Axelrod & Hamilton 1981). In these games, the two players have two possible strategies, cooperate or defect. The behavior we expect to be evolutionarily stable depends on the value of the payoffs in the matrix (Fig. 14.6a).

## Mutualism

Consider two lions hunting a gazelle. If each has a small chance of catching it on its own (but will eat the whole thing if it can catch it) but the two of them hunting together have a much larger chance of catching and sharing the prey, they will do better by cooperating. In this case in the payoff matrix, R (reward for cooperating) is greater than T (temptation to defect), S (sucker's payoff), and P (punishment for mutual defection), and the **evolutionarily stable strategy** is to cooperate (Fig. 14.6b). This kind of cooperation is sometimes called **byproduct mutualism** or short-term mutualism, because the best strategy is to cooperate regardless of what the other individual does. This kind of **mutualism** can explain cooperation in situations such as predator mobbing, and is probably a common explanation for much cooperation observed in nature.

## Reciprocity

Trivers (1971) suggested that altruism between nonrelatives could evolve if an altruistic act of individual A to B was repaid by B in the future, a phenomenon he called **reciprocal altruism**. This could work as long as the benefits of the act outweighed the costs (so that by cooperating repeatedly the participants would gain a net benefit), the participants had the opportunity to exchange acts, and cheaters (that accepted altruistic acts but did not repay them) could be identified and excluded. These ideas can be analyzed by studying a two-person game called the **prisoner's dilemma** (Axelrod & Hamilton 1981). The payoffs in the prisoner's dilemma differ in important ways from those described for mutualism. Here if both players cooperate, they each gain a reward R; if they both defect, they each get a punishment (P). However, the payoff to an individual that defects when its companion cooperates (T) is even greater than R, and the cooperator in this case gets the sucker's payoff (S), which is less than P. Thus $T > R > P > S$ (Fig. 14.6c). In this case, there is a temptation to cheat (defect when your companion cooperates) rather than cooperate. In the example of two lions hunting a gazelle, the meat may be divided in a different way that gives rise to these kinds of payoffs. If both cooperate to make the kill, they both incur the energetic cost of the hunt but gain half the meat (R). But if one catches the gazelle and the other cheats by not participating in the hunt and snatching the whole gazelle because the hunter is too exhausted to defend it, the payoff to cheating (T) would be even greater than the reward (R) from both catching the gazelle; and the sucker's payoff (S), exhaustion from the hunt and no meat, would be more costly than (P), the hunger experienced when neither lion hunts or gets meat. With these kinds of payoffs, both individuals would do best in the long term if they cooperated, because each would get the reward R in each interaction. However, there is always a short-term temptation to cheat and gain an even higher payoff (T). Axelrod and Hamilton (1981) showed theoretically that when the payoffs are set as a prisoner's dilemma, cooperation can pay if the two participants start by cooperating, have a large number of subsequent interactions, and make cooperation conditional on the previous cooperation of their companion. A variety of reciprocating strategies fulfill these requirements (Nowak & Sigmund 1993), including **tit-for-tat**, when the individual cooperates on the first move and then copies whatever the opponent did in the previous move. However, the requirements are still quite restrictive, and it has proved very difficult to find unambiguous empirical examples of animals following these strategies (Pusey & Packer 1997). A major difficulty is measuring the real payoffs involved and showing that they conform to a prisoner's dilemma.

## Long-term mutualism

Even when $T > R$ and there is a short-term temptation to defect, it may still pay to cooperate because of longer-term advantages of the presence of companions (Pusey & Packer 1997). For example, in a model of cooperative vigilance Lima (1989) has shown that when animals benefit greatly from living in groups from the dilution effect and group members are not easily replaced, although individuals will benefit in the short term by defecting (feeding and relying on their companions' vigilance), in the long term they will benefit by cooperating (being vigilant also) because this behavior will contribute to the survival of their companions, which will increase their own survival through the dilution effect. Another example is a model of group augmentation (Kokko et al. 2001). Suppose that survival and productivity of individuals in a group is strongly dependent on group size, and that group extinction of small groups is likely (as is true of some species of cooperative breeders such as meerkats; Clutton-Brock et al. 1999b). Individuals can increase group size by helping raise infants to maturity. Kokko et al.'s model shows that even costly **helping behavior** by nonrelatives can be stable if the helping has a large effect on recruitment because the **helpers** will reap the benefits of a larger group in the future. Their long-term survival will be higher, they will inhabit a large group if and when they become breeders, and the group members will help them for the same reasons. Although active cooperation in these models is sometimes called delayed reciprocity, an important feature of these models is that **unconditional cooperation** is stable. There is no temptation to cheat by not helping because the resulting lower group size will have negative effects on the individual. Although helpers may benefit in the future from the cooperative behavior of individuals they helped, strict tit-for-tat reciprocity from the same individuals is not required for cooperation to persist.

### *Coerced cooperation*

Another possible route to cooperation is if some individuals in the group coerce others to cooperate (Boyd & Richerson 1992; Clutton-Brock & Parker 1995). If there are differences in dominance among individuals in the group, as is often the case (see below), the dominant may be able to punish the subordinate for defecting at little cost to itself and thus force the subordinate to cooperate. Several examples of conflict have been described that might fit this model. When bee-eaters start nesting, dominants, especially males, are sometimes seen harassing males at neighboring nests and preventing them from breeding. The harassed male often gives up his own nesting attempt and helps at the harassing male's nest. This is particularly the case between fathers and their yearling sons. There is a strong dominance differential between the two males, so the father has little to fear in terms of aggressive retaliation. Also, the son does not lose much in terms of inclusive fitness because the extra number of his full siblings $(r = {}^1\!/_2)$ that survive because of his help is almost the same as the number of offspring $(r = {}^1\!/_2)$ he is likely to raise in his own nest without helpers (Emlen & Wrege 1992).

Superb fairy wrens (*Malurus cyaneus*) are small, cooperatively breeding birds in Australia. The presence of helpers greatly decreases the workload of the dominant male in caring for the young. Mulder and Langmore (1993) experimentally removed helpers from groups for 24 h and then returned them. They found that the breeding male often showed intense and prolonged aggression toward the helpers on their return and the authors interpreted this as punishment for defection from helping.

## Conflict

Although there are many ways that individuals can benefit by living in groups, conflict is an inevitable part of group life, even between relatives. For example, although baboons might benefit from living in groups by avoiding predation through increased vigilance, dilution, and sometimes group defense, their close proximity often leads to competition over items or patches of food. They may also compete for safe places to sleep. In addition, when only one female in the group is ready to mate, all the males in the group are in competition to mate with her. How are disputes settled?

## Dominance

Early theory of competition was based on behavior during single encounters between two contestants (see Chapter 9), but in social groups individuals have the opportunity for many repeated interactions (Pusey & Packer 1997). Rather than fighting over every item, individuals usually use some kind of assessment rule, giving way if their opponent is superior to themselves in size, age, or another measure of competitive ability (Parker 1974). This mode of responding to a dispute is called the **Assessor strategy** (similar to that seen in Chapter 9). A common result of repeated pairwise interactions within a group is that the individuals come to be ranked in a pecking order or **dominance hierarchy** in which individual A dominates all others, B dominates all except A, and so on. Rank between even the most evenly matched group members becomes differentiated and stable. Dominance hierarchies are based on age in most species of cooperative breeders, with the oldest individuals dominating younger, and relationships within cohorts of siblings often sorted out during early life, for example by play fighting. In other species, particularly among males, dominance rank depends on competitive ability and takes an inverted U-shaped form, with individuals gaining dominance as they reach their prime, then losing dominance as they age. Male baboons are a classic example. In contrast, female baboons, females of many other species of primates, and female hyenas (*Crocuta crocuta*) inherit their dominance rank from the mother. Each female helps her youngest daughter rise in rank to a position just above her sisters and below her mother. The close relatives within each matriline support each other in contests with members of other matrilines, and matrilines are ranked in order.

## Ownership

Another less common way for disputes to be settled is by the owner of the resource winning. Respect of ownership is named the **bourgeois strategy** (Hammerstein 1981; Maynard Smith 1982). Here, when two individuals contest a resource, the prior owner wins and the other respects its rival's ownership and gives up. This strategy can beat the Assessor strategy in a game-theory model when the costs of fighting are high and the opponents are equal in competitive ability. Female lions exemplify this strategy (Packer et al. 2001). Rank differences do not occur among female lions. Instead, whichever reaches a food source (e.g., position on a carcass) first defends her possession from others and they respect her ownership. If she stops feeding and another claims the site, then the previous female in turn respects the new female's ownership. In lions, the costs of fighting are very high. Not only do they have great strength and sharp teeth, but even a small lion can severely wound or blind a companion with her claws.

# Philopatry and Dispersal

Given the various advantages of group living that we have discussed, we might often expect individuals born in a group to remain there (i.e., show **philopatry**) unless there is such an overproduction of offspring that the optimal group size is exceeded, in which case competition might lead to some leaving and settling elsewhere. One population of killer whales (*Orcinus orca*) actually does live in very closed groups (pods). They travel and feed together and sometimes show highly coordinated hunting. Calves of both sexes that are born in the pod remain there for life (Baird 2000). However, this situation turns out to be highly unusual. In most animals that live in permanent groups, most or all of the members of one sex leave their group and breed elsewhere whereas members of the other sex remain in the group. In baboons, all females remain in the group in which they are born, but all males move to other groups as young adults. In chimpanzees (*Pan troglodytes*), males remain in the community in which they are born whereas most females join other groups in adolescence. Overall, there is a strong tendency for female mammals to remain philopatric and for males to disperse, and for male birds to remain philopatric and females disperse (Greenwood 1980).

How can we explain the evolution of these marked patterns of sex-biased **dispersal**? Why should individuals leave the safety of their own group and travel to find another group and make their way into it, often against the opposition of like-sexed adults in the new group? A likely selection pressure is inbreeding avoidance. When close relatives mate, their young usually suffer from inbreeding depression, a reduction in fitness that in large part is caused by the expression in the homozygous form of deleterious recessive alleles shared by common descent. Inbreeding between full siblings or parents and offspring commonly results in a reduction in fitness of at least one-third. A game-theory model that takes into account what members of the other sex are doing shows that when the costs of dispersal and inbreeding are identical for each sex, and inbreeding costs are set at realistic levels, two evolutionarily stable strategies exist: complete dispersal by either males or females (Perrin & Mazalov 1999). However, it is often the case that costs for the two sexes are asymmetric (Perrin & Mazalov 2000). Because of sex differences in reproductive potential, male mammals are likely to suffer more from local mate competition with their male relatives than females are with theirs. They will thus do better to avoid competing with their relatives by dispersing. Only when females suffer strong within-sex costs of competition over resources, as for example in monogamous systems, are significant proportions of females then likely to disperse as well. There can also be positive effects from living with kin (local resource enhancement). For example, female bank voles (*Clethrionomys glareolus*) survive better in kin groups. In male red grouse (*Lagopus lagopus*), males are better able to acquire territories near kin because of lower levels of aggression. Such benefits will increase costs of dispersal for that sex (Perrin & Mazalov 2000).

If inbreeding avoidance is a major factor in sex-biased dispersal, why do not killer whales disperse too? It turns out that these manage to avoid inbreeding by mating with individuals in other pods while remaining members of their own pod (Baird 2000), but this is not a common pattern.

# Reproductive Skew Models: Toward a General Theory of Social Evolution?

Animal societies differ greatly in the extent to which individuals in the group are able to reproduce. **Reproductive skew** is a measure of the extent to which reproduction in a group is restricted to one or a few breeding individuals. Extreme reproductive skew occurs in some societies such as most ants, where there is just one breeding female, the queen, and thousands of nonbreeding adult females that altruistically help the queen. In other societies such as lions (see below), all females in the group reproduce and thus there is no reproductive skew. Other societies fall on a continuum between these two extremes.

Much recent research has focused on identifying the factors that can explain variation in reproductive skew and creating models that combine these factors and predict skew (Keller & Reeve 1994b; Johnstone 2000). Reproductive skew models start by considering a dominant breeding individual and a subordinate individual of the same sex, and estimate whether the subordinate should join the dominant in a group, what share of the group's reproduction the subordinate will achieve, and the degree of aggressive behavior shown. The models identify several critical parameters.

1 *Chance the subordinate has of breeding on its own.* If the chances of breeding alone are low, an individual should be more likely to stay in or join a group even if reproductive skew exists and its share of reproduction is low. Reasons why this chance might be low are generally considered under the heading "ecological constraints." These include a shortage of breeding spaces, a shortage of mates of the opposite sex, or a high cost of dispersing (e.g., from predation) to find a breeding opportunity. The other side of the same coin is benefits to the subordinate of group living. Even if a subordinate can breed on its own, it may benefit by staying in the group if there are strong advantages, such as access to food stores or a nest that are costly to create, or a high likelihood of inheriting the breeding spot in a high-quality territory in the future such that its lifetime inclusive fitness would be higher if it stayed.

2 *Increase in group productivity that the subordinate's presence in the group will achieve relative to the productivity of a single breeding adult.* A dominant should tolerate a subordinate in the group if its presence increases group productivity and the dominant's own inclusive fitness. Group productivity may increase for several of the reasons discussed earlier in this chapter, such as better defense from predators or better acquisition of food, but in most models it is assumed that the subordinate will in some way help the dominant raise young and that skew will increase when productivity increases.

3 *Relatedness of the dominant and the subordinate.* If the dominant and subordinate are closely related, the subordinate might benefit by joining a group and helping even if it does not achieve much reproduction, because it will still gain indirect fitness benefits. If it is not related to the dominant, it should only join if it can eventually achieve direct fitness through personal reproduction. On the other hand, the dominant should be less likely to evict a close relative because of the loss in inclusive fitness due to the relative's poor breeding prospects.

4 *Difference in fighting ability between dominant and subordinate.* If the dominant can easily dominate the subordinate, it can take a larger share of the reproduction without suffering the risk of challenge by the subordinate. If the two are evenly matched, the subordinate can fight for a more equal share.

Skew models have become complex and may be divided into two main types, although these may each be special cases of a more general model (Johnstone 2000). Concession (or transactional) models assume that the dominant has total control of reproduction in the group, but concedes some reproduction to the subordinate under certain circumstances in return for the subordinate staying in the group and helping. Compromise (or incomplete control) models view the division of reproduction as the outcome of a conflict between group members in which each struggles to achieve its optimal level of reproduction. We apply these ideas to three animal societies.

## Paper wasps (*Polistes fuscatus*)

Hudson Reeve and his associates studied *Polistes fuscata* near Cornell University in New York State (Reeve et al. 2000). Mated females overwinter and then build a nest the following spring, and lay eggs. They stay on the nest and care for the brood. The early brood develops into females, some of which work on the nest but most of which become foundresses the following year. Later in the season the brood contains males and late females that also become foundresses the following year. Often, females cooperate to found a nest in which they both lay eggs. Why? It turns out that mortality of foundress females is high, and nests with multiple females have a much better chance that at least one adult will survive until the workers emerge. Therefore there is an advantage to a lone female to cooperate with others, even as a subordinate.

When there is more than one queen on the nest, a dominance hierarchy develops among the females. Reeve et al. believe that in this species the **alpha** female has complete control of reproduction, and concedes a certain amount of reproduction in return for help, this amount varying with the values of the four factors listed above. They measured the degree of relatedness between females and the degree of reproductive skew using genetic analysis (by examining similarity of genetic markers from DNA between females and between females and brood). First, they found that as nest productivity (number of cells) increases, reproductive skew increases (Fig. 14.7a) and suggest that once the subordinate has achieved reproduction above the amount that she would have achieved on her own, the dominant can retain the additional reproduction for herself. Second, relatedness among the females is positively correlated with degree of skew (Fig. 14.7b). Reeve et al. argue that the dominant need cede less reproduction to a close relative because she will gain indirect fitness from helping the dominant. Finally, they found that patterns of aggressive behavior among the females also supported the idea that the alpha is in control of reproduction and is ceding a share to the subordinate. In general, there is some level of aggression between the females and the dominant may even destroy the subordinate's eggs. The researchers simulated egg destruction by removing a proportion of the eggs and observed the behavior of each female. They found that the subordinate female greatly increased her aggression to the dominant female

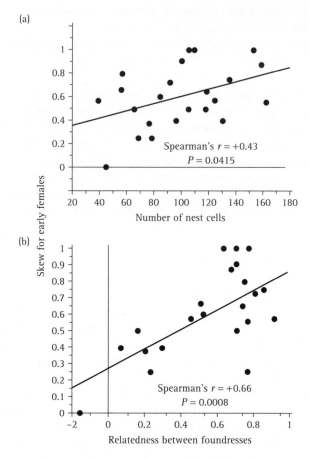

**Fig. 14.7** Reproductive skew (dominant's share of production of early females) versus (a) group output as measured by the number of nest cells at colony collection and (b) relatedness between foundresses. (From Reeve et al. 2000.)

following egg removal, but that the dominant female did not increase her level of aggression. Thus although the alpha is capable of being aggressive to the subordinate all the time, she does not indulge in aggressive egg-laying when the subordinate's reproductive chances reach such a low level that she might leave. This interpretation is also in accord with observations that in intact nests during the early period of egg-laying, when the subordinate's help is important to the alpha, alphas sometimes show submissive behavior to subordinates.

## Meerkats

Tim Clutton-Brock and his associates have spent 7 years studying meerkats, small **diurnal** carnivores that live in arid parts of southern Africa (Clutton-Brock et al. 2001).

Meerkats live in groups of 2–30 consisting of roughly equal numbers of adults of each sex, assorted subadults, and young. A dominant female does all or most of the breeding and a dominant male fathers most of her young, and the other individuals help raise the young. Subordinate females sometimes breed, but at low rates. Meerkats thus show strong reproductive skew. Helpers help by babysitting the young and protecting them from aerial and terrestrial predators at the den while the rest of the group is feeding. This is costly behavior because the babysitter is not able to feed and loses weight. Why do subordinates live in the group and help rather than attempting to breed themselves? Meerkats live in open areas containing a great many predators. Pup and adult survival increase markedly with group size up to group sizes of 11, mostly because of better predator detection and avoidance. Small groups often go extinct. So subordinates have low chances of breeding on their own and their presence in the group contributes significantly to group productivity.

Clutton-Brock does not believe that patterns of subordinate reproduction support the idea that the dominant female has full control of reproduction in the group, as assumed by concession models of reproductive skew. Instead he believes that there is a struggle over reproduction. Dominant females do attempt to control subordinates' reproduction by infanticide, but are not always able to do so. For example, more subordinates breed:

1  in the first few months after the dominant has assumed alpha status and is less secure in this position;
2  if they are of the same generation as the alpha (and thus of more similar rank); and
3  if they are large in body size (and thus more difficult to control by force).

Concession models predict that alphas should cede reproduction to subordinates when they are most needed. Therefore, they should be more likely to allow subordinate females in small groups to breed because their help is more crucial, but this is not observed. Finally, unlike in the wasps, there was no relationship between degree of relatedness and reproductive skew. Less related females were not more likely to breed. Meerkats thus conform more to compromise models.

Another important factor influencing skew in this species is inbreeding avoidance. Subordinate females were less likely to breed if the only males available in their group were relatives (father and brothers). The importance of this factor in preventing subordinate females from breeding and thus increasing skew has also been recognized in many other cooperatively breeding species, but has not yet been incorporated into formal models of reproductive skew.

## Egalitarian lions

Unlike wasps and meerkats, each female lion in the pride is as likely to reproduce as successfully as any other (Packer et al. 2001). Do the same four factors help to explain lion social structure? Lions in northern Tanzania have been studied for more than 30 years. Prides contain 3–10 adult females (range 1–18) and their young and a group of one to three (range, one to eight) adult males (Packer et al. 1988). Females remain in the pride in which they are born, or emigrate with pride-mates to form new prides when pride size becomes large. All males leave their natal prides as subadults and cooperate with their male pride-mates or sometimes single males from other prides to take over another pride. At takeovers the new coalition evicts all the previous adult males, subadult males, and subadult females too young to mate, and kills the unweaned cubs. The result is that the females of the pride resume breeding with the new males more quickly.

As in wasps and meerkats, solitary females have much lower chances of survival and reproduction than those in groups (Packer et al. 1988). Although it used to be assumed that a major advantage of grouping for lions is the gain from cooperating to kill large prey, a careful study of the meat acquired by each female when hunting in different-sized groups showed that hunting efficiency is inadequate to explain common grouping patterns. Compared with single females and females in groups of five, females in groups of two to four did very poorly during the lean hunting season, although these are group sizes in which lions are commonly found (Packer et al. 1990). Instead, they gain advantages in grouping to defend resources. Lions differ from solitary cat species such as tigers and leopards in that they live at much higher densities, presumably because of the high density of prey species in their savannah habitat (Packer 1986). Although each lion needs a territory with adequate space to hunt and a good place to hide its cubs, intruder pressure is likely to be high because of high density and they appear to do better by cooperating with others to defend a joint territory. Single females and pairs are unable to defend a territory against their neighbors, whereas females living in prides of three to seven have higher reproductive success and survive better (Packer et al. 1988). Another factor contributing to female sociality is cooperative defense against infanticidal males. Females with cubs band together more closely and females in groups are better able to defend their cubs from intruding males (Packer et al. 1990).

Lack of relatedness cannot account for the lack of reproductive skew in female lions because pride-mates are usually closely related. However, the fourth factor, relative fighting abilities, is consistent with lack of skew. As argued above, the costs to lions of fighting are extremely high and thus they rely on ownership rather than dominance to settle disputes. Even a small female can inflict serious damage on a large female with her claws. This reduces the ability of a despotic female to control the reproduction of others. Another feature of lion behavior is that they hide their newborn cubs in a solitary den for the first few weeks of life, unlike meerkats and most cooperatively breeding birds and insects that put their young in the same communal den or nest. Therefore, other females are unable to manipulate the size of their companions' litters by infanticide.

A final feature of lion society that relates to the second factor in the model, group productivity, is the fact that per-capita cub survival in lions is best when several females raise their cubs at the same time in a **communal crèche**. If females lose their cubs, they stop associating and cooperating with the rest of the females in the crèche. Therefore, unlike wasps or meerkats, a female will not gain help by preventing another's reproduction. This may also be true for a number of other animals that form nursery groups such as antelope and bats, and raises questions about the generality of skew models that assume a benefit to dominant individuals of manipulating others' reproduction.

Proponents of reproductive skew models believe they hold the promise of developing into a general model of social evolution that can predict features of social systems, including group size, reproductive skew, and quality of social behavior, on the basis of just a few key parameters (Johnstone 2000; Reeve 2001). The idea is very appealing but it remains to be seen if these models will comfortably fit all animal societies.

## SUMMARY AND CONCLUSIONS

Although many animals live largely solitary lives, some live in groups. Groups vary from anonymous collections of individuals such as fish shoals to the highly structured societies of the social insects, in which specialized castes of sterile workers maintain the nest and help the queen raise her young. Important selection pressures that favor group living include advantages from predator evasion and resource acquisition. By living in groups animals may reduce their chances of being captured by a predator through dilution, hiding in the herd, the benefit of increased vigilance from many eyes and ears, and group defense. They may locate, capture, or defend food more successfully. Group members often cooperate. Kin selection is an important evolutionary explanation of altruistic behavior, when an individual helps another at a cost to itself. By helping relatives, including nondescendant kin as well as their offspring, individuals can pass on more copies of their genes to future generations. Much altruism observed in nature occurs between relatives. Sterile workers in social insects are sometimes more closely related to the individuals that they rear than they would be to their own offspring. Individuals may also show altruistic behavior to nonrelatives if by doing so they gain future benefits such as a viable group in which to live and breed. Conflict is an inevitable part of group life and competition often leads to the development of stable dominance hierarchies. In rare cases, where the costs of fighting are high, conflict may be settled by respect of prior ownership of resources. Although we might expect most individuals to remain in the group in which they are born, in most societies the members of one sex or the other leave the group. In this way they avoid the deleterious consequences of inbreeding depression. In many societies there is strong reproductive skew, where only one or a few members of the group reproduce. Current models attempt to explain differences in reproductive skew among species on the basis of a few key parameters, and these models may lead to a general theory of social evolution.

## FURTHER READING

Cooperatively breeding birds have been the subject of much study. Brown (1987) is an important review of the field, and Stacey and Koenig (1990) is an interesting compendium of long-term studies. Naked mole-rats are extraordinary mammals that live in groups in underground burrows and come closest to the eusocial insects in terms of social structure (see Sherman et al. 1991; O'Riain et al. 2000). Several chapters in Dugatkin (2001) are wonderful, personal introductions to long-term studies of social animals. These include Uetz on colonial spiders, Connor on cooperative alliances between male dolphins, Creel on cooperative hunting in wild dogs, Silk on social relationships among female bonnet macaques, and Harcourt on gorilla social structure.

# animal behavior and human society

# 15

# applied animal behavior and animal welfare

DAVID FRASER AND DANIEL M. WEARY

## INTRODUCTION

Why do captive tigers pace for hours, tracing and retracing the same path in their pens? Does the presence of tourists drive grizzly bears away from their spring feeding areas? Why do some pigs chew the tails of their pen-mates? Why is it so hard to get wild rats to eat poisoned bait? Is it frustrating for a hen to live in a cage with no secluded place to lay her eggs? Why do certain dogs never become fully socialized with their human families? Since animals cannot talk, how do we know when they are in pain? These are a small sample of the questions that the field of applied animal behavior has tried to answer as it grapples with practical problems and **animal welfare** issues arising in the management of wild, farmed, companion, and laboratory animals.

## An Old or New Field?

In one sense, applied animal behavior is one of the oldest fields of science. In the foothills of the Rocky Mountains is a historic site named "Head-Smashed-In Buffalo Jump" where the native people of the plains hunted American buffalo (*Bison bison*) on foot for more than 5000 years. In the autumn the people would locate a group of buffalo grazing in the vicinity of a particular clifftop. They would then begin the slow process, perhaps extending over several days, of moving the buffalo gradually closer to the cliff. Some of the hunters dressed in the skins of buffalo calves and positioned themselves between the herd and the cliff, taking advantage of the buffaloes' poor eyesight and natural tendency to maintain protective contact with calves. Others would dress in wolf skins and menace the buffalo from the other side to assist the gradual movement of the herd. Eventually this would bring the buffalo into the final valley where they entered a configuration of rock cairns, each large enough to conceal a person, arranged in a funnel-shaped pattern leading to the clifftop. As the buffalo passed each cairn, a hunter would leap into view, frightening the animals to create panic and keep them bunched together until the herd was thundering at full gallop toward the cliff. The site had been carefully chosen: it had a slight rise before the precipice so that the lead animals would not see the drop until it was too late, and many would fall to their death. In this way, people were able to move and kill herds of wild animals much larger and stronger than themselves using little more than a highly developed understanding of animal behavior.

In modern science, however, applied animal behavior is a remarkably new field (Box 15.1). Before 1900, practical problems of hunting and game management stimu-lated some early observational work on animal behavior (Thorpe 1979), and animals of social and economic importance played a significant role in basic behavioral research. Most notably, Pavlov (1927) used domestic dogs in his research on **classical conditioning** (see Chapter 7); von Frisch (1967) studied domestic honeybees in his pioneering work on insect communication (see Chapter 10); and domestic chickens served as a model in early research on social organization (Allee *c.* 1938). Nonetheless, it was not until the 1950s and 1960s that scientific books on the application of animal behavior to practical problems of animal management were published; the first textbook of domestic animal behavior appeared in 1962 (Hafez 1962), followed by specialist books on the reproduct-ive and abnormal behavior of animals (Fox 1968; A.F. Fraser 1968). The first scientific society in the field was founded in 1966 and the first journal in 1974. After this late beginning, however, the field has grown rapidly, with an extensive scientific literature, numerous textbooks, and growing educational opportunities for biologists, animal scientists, veterinarians, and other animal care professionals to study animal behavior and its applications.

Just when applied animal behavior was developing as a field of study, an emerging social issue catapulted it into prominence. In 1964 an English animal welfare advocate published *Animal Machines*, a book describing "intensive" systems of animal produc-tion such as cages for hens and crates for veal calves, which were then becoming common (Harrison 1964). The book argued that these systems are so restricting and unnatural for animals that they cause widespread suffering. *Animal Machines* created such a strong public reaction that the British government set up a technical committee to investigate the welfare of farm animals. Included on the committee was the eminent **ethologist** William Thorpe, a scholarly Quaker pacifist who had brought the German and non-German ethologists together after the Second World War. Thorpe realized that scientific research on animal behavior and related fields could do much to help answer the many questions that arose over the welfare of animals in captivity. In an essay that appeared as an appendix to the committee report, Thorpe (1965) proposed how beha-vioral research could be used to detect pain and discomfort, understand the cognitive powers of animals, and identify **motivations** that are thwarted in captivity; he also noted that physiological studies can indicate stress in animals, and that preference tests could be used to identify environments that animals prefer. The committee, clearly impressed by these ideas, called for research into the welfare of animals, especially through studies

## Box 15.1 Development of applied animal behavior and animal welfare science

### Applied animal behavior

Before 1950 domestic animals were often used in basic research on animal behavior (Pavlov 1927; von Frisch 1967; Allee c. 1938), and research on applied and abnormal animal behavior was increasing. The 1950s and 1960s saw a steady increase in scientific papers on applied animal behavior together with books such as *Wild Animals in Captivity* (Hediger 1950), the first textbook of domestic animal behavior (Hafez 1962), and specialist books on reproductive behavior (A.F. Fraser 1968) and abnormal behavior (Fox 1968). The Society for Veterinary Ethology (now called the International Society for Applied Ethology) was founded in 1966 and the journal *Applied Animal Ethology* (now called *Applied Animal Behaviour Science*) in 1974. The 1970s saw additional books on the behavior of farm animals (A.F. Fraser 1974) and chickens (Wood-Gush 1971), followed in the 1980s by a rapid increase in the research literature and many new books (Craig 1981; Houpt & Wolski 1982; Waring 1983; Kilgour & Dalton 1984). By the 1990s the field was well established and taught at many universities.

### Animal welfare concerns

Concern over animal welfare dates to ancient times, and regained prominence in Western countries after the Second World War, with particular emphasis on the use of laboratory animals and humane slaughter. In the 1960s public concern about living conditions for farm animals was catalyzed in the UK by *Animal Machines* (Harrison 1964) followed by the Brambell Committee (1965), which called for evaluation and improvements in the welfare of farm animals kept in intensive production systems. The 1970s saw other books on animal ethics and advocacy such as *Animal Liberation* (Singer 1975) and *Slaughter of the Innocent* (Ruesch 1978), and welfare codes and guidelines for farm animals were written in several countries. The 1980s saw many additional books (Rollin 1981; Midgley 1983; Regan 1983) and the formation of many new animal advocacy organizations. By the 1990s animal welfare and ethics were receiving major media attention, and farm animal welfare standards were being enshrined in legislation and international agreements.

### Animal welfare research

Beginning in the 1960s, concerns about animal welfare led to calls for scientific research to assess and improve animal welfare, with Thorpe's (1965) essay playing a key role. The 1970s saw early research papers with titles like "Frustration in the fowl" (Duncan

1970) and "Do hens suffer in battery cages?" (Dawkins 1977), together with the first textbook chapter on farm animal welfare (Wood-Gush et al. 1975). The 1980s saw the first book on animal welfare science, *Animal Suffering: The Science of Animal Welfare* (Dawkins 1980), and the creation of the first university chair in animal welfare science (held by D.M. Broom) at Cambridge in 1986. In the 1990s, two scientific journals were founded (*Animal Welfare* in 1992 and *Journal of Applied Animal Welfare Science* in 1998), numerous books were published (Webster 1994; Rollin 1995; Appleby & Hughes 1997; Fraser & Broom 1997), and the role of scientific research in the emerging animal welfare standards was clear.

of animal behavior. Such research began in the 1960s and 1970s, especially in the UK, and spread rapidly to other countries, mainly in Europe and the English-speaking world. Thus, barely three years after its first textbook had been published, the field of applied animal behavior was cited as a primary source of guidance on high-profile and highly contentious issues of animal welfare.

As a result of these developments, the field of applied animal behavior has acquired two somewhat distinct but overlapping mandates: more conventionally, to understand the behavior of animals in order to solve practical problems of animal housing, management, and health; and more controversially, to contribute to "animal welfare science," which seeks to improve our understanding of the welfare of animals, partly as a basis for humanitarian action and social policy.

## Practical Problems, Practical Solutions

### Using the abilities of animals

For thousands of years, humans have used certain abilities of animals, such as the horse's strength and the dog's powerful sense of smell, to complement human talents and to accomplish tasks that humans alone could not do. For such use of animals to be successful, handlers need to understand and shape the behavior of the animals. For example, "detector" dogs can find narcotics concealed in luggage and other parcels (Fig. 15.1). In the Australian Customs Service, dogs are trained for this task in a series of stages that make use of the animals' fondness for playing tug-of-war. Initially the dogs are trained to retrieve a stick or ball, with praise and a game of tug-of-war as the reward. The stick is then replaced by a cloth tug-of-war toy, which is subsequently hidden in open cardboard boxes; at this stage, the dog must search for the toy and bring it to the trainer for the reward. Next, the cloth is impregnated with the scents of various narcotics, and the toy is concealed in closed boxes. The dogs thus learn to use the scent to find the toy, and subsequently they search eagerly for narcotic scents in luggage and other containers. While the dog is working in this way, the trainer keeps the dog's toy

**Fig. 15.1** A dog in the Australian Customs Service trained to search for narcotics. (Photograph by Peter Sanderson, courtesy of Dr G.J. Adams.)

close by, and continues to play tug-of-war as a reward for successful detection (Adams & Johnson 1994).

Scent detection is one of the simpler animal talents that humans exploit. Animals, dogs in particular, are also used for complicated tasks such as herding sheep or apprehending criminals. These tasks require extensive training and a complex combination of cognitive skills and temperament traits; consequently, applied researchers have developed procedures to identify animals with good aptitude for various types of work. Since the early 1900s, for example, there has been increasing use of "service" dogs, initially to assist the blind but now increasingly used to help people with a range of physical or mental disabilities. However, many dog trainers report a high failure rate among dogs that begin the long and costly training process. After years of experience with dogs, Emily Weiss (2002) developed a series of tests that can be used to screen adult dogs from animal shelters for suitability as service animals. The tests involve training dogs to follow simple instructions and exposing them to a wide range of situations, including other dogs, strange people, and fear-producing events. Dogs fail the test if they are fearful, unruly, or slow to learn, if they overreact to other dogs or to a sudden noise or visual stimulus (an opened umbrella), or if they react aggressively to mild pain. By identifying better and worse candidates, the test procedure can allow animal trainers to focus on animals with a high probability of success.

## Preventing undesirable behavior

As well as beneficial behavior that people try to exploit, animals often perform harmful behavior that people try to prevent. Rodents can be serious crop pests; deer can destroy orchards; introduced species can cause significant damage to ecological systems. Instead of killing such animals, we can sometimes find less drastic solutions through knowledge of their behavior. In western North America, deer (*Odocoileus hemionus*) and elk (*Cervus elephas*) sometimes cause severe damage to plantations of seedling trees. In a search for an effective repellent, researchers assembled 225 candidate chemicals and screened them for repellency by spraying them on samples of feed that were then presented to captive deer. They found that decomposed protein-rich material was highly repugnant to deer. On this basis they developed a fermented egg product treated so as to give off a rotting odor, which repelled deer even in minute concentrations, likely because these ruminant herbivores, which might be harmed by eating rotting animal protein, may have evolved a strong capacity to detect and avoid such material. The compound formed the basis of a commercial repellent for the protection of conifer plantation seedlings (Bullard et al. 1978).

As a more sophisticated approach, scientists have used **conditioned taste aversion** (a form of classical conditioning; see Chapter 7) to prevent certain undesirable behavior. On the island ecosystems of New Zealand, introduced predators have brought certain species of birds to the brink of extinction. A famous example is the kakapo (*Strigops habroptilus*), a large flightless parrot, whose decline has occurred partly because its eggs are eaten by introduced rats. An ingenious approach to controlling such predation has been to add nonlethal toxins to some eggs so that predators learn that this type of prey makes them ill. In an experimental demonstration of this effect, researchers inoculated chicken eggs with toxins and painted these eggs green. The researchers found that crows (*Corvus brachyrhynchos*) quickly learned to avoid these eggs and subsequently avoided green eggs without the toxin (Nicolaus et al. 1983).

Some captive animals direct harmful behavior to themselves or their pen-mates. Some pigs chew each others' tails to the point of causing serious injury. Some chickens peck their cage-mates to the point of denuding, injuring, or even killing them. Certain zoo or laboratory animals mutilate themselves or attack their newborn young.

By understanding the **causes** of such behavior, applied ethologists can often find ways to prevent or mitigate the problem. One of the most intractable examples is "cross-sucking" by young calves. Dairy calves are normally removed from the mother within the first day after birth, at an age when they still have high motivation to suck, and are generally fed a milk-based or milk-like diet from a bucket. If young calves are housed in groups, they will often suck avidly on the navel, ears, or prepuce of other calves, sometimes to the point of causing damage. The most common solution has been to house calves in individual cubicles, but the practice deprives the young animals of social contact. However, if the calves obtain their milk by sucking from artificial teats, this appears to satisfy their motivation for both milk and the act of sucking, and allows the animals to be raised in groups. Even for calves in stalls, dummy teats attached to the wall allow the animals to suck in a harmless way, and has the additional advantage of causing a release of digestive enzymes that are not released to the same extent when animals drink from a bucket (de Passillé & Rushen 1997).

## Improving animal handling

A better understanding of animal behavior often allows humans to be more effective in handling animals. Early in his research career, Australian researcher Paul Hemsworth studied a group of 12 small, one-operator pig farms in the Netherlands; the farms used the same genetic line of pigs, the same diet, and the same building design, but the number of piglets born per sow each year differed considerably from farm to farm. Hemsworth found a striking behavioral difference between animals on farms with the greatest and least number of piglets born. On the more productive farms the breeding sows would more readily approach a human visitor, whereas on the less productive farms the animals tended to shy away. This observation and a large body of subsequent research (Hemsworth & Coleman 1998) led to the theory that rough, unskillful, or inconsistent handling by people can create fear responses in animals that interfere with the basic endocrine processes underlying reproduction and growth. In one striking demonstration, inappropriate handling of dairy cows interfered with milk yield. In this experiment, cows received rough handling, including slaps and shouts, from one handler, and more gentle handling from another. When later tested in the milking parlor, cows in the presence of the rough handler "retained" more milk (i.e., they failed to release the milk during milking), likely because at a physiological level the neuroendocrine responses associated with fear can counteract the milk-releasing action of the hormone oxytocin (Rushen et al. 1999).

## Mitigating harm to animals

Animal behavior has also been applied in efforts to reduce harmful impacts of humans on animals, especially wildlife. In forested areas of Canada, many moose (*Alces alces*) are killed in highway accidents every year, with most of the accidents occurring in

**Fig. 15.2** A moose (*Alces alces*) drinking from one of several plastic pails sunk into the ground at a natural mineral spring in Canada, as part of a preference experiment to determine which chemicals attract moose to the springs. (Photograph by Hank Hristienko.)

May–July. During these months moose show a remarkable change in their feeding behavior. In May, moose in the area show a sudden strong attraction to naturally occurring mineral-rich springs where they drink huge volumes of water. Once new aquatic vegetation develops in lakes and ponds, the moose appear to shift from using mineral springs and begin consuming large amounts of aquatic plants. "Cafeteria" experiments, using pails of pure salt solutions presented at mineral springs, showed that of the various minerals available in the springs, it is sodium that attracts the animals (Fig. 15.2). Similar research offering selections of aquatic plants showed that sodium-rich species are highly preferred over others. Hence, the use of both mineral springs and aquatic vegetation seem motivated by a search for sodium, perhaps to cope with the change in electrolyte balance caused by the newly green vegetation in the spring and early summer. Subsequent research on highway accidents showed that the majority occurred near poorly drained areas of the roadside where highway deicing salt, applied during the winter, remained dissolved in stagnant pools of sodium-rich water. The problem was managed by eliminating some of the stagnant pools with better roadside drainage, and by placing warning signs in the immediate vicinity of wet salty areas that could not be drained successfully (Fraser & Thomas 1982).

## Designing Better Environments for Animals

One of the major applications of animal behavior is the design of better environments for captive, farmed, and laboratory animals, partly for the practical goal of making the environments function better, and partly to improve the welfare of the animals that live in them.

### Accommodating animals' natural behavior

One strategy for improving animal housing has been to devise environments where animals can carry out elements of their natural behavior. As primatologist Jane Goodall (1971) discovered during her field studies, wild chimpanzees (*Pan troglodytes*) will use long twigs as "fishing rods" for termites (see also Chapter 8). A chimpanzee pokes the twig into a hole in a termite mound, and when the termites react by biting the twig, the chimpanzee withdraws the twig and eats the termites. Real termite fishing would be difficult to re-create in most zoos, but if chimpanzees are provided with a large container with holes and some long sticks, they will occupy a good deal of time fishing for a taste-treat such as honey or mustard.

Servals (*Felis serval*) are long-legged cats of west central Africa that hunt by leaping on their prey, sometimes flushing birds from low vegetation and catching them by spectacular jumps into the air. When kept and fed in a standard zoo cage, servals spend much of their time inactive or pacing repetitively in the cage. In his classic account of **behavioral enrichment** for zoo animals, Hal Markowitz (1982) described how the servals became much more animated, and more interesting to zoo visitors, when fed "flying meatballs" attached to a rope or rod and swung over the heads of the cats (Fig. 15.3). Servals fed in this way would leap vertically twice their body length to capture the prey.

### Testing environmental preferences

Another common strategy for improving animal environments is to "ask" the animals what environments they themselves prefer. William Thorpe, in his initial proposal for using science to help improve animal welfare, cited an early anecdotal example:

> In the early part of 1964 a group of African buffalo were captured in a region of Kenya where their natural existence was no longer tolerable or possible, and were taken for release in the Nairobi National Park.... During the process of transport and preparation for release, they were of course kept in pens or yards much like those in which domestic cattle are kept. When the time came for their release in the new environment, they showed many signs of distaste for it. They would return toward human habitations toward nightfall and try to enter the paddocks where they had been. One even tried to walk through the french windows of the office of the Director of the Kenya National Parks. The natural

**Fig. 15.3** A serval (*Felis serval*) leaping into the air to capture a "flying meatball" in the San Diego Zoo. (Photograph by Dr Hal Markowitz; from Markowitz 1982.)

assumption is that the unfamiliar National Park, reeking of lion, leopard and other dangerous and uncomfortable neighbours, must have seemed a very unfriendly place; far inferior to the luxurious though restricted quarters they had become used to inhabiting! (Thorpe 1965, pp. 73–74)

Since that unplanned experiment, scientists have used **environmental preference research** with many animal species to identify preferred levels of temperature, illumination, social contact and space allowance, preferred flooring and bedding materials, and preferred design features for pens, cages, and animal handling equipment (Fraser & Matthews 1997). In one experiment, for example, Farmer and Christison (1982) housed pigs in an experimental pen with two compartments, identical except that they were floored with different materials. In a series of pairwise choice experiments, the researchers monitored the amount of time the pigs spent on the different types of flooring, and were then able to rank the products from most preferred to least preferred. The researchers then measured numerous physical properties of the flooring products, such as coefficient of friction and thermal conductance. By comparing the preference rankings and the physical measurements, they found that young piglets generally preferred flooring that would not conduct heat away from the body, whereas older pigs chose floors that provide good traction. Thus, in addition to providing practical guidance to pig producers on specific flooring products, the experiment helped clarify the features that are important to the animals at different ages.

## Testing motivation strength

By themselves, simple preferences do not indicate the degree of importance that the animal attaches to the preferred option. This weakness led to attempts to measure the strength of animals' motivation (see Chapter 3) to obtain preferred options or to avoid unpreferred ones. In an influential paper called "Battery hens name their price," British ethologist Marian Dawkins (1983) proposed a way to "titrate" an unknown motivation against a known one. As we saw in Chapter 3, dustbathing is a natural behavior whereby chickens work dust, sand, or other loose material into their feathers, thus keeping the feathers in good condition by absorbing excess oil. Because the behavior is impossible to perform in standard commercial cages, a debate arose over how strongly birds are motivated to perform it. In one experiment Dawkins trained hens to enter two cages from a common choice point; one cage contained dustbathing material and the other contained food. The hens were then required to choose between the two cages after different periods of food deprivation. The experiment showed that the hens' motivation to dustbathe (under the conditions tested) appeared to be about as strong as their motivation to eat when deprived of food for several hours.

As a further refinement, animals can be trained to perform an **operant** task (see Chapter 7), such as pressing a lever or pecking a key, in order to obtain a reward; researchers can then compare how much work animals are willing to perform in order to obtain access to various environmental features as rewards. American mink (*Mustela vison*) are active, partially aquatic carnivores raised commercially for fur. In the wild, mink perform a wide range of behavior that is impossible in captivity; for example, they swim, rest in several nest sites, survey the environment from raised perching places, and explore the burrows of potential prey animals. But how important is it to mink to be able to carry out these types of behavior? In one study, mink in standard cages were trained to push against weighted doors for access to various rewards, including a tunnel, a raised platform, an alternative nest box, and a small pool of water where they could swim. The experimenters then varied the amount of weight that the animals had to lift to open the different doors. The amount of work the animals performed, expressed as the total amount of weight they lifted per unit of time, was much greater for access to the pool of water than for the raised platform, the tunnel, and other rewards (Fig. 15.4; Mason et al. 2001).

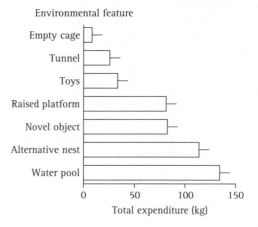

**Fig. 15.4** The price caged American mink (*Mustela vison*) will pay for access to various environmental features. Price is expressed as the total weight (kg) lifted by mink over a 6-week test. Values are means (+SE) from 16 animals tested. (Data from Mason et al. 2001.)

Thus we see, in a sense, two main variations of a research paradigm: (i) measures of preference for environmental features; and (ii) measures of motivation for access to these features, including the titration of an unknown motivation against a known one and measures of the effort an animal will expend for access to a reward. These types of research have led to many refinements in animal housing and handling equipment. For example, research on laying hens has shown that the birds seek out four environmental features: a nest box, sand or other loose material for dustbathing, a perch for resting, and more space than is provided in standard commercial cages. Based on this research, in 1999 when the European Union agreed to phase out the standard battery cage, it approved an "enriched" cage containing these four features as a replacement.

## Behavioral Genetics and Animal Welfare

Instead of designing environments that suit the animals' behavior, could we solve animal welfare problems by the reverse strategy? In other words, could we use genetic selection to create animals that are so well adapted to restrictive artificial environments that their welfare is not compromised? In fact, has the artificial selection of domestic animals already achieved this result?

In some cases, the answer is no. A wild sow (*Sus scrofa*), in the days before she gives birth, seeks out a suitable nesting site, digs a shallow depression, and builds a nest of branches and grass which creates a soft protected area for the newborn piglets. Presumably the behavior has been important for the survival of the young under natural conditions, and evolution appears to have equipped sows with strong motivation, probably under the control of the hormonal changes leading to parturition, to find and prepare a nest. Domestic sows, however, have been bred for many decades in protected indoor environments where nesting behavior is impossible to perform and is no longer needed for piglet survival. Nonetheless, when British and Swedish researchers released domestic sows in forested areas, the animals behaved much like their wild cousins, suddenly performing elaborate nesting behavior that had not been seen for many generations (Jensen 1986). Moreover, when kept in indoor stalls, sows show intense restlessness during the day before parturition, changing posture repeatedly, performing digging movements against the hard floor, biting the bars of the stall, and showing an intense interest in straw or other loose material. Evidently, the motivation to find and prepare a nest site is still strong in the domestic sow, and an inability to perform the behavior remains an animal welfare concern despite many generations of artificial selection.

In other cases, especially involving general temperament rather than specific behavior patterns, fairly rapid genetic change may be possible. One of the welfare concerns in the caging of fur-bearing carnivores is that these animals remain fearful of humans and may experience substantial stress from close human proximity. In Denmark, where there is extensive commercial breeding of mink, applied ethologists have devised a rapid test for temperament differences: they put a stick into the front of the mink's cage and note whether the animal approaches and investigates the stick, attacks it, or retreats from it. By breeding selectively from mink that approach and investigate the stick, scientists have produced, within just a few generations, animals that appear to remain calm in the presence of humans. The animals' welfare is presumably improved because they show little fear of people and a less pronounced physiological stress response to handling. There are also commercial advantages because the animals, being calmer, can be mated at a younger age than fearful ones (Malmkvist & Hansen 2001).

In yet other cases, selective breeding may help reduce welfare problems that likely arose in part through previous genetic selection. On commercial egg farms, where laying hens are typically housed in cages of 3–10 birds, the hens sometimes peck each other to the point of causing feather loss and occasionally more severe injuries or even death. The problem has likely been accentuated because geneticists, in breeding selectively from birds with the highest egg production, may inadvertently have favored the more competitive aggressive birds. As an alternative breeding strategy, some poultry geneticists have housed hens in cages of closely related birds, and then bred selectively from those groups where the birds achieved a high level of production on average. After only six generations of such group-based selection, egg production increased by 160%, partly because of reduced aggression and fewer deaths among the birds (Muir & Craig 1998).

## Animal Welfare and Affective States

Many concerns about animal welfare are primarily concerns about the **affective states** of animals, their "emotions," "feelings," and other pleasant or unpleasant experiences. Are the animals in our care experiencing fear, pain, hunger, and other negative states, or alternatively are they comfortable and contented? If scientists are to provide guidance on animal welfare, they must do their best to confront these difficult issues (Duncan 1993).

# Assessing negative states

Of the various affective states, fear is one of the most widely studied. An intriguing example arose over the mechanical "harvesting" of chickens that are raised for meat. These birds, unlike caged laying hens, are normally housed in large open buildings; when they reach market weight, crews of people are employed to catch the birds, usually grabbing them by the legs and carrying them upside-down to the shipping crates. A newer alternative is a mechanical "chicken harvester," a large machine that moves through the pens, gathers the birds in counter-rotating rubber fingers, and transfers them to the shipping crates via a conveyor belt. When chicken harvesters first appeared, there was concern that they would cause unnecessary fear in the birds. To investigate this concern, Ian Duncan, one of the pioneers of animal welfare research, monitored the heart rate of birds when they were captured by hand or by machine, and found (perhaps surprisingly) that the rapid heart rate of newly caught birds returned to normal much more quickly if they had been caught by machine rather than by hand. A widely used behavioral test for fear in chickens involves flipping the bird suddenly onto its back, whereupon it will often stay totally immobile for many minutes in a reaction called **tonic immobility**. It can be shown experimentally that chickens tend to remain in tonic immobility longer if they have been frightened before the test. Duncan and coworkers found that chickens that had been loaded by hand maintained tonic immobility for over 10 min on average, whereas those that had been loaded by machine righted themselves much sooner. The evidence thus suggested that machine catching actually caused less fear than manual catching, probably because the mechanical device, being so foreign to the birds, did not trigger any form of predator recognition (Duncan et al. 1986).

Pain is another state that animal welfare scientists have often tried to quantify. Many routine procedures performed on animals, including ear-cropping of puppies, castration of piglets, and dehorning of calves, are likely painful, and much recent research has been directed at developing measures of this pain so that less painful procedures can be identified. An interesting example comes from pediatric medicine. Circumcision of babies, like many of the procedures done to farm animals, has typically been performed without any intervention to control pain. In one influential study, infant boys were observed during circumcision with and without a local anesthetic applied to the foreskin. The researchers evaluated pain responses using facial actions scored from videotape. These included bulging of the brow, squeezing the eyes closed, opening the mouth, pursing the lips, holding the tongue taut, quivering of the chin, and protrusion of the tongue (Fig. 15.5). Babies that received the analgesic showed 12–49% less facial activity than those that received a placebo. Measures of vocal activity and heart rate showed similar effects: the analgesic-treated infants cried for half as long, and their heart rate increased less than that of the placebo-treated controls (Taddio et al. 1997). These results helped lead to the recommendation that infants should receive analgesics before circumcision.

With farm and laboratory animals, management practices often involve disrupting the animals' normal social relationships. For example, dairy calves are typically separated from the mother soon after birth; piglets are often weaned by sudden removal from the mother at only 2–4 weeks of age; laboratory animals may be housed individually for experimental purposes. Such situations give rise to concerns over separation

**Fig. 15.5** Facial expressions of a newborn human infant before and immediately after heel-lancing for a blood sample. Characteristics of the facial response to pain include bulging of the brow, squeezing the eyes closed, opening the mouth, pursing the lips, holding the tongue taut, quivering of the chin, and protrusion of the tongue. (From Grunau & Craig 1987, with permission from Elsevier Science.)

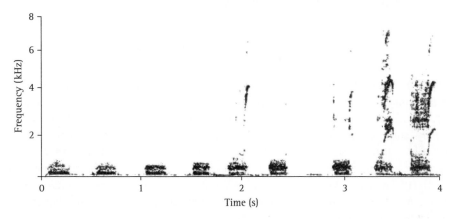

**Fig. 15.6** Sonogram of a sequence of nine "separation calls" given by a piglet separated from its mother.

distress (see Chapter 6), and measures have been used to assess such distress and test ways of reducing it. If an unweaned piglet is removed to an isolated pen, it gives a characteristic set of calls, beginning with quiet closed-mouth grunts and progressing to loud high-pitched squeaks and squeals (Fig. 15.6). The calls are so characteristic that experienced pig-keepers immediately recognize them as coming from a lost piglet. Experiments have shown that newly isolated piglets give more calls, especially of the loud high-pitched variety, if they have not been fed recently or if they are in a cool environment, both conditions that presumably increase their need to be reunited with the mother. Moreover, sows respond more vigorously to calls given by piglets in conditions of greater need. The current thinking is that these calls form a communication system that helps to reunite isolated piglets with their mothers, and that the number and type of calls reflect the animals' level of distress at being separated (Weary & Fraser 1995). Hence the calls may be useful for testing ways to mitigate separation distress. For example, experiments show that piglets separated from the sow call much less if they are kept with several familiar litter-mates; hence, maintaining intact litters at weaning may help reduce the distress caused by the practice (D. Fraser 1975).

Avoidance **learning** has proven a useful means of assessing how strongly animals avoid management practices suspected of being unpleasant. One example arose over the electroimmobilization of sheep. Electroimmobilization involves passing a pulsed low-voltage current through the body to immobilize animals temporarily for procedures such as shearing their wool. The electrical current had been claimed to function as an analgesic, making procedures such as shearing less unpleasant for the animals. But does it really prevent discomfort or does it merely render the animals unable to move? To test these claims, Australian–Canadian researcher Jeffrey Rushen (1986) trained sheep to move along a runway to a pen where they received mildly **aversive** treatments such as rough shearing, with and without electroimmobilization. The results showed that over repeated trials, sheep that received the electrical treatment became more difficult to move along the runway compared with those that received the mildly aversive treatments without electroimmobilization. Rushen concluded that electroimmobilization actually made unpleasant procedures more aversive, not less.

## Interpreting abnormal behavior

Abnormal animal behavior has provided a strong stimulus for understanding affective states of animals. In a classic article on behavioral disturbances, psychiatrist David Levy (1944) described the repeated rocking movements and other **stereotyped behavior** shown by some emotionally disturbed children. In the same article Levy described similar behavior in farm animals, including repetitive weaving by horses in stables and stereotyped head movements by caged chickens. Levy proposed that these abnormalities reflect the same kinds of problems seen with children in severely deprived environments. The idea generated enormous interest in abnormal animal behavior and its implications for the welfare of animals.

One of the most striking examples is seen with pregnant sows. During pregnancy most sows must have their food intake limited in order to prevent excessive weight gain and later health problems, but the restricted diet can lead to serious aggression if the animals are fed in groups. A common solution is to house sows individually, usually in narrow stalls where they are sometimes tethered by a collar around the neck. Some such sows develop stereotyped movement patterns; for example, a sow may make three rooting movements to the left, swing her head to the right, and bite the bar of the stall, and then repeat the same sequence of movements for several hours every day. But what is the significance of these bizarre movements? Various scientists have proposed that the behavior develops from exploratory motivation or from attempts to escape from a confined space, or that the behavior helps animals to "cope" with an aversive environment, for example by causing a release of endogenous opioids (see Lawrence & Rushen 1993). However, research in Scotland showed that food restriction plays a large role in the development of stereotyped behavior of sows. One hypothesis is that food restriction causes a motivation to forage for food, but in a barren environment where normal foraging is impossible, elements of foraging behavior become fused together into stereotyped sequences of behavior, and because the behavior never leads to actual eating it does not stop in the normal manner. In a critical experiment, Claudia Terlouw et al. (1991) tested the food-restriction theory. They housed some sows in narrow stalls where they were tethered by a chain, whereas others were loose-housed in larger pens equipped with chains hanging from the walls. In each housing treatment, half the animals were fed a restricted diet typical of commercial practice whereas the others received nearly twice as much. In both pens and stalls, the restricted-fed animals spent considerable time in chewing, biting, and rooting the chain and in other seemingly functionless and stereotyped behavior, whereas these activities were much less common among the generously fed animals. Terlouw et al. (1991) concluded that chain manipulation and other stereotyped behavior of sows are more related to restricted feeding than to restraint itself, but they noted that none of the available theories adequately explains this behavior.

Fear, pain, separation distress, avoidance learning, and stereotyped behavior are some of the simpler issues being studied by animal welfare scientists. At the frontier of the field, scientists are asking more unconventional questions. Can we operationalize "boredom" in animals (Wemelsfelder 1993)? Can we find indices of positive states ("well-being") that will apply to both humans and nonhuman species (Broom 2002)? What species possess what types and degrees of **consciousness** (see Chapter 8), and how does this affect their capacity to suffer (Kirkwood et al. 2001)?

## Probing the Limits of Science

### Science and the mental experience of animals

Can science really help us understand the affective states of other species? A century ago biological scientists had little doubt on this issue. The last great work of Charles Darwin (1872) was called *The Expression of the Emotions in Man and the Animals*. Darwin's friend and contemporary George Romanes, in his book *Animal Intelligence*, assembled narrative accounts of animal behavior from what he regarded as reliable sources. From these he tried to infer the emotional capacity of many species; he argued, for example, that elephants are capable of vindictiveness toward humans or elephants that have harmed them, and sympathy toward the injured (Romanes 1904). The pioneering ethologist Julian Huxley (1914, quoted by Burkhardt 1997, p. 8) proposed that through the study of behavior "we can deduce the bird's emotions with much more probability of accuracy than we can possibly have about their nervous processes."

However, at the time when Darwin was pondering the evolution of emotions, another influential scientist was proposing a view of science that excluded such interests from science altogether. Auguste Comte was the nineteenth-century French thinker whose "Philosophie Positive" gave us the school of thought that we call Positivism. Comte was attempting to draw a clear distinction between science, interpreted as the study of the material world, and other branches of thought such as theology and metaphysics. Science, as seen by the Positivists, is concerned only with what we can observe. With this emphasis on the tangible, Positivist thinkers held that we should not postulate unobservable processes to explain observable ones, and that processes that cannot be observed fall outside the realm of scientific enquiry. On this basis, some early Positivists ruled that the origin of the universe, the atomic theory of matter, and the theory of evolution are not part of science. These ideas have now faded from memory, but Positivism had a more lasting influence on the study of animal behavior, with behaviorists such as John Watson and ethologists such as Niko Tinbergen persuading many animal behavior researchers that the mental states of animals should play no role in the scientific study of behavior (Rollin 1989; Burkhardt 1997). In the words of Tinbergen (1951, p. 4), "Because subjective phenomena cannot be observed objectively in animals, it is idle either to claim or to deny their existence."

Arguably, this attitude imposed a valuable discipline on behavioral science. It helped prevent scientists from unrestrained speculation about the mental lives of animals, from assuming that the mental experiences of nonhumans are the same as those of humans, and from believing that behavior is explained when it is merely rephrased in mentalistic terms. These errors are all too easily made by writers purporting to describe the subjective lives of animals. For example one popular writer, after seeing a televised sequence of a puma that had just killed a bighorn sheep, described the puma as gazing "fondly" into the sheep's eyes and "tenderly" patting the sheep's face (Thomas 1994, p. 25). This was subsequently presented by other popular writers as evidence that predators feel "gratitude" toward their prey (Masson & McCarthy 1995, p. 174). The moral is that when we use scientific methods to probe the affective states of animals, we will need rigorous thinking and clever means of testing our ideas, or else we will see all manner of gratuitous speculation jumbled together with science. Nonetheless, Marian Dawkins, while fully recognizing the need for intellectual discipline, proposes that we not shrink from the challenge of understanding the mental states of animals:

> Consciousness is the greatest remaining mystery in biology . . . Ethical concerns about the welfare of animals come from many people's deeply held conviction that many non-human animals consciously experience emotions such as fear, anxiety, and boredom . . . So the study of animal welfare, by its very nature . . . is forced to confront the greatest remaining mystery in biology. (Dawkins 2001, p. S19)

The philosopher Daniel Dennett has given us a vocabulary for understanding the different approaches to the issue of animal consciousness. Dennett (1987) refers to a "stance" as a conceptual framework or set of working presuppositions that scientists adopt to interpret observations and guide further empirical study. The view of the animal welfare scientist, that higher vertebrates can consciously experience states such as pain, fear, and hunger, is not a hypothesis that we can expect to either prove or disprove; rather, it is a stance adopted by animal welfare scientists (in contrast to the Positivist stance adopted by Watson and Tinbergen) that will ultimately be judged by its usefulness in suggesting interesting questions, in leading to correct predictions, and in providing satisfying explanations.

Apart from its role in the study of animal welfare, could efforts to understand the affective states of animals also give us better explanatory models and predictive theories of behavior? Jane Goodall (1971) gave many narrative descriptions of the behavior of free-living chimpanzees. She described, for example, how an adult male repeatedly collected empty paraffin cans and banged them together while charging toward other, more dominant chimpanzees; this caused the others to scatter, and was followed by a distinct rise in the male's dominance status within the group. Can we provide a satisfactory explanation of this behavior without postulating certain mental processes such as a desire for dominance and planning of the display? Psychologist Ronald Baenninger (1990, p. 257) used the simpler example of the behavior of a hungry dog to provide a thought-provoking commentary on the place of mental states in the scientific explanation of behavior:

> Positive or negative **reinforcement** may be adequate to explain a dog's movement to a place where food . . . has previously occurred. But what of the responses that were not even present during the acquisition trials? Why does the dog perk up its ears, whimper, turn its head and eyes toward the learned location, and prepare to spring toward it?

As Baenninger suggested, we could try to explain this behavior without reference to any mental state of the dog. We could, for example, postulate a number of learned stimulus–response chains for each of these movements, but would it not be simpler and less cumbersome to postulate a single mediating mental event ("expectation") which influences behavior in certain ways? As long as we confine ourselves to generalized quantitative response measures, such as the speed with which a food-deprived animal moves to a location where it is fed, then explanations are not likely to be improved by postulating that the animal *feels* hunger and *expect*s food. However, when we observe behavior in narrative detail, as in the examples from Goodall and Baenninger, theories that include the affective and cognitive processes of animals may provide more complete and **parsimonious** explanations of behavior than those that do not. In other fields, such as physics and organismal biology, scientists reached a point where they needed to postulate the existence and properties of phenomena such as electron spin and **speciation** by **natural selection** that could not be observed directly. Has animal behavior reached a similar stage, or are there more fundamental reasons why we cannot, or should not try to, understand the mental states of animals?

## Animal welfare, science, and ethics

The application of science to animal welfare also raises important questions about the relationship of science and ethics. Philosopher David Hume (1711–76) famously pointed out that we cannot derive an "ought" from an "is," in other words, that we cannot use facts to answer ethical questions. Questions about animal welfare are ultimately motivated by concerns over how we ought to treat animals, whereas science deals with questions of fact. How, then, can there be a science of animal welfare?

One response has been to draw a clear line between research on variables associated with animal welfare, such as signs of fear, pain, and disease, and ethical decisions about what constitutes an acceptable level of these variables. The distinction is important, but the interplay between science and values is more subtle than this simple compartmentalization would suggest.

Table 15.1 Three conceptions of animal welfare and typical measures used to provide positive or negative evidence of animal welfare.

| Conception of animal welfare | Typical measures |
| --- | --- |
| Biological function | Increase in stress hormones (–) |
| | Reduction in immune competence (–) |
| | Incidence of disease and injury (–) |
| | Survival rate (+) |
| | Growth rate (+) |
| | Reproductive success (+) |
| Affective states | Behavioral signs of fear, pain, frustration, etc. (–) |
| | Physiological changes thought to reflect fear, pain, etc. (–) |
| | Behavioral signs of aversion or learned avoidance (–) |
| | Behavioral indicators of comfort/contentment (+) |
| | Performance of behavior (e.g., play) thought to be pleasurable (+) |
| | Behavioral signs of approach/preference (+) |
| Natural living | Performance of natural behavior (+) |
| | Behavioral/physiological indicators of thwarted natural behavior (–) |
| | Performance of abnormal behavior (–) |

The variables that scientists choose to study in assessing animal welfare, and the interpretation they attach to these variables, are underlain by value-laden ideas about what constitutes a good life for animals. Some scientists, including some veterinarians and agriculturalists, tend to emphasize the biological functioning of animals (health, growth, etc.) as fundamental to animal welfare; in assessing animal welfare, these scientists are likely to use traditional measures such as disease incidence, reproductive success, and stress physiology (Table 15.1). Other scientists tend to emphasize affective states as the basis for animal welfare, and their scientific measures of welfare include indicators of pain, distress, and related states. Yet others see satisfactory animal welfare as requiring that animals can live relatively natural lives, in accordance with their evolved **adaptations**; in studying animal welfare these scientists tend to use the occurrence of natural behavior (body care, normal social interaction) as indicators of good animal welfare, and abnormal behavior (stereotyped behavior, self-mutilation, excessive aggression) as denoting impaired welfare.

These different views of animal welfare sometimes lead to similar conclusions. For example, allowing a sow to wallow in cool mud when the weather is hot should be good for animal welfare because the sow should avoid stress and disease problems caused by heat (a biological functioning criterion), should not suffer from the heat (an affective state criterion), and because wallowing is the animal's natural way of cooling off (a natural living criterion). Nonetheless, the three views involve quite different areas of emphasis in assessing animal welfare and sometimes lead to conflicting conclusions.

For example, hens in a confined, high-health flock may have little disease and high rates of growth and production, whereas hens kept outdoors are more free to perform natural behavior but they may also have more parasites, lay fewer eggs, and be more prone to fear of predators. In many cases there is no logically or empirically correct way of weighing these different elements. Hence, in the scientific assessment of animal welfare our empirical studies are underlain by a conceptual framework where values play a key and sometimes subtle role in the selection and interpretation of variables (Fraser et al. 1997). From its beginnings, therefore, animal welfare research has included debate about the values underlying the science, the interplay between values and science, and the ethical implications of the results.

In writing this chapter, we found a pleasant irony in these last few pages. Applied animal behavior began as an attempt to solve real-life problems through an understanding of animal behavior. The field thus tended to be strong on practical ingenuity but light on theory, a kind of rough-and-ready country cousin of theoretical science. As it has developed, however, applied animal behavior has found itself probing the conceptual frontiers of animal behavior research, rethinking whether and how to study affective experience in animals, confronting fundamental questions about animal consciousness, and articulating the often subtle interplay between empirical and value issues in the conduct and interpretation of research.

## SUMMARY AND CONCLUSIONS

Applied animal behavior science began through the application of animal behavior to practical problems: improved handling and raising of animals, designing better housing for animals in captivity, prevention of abnormal or undesirable behavior, genetic manipulation of behavioral traits, and more effective use and training of animals. Since the 1960s the field has also provided a means of assessing and improving animal welfare through studying the preferences and motivations of captive animals, abnormal behavior, and affective states such as fear, pain, and distress. Both goals have given rise to a suite of research approaches that tend to combine behavioral observations and experiments with elements of stress physiology, veterinary medicine, animal production, and environmental design. In dealing with animal welfare issues, the field has been stretched beyond the traditional boundaries of animal behavior research into probing the affective states of animals and understanding the interplay of empirical and ethical elements that occurs when we apply science to an area of social action.

## FURTHER READING

The major scientific journal dealing with applied animal behavior is *Applied Animal Behaviour Science*, now in its thirtieth year; however, papers on animal behavior applied to practical problems appear in many journals covering animal, poultry and dairy science, animal behavior, veterinary medicine, zoo biology, laboratory animal science, and other fields. Journals specializing in the scientific study of animal welfare are *Animal Welfare* and *Journal of Applied Animal Welfare Science*; journals dealing with human–animal interaction and animals in society include *Animals and Society* and *Anthrozoös*. Recent books providing a general introduction to farm or domestic animal behavior include Jensen (2002), Fraser and Broom (1997), and Houpt (1998). Recent books on animal behavior have been written about many individual species including cats (Turner & Bateson 2000), dogs (Serpell 1995), cattle (Albright & Arave 1997), and horses (Waring 2003). Specialized topics that have received book-length treatment include stereotyped behavior (Lawrence & Rushen 1993), transportation and handling of animals (Grandin 2000), human–animal interaction (Hemsworth & Coleman 1998), and the application of behavior to conservation (Clemmons & Buchholz 1997). Recent works approaching animal welfare from a scientific viewpoint include Appleby and Hughes (1997), Moberg and Mench (2000), Rollin (1995), and Broom (2002). Works about animal consciousness and its implications for animal ethics are covered in Dawkins (1993), Dol et al. (1997), and Kirkwood et al. (2001). The interplay of values and ethics in the study of animal welfare are covered by Rollin (1995) and D. Fraser (1999).

## ACKNOWLEDGMENTS

We would like to dedicate this chapter to Andrew Fergusson Fraser, one of the founders of the (now) International Society for Applied Ethology, founding editor of *Applied Animal Behaviour Science*, and vigorous promoter of the field. We are grateful to colleagues Ruth Grunau, Hal Markowitz, Georgia Mason, Cheryl O'Connor, Sarah Murphy, Hank Hristienko, and Peter Sanderson (courtesy of Dr G.J. Adams) for kindly supplying material and photographs, and for the financial support of the Natural Sciences and Engineering Research Council of Canada, the British Columbia SPCA, the British Columbia Veterinary Medical Association, and the many other sponsors of the UBC Animal Welfare Program listed on our website at www.agsci.ubc.ca/animalwelfare.

# 16
# animal behavior and conservation biology

TIM CARO AND JOHN EADIE

## INTRODUCTION

Whereas the study of animal behavior is mainly concerned with the **causes**, **development**, and adaptive significance of variation in behavior of individuals, conservation biology is concerned with the behavior of populations, especially their response to disturbance caused by humans, and in preventing their extinction. Nonetheless, an increasing number of people studying animal behavior have become concerned about species' extinctions and habitat loss, sometimes for professional reasons because their study populations are under threat, or for personal reasons (Rubenstein 1998). Consequently, since 1995, there have been several attempts to point out the relevance of animal behavior to the field of conservation biology. The purpose of this chapter is to:

1 outline briefly the history of these attempts;
2 describe the major areas of animal behavior that have the potential to address conservation problems; and
3 discuss why connections between these disciplines have failed to solidify as quickly as expected.

At the end of the chapter, we suggest ways in which those embarking on new studies in animal behavior can tailor their research to solving urgent conservation problems.

## Attempts to Link Animal Behavior to Conservation Biology

Although interest in conservation increased steadily from 1950 onwards (see articles in the journals *Oryx*, *Journal of Wildlife Management*, *Environmental Conservation*, and *Biological Conservation*), one can argue that the discipline of conservation biology was born officially in 1987 when the first issue of an influential journal of that name appeared. Conservation biology is a multidisciplinary science that documents the extent and distribution of biodiversity; examines the nature, causes and consequences of loss of genes, populations, species, and habitats; and attempts to develop practical methods for stemming species' extinctions and allow for continuation of functioning ecosystems (Wilson 1992; Meffe & Carroll 1997). Initially, it used principles from ecology, population genetics, and systematics to describe biological diversity and seek ways to conserve it (Simberloff 1988) but as the discipline grew it embraced economic, sociological, anthropological, and philosophical constructs to understand and change the impacts of human activity on species and habitats. Animal behavior was deemed to have little relevance to the study of changes in population size and composition since the behavior of a population necessarily encompassed the sum of the behavior of individuals within that population. Two exceptions were zoo managers, who recognized that individual behavioral idiosyncrasies could influence breeding success in very small captive populations, and those in charge of reintroduction programs, who saw behavior following release as a key element of success (Kleiman 1989).

Recognition that advances in animal behavior might be pertinent to conservation issues came with the realization that a species' biology could predispose it to changes in habitat, to predation or competition from introduced animals, or to hunting (Caughley & Gunn 1996); that knowledge about **mating systems** (see Chapters 11 & 12) and social organization (see Chapter 14) could influence **effective population size** and population growth (Caro & Durant 1995); and that knowledge of **learning** mechanisms (see Chapters 7 & 8) could revise predictions about breeding success in captivity (Curio 1996) and prey species reintroductions (McLean et al. 1994). These and other ideas were brought together in a special edition of the journal *Oikos* (volume 77) and in three wide-ranging edited volumes by Clemmons and Buchholz (1997), Caro (1998a) and Gosling and Sutherland (2000), in short syntheses that championed the importance of behavior for conservation (Martin 1998; Sutherland 1998; Caro 1999), and in taxonomically restricted review articles (Strier 1997; Reed 1999; Shumway 1999; Colishaw & Dunbar 2000). This sudden burst of interest signifies a new awareness of the way in which principles of animal behavior can be used to redirect conservation programs (Caro 1998b).

## Conceptual Links Between Animal Behavior and Conservation Biology

### Behavioral methodology

In order to monitor populations so that conservation action can be implemented well in advance of crises, it is necessary to estimate population size and growth rate regularly. Although ecologists have developed many indirect methods of doing this (e.g., catch per unit effort, transects, acoustic surveys, point counts, and live trapping), fieldworkers studying behavior have needed to develop specific techniques to identify individuals since behavioral biologists are interested in causes and consequences of individual variation. Their techniques fall into two categories (McGregor & Peake 1998).

1 Artificial markers, such as leg bands placed on birds, numbered collars on mammals, radio and satellite transmitters, and modifying the appearance of individuals using fur dyes and bleaches, freeze branding, ear notching, and toe clipping.

2 Using natural markings for field identification, such as coat markings in cheetahs (*Acinonyx jubatus*), facial characteristics in Bewick's swans (*Cygnus columbianus*), scars in dolphins (*Tursiops truncates*), footprints in cougars (*Puma concolor*), acoustic **signals** in blue monkeys (*Cercopithecus mitis*), and genetic markers in marine turtles. Natural markings are superior to artificial techniques in that they avoid risks inherent in capturing and marking animals (Cuthill 1991; McGregor & Peake 1998).

Individual identification has several advantages. First, the researcher sometimes knows all the individuals in the population instead of a sample, and can thereby assess the resolution of more conventional and widely used ecological census techniques. For example, Gros et al. (1996) were able to gauge the accuracy of interviewing people about cheetah numbers against known population sizes of cheetahs gleaned from long-running behavioral studies. Second, if individuals' reproductive careers and survival are followed over time, the causes of changes in population size can be discerned. Third, if properties of calls can be individually recognized, researchers can estimate the population size of secretive species such as corncrakes (*Crex crex*) or bitterns (*Botaurus stellaris*) (McGregor et al. 2000).

Other methods, such as playing back the recorded songs of birds, can also be employed to calculate population size (Baptista & Gaunt 1997). Although ornithologists have long used birds' vocalizations to elicit answering calls and count individuals in thick vegetation, mammalogists now use similar techniques, for example playing whooping calls to call in spotted hyenas (*Crocuta crocuta*) from a known radius (Mills et al. 2001). This method is well suited to censusing rare species at low densities, the very populations of concern to conservation biologists.

## Ontogeny

Two elements of behavioral development (see Chapter 6) have a direct bearing on restoration projects in conservation biology: acquiring antipredator behavior and **imprinting**. Ability to recognize predators is influenced by genetic processes (Hobson et al. 1988) and learning processes (Curio et al. 1987). For example, New Zealand robins (*Petroica australis*) from mainland New Zealand that have been exposed to (introduced) small carnivores for over 100 years respond immediately to stoats (*Mustela erminea*) whereas those from an outlying island with no such experience do not. Yet after only one exposure to a stoat, the naive robins show full response intensity (Maloney & McLean 1995).

Practical methods have been used to train naive birds and mammals prior to reintro-duction, particularly in Australia where remnant native fauna has been subject to intense predation from introduced placental carnivores (Short et al. 2002). Mammalian examples include rufous bettongs (*Aepypyrmnus rufescens*) and quokkas (*Setonix brachyurus*) being **conditioned** to respond fearfully to a fox (*Vulpes vulpes*) by pairing a stuffed fox with a live domestic dog (*Canis familiaris*) that harassed them (McLean et al. 2000), and rufous hare-wallabies (*Lagorchestes hirsutus*) being trained to avoid a model fox or cat (*Felis catus*) by pairing the predator's appearance with a conspecific alarm call or loud noise or, alternatively, with a moving predator puppet and squirt of water (McLean et al. 1995). These and other studies (Griffin et al. 2000) raise a host of applied developmental questions, including how frequent and for how long should training last, how natural should it be, will it transfer to future generations, and whether responses are specific to different predators (McLean et al. 1994; Griffin et al. 2001). Currently, the beneficial consequences of predator avoidance training on survival fol-lowing reintroduction are equivocal; for example, rufous hare-wallabies (*Lagorchestes hirsutus*) failed to respond to the predators 8 months later, and the very small number of studies that have monitored long-term survival have yet to reach any consensus (McLean et al. 1994).

More generally, animals reared in isolation or in peer groups without parents face problems if they are reintroduced into the wild, including loss of dominance (Marshall & Black 1992) and lack of knowledge about poisonous foods (Beck et al. 1994) and migratory routes (Baskin 1993). Furthermore, captive-reared individuals can imprint (see Chapter 6) on their human caretakers, heterospecific foster parents, or even on their captive surroundings, resulting in inappropriate breeding behavior. Captive-rearing institutions have known about these problems for years and have developed elaborate programs to deal with them (McLean 1997; Curio 1998). There are many examples. California condor (*Gymnogyps californianus*) chicks are fed in the nest using hand-held puppets of a parent's bill and head to avoid chicks making attachments to humans (Toone & Wallace 1994). Endangered whooping cranes (*Grus americana*) cross-fostered to sandhill cranes (*Grus canadensis*), so as to induce the whooping crane parents to produce a second clutch, have difficulty in forming pair bonds (Kepler 1977) and there-fore workers disguised as whooping cranes (dressed in sheets with a puppet head on one hand) feed the chicks in the field. To prevent released California condors from roost-ing on power lines, chicks are fledged in large flight pens with tree branches and are conditioned to avoid a model power pole that gives moderate electric shocks (Wallace 2000).

Unfortunately, most of the progress in the area of reintroductions has been on a case-by-case basis, dealing with developmental problems as they arise. Progress in understanding behavioral development, on the other hand, has been based on studies of relatively few model species. Consequently, there are few guidelines to inform us about relatively unknown endangered species other than obvious concerns about pre-dators needing to acquire hunting skills and migratory species requiring knowledge of migratory routes. At present, application of knowledge of behavioral ontogeny to con-servation is largely by trial and error.

# Mechanisms

## *Hormones*

Environmental stressors can trigger a cascade of hormone secretions (Wingfield et al. 1997). For example, glucocorticosteroids play a central role in physiological and behavioral responses to stress and field assays of these hormones have been used to evaluate levels of stress in wild populations. In the Western fence lizard (*Sceloporus occidentalis*), adrenal responsiveness was higher in individuals from populations on the periphery of the species' range (Dunlap & Wingfield 1995); **habitat fragmentation** may cause similar effects (Wingfield et al. 1997). Following an oil spill near a colony of Magellanic penguins (*Spheniscus magellanicus*) in Argentina, birds with light oil contamination (< 5% of body surface) returned to the colony but did not breed (Fowler et al. 1995). Field assays revealed a reduction in sex steroids and an increase in stress hormones. Heavily oiled birds that were rescued and washed not only exhibited higher levels of corticosterone than nonoiled birds but also significantly higher levels than oiled birds that were not washed, indicating that considerable stress is involved in restraining and cleaning oiled birds (Fowler et al. 1995).

Hormonal therapy can be used to enhance breeding in captive animals or in populations that exhibit low reproductive rates in the wild (Wingfield et al. 1997). Conversely, hormone therapy could be used to suppress reproduction in overcrowded populations or in predators or parasites of species in peril (Seal 1991). Finally, some pollutants may mimic natural hormones and have unanticipated impacts on wild populations. Several components of petroleum-related products have estrogenic properties and have potent effects on reproductive behavior and development (Hose & Guillette 1995).

## *Behavioral toxicology*

Direct assays of behavior have been used to measure stress. Behavioral assessments are rapid and sensitive, and are likely to detect sublethal effects of an environmental perturbation before impacts at the population level are manifest (Smith & Logan 1997). Most applications of **behavioral toxicology** involve controlled laboratory studies of chemical contaminants and focus on behaviors such as orientation, locomotion, or preference/avoidance (reviews in Little et al. 1993; Smith & Logan 1997), although the methodology can be readily applied in the field. For example, Krebs and Burns (1977) documented the long-term effects of an oil spill on the population dynamics and behavior of a saltmarsh crab (*Uca pugnax*). Many crabs died or left the area; those that remained displayed aberrant locomotor and burrowing responses, slow or impaired escape behavior, and molted and developed mating colors at the wrong time of the year. These changes impaired successful reproduction and increased exposure to predators. Consequently, densities were reduced for at least 7 years after the spill. Understanding behavioral abnormalities induced by oil provides insights as to why this population failed to recover.

## Behavioral flexibility

Information on the **behavioral flexibility** of a species may be useful in predicting the degree to which a population would be placed at risk by environmental change, since **specialists** may be more vulnerable to disturbance than **generalists** (Arcese et al. 1997). Nonetheless, species with highly specialized behaviors may be able to expand their repertoire when opportunity or necessity dictate. For example, the Mauritius kestrel (*Falco punctatus*) is an obligate cavity-nesting bird requiring large tree holes in which to nest. Loss of nest sites and increased nest predation by introduced macaques (*Macaca fascicularis*) resulted in the population being reduced to only two pairs in the wild. In 1974, however, one pair nested on a cliff and was successful. Offspring from this pair also nested on cliffs and recruits to the population have come predominantly from cliff-nesting birds (Temple 1986). This example illustrates that shifts in behavioral preferences may be transferred between generations, highlighting the importance of learning and imprinting. Understanding whether a species is capable of such behavioral flexibility and determining how such shifts occur and are maintained may be critical for conservation efforts, especially for species where it is impossible to restore specialized resources upon which they depend.

Behavioral flexibility may also predict whether a species is likely to invade novel environments and thus become a conservation concern for other species. Sol et al. (2002) found that bird species with relatively large brains and which exhibited foraging innovations were more likely to become established when they were released into a new region.

## Interference with sensory modalities

Introduction of detrimental light into the environment (**photopollution**) can disrupt behaviors such as orientation, timing of periodic behavior, and visual communication. Eggs of endangered sea turtles hatch at night and young turtles move immediately to sea using a complex phototaxis toward the brightest horizon (the open ocean on unlit beaches; Witherington 1997). Artificial lighting from roads or houses along the beach disrupts this orientation mechanism; in Florida alone, approximately 1 million hatchling sea turtles are misdirected by lighting each year, resulting in hundreds of thousands of hatchling deaths. Changing the spectra of artificial lights could reduce misorientation deaths of hatchlings (Witherington 1997).

Orientation behaviors of large numbers of **nocturnally** migrating birds are also affected by artificial light sources such as lighthouses, aircraft beacons, and office towers (Reed et al. 1985). Interference with visual systems impacts many other behaviors, particularly those that rely on color for signaling or **display**, such as birds **lekking** in fragmented forests (Endler 1997). Altered light has also interfered with the mating displays of cichlid fishes in the African Great Lakes. Members of this speciose group are sexually isolated by mate choice, determined on the basis of body coloration. Increased turbidity of the water, brought about by increases in lake productivity, deforestation, and agriculture, constrains color vision such that the mating displays maintaining reproductive isolation are no longer functional. Accordingly, there has been a drastic loss of species in areas of the lakes with high turbidity due to the breakdown of reproductive barriers (Seehausen et al. 1997).

Interference with animal auditory systems can have similar effects (McGregor et al. 2000). Density of breeding birds was reduced by 20–95% in areas adjacent to busy roads and highways in the Netherlands (Reijnen et al. 1995) and there was a negative correlation between noise level and bird density (Reijnen et al. 1997). Male willow warblers (*Phylloscopus trochilus*) experienced difficulties attracting or keeping females near roads, possibly due to distortion of male song (Reijnen & Foppen 1994). Underwater noise may affect marine mammals in a comparable manner. Some whales communicate vast distances underwater using vocalizations, but the present level of anthropogenic oceanic noise now precludes such communication (McGregor et al. 2000). The effects of this interference on the population and social structure of marine mammals are unknown.

## Habitat selection

Understanding the habitat needs for a species is a basic requirement of any conservation program. However, the study of **habitat selection** has been fraught with difficulties, including debate over operational definitions of habitat use, preference, selection, availability or suitability (Hall et al. 1997), concerns over methodology used to measure habitat selection (Garshelis 2000), and uncertainty about the appropriate scale at which to do so (Arthur et al. 1996). Most empirical studies of habitat selection involve a comparison of the habitat types used to those available (Garshelis 2000). Assessments of "availability" assume that researchers can measure habitat in the same way as that perceived by the study animal. This is problematic because different estimates of availability can lead to very different (even opposite) indices of habitat selection for the same species (Arthur et al. 1996; McClean et al. 1998; Mysterud & Ims 1998). Uncertainty over the scale at which to measure habitat use and availability has further resulted in debate over habitat needs for threatened species, such as the northern spotted owl (*Strix occidentalis*) (Buchanan et al. 1995; Meyer et al. 1998; Folliard et al. 2000).

Efforts to link habitat selection to **fitness** consequences have centered on the concept of habitat **sources** and **sinks** (Pulliam & Danielson 1991; Pulliam 1996). Animals experience different local birth and death rates in different areas and reproductive surpluses from productive habitats (sources) could maintain populations in unproductive habitats (sinks). A critical question for conservation biologists is whether animals are able to discriminate between the two types of habitats.

Delibes et al. (2001) examined the effects of habitat selection on the degree to which increasing amounts of sink habitat would impact population growth rates. When animals use source and sink habitats at random (no habitat preference), population growth rate declines once a critical amount of sink habitat is exceeded. However, when animals can identify and avoid sink habitats, population growth rates remain high until most of the habitat is converted to sinks. There is a third, more worrisome possibility: animals can be attracted to sink habitats. In this case, there may be dramatic impacts on population growth rates, causing rapid reductions once a critical level of sink habitat is reached. Such attractive sinks, or **ecological traps** (Donovan & Thompson 2001;

Woodward et al. 2001), exist because the cues that animals use to select habitat are indirect; animals cannot predict breeding success directly and must use other cues to assess habitat quality (Kokko & Sutherland 2001). When those cues become uncoupled from the underlying fitness value of a habitat (by changes in the quality of a site but not its appearance), attractive sinks can develop. Understanding the cues animals use to assess habitat quality, and the degree to which such preferences can be altered, may be critical in evaluating the consequences of anthropogenic habitat change.

## Foraging and patch choice

The conceptual framework for the study of foraging behavior has a long theoretical history and strong links with **behavioral ecology** (Stephens & Krebs 1986; Giraldeau & Caraco 2000). The most effective use of foraging theory in a conservation context has come from efforts to link foraging behavior and density-dependent habitat selection using the **ideal free distribution** and ideal despotic distribution (Sutherland 1996). For example, Goss-Custard et al. (1995a,b) developed individual-based models for the oystercatcher (*Haematopus ostralegus*) in which the location, behavior, and body condition of each individual was tracked. A **game-theory** approach was then used to determine where each individual feeds, its body reserves, and the survival consequences for the individual and all others in the population (Stillman et al. 2000). Using this model, the effect of habitat loss to oystercatchers can be calculated and the most vital habitats determined. Stillman et al. (2001) extended this approach to examine the impact of shellfish harvest and found that although current levels of harvest were sustainable, increased fishing effort would greatly affect oystercatcher mortality and population size. Parallel studies have examined loss of winter habitat, breeding habitat, and migratory strategies on bird populations (Dolman & Sutherland 1995; Sutherland 1996) and have used foraging models to develop baseline expectations of habitat use against which effects of disturbance can be evaluated (Gill & Sutherland 2000).

Foraging behavior has also been used in other conservation contexts, such as examining the influence of human hunters on animal populations, including indigenous peoples (Winterhalder & Lu 1997), fishermen (Abrahams & Healey 1990), and whalers (Whitehead & Hope 1991). Studies of the foraging success of seabirds provide reliable indices of the abundance and distribution of commercially important fish species and do so less expensively than conventional fisheries surveys (Monaghan 1996).

## Allee effect and conspecific attraction

When populations decline to exceptionally low densities or groups dwindle to very small numbers of individuals, per-capita rates of increase can decline to zero or become negative (Fig. 16.1). This is called the **Allee effect** and it arises for a number of reasons: (i) genetic inbreeding and loss of **heterozygosity** leading to reduced fitness; (ii) random demographic stochastic effects that include highly skewed **sex ratios**, resulting in a paucity of mates; or (iii) a loss or reduction in opportunities for cooperative interactions

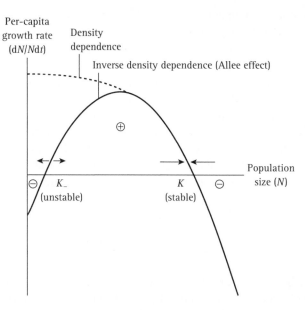

**Fig. 16.1** Illustration of the Allee effect from a very simple mathematical model of population dynamics: $dN/dt = rN(1 - N/K)(N/K - 1)$. The per-capita growth rate ($dN/dt$) is negative above the carrying capacity ($K$) and positive below. However, in the presence of the Allee effect, it also decreases below a given population size, and can even become negative below a critical threshold ($K_-$). When a population displaying this type of population dynamics is driven below the critical threshold, the low, sometimes negative, per-capita growth rate may lead it to extinction. (From Courchamp et al. 1999.)

between individuals, for example the inability to find receptive mates (e.g., African elephants, *Loxondata africana*, Dobson & Poole 1998; Glanville fritillary butterfly, *Melitaea cinxia*, Kuussaari et al. 1998) or lack of group defense (Courchamp et al. 1999; Stephens & Sutherland 1999).

Once regarded as idiosyncratic and of limited relevance to natural populations, the Allee effect is now seen as potentially significant when populations dwindle to very low densities, when populations are heavily harvested, when reductions in group sizes of susceptible hosts prevent disease from spreading (Dobson & Poole 1998), when small numbers of individuals are reintroduced in the course of a restoration project, and when individuals are encouraged to congregate and breed in safe habitats (Jeffries & Brunton 2001).

One of the ways in which an Allee effect might be mitigated is through **conspecific attraction**. Here, animals use the presence of conspecifics to select a habitat in which to live or breed. For example, pelagic marine invertebrates use chemicals released by conspecifics to settle close to established conspecifics (Meadows & Campbell 1972), and juvenile lizards (*Anolis aeneus*) settle next to areas where they have seen conspecifics in experiments that control for habitat quality (Stamps 1988). Conspecific attraction is thought to be particularly important in colonial seabirds choosing where to nest (Danchin & Wagner 1997). Using presence of conspecifics as a proxy for suitable habitat may also serve to reduce settlement costs if it is difficult or time-consuming to assess components of habitat quality, or, at a coarser level, conspecifics may simply be used to locate suitable habitat (e.g., listening for and moving toward frogs chorusing at an ephemeral pond; Greene & Stamps 2001).

Conspecific attraction is an important tool in reintroduction programs because it can be employed to draw released individuals into a safe target area; thus the use of decoys, artificial droppings, and tape lures are common in bird reintroduction attempts (Jeffries & Brunton 2001). It is also important in reserves designed to protect **metapopulations** (spatially discrete subpopulations connected by occasional **dispersal**). Without knowledge about conspecific attraction, suitable habitats may appear to be unsuitable simply due to an absence of conspecifics and unwittingly be omitted from inclusion in a reserve (Smith & Peacock 1990).

## Movement, ranging, and dispersal

If habitats differ in risk, for example if one lies inside a reserve but the other does not, movement of individuals between habitat **patches** will dictate patterns of mortality and reproduction inside and outside the protected area. Unfortunately, we know surprisingly little about the permeability of habitat edges, let alone about individual movements in their vicinity. Edges are detrimental to many forest-loving species because forest edges receive more sunlight, are less humid, and suffer greater wind shear than forest interiors. Edges are also detrimental to some specialists that cannot compete with generalist and commensal species that make forays in from the surrounding area. From this follow two predictions: certain species should avoid edges, and species that range widely will be more likely to encounter and cross boundaries and suffer problems there. Regarding the second point, Woodroffe and Ginsberg (2000) documented very high levels of human-induced mortality among large carnivores living in protected areas and reasoned that species with large **home ranges** would be more likely to encounter human activities because they were more likely to leave reserves than those species with smaller ranges. Woodroffe and Ginsberg then derived a measure of **critical reserve size** necessary to maintain each carnivore species. Critical reserve size correlated positively with female home range size after controlling for **phylogeny** (see Chapter 13) and population size. Moreover, female home range size was larger in species listed as threatened by the International Union of Nature and Natural Resources (IUCN) and was correlated with proneness to extinction (Woodroffe 2001). Thus, patterns of ranging are an important predictor of **effective reserve size** and extinction risk (see also Harcourt 1998 for a parallel finding in primates).

Reserve design has been a central focus in conservation biology for 25 years, with early debates focusing on the appropriate size and number of reserves and current interest on the importance of connecting reserves. Since large reserves are preferable to smaller reserves, an important conceptual question is whether to sacrifice reserve size for a **corridor** (narrow strips of land that differ from the habitat on either side and are attached to somewhat similar patches of vegetation; Fig. 16.2). Benefits of corridors include exchange of individuals among previously connected populations, which could lower regional

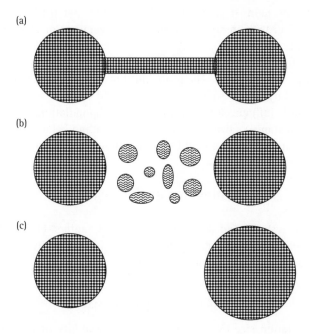

**Fig. 16.2** Comparison of tradeoffs in reserve design. (a) Linear patch has similar vegetation to habitat patches. (b) Moderate-quality patches through matrix. (c) Patch size increased by including area formerly allocated to corridor. (From Rosenberg et al. 1997.)

extinctions, reduce inbreeding depression, and increase recolonization in unoccupied patches. Corridors may also act as suitable habitats in their own right. Disadvantages include facilitating spread of disease or fire between patches, and attracting edge-loving and introduced species (Hobbs 1992; Rosenberg et al. 1997).

A key issue in this debate is whether corridors facilitate movement between patches and, as a consequence, increase population viability within those patches (Beier & Noss 1998). The problem has been addressed either demographically, by comparing patch occupancy and abundance in patches that are or are not connected (but usually failing to observe whether animals move down corridors), or behaviorally, by observing whether animals are found in, or better still, move along corridors (but often failing to document whether movements occur across the surrounding habitat as well). Studies that have observed animal movements in corridors are beginning to paint a complicated picture that includes closely related species using corridors but not others (e.g., butterflies, Sutcliffe & Thomas 1996; vole species, Mech & Hallett 2001), some species refusing to cross even small gaps (e.g., dormice, *Muscardinus avellanarius*, Bright 1998) but others doing so easily (e.g., tigers *Panthera tigris*, Johnsingh et al. 1990), and juveniles using corridors for dispersal but adults of the same species settling there (e.g., songbirds, Machtans et al. 1996). Only a few generalizations can be made at this stage: animals are more likely to select pathways that include components of their habitat, to move more rapidly through low- than high-quality habitat, and to avoid using the surrounding area the more it contrasts with their own patch (Rosenberg et al. 1997). We foresee a rapid growth in studies observing movements of animals in corridors in the next few years.

Movement and dispersal are also important for discrete populations connected by migration (a so-called metapopulation). The probability of extinction of a metapopulation can be highly influenced by factors such as habitat loss and emigration rates between patches. In turn, emigration is influenced by the size of the subpopulation, the suitability of each habitat patch, and distance between patches. Understanding behavioral patterns of movement between subpopulations is critical for maintaining the metapopulation (Hanski 1998).

# Mating and social systems

Studies of mating systems and social systems (see Chapters 11, 12 & 14) have contributed to two areas in conservation biology: determining effective population size, and evaluating effects of exploitation on harvested species.

## Effective population size

The effective population size ($N_e$) is a measure of the ability of a population to maintain genetic diversity (defined as the size of an ideal population that would lose genetic variation via genetic drift at the same rate) and has been a central component of conservation planning for small populations (using population viability analysis). $N_e$ can be substantially lower than the actual population size due to variance in sex ratio, variance in reproductive success among individuals, or changes in population size over time which can be influenced by the mating system.

Parker and Waite (1997) examined the effect of mating system and reproductive failure on $N_e$. With increasing levels of failure (as might occur in a declining population), $N_e$ declines (Fig. 16.3a). However, $N_e$ is also strongly affected by the mating system. As the mating system deviates from **monogamy** to increasing extremes of **polygyny** or **polyandry**, $N_e$ is reduced substantially because fewer males (polygyny) or females (polyandry) contribute genetically to the next generation. Conversely, increased **promiscuity** leads to larger $N_e$ than would be expected under monogamy because members of the more abundant sex have greater opportunities to breed. The influence of mating system applies across most ranges of failure, although the rate at which $N_e$ is impacted differs with mating system.

Application of molecular genetic techniques to studies of mating systems has revealed the presence of extrapair young in many vertebrates. A consequence of increased extrapair young is increased **reproductive skew** (see Chapter 14) because fewer males dominate more of the breeding opportunities. Increased reproductive skew, in turn, leads to a reduction in $N_e$ (Fig. 16.3b). Patterns of mate choice can further impact $N_e$ (Blumstein 1998). Females rarely chose mates randomly; typically, females select males on the basis of one or more traits and they may do so using a relative or an absolute assessment rule. Females using absolute threshold assessment rules select mates which exceed some threshold, and reject males falling below. Blumstein (1998) examined

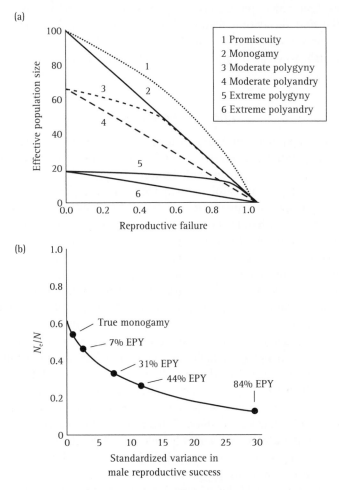

**Fig. 16.3** (a) Influence of the mating system on the relationship between the rate of reproductive error (proportion of unsuccessful breeding attempts) and the annual effective population size. Mating systems: 1, promiscuity; 2, monogamy; 3, moderate polygyny; 4, moderate polyandry; 5, extreme polygyny; 6, extreme polyandry. (b) The effects of reproductive skew, as indicated by the degree of extrapair young (EPY) and measured as the standardized variance in male reproductive success, on the relative reduction in effective population size ($N_e/N$). (From Parker & Waite 1997.)

situations where the distribution of male trait values was reduced, as might occur following disease or environmental hardship that reduced animals' body condition. This, in turn, resulted in a smaller proportion of males being "acceptable" to females and a consequent reduction in $N_e$.

Despite the growing number of models examining the effects of mating and social systems on $N_e$, empirical data are scarce. However, Creel (1998) collected data from species of African carnivores in order to examine the relative influence on $N_e$ of variance in population size, sex ratio, and reproductive success, as well as social and behavioral factors such as dominance, reproductive suppression, reproductive skew, and dispersal behavior. Social and behavioral features had the greatest impact on $N_e$. Variance in population size or sex ratio resulted in $N_e$ being reduced to 75–95% that of the actual population size ($N$), whereas incorporation of behavioral factors reduced $N_e$ to 15% of $N$ for some species.

## Effects of exploitation

The study of social systems provides insight into the effects of harvest and over-exploitation on populations in the wild. For example, Greene et al. (1998) considered the interaction of breeding systems with hunting intensity and harvest strategies for several African ungulates and carnivores. In their baseline population (assumed to be polygynous), the population growth rate was related to harem size. Population growth rates were lower for small harems because of low male survivorship and an insufficient number of males to fertilize all females (Allee effect). Fecundity also decreased in very large harems because of competition among females. The authors examined the effects of three different hunting regimes (on adult males, all adults, or adults and juveniles) and found similar effects on population growth. Under baseline conditions, the model population could sustain hunting intensities of 30–40% and was resilient to the hunting of males when harem size was large (Fig. 16.4a). When infanticide by males was included in the model, the population could no longer sustain the same levels of hunting and now the removal of males resulted in reductions in population growth because replacement males killed offspring (Fig. 16.4b). If the effects of reproductive suppression were included (i.e., dominant individuals prevent reproduction by subordinates), the population could sustain only very low levels of hunting for the adult and adult-and-juvenile harvest regimes. Conversely, if the harvest was restricted to only males, much higher intensities could be tolerated (Fig. 16.4c). Greene et al.'s study illustrates how breeding system attributes can significantly influence the magnitude of a population response to hunting pressure.

Other studies have examined the relationship between the degree of plumage dimorphism and introduction success on islands. McLain et al. (1995, 1999) found that introduction success rate was lower for species of birds with sexually dichromatic plumage than for species with monochromatic plumage. They argued that species subjected to intense **sexual selection** (i.e., those with dichromatic plumage) may have a reduced evolutionary potential to respond to **natural selection** pressures and so may be at greater risk of extinction when populations are small.

## Demography and life histories

Overexploitation can also impact life histories, as illustrated by coho salmon (*Oncorhynchus kisutch*). Male salmon have two life-history tactics: jacks mature precociously (6 months in the ocean) at small size, whereas hooknose males delay maturity until they reach a larger size (18 months in the ocean). These alternative life histories correlate with different behavioral tactics to obtain mates: large hooknose males fight

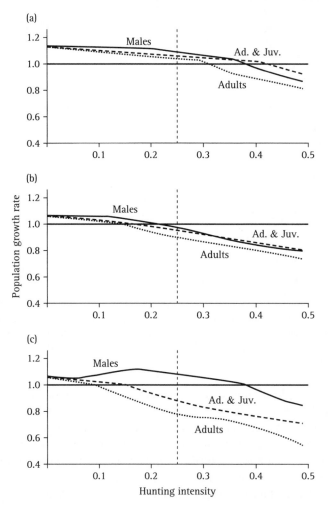

**Fig. 16.4** Population growth rate as a function of hunting intensity when adult males (Males), adults of either sex (Adults), or juveniles and adults (Ad. & Juv.) are hunted. (a) Growth rate of a population assuming polygyny and a constant harem size of five females; (b) population growth rate of an infanticidal species; (c) population growth rate of a species with reproductive suppression. (From Greene et al. 1998.)

for access to females whereas small jacks attempt to sneak matings (Gross 1991). Each tactic does better when rare and the relative value of the two life histories is negatively frequency-dependent (Fig. 16.5). In undisturbed conditions, an equilibrium balance of jacks and hooknoses could be maintained at the frequency $p_1^*$ where the fitness of the two tactics is equal. Humans, however, have altered this relationship through harvest. Fishing removes the largest individuals, typically the hooknose males. Accordingly, the survivorship of hooknose males is reduced, lowering the fitness surface for that life-history tactic (Fig. 16.5). This results in a shift in the equilibrium frequency of jacks in the population (from $p_1^*$ to $p_2^*$ or $p_3^*$, depending on fishing pressure). Hence,

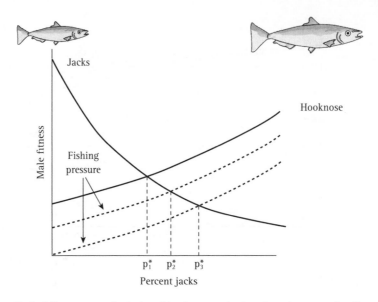

**Fig. 16.5** Hypothetical fitness curves for jack and hooknose males in coho salmon as a function of the frequency of jacks in the population. Selective harvesting of large hooknose males decreases their relative fitness and favors an evolutionary increase in the frequency of jacks; $p_1^*$, frequency of jacks with no harvesting; $p_2^*$ and $p_3^*$, frequency of jacks with increasing levels of selective harvest. (From Gross 1991.)

size-selective fishing leads not only to changes in the demographic dynamic (reduced population size, especially of large males) but possibly the evolutionary dynamic as well. Overexploitation of the large males could result in an evolutionary shift favoring the jack life history and in doing so would reduce the proportion of large economically desirable males. This situation is further complicated by the observation that being a jack or hooknose may be conditional, with faster-growing fish turning into jacks and slow growers into hooknoses. Artificial selection in fish hatcheries for fast growth may actually increase numbers of small animals because managers were unknowingly selecting for jacks.

Consideration of alternative reproductive behaviors may have important consequences for population dynamics as well. For example, conspecific brood parasitism in birds can lead to population fluctuations, cycles, or even local extinction (Eadie & Fryxell 1992; Nee & May 1993). Provision of high densities of artificial nest sites, a common restoration practice, may exacerbate this problem (Semel & Sherman 1995; Eadie et al. 1998).

The study of life histories has also been used in conservation biology to identify species that may be vulnerable to perturbation. Detailed demographic data are frequently unavailable for many species, yet conservation managers require some method to evaluate species at risk. One possibility is to employ ecological characteristics that correlate with some measure of vulnerability. For example, Harcourt (1998) examined the response to logging of a number of primate species and evaluated the utility of ecological traits in predicting whether a species was impacted (as measured by an index of density before and after logging). Of the variables examined, only home range size was a strong predictor; species with large home ranges were vulnerable to the effects of logging (Harcourt 1998).

## Relaxed selection

Recolonization is a fundamental goal of conservation biology and endangered carnivores are being reintroduced regularly around the world (Gittleman & Gompper 2001) despite a persistent worry that prey populations may suffer reductions or extinctions without knowledge of contemporary predators. In the absence of predation, selection for predator evasion strategies may become diminished or relaxed.

For example, populations of California ground squirrels (*Spermophilus beecheyi*) are more resistant to northern Pacific rattlesnake (*Crotalus viridis*) venom where snakes are abundant than where they are absent (Poran et al. 1987) even though all California populations are able to recognize snakes (Coss 1999). Estimated maximum time since release from snake predation ranges from 70,000 to 300,000 years. In contrast, Arctic ground squirrels (*Spermophilis parryii*), whose ancestors have experienced **relaxed selection** for 3–5 million years, show an inability to recognize snakes and exhibit inappropriate antipredator behavior (Goldthwaite et al. 1990). Similarly, Byers (1997) noted that specific forms of antipredator behavior of pronghorn (*Antilocapra americana*) have persisted despite the extinction of predators such as North American cheetahs (*Miracinonyx* sp.) in the last ice age (10,000 years ago). Furthermore, in laboratory experiments, tammar wallabies (*Macropus eugenii*) that had been isolated from mammalian predators since the last ice age responded to visual presentations of evolutionarily and ontogenetically novel predators (fox and cat) by reducing their foraging and increasing their **vigilance** in comparison with controls. However, they did not respond to acoustic signals, such as howls of dingoes (*Canis lupus*) (Blumstein et al. 2000).

In contrast to these studies, Berger (1998; Berger et al. 2001) found a rapid decrease in predator recognition abilities of North American ungulates isolated from large predators for only 40–75 years (10 generations). Specifically, moose (*Alces alces*) living in areas where predators have been recently extirpated reduced their feeding rate in response to wolf urine, wolf howls, and raven (*Corvus corax*) calls (ravens are associated with carcasses) compared with moose in predator-rich habitats, although all populations reduced their feeding rate in response to grizzly bear (*Ursus arctos*) feces. Thus we currently face a complicated picture where responses to novel predators vary across species, across populations of the same species, differ according to the behavior under consideration (Table 16.1), differ between predators, and even between different cues provided by the same predator.

From a conservation perspective, however, it is clear that individuals can learn about predators rapidly. Predator-naive moose mothers whose calves were killed by wolves during the recent wolf recolonization in Wyoming elevated their vigilance in response to playbacks of wolf howls by 500% in years after the predation event and were four times as likely to abandon their feeding sites following playbacks (Berger et al. 2001). In some species, at least, offspring loss causes hypersensitive maternal behavior that must ameliorate actions of novel predators.

Table 16.1 Summary of the behavioral consequences of relaxation of predation in North American ungulates.

| Species | Location | Extinct predators | Effects* | Repeated at other sites | Time frame (years) |
|---|---|---|---|---|---|
| **Group size** | | | | | |
| Pronghorn | National Bison Range, Montana | Cheetah, short-faced bear, lion† | No change | No | 10,000+ |
| Pronghorn | Great Basin Desert, Nevada (paired sites) | Human‡ vs. none | Smaller | No | 25 |
| Musk ox | Alaska, Canada and Greenland (19 sites) | Wolf | Smaller | Yes | 25–50 |
| **Vigilance** | | | | | |
| Caribou | Peninsula, Alaska and Kangerlussuag, Greenland | Wolf | Reduced | No | 4000+ |
| Bison | Badlands, South Dakota and Wood Buffalo, Canada | Wolf | No change | No | 75 |
| **Location in group** | | | | | |
| Pronghorn | Badlands, South Dakota | Wolf, grizzly bear | Vigilance differs | No | 75 |
| Bison | Badlands, South Dakota and Wood Buffalo, Canada | Wolf, grizzly bear | No change | No | 75 |
| **Raven response** | | | | | |
| Moose | Alaska and Wyoming | Wolf, grizzly bear | Decreased | Yes | 40–75 |

* Changes at sites lacking in predation.
† Pleistocene extinctions.
‡ Modern humans.
*Source*: Berger (1999).

Relaxed selection is also seen as a separate problem confronting breeding institutions (Wallace 2000). Here there is concern that species bred for generations in zoos may lose their ability to cope with environmental stresses, including food shortages, competition over resources, challenges from conspecifics, as well as appropriate antipredator behavior outlined above. At present, there has been no systematic study of this topic.

## Human behavioral ecology

Until recently, indigenous people hunting wild vertebrates or harvesting wild plants were seen as good conservationists (and termed "ecologically noble savages"), but this view has come under sharp scrutiny from anthropologists using sophisticated behavioral, ecological, and economic theory. One problem is that claims of resource conservation were often made on the basis of reports, about food taboos for instance, rather than from empirical data. Another problem is that it cannot be concluded that native groups are conservationists because they are not overexploiting their resources; they may simply live at a low density that is not yet resource limited (Alvard 1998a; FitzGibbon 1998). Clearly, conservation needs to be defined carefully and must incorporate two criteria. It must prevent or mitigate resource depletion, species extirpation, or habitat degradation, and it must be designed to do so in order to separate it from epiphenomenal conservation such as exploiting males from a polygynous species simply because males are easier to catch (Alvard 1998a). Conservation, thus defined, often involves a short-term loss in order to reap a long-term gain (Smith & Wishnie 2000).

Accordingly, human behavioral ecologists have generated predictions that contrast true conservation with behavior designed to maximize food intake based on optimal foraging theory (Alvard 1998b). To illustrate, a conservation hypothesis predicts that hunters will choose species that are less vulnerable to local extinction, and will choose young and old age classes that have lower reproductive value than prime-aged individuals. In contrast, an **optimal foraging model** (the prey model discussed in Chapter 9) predicts that choice will be based on prey types that maximize return rates and that hunters will select any age class that they encounter but ignore immatures if they fall below the range in body size as predicted by the diet breadth model. In the first instance, prey species can now be ranked according to (i) their maximum intrinsic rate of increase ($r_{max}$) (Robinson & Redford 1991) or (ii) according to their profitability based on **handling** (pursuing, killing, and processing) prey or on mean return rates from continued search for higher ranked prey (i.e., return in calories for higher ranked prey divided by both handling and search time). All these variables can be estimated or measured empirically.

Among the Piro of south-eastern Peru who use shotguns, prey items closely matched those predicted by optimal foraging theory. Thus, large species such as spider monkeys (*Ateles paniscus*), howler monkeys (*Alouatta seniculus*), capybara (*Hydrochaeris hydrochaeris*), deer (*Mazama americana*), and tapir (*Tapirus terrestris*) were pursued at nearly every encounter despite monkeys and tapir having a low $r_{max}$. Similarly, the ratio of immatures to adults killed was indistinguishable from that in the census population for peccaries, deer, and capybara, whereas primate prey were significantly biased toward adults; old prey made up a small proportion of kills (Alvard 1995). Thus predictions of optimal foraging were better supported than those of conservation. More generally, field studies from many different parts of the world show that humans follow the predictions of optimal foraging theory rather than conservation (Table 16.2).

Another branch of human behavioral ecology is examining apparently **altruistic** conservation acts among people in production systems where they have control over resources.

**Table 16.2** Field studies using optimal foraging theory (OFT) with results that bear on the issue of conservation.

| People | Primary hunting technology | Prey | Location | Results |
|---|---|---|---|---|
| Ache | Shotgun and bow | Large/medium-sized ungulates, rodents, primates | Paraguay; rainforest | OFT predictions upheld |
| Cree | Rifle and trap | Large ungulates, small mammals, birds, fish | N. Ontario; boreal forest | OFT predictions upheld |
| Wana | Trap, spear, blowgun, and dog | Large ungulates, primates, rodents, birds, bats, fish | Sulawesi, Indonesia; rainforest | No obvious conservation |
| Piro | Shotgun and bow | Large/medium-sized ungulates, rodents, primates, birds | Amazonian Peru; rainforest | OFT predictions unpheld |
| Inujjuamiut | Rifle and trap | Large marine and terrestrial mammals, birds, fish | Canadian arctic; tundra | OFT predictions upheld |
| Yanamomo, Ye'kwana | Shotgun and bow Bow | Large/medium-sized ungulates, rodents, primates, birds, fish | Venezuela; rainforest | "Hunters and fishers that have depleted resources hunt and fish more intensively" |
| Hadza | Bow | Large terrestrial mammals | Tanzania; savannah woodland | "A hunter maximizes average rate of meat acquisition by ignoring small prey" |

*Source*: Adapted from Alvard (1998b).

Pastoralists, who graze cattle, have long been credited with protecting grasslands from overuse by means of grazing regimes, stocking regulations, and institutional land-use practices. Borgerhoff Mulder and Ruttan (2000) used game theory to model the payoffs of rich and poor herders grazing their cattle between wet and sensitive dry season pastures. Payoffs are asymmetrical because their value depends on the number of cattle owned by the herder. Borgerhoff Mulder and Ruttan found situations in which poor and rich herders should cooperate in reducing grazing in dry-season areas, in which neither poor nor rich should cooperate, and a large number of situations in which the rich should cooperate but poor should defect. In this modeling space, rich herders could obtain even higher payoffs if they coerced poor herders to leave the dry-season reserve when the wet season begins. The importance of this work is that, in contrast to the hunter-gatherer studies, it shows that some people (here the rich) can be good conservationists while pursuing selfish goals.

In both the foraging and pastoralist context, a dispassionate understanding of the conditions under which people switch to and away from conservation strategies is central to programs designed to develop sustainable patterns of resource use, conservation of biodiversity, and protection of human rights (Robinson & Bennett 2000).

## Impediments to Applying Animal Behavior to Conservation Biology

Although the number of connections between animal behavior and conservation biology is impressive, many of the links take the form of "how knowledge of animal behavior might influence conservation." There are remarkably few examples that meet three criteria: (i) how behavior varies in response to social or environmental factors, (ii) how this variation changes the way a population responds to exploitation or to a restoration project, and (iii) how management takes note and alters its conservation program as a consequence. We regard this three-stage process as the yardstick of success in linking these disciplines. There are three classes of problems that impede rapid integration of these two fields.

## Conceptual problems

Many studies of animal behavior are interested in how natural selection shapes the behavior of individuals and how this affects reproductive success and survival. Conservation biologists and managers, on the other hand, focus on population size and structure and are interested in individual fitness only if it directly influences the response of populations to anthropogenic disturbance (Fig. 16.6). Differential emphases on individuals and populations remain a key impediment to linking these fields (Beissinger 1997).

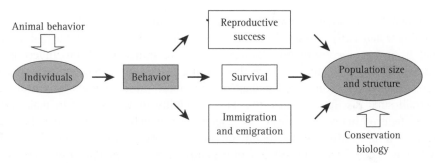

**Fig. 16.6** Principal foci of attention (ovals) of studies of animal behavior and conservation biology. Connections between foci are also shown.

Table 16.3 Areas of conservation biology that are likely or unlikely to benefit from animal behavior.

| Area | Likely to benefit | Unlikely to benefit |
| --- | --- | --- |
| Extent of biodiversity | | ✔ |
| Loss of biodiversity | | ✔ |
| Genetic stochasticity and $N_e$ | ✔ | |
| Demographic stochasticity and PVA | ✔ | |
| Environmental stochasticity | ✔ | |
| Habitat fragmentation and metapopulations | ✔ | |
| Prioritizing management plans | | ✔ |
| Reserve connectivity | ✔ | |
| Extractive reserves | ✔ | |
| Managing reserves | | ✔ |
| Trade in wildlife | | ✔ |
| Captive breeding | ✔ | |
| Species reintroductions | ✔ | |
| Philosophical issues | | ✔ |

PVA denotes population viability analysis.
*Source*: Adapted from Caro (1998a).

In addition, many aspects of animal behavior do not have direct consequences for populations. For example, grooming, song learning, and play are almost irrelevant to decision-makers trying to save a dwindling population. Moreover, many issues in conservation biology are simply unlikely to benefit from knowledge of animal behavior (Table 16.3).

## Social problems

Many population biologists view behavior studies as difficult to conduct or as too time-consuming when conservation decisions need to be made rapidly. Interest in relating animal behavior to conservation biology has come principally from undergraduates and graduates, who do not yet have the training to develop sophisticated or rigorous analyses. University faculty and managers who guide these students have training in more traditional disciplines and often lack the ability or willingness to make bridges between fields. Finally, the short time span over which tentative links have been made has been insufficient for many intellectually rich areas to have surfaced, let alone to have been debated or tested; consequently there are remarkably few well-worked examples demonstrating how knowledge of behavior is important for conservation management.

## Institutional problems

Last, animal behaviorists come from a different "culture" than managers and, to a lesser extent, conservation biologists. Managers view behavioral research as too esoteric whereas animal behaviorists view conservation as being too applied. They do not go to each other's meetings, nor do they read each other's journals (Sutherland 1998). Most damaging, there are very few sources of funding available to provide graduate training to link the two fields. Indeed, in the USA the National Science Foundation does not even have a panel that specifically considers or funds conservation research.

## How to Move Forward

For a study of animal behavior to be taken seriously by conservation biologists, it must help solve a conservation problem. The onus is on animal behaviorists to be aware of, and take an active interest in, conservation issues so that they can grasp research and management opportunities as they arise. Aside from being conservation "savvy," we suggest future animal behavior studies stay mindful of five issues.

## Focus on a species or system of conservation concern

### Choose a study animal of conservation concern

Studies of animal behavior conducted on endangered or rare species have a better chance of being relevant to conservation than studies on common species, all else being equal (Caro 1998c). What are the advantages and disadvantages of this research gambit? First, with endangered species there may be questions relating to population size or restoration to which managers need answers. Thus, from the onset, the behaviorist will be working in collaboration with, and under the auspices of, a conservation team: hence behavioral findings will have a greater chance of being acted upon. Second, any findings about behavior that affect juvenile survival and reproductive rates and hence population size and structure (Fig. 16.6) are likely to be important in helping bolster populations that are, by definition, at risk. Against these benefits, there will be difficulties in obtaining large samples (although any results are likely to be interesting; Bunin & Jamieson 1996), animals may be difficult to observe if they are sensitive to disturbance or have been hunted, and permits may be difficult to obtain.

### Work on several species simultaneously

Although it is unusual for an observational behavioral study to focus on more than one species, conservation biologists often do so in order to make better management decisions. Working on several species allows researchers to maximize behavioral data collected during a period of fieldwork. If responses to, say, an environmental perturbation are common to several species, it highlights the importance and robustness of the results; if they are different, it alerts researchers and managers to additional causal factors affecting behavior, or the need to consider differences in species' behavioral ecology.

### Choose a study area of conservation relevance

Given that habitat fragmentation, pollution, direct exploitation, and the introduction of exotic species are the four most devastating forces affecting habitats and species, we advocate research that compares behavior of animals in such areas to control areas. For example, one might compare behavior before and after a perturbation such as habitat fragmentation or impending translocation. Or one might contrast behavior in areas impacted by oil slicks or in populations suffering from disease or overharvesting with control sites. At a broader scale, we would welcome more research in the tropics since this is where most of the world's biodiversity is found, where habitats are disappearing most rapidly, and where fewest researchers work.

### Avoid surrogate species

Several colleagues have advocated the use of **surrogate species** to explore processes by which animal behavior affects conservation but we are leery of transferring results between even closely related species. For example, our own work shows that ungulate species with slightly different breeding systems respond quite differently to hunting pressure (Greene et al. 1998). Similarly, conspecific brood parasitism occurs frequently in wood ducks (*Aix sponsa*), which compromises the efficacy of using nest boxes to bolster populations, but occurs to a lesser extent in Barrow's goldeneye (*Bucephala islandica*) because of territoriality, enabling nest boxes to be used (Eadie et al. 1998). A further limitation of studying substitute species is that some managers are not comfortable or willing to draw comparisons between systems and will only utilize behavioral data if they come from the species at risk. Finally, and more worrying, we perceive a growing trend in which researchers attempt to relate a behavioral project on a common species to conservation in an offhand and indirect fashion on grounds that *any* findings about, say, dispersal, mating systems, or antipredator behavior are relevant to population persistence; such an approach avoids responsibility for making firm and useful connections to a specific conservation problem.

## Focus on behavioral factors that influence population dynamics

Any attempt to integrate animal behavior with conservation biology must link behavior with fundamental demographic processes (birth, death, immigration, emigration; see Fig. 16.6). It is not sufficient to suggest that a given behavior "might" impact population growth rates; rather, one must demonstrate that it does, and specifically how. Behaviors that affect age at first reproduction (e.g., dominance), clutch size (e.g., life-history tradeoffs), offspring sex ratio (e.g., age or dominance), or survival (e.g., mating or resource competition) and which are conditional on environmental or social circumstances will modify population growth rates and can be incorporated into a population viability analysis. Similarly, behavioral factors that alter breeding sex ratios, mating system, or variance in family size will influence $N_e$. Conditions under which infanticide, siblicide, and intrasexual competition over mating opportunities are expressed each bear on this important parameter in conservation biology.

## Identify the specific behaviors involved and determine the effect size

Even when it can be demonstrated that behavior has an influence on the demography of a population of conservation concern, it is not always clear what specific component of the **behavior system** has been affected. For example, debate on the effect of dehorning black rhinos (*Diceros bicornis*) as a conservation measure was swayed only when Berger and Cunningham (1994) were able to highlight specifically how dehorning reduced a female's ability to defend her young against predators. To be most useful to conservation efforts, animal behaviorists need also to determine the effect size of a given behavioral perturbation to help prioritize conservation efforts. Simulation models provide one method (e.g., Greene et al. 1998); an alternative approach is to compare populations in areas where they have been impacted to those where they have not (Berger & Cunningham 1994).

## Identify possible solutions

If there is a case that behavior influences a conservation problem, then animal behaviorists are likely to be in a good position to propose or develop possible solutions. The same training that allows an animal behaviorist to identify a behavioral problem can equally be applied to finding practical ways to alleviate that behavioral perturbation. Moreover, the personal experience than an animal behaviorist may have through several years of field study may prove invaluable to a conservation planning team (Arcese et al. 1997).

## Get the data into the hands of those who need it and will use it

Academic researchers are trained that the culmination of a research project is publication in a peer-reviewed journal, with the assumption that those who need the information can find it easily there. Unfortunately, conservation managers rarely read journals such as *Animal Behaviour* and, even if they do, the time delay between the behavioral study and applying its findings to a field situation may be too great. It often takes more than a year between submission and publication. Populations can become extinct in less time. If animal behaviorists are serious about playing an active participatory role in conservation biology, they must become engaged in the process at the outset.

## SUMMARY AND CONCLUSIONS

Animal behavior is concerned with variation in the behavior of individuals, whereas conservation biology is concerned with the response of populations to environmental factors, often anthropogenic disturbance. Nonetheless, knowledge of how animal behavior varies in response to environmental or social factors, and how such variation changes the way a population responds to exploitation or a restoration project, can alter management decisions about a conservation program. In this chapter, we explore how the study of animal behavior can play an important role in conservation biology. For example, we consider how knowledge of behavioral methods and behavioral ontogeny can provide practical tools to aid monitoring programs and to develop successful captive-rearing and release efforts. We also consider how a greater understanding of the **proximate** mechanisms underlying behavior may help develop useful assays for populations under stress and enable us to predict which species may be most vulnerable to the effects of anthropogenic change. We then examine how habitat selection, foraging and patch choice, the Allee effect and conspecific attraction, movement, ranging and dispersal behavior may be critical elements in determining why some populations decline and what must be done to remedy the situation. Similarly, we consider how analysis of mating and social systems, demography and life histories, and relaxed selection bear on contemporary conservation issues. Finally, we examine how human behavior relates to conservation. It is clear from even a cursory review that the study of animal behavior has much to offer conservation biology; indeed, we believe that many conservation plans may be at best incomplete and at worst misleading without a more careful consideration of how individual behavior influences population dynamics in species of concern. Nevertheless, there are still conceptual difficulties in applying animal behavior to conservation biology, as well as social and institutional problems. The way forward may be to focus behavioral research more closely on conservation problems, especially those that relate to important demographic parameters. Animal behaviorists need to form a new dialogue with conservation managers.

## FURTHER READING

For those who have interest in the topic of conservation and behaviour we recommend the following three books: *Behavioral Ecology and Conservation Biology* (Caro 1998a), *Behaviour and Conservation* (Gosling & Sutherland 2000), and *Animal Behavior and Wildlife Conservation* (Festa-Bianchet & Apollonio 2003). These three books together present a series of subject areas where scientists have tried to relate animal behavior to conservation biology. We recommend readers think carefully as to whether the chapter authors have actually demonstrated that knowledge of a behavioral system changes the way that conservationists think about a problem and that, as a consequence, alters management strategy, or whether the authors simply indicate that behavior might be relevant to conservation.

## ACKNOWLEDGMENTS

We thank Judy Stamps and the editors for comments.

# 17

# human behavior as animal behavior

## Martin Daly and Margo Wilson

## INTRODUCTION

Why discuss the human animal in a book on animal behavior? After all, *Homo sapiens* has a science all its own, namely anthropology, and the other "social sciences" (not to mention the "humanities") are almost exclusively concerned with this one species too. Nevertheless, many animal behavior researchers, undaunted by all these specialists, have made *H. sapiens* one of their study species, a choice justified by the fact that theories and methods developed by students of nonhuman animals can often illuminate human affairs in ways that escape scientists whose training and focus is exclusively **anthropocentric** (see, for example, Chapter 16).

The continuity of anatomy, physiology, brain, and behavior between people and other animals clearly implies that nonhuman research can shed light on human nature. Medical researchers rely on this continuity, using "animal models" whenever human research would be premature, too intrusive, or too risky. The same is true in basic behavioral research.

Consider, for example, the study of hormonal influences on behavior (see Chapter 3). The "activating" (i.e., immediate **causal**) effects of circulating steroid hormones on sexual **motivation**, aggression, persistence, and other behavioral phenomena were first established in other species and only then investigated in human beings. Similarly, nonhuman research on the "organizing" (**developmental**) effects of these same gonadal hormones has motivated and guided human research on the behavioral consequences of endocrine disorders (Hines 2002). In a more recent example, discoveries concerning the role of androgens in mediating tradeoffs between mating effort and male parental effort in animals with biparental care (Wingfield et al. 1990; Wynne-Edwards 2001) have inspired studies of the same phenomena in human fathers (Storey et al. 2000).

The situation is similar, but much more richly developed, in **behavioral neuroscience** (see Chapter 5), where virtually everything now known about the human brain was discovered with crucial inspiration and support from experimental research on **homologous structures** and processes that serve similar perceptual and cognitive functions in other species.

The fact that *H. sapiens* is a member of the animal kingdom also means that it is both possible and enlightening to include our species in **comparative** analyses. A famous example, discussed in Chapters 12 and 13, is the association between testis size and **mating systems**. If a female mates **polyandrously**, i.e., with more than one male, and if she does so within a sufficiently short interval, then the different males' ejaculates must "compete" for the paternity of her offspring. Where such **sperm competition** has been chronic, there has been selection for increases in sperm count, ejaculate volume, and testis size. Within the order Primates, the resultant tendency for males to have relatively large testes in species in which females often mate polyandrously is sufficiently consistent (see Fig. 12.5) that one can make a good guess about the mating system of an unstudied species on the basis of this anatomical feature alone. Thus, although human testes are smaller than those of the most **promiscuous** primates, they are nevertheless larger than would be expected under **monogamy**; this observation has substantially bolstered the notion that ancestral women were not strictly monogamous in their sexual behavior and hence that selection may have equipped the human female with facultative inclinations to cuckold their primary partners by clandestine adultery, or maintain multiple simultaneous sexual relationships, or both. These ideas, which run contrary to the previous notion that only males would be expected to possess adaptive tendencies to mate polygamously, have had substantial impact on recent research into women's sexuality (Gangestad & Simpson 2000; Greiling & Buss 2000; Scheib 2001; Little et al. 2002).

## Study of *Homo sapiens* as "Just Another Animal"

The human animal is undoubtedly special by virtue of language and complex culture, to which we shall return, but before we focus on the things that make our species unique, it is first worth asking to what extent we can illuminate human affairs by treating *H. sapiens* as an animal like any other.

### Discoveries in other species inspire directly analogous human research

There are many cases in which theories and findings from the field of animal behavior have inspired human research on the basis of the same logic that might be applied to any other creature (Daly & Wilson 1999). Research on the effects of shared major histocompatibility complex (MHC) alleles in mate assessment provides one interesting example. The MHC is a group of linked polyallelic genes whose products play roles in cell-surface recognition and immune function (see Chapter 2). Estrous female mice preferentially approach males who are genetically different from themselves at MHC loci, whereas when pregnant they prefer to aggregate with females who share their MHC alleles (Penn & Potts 1999). These preferences are mediated by odors, and invite a **functional** interpretation: approaching MHC-dissimilar males when in estrus should promote adaptive mate choice with respect to outbreeding and/or immune function of the young, whereas the switch to a preference for MHC-similar others during pregnancy should tend to promote selective affiliation with kin.

The Swiss behavioral ecologist Claus Wedekind and colleagues wondered if a comparable pattern of preferences might be observed in our own species, and therefore asked women to assess men's bodily odors in experimental T-shirt sniffing tests. What they found was that women in the potentially fertile phase of their ovarian cycle indeed rated the odors of MHC-dissimilar men as more pleasant (or at least as less *un*pleasant) than those of men with whom the raters shared MHC alleles; moreover, in striking parallel with the mouse results, these preferences were reversed among women taking oral contraceptives that work by inducing a hormonal condition of pseudopregnancy (Wedekind et al. 1995; Wedekind & Füri 1997). Although the robustness of these findings remains to be established and much more work is needed, this approach has opened up a hitherto unsuspected realm of human social information processing, which apparently exerts some influence on mate choice in the real world (Ober et al. 1997), as well as raising the important issue of whether modern contraceptive practices may be having subtle effects on mate selection that might in turn affect rates of infertility and/or marital success.

Some related work provides an even more direct example of human research inspired by findings in another animal, in this case an insect. Recall from Chapter 11 that "**fluctuating asymmetry**" (FA) refers to departures from bilateral symmetry in structures that are symmetrical "by design," as is usually the case in such bilateral structures as left–right pairs of limbs or wings. There has been a great deal of recent research on FA because it reflects (albeit noisily) the extent to which individual development has been disrupted by environmental or other stressors, and hence is a predictor (albeit a weak one) of many aspects of phenotypic quality, including fertility, metabolic efficiency, and longevity (Polak 2002). Having relatively low FA can thus be one criterion of a good mate, not least because lower than average FA is indicative of higher than average resistance to locally prevalent strains of diseases that might compromise development, and such resistance is usually somewhat **heritable** (see Chapter 11).

When we indeed observe that symmetrical individuals are preferred as mates, this should not imply assessment of symmetry per se, because other correlates of phenotypic quality are likely to be correlated with FA too. Randy Thornhill (1992), a behavioral ecologist from the USA, proved this point by showing that female scorpionflies (*Panorpa japonica*) can and do discriminate in favor of low-FA males solely on the basis of the **pheromones** that the males release in order to advertise prey capture and thereby attract a female, and this result led Thornhill to wonder whether women might also prefer relatively symmetrical men on the basis of scent alone. In order to find out, he conducted T-shirt-sniffing studies much like those that Wedekind had used to assess

MHC preferences, and found that women indeed prefer the odors of low-FA men. Moreover, just as in the MHC experiments, these preferences have proven to be most pronounced when women are near the point in their menstrual cycle at which ovulation occurs and hence when they are most likely to be fertile (Gangestad & Thornhill 1998; Rikowski & Grammer 1999; Thornhill & Gangestad 1999).

Other applications of nonhuman research to the human case are less direct, entailing a more abstract conceptual commonality. Our own work on family violence provides an example. There are many well-studied cases of animals who care solicitously for their own young (or for those who present the parents with cues that they *might* be their own young), while treating other conspecific young with indifference or even aggression (see Chapter 14). It is obvious to an evolutionist why parents should be discriminative in this way: selection must typically favor parental inclinations that selectively promote the survival and reproduction of the parent's own young rather than the young of their competitors. Thus, both evolutionary reasoning and research on discriminative parental solicitude in other animals led us to wonder whether human stepchildren might be overrepresented as victims of child abuse (Daly & Wilson 1998). Obvious though this hypothesis may seem, it had never been examined by child abuse researchers, so we tested and confirmed it (Wilson et al. 1980). This discovery has led to a substantial body of further research on step relationships in the light of a Darwinian perspective on parental and marital sentiments, and we now know that human parents treat their (putative) genetic offspring better than their stepchildren in ways that cover the gamut from assaults and exploitation to differential investments of time and money. Anthropologist Mark Flinn (1988), for example, used **behavioral scan samples** of the sort that one might use in observational studies of other species to show that stepparents in a Caribbean village interact with the children less frequently and more agonistically than (presumed) genetic parents; he has also shown that stepchildren have chronically higher circulating levels of the stress hormone cortisol than children living in the same villages with just their birth parents (Flinn & England 1995). Princeton University economist Anne Case and colleagues have used a very different approach, analyzing various sorts of US national survey data to demonstrate that stepchildren are the recipients of less parental investment than other children, in domains ranging from dental care and health monitoring to expenditures on food, and that differences in parental wealth or other possible confounding factors cannot explain this disadvantage (Case et al. 2000; Case & Paxson 2001). Most dramatically, stepchildren incur vastly higher risk of being severely assaulted or killed by stepparents than is the case in other parent–child relationships (Daly & Wilson 1996, 2001a) (Fig. 17.1).

In light of the above discussion, it is important to stress that most stepparent-stepchild relationships are not abusive. Human behavior and inclinations in this domain are clearly not analogous to what we see in species in which replacement mates routinely commit "sexually selected infanticide." But as behavioral ecologist Sievert Rohwer has noted, there are many species in which replacement mates ("stepparents") are to varying degrees tolerant of their predecessors' offspring, and if we therefore ask why parents invest in stepchildren at all, a comparative perspective is again illuminating. Avian stepparents of some species routinely kill their predecessors' young, while those of other species ignore them and wait for them to fledge, and still others actively care

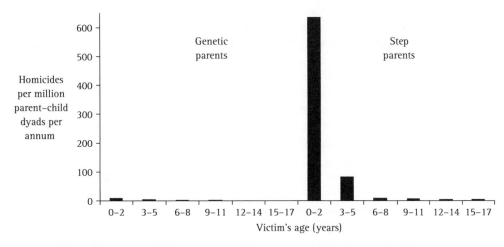

**Fig. 17.1** Age-specific rates of child homicide perpetrated by genetic parents versus stepparents in Canada, 1974–90, based on all cases known to Canadian police forces.

for them. A comparative analysis thus supports an interpretation of active stepparental care as a component of mating effort, occurring primarily in those species in which mateships have a long potential future and courtship expenditures are relatively high (Rohwer et al. 1999).

## Many ethologists have been drawn to human research

Getting involved in human research appears to be an occupational hazard for animal behavior researchers. In his 1973 Nobel Prize autobiography, Niko Tinbergen revealed that he had long harbored a "dormant desire to make **ethology** apply its methods to human behaviour," a desire that he acted upon, late in his research career, by studying autistic children (Tinbergen & Tinbergen 1972). Others made the move earlier in their careers, with greater impact. The British ethologist Nicholas Blurton Jones, one of the founders of "human ethology" (Blurton Jones 1972) and now a major figure in hunter-gatherer studies (Blurton Jones et al. 2000), did his PhD work on threat **displays** in the great tit (*Parus major*) but then began almost immediately to study human children. He writes:

> I studied at Oxford with Niko Tinbergen [who] shared the Nobel Prize with Konrad Lorenz for their demonstration that behavior should be studied in the same way as any other feature of an animal – as a product of evolution by **natural selection**. My career has been devoted to extending that idea into human behavior. (Blurton Jones 1998)

Perhaps the most energetic practitioner of human ethology has been the German ethologist Irenäus Eibl-Eibesfeldt (1989) who began his observational studies of human interaction and his efforts to document cross-cultural universals therein only after a 20-year career of ethological research on a wide variety of other animals.

Just as they had done in their studies of other animals, Blurton Jones, Eibl-Eibesfeldt, and others who had begun to call their field of research human ethology initially concentrated on categorizing overt motor patterns (generating a human "ethogram") and counting how often each behavioral act was executed. This approach elicited some mockery from social scientists as the "study of people as if they could not talk" (Washburn 1978), but the ethologists were surely correct in seeing the human sciences as badly in need of a more detached observational approach that could avoid the excesses of, on the one hand, research relying on self-reports and, on the other, sterile **"behaviorism"** (see Chapters 1 & 7). Indeed, other scientists without animal behavior training were coming to similar views about the need for a more objective observational approach at about this time, and a few even turned to Darwin for inspiration. An interesting example is the work of Paul Ekman, an American psychologist who traveled to highland New Guinea and other remote places to prove that facial expressions of emotion and their interpretations by observers are cross-culturally universal rather than exhibiting arbitrary cultural variation from place to place, as many anthropologists had supposed (Ekman et al. 1969). This research program was akin to that of Eibl-Eibesfeldt in its questions, its theoretical foundations, and its results, but perhaps because Ekman was trained in psychology, he was less reluctant than the ethologist to use elicited verbal data as his test of universality.

Despite some successes, especially in the realms of emotional expression and child development, the classical ethological approach to the study of human behavior has not flourished. In its 17-year history (1980–96), the human-focused journal *Ethology and Sociobiology* published fewer than 50 research reports in which observation of naturally occurring behavior outside the laboratory was the primary data source, and such papers decreased in prevalence from eight in volume 1 to fewer than one per year in the last few volumes. When we (Daly & Wilson) became the journal's editors in 1997, its subscribers (members of the Human Behavior and Evolution Society) voted overwhelmingly to rename it *Evolution and Human Behavior*, to better reflect its actual content; submissions based on observational data remain rare, comprising less than 2% of the total. Of course, one might say that the classical ethological approach has withered in nonhuman research too, with the ascendancy of **behavioral ecology** (see Chapter 1), but the hallmark of classical ethology, namely observational study of behavior in its natural context, has not been forsaken. What distinguishes human research is only partly the fact that we cannot ignore the centrality of complex linguistic communication in human social life. An even more pervasive problem for human ethology is the fact that observational study of behavior in its natural context is ethically problematic when the animals of interest are people. We will return to these topics later.

## Applying an evolutionary ecological approach to human behavior

In general, animal behavior researchers have been even more insistent that the human sciences need an evolutionary and ecological theoretical framework than that they need ethological methods. The fact that entomologists should write books with titles such as *On Human Nature* (Wilson 1978) or *Darwinism and Human Affairs* (Alexander 1979) has struck many nonbiologists as worse than hubristic. Readers of these books, however, have encountered insights about the human animal that mainstream social scientists had never imagined, and the reason seems clearly to be that Wilson, Alexander, and other biologists had the benefit of possessing imaginations informed by a sound theory of the origins of human **adaptations**, namely the theory of evolution by natural selection.

How have more specific lower-level theories imported from animal behavior informed research on human beings? The question is best answered with some specific examples. One such is anthropologist Monique Borgerhoff Mulder's (1990) use of the Orians–Verner–Willson **polygyny threshold model**, described in Chapter 11, to make sense of marital transactions in an African society in which **polygynous** marriage is legitimate and customary: as would be expected from the polygyny threshold theory, women and their relatives opt for marriage to men who are already married, rather than available bachelors, when the polygynist's resources are sufficient to predict a higher reproductive rate. A different sort of example is provided by psychologist Nicholas Pound's (2002) use of sperm competition theory, described in Chapter 12, to account for the surprising prevalence and popularity of scenes of polyandrous sexual behavior in pornography designed for male audiences. Yet another example is provided by psychologist Catherine Salmon's use of parental investment theory to predict that firstborn and last-born children will be relatively strongly attached to their parents, whereas middleborns (those with both older and younger siblings) will focus more on reciprocity-based relationships with nonrelatives (Salmon 1998; Salmon & Daly 1998).

In addition to such particular examples as those in the preceding paragraph, whole fields of research have been launched by applying evolutionary ecological models to the human case. For example, **optimal foraging models** originating in nonhuman behavioral ecology (see Chapter 9) have inspired a substantial body of research on human hunter-gatherers, aimed at elucidating why men hunt in situations in which gathering plant foods would provide a higher rate of caloric returns, and why they hunt the particular prey they do (Winterhalder & Smith 2000). Similarly, Trivers and Willard's (1973) theory of **condition-dependent** parental preferences for sons versus daughters (see Chapters 11 & 14) has inspired dozens of human studies, using a wide variety of measures and methods (Lazarus 2002).

Most importantly, certain major theories have had very broad general effects on human research, much as they have had on nonhuman research. The most noteworthy cases in point are Hamilton's (1964) **inclusive fitness** theory (see Chapter 14) and Trivers's (1972) theory that sex differences in parental investment underpin **sexual selection** and the evolution of other sex differences (see Chapter 11).

The breadth of influence of Hamilton's theory can be seen by considering a few examples. In one early application, anthropologists Napoleon Chagnon and Paul Bugos (1979) analyzed men's actions during a violent melee in a Yanomamö village in Amazonia, and demonstrated nepotistic biases in who sided with whom. In fact, the researchers' estimates of genetic **relatedness** on the basis of genealogical reconstructions predicted men's alliances better than did mere kinship terminology, which, in the Yanomamö language, does not distinguish brothers from certain more distant kin who are related by a series of patrilineal links. Taking a different approach to address much the same issue, Daly and Wilson (1982a) analyzed homicide case data from a variety of societies and showed that collaborating killers are always much more closely related, on average, than are killers and their victims, findings that refuted a prevalent criminological hypothesis that both violent conflict and cooperation arise within particular relationships in proportion to the frequency and intensity of relationship-specific interaction. Fratricide (the killing of one's brother), for example, constitutes a tiny proportion of homicides, but brothers comprise a much larger proportion of the relationships among co-offenders who act together to kill a third party. Both of these studies illustrate the fact that kinship is associated with a reduction in conflict and an increase in cooperation, in dangerous situations of male rivalry.

Other research programs inspired by Hamilton's theory have focused on purely cooperative, rather than violent, actions. For example, using behavioral scan sample methods anthropologist Ray Hames (1987) demonstrated that the Yek'wana Indians of Venezuela will help close relatives repeatedly even when those who are helped have not had a chance to reciprocate, and thus will allow "labor debts" to accumulate among kin, whereas the same sorts of cooperative labor on behalf of unrelated friends must be reciprocated before further help will be volunteered.

Additional research inspired by Hamilton's theory has addressed the question of possible kin recognition cues. Using both interview and unobtrusive observational methods, Daly and Wilson (1982b) and Regalski and Gaulin (1993) showed that all interested parties pay more attention to patrilineal than to matrilineal phenotypic resemblances of infants, and that the distribution of remarks about such resemblance is in accordance with the hypothesis that mothers and mothers' relatives have an interest in promoting the putative fathers' confidence that they really are the fathers. Another method was devised by Oates and Wilson (2002), who used email solicitations to show that rates of providing help to unseen strangers increase considerably when the potential helper and the person to be helped have a name in common, especially a surname. Finally, in two recent studies in which the researchers used computer "morphing" to generate realistic facial images varying in their similarity to research participants, DeBruine (2002) has shown that people are more likely to entrust a real financial decision to strangers who resemble them than to strangers who do not, while Platek et al. (2002) demonstrated that men's, but not women's, responses to pictures of babies are positively affected by resemblance to themselves.

Trivers's theory of sexually selected sex differences has had an even greater impact on human research than Hamilton's inclusive fitness theory. Trivers (see Chapter 11) proposed that psychological and behavioral sex differences are largely predictable from the degree to which mothers make a greater investment of time and energy in the rearing of each individual offspring than fathers, with the sex that makes the lesser parental investment being more polygamously inclined, more intensely competitive, and less choosy about potential mates. Although both theory and observation indicate that these sex differences are less dramatic in biparental mammals, such as human beings, than in species in which females care for young without male help, the minimal investment required of a man for successful reproduction is still much less than that required of a woman, so sex differences that are directionally similar to those seen in other mammals are to be expected in the human case as well.

This line of thinking has inspired researchers to investigate sex differences in human courtship behavior, mate-choice criteria and selectivity, sexual advertisement, sexual fantasies, intrasexual competition, jealousy, **deception**, and how women and men disparage rivals, among other things. In general, the results are strongly supportive of expectations from parental investment theory. For example, men have consistently been found to be more interested in polygamy and in casual sexual opportunity than women, and to be less choosy about acceptable sexual partners. Both sexes do exercise selectivity, of course, but Trivers's theory garners support here too, for it turns out that the sexes' mate-choice criteria are predictably distinct, with men paying greater attention to cues of fertility and reproductive value and women paying greater attention to cues of resource accrual capability. There is also considerable evidence that intrasexual competition is more intense and dangerous among men than among women and, moreover, that women and men compete with their same-sex rivals in different ways that reflect the above mate-choice criteria, as individuals of each sex strive to enhance their own attractiveness relative to that of rivals (Buss & Dedden 1990). The sexes also exhibit differences in the qualitative nature of jealousy in ways that make sense in light of the distinct threats to **fitness** that infidelity poses: men, who differ from women in being vulnerable to cuckoldry, are relatively concerned about specifically sexual infidelity on the part of their mates, whereas women, who suffer negative fitness consequences from the loss of a mate's help and resources, are relatively concerned about retaining their mates' emotional commitment (Pietrzak et al. 2002). The literature on these topics is now so large that we cannot cite even a fraction of the original research reports; interested readers can find fuller descriptions of this research area in four very different, but complementary, reviews (Buss 1994; Geary 1998; Mealey 2000; Daly & Wilson 2001b).

## Limitations to the Study of *Homo sapiens* as "Just Another Animal"

### Ethical problems

As we have seen, the proposition that human behavior can be approached like that of any other animal has led to many novel discoveries. Nevertheless, several complications threaten this enterprise. Some of the impediments to such research are ethical. Many experiments that would be enlightening obviously cannot be performed on human beings: we cannot place subjects in a genuine mate-choice situation, cannot manipulate the sociosexual experience of a randomly selected subset of our subjects, and so forth. We therefore rely heavily on correlational data, and when we do conduct experiments they often have an "as if" flavor, with the research participants being invited to evaluate hypothetical partners, or to report on their preferences, or to recall an event while physiological reactions are monitored.

Moreover, notions of what constitutes ethically acceptable research are in flux, and have generally been moving in the direction of greater stringency. Not so long ago, psychologists routinely conducted experiments in which subjects might feel embarrassed or diminished. Such research is increasingly forbidden, and those earlier researchers might be astonished to learn that controversy has now been enjoined about such issues as what constitutes truly informed consent, whether recording people's behavior without asking their permission to do so constitutes an invasion of privacy even when the behavior occurs in public, whether giving some sort of academic credit for experimental participation constitutes undue coercion, and whether deception of any sort can be justified. Ethical concerns are becoming increasingly prominent in other areas as well, including the legitimate uses of archival data such as police and governmental records that contain potentially identifying information, and contested claims of stakeholder standing in archaeological research, especially when aboriginal peoples protest against research activities in places that they believe to have been occupied by their ancestors.

## Uniqueness of human culture

Another reason why treating human beings as "just another animal" can be problematic is that in many ways we are very exceptional animals indeed. Although other creatures can learn from conspecifics and may even have local traditions, human cultural transmission and the diversity of practices that it has engendered are unique, and how we should approach the study of human behavior from an evolutionary adaptationist perspective is therefore controversial. When we watch an animal foraging in its natural habitat, it seems reasonable to ask what adaptive functions are served by measurable aspects of its behavior, and to attempt to determine whether the parameters of relevant **decision** processes have been optimized by past selection (see Chapter 9). But when we observe different human groups raising different domesticated plants and processing them in diverse ways, hunting with radically different technologies, refusing foodstuffs that people from other societies consider delicacies, and so forth, what questions should we ask? We can certainly attempt to assess whether the people we observe are behaving like "optimal foragers" within the constraints of their preferences, technical knowledge, and taboos (Kaplan & Hill 1992), but what can an evolutionist say about the cross-cultural diversity itself?

One approach to the issue of cultural diversity is to attempt to make sense of the distinct practices of people in different parts of the world as representing facultative adaptation to the diversity in local ecological circumstances. A nice example is provided by demonstrations that cross-cultural variation in the use of spices is partly to be understood as response to variation in local and foodstuff-specific rates at which unrefrigerated foods spoil and in the antimicrobial effectiveness of particular spices (Billing & Sherman 1998; Sherman & Hash 2001). Presumably, such **cultural adaptations** are usually the product of an "evolutionary" process that does not entail cumulative change in gene pools but only in socially transmitted information and practices, although there are certainly some cases in which there has been **gene–culture coevolution** (Richerson

& Boyd 2004). The best-known example of the coevolution of human genes and human culture concerns the variable prevalence of genes that permit people to digest milk and milk products beyond early childhood. In populations that lack dairying traditions, most adults are lactose-intolerant and suffer indigestion if they drink milk, because they no longer produce lactase, the enzyme that permits us to metabolize lactose. But in populations with a long history of dairying, genotypes that engender persistent lactase production into adulthood predominate, apparently as a result of natural selection favoring those able to derive nutrition from their herds.

There have been many successful adaptationist analyses of cultural diversity, using comparative methods much as one would do in cross-species analysis. Several authors have discerned patterns in the considerable cultural diversity of inheritance practices, for example, by seeking evidence of flexible fitness-promoting strategies: it turns out that the variations are largely intelligible in terms of probabilities of relatedness, with men transmitting their wealth to their descendants in societies in which their probability of paternity is high, and to nondescendant kin who are known to be related through the mother in societies in which women's sexuality is less controlled and paternity confidence is lower (Flinn 1981). In another example, anthropologists Steve Gaulin and Jim Boster (1990) have made sense of the seemingly arbitrary difference between bridewealth (transfer of economic resources from the groom's kin to the bride's) and dowry (transfer of resources in the opposite direction) by showing that bridewealth occurs in societies where polygynous marriage is legitimate, whereas dowry is confined to those relatively rare societies in which disparities in wealth *would* be sufficient to surpass the "polygyny threshold" were it not for the fact that monogamous marriage is socially enforced, a situation that encourages families to vie to marry their daughters up the social hierarchy and to pay for the privilege.

Enlightening as such approaches may be, however, they can never make functional sense of every particular cultural phenomenon, for it is certain that a great deal of cultural variability is functionally arbitrary in its details, and at least a few culturally prescribed practices have disastrous fitness consequences. A famous example of such a disastrous cultural practice is the transmission of kuru, a fatal prion-induced brain disease akin to Creutzfeldt–Jakob (human BSE or "mad cow") disease, among the Fore people of highland New Guinea. Like other prion-induced diseases, kuru is not easily transmitted under most circumstances, but as a result of funerary practices that included intimate handling of corpses and ritual cannibalism of parts of deceased kinsmen, the Fore suffered an epidemic resulting in high levels of mortality (Klitzman et al. 1984).

In response to culture's seemingly arbitrary aspects, evolutionists have tackled the subject in three distinct but complementary ways: as a second system of phenotypic inheritance and evolution that is partially independent of genetic transmission and evolution, as discussed above; as an inevitable but functionless byproduct of our evolved capacity for **social learning**; and as compromise outcomes of struggles between individuals and groups with conflicting interests. The resultant literature is beyond our present scope, but for rather different perspectives on this enterprise see Richerson and Boyd (2004), Flinn (1997), and Blackmore (1999).

## Uniqueness of human language

Closely linked to humankind's unparalleled degree of social learning and cultural diversity is the unique phenomenon of language (Pinker 1994). Great efforts have been made to train some sort of linguistic performance in other species, and the results sometimes provide impressive evidence of complex cognitive ability (Pepperberg 2000). However, these efforts have also proven beyond doubt that human language, which is acquired without instruction by every normal toddler, entails an unmatched ability to **learn** and manipulate arbitrary symbols and to communicate an unlimited diversity of messages, both concrete and abstract.

Does the unique role of language in human communication and cognition imply that our sociality and behavioral decision-making are qualitatively different from those of other animals and require a different conceptual arsenal? Yes and no. On the one hand, fields like psycholinguistics have appropriately developed their own concepts and theories for dealing with phenomena that are uniquely human, and the same can be said about such broader disciplines as economics, political science, and history. On the other hand, consideration of the role of natural selection in shaping human nature is contributing to these uniquely human sciences (Alexander 1979; Betzig 1986; McCabe et al. 1998; Hirshleifer 1999; Sigmund et al. 2002), and will surely contribute more in the future.

Not only is our language faculty of interest as a crucial component of human nature, but it also affects how we can study this strange species. The fact that people can talk provides an irresistible source of data: we can simply ask our subjects their ages, numbers of children, and so forth, indeed everything from matrilineal kinship links, sexual histories, and the bride prices paid for women of different reproductive values to desires, preferences, attentional priorities, beliefs, and grievances. But this list should make it apparent that even though having speaking research subjects makes it possible to ask questions that one can scarcely imagine how to address in other animals, it can also be a source of error.

One obvious problem with relying on utterance as a primary data source is that people tell lies. A cautionary tale is that of Margaret Mead, whose distinguished anthropological career was built largely upon her credulous acceptance of Samoan schoolgirls' tall tales. Mead became famous for doctoral research that allegedly showed that Samoa is a paradise in which sex is unrestricted, and jealousy, rape, and adolescent adjustment problems are unknown. But none of it was true. Mead never actually learned the Samoan language and she interviewed only schoolgirls, who later acknowledged that they had deceived her for their amusement (Freeman 1999). Such gullibility may be especially problematic for researchers operating in exotic settings, but it would be foolish to assume that sharing a culture with one's interviewees is a guarantee against being duped. More subtle than simple mendacity is the fact that even an honestly reported memory may be untrue, and memory's failings are not random but systematically biased (Weingardt et al. 1995). Moreover, even cooperative interviewees have introspective access to only a fraction of the workings of their minds, indeed a smaller part than either they or the scientist questioning them may imagine: a good deal of clever psychological research has shown that people often attribute their behavioral choices (with great confidence) to variables that are demonstrably irrelevant, while vehemently denying the relevance of factors that can be shown experimentally to be the real determinants of their choices (Nisbett & Wilson 1977).

Recognizing that speech is not always truthful, we can proceed to study its content, and some of the most interesting recent work by evolutionists has done just that. One example is Chagnon's (1988) demonstration that the Yanomamö "manipulate kinship" by stressing those particular genealogical links that bring their acquaintances into useful (e.g., marriage-eligible) categories while ignoring others. Another example is provided by Buss and Dedden's (1990) demonstration that women and men disparage their rivals in distinct ways that are customized to fit the opposite sex's mate-choice criteria: men disparage other men by calling them lazy and predicting that they will never amount to anything, whereas women disparage other women by pointing out that their physical charms have been artificially enhanced and by calling them promiscuous. A third example is provided by Salmon's (1998) experimental demonstration that the metaphorical use of kinship terminology, such as calling an unrelated acquaintance "brother," has persuasive impact on firstborns and lastborns, who also exhibit other signs of a strongly familial social orientation, but has no such impact on middleborns, whose strongest social ties tend to be reciprocal relationships with nonrelatives. In these and other studies, what people say has been treated as social behavior in its own right, perhaps representing sincerely informative cooperative acts in some cases and more deceptive acts of disinformation, persuasion, and impression management in others. The conceptual framework of these studies is therefore much like the contemporary adaptationist approach to nonhuman communication (see Chapter 10), notwithstanding the much richer information content of human utterances.

Reliance on verbal data begins to get researchers into trouble when they treat the subjects' recollections as if they were unproblematic records of past behavior. In areas such as the study of sexual behavior, we can often do little more than collect self-reports, but we should always be suspicious about their validity. Survey data regularly indicate, for example, that the average man has had heterosexual relations with more partners than the average woman, but as long as the sexes are about equally numerous this obviously cannot be true, and it is not easy to determine whether men are exaggerating upward, women are exaggerating downward, or both. The mistake of assuming that recall data provide an unbiased record of actual behavior is surprisingly prevalent in some areas of the social sciences (see Daly & Wilson 1999), but fortunately not in the work of evolutionists, who may derive some protection against such gullibility from their long-standing interests in deceptive self-presentation (Alexander 1987) and self-deception (Lockard & Paulhus 1988). Nevertheless, evolution-minded students of human behavior have not been entirely immune to the siren song of abundant verbal data. For example, in an ambitious and widely cited multinational study, Buss (1989) asked questionnaire respondents in 37 different societies to rank the importance of a given list of mate-choice criteria, and found that several aspects of the data were cross-culturally consistent: the sexes were consistently alike in ranking a pleasant nature and intelligence highly, and consistently differed in that men ranked physical attractiveness more highly than women did, whereas women ranked resource accrual capabilities more highly than men. These results are both interesting and readily interpretable, but we should not assume that they provide direct testimony about actual mate-choice criteria, for although people may sincerely believe that they place great weight on certain factors, such as pleasant personality traits, they do not necessarily *know* what factors really influence their judgments.

So what should researchers do about these problems with self-report data? The answer is clearly not to avoid collecting verbal information from research subjects altogether. Verbal data, including retrospective behavioral data, are too valuable to justify such a drastic remedy. In human research, even observational studies that rely primarily on behavioral scan samples almost always make use of supplementary verbal data, and any study that tests for effects of age or education or birth order or marital status will generally depend on hearsay rather than observation for at least some of its measures. A researcher's confidence in data of this sort can often be enhanced by cross-checking with multiple informants. Moreover, mismatches in the information provided by people with distinct interests are potentially interesting in their own right: if A and B tell conflicting stories, we can sometimes hope to make sense of that fact in terms of conflicting social agendas.

## Controversies in the Study of Evolution and Human Behavior

There are a number of current controversies in the study of human behavior from an evolutionary perspective, and most of them closely parallel ongoing controversies in animal behavior more generally.

One perennial point of discussion is whether measures of reproductive success are essential for testing adaptationist hypotheses. Evolutionary anthropologists who reported that wealth and/or status is positively related to reproductive success in certain societies presented these correlations as testimony to the relevance of Darwinism for the human sciences (Irons 1979; Turke & Betzig 1985), and this invited the rejoinder that a failure to find such a correlation in modern industrialized societies must then constitute evidence of Darwinism's *ir*relevance (Vining 1986). Anthropologist Donald Symons (1989, 1992) then entered the fray with a forceful counterargument to the effect that measures of reproductive attainment are virtually useless for testing adaptationist hypotheses, which should instead be tested on the basis of "design" criteria (see Chapter 9). These arguments sometimes read as if the issue applies only to the cultural animal *H. sapiens* but, as Thornhill (1997) has pointed out, the same debate can be found in the nonhuman literature, with writers like Wade (1987) and Reeve and Sherman (1993) arguing that fitness consequences provide the best test of adaptationist hypotheses, whereas Thornhill (1990) and Williams (1992) defend the opposing view.

A related point of contention concerns the characterization of the human "**environment of evolutionary adaptedness**" (EEA). This concept is often invoked in attempts to understand the prevalence of some unhealthy or otherwise unfit practice in the modern world, such as damaging levels of consumption of refined sugar or psychoactive drugs. The point is simply that these substances did not exist in the selective environment that shaped the human adaptations they now exploit, and that this is why we lack defenses against their harmful effects. Essentially the same point can be made about more benign modern novelties, such as effective contraceptive devices, telephones, and erotica: there is little reason to expect that we will use these inventions in ways that promote our fitness, since they have, in a sense, been designed to "parasitize" our adaptations, and there has not been sufficient time for natural selection to have crafted countermeasures to their effects. The EEA concept has become controversial because several writers believe that it entails untestable assumptions about the past; presupposes that human evolution stopped in the Pleistocene; and is invoked in a pseudo-explanatory post-hoc fashion to dispose of puzzling failures of adaptation (Foley 1996; Irons 1998; Smith et al. 2001). Yet it is surely not controversial that a world with novel chemical pollutants, televised violence, internet pornography, and exogenous opiates is very different from that in which the characteristic features of human psychophysiology evolved (Daly & Wilson 1999).

Once again, these debates about the utility of the EEA concept read as if the issue were peculiar to the human case. But in fact, any adaptation in any species has its "environment of evolutionary adaptedness," and the notion that some adaptations are tuned to aspects of past environments which no longer exist is as relevant to the behavior of other animals as it is to our own. Byers (1997), for example, has argued that various aspects of the behavior of the pronghorn, a social ungulate of North American grasslands, can only be understood as adaptations to predators that are now extinct. Similarly, Coss et al. (1993) have demonstrated that California ground squirrels from different populations, none of which presently live in sympatry with rattlesnakes, may or may not exhibit adaptive antipredator responses to introduced snakes and that the difference reflects how many millennia have passed since the squirrel populations lost contact with the rattlesnakes.

Yet another issue of current controversy concerns the reasons why there is so much genetic diversity affecting behavioral diversity within human populations. Personality dimensions in which there are stable individual differences consistently prove to have heritabilities of around 0.5, which means that about half the variability among individuals in things like extroversion, shyness, and willingness to take risks can be attributed to differences in genotype. The puzzle is why selection "tolerates" this variability: if selection works by weeding out suboptimal variants and thereby optimizing quantitative traits (see Chapter 9), how can all this heritable diversity persist? One possibility is that the diversity is a functionless byproduct of the fact that selection on many traits is weak relative to mutation pressure; in finite populations, not all attributes can be optimized by selection simultaneously. Another possibility is that heritable diversity in personality represents the expression of formerly neutral variants in evolutionarily novel environments (e.g., in the presence of novel synthetic chemicals). Still another view, argued by Tooby and Cosmides (1990), is that heritable personality diversity is indeed functionless "noise" but is nevertheless maintained by frequency-dependent selection favoring rare genotypes in a never-ending "**arms race**" with polymorphic rapidly evolving pathogen strains. Finally, Wilson (1994) has defended the possibility that there is a substantial prevalence of adaptive behavioral polymorphisms maintained by selection on the behavioral **phenotypes** themselves. As shown in

Chapter 9, the "evolutionarily stable" state in **game-theory** models of social behavior is often a mix of different types. If most individuals are **honest** reciprocators, for example, this creates a niche for exploitative "cheaters" whose success is maximal when they are extremely rare and declines as they become more prevalent (**producer–scrounger game** of Chapter 9).

Once again, this is obviously an issue of relevance in other species as well as human beings, and it is not an easy issue to resolve (see Barton & Keightley 2002). However, the right answer will influence how we should look at matters ranging from sexual selection to psychopathology. Gangestad (1997) has argued that there is an evolutionarily stable mix of women with distinct sexualities such that some are inclined to long-term monogamy and others are not. Lalumière et al. (2001) present evidence that "psychopaths," socially exploitative people who are lacking in empathy for others, are not suffering from a pathology but are instead a discrete type of person that is maintained at low frequencies by selection. How such ideas will fare in the light of future theorizing and research is an open question.

## SUMMARY AND CONCLUSIONS

In this chapter we hope to have convinced you that there is no real antithesis of evolutionary versus other "nonevolutionary" alternatives in the human sciences. Because humans, just as much as any other living organism, have been produced by evolutionary mechanisms, the only available "alternative" would be creationism, which is devoid of testable scientific implications and hence not a true scientific alternative. This is not to say that alternative, nonevolutionary approaches to human behavior are useless. Rather we hope to have convinced readers that evolutionary approaches provide a strong heuristic complement to traditional nonevolutionary approaches in the social sciences, helping us to generate testable hypotheses about the **proximate** causal factors that psychologists investigate, the cross-cultural diversity that anthropologists document, and the utility functions that economists accept as givens. And that is what evolutionary (selectionist, adaptationist, "functional") theories do for animal behavior generally: they help direct research on causation.

## FURTHER READING

The latest edition of Rob Boyd and Joan Silk's (2003) human evolution textbook is very good. Ian Pitchford's "evolutionary psychology" website (http://human-nature.com/) is full of material that you might enjoy while keeping a critical mind. For more formal research results on the topics covered in this chapter you should consult the journals of greatest relevance to the study of humans from an animal behaviourist's perspective: *Evolution and Human Behavior, Evolutionary Anthropology*, and *Human Nature*.

# references

Abrahams, M.V. & Healey, M.C. 1990. Variation in the competitive abilities of fishermen and its influence on the spatial distribution of British Columbian salmon troll fleet. *Canadian Journal of Fish and Aquatic Sciences*, 6, 1116–21.

Adams, C.D. & Dickinson, A. 1981. Instrumental responding following reinforcer devaluation. *Quarterly Journal of Experimental Psychology B*, 33, 109–21.

Adams, G.J. & Johnson, K.G. 1994. Sleep, work, and the effects of shift work in drug detector dogs *Canis familiaris. Applied Animal Behaviour Science*, 41, 115–26.

Ainsworth, M.D.S., Blehar, M.C., Waters, E. & Wall, S. 1978. *Patterns of Attachment: Assessed in the Strange Situation and at Home.* Hillsdale, NJ: Erlbaum.

Albright, J.L. & Arave, C.W. 1997. *The Behaviour of Cattle.* Wallingford, UK: CAB International.

Alexander, J. & Stimson, W.H. 1989. Sex hormones and the course of parasitic infection. *Parasitology Today*, 4, 1891–3.

Alexander, R.D. 1979. *Darwinism and Human Affairs.* Seattle: University of Washington Press.

Alexander, R.D. 1987. *The Biology of Moral Systems.* Hawthorne, NY: Aldine de Gruyter.

Alexander, R.D., Hoogland, J.L., Howard, R.D., Noonan, K.M. & Sherman, P.W. 1979. Sexual dimorphisms and breeding systems in pinnipeds, ungulates, primates, and humans. In: N.A. Chagnon & W. Irons (eds.), *Evolutionary Biology and Human Social Behavior*, pp. 402–35. North Scituate, MA: Duxbury Press.

Allee, W.C. 1926. Studies in animal aggregations: causes and effects of bunching in land isopods. *Journal of Experimental Zoology*, 45, 255–77.

Allee, W.C. 1938. *The Social Life of Animals.* New York: W.W. Norton.

Allen, G., Rappe, J., Earnest, D.J. & Cassone, V.M. 2001. Oscillating on borrowed time: diffusible signals from immortalized suprachiasmatic nucleus cells regulate circadian rhythmicity in cultured fibroblasts. *Journal of Neuroscience*, 21, 7937–43.

Altman, J. 1962. Are neurons formed in the brains of adult mammals? *Science*, 135, 1127–8.

Alvard, M.S. 1995. Intraspecific prey choice by Amazonian hunters. *Current Anthropology*, 36, 789–818.

Alvard, M.S. 1998a. Evolutionary ecology and resource conservation. *Evolutionary Anthropology*, 7, 62–74.

Alvard, M. 1998b. Indigenous hunting in the neotropics: conservation or optimal foraging? In: T. Caro (ed.), *Behavioral Ecology and Conservation Biology*, pp. 474–500. New York: Oxford University Press.

Alvarez-Buylla, A., Theelen, M. & Nottebohm, F. 1990. Proliferation "hotspots" in adult avian ventricular zone reveal radial cell division. *Neuron*, 5, 101–9.

Andersson, M. 1994. *Sexual Selection*. Princeton, NJ: Princeton University Press.

Andrade, M.B.C. 1996. Sexual selection for male sacrifice in the Australian redback spider. *Science*, 271, 70–2.

Andrés, J.A. & Cordero Rivera, A. 2000. Copulation duration and fertilization success in a damselfly: an example of cryptic female choice? *Animal Behaviour*, 59, 695–703.

Appleby, M.C. & Hughes, B.O. (eds.) 1997. *Animal Welfare*. Wallingford, UK: CAB International.

Arak, A. 1988a. Callers and satellites in the natterjack toad: evolutionarily stable decision rules. *Animal Behaviour*, 36, 416–32.

Arak, A. 1988b. Sexual dimorphism in body size: a model and a test. *Evolution*, 42, 820–5.

Arcese, P., Keller, L.F. & Cary, J.R. 1997. Why hire a behavioral ecologist into a conservation or management team? In: J.R. Clemmons & R. Buchholz (eds.), *Behavioural Approaches to Conservation in the Wild*, pp. 48–71. Cambridge: Cambridge University Press.

Archer, M.S. & Elgar, M.A. 1999. Female preference for multiple partners: sperm competition in the hide beetle, *Dermestes maculatus*. *Animal Behaviour*, 58, 669–75.

Arnold, S.J. 1976. Sexual behavior, sexual interference and sexual defense in the salamanders *Ambystoma maculatum*, *Ambystoma tigrinum* and *Plethodon jordani*. *Zeitschrift für Tierpsychologie*, 42, 247–300.

Arnqvist, G. 1989. Sexual selection in the water strider: the function, mechanism of selection and heritability of a male grasping organ. *Oikos*, 56, 344–50.

Arnqvist, G. 1992. Spatial variation in selective regimes: sexual selection in the water strider, *Gerris odontogaster*. *Evolution*, 46, 914–29.

Arnqvist, G. 1998. Comparative evidence for the evolution of genitalia by sexual selection. *Nature*, 393, 784–8.

Arnqvist, G. & Nilsson, T. 2000. The evolution of polyandry: multiple mating and female fitness in insects. *Animal Behaviour*, 60, 145–64.

Arnqvist, G. & Rowe, L. 2002. Antagonistic coevolution between the sexes in a group of insects. *Nature*, 415, 787–9.

Arthur, S.M., Manly, B.F.J., McDonald, L.L. & Garner, G.W. 1996. Assessing habitat selection when availability changes. *Ecology*, 77, 215–27.

Aschoff, J. (ed.) 1981. *Biological Rhythms: Handbook of Behavioral Neurobiology*, vol. 4. New York: Plenum Press.

Aschoff, J., Daan, S. & Groos, G.A. (eds.) 1982. *Vertebrate Circadian Systems*. Berlin: Springer.

Autumn, K., Ryan, M.J. & Wake, D.B. 2002. Integrating historical and organismal biology enhances the study of adaptation. *Quarterly Review of Biology*, 77, 383–408.

Axelrod, R. & Hamilton, W.D. 1981. The evolution of cooperation. *Science*, 211, 1390–6.

Bachmann, C. & Kummer, H. 1980. Male assessment of female choice in Hamadryas baboons. *Behavioral Ecology and Sociobiology*, 6, 315–21.

Baddeley, A.D. 1976. *The Psychology of Memory*. New York: Basic Books.

Baenninger, R. 1990. Consciousness and comparative psychology. In: M.G. Johnson & T.B. Henley (eds.), *Reflections on the Principles of Psychology: William James after a Century*, pp. 249–69. Hillsdale, NJ: Erlbaum.

Baer, B. & Schmid-Hempel, P. 1999. Experimental variation in polyandry affects parasite loads and fitness in a bumble-bee. *Nature*, 397, 151–4.

Baerends, G.P. 1976. The functional organization of behaviour. *Animal Behaviour*, 24, 726–38.

Baerends, G.P. 1982. Supernormality. *Behaviour*, 82, 358–63.

Baerends, G.P. 1987. Ethology and physiology: a happy marriage. *Behavior and Brain Sciences*, 10, 369–70.

Baerends, G.P., Brouwer, R. & Waterbolk, H.T. 1955. Ethological studies on *Lebistes reticulatus* (Peters): I. An analysis of the male courtship pattern. *Behaviour*, 8, 249–334.

Baerends-van Roon, J.M. & Baerends, G.P. 1979. The morphogenesis of the behaviour of the domestic cat, with a special emphasis on the development of prey-catching. *Verhandelingen der Koninklijke Nederlandse Akademie van Wetenschappen: Afd. Natuurkunde* (Tweede Reeks) [*Proceedings of the Royal Netherlands Academy of Sciences: Section Physics* (Second Series)], Part 72.

Baird, R. 2000. The killer whale: foraging specializations and group hunting. In: J. Mann, R.C. Connor, P.L. Tyack & H. Whitehead (eds.), *Cetacean Societies*, pp. 127–53. Chicago: University of Chicago Press.

Bakker, T.C.M. & Pomiankowski, A. 1995. The genetic basis of female mate preferences. *Journal of Evolutionary Biology*, 8, 129–81.

Bakker, T.C.M., Kunzler, R. & Mazzi, K. 1999. Condition-related mate choice in sticklebacks. *Nature*, 401, 234.

Balsalobre, A. 2001. Clock genes in mammalian peripheral tissues. *Cell and Tissue Research*, 309, 193–9.

Baptista, L.F. & Gaunt, S.L.L. 1997. Bioacoustics as a tool in conservation studies. In: J.R. Clemmons & R. Buchholz (eds.), *Behavioural Approaches to Conservation in the Wild*, pp. 212–42. Cambridge: Cambridge University Press.

Barinaga, M. 1997. Visual system provides clues to how the brain perceives. *Science*, 275, 1583–5.

Barker, L.M., Best, M. & Domjan, M. (eds.) 1977. *Learning Mechanisms in Food Selection*. Waco, TX: Baylor University Press.

Barlow, H.B. 1953. Summation and inhibition in the frog's retina. *Journal of Physiology London*, 173, 377–407.

Barlow, H.B. 1985. The role of single neurones in the psychology of perception. *Quarterly Journal of Experimental Psychology A*, 37, 121–45.

Barnard, C.J. 1984. *Producers and Scroungers: Strategies of Exploitation and Parasitism*. London: Croom Helm.

Barnard, C.J. & Sibly, R.M. 1981. Producers and scroungers: a general model and its application to captive flocks of house sparrows. *Animal Behaviour*, 29, 543–50.

Barnett, M., Telford, S.R. & Tibbles, B.J. 1995. Female mediation of sperm competition in the millipede *Alloporas unicatus* (Diplopoda: Spirostreptidae). *Behavioral Ecology and Sociobiology*, 36, 413–19.

Barrette, C. 2000. *Le Miroir du Monde: Évolution par Sélection Naturelle et Mystère de la Nature Humaine*. Sainte-Foy: Éditions MultiMondes.

Barta, Z. & Giraldeau, L.-A. 2001. Breeding colonies as information centers: a reappraisal of information-based hypotheses using the producer–scrounger game. *Behavioral Ecology*, 12, 121–39.

Barton, N.H. & Keightley, P.D. 2002. Understanding quantitative genetic variation. *Nature Reviews Genetics* 3, 11–21.

Baskin, Y. 1993. Trumpeter swans relearn migration. *BioScience*, 43, 76–9.

Basolo, A.L. 1990. Female preference predates the evolution of the sword in swordtail fish. *Science*, 250, 808–10.

Basolo, A.L. 1995. A further examination of a pre-existing bias favouring a sword in the genus *Xiphophorus*. *Animal Behaviour*, 50, 365–75.

Bateman, A.J. 1948. Intra-sexual selection in *Drosophila*. *Heredity*, 2, 349–68.

Bateson, P.P.G. 1966. The characteristics and context of imprinting. *Biological Reviews*, 41, 177–220.

Bateson, P.P.G. 1978. Sexual imprinting and optimal outbreeding. *Nature*, 273, 659–60.

Bateson, P. 1979. How do sensitive periods arise and what are they for? *Animal Behaviour*, 27, 470–86.

Bateson, P. 1987. Imprinting as a process of competitive exclusion. In: J.P. Rauschecker & P. Marler (eds.), *Imprinting and Cortical Plasticity: Comparative Aspects of Sensitive Periods*, pp. 151–68. New York: John Wiley & Sons.

Bateson, P. 1999. Foreword. In: J.J. Bolhuis & J.A. Hogan (eds.), *The Development of Animal Behavior: A Reader*. Oxford: Blackwell Publishers.

Beach, F.A. 1948. *Hormones and Behavior*. New York: Hoeber.

Beach, F.A. 1956. Characteristics of the masculine "sex drive." In: M.R. Jones (ed.), *The Nebraska Symposium on Motivation*, pp. 1–32. Lincoln, NE: University of Nebraska Press.

Beauchamp, G. 2000. Learning rules for social foragers: implications for the producer–scrounger game and ideal free distribution theory. *Journal of Theoretical Biology*, 207, 21–35.

Beck, B.B., Rapaport, L.G., Stanley Price, M.R. & Wilson, A.C. 1994. Reintroduction of captive-born animals. In: P.J.S. Olney, G.M. Mace & A.T.C. Feistner (eds.), *Creative Conservation*, pp. 265–86. London: Chapman & Hall.

Beier, P. & Noss, R. 1998. Do habitat corridors provide connectivity? *Conservation Biology*, 12, 1241–52.

Beissinger, S.R. 1997. Integrating behavior into conservation biology: potentials and pitfalls. In: J.R. Clemmons & R. Buchholz (eds.), *Behavioural Approaches to Conservation in the Wild*, pp. 23–47. Cambridge: Cambridge University Press.

Bensch, S. & Hasselquist, D. 1992. Evidence for active female choice in a polygynous warbler. *Animal Behaviour*, 44, 301–12.

Benus, R.F., Den Daas, S., Koolhaas, J.M. & Van Oortmerssen, G.A. 1990. Routine formation and flexibility in social and nonsocial behavior of aggressive and nonaggressive male mice. *Behaviour*, 112, 176–93.

Berger, J. 1998. Future prey: some consequences of the loss and restoration of large carnivores. In: T. Caro (ed.), *Behavioral Ecology and Conservation Biology*, pp. 80–100. New York: Oxford University Press.

Berger, J. 1999. Anthropogenic extinction of top carnivores and interspecific animal behaviour: implications of the rapid decoupling of a web involving wolves, bears, moose and ravens. *Proceedings of the Royal Society of London Series B*, 266, 2261–7.

Berger, J. & Cunningham, C. 1994. Phenotypic alterations, evolutionary significant structures, and rhino conservation. *Conservation Biology*, 8, 833–40.

Berger, J., Swenson, J.E. & Persson, I.-L. 2001. Recolonizing carnivores and naïve prey: conservation lessons from Pleistocene extinctions. *Science*, 291, 1036–9.

Berglund, A., Rosenqvist, G. & Svensson, I. 1989. Reproductive success of females limited by males in two pipefish species. *American Naturalist*, 133, 506–16.

Berlyne, D.E. 1960. *Conflict, Arousal, and Curiosity*. New York: McGraw-Hill.

Bessa-Gomes, C., Legendre, S., Clobert, J. & Møller, A.P. 2003. Modeling mating patterns given mutual mate choice: the importance of individual mating preferences and mating system. *Journal of Biological Systematics*, 11, 205–19.

Betzig, L.L. 1986. *Despotism and Differential Reproduction: A Darwinian View of History*. New York: Aldine.

Betzig, L.L. & Weber, S. 1995. Presidents preferred sons. *Politics and the Life Sciences*, 14, 61–4.

Billing, J. & Sherman, P.W. 1998. Antimicrobial function of spices: why some like it hot. *Quarterly Review of Biology*, 73, 3–49.

Birkhead, T.R. 1998a. Cryptic female choice: criteria for establishing female sperm choice. *Evolution*, 52, 1212–18.

Birkhead, T.R. 1998b. Sperm competition in birds: mechanisms and function. In: T.R. Birkhead & A.P. Møller (eds.), *Sperm Competition and Sexual Selection*, pp. 579–622. London: Academic Press.

Birkhead, T.R. 2000. *Promiscuity*. London: Faber and Faber.

Birkhead, T.R. & Møller, A.P. 1992. *Sperm Competition in Birds: Evolutionary Causes and Consequences*. London: Academic Press.

Birkhead, T.R. & Møller, A.P. (eds.) 1998. *Sperm Competition and Sexual Selection*. London: Academic Press.

Biro, D. & Matsuzawa, T. 1999. Numerical ordering in a chimpanzee (*Pan troglodytes*): planning, executing and monitoring. *Journal of Comparative Psychology*, 113, 178–85.

Bischof, H.-J. 1994. Sexual imprinting as a two-stage process. In: J.A. Hogan & J.J. Bolhuis (eds.), *Causal Mechanisms of Behavioural Development*, pp. 82–97. Cambridge: Cambridge University Press.

Blackmore, S. 1999. *The Meme Machine*. Oxford: Oxford University Press.

Bliss, T.V.P. & Lømo, T. 1973. Long-lasting potentiation of synaptic transmission in the dentate area of the unanaesthetized rabbit following stimulation of the perforant path. *Journal of Physiology London*, 232, 331–56.

Blough, D.S. 1959. Delayed matching in the pigeon. *Journal of the Experimental Analysis of Behavior*, 2, 151–60.

Blüm, V. & Fiedler, K. 1965. Hormonal control of reproductive behavior in some cichlid fish. *General and Comparative Endocrinology*, 5, 186–96.

Blumstein, D.T. 1998. Female preference and effective population size. *Animal Conservation*, 1, 173–7.

Blumstein, D.T., Daniel, J.C., Griffin, A.S. & Evans, C.S. 2000. Insular tammar wallabies (*Macropus eugenii*) respond to visual but not acoustic cues from predators. *Behavioral Ecology*, 11, 528–35.

Blurton Jones, N.G. (ed.) 1972. *Ethological Studies of Child Behavior*. London: Cambridge University Press.

Blurton Jones, N.G. 1998. Autobiographical notes on the AfricaQuest website:
http://quest.classroom.com/archive/africaquest1998/footer/about/pg00150.htm

Blurton Jones, N.G., Marlowe, F., Hawkes, K. & O'Connell, J.F. 2000. Hunter-gatherer divorce rates and the paternal provisioning theory of human monogamy. In: L. Cronk, N. Chagnon & W. Irons (eds.), *Adaptation and Human Behavior*, pp. 69–90. Hawthorne, NY: Aldine de Gruyter.

Boakes, R.A. 1984. *From Darwin to Behaviorism: Psychology and the Minds of Animals*. Cambridge: Cambridge University Press.

Bolhuis, J.J. 1991. Mechanisms of avian imprinting: a review. *Biological Reviews*, 66, 303–45.

Bolhuis, J.J. 1996. Development of perceptual mechanisms in birds: predispositions and imprinting. In: C.F. Moss & S.J. Shettleworth (eds.), *Neuroethological Studies of Cognitive and Perceptual Processes*, pp. 158–84. Boulder, CO: Westview Press.

Bolhuis, J.J. 1999. The development of animal behavior. From Lorenz to neural nets. *Naturwissenschaften*, 86, 101–11.

Bolhuis, J.J. & Bateson, P.P.G. 1990. The importance of being first: a primacy effect in filial imprinting. *Animal Behaviour*, 40, 472–83.

Bolhuis, J.J. & Eda-Fujiwara, H. 2003. Bird brains and songs: neural mechanisms of birdsong perception and memory. *Animal Biology*, 53, 129–45.

Bolhuis, J.J. & Hogan, J.A. (eds.) 1999. *The Development of Animal Behavior: A Reader*. Oxford: Blackwell Publishers.

Bolhuis, J.J. & Honey, R.C. 1998. Imprinting, learning and development: from behaviour to brain and back. *Trends in Neurosciences*, 21, 306–11.

Bolhuis, J.J. & Macphail, E.M. 2001. A critique of the neuroecology of learning and memory. *Trends in Cognitive Sciences*, 5, 426–33.

Bolhuis, J.J., De Vos, G.J. & Kruijt, J.P. 1990. Filial imprinting and associative learning. *Quarterly Journal of Experimental Psychology*, 42B, 313–29.

Bolhuis, J.J., Zijlstra, G.G.O., Den Boer-Visser, A.M. & Van der Zee, E.A. 2000. Localized neuronal activation in the zebra finch brain is related to the strength of song learning. *Proceedings of the National Academy of Sciences USA*, 97, 2282–5.

Bolles, R.C. 1979. *Learning Theory*, 2nd edn. New York: Holt, Rinehart and Winston.

Borbély, A.A. 1982. A two-process model of sleep. *Human Neurobiology*, 1, 195–204.

Borbély, A.A., Dijk, D.-J., Achermann, P. & Tobler, I. 2001. Processes underlying the regulation of the sleep–wake cycle. In: J.S. Takahashi, F.W. Turek & R.Y. Moore (eds.), *Circadian Clocks: Handbook of Behavioral Neurobiology*, vol. 12, pp. 458–79. New York: Kluwer Academic/Plenum.

Borgerhoff Mulder, M. 1990. Kipsigis women's preferences for wealthy men: evidence for female choice in mammals? *Behavioral Ecology and Sociobiology*, 27, 255–64.

Borgerhoff Mulder, M. & Ruttan, L. 2000. Grassland conservation and the pastoralist commons. In: L.M. Gosling & W.J. Sutherland (eds.), *Behaviour and Conservation*, pp. 34–50. Cambridge: Cambridge University Press.

Bourke, A.F.G. 1997. Sociality and kin selection in insects. In: J.R. Krebs & N.B. Davies (eds.), *Behavioural Ecology: An Evolutionary Approach*, 4th edn, pp. 203–27. Oxford: Blackwell Science.

Bowlby, J. 1969. *Attachment and Loss*, vol. 1. *Attachment*. London: Hogarth Press.

Boyd, R. & Richerson, P. 1992. Punishment allows the evolution of cooperation (or anything else) in sizable groups. *Ethology and Sociobiology*, 13, 171–95.

Boyd, R. & Silk, J.B. 2003. *How Humans Evolved*, 3rd edn. New York: W.W. Norton.

Boysen, S.T. & Berntson, G.G. 1989. Numerical competence in a chimpanzee (*Pan troglodytes*). *Journal of Comparative Psychology*, 103, 23–31.

Bradbury, J.W. & Vehrencamp, S.L. 1998. *The Principles of Animal Communication*. Sunderland, MA: Sinauer.

Brambell, F.W.R. (chairman) 1965. *Report of the Technical Committee to Enquire into the Welfare of Animals Kept under Intensive Livestock Husbandry Systems*. London: HMSO.

Brennan, S. E. 1985. The caricature generator. *Leonardo*, 18, 170–8.

Bright, P.W. 1998. Behaviour of specialist species in habitat corridors: arboreal dormice avoid corridor gaps. *Animal Behaviour*, 56, 1485–90.

Broadbent, D.E. 1958. *Perception and Communication*. London: Pergamon.

Brockmann, H.J., Grafen, A. & Dawkins, R. 1979. Evolutionarily stable nesting strategy in a digger wasp. *Journal of Theoretical Biology*, 77, 473–96.

Brooks, D.R. & McLennan, D.A. 1991. *Phylogeny, Ecology, and Behavior*. Chicago: University of Chicago Press.

Broom, D.M. (ed.) 2002. *Coping with Challenge: Welfare in Animals including Humans*. Berlin: Dahlem University Press.

Brown, J.L. 1980. Fitness in complex avian social systems. In: H. Markl (ed.), *Evolution of Social Behaviour*, pp. 115–28. Weinheim: Verlag-chemie.

Brown, J.L. 1987. *Helping and Communal Breeding in Birds*. Princeton, NJ: Princeton University Press.

Brown, J.L. & Eklund, A. 1994. Kin recognition and the major histocompatibility complex: an integrative review. *American Naturalist*, 143, 435–61.

Brown, J.S. 1948. Gradients of approach and avoidance responses and their relation to level of motivation. *Journal of Comparative and Physiological Psychology*, 41, 450–85.

Bshary, R. & D'Souza, A. 2004. Cooperation in communication networks: indirect reciprocity in interactions between cleaner fish and client reef fish. In: P.K. McGregor (ed.), *Animal Communication Networks*, pp. 1160–99. Cambridge: Cambridge University Press.

Buchanan, J.B., Irwin, L.L. & McCutchen, E.L. 1995. Within-stand nest site selection by spotted owls in the eastern Washington Cascades. *Journal of Wildlife Management*, 59, 301–10.

Bugnyar, T. & Kotrschal, K. 2002. Observational learning and the raiding of food caches in ravens, *Corvus corax*: is it "tactical" deception? *Animal Behaviour*, 64, 185–95.

Bull, J.J. & Wichman, H.A. 2001. Applied evolution. *Annual Review of Ecology and Systematics*, 32, 183–217.

Bullard, R.W., Leiker, T.J., Peterson, J.E. & Kilburn, S.R. 1978. Volatile components of fermented egg, an animal attractant and repellent. *Journal of Agricultural and Food Chemistry*, 26, 155–9.

Bunin, J.S. & Jamieson, I.G. 1996. Responses to a model predator of New Zealand's endangered takahe and its closest relative, the pukeko. *Conservation Biology*, 10, 1463–6.

Buntin, J.D. 1996. Neural and hormonal control of parental behavior in birds. *Advances in the Study of Behavior*, 25, 161–213.

Burgess, H.J., Sharkey, K.M. & Eastman, C.I. 2002. Bright light, dark and melatonin can promote circadian adaptation in night shift workers. *Sleep Med Rev*, 6, 407–20.

Burke, T., Davies, N.B., Bruford, M.W. & Hatchwell, B.J. 1989. Parental care and mating behaviour of polyandrous dunnocks *Prunella modularis* related to paternity by DNA fingerprinting. *Nature*, 338, 249–51.

Burkhardt, R.W. Jr. 1997. The founders of ethology and the problem of animal subjective experience. In: M. Dol, S. Kasanmoentalib, S. Lijmbach, E. Rivas & R. van den Bos (eds.), *Animal Consciousness and Animal Ethics*, pp. 1–16. Assen, The Netherlands: Van Gorcum.

Burley, N. 1981. Sex ratio manipulation and selection for attractiveness. *Science* 211, 721–2.

Burley, N. 1986. Sexual selection for aesthetic traits in species with biparental care. *American Naturalist*, 127, 415–45.

Buss, D.M. 1989. Sex differences in human mate preferences: evolutionary hypotheses tested in 37 cultures. *Behavioral and Brain Sciences*, 12, 1–49.

Buss, D.M. 1994. *The Evolution of Desire*. New York: Basic Books.

Buss, D.M. & Dedden, L. 1990. Derogation of competitors. *Journal of Social and Personal Relationships*, 7, 395–422.

Butler, R.A. & Harlow, H.F. 1954. Persistence of visual exploration in monkeys. *Journal of Comparative and Physiological Psychology*, 47, 257–63.

Butlin, R.K., Guilford, T. & Krebs, J.R. 1993. The evolution and design of animal signalling systems. *Philosophical Transactions of the Royal Society of London Series B*, 340, 161–225.

Byers, J.A. 1997. *American Pronghorn: Social Adaptations and Ghosts of Predators Past*. Chicago: University of Chicago Press.

Cade, W.H. 1975. Acoustically orienting parasitoids: fly phonotaxis to cricket song. *Science*, 190, 1312–13.

Cade, W.H. 1978. Of cricket song and sex. *Natural History*, 87, 64–72.

Capranica, R.R. 1976. Morphology and physiology of the auditory system. In: R. Llinás & W. Precht (eds.), *Frog Neurobiology*, pp. 551–75. Berlin: Springer.

Carew, T.J. 2000. *Behavioral Neurobiology*. Sunderland, MA: Sinauer.

Caro, T. (ed.) 1998a. *Behavioral Ecology and Conservation Biology*. New York: Oxford University Press.

Caro, T. 1998b. The significance of behavioral ecology for conservation biology. In: T. Caro (ed.), *Behavioral Ecology and Conservation Biology*, pp. 3–26. New York: Oxford University Press.

Caro, T. 1998c. How do we refocus behavioral ecology to address conservation issues more directly? In: T. Caro (ed.), *Behavioral Ecology and Conservation Biology*, pp. 557–65. New York: Oxford University Press.

Caro, T.M. 1999. The behaviour–conservation interface. *Trends in Ecology and Evolution*, 14, 366–9.

Caro, T.M. & Durant, S.M. 1995. The importance of behavioral ecology for conservation biology: examples from Serengeti carnivores. In: A.R.E. Sinclair & P. Arcese (eds.), *Serengeti II: Dynamics,*

*Management, and Conservation of an Ecosystem*, pp. 451–72. Chicago: University of Chicago Press.

Carr, C.E. & Konishi, M. 1990. A circuit for detection of interaural time differences in the brain stem of the barn owl. *Journal of Neuroscience*, 10, 3227–46.

Carskadon, M.A., Acebo, C., Richardson, G.S., Tate, B.A. & Seifer, R. 1997. An approach to studying circadian rhythms of adolescent humans. *Journal of Biological Rhythms*, 12, 278–89.

Cartwright, B.A. & Collett, T.S. 1983. Landmark learning in bees. *Journal of Comparative Physiology A*, 151, 521–43.

Case, A.C. & Paxson, C. 2001. Mothers and others: who invests in children's health? *Journal of Health Economics*, 20, 301–28.

Case, A.C., Lin, I.F. & McLanahan, S. 2000. How hungry is the selfish gene? *Economic Journal*, 110, 781–804.

Catchpole, C.K. & Slater, P.J.B. 1995. *Bird Song: Biological Themes and Variations*. Cambridge: Cambridge University Press.

Caughley, G. & Gunn, A. 1996. *Conservation Biology in Theory and Practice*. Cambridge, MA: Blackwell Scientific Publications.

Chadwick, D.J. & Ackrill, K. (eds.) 1995. *Circadian Clocks and Their Adjustment*. Ciba Foundation Symposium 183. Chichester: John Wiley.

Chagnon, N.A. 1988. Male Yanomamö manipulations of kinship classifications of female kin for reproductive advantage. In: L. Betzig, M. Borgerhoff Mulder & P. Turke (eds.), *Human Reproductive Behavior: A Darwinian Perspective*, pp. 23–48. New York: Cambridge University Press.

Chagnon, N.A. & Bugos, P. 1979. Kin selection and conflict: an analysis of a Yanomamo ax fight. In: N.A. Chagnon & W. Irons (eds.), *Evolutionary Biology and Human Social Behavior: An Anthropological Perspective*, pp. 213–38. North Scituate, MA: Duxbury Press.

Chain, D.G., Schwartz, J.H. & Hegde, A.N. 2000. Ubiquitin-mediated proteolysis in learning and memory. *Molecular Neurobiology*, 20, 125–42.

Chapman, T., Arnqvist, G., Bangham, J. & Rowe, L. 2003. Sexual conflict. *Trends in Ecology and Evolution*, 18, 41–7.

Cheney, D.L. & Seyfarth, R.M. 1990. *How Monkeys See the World: Inside the Mind of Another Species*. Chicago: University of Chicago Press.

Chomsky, N. 1959. A review of B.F. Skinner's *Verbal Behavior*. *Language*, 35, 26–58.

Chovnick, A. (ed.) 1960. *Biological Clocks*. Cold Spring Harbor Symposium on Quantitative Biology, vol. 25. New York: Cold Spring Harbor.

Clayton, N.S. & Dickinson, A. 1998. Episodic-like memory during cache recovery by scrub jays. *Nature*, 395, 272–4.

Clemmons, J.R. & Buchholz, R. (eds.) 1997. *Behavioural Approaches to Conservation in the Wild*. Cambridge: Cambridge University Press.

Clutton-Brock, T.H. & Parker, G.A. 1995. Punishment in animal societies. *Nature*, 373, 209–16.

Clutton-Brock, T.H. & Vincent, A.C.J. 1991. Sexual selection and the potential reproductive rates of males and females. *Nature*, 351, 58–60.

Clutton-Brock, T.H., O'Riain, M.J., Brotherton, P.N.M. et al. 1999a. Selfish sentinels in cooperative mammals. *Science*, 284, 1640–4.

Clutton-Brock, T.H., Gaynor, D., McIlrath, G.M. et al. 1999b. Predation, group size and mortality in a cooperative mongoose, *Suricata suricata*. *Journal of Animal Ecology*, 68, 672–83.

Clutton-Brock, T.H., Brotherton, P.N.M., Russell, A.F. et al. 2001. Cooperation, control, and concession in meerkat groups. *Science*, 291, 478–81.

Cohen, J.D. & Tong, F. 2001. The face of controversy. *Science*, 293, 2405–7.

Cohen, L.G., Celnik, P., Pascual-Leone, A. et al. 1997. Functional relevance of cross-modal plasticity in blind humans. *Nature*, 389, 180–3.

Colishaw, G. & Dunbar, R. 2000. *Primate Conservation Biology*. Chicago: University of Chicago Press.

Collett, T.S., Cartwright, B.A. & Smith, B.A. 1986. Landmark learning and visuospatial memories in gerbils. *Journal of Comparative Psychology A*, 158, 835–51.

Conner, J. 1988. Field measurements of natural and sexual selection in the fungus beetle, *Bolitotherus cornutus*. *Evolution*, 42, 735–49.

Conner, J. 1989. Density-dependent sexual selection in the fungus beetle *Bolitotherus cornutus*. *Evolution*, 43, 1378–86.

Cook, P.A. & Wedell, N. 1999. Non-fertile sperm delay female remating. *Nature*, 397, 486.

Coss, R.G. 1999. Effects of relaxed natural selection in the evolution of behavior. In: S.A. Foster & J.A. Endler (eds.), *Geographic Variation in Behavior: Perspectives on Evolutionary Mechanisms*, pp. 180–208. New York: Oxford University Press.

Coss, R.G., Gusé, K.L., Poran, N.S. & Smith, D.G. 1993. Development of antisnake defenses in California ground squirrels (*Spermophilus beecheyi*) II. Microevolutionary effects of relaxed selection from rattlesnakes. *Behaviour*, 124, 137–64.

Courchamp, F., Clutton-Brock, T. & Grenfell, B. 1999. Inverse density dependence and the Allee effect. *Trends in Ecology and Evolution*, 14, 405–10.

Craig, J.V. 1981. *Domestic Animal Behavior: Causes and Implications for Animal Care and Management*. Englewood Cliffs, NJ: Prentice-Hall.

Creel, S. 1998. Social organization and effecvtive population size in carnivores. In: T. Caro (ed.), *Behavioral Ecology and Conservation Biology*, pp. 246–70. New York: Oxford University Press.

Cresswell, W. 1994. Flocking is an effective anti-predation strategy in redshanks, *Tringa totanus*. *Animal Behaviour*, 47, 433–42.

Cristol, D.A., Switzer, V.P., Johnson, K.L. & Walke, L.S. 1997. Crows do not use automobiles as nutcrackers: putting an anecdote to the test. *Auk*, 114, 296–8.

Crudgington, H.S. & Siva-Jothy, M.T. 2000. Genital damage, kicking and early death. *Nature*, 407, 855–6.

Cumming, J.M. 1994. Sexual selection and the evolution of dance fly mating systems (Diptera: Empdidae: Empidinae). *Canadian Entomologist*, 126, 907–20.

Curio, E. 1996. Conservation needs ethology. *Trends in Ecology and Evolution*, 11, 260–3.

Curio, E. 1998. Behavior as a tool for management intervention in birds. In: T. Caro (ed.), *Behavioral Ecology and Conservation Biology*, pp. 163–87. New York: Oxford University Press.

Curio, E., Ernst, U. & Vieth, W. 1987. Cultural transmission of enemy recognition: one function of mobbing. *Science*, 202, 899–901.

Cuthill, I. 1991. Field experiments in animal behaviour, methods and ethics. *Animal Behaviour*, 42, 1007–14.

Cuthill, I.C., Partridge, J.C. & Bennett, A.T.D. 2000. Avian UV vision and sexual selection. In: Y. Espmark, T. Amundsen & G. Rosenqvist (eds.), *Animal Signals: Signalling and Signal Design in Animal Communication*, pp. 61–82. Trondheim: Tapir Academic Press.

Czeisler, C.A. & Dijk, D.-J. 2001. Human circadian physiology and sleep–wake regulation. In: J.S. Takahashi, F.W. Turek & R.Y. Moore (eds.), *Circadian Clocks. Handbook of Behavioral Neurobiology*, vol. 12, pp. 531–69. New York: Kluwer Academic/Plenum.

Daan, S. 1981. Adaptive daily strategies in behavior. In: J. Aschoff (ed.), *Biological Rhythms. Handbook of Behavioral Neurobiology*, vol. 4, pp. 275–98. New York: Plenum Press.

Daan, S., Beersma, D.G.M. & Borbély, A.A. 1984. Timing of human sleep: recovery process gated by a circadian pacemaker. *American Journal of Physiology*, 246, R161–R178.

Dabelsteen, T. 1992. Interactive playback: a finely tuned response. In: P.K. McGregor (ed.), *Playback and Studies of Animal Communication*, pp. 97–109. New York: Plenum Press.

Dabelsteen, T. 2004. Public, private or anonymous? Facilitating and countering eavesdropping: In P.K. McGregor (ed.), *Animal Communication Networks*, pp. 97–149. Cambridge: Cambridge University Press.

Daly, M. & Wilson, M.I. 1982a. Homicide and kinship. *American Anthropologist*, 84, 372–8.

Daly, M. & Wilson, M.I. 1982b. Whom are newborn babies said to resemble? *Ethology and Sociobiology*, 3, 69–78.

Daly, M. & Wilson, M.I. 1996. Violence against stepchildren. *Current Directions in Psychological Science*, 5, 77–81.

Daly, M. & Wilson, M.I. 1998. *The Truth About Cinderella*. London: Weidenfeld & Nicolson.

Daly, M. & Wilson, M.I. 1999. Human evolutionary psychology and animal behaviour. *Animal Behavior*, 57, 509–19.

Daly, M. & Wilson, M.I. 2001a. An assessment of some proposed exceptions to the phenomenon of nepotistic discrimination against stepchildren. *Annales Zoologici Fennici*, 38, 287–96.

Daly, M. & Wilson, M.I. 2001b. Risk-taking, intrasexual competition, and homicide. *Nebraska Symposium on Motivation*, 47, 1–36.

Damasio, A.R. 1990. Category-related recognition defects as a clue to the neural substrates of knowledge. *Trends in Neurosciences*, 13, 95–8.

Damiola, F., Le Minh, N., Preitner, N., Kornmann, B., Fleury-Olela, F. & Schibler, U. 2000. Restricted feeding uncouples circadian oscillators in peripheral tissues from the central pacemaker in the suprachiasmatic nucleus. *Genes and Development*, 14, 2950–61.

Danchin, E. & Wagner, R.H. 1997. The evolution of coloniality: the emergence of new perspectives. *Trends in Ecology and Evolution*, 12, 342–7.

Darwin, C. 1859. *On the Origin of Species by Means of Natural Selection, or the Preservation of Favoured Races in the Struggle for Life*. London: John Murray.

Darwin, C. 1862. *On the Various Contrivances by which Orchids are Fertilized by Insects*. London: John Murray.

Darwin, C. 1872. *The Expression of the Emotions in Man and the Animals*. London: John Murray.

Dasser, V. 1988. A social concept in Java monkeys. *Animal Behaviour*, 36, 225–30.

Davies, N.B. 1983. Polyandry, cloaca-pecking and sperm competition in dunnocks. *Nature*, 302, 334–6.

Davies, N.B. 1992. *Dunnock Behaviour and Social Evolution*. Oxford: Oxford University Press.

Davies, N.B. & Houston, A.L. 1981. Owners and satellites: the economics of territory defence in the pied wagtail, *Motacilla alba*. *Journal of Animal Ecology*, 50, 157–80.

Davis, H. & Bradford, S.A. 1986. Counting behavior by rats in a simulated natural environment. *Ethology*, 73, 265–80.

Davis, R.B., Herreid, C.F.I. & Short, H.L. 1962. Mexican free-tailed bats in Texas. *Ecological Monographs*, 32, 311–46.

Dawkins, M.S. 1977. Do hens suffer in battery cages? Environmental preferences and welfare. *Animal Behaviour*, 25, 1034–46.

Dawkins, M.S. 1980. *Animal Suffering: The Science of Animal Welfare*. London: Chapman & Hall.

Dawkins, M.S. 1983. Battery hens name their price: consumer demand theory and the measurement of ethological "needs." *Animal Behaviour*, 31, 1195–205.

Dawkins, M.S. 1993. *Through Our Eyes Only? The Search for Animal Consciousness*. Oxford: W.H. Freeman.

Dawkins, M.S. 1995. *Unravelling Animal Behaviour*, 2nd edn. Harlow, UK: Longman.

Dawkins, M.S. 2001. Who needs consciousness? *Animal Welfare*, 10 (Suppl.), S19–S29.

Dawkins, R. 1996. *Climbing Mount Improbable*. New York: W.W. Norton.

Dawkins, R. & Krebs, J.R. 1978. Animal signals: information or manipulation? In: J.R. Krebs & N.B. Davies (eds.), *Behavioural Ecology: An Evolutionary Approach*, pp. 282–309. Oxford: Blackwell Scientific Publications.

DeBruine, L.M. 2002. Facial resemblance enhances trust. *Proceedings of the Royal Society of London Series B*, 269, 1307–12.

DeCoursey, P.J. 1986. Light-sampling behavior in photoentrainment of a rodent circadian rhythm. *Journal of Comparative Physiology A*, 159, 161–9.

DeCoursey, P.J., Krulas, J.R., Mele, G. & Holley, D.C. 1997. Circadian performance of suprachiasmatic nuclei (SCN)-lesioned antelope ground squirrels in a desert enclosure. *Physiology and Behavior*, 62, 1099–108.

DeCoursey, P.J., Walker, J.K. & Smith, S.A. 2000. A circadian pacemaker in free-living chipmunks: essential for survival? *Journal of Comparative Physiology A*, 186, 169–80.

Delcomyn, F. 1998. *Foundations of Neurobiology*. San Francisco: Freeman.

Delibes, M., Gaona, P. & Ferreras, P. 2001. Effects of an attractive sink leading into maladaptive habitat selection. *American Naturalist*, 158, 277–85.

de Lope, F. & Møller, A.P. 1993. Female reproductive effort depends on the degree of ornamentation of their mates. *Evolution*, 47, 1152–60.

Dennett, D.C. 1987. *The Intentional Stance*. Cambridge, MA: MIT Press.

de Passillé, A.M. & Rushen, J. 1997. Motivational and physiological analysis of the causes and consequences of non-nutritive sucking by calves. *Applied Animal Behaviour Science*, 53, 15–31.

Desimone, R. & Duncan, J. 1995. Neural mechanisms of selective visual attention. *Annual Review of Neuroscience*, 18, 193–222.

DeVoogd, T.J. 1994. The neural basis for the acquisition and production of bird song. In: J.A. Hogan & J.J. Bolhuis (eds.), *Causal Mechanisms of Behavioural Development*, pp. 49–81. Cambridge: Cambridge University Press.

Deweer, B., Sara, S.J. & Hars, B. 1980. Contextual cues and memory retrieval in rats: alleviation of forgetting by a pretest exposure to background stimuli. *Animal Learning and Behavior*, 8, 265–72.

Dewsbury, D. 1989. A brief history of the study of animal behavior in North America. In: P.P.G. Bateson & P.H. Klopfer (eds.), *Perspectives in Ethology*, pp. 85–122. London: Plenum Press.

Dobson, A. & Poole, J. 1998. Conspecific aggregation and conservation biology. In: T. Caro (ed.), *Behavioral Ecology and Conservation Biology*, pp. 193–208. New York: Oxford University Press.

Dol, M., Kasanmoentalib, S., Lijmbach, S., Rivas, E. & van den Bos, R. (eds.) 1997. *Animal Consciousness and Animal Ethics*. Assen, The Netherlands: Van Gorcum.

Dolman, P.M. & Sutherland, W.J. 1995. The response of bird populations to habitat loss. *Ibis*, 137, S38–S46.

Donovan, T.M. & Thompson, F.R. 2001. Modeling the ecological trap hypothesis: a habitat and demographic analysis for migrant songbirds. *Ecological Applications*, 11, 871–82.

Douglas, R.H., Partridge, J.C., Dulai, K. et al. 1998. Dragon fish see using chlorophyll. *Nature*, 393, 423–4.

Doupe, A.J. & Kuhl, P.K. 1999. Birdsong and human speech: common themes and mechanisms. *Annual Review of Neuroscience*, 22, 567–631.

Downes, J.A. 1978. Feeding and mating in the insectivorous ceratopogoninae (Diptera). *Memoirs of the Entomological Society of Canada*, 104, 1–62.

Dugatkin, L.A. (ed.) 2001. *Model Systems in Behavioral Ecology*. Princeton, NJ: Princeton University Press.

Dugatkin, L.A. & Reeve, H.K. 1998. *Game Theory and Animal Behavior*. New York: Oxford University Press.

Dukas, R. (ed.) 1998. *Cognitive Ecology: The Evolutionary Ecology of Information Processing and Decision Making.* Chicago: University of Chicago Press.

Dunbar, R.I.M. 1992. Neocortex size as a constraint on group size in primates. *Journal of Human Evolution*, 20, 469–93.

Duncan, C.P. 1949. The retroactive effect of electroshock on learning. *Journal of Comparative and Physiological Psychology*, 42, 32–44.

Duncan, I.J.H. 1970. Frustration in the fowl. In: B.M. Freeman & R.F. Gordon (eds.), *Aspects of Poultry Behaviour*, pp. 15–31. Edinburgh: British Poultry Science Ltd.

Duncan, I.J.H. 1993. Welfare is to do with what animals feel. *Journal of Agricultural and Environmental Ethics*, 6 (Suppl. 2), 8–14.

Duncan, I.J.H., Slee, G., Kettlewell, P., Berry, P. & Carlisle, A.J. 1986. Comparison of the stressfulness of harvesting broiler chickens by machine and by hand. *British Poultry Science*, 27, 109–14.

Duncan, I.J.H., Widowski, T.M., Malleau, A.E., Lindberg, A.C. & Petherick, J.C. 1998. External factors and causation of dustbathing in domestic hens. *Behavioural Processes*, 43, 219–28.

Dunlap, J.C., Loros, J.J. & DeCoursey, P.J. (eds.) 2004. *Chronobiology: Biological Timekeeping.* Sunderland, MA: Sinauer.

Dunlap, K.D. & Wingfield, J.C. 1995. External and internal influences on indices of physiological stress. 1. Seasonal and population variation in adrenocortical secretion of free-living lizards, *Sceloporus occidentalis. Journal of Experimental Zoology*, 271, 36–46.

Eadie, J.M. & Fryxell, J.M. 1992. Density dependence, frequency dependence, and alternative nesting strategies in goldeneyes. *American Naturalist*, 140, 621–41.

Eadie, J., Sherman, P. & Semel, B. 1998. Conspecific brood parasitism, population dynamics, and the conservation of cavity-nesting birds. In: T. Caro (ed.), *Behavioral Ecology and Conservation Biology*, pp. 306–40. New York: Oxford University Press.

Eaton, R.C. 2001. The Mauthner cell and other identified neurons of the brainstem escape network of fish. *Progress in Neurobiology*, 63, 467–85.

Eberhard, W.G. 1996. *Female Control: Sexual Selection by Cryptic Female Choice.* Princeton, NJ: Princeton University Press.

Edwards, D.H., Heitler, W.J. & Krasne, F.B. 1999. Fifty years of a command neuron: the neurobiology of escape behavior in the crayfish. *Trends in Neurosciences*, 22, 153–61.

Ehrlich, P.R. & Raven, P.H. 1964. Butterflies and plants: a study in coevolution. *Evolution*, 18, 586–608.

Eibl-Eibesfeldt, I. 1989. *Human Ethology.* New York: Aldine de Gruyter.

Ekman, P., Sorensen, E.R. & Friesen, W.V. 1969. Pan-cultural elements in facial displays of emotion. *Science*, 164, 86–8.

Elbert, T., Pantev, C., Wienbruch, C., Rockstroh, B. & Taub, E. 1995. Increased cortical representation of the fingers of the left hand in string players. *Science*, 270, 305–7.

Elgar, M.A., Schneider, J.M. & Herberstein, M.E. 2000. Females control paternity in a sexually cannibalistic spider. *Proceedings of the Royal Society of London Series B*, 267, 2439–43.

Emery, N.J. 2000. The eyes have it: the neuroethology, function and evolution of social gaze. *Neuroscience and Biobehavioral Reviews*, 24, 581–604.

Emery, N.J. & Clayton, N.S. 2001. Effects of experience and social context on prospective caching strategies by scrub jays. *Nature*, 414, 443–6.

Emlen, S.T. & Oring, L.W. 1977. Ecology, sexual selection, and the evolution of mating systems. *Science*, 197, 215–23.

Emlen, S.T. & Wrege, P.H. 1988. The role of kinship in helping decisions among white-fronted bee-eaters. *Behavioral Ecology and Sociobiology*, 23, 305–15.

Emlen, S.T. & Wrege, P.H. 1992. Parent–offspring conflict and the recruitment of helpers among bee-eaters. *Nature*, 356, 331–3.

Emmerton, J. 1998. Numerosity differences and effects of simulus density on pigeons' discrimination performance. *Animal Learning and Behavior*, 26, 243–56.

Endler, J.A. 1997. Light, behavior and the conservation of forest-dwelling organisms. In: J.R. Clemmons & R. Buchholz (eds.), *Behavioural Approaches to Conservation in the Wild*, pp. 329–55. Cambridge: Cambridge University Press.

Endler, J.A. 2000. Evolutionary implications of the interaction between animal signals and the environment. In: Y. Espmark, T. Amundsen & G. Rosenqvist (eds.), *Animal Signals: Signalling and Signal Design in Animal Communication*, pp. 11–46. Trondheim: Tapir Academic Press.

Enquist, M. & Arak, A. 1993. Selection of exaggerated male traits by female aesthetic senses. *Nature*, 361, 446–8.

Enquist, M. & Arak, A. 1998. Neural representation and the evolution of signal form. In: R. Dukas (ed.), *Cognitive Ecology*, pp. 21–87. Chicago: University of Chicago Press.

Espmark, Y., Amundsen, T. & Rosenqvist, G. (eds.) 2000. *Animal Signals: Signalling and Signal Design in Animal Communication*. Trondheim: Tapir Academic Press.

Ewert, J.-P. 1980. *Neuroethology: An Introduction to the Neurophysiological Fundamentals of Behavior*. Berlin: Springer-Verlag.

Ewert, J.-P. 1985. The Niko Tinbergen Lecture 1983: Concept in vertebrate neuroethology. *Animal Behaviour*, 33, 1–29.

Ewert, J.-P. 1987. Neuroethology of releasing mechanisms. *Behavior and Brain Sciences*, 10, 337–405.

Ewert, J.-P. 1997. Neural correlates of key stimulus and releasing mechanism. *Trends in Neurosciences*, 20, 332–9.

Ewert, J.-P. 2002. Command neurons and command systems. In: M.A. Arbib (ed.), *Handbook of Neural Networks*, pp. 233–8. Cambridge, MA: MIT Press.

Ewert, J.-P. 2004. Motion perception shapes the visual world of amphibians. In: F.R. Prete (ed.), *Complex Worlds from Simpler Nervous Systems*, pp. 117–60. Cambridge, MA: MIT Press.

Ewert, J.-P. & Traud, R. 1979. Releasing stimuli for antipredator behavior in the common toad *Bufo bufo* (L.). *Behaviour*, 68, 170–80.

Ewert, J.-P., Buxbaum-Conradi, H., Dreisvogt, F. et al. 2001. Neural modulation of visuomotor functions underlying prey-catching behaviour in anurans. *Comparative Biochemistry and Physiology A*, 128, 417–61.

Ewing, A.E. & Miyan, J.A. 1986. Sexual selection, sexual isolation and the evolution of song in the *Drosophila repelata* group of species. *Animal Behaviour*, 34, 421–9.

Farmer, C. & Christison, G.I. 1982. Selection of perforated floors by newborn and weanling pigs. *Canadian Journal of Animal Science*, 62, 1229–36.

Feekes, F. 1972. "Irrelevant" ground pecking in agonistic situations in Burmese red junglefowl (*Gallus gallus spadiceus*). *Behaviour*, 43, 186–326.

Felsenstein, J. 1985. Phylogenies and the comparative method. *American Naturalist*, 125, 1–15.

Festa-Bianchet, M. & Apollonio, M. 2003. *Animal Behavior and Wildlife Conservation*. Washington, DC: Island Press.

Fiala, A., Müller, U. & Menzel, R. 1999. Reversible downregulation of protein kinase A during olfactory learning using antisense technique impairs long-term memory formation in the honeybee, *Apis mellifera*. *Journal of Neuroscience*, 19, 10125–34.

Fisher, R.A. 1930. *The Genetical Theory of Natural Selection*. Oxford: Clarendon Press.

Fitch, W.T. 2000. The evolution of speech: a comparative review. *Trends in Cognitive Sciences*, 4, 258–66.

FitzGibbon, C.D. 1998. The management of subsistence harvesting: behavioral ecology of hunters and their mammalian prey. In: T. Caro (ed.), *Behavioral Ecology and Conservation Biology*, pp. 449–73. New York: Oxford University Press.

Fleming, A.S. & Blass, E.M. 1994. Psychobiology of the early mother–young relationship. In: J.A. Hogan & J.J. Bolhuis (eds.), *Causal Mechanisms of Behavioural Development*, pp. 212–41. Cambridge: Cambridge University Press.

Fleming, A.S., Ruble, D., Krieger, H. & Wong, P.Y. 1997. Hormonal and experiential correlates of maternal responsiveness during pregnancy and the puerperium in human mothers. *Hormones and Behavior*, 31, 145–58.

Flinn, M.V. 1981. Uterine vs. agnatic kinship variability and associated cousin marriage preferences: an evolutionary biological analysis. In: R.D. Alexander & D.W. Tinkle (eds.), *Natural Selection and Social Behavior*, pp. 439–75. New York: Chiron Press.

Flinn, M.V. 1988. Step- and genetic parent–offspring relations in a Caribbean village. *Ethology and Sociobiology*, 9, 335–69.

Flinn, M.V. 1997. Culture and the evolution of social learning. *Evolution and Human Behavior*, 18, 23–67.

Flinn, M.V. & England, B.G. 1995. Childhood stress and family environment. *Current Anthropology*, 36, 854–66.

Foley, R. 1996. The adaptive legacy of human evolution: a search for the environment of evolutionary adaptedness. *Evolutionary Anthropology*, 4, 194–203.

Folliard, L.B., Reese, K.P. & Diller, L.V. 2000. Landscape characteristics of Northern Spotted Owl nest sites in managed forests of northwestern California. *Journal of Raptor Research*, 34, 75–84.

Folstad, I. & Karter, A.J. 1992. Parasites, bright males, and the immunocompetence handicap. *American Naturalist*, 139, 603–22.

Fowler, G.S., Wingfield, J.C. & Boersma, P.D. 1995. Hormonal and reproductive effects of low level of petroleum fouling in Magellanic penguins (*Spheniscus magellanicus*). *Auk*, 112, 382–9.

Fox, M.W. (ed.) 1968. *Abnormal Behavior in Animals*. Philadelphia: Saunders.

Fraser, A.F. 1968. *Reproductive Behaviour in Ungulates*. London: Academic Press.

Fraser, A.F. 1974. *Farm Animal Behaviour*. London: Baillière Tindall.

Fraser, A.F. & Broom, D.M. 1997. *Farm Animal Behaviour and Welfare*, 3rd edn. Wallingford, UK: CAB International.

Fraser, D. 1975. Vocalizations of isolated piglets. II. Some environmental factors. *Applied Animal Ethology*, 2, 19–24.

Fraser, D. 1999. Animal ethics and animal welfare science: bridging the two cultures (D.G.M. Wood-Gush Memorial Lecture). *Applied Animal Behaviour Science*, 65, 171–89.

Fraser, D. & Matthews, L.R. 1997. Preference and motivation testing. In: M.C. Appleby & B.O. Hughes (eds.), *Animal Welfare*, pp. 159–73. Wallingford, UK: CAB International.

Fraser, D. & Thomas, E.R. 1982. Moose–vehicle accidents in Ontario: relation to highway salt. *Wildlife Society Bulletin*, 10, 261–5.

Fraser, D., Weary, D.M., Pajor, E.A. & Milligan, B.N. 1997. A scientific conception of animal welfare that reflects ethical concerns. *Animal Welfare*, 6, 187–205.

Freeman, D. 1999. *The Fateful Hoaxing of Margaret Mead*. Boulder, CO: Westview Press.

Fretwell, S.D. 1972. *Populations in a Seasonal Environment*. Princeton, NJ: Princeton University Press.

Freud, S. 1940/1949. *An Outline of Psycho-analysis*. New York: Norton.

Futuyma, D.J. & Mitter, C. 1996. Insect–plant interactions: the evolution of component communities. *Philosophical Transactions of the Royal Society of London Series B*, 351, 1361–6.

Gage, M.J.G. 1995. Continuous variation in reproductive strategy as an adaptive response to population density in the moth *Plodia interpunctella*. *Proceedings of the Royal Society of London Series B*, 261, 25–30.

Galef, B.G. Jr. 1996. Social enhancement of food preferences in Norway rats: a brief review. In: C.M. Heyes & B.G. Galef Jr (eds.), *Social Learning in Animals: The Roots of Culture*, pp. 49–64. New York: Academic Press.

Gallese, V., Fadiga, L., Fogassi, L. & Rizzolatti, G. 1996. Action recognition in the premotor cortex. *Brain*, 119, 593–609.

Gallup, G.G. Jr. 1970. Chimpanzees: self-recognition. *Science*, 167, 341–3.

Gangestad, S.W. 1997. Evolutionary psychology and genetic variation: non-adaptive, fitness-related and adaptive. In: G.R. Bock & G. Cardew (eds.), *Characterizing Human Psychological Adaptations*, pp. 212–30. Chichester: John Wiley & Sons.

Gangestad, S.W. & Simpson, J.A. 2000. The evolution of human mating: trade-offs and strategic pluralism. *Behavioral and Brain Sciences*, 23, 573–624.

Gangestad, S.W. & Thornhill, R. 1998. Menstrual cycle variation in women's preferences for the scent of symmetrical men. *Proceedings of the Royal Society of London Series B*, 265, 927–33.

Garcia, J. & Koelling, R.A. 1966. The relation of cue to consequence in avoidance learning. *Psychonomic Science*, 5, 123–4.

Garshelis, D.L. 2000. Delusions in habitat evaluation: measuring use, selection and importance. In: L. Boitani & T.K. Fuller (eds.), *Research Techniques in Animal Ecology: Controversies and Consequences*, pp. 111–64. New York: Columbia University Press.

Gaulin, S.J.C. & Boster, J.S. 1990. Dowry as female competition. *American Anthropologist*, 92, 994–1005.

Gazzaniga, M.S. (ed.) 2000. *The New Cognitive Neurosciences*. Cambridge, MA: MIT Press.

Geary, D.C. 1998. *Male/Female: The Evolution of Human Sex Differences*. Washington, DC: American Psychological Association.

Gerhardt, H.C. 1981. Mating call recognition in the green tree frog (*Hyla cinerea*). *Journal of Comparative Physiology*, 144, 9–16.

Gerhardt, H.C. & Huber, F. 2002. *Acoustic Communication in Insects and Anurans: Common Problems and Diverse Solutions*. Chicago: Chicago University Press.

Gerkema, M.P., Daan, S., Wilbrink, M., Hop, M.W. & van der Leest, F. 1993. Phase control of ultradian feeding rhythms in the common vole (*Microtus arvalis*): the roles of light and the circadian system. *Journal of Biological Rhythms*, 8, 151–71.

Getty, T. 1998. Reliable signalling need not be a handicap. *Animal Behaviour*, 56, 253–5.

Getty, T. 2002. The discriminating babbler meets the optimal diet hawk. *Animal Behaviour*, 63, 397–402.

Getty, T. & Krebs, J.R. 1985. Lagging partial preferences for cryptic prey: a signal detection analysis of great tit foraging. *American Naturalist*, 125, 39–60.

Gil, D., Graves, J., Hazon, N. & Wells, A. 1999. Male attractiveness and differential testosterone investment in zebra finch eggs. *Science*, 286, 126–8.

Gill, J.A. & Sutherland, W.J. 2000. Predicting the consequences of human disturbance from behavioural decisions. In: L.M. Gosling & W.J. Sutherland (eds.), *Behaviour and Conservation*, pp. 51–64. Cambridge: Cambridge University Press.

Giraldeau, L.-A. & Beauchamp, G. 1999. Food exploitation: searching for the optimal joining policy. *Trends in Ecology and Evolution*, 14, 102–6.

Giraldeau, L.-A. & Caraco, T. 2000. *Social Foraging Theory*. Princeton, NJ: Princeton University Press.

Giraldeau, L.-A. & Kramer, D.L. 1982. The marginal value theorem: a quantitative test using load size variation in a central place forager the eastern chipmunk, *Tamias striatus*. *Animal Behaviour*, 30, 1036–42.

Giraldeau, L.-A. & Livoreil, B. 1998. Game theory and social foraging. In: L.A. Dugatkin & H.K. Reeve (eds.), *Game Theory and Animal Behavior*, pp. 16–37. New York: Oxford University Press.

Giraldeau, L.-A., Kramer, D.L., Deslandes, I. & Lair, H. 1994. The effect of competitors and distance on central place foraging in eastern chipmunks, *Tamias striatus*. *Animal Behaviour*, 47, 621–32.

Gittleman, J.L. & Gompper, M.E. 2001. The risk of extinction: what you don't know will hurt you. *Science*, 291, 997–9.

Goldman, S.A. & Nottebohm, F. 1983. Neuronal production, migration, and differentiation in a vocal control nucleus of the adult female canary brain. *Proceedings of the National Academy of Sciences USA*, 80, 2390–4.

Goldthwaite, R.O., Coss, R.G. & Owings, D.H. 1990. Evolutionary dissipation of an antisnake system: differential behaviour by California and Arctic ground squirrels in above- and below-ground contexts. *Behaviour*, 112, 246–69.

Goodall, J. 1971. *In the Shadow of Man*. London: Collins.

Gorman, M., Borman, B.D. & Zucker, I. 2001. Mammalian photoperiodism. In: J.S. Takahashi, F.W. Turek & R.Y. Moore (eds.), *Circadian Clocks. Handbook of Behavioral Neurobiology*, vol. 12, pp. 481–510. New York: Kluwer Academic/Plenum.

Gosling, L.M. & Sutherland, W.J. (eds.) 2000. *Behaviour and Conservation*. Cambridge: Cambridge University Press.

Goss-Custard, J.D. & Sutherland, W.J. 1997. Individual behaviour, populations and conservation. In: J.R. Krebs & N.B. Davies (eds.), *Behavioural Ecology: An Evolutionary Approach*, 4th edn, pp. 373–95. Oxford: Blackwell Science.

Goss-Custard, J.D., Caldow, R.W.G., Clarke, R.T., Durell, S.E.A.Le V. dit, Urfi, J. & West, A.D. 1995a. Consequences of habitat loss and change to populations of wintering migratory birds: predicting the local and global effects from studies of individuals. *Ibis*, 137, S56–S66.

Goss-Custard, J.D., Clarke, R.T., Durell, S.E.A.Le V. dit, Caldow, R.W.G. & Ens, B.J. 1995b. Population consequences of winter habitat loss in a migratory shorebird. II. Model predictions. *Journal of Applied Ecology*, 32, 337–51.

Gottlieb, G. 1976. The roles of experience in the development of behavior and the nervous system. In: G. Gottlieb (ed.), *Neural and Behavioral Specificity: Studies in the Development of Behavior and the Nervous System*, pp. 237–80. New York: Academic Press.

Gottlieb, G. 1980. Development of species identification in ducklings: VI. Specific embryonic experience required to maintain species-typical perception in Peking ducklings. *Journal of Comparative and Physiological Psychology*, 94, 579–87.

Gottlieb, G. 2002a. On the epigenetic evolution of species specific perception: the developmental manifold concept. *Cognitive Development*, 17, 1287–300.

Gottlieb, G. 2002b. *Individual Development and Evolution: The Genesis of Novel Behavior*. Mahwah, NJ: Erlbaum.

Gould, E., Tanapat, P., Hastings, N.B. & Shors, T.J. 1999. Neurogenesis in adulthood: a possible role in learning. *Trends in Cognitive Sciences*, 3, 186–92.

Gould, S.J. & Lewontin, R.C. 1979. The spandrels of San Marco and the Panglossian paradigm: a critique of the adaptationist programme. *Proceedings of the Royal Society of London Series B*, 205, 581–98.

Grafe, T.U. 2004. Anuran choruses as communication networks. In: P.K. McGregor (ed.), *Animal Communication Networks*, pp. 617–70. Cambridge: Cambridge University Press.

Grandin, T. (ed.) 2000. *Livestock Handling and Transport*, 2nd edn. Wallingford, UK: CAB International.

Grant, D.S. 1976. Effect of sample presentation time on long-delay matching in the pigeon. *Learning and Motivation*, 7, 580–90.

Greene, C.M. & Stamps, J.A. 2001. Habitat selection at low population densities. *Ecology*, 82, 2091–100.

Greene, C., Umbanhowar, J., Mangel, M. & Caro, T. 1998. Animal breeding systems, hunter selectivity, and consumptive use in wildlife conservation. In: T. Caro (ed.), *Behavioral Ecology and Conservation Biology*, pp. 271–305. New York: Oxford University Press.

Greene, H.W. 1994. Homology and behavioral repertoires. In: B.K. Hall (ed.), *Homology: The Hierarchical Basis of Comparative Biology*, pp. 369–92. San Diego: Academic Press.

Greenfield, M.D. 2002. *Signalers and Receivers: Mechanisms and Evolution of Arthropod Communication.* Oxford: Oxford University Press.

Greenough, W.T., Black, J.E. & Wallace, C.S. 1987. Experience and brain development. *Child Development*, 58, 539–59.

Greenwood, P.J. 1980. Mating systems, philopatry, and dispersal in birds and mammals. *Animal Behaviour*, 28, 1140–62.

Greiling, H. & Buss, D.M. 2000. Women's sexual strategies: the hidden dimension of extra-pair mating. *Personality and Individual Differences*, 28, 929–63.

Griffin, A.S., Blumstein, D.T. & Evans, C.S. 2000. Training captive-bred or translocated animals to avoid predators. *Conservation Biology*, 14, 1317–26.

Griffin, A.S., Evans, C.S. & Blumstein, D.T. 2001. Learning specificity in acquired predator recognition. *Animal Behaviour*, 62, 577–89.

Griffin, D.R. 2001. *Animal Minds: Beyond Cognition to Consciousness*, 2nd edn. Chicago: Chicago University Press.

Grobstein, P. 1991. Directed movement in the frog: a closer look at a central representation of spacial location. In: M.A. Arbib & J.-P. Ewert (eds.), *Visual Structures and Integrated Functions*, pp. 125–38. Berlin: Springer.

Gros, P.M., Kelly, M.J. & Caro, T.M. 1996. Estimating carnivore densities for conservation purposes: indirect methods compared to baseline demographic data. *Oikos*, 77, 197–206.

Gross, M.R. 1985. Disruptive selection for alternative life histories in salmon. *Nature*, 313, 47–8.

Gross, M.R. 1991. Salmon breeding behavior and life history evolution in changing environments. *Ecology*, 72, 1180–6.

Grunau, R.V.E. & Craig, K.D. 1987. Pain expression in neonates: facial action and cry. *Pain*, 28, 395–410.

Gwinner, E. & Brandstatter, R. 2001. Complex bird clocks. *Philosophical Transactions of the Royal Society of London Series B*, 356, 1801–10.

Hafez, E.S.E. (ed.) 1962. *The Behaviour of Domestic Animals.* Baltimore: Williams & Wilkins.

Hall, G. 1979. Exposure learning in young and adult laboratory rats. *Animal Behaviour*, 27, 586–91.

Hall, G. 1994. Pavlovian conditioning: laws of association. In: N.J. Mackintosh (ed.), *Animal Learning and Cognition. Handbook of Perception and Cognition*, vol. 9, pp. 15–43. San Diego: Academic Press.

Hall, L.S., Krausman, P.R. & Morrison, M.L. 1997. The habitat concept and a plea for standard terminology. *Wildlife Society Bulletin*, 25, 173–82.

Hall, W.G. 1979. Feeding and behavioral activation in infant rats. *Science*, 190, 1313–15.

Hall, W.G. & Williams, C.L. 1983. Suckling isn't feeding, or is it? A search for developmental continuities. *Advances in the Study of Behavior*, 13, 219–54.

Hames, R.B. 1987. Relatedness and garden labor exchange among the Ye'kwana. *Ethology and Sociobiology*, 8, 354–92.

Hamilton, W.D. 1964. The genetical evolution of social behavior. *Journal of Theoretical Biology*, 7, 1–51.

Hamilton, W.D. 1971. Geometry for the selfish herd. *Journal of Theoretical Biology*, 31, 295–311.

Hamilton, W.D. & Zuk, M. 1982. Heritable true fitness and bright birds: a role for parasites? *Science*, 218, 384–7.

Hammerstein, P. 1981. The role of asymmetries in animal contests. *Animal Behaviour*, 29, 193–205.

Hansen, K. 1984. Discrimination and production of disparlure enantiomers by the gypsy moth and the nun moth. *Physiological Entomology*, 9, 9–18.

Hanski, I. 1998. Metapopulation dynamics. *Nature*, 396, 41–9.

Harcourt, A.H. 1998. Ecological indicators of risk for primates, as judged by species' susceptibility to logging. In: T. Caro (ed.), *Behavioral Ecology and Conservation Biology*, pp. 56–79. New York: Oxford University Press.

Harcourt, A.H., Harvey, P.H., Larson, S.G. & Short, R.V. 1981. Testis weight, body weight and breeding season in primates. *Nature*, 293, 55–7.

Harcourt, A.H., Purvis, A. & Liles, L. 1996. Sperm competition: mating system, not breeding season, affects testes size of primates. *Functional Ecology*, 9, 468–76.

Hare, B. & Tomasello, M. 1999. Domestic dogs (*Canis familiaris*) use human and conspecific social cues to locate hidden food. *Journal of Comparative Psychology*, 113, 173–7.

Hare, B., Call, J. & Tomasello, M. 2001. Do chimpanzees know what conspecifics know? *Animal Behaviour*, 61, 139–51.

Harlow, H.F. 1950. Learning and satiation of response in intrinsically motivated complex puzzle performance by monkeys. *Journal of Comparative and Physiological Psychology*, 43, 289–94.

Harlow, H.F. 1958. The nature of love. *American Psychologist*, 13, 573–685.

Harlow, H.F. & Harlow, M.K. 1962. Social deprivation in monkeys. *Scientific American*, 207, 136–46.

Harnad, S. 1987. Category induction and representation. In: S. Harnad (ed.), *Categorial Perception: The Groundwork of Cognition*, pp. 535–65. Cambridge: Cambridge University Press.

Harper, D.G.C. 1982. Competitive foraging in mallards: "ideal free" ducks. *Animal Behaviour*, 30, 575–84.

Harper, D.N., McLean, A.P. & Dalrymple-Alford, J.C. 1993. List item memory in rats: effects of delay and task. *Journal of Experimental Psychology: Animal Behavior Processes*, 19, 307–16.

Harrison, R. 1964. *Animal Machines*. London: Vincent Stuart.

Hartiline, H.K. & Ratliff, E. 1957. Inhibitory interaction of receptor units in the eye of *Limulus*. *Journal of General Physiology*, 40, 357–76.

Harvey, P.H. & May, R.M. 1989. Out for the sperm count. *Nature*, 337, 508–9.

Harvey, P.H. & Pagel, M.D. 1991. *The Comparative Method in Evolutionary Biology*. Oxford: Oxford University Press.

Hauser, M.D. 1996. *The Evolution of Communication*. Cambridge, MA: MIT Press.

Hauser, M.D. & Konishi, M. (eds.) 1999. *The Design of Animal Communication*. Cambridge, MA: MIT Press.

Hebb, D.O. 1946. On the nature of fear. *Psychological Review*, 53, 259–76.

Hebb, D.O. 1949. *The Organization of Behavior: A Neuropsychological Theory*. New York: John Wiley & Sons.

Hediger, H. 1950. *Wild Animals in Captivity* (translated by G. Sircom). London: Butterworth.

Heiligenberg, W. 1974. Processes governing behavioral states of readiness. *Advances in the Study of Behavior*, 5, 173–200.

Heiligenberg, W. & Rose, G. 1985. Neural correlates of the jamming avoidance response (JAR) in the weakly electric fish *Eigenmannia*. *Trends in Neurosciences*, 8, 442–9.

Heinrich, B. 1996. An experimental investigation of insight in common ravens, *Corvus corax. Auk*, 112, 994–1003.

Hemsworth, P.H. & Coleman, G.J. 1998. *Human–Livestock Interactions: The Stockperson and the Productivity and Welfare of Intensively Farmed Animals*. London: CAB International.

Herman, L.M., Richards, D.G. & Wolz, J.P. 1984. Comprehension of sentences by bottlenosed dolphins. *Cognition*, 16, 129–219.

Heyes, C.M. 1994. Reflections of self-recognition in primates. *Animal Behaviour*, 47, 909–19.

Hinde, R.A. 1954. Changes in responsiveness to a constant stimulus. *Behaviour*, 2, 41–54.

Hinde, R.A. 1960. Energy models of motivation. *Symposia of the Society for Experimental Biology*, 14, 199–213.

Hinde, R.A. 1970. *Animal Behaviour: A Synthesis of Ethology and Comparative Psychology*, 2nd edn. New York: McGraw-Hill.

Hinde, R.A. 1977. Mother–infant separation and the nature of inter-individual relationships: experiments with rhesus monkeys. *Proceedings of the Royal Society of London Series B*, 196, 29–50.

Hinde, R.A. & Bateson, P. 1984. Discontinuities versus continuities in behavioural development and the neglect of process. *International Journal of Behavioral Development*, 7, 129–43.

Hines, M. 2002. Sexual differentiation of human brain and behavior. In: D.W. Pfaff, A.P. Arnold, A.M. Etgen, S.E. Fahrbach & R.T. Rubin (eds.), *Hormones, Brain and Behavior*, vol. 4, pp. 425–62. San Diego: Academic Press.

Hirshleifer, J. 1999. There are many evolutionary pathways to cooperation. *Journal of Bioeconomics*, 1, 73–93.

Hobbs, R.J. 1992. The role of corridors in conservation: solution or bandwagon. *Trends in Ecology and Evolution*, 7, 389–92.

Hobson, K.A., Bouchart, M.L. & Sealy, G.S. 1988. Responses of naive yellow warblers to a novel test predator. *Animal Behaviour*, 36, 1823–30.

Hogan, J.A. 1965. An experimental study of conflict and fear: an analysis of behavior of young chicks toward a mealworm. Part I. The behavior of chicks which do not eat the mealworm. *Behaviour*, 25, 45–97.

Hogan, J.A. 1971. The development of a hunger system in young chicks. *Behaviour*, 39, 128–201.

Hogan, J.A. 1984. Pecking and feeding in chicks. *Learning and Motivation*, 15, 360–76.

Hogan, J.A. 1988. Cause and function in the development of behavior systems. In: E.M. Blass (ed.), *Handbook of Behavioral Neurobiology*, vol. 9, pp. 63–106. New York: Plenum Press.

Hogan, J.A. 1994. The concept of cause in the study of behaviour. In: J.A. Hogan & J.J. Bolhuis (eds.), *Causal Mechanisms of Behavioural Development*, pp. 3–15. Cambridge: Cambridge University Press.

Hogan, J.A. 1997. Energy models of motivation: a reconsideration. *Applied Animal Behaviour Science*, 53, 89–105.

Hogan, J.A. 1998. Motivation. In: G. Greenberg & M.M. Haraway (eds.), *Comparative Psychology: A Handbook*, pp. 164–75. New York: Garland.

Hogan, J.A. 2001. Development of behavior systems. In: E.M. Blass (ed.), *Handbook of Behavioral Neurobiology*, vol. 13, pp. 229–79. New York: Kluwer Academic/Plenum.

Hogan, J.A. & Bolhuis, J.J. (eds.) 1994. *Causal Mechanisms of Behavioural Development*. Cambridge: Cambridge University Press.

Hogan, J.A. & Bols, R.J. 1980. Priming of aggressive motivation in *Betta splendens*. *Animal Behaviour*, 28, 135–42.

Hogan, J.A. & Roper, T.J. 1978. A comparison of the properties of different reinforcers. *Advances in the Study of Behavior*, 8, 155–255.

Holland, B. & Rice, W.R. 1998. Chase-away sexual selection: antagonistic seduction versus resistance. *Evolution*, 52, 1–7.

Holland, B. & Rice, W.R. 1999. Experimental removal of sexual selection reverses intersexual antagonistic coevolution and removes a reproductive load. *Proceedings of the National Academy of Sciences USA*, 96, 5083–8.

Holland, P.C. & Straub, J.J. 1979. Differential effects of two ways of devaluing the unconditioned stimulus after Pavlovian appetitive training. *Journal of Experimental Psychology: Animal Behavior Processes*, 5, 65–78.

Hölldobler, B. 1999. Multimodal signals in ant communication. *Journal of Comparative Physiology A*, 184, 129–41.

Holmes, W.G. & Sherman, P.W. 1982. The ontogeny of kin recognition in two species of ground squirrels. *American Zoologist*, 22, 491–517.

Hoogland, J. 1998. Why do female Gunnison prairie dogs copulate with more than one male? *Animal Behaviour*, 55, 351–9.

Horn, G. 1985. *Memory, Imprinting, and the Brain*. Oxford: Clarendon Press.

Horn, G. 1998. Visual imprinting and the neural mechanisms of recognition memory. *Trends in Neurosciences*, 21, 300–5.

Hose, J.E. & Guillette, L.J. 1995. Defining the role of pollutants in the disruption of reproduction in wildlife. *Environmental Health Perspectives*, 103, 87–91.

Houck, L.D. & Drickamer, L.C. (eds.) 1996. *Foundations of Animal Behaviour: Classic Papers with Commentaries*. Chicago: University of Chicago Press.

Houde, A.E. 1997. *Sex, Color and Mate Choice in Guppies*. Princeton, NJ: Princeton University Press.

Houpt, K.A. 1998. *Domestic Animal Behavior for Veterinarians and Animal Scientists*, 3rd edn. Ames: Iowa State University Press.

Houpt, K.A. & Wolski, T.R. 1982. *Domestic Animal Behavior for Veterinarians and Animal Scientists*. Ames: Iowa State University Press.

Hubel, D.H. & Livingstone, M.S. 1987. Segregation of form, colour, and stereopsis in primate area 18. *Journal of Neuroscience*, 7, 3378–415.

Hubel, D.H. & Wiesel, T.N. 1977. Functional architecture of macaque monkey visual cortex. *Proceedings of the Royal Society of London B*, 198, 1–59.

Humphrey, G. 1933. *The Nature of Learning*. London: Kegan Paul.

Humphrey, N.K. 1976. The social function of intellect. In: P.P.G. Bateson & R.A. Hinde (eds.), *Growing Points in Ethology*, pp. 303–17. Cambridge: Cambridge University Press.

Hunt, G.R. 1996. Manufacture and use of hook-tools by New Caledonian crows. *Nature*, 379, 249–51.

Hunter, W.S. 1913. The delayed reaction in animals and children. *Behavior Monographs*, 2, 1–86.

Huxley, J. 1914. The courtship habits of the great crested grebe *Porpodiceps cristatus*. *Proceedings of the Zoological Society of London*, 2, 491–562.

Inglis, I.R. 2000. The central role of uncertainty reduction in determining behaviour. *Behaviour*, 137, 1567–99.

Irons, W. 1979. Cultural and biological success. In: N.A. Chagnon & W. Irons (eds.), *Evolutionary Biology and Human Social Behavior: An Anthropological Perspective*, pp. 257–72. North Scituate, MA: Duxbury Press.

Irons, W. 1998. Adaptively relevant environments versus the environment of evolutionary adaptedness. *Evolutionary Anthropology*, 6, 194–204.

Ishai, A. & Sagi, D. 1995. Common mechanisms of visual imagery and perception. *Science*, 268, 1719–20.

Janetos, A.C. 1980. Strategies for female mate choice: a theoretical analysis. *Behavioral Ecology and Sociobiology*, 7, 107–12.

Jarman, P.J. 1974. The social organization of antelope in relation to their ecology. *Behaviour*, 48, 215–56.

Jarman, P.J. 1989. On being thick-skinned: dermal shields in large mammalian herbivores. *Biological Journal of the Linnean Society*, 36, 169–91.

Jarvis, E.D. & Nottebohm, F. 1997. Motor-driven gene expression. *Proceedings of the National Academy of Sciences USA*, 94, 4097–102.

Jeannerod, M., Arbib, M.A., Rizzolatti, G. & Sakata, H. 1995. Grasping objects: the cortical mechanism of visuomotor transformation. *Trends in Neurosciences*, 18, 314–20.

Jeffress, L.A. 1948. A place theory of sound localization. *Journal of Comparative and Physiological Psychology*, 41, 35–9.

Jeffries, D.S. & Brunton, D.H. 2001. Attracting endangered species to "safe" habitats: responses of fairy wrens to decoys. *Animal Conservation*, 4, 301–5.

Jellema, T., Baker, C.I., Wicker, B. & Perrett, D.I. 2000. Neural representation for the perception of the intentionality of actions. *Brain and Cognition*, 44, 280–302.

Jennions, M.D. & Petrie, M. 2000. Why do females mate multiply? A review of the genetic benefits. *Biological Reviews*, 75, 21–64.

Jennions, M.D., Møller, A.P. & Petrie, M. 2001. Sexually selected traits and adult survival: a meta-analysis of the phenotypic relationship. *Quarterly Review of Biology*, 76, 3–36.

Jensen, P. 1986. Observations on the maternal behaviour of free-ranging domestic pigs. *Applied Animal Behaviour Science*, 16, 131–42.

Jensen, P. (ed.) 2002. *The Ethology of Domestic Animals: An Introductory Text*. Wallingford, UK: CAB International.

Johnsingh, A.J.T., Narenda Prasad, S. & Goyal, S.P. 1990. Conservation status of the Chila-Motichur corridor for elephant movement in Rajaji-Corbett National Parks area, India. *Biological Conservation*, 51, 125–38.

Johnson, K.P., McKinney, F., Wilson, R. & Sorenson, M.D. 2000. The evolution of postcopulatory displays in dabbling ducks (Anatini): a phylogenetic perspective. *Animal Behaviour*, 59, 953–63.

Johnson, M.H. 1997. *Developmental Cognitive Neuroscience: An Introduction*. Oxford: Blackwell Publishers.

Johnson, M.H. & Horn, G. 1988. Development of filial preferences in dark-reared chicks. *Animal Behaviour*, 36, 675–83.

Johnson, M.H. & Morton, J. 1991. *Biology and Cognitive Development: The Case of Face Recognition*. Oxford: Blackwell Publishers.

Johnson, M.H., Bolhuis, J.J. & Horn, G. 1985. Interaction between acquired preferences and developing predispositions during imprinting. *Animal Behaviour*, 33, 1000–6.

Johnson, M.H., Davies, D.C. & Horn, G. 1989. A sensitive period for the development of a predisposition in dark-reared chicks. *Animal Behaviour*, 37, 1044–6.

Johnson, M.H., Munakata, Y. & Gilmore, R.O. 2002. *Brain Development and Cognition: A Reader*, 2nd edn. Oxford: Blackwell Publishers.

Johnstone, R.A. 1997. The evolution of animal signals. In: J.R. Krebs & N.B. Davies (eds.), *Behavioural Ecology: An Evolutionary Approach*, pp. 155–78. Oxford: Blackwell Scientific Publications.

Johnstone, R.A. 2000. Models of reproductive skew: a review and synthesis. *Ethology*, 106, 5–26.

Jones, T.M. 2001. A potential cost of monandry in the lekking sandfly *Lutzomyia longipalpis*. *Journal of Insect Behavior*, 14, 385–99.

Kaas, J.H. 1991. Plasticity of sensory and motor maps in adult mammals. *Annual Review of Neuroscience*, 14, 137–67.

Kafka, W.A. 1970. Molekulare Wechselwirkungen bei der Erregung einzelner Riechzellen. *Zeitschrift für Vergleichende Physiologie*, 70, 105–43.

Kaissling, K.E. 1987. *R.H. Wright Lectures on Insect Olfaction* (K. Colbow ed.), pp. 1–190. Burnaby, BC: Simon Fraser University.

Kamil, A.C. & Cheng, K. 2001. Way-finding and landmarks: the multiple-bearings hypothesis. *Journal of Experimental Biology*, 204, 101–13.

Kamin, L.J. 1968. "Attention-like" processes in classical conditioning. In: M.R. Jones (ed.), *Miami Symposium on the Prediction of Behavior: Aversive Stimulation*, pp. 9–33. Miami: University of Miami Press.

Kaplan, H. & Hill, K. 1992. The evolutionary ecology of food acquisition. In: E.A. Smith & B. Winterhalder (eds.), *Evolutionary Ecology and Human Behavior*, pp. 167–201. Hawthorne, NY: Aldine de Gruyter.

Kapsalis, E. & Berman, C.M. 1996. Models of affiliative relationships among free-ranging rhesus monkeys (*Macaca mulatta*) I. Criteria for kinship. *Behaviour*, 133, 1209–34.

Kastner, S., De Weerd, P., Desimone, R. & Ungerleider, L.G. 1998. Mechanisms of directed attention in the human extrastriate cortex as revealed by functional MRI. *Science*, 282, 108–11.

Keller, L. & Reeve, H.K. 1994a. Genetic variability, queen number, and polyandry in social hymenoptera. *Evolution*, 48, 694–704.

Keller, L. & Reeve, H.K. 1994b. Partitioning of reproduction in animal societies. *Trends in Ecology and Evolution*, 12, 99–102.

Kempenaers, B., Verheyen, G.R., Van den Broeck, M., Burke, T., van Broekhoven, C. & Dhondt, A.A. 1992. Extra-pair paternity results from female preference for high-quality males in the blue tit. *Nature*, 357, 494–6.

Kendrick, K.M. 1994. Neurobiological correlates of visual and olfactory recognition in sheep. *Behavioral Processes*, 33, 89–112.

Kennedy, M. & Gray, R.D. 1993. Can ecological theory predict the distribution of foraging animals? A critical evaluation of experiments on the ideal free distribution. *Oikos*, 68, 158–66.

Kepler, C.B. 1977. Captive propagation of whooping cranes: a behavioral approach. In: S.A. Temple (ed.), *Endangered Birds: Management Techniques for Preserving Threatened Species*, pp. 231–41. Wisconsin: University of Wisconsin Press.

Kessel, E.L. 1955. The mating activities of balloon. *Systematic Zoology*, 4, 97–104.

Kilgour, R. & Dalton, C. 1984. *Livestock Behaviour: A Practical Guide*. Boulder, CO: Westview Press.

Kim, J.H., Udo, H., Li, H.L. et al. 2003. Presynaptic activation of silent synapses and growth of new synapses contribute to intermediate and long-term facilitation in *Aplysia*. *Neuron*, 25, 151–65.

Kirkwood, J.K., Hubrecht, R.C., Wickens, S., O'Leary, H. & Oakeley, S. (eds.) 2001. *Consciousness, Cognition and Animal Welfare*. Supplement to *Animal Welfare*, vol. 10. Wheathampstead, UK: Universities Federation for Animal Welfare.

Kitchen, D.M. & Packer, C. 1999. Complexity in vertebrate societies. In: L. Keller (ed.), *Levels of Selection in Evolution*, pp. 176–96. Princeton, NJ: Princeton University Press.

Kleiman, D.G. 1989. Reintroduction of captive mammals for conservation. *BioScience*, 39, 152–61.

Klein, D.C., Moore, R.Y. & Reppert, S.M. 1991. *Suprachiasmatic Nucleus: The Mind's Clock*. New York: Oxford University Press.

Kleitman, N. 1963. *Sleep and Wakefulness*. Chicago: University of Chicago Press.

Kleitman, N. 1993. Basic rest–activity cycle. In: M.A. Carskadon (ed.), *Encyclopedia of Sleep and Dreaming*, pp. 65–6. New York: Macmillan.

Klitzman, R.L., Alpers, M.P. & Gajdusek, D.C. 1984. The natural incubation period of kuru and the episodes of transmission in three clusters of patients. *Neuroepidemiology*, 3, 3–20.

Klump, G.M., Kretzschmar, E. & Curio, E. 1986. The hearing of an avian predator and its avian prey. *Behavioral Ecology and Sociobiology*, 18, 317–23.

Knapp, R.A. & Kovach, J.T. 1991. Courtship as an honest indicator of male parental quality in the bicolor damselfish, *Stegastes partitus*. *Behavioral Ecology*, 2, 295–300.

Köhler, W. 1925. *The Mentality of Apes*. London: Routledge & Kegan Paul (original work published in 1917, English translation by E. Winter 1925).

Kokko, H. & Sutherland, W.J. 2001. Ecological traps in changing environments: ecological and evolutionary consequences of a behaviourally mediated Allee effect. *Evolutionary Ecology Research*, 3, 537–51.

Kokko, H., Johnstone, R.A. & Clutton-Brock, T.H. 2001. The evolution of cooperative breeding through group augmentation. *Proceedings of the Royal Society of London Series B*, 268, 187–96.

Konishi, M. 1993. Listening with two ears. *Scientific American*, 268, 66–73.

Konishi, M. 1995. Neural mechanisms of auditory image formation. In: M.S. Gazzaniga (ed.), *The Cognitive Neurosciences*, pp. 269–77. Cambridge, MA: MIT Press.

Köppl, C., Manley, G.A. & Konishi, M. 2000. Auditory processing in birds. *Current Opinion in Neurobiology*, 10, 474–81.

Kortlandt, A. 1940. Wechselwirkung zwischen Instinkten. *Archives Néerlandaises de Zoologie*, 4, 443–520.

Kosslyn, S.M., Pascual-Leone, A., Felician, O. et al. 1999. The role of area 17 in visual imagery: convergent evidence from PET and rTMS. *Science*, 284, 167–70.

Kotiaho, J.S., Alatalo, R.V., Mappes, J. & Parri, S. 1999. Sexual signalling and viability in a wolf spider (*Hygrolycosa rubrofasciata*): measurements under laboratory and field conditions. *Behavioral Ecology and Sociobiology*, 46, 123–8.

Krebs, C.T. & Burns, K.A. 1977. Long-term effects of an oil-spill on populations of the salt-marsh crab *Uca pugnax*. *Science*, 179, 484–7.

Krebs, J.R. 1978. Optimal foraging: decision rules for predators. In: J.R. Krebs & N.B. Davies (eds.), *Behavioural Ecology: An Evolutionary Approach*, pp. 23–63. Sunderland, MA: Sinauer.

Krebs, J.R. & Davies, N.B. (eds.) 1978. *Behavioural Ecology: An Evolutionary Approach*. Sunderland, MA: Sinauer.

Krebs, J.R. & Davies, N.B. 1993. *An Introduction to Behavioural Ecology*. Oxford: Blackwell Scientific Publications.

Krebs, J.R. & Davies, N.B. (eds.) 1997. *Behavioural Ecology: An Evolutionary Approach*, 4th edn. Oxford: Blackwell Science.

Krebs, J.R., Erichsen, J.T., Webber, M.I. & Charnov, E.L. 1977. Optimal prey-selection by the great tit (*Parus major*). *Animal Behaviour*, 25, 30–8.

Kroodsma, D.E. & Miller, E.H. 1996. *Ecology and Evolution of Acoustic Communication in Birds*. Ithaca, NY: Cornell University Press.

Kruijt, J.P. 1964. Ontogeny of social behaviour in Burmese red junglefowl (*Gallus gallus spadiceus*). *Behaviour*, Suppl. 9, 1–201.

Kruijt, J.P. & Meeuwissen, G.B. 1991. Sexual preferences of male zebra finches: effects of early and adult experience. *Animal Behaviour*, 42, 91–102.

Kupfermann, I. & Weiss, K.R. 1978. The command neuron concept. *Behavior and Brain Sciences*, 1, 3–39.

Kuussaari, M., Saccheri, I., Camara, M. & Hanski, I. 1998. Allee effect and population dynamics in the Glanville fritillary butterfly. *Oikos*, 82, 384–92.

Lack, D. 1968. *Ecological Adaptations for Breeding Birds*. London: Methuen.

Lagerspetz, K. 1964. Studies on the aggressive behaviour of mice. *Annales Academiae Scientiarum Fennicae, Series B*, 131, 1–131.

Laland, K.N. & Brown, G.R. 2002. *Sense and Nonsense: Evolutionary Perspectives on Human Behaviour*. Oxford: Oxford University Press.

Lalumière, M.L., Harris, G.T. & Rice, M.E. 2001. Psychopathy and developmental instability. *Evolution and Human Behavior*, 22, 75–92.

Lam, R. 1998. *Seasonal Affective Disorder and Beyond. Light Treatment for SAD and Non-SAD Conditions*. Washington, DC: American Psychiatric Press.

Lande, R. 1982. Rapid origin of sexual isolation and character divergence in a cline. *Evolution*, 36, 213–23.

Langemann, U. & Klump, G.M. 2004. Perception and acoustic communication networks. In: P.K. McGregor (ed.), *Animal Communication Networks*, pp. 1003–64. Cambridge: Cambridge University Press.

Langley, C.M., Riley, D.A., Bond, A.B. & Goel, N. 1996. Visual search and natural grains in pigeons (*Columba livia*): search images and selective attention: *Journal of Experimental Psychology: Animal Behavior Processes*, 22, 139–51.

Lashley, K.S. 1929. *Brain Mechanisms and Intelligence.* Chicago: University of Chicago Press.

Lashley, K.S. 1938. Experimental analysis of instinctive behavior. *Psychological Review*, 45, 445–71.

Lawrence, A.B. & Rushen, J. (eds.) 1993. *Stereotypic Animal Behaviour: Fundamentals and Applications to Welfare.* Wallingford, UK: CAB International.

Lazarus, J. 2002. Human sex ratios: adaptations and mechanisms, problems and prospects. In: I.C.W. Hardy (ed.), *Sex Ratios: Concepts and Research Methods*, pp. 287–311. Cambridge: Cambridge University Press.

LeBoeuf, B.J. & Briggs, K.T. 1977. The costs of living in a seal harem. *Mammalia*, 41, 167–95.

Lee, S.-H. & Blake, R. 1999. Visual form created solely from temporal structure. *Science*, 284, 1165–8.

Lehrman, D.S. 1953. A critique of Konrad Lorenz's theory of instinctive behavior. *Quarterly Review of Biology*, 28, 337–63.

Lehrman, D.S. 1955. The physiological basis of parental feeding behaviour in the ring dove (*Streptopelia risoria*). *Behaviour*, 7, 241–86.

Lehrman, D.S. 1965. Interaction between internal and external environments in the regulation of the reproductive cycle of the ring dove. In: F.A. Beach (ed.), *Sex and Behavior*, pp. 355–80. New York: John Wiley & Sons.

Lehrman, D.S. 1970. Semantic and conceptual issues in the nature–nurture problem. In: L.R. Aronson, E. Tobach, D.S. Lehrman & J.S. Rosenblatt (eds.), *Development and Evolution of Behavior*, pp. 17–52. San Francisco: Freeman.

Lettvin, J.Y., Maturana, H.R., McCulloch, W.S. & Pitts, W.H. 1959. What the frog's eye tells the frog's brain. *Proceedings of the Institute for Radio Engineering*, 47, 1940–51.

Levy, D.M. 1944. On the problem of movement restraint: tics, stereotyped movements, hyperactivity. *American Journal of Orthopsychiatry*, 14, 644–71.

Lewis, D.J. 1979. Psychobiology of active and inactive memory. *Psychological Bulletin*, 86, 1054–83.

Lima, S.L. 1989. Iterated prisoner's dilemma: an approach to evolutionarily stable cooperation. *American Naturalist*, 134, 828–44.

Little, A.C., Burt, D.M., Penton-Voak, I.S. & Perrett, D.I. 2001. Self-perceived attractiveness influences human female preferences for sexual dimorphism and symmetry in male faces. *Proceedings of the Royal Society of London Series B*, 268, 39–44.

Little, A.C., Jones, B.C., Penton-Voak, I.S., Burt, D.M. & Perrett, D.I. 2002. Partnership status and the temporal context of relationships influence female preferences for sexual dimorphism in male face shape. *Proceedings of the Royal Society of London Series B*, 269, 1095–100.

Little, E.E., Fairchild, J.F. & DeLonay, A.J. 1993. Behavioral methods for assessing impacts of contaminants on early life stage fishes. *American Fisheries Society Symposium*, 14, 67–76.

Lloyd, J.E. 1984. On deception, a way of all flesh, and firefly signalling and systematics. *Oxford Surveys in Evolutionary Biology*, 1, 48–84.

Lockard, J.S. & Paulhus, D.L. (eds.) 1988. *Self-deception: An Adaptive Mechanism?* Englewood Cliffs, NJ: Prentice Hall.

Lohmann, K.J., Cain, S.D., Dodge, S.A. & Lohmann, C.M.F. 2001. Regional magnetic fields as navigational markers for sea turtles. *Science*, 294, 364–6.

Lorenz, K. 1935. Der Kumpan in der Umwelt des Vogels. *Journal für Ornithologie*, 83, 137–213, 289–413.

Lorenz, K. 1937a. The companion in the bird's world. *Auk*, 54, 245–73.

Lorenz, K. 1937b. Uber die Bildung des Instinkbegriffes. *Naturwissenschaften*, 25, 289–300, 307–18, 324–31.

Lorenz, K. 1950. The comparative method in studying innate behaviour patterns. *Symposia of the Society for Experimental Biology*, 4, 221–68.

Lorenz, K. 1965. *Evolution and Modification of Behavior*. Chicago: University of Chicago Press.

Lorenz, K. 1966. *On Aggression*. London: Methuen.

Lorenz, K. 1967. The evolution of behavior. In: J.L. McGaugh, N.M. Weinberger & R.E. Whalen (eds.), *Psychobiology: The Biological Bases of Behavior. Readings from Scientific American*, pp. 33–42. San Francisco: W.H. Freeman.

Lorenz, K. 1971. Comparative studies of the motor patterns of Anatinae. In: *Studies on Animal and Human Behavior, vol. 2* (translated by R. Martin), pp. 14–114. London: Methuen.

Low, B.S. 2000. *Why Sex Matters*. Princeton, NJ: Princeton University Press.

Luchin, A.S. 1942. Mechanization in problem solving. *Psychological Monographs*, 45, no. 28.

Macaluso, E., Frith, C.D. & Driver, J. 2000. Modulation of human visual cortex by crossmodal spatial attention. *Science*, 289, 1206–8.

MacArthur, R.H. & Pianka, E.R. 1996. On optimal use of a patchy environment. *American Naturalist*, 100, 603–9.

McCabe, K., Hoffman, E. & Smith, V.L. 1998. Behavioral foundations of reciprocity: experimental economics and evolutionary psychology. *Economic Inquiry*, 36, 335–52.

McClean, S.A., Rumble, M.A., King, R.M. & Baker, W.L. 1998. Evaluation of resource selection methods with different definitions of availability. *Journal of Wildlife Management*, 62, 793–801.

McFarland, D.J. 1974. Time-sharing as a behavioral phenomenon. *Advances in the Study of Behavior*, 5, 201–25.

McFarland, D.J. & Houston, A. 1981. *Quantitative Ethology: The State Space Approach*. London: Pitman.

McGregor, P.K. (ed.) 1992. *Playback and Studies of Animal Communication*. New York: Plenum Press.

McGregor, P.K. (ed.) 2004. *Animal Communication Networks*. Cambridge: Cambridge University Press.

McGregor, P. & Peake, T. 1998. The role of identification in conservation biology. In: T. Caro (ed.), *Behavioral Ecology and Conservation Biology*, pp. 31–55. New York: Oxford University Press.

McGregor, P., Peake, T.M. & Gilbert, G. 2000. Communication behaviour and conservation. In: L.M. Gosling & W.J. Sutherland (eds.), *Behaviour and Conservation*, pp. 261–80. Cambridge: Cambridge University Press.

Machacado, C.A., Jousselin, E., Kjellberg, F., Comptom, S.G. & Herre, E.A. 2001. Phylogenetic relationships, historical biogeography and character evolution of fig-pollinating wasps. *Proceedings of the Royal Society of London Series B*, 268, 685–94.

Machtans, C.S., Villard, M.-A. & Hannon, S.J. 1996. Use of riparian buffer strips as movement corridors by forest birds. *Conservation Biology*, 10, 1366–79.

Mackintosh, N.J. (ed.) 1994. *Animal Learning and Cognition. Handbook of Perception and Cognition*, vol. 9. San Diego: Academic Press.

McLain, D.K., Moulton, M.P. & Redfearn, T.P. 1995. Sexual selection and the risk of extinction of introduced birds on oceanic islands. *Oikos*, 74, 27–34.

McLain, D.K., Moulton, M.P. & Sanderson, J.G. 1999. Sexual selection and extinction: the fate of plumage-dimorphic and plumage-monomorphic birds introduced onto islands. *Evolutionary Ecology Research*, 1, 549–65.

McLean, I.G. 1997. Conservation and the ontogeny of behavior. In: J.R. Clemmons & R. Buchholz (eds.), *Behavioural Approaches to Conservation in the Wild*, pp. 132–56. Cambridge: Cambridge University Press.

McLean, I.G., Lundie-Jenkins, G. & Jarman, P.J. 1994. Teaching captive rufous hare-wallabies to recognize predators. In: M. Serena (ed.), *Reintroduction Biology of Australian and New Zealand Fauna*, pp. 177–82. Chipping Norton, Australia: Surrey Beatty & Sons.

McLean, I.G., Lundie-Jenkins, G. & Jarman, P.J. 1995. Teaching an endangered mammal to recognize predators. *Biological Conservation*, 75, 51–62.

McLean, I.G., Schmitt, N.T., Jarman, P.J., Duncan, C. & Wynne, C.D.L. 2000. Learning for life: training marsupials to recognize introduced predators. *Behaviour*, 137, 1361–76.

Macphail, E.M. 1982. *Brain and Intelligence in Vertebrates*. Oxford: Clarendon Press.

Macphail, E.M. & Bolhuis, J.J. 2001. The evolution of intelligence: adaptive specialisations versus general process. *Biological Reviews*, 76, 341–64.

Maki, W.S. & Hegvik, D.K. 1980. Directed forgetting in pigeons. *Animal Learning and Behavior*, 8, 567–74.

Malmkvist, J. & Hansen, S.W. 2001. The welfare of farmed mink (*Mustela vison*) in relation to behavioural selection: a review. *Animal Welfare*, 10, 41–52.

Maloney, R.F. & McLean, I.G. 1995. Historical and experimental learned predator recognition in free-living New Zealand robins. *Animal Behaviour*, 50, 1193–201.

Manning, A. & Dawkins, M.S. 1998. *Animal Behaviour*, 4th edn. Cambridge: Cambridge University Press.

Markl, H. & Hölldobler, B. 1978. Recruitment and food-retrieving behavior in *Novomessor* (Formicidae, Hymenoptera). II. Vibration signals. *Behavioral Ecology and Sociobiology*, 4, 183–216.

Markowitz, H. 1982. *Behavioral Enrichment in the Zoo*. New York: Van Nostrand Reinhold.

Marler, P. 1976. Sensory templates in species-specific behavior. In: J. Fentress (ed.), *Simpler Networks and Behavior*, pp. 314–29. Sunderland, MA: Sinauer.

Marler, P. 1987. Sensitive periods and the roles of specific and general sensory stimulation in birdsong learning. In: J.P. Rauschecker & P. Marler (eds.), *Imprinting and Cortical Plasticity: Comparative Aspects of Sensitive Periods*, pp. 99–135. New York: John Wiley.

Marler, P. 1991. Song-learning behavior: the interface with neuroethology. *Trends in Neurosciences*, 14, 199–206.

Marler, P. & Peters, S. 1987. A sensitive period for song acquisition in the song sparrow, *Melospiza melodia*: a case of age-limited learning. *Ethology*, 76, 89–100.

Marshall, A.P. & Black, J.M. 1992. The effect of rearing experience on subsequent behavioural traits in Hawaiian geese *Branta sandvicensis*: implications for the recovery programme. *Bird Conservation International*, 2, 131–47.

Marshall, N.J. 2000. The visual ecology of reef fish colours. In: Y. Espmark, T. Amundsen & G. Rosenqvist (eds.), *Animal Signals: Signalling and Signal Design in Animal Communication*, pp. 83–120. Trondheim: Tapir Academic Press.

Martin, K. 1998. The role of animal behavior studies in wildlife science and management. *Wildlife Society Bulletin*, 26, 911–20.

Martins, E. (ed.) 1996. *Phylogenies and the Comparative Method in Animal Behavior*. Oxford: Oxford University Press.

Mason, G.J., Cooper, J. & Clarebrough, C. 2001. Frustrations of fur-farmed mink. *Nature*, 410, 35–6.

Masson, J.M. & McCarthy, S. 1995. *When Elephants Weep: The Emotional Lives of Animals*. New York: Delacorte Press.

Maynard Smith, J. 1964. Group selection and kin selection. *Nature*, 201, 1145–7.

Maynard Smith, J. 1976. Group selection. *Quarterly Review of Biology*, 51, 277–83.

Maynard Smith, J. 1982. *Evolution and the Theory of Games*. Cambridge: Cambridge University Press.

Maynard Smith, J. 1994. Must reliable signals always be costly? *Animal Behaviour*, 47, 1115–20.

Maynard Smith, J. & Price, G.R. 1973. The logic of animal conflict. *Nature*, 246, 15–18.

Mayr E. 1942. *Systematics and the Origin of Species*. New York: Columbia University Press.

Meadows, P.S. & Campbell, J.I. 1972. Habitat selection by aquatic invertebrates. In: F.S. Russell & M. Yonge (eds.), *Advances in Marine Biology*, vol. 10, pp. 271–382. New York: Academic Press.

Mealey, L. 2000. *Sex Differences: Developmental and Evolutionary Strategies*. San Diego: Academic Press.

Mech, S.G. & Hallett, J.G. 2001. Evaluating the effectiveness of corridors: a genetic approach. *Conservation Biology*, 15, 467–74.

Meffe, G.K. & Carroll, R.C. 1997. *Principles of Conservation Biology*, 2nd edn. Sunderland, MA: Sinauer.

Menzel, E.W. Jr. 1974. A group of young chimpanzees in a one-acre field: leadership and communication. In: A.M. Schrier & F. Stollnitz (eds.), *Behavior of Nonhuman Primates*, pp. 83–153. New York: Academic Press.

Menzel, R. & Müller, U. 1996. Learning and memory in honeybees: from behavior to neural substrates. *Annual Review of Neuroscience*, 19, 379–404.

Menzel, R., Giurfa, M., Gerber, B. & Hellstern, F. 2001. Cognition in insects: the honeybee as a study case. In: G. Roth & M.F. Wullimann (eds.), *Brain Evolution and Cognition*, pp. 333–66. New York: John Wiley & Sons.

Meyer, A., Morrissey, J.M. & Schartl, M. 1994. Recurrent origin of a sexually selected trait in *Xiphophorus* fishes inferred from a molecular phylogeny. *Nature*, 368, 539–42.

Meyer, J.S., Irwin, L.L. & Boyce, M.S. 1998. Influence of habitat abundance and fragmentation on northern spotted owls in western Oregon. *Wildlife Monographs*, 139, 5–51.

Midgley, M. 1983. *Animals and Why They Matter*. Athens, GA: University of Georgia Press.

Milinski, M. & Parker G.A. 1991. Competition for resources. In: J.R. Krebs & N.B. Davies (eds.), *Behavioural Ecology: An Evolutionary Approach*, pp. 137–68. Sunderland, MA: Sinauer.

Miller, G.A. 1956. The magical number seven plus or minus two: some limits on our capacity for processing information. *Psychological Review*, 63, 81–97.

Miller, N.E. 1959. Liberalization of basic S-R concepts: extensions to conflict behavior, motivation, and social learning. In: S. Koch (ed.), *Psychology: A Study of a Science*, vol. 2, pp. 196–292. New York: McGraw-Hill.

Mills, M.G.L., Juritz, J.M. & Zucchini, W. 2001. Estimating the size of spotted hyaena (*Crocuta crocuta*) populations through playback recordings allowing for non-response. *Animal Conservation*, 4, 335–43.

Mineka, S. & Cook, M. 1988. Social learning and the acquisition of snake fear in monkeys. In: T.R. Zentall & B.G. Galef (eds.), *Social Learning: Psychological and Biological Perspectives*, pp. 51–73. New York: Lawrence Erlbaum.

Mistlberger, R.E. 1994. Circadian food anticipatory activity: formal models and physiological mechanisms. *Neuroscience and Biobehavioral Reviews*, 189, 171–95.

Mistlberger, R.E. & Skene, D.J. 2004. Social influences on circadian rhythms in mammals: animal and human studies. *Biological Reviews*, 79, 1–23.

Miyashita, Y. 1995. How the brain creates imagery. *Science*, 268, 1719–20.

Moberg, G.P. & Mench, J.A. (eds.) 2000. *The Biology of Animal Stress: Basic Principles and Implications for Animal Welfare*. Wallingford, UK: CAB International.

Moiseff, A. 1989. Bi-coordinate sound localization by the barn owl. *Journal of Comparative Physiology A*, 164, 637–44.

Moiseff, A. & Konishi, M. 1981. Neuronal and behavioral sensitivity to binaural time differences in the owl. *Journal of Neuroscience*, 1, 40–8.

Moiseff, A. & Konishi, M. 1983. Binaural characteristics of units in the owl's brainstem auditory pathway: precursors of restricted spatial receptive fields. *Journal of Neuroscience*, 3, 2553–62.

Møller, A.P. 1987. Extent and duration of mate guarding in swallows *Hirundo rustica*. *Ornis Scandinavica*, 18, 95–100.

Møller, A.P. 1994. *Sexual Selection and the Barn Swallow*. Oxford: Oxford University Press.

Møller, A.P. 2000. Sexual selection and conservation. In: M. Gosling & W.J. Sutherland (eds.), *Behaviour and Conservation*, pp. 172–97. Cambridge: Cambridge University Press.

Møller, A.P. & Alatalo, R.V. 1999. Good genes effects in sexual selection. *Proceedings of the Royal Society of London Series B*, 266, 85–91.

Møller, A.P. & Cuervo, J.J. 2003. Asymmetry, size and sexual selection: factors affecting heterogeneity in relationships between asymmetry and sexual selection. In: M. Polak (ed.), *Developmental Instability*, pp. 262–75. New York: Oxford University Press.

Møller, A.P. & de Lope, F. 1994. Differential costs of a secondary sexual character: an experimental test of the handicap principle. *Evolution*, 48, 1676–83.

Møller, A.P. & Jennions, M.D. 2001. How important are direct fitness benefits of sexual selection? *Naturwissenschaften*, 88, 401–15.

Møller, A.P. & Legendre, S. 2001. Allee effect, sexual selection and demographic stochasticity. *Oikos*, 92, 27–34.

Møller, A.P. & Pomiankowski, A. 1993. Why have birds got multiple sexual ornaments? *Behavioral Ecology and Sociobiology*, 32, 167–76.

Møller, A.P. & Thornhill, R. 1998. Bilateral symmetry and sexual selection: a meta-analysis. *American Naturalist*, 151, 174–92.

Møller, A.P., Sorci, G. & Erritzøe, J. 1998. Sexual dimorphism in immune defense. *American Naturalist*, 152, 605–19.

Møller, A.P., Christe, P. & Lux, E. 1999. Parasite-mediated sexual selection: effects of parasites and host immune function. *Quarterly Review of Biology*, 74, 3–20.

Møller, A.P., Biard, C., Blount, J.D. et al. 2000. Carotenoid-dependent signals: indicators of foraging efficiency, immunocompetence or detoxification ability? *Poultry and Avian Biology Reviews*, 11, 137–59.

Monaghan, P. 1996. Relevance of the behavior of seabirds to the conservation of marine environments. *Oikos*, 77, 227–37.

Montminy, M.R. & Bilezikjian, L.M. 1987. Binding of a nuclear protein to the cyclic-AMP response element of the somatostatin gene. *Nature*, 328, 175–8.

Moore-Ede, M.C. 1986. Physiology of the circadian timing system: predictive versus reactive homeostasis. *American Journal of Physiology*, 250, R737–R752.

Moore-Ede, M.C., Sulzman, F.K. & Fuller, C. 1982. *The Clocks That Time Us*. Cambridge, MA: Harvard University Press.

Morgan, C.L. 1894. *Introduction to Comparative Psychology*. London: Scott.

Morris, R.G.M. 1981. Spatial localization does not require the presence of local cues. *Learning and Motivation*, 12, 239–60.

Motter, B.C. 1994. Neural correlates of attentive selection for color or luminance in extrastriate area V4. *Journal of Neuroscience*, 14, 2178–89.

Mottley, K. & Giraldeau, L.-A. 2000. Experimental evidence that group foragers can converge on predicted producer–scrounger equilibria. *Animal Behaviour*, 60, 341–50.

Mountcastle, V.B., Lynch, J.C., Georgopoulos, A., Sakata, H. & Acuna, C. 1975. Posterior parietal association cortex of the monkey: command functions operations within extrapersonal space. *Journal of Neurophysiology*, 38, 871–908.

Mrosovsky, N. 1999. Masking: history, definitions, and measurement. *Chronobiology International*, 16, 415–29.

Muir, W.M. & Craig, J.V. 1998. Improving animal well-being through genetic selection. *Poultry Science*, 77, 1781–8.

Mulder, R.A. & Langmore, N.E. 1993. Dominant males punish helpers for temporary defection in superb fairy wrens. *Animal Behaviour*, 45, 830–3.

Mulder, R.A., Dunn, P.O., Cockburn, A., Lazenby-Cohen, K.A. & Howell, M.J. 1994. Helpers liberate female fairy-wrens from constraints on extra-pair male choice. *Proceedings of the Royal Society of London Series B*, 255, 223–9.

Mysterud, A. & Ims, R.A. 1998. Functional responses in habitat use: availability influences relative use in trade-off situations. *Ecology*, 79, 1435–41.

Nader, K., Bechara, A. & van der Kooy, D. 1997. Neurobiological constraints on behavioral models of motivation. *Annual Review of Psychology*, 48, 85–114.

Nagell, K., Olguin, K. & Tomasello, M. 1993. Processes of social learning in the tool use of chimpanzees (*Pan troglodytes*) and human children (*Homo sapiens*). *Journal of Comparative Psychology*, 107, 174–86.

Nee, S. & May, R.M. 1993. Population-level consequences of conspecific brood parasitism in birds and insects. *Journal of Theoretical Biology*, 161, 95–109.

Nelson, K.R. & Wasserman, E.A. 1978. Temporal factors influencing the pigeon's successive matching-to-sample performance: sample duration, intertrial interval, and retention interval. *Journal of the Experimental Analysis of Behavior*, 30, 153–62.

Nelson, R.J. 1999. *An Introduction to Behavioral Endocrinology*, 2nd edn. Sunderland, MA: Sinauer.

Nicolaus, L.K., Cassel, J.F., Carlson, R.B. & Gustavson, C.R. 1983. Taste-aversion conditioning of crows to control predation on eggs. *Science*, 22, 212–14.

Nisbett, R.E. & Wilson, T. 1977. Telling more than we know: verbal reports on mental processes. *Psychological Review*, 84, 231–59.

Nonacs, P. 2001. State dependent behavior and the marginal value theorem. *Behavioral Ecology*, 12, 71–83.

Nottebohm, F. 1981. A brain for all seasons: cyclical anatomical changes in song control nuclei of the canary brain. *Science*, 214, 1368–70.

Nottebohm, F. 1999. The anatomy and timing of vocal learning in birds. In: M.D. Hauser & M. Konishi (eds.), *The Design of Animal Communication*, pp. 63–110. Cambridge, MA: MIT Press.

Nowak, M. & Sigmund, K. 1993. A strategy of win–stay, lose–shift that outperforms tit-for-tat in the prisoner's dilemma game. *Nature*, 364, 56–8.

Oates, K. & Wilson, M. 2002. Nominal kinship cues promote altruism. *Proceedings of the Royal Society of London Series B*, 269, 105–9.

Ober, C., Weitkamp, L.R., Cox, N., Dytch, H., Kostyu, D. & Elias, S. 1997. HLA and mate choice in humans. *American Journal of Human Genetics*, 61, 497–504.

Oppenheim, R.W. 1981. Ontogenetic adaptations and retrogressive processes in the development of the nervous system and behaviour: a neuroembryological perspective. In: K.J. Connolly & H.F.R. Prechtl (eds.), *Maturation and Development: Biological and Psychological Perspective*, pp. 73–109. Philadelphia: Lippincott.

O'Riain, M.J., Jarvis, J.U.M., Alexander, R.D., Buffenstein, R. & Peeters, C. 2000. Morphological castes in a vertebrate. *Proceedings of the Royal Society of London Series B*, 97, 13194–7.

Orians, G.H. 1969. On the evolution of mating systems in birds and mammals. *American Naturalist*, 103, 589–603.

Packer, C. 1983. Sexual dimorphism: the horns of African antelopes. *Science*, 221, 1191–3.

Packer, C. 1986. The ecology of sociality in felids. In: D.I. Rubenstein & R.W. Wrangham (eds.), *Ecological Aspects of Social Evolution*, pp. 429–51. Princeton, NJ: Princeton University Press.

Packer, C. & Ruttan, L.M. 1988. The evolution of cooperative hunting. *American Naturalist*, 132, 159–98.

Packer, C., Herbst, L., Pusey, A.E. et al. 1988. Reproductive success of lions. In: T.H. Clutton-Brock (ed.), *Reproductive Success*, pp. 363–83. Chicago: University of Chicago.

Packer, C., Scheel, D. & Pusey, A.E. 1990. Why lions form groups: food is not enough. *American Naturalist*, 136, 1–19.

Packer, C., Pusey, A.E. & Eberly, L.E. 2001. Egalitarianism in female lions. *Science*, 293, 690–3.

Page, R.E. Jr. 1986. Sperm utilization in social insects. *Annual Review of Entomology*, 31, 297–320.

Panda, S., Hogenesch, J.B. & Kay, S.A. 2002. Circadian rhythms from flies to human. *Nature*, 417, 329–35.

Parker, G.A. 1970. Sperm competition and its evolutionary consequences in the insects. *Biological Reviews*, 45, 525–67.

Parker, G.A. 1974. Assessment strategy and the evolution of fighting behavior. *Journal of Theoretical Biology*, 47, 223–43.

Parker, G.A. 1984. Evolutionary stable strategies. In: J.R. Krebs & N.B. Davies (eds.), *Behavioural Ecology: An Evolutionary Approach*, pp. 30–61. Sunderland, MA: Sinauer.

Parker, G.A. 1998. Sperm competition and the evolution of ejaculates: towards a theory base. In: T.R. Birkhead & A.P. Møller (eds.), *Sperm Competition and Sexual Selection*, pp. 3–54. London: Academic Press.

Parker, G.A. 2001. Golden flies, sunlit meadows: a tribute to the yellow dungfly. In: L.A. Dugatkin (ed.), *Model Systems in Behavioral Ecology*, pp. 3–26. Princeton, NJ: Princeton University Press.

Parker, P.G. & Waite, T.A. 1997. Mating systems, effective population size, and conservation of natural populations. In: J.R. Clemmons & R. Buchholz (eds.), *Behavioural Approaches to Conservation in the Wild*, pp. 243–61. Cambridge: Cambridge University Press.

Parr, L.A. & de Waal, F.B.M. 1999. Visual kin recognition in chimpanzees. *Nature*, 399, 647–8.

Pascalis, O., de Haan, M. & Nelson, C.A. 2002. Is face processing species-specific during the first year of life? *Science*, 296, 1321–3.

Pavlov, I.P. 1927. *Conditioned Reflexes: An Investigation of the Physiological Activity of the Cerebral Cortex* (translated by G.V. Anrep, 1960 reprint). New York: Dover Publications.

Peake, T.M. 2004. Eavesdropping in communication networks. In. P.K. McGregor (ed.), *Animal Communication Networks*, pp. 42–96. Cambridge: Cambridge University Press.

Pearce, J.M. 1997. *Animal Learning and Cognition: An Introduction*, 2nd edn. Hove, UK: Psychology Press.

Peña, J.L., Viete, S., Funabiki, K., Saberi, K. & Konishi, M. 2001. Cochlear and neural delays for coincidence detection in owls. *Journal of Neuroscience*, 21, 9455–9.

Penn, D.J. & Potts, W.K. 1999. The evolution of MHC-disassortative mating preferences. *American Naturalist*, 153, 145–64.

Pepperberg, I.M. 1999. *The Alex Studies: Communication and Cognitive Capacities of an African Grey Parrot*. Cambridge, MA: Harvard University Press.

Perret, D.I. & Rolls, E.T. 1983. Neural mechanisms underlying the visual analysis of faces. In: J.-P. Ewert, R.R. Capranica & D.J. Ingle (eds.), *Advances in Vertebrate Neuroethology*, pp. 543–66. New York: Plenum Press.

Perrin, N. & Mazalov, V. 1999. Dispersal and inbreeding avoidance. *American Naturalist*, 154, 282–92.

Perrin, N. & Mazalov, V. 2000. Local competition, inbreeding, and the evolution of sex-biased dispersal. *American Naturalist*, 155, 116–27.

Petherick, J.C., Seawright, E., Waddington, D., Duncan, I.J.H. & Murphy, L.B. 1995. The role of perception in the causation of dustbathing behaviour in domestic fowl. *Animal Behaviour*, 49, 1521–30.

Petrie, M. 1992. Peacocks with low mating success are more likely to suffer predation. *Animal Behaviour*, 44, 485–6.

Petrie, M., Schwabl, H., Brande-Lavridsen, N. & Burke, T. 2001. Sex differences in avian yolk hormone levels. *Nature*, 412, 498–9.

Phelps, S.M. & Ryan, M.J. 2000. History influences signal recognition: neural network models of túngara frogs. *Proceedings of the Royal Society of London Series B*, 267, 1633–9.

Pietrzak, R.H., Laird, J.D., Stevens, D.A. & Thompson, N.S. 2002. Sex differences in human jealousy: a coordinated study of forced-choice, continuous rating-scale, and physiological responses in the same subjects. *Evolution and Human Behavior*, 23, 83–94.

Pinker, S. 1994. *The Language Instinct.* New York: William Morrow.

Pittendrigh, C.S. 1993. Temporal organization: reflections of a Darwinian clock-watcher. *Annual Review of Physiology*, 55, 16–54.

Pittendrigh, C.S. & Daan, S. 1976. A functional analysis of circadian pacemakers in nocturnal rodents: IV. Entrainment: pacemaker as clock. *Journal of Comparative Physiology A*, 106, 291–331.

Pittenger, C. & Kandel, E.R. 2003. In search of general mechanisms for long-lasting plasticity: *Aplysia* and the hippocampus. *Philosophical Transactions of the Royal Society of London Series B*, 358, 757–67.

Pizzari, T. & Birkhead, T.R. 2000. Female feral fowl eject sperm of subdominant males. *Nature*, 405, 787–9.

Platek, S.M., Burch, R.L., Panyavin, I.S., Wasserman, B.H. & Gallup, G.G. 2002. Reactions to children's faces: resemblance affects males more than females. *Evolution and Human Behavior*, 23, 159–66.

Polak, M. (ed.) 2002. *Developmental instability: causes and consequences.* New York: Oxford University Press.

Polsky, R.H. 1975. Hunger, prey feeding, and predatory aggression. *Behavioral Biology*, 13, 81–93.

Poran, N.S., Coss, R.G. & Benjamini, E. 1987. Resistance of California ground squirrels (*Spermophilus beecheyi*) to the venom of the Northern Pacific rattlesnake (*Crotalus viridis oreganus*). A study of adaptive variation. *Toxicon*, 25, 767–77.

Pound, N. 2002. Male interest in visual cues of sperm competition risk. *Evolution and Human Behavior*, 23, 443–66.

Povinelli, D.J. & Eddy, T.J. 1996a. Chimpanzees: joint visual attention. *Psychological Science*, 7, 129–35.

Povinelli, D.J. & Eddy, T.J. 1996b. What young chimpanzees know about seeing. *Monographs of the Society of Research in Child Development*, 61(3).

Povinelli, D.J., Nelson, K.E. & Boysen, S.T. 1990. Inferences about guessing and knowing by chimpanzees (*Pan troglodytes*). *Journal of Comparative Psychology*, 104, 203–10.

Povinelli, D.J., Gallup, G.G. Jr, Eddy, T.J. et al. 1997. Chimpanzees recognize themselves in mirrors. *Animal Behaviour*, 53, 1083–8.

Premack, D. & Woodruff, G. 1978. Does the chimpanzee have a theory of mind? *Behavioral and Brain Sciences*, 1, 515–26.

Prete, F.R. 1992. Discrimination of visual stimuli representing prey versus non-prey by the praying mantis, *Sphodromantis lineola* (Burr.). *Brain, Behavior and Evolution*, 39, 285–8.

Prete, F.R. (ed.) 2004. *Complex Worlds from Simpler Nervous Systems.* Cambridge, MA: MIT Press.

Pribil, S. & Searcy, W.A. 2001. Experimental confirmation of the polygyny threshold model for red-winged blackbirds. *Proceedings of the Royal Society of London Series B*, 268, 1643–6.

Priesner, E. 1980. Sex attractant system in *Polia pisi* (Lepidoptera: Noctuidae). *Zeitschrift für Naturforschung. Section C, A Journal of Biosciences*, 35, 990–4.

Promislow, D.E.L., Montgomerie, R. & Martin, T.E. 1992. Mortality costs of sexual dimorphism in birds. *Proceedings of the Royal Society of London Series B*, 250, 143–50.

Promislow, D.E.L., Montgomerie, R. & Martin, T. E. 1994. Sexual selection and survival in North American waterfowl. *Evolution*, 48, 2045–50.

Pulliam, H.R. 1996. Sources and sinks: empirical evidence and population consequences. In: O.E. Rhodes Jr, R.K. Chesser & M.H. Smith (eds.), *Population Dynamics in Ecological Space and Time*, pp. 45–69. Chicago: University of Chicago Press.

Pulliam, R.H. & Caraco, T. 1984. Living in groups: is there an optimal group size? In: J.R. Krebs & N.B. Davies (eds.), *Behavioural Ecology: An Evolutionary Approach*, pp. 122–47. Sunderland, MA: Sinauer.

Pulliam, H.R. & Danielson, B.J. 1991. Sources, sinks and habitat selection: a landscape perspective on population dynamics. *American Naturalist*, 137, S50–S66.

Pusey, A.E. & Packer, C. 1994. Non-offspring nursing in social carnivores: minimizing the costs. *Behavioral Ecology*, 5, 362–74.

Pusey, A.E. & Packer, C. 1997. The ecology of relationships. In: J.R. Krebs & N.B. Davies (eds.), *Behavioural Ecology: An Evolutionary Approach*, 4th edn, pp. 254–83. Oxford: Blackwell Science.

Queller, D.C. & Strassmann, J.E. 1998. Kin selection and social insects. *BioScience*, 48, 165–75.

Ralph, M.R. & Lehman, M.N. 1991. Transplantation: a new tool in the analysis of the mammalian hypothalamic circadian pacemaker. *Trends in Neurosciences*, 14, 362–6.

Read, A.F. & Harvey, P.H. 1989. Reassessment of comparative evidence for Hamilton and Zuk theory on the evolution of secondary sexual characters. *Nature*, 339, 618–20.

Reed, J.M. 1999. The role of behavior in recent avian extinctions and endangerments. *Conservation Biology*, 13, 232–41.

Reed, J.M., Sincock, J.L. & Hailman, J.P. 1985. Light attraction in procellariiform birds: reduction by shielding upward radiation. *Auk*, 102, 377–83.

Reeve, H.K. 2001. In search of unified theories in sociobiology: help from social wasps. In: L.A. Dugatkin (ed.), *Model Systems in Behavioral Ecology*, pp. 57–71. Princeton, NJ: Princeton University Press.

Reeve, H.K. & Sherman, P.W. 1993. Adaptation and the goals of evolutionary research. *Quarterly Review of Biology*, 68, 1–32.

Reeve, H.K., Starks, P.T., Peters, J.M. & Nonacs, P. 2000. Genetic support for the evolutionary theory of reproductive transactions in social wasps. *Proceedings of the Royal Society of London Series B*, 267, 75–9.

Refinetti, R. 2000. *Circadian Physiology*. Boca Raton, FL: CRC Press.

Regalski, J.M. & Gaulin, S.J.C. 1993. Whom are newborn Mexican babies said to resemble? Monitoring and fostering paternal confidence in the Yucatan. *Ethology and Sociobiology*, 14, 97–113.

Regan, T. 1983. *The Case for Animal Rights*. Berkeley: University of California Press.

Reijnen, R. & Foppen, R. 1994. The effects of car traffic on breeding bird populations in woodland: I. Evidence of reduced habitat quality for willow warblers (*Phylloscopus trochilus*) breeding close to a highway. *Journal of Applied Ecology*, 31, 85–94.

Reijnen, R., Foppen, R., Ter Braak, C. & Thissen, J. 1995. The effects of car traffic on breeding bird populations in woodland: III. Reduction of density in relation to the proximity of main roads. *Journal of Applied Ecology*, 32, 187–202.

Reijnen, R., Foppen, R. & Veenbaas, G. 1997. Disturbance by traffic of breeding birds: evaluation of the effect and considerations in planning and managing road corridors. *Biodiversity and Conservation*, 6, 567–81.

Reiss, D. & Marino, L. 2001. Mirror self-recognition in the bottlenose dolphin: a case of cognitive convergence. *Proceedings of the National Academy of Sciences USA*, 98, 5937–42.

Reppert, S.M. & Weaver, D.R. 2002. Coordination of circadian timing in mammals. *Nature*, 418, 935–41.

Rescorla, R.A. & Wagner, A.R. 1972. A theory of Pavlovian conditioning: variations in the effectiveness of reinforcement and nonreinforcement. In: A.H. Black & W.F. Prokasy (eds.), *Classical Conditioning II: Current Research and Theory*, pp. 64–99. New York: Appleton-Century-Crofts.

Rice, W.R. 1996. Sexually antagonistic male adaptation triggered by experimental arrest of female evolution. *Nature*, 361, 232–4.

Rice, W.R. 1996. Sexually antagonistic male adaptation triggered by experimental arrest of female evolution. *Nature*, 381, 232–4.

Richard-Yris, M.-A., Sharp, P.J., Wauters, A.-M., Guémené, D., Richard, J.-P. & Forasté, M. 1998. Influence of stimuli from chicks on behavior and concentrations of plasma prolactin and luteinizing hormone in incubating hens. *Hormones and Behavior*, 33, 139–48.

Richerson, P.J. & Boyd, R. 2004. *The Nature of Cultures*. Chicago: University of Chicago Press.

Rikowski, A. & Grammer, K. 1999. Human body odour, symmetry, and attractiveness. *Proceedings of the Royal Society of London Series B*, 266, 869–74.

Rizzolatti, G., Fadiga, L., Gallese, V. & Fogassi, L. 1996. Premotor cortex and the recognition of motor actions. *Cognitive Brain Research*, 3, 131–41.

Roberts, W.A. 1998. *Principles of Animal Cognition*. Boston: McGraw Hill.

Roberts, W.A. & Grant, D.S. 1976. Studies of short-term memory in the pigeon using the delayed matching to sample procedure. In: D.L. Medin, W.A. Roberts & R.T. Davis (eds.), *Processes of Animal Memory*, pp. 79–112. Hillsdale, NJ: Erlbaum.

Robinson, J.G. & Bennett, E.L. (eds.) 2000. *Hunting for Sustainability in Tropical Forests*. New York: Columbia University Press.

Robinson, J.G. & Redford, K.H. 1991. Sustainable harvest of neotropical forest mammals. In: J.G. Robinson & K.H. Redford (eds.), *Neotropical Wildlife Use and Conservation*, pp. 415–29. Chicago: University of Chicago Press.

Roeder, K.D. 1967. *Nerve Cells and Insect Behavior*, 2nd edn. Cambridge, MA: Harvard University Press.

Roenneberg, T. & Aschoff, J. 1990. Annual rhythm of human reproduction: I. Biology, sociology, or both? *Journal of Biological Rhythms*, 5, 195–216.

Rohwer, S., Herron, J.C. & Daly, M. 1999. Stepparental behavior as mating effort in birds and other animals. *Evolution and Human Behavior*, 20, 367–90.

Rollin, B.E. 1981. *Animal Rights and Human Morality*. Buffalo: Prometheus Books.

Rollin, B.E. 1989. *The Unheeded Cry: Animal Consciousness, Animal Pain and Science*. Oxford: Oxford University Press.

Rollin, B.E. 1995. *Farm Animal Welfare: Social, Bioethical, and Research Issues*. Ames: Iowa State University Press.

Rolls, E.T. 1994. Brain mechanisms for invariant visual recognition and learning. *Behavioral Processes*, 33, 113–39.

Romanes, G.J. 1904. *Animal Intelligence*, 8th edn. London: Kegan Paul, Trench, Trübner & Co.

Rosenberg, D.K., Noon, B.R. & Meslow, E.C. 1997. Biological corridors: form, function, and efficacy. *BioScience*, 47, 677–87.

Rowe, R., Arnqvist, G., Sih, A. & Krupa, J.J. 1994. Sexual conflict and the evolutionary ecology of mating patterns: water striders as a model system. *Trends in Ecology and Evolution*, 9, 289–93.

Rowland, W.J. 1989. Mate choice and the supernormality effect in female sticklebacks (*Gasterosteus aculeatus*). *Behavioral Ecology and Sociobiology*, 24, 433–8.

Rubenstein, D.I. 1998. Behavioral ecology and conservation policy: on balancing science, applications, and advocacy. In: T. Caro (ed.), *Behavioral Ecology and Conservation Biology*, pp. 527–53. New York: Oxford University Press.

Ruesch, H. 1978. *Slaughter of the Innocent*. New York: Bantam Books.

Rushen, J. 1986. Aversion of sheep to electro-immobilization and physical restraint. *Applied Animal Behaviour Science*, 15, 315–24.

Rushen, J., de Passillé, A.M. & Munksgaard, L. 1999. Fear of people by cows and effects on milk yield, behavior and heart rate at milking. *Journal of Dairy Science*, 82, 720–7.

Russell, P.A. 1973. Relationships between exploratory behaviour and fear: a review. *British Journal of Psychology*, 64, 417–33.

Rutter, M. 2002. Nature, nurture, and development: from evangelism through science toward policy and practice. *Child Development*, 73, 1–21.

Ryan, M.J. 1985. *The Túngara Frog*. Chicago: University of Chicago Press.

Ryan, M.J. & Rand, A.S. 1993. Sexual selection and signal evolution: the ghost of biases past. *Philosophical Transactions of the Royal Society of London Series B*, 340, 187–95.

Ryan, M.J. & Rand, A.S. 1995. Female responses to ancestral advertisement calls in the túngara frog. *Science*, 269, 390–2.

Ryan, M.J. & Rand, A.S. 1999. Phylogenetic influences on mating call preferences in female túngara frogs (*Physalaemus pustulosus*). *Animal Behaviour*, 57, 945–56.

Ryan, M.J., Fox, J.H., Wilczynski, W. & Rand, A.S. 1990. Sexual selection for sensory exploitation in the frog *Physalaemus pustulosus*. *Nature*, 343, 66–7.

Sachs, B.D. & Barfield, R.J. 1976. Functional analysis of masculine copulatory behavior in the rat. *Advances in the Study of Behavior*, 7, 92–154.

Saino, N., Bolzern, A.M. & Møller, A.P. 1997. Immunocompetence, ornamentation and viability of male barn swallows (*Hirundo rustica*). *Proceedings of the National Academy of Sciences USA*, 94, 549–52.

Salmon, C.A. 1998. The evocative nature of kin terminology in political rhetoric. *Politics and the Life Sciences*, 17, 51–7.

Salmon, C.A. & Daly, M. 1998. Birth order and familial sentiment: middleborns are different. *Evolution and Human Behavior*, 19, 299–312.

Salzen, E.A. & Meyer, C.C. 1967. Imprinting: reversal of a preference established during the critical period. *Nature* 215, 785–6.

Savage-Rumbaugh, E.S. & Lewin, R. 1994. *Kanzi: The Ape at the Brink of the Human Mind*. New York: John Wiley & Sons.

Schacter, D.L. 1996. *Searching for Memory*. New York: Basic Books.

Scheib, J.E. 2001. Context-specific mate choice criteria: women's trade-offs in the contexts of long-term and extra-pair mateships. *Personal Relationships*, 8, 371–89.

Schleidt, W. 1961. Über die Auslösung der Flucht vor Raubvögeln bei Truthühnern. *Naturwissenschaften*, 48, 141–2.

Schneider, J.M. 1999. Delayed oviposition: a female strategy to counter infanticide by males? *Behavioral Ecology*, 10, 567–71.

Schneider, J.M. & Elgar, M.A. 2001. Sexual cannibalism and sperm competition in the golden orb-web spider *Nephila plumipes* (Araneoidea): female and male perspectives. *Behavioral Ecology*, 12, 547–52.

Schradin, C. 2000. Confusion effect in a reptilian and a primate predator. *Ethology*, 106, 691–700.

Schürg-Pfeiffer, E., Spreckelsen, C. & Ewert, J.-P. 1993. Temporal discharge patterns of tectal and medullary neurons chronically recorded during snapping toward prey in toads *Bufo bufo spinosus*. *Journal of Comparative Physiology A*, 173, 363–76.

Schusterman, R.J. & Krieger, K. 1984. California sea lions are capable of semantic comprehension. *Psychological Record*, 34, 3–23.

Schwabl, H. 1993. Yolk is a source of testosterone for developing birds. *Proceedings of the National Academy of Sciences USA*, 90, 11446–50.

Seal, U.S. 1991. Fertility control as a tool for regulating captive and free-ranging wildlife. *Journal of Zoo and Wildlife Medicine*, 22, 1–5.

Searcy, W.A. & Nowicki, S. 2000. Male–male competition and female choice in the evolution of vocal signaling. In: Y. Espmark, T. Amundsen & G. Rosenqvist (eds.), *Animal Signals: Signalling and Signal Design in Animal Communication*, pp. 301–15. Trondheim: Tapir Academic Press.

Seehausen, O., van Alphen, J.J.M. & Witte, F. 1997. Cichlid fish diversity threatened by eutrophication that curbs sexual selection. *Science*, 277, 1808–11.

Seghers, B.H. 1974. Schooling behaviour in the guppy *Poecilia reticulata*: an evolutionary response to predation. *Evolution*, 28, 486–9.

Semel, B. & Sherman, P.W. 1995. Alternative placement strategies for wood duck nest boxes. *Wildlife Society Bulletin*, 23, 463–71.

Serpell, J. (ed.) 1995. *The Domestic Dog: Its Evolution, Behaviour, and Interactions with People.* Cambridge: Cambridge University Press.

Sevenster, P. 1961. A causal analysis of a displacement activity (fanning in *Gasterosteus aculeatus* L.). *Behaviour*, Suppl. 9, 1–170.

Sevenster-Bol, A.C.A. 1962. On the causation of drive reduction after a consummatory act. *Archives Néerlandaises de Zoologie*, 15, 175–236.

Sherman, P.W. & Hash, G.A. 2001. Why vegetable recipes are not very spicy. *Evolution and Human Behavior*, 22, 147–63.

Sherman, P.W., Jarvis, J.U.M. & Alexander, R.D. 1991. *The Biology of the Naked Mole-rat.* Princeton, NJ: Princeton University Press.

Sherman, P.W., Reeve, H.K. & Pfennig, D.W. 1997. Recognition systems. In: J.R. Krebs & N.B. Davies (eds.), *Behavioural Ecology: An Evolutionary Approach*, 4th edn, pp. 69–96. Oxford: Blackwell Science.

Sherry, D.F., Mrosovsky, N. & Hogan, J.A. 1980. Weight loss and anorexia during incubation in birds. *Journal of Comparative and Physiological Psychology*, 94, 89–98.

Shettleworth, S.J. 1975. Reinforcement and the organization of behavior in golden hamsters: hunger, environment, and food reinforcement. *Journal of Experimental Psychology: Animal Behavior Processes*, 104, 56–87.

Shettleworth, S.J. 1998. *Cognition, Evolution, and Behavior.* New York: Oxford University Press.

Short, J., Kinnear, J.E. & Robley, A. 2002. Surplus killing by introduced predators in Australia: evidence for ineffective anti-predator adaptations in native prey species? *Biological Conservation*, 103, 283–301.

Shumway, C.A. 1999. A neglected science: applying behavior to aquatic conservation. *Environmental Biology of Fishes*, 55, 183–201.

Sigmund, K., Fehr, E. & Nowak, M.A. 2002. The economics of fair play. *Scientific American*, 286(1), 83–7.

Sih, A. & Christensen, B. 2001. Optimal diet theory: when does it work, and when and why does it fail? *Animal Behaviour*, 61, 379–90.

Silver, R. 1990. Biological timing mechanisms with special emphasis on the parental behavior of doves. In: D.A. Dewsbury (ed.), *Contemporary Issues in Comparative Psychology*, pp. 252–77. Sunderland, MA: Sinauer.

Silver, R., LeSauter, J., Tresco, P.A. & Lehman, M.N. 1996. A diffusible coupling signal from the transplanted suprachiasmatic nucleus controlling circadian locomotor rhythms. *Nature*, 382, 810–13.

Simberloff, D. 1988. The contribution of population and community biology to conservation science. *Annual Review of Ecology and Systematics*, 19, 473–511.

Simmons, L.W. 2001. *Sperm Competition and its Evolutionary Consequences in the Insects*. Princeton, NJ: Princeton University Press.

Simmons, L.W. & Gwynne, D.T. 1991. The refractory period of female katydids (Orthoptera: Tettigoniidae): sexual conflict over the remating interval? *Behavioral Ecology*, 2, 276–82.

Simmons, L.W., Llorens, T., Schinzig, M., Hosken, D. & Craig, M. 1994. Sperm competition selects for male mate choice and protandry in the bushcricket, *Requena verticalis* (Orthopera: Tettigoniidae). *Animal Behaviour*, 47, 117–22.

Singer, P. 1975. *Animal Liberation*. New York: Avon Books.

Singer, W. 1995. Development and plasticity of cortical processing architectures. *Science*, 270, 758–64.

Skinner, B.F. 1938. *The Behavior of Organisms*. New York: Appleton-Century-Crofts.

Skinner, B.F. 1957. *Verbal Behavior*. Englewood Cliffs, NJ: Prentice Hall.

Slater, P.J.B. 1983. The development of individual behaviour. In: T.R. Halliday & P.J.B. Slater (eds.), *Genes, Development and Learning. Animal Behaviour*, vol. 3. New York: W.H. Freeman.

Sluckin, W. 1972. *Imprinting and Early Learning*. London: Methuen.

Smith, A.T. & Peacock, M.M. 1990. Conspecific attraction and the determination of metapopulation colonization rates. *Conservation Biology*, 4, 320–3.

Smith, E.A. & Wishnie, M. 2000. Conservation and subsistence in small-scale societies. *Annual Review of Anthropology*, 29, 493–524.

Smith, E.A., Borgerhoff Mulder, M. & Hill, K. 2001. Controversies in the evolutionary social sciences: a guide for the perplexed. *Trends in Ecology and Evolution*, 16, 128–35.

Smith, E.H. & Logan, D.T. 1997. Linking environmental toxicology, ethology, and conservation. In: J.R. Clemmons & R. Buchholz (eds.), *Behavioural Approaches to Conservation in the Wild*, pp. 277–302. Cambridge: Cambridge University Press.

Snowdon, C.T. & Hausberger, M. (eds.) 1997. *Social Influences on Vocal Development*. Cambridge: Cambridge University Press.

Sol, D., Timmermans, S. & Lefebvre, L. 2002. Behavioural flexibility and invasion success in birds. *Animal Behaviour*, 63, 495–502.

Spalding, D.A. 1873. Instinct, with original observations on young animals. *Macmillan's Magazine*, 27, 282–93. Reprinted in 1954 in *British Journal of Animal Behaviour*, 2, 2–11.

Spear, N.E. 1973. Retrieval of memory in animals. *Psychological Review*, 80, 163–75.

Spear, N.E., Miller, J.S. & Jagielo, J.A. 1990. Animal memory and learning. *Annual Review of Psychology*, 41, 169–211.

Squire, L.R. & Fox, M.M. 1980. Assessment of remote memory: validation of the television test by repeated testing during a seven-day period. *Behavioral Research Methods, Instruments and Computers*, 12, 583–6.

Squire, L.R. & Slater, P.C. 1975. Forgetting in very long-term memory as assessed by an improved questionnaire technique. *Journal of Experimental Psychology: Human Learning and Performance*, 104, 50–4.

Stacey, P.B. & Koenig, W.D. 1990. *Cooperative Breeding in Birds*. Cambridge: Cambridge University Press.

Staddon, J.E.R. 1975. A note on the evolutionary significance of "supernormal" stimuli. *American Naturalist*, 109, 541–5.

Stamps, J.A. 1988. Conspecific attraction and aggregation in territorial species. *American Naturalist*, 131, 329–47.

Stander, P.E. 1992. Cooperative hunting in lions: the role of the individual. *Behavioral Ecology and Sociobiology*, 29, 445–54.

Stephens, D.W. & Krebs, J.R. 1986. *Foraging Theory*. Princeton, NJ: Princeton University Press.

Stephens, P.A. & Sutherland, W.J. 1999. Consequences of the Allee effect for behaviour, ecology and conservation. *Trends in Ecology and Evolution*, 14, 401–5.

Stillman, R.A., Goss-Custard, J.D., West, A.D. et al. 2000. Predicting mortality in novel environments: tests and sensitivity of a behaviour-based model. *Journal of Applied Ecology*, 37, 564–88.

Stillman, R.A., Goss-Custard, J.D., West, A.D. et al. 2001. Predicting shorebird mortality and population size under different regimes of shellfishery management. *Journal of Applied Ecology*, 38, 857–68.

Storey, A.E., Walsh, C.J., Quinton, R.L. & Wynne-Edwards, K.E. 2000. Hormonal correlates of paternal responsiveness in new and expectant fathers. *Evolution and Human Behavior*, 21, 71–95.

Strausfeld, N.J., Hansen, L., Yongsheng, L., Gomez, R.S. & Ito, K. 1998. Evolution, discovery, and interpretations of arthropod mushroom bodies. *Learning and Memory*, 5, 11–37.

Strier, K.B. 1997. Behavioral ecology and conservation biology of primates and other animals. *Advances in the Study of Behaviour*, 26, 101–58.

Suga, N. 1990. Biosonar and neural computation in bats. *Scientific American*, 262, 60–8.

Sutcliffe, O.L. & Thomas, C.D. 1996. Open corridors appear to facilitate dispersal by ringlet butterflies (*Aphantopus hyperantus*) between woodland clearings. *Conservation Biology*, 10, 1359–65.

Sutherland, W.J. 1983. *From Individual Behaviour to Population Ecology*. Oxford: Oxford University Press.

Sutherland, W.J. 1985. Chance can produce a sex difference in variance in mating success and explain Bateman's data. *Animal Behaviour*, 33, 1349–52.

Sutherland, W.J. 1996. Predicting the consequences of habitat loss for migratory populations. *Proceedings of the Royal Society of London Series B*, 263, 1325–7.

Sutherland, W.J. 1998. The importance of behavioural studies in conservation biology. *Animal Behaviour*, 56, 801–9.

Symons, D. 1989. A critique of Darwinian anthropology. *Ethology and Sociobiology*, 10, 131–44.

Symons, D. 1992. On the use and misuse of Darwinism in the study of human behavior. In: J. Barkow, L. Cosmides & J. Tooby (eds.), *The Adapted Mind*, pp. 137–59. New York: Oxford University Press.

Taddio, A., Stevens, B., Craig, K. et al. 1997. Efficacy and safety of lidocaine-prilocaine cream for pain during neonatal circumcision. *New England Journal of Medicine*, 336, 1197–201.

Takahashi, J.S., Turek, F.W. & Moore, R.Y. (eds.) 2002. *Circadian Clocks. Handbook of Behavioral Neurobiology*, vol. 12. New York: Kluwer Academic/Plenum.

Takahashi, T., Moiseff, A. & Konishi, M. 1984. Time and intensity cues are processed independently in the auditory system of the owl. *Journal of Neuroscience*, 4, 1781–6.

Temple, S.A. 1986. Recovery of the endangered Mauritius Kestrel *Falco punctatus* from an extreme population bottleneck. *Auk*, 103, 632–3.

ten Cate, C. 1989. Behavioral development: toward understanding processes. In: P.P.G. Bateson & P.H. Klopfer (eds.), *Perspectives in Ethology*, vol. 8, pp. 243–69. New York: Plenum Press.

Terlouw, E.M.C., Lawrence, A.B. & Illius, A.W. 1991. Influences of feeding level and physical restriction on development of stereotypies in sows. *Animal Behaviour*, 42, 981–91.

Ter Pelkwijk, J.J. & Tinbergen, N. 1937. Eine reizbiologische Analyse einiger Verhaltensweisen von *Gasterosteus aculeatus*. *Zeitschrift für Tierpsychologie*, 1, 194–200.

Terrace, H.S. 1991. Chunking during serial learning by a pigeon: I. Basic evidence. *Journal of Experimental Psychology: Animal Behavior Processes*, 17, 81–93.

Terrace, H.S., Pettito, L.A., Sanders, R.J. & Bever, T.G. 1979. Can an ape create a sentence? *Science*, 206, 891–902.

Thomas, E.M. 1994. *The Tribe of the Tiger.* New York: Simon & Schuster.

Thorndike, E.L. 1911. *Animal Intelligence.* New York: Macmillan.

Thornhill, R. 1983. Cryptic female choice and its implications in the scorpionfly *Harpobittacus nigriceps. American Naturalist*, 122, 765–88.

Thornhill, R. 1990. The study of adaptation. In: M. Bekoff & D. Jamieson (eds.), *Interpretation and Explanation in the Study of Behavior*, vol. 2, pp. 31–62. Boulder, CO: Westview Press.

Thornhill, R. 1992. Females prefer the pheromone of males with low fluctuating asymmetry in the Japanese scorpionfly (*Panorpa japonica*). *Behavioral Ecology*, 3, 277–83.

Thornhill, R. 1997. The concept of an evolved adaptation. In: G.R. Bock & G. Cardew (eds.), *Characterizing Human Psychological Adaptations*, pp. 4–22. Chichester: John Wiley & Sons.

Thornhill, R. & Gangestad, S.W. 1999. The scent of symmetry: a human sex pheromone that signals fitness? *Evolution and Human Behavior*, 20, 175–201.

Thornhill, R. & Møller, A.P. 1998. The relative importance of size and asymmetry in sexual selection. *Behavioral Ecology*, 9, 546–51.

Thornton, J.W., Need, E. & Crews, D. 2003. Resurrecting the ancestral steroid receptor: ancient origin of estrogen signaling. *Science*, 301, 1714–17.

Thorpe, W.H. 1956. *Learning and Instinct in Animals.* London: Methuen.

Thorpe, W.H. 1965. The assessment of pain and distress in animals. In: F.W. Rogers Brambell, chairman (ed.), *Report of the Technical Committee to Enquire into the Welfare of Animals Kept Under Intensive Livestock Husbandry Systems*, pp. 71–9. London: HMSO.

Thorpe, W.H. 1979. *The Origins and Rise of Ethology: The Science of the Natural Behaviour of Animals.* London: Heinemann Educational.

Tinbergen, N. 1940. Die Übersprungbewegung. *Zeitschrift für Tierpsychologie*, 4, 1–40.

Tinbergen, N. 1951. *The Study of Instinct.* Oxford: Clarendon Press.

Tinbergen, N. 1952. The curious behavior of the stickleback. *Scientific American*, 187, 2–6.

Tinbergen, N. 1959. Comparative studies of the behaviour of gulls (Laridae): a progress report. *Behaviour*, 15, 1–70.

Tinbergen, L. 1960. The natural control of insects in pinewoods. *Archives Neerlandaise de Zoologie*, 13, 265–343.

Tinbergen, N. 1963. On aims and methods of ethology. *Zeitschrift für Tierpsychologie*, 20, 410–33.

Tinbergen, N. & Kuenen, D.J. 1939. Über die auslösenden und die richtunggebenden Reizsituationen der Sperrbewegung von jungen Drosseln (*Turdus m. merula* L. und *T. e. ericetorum* Turton). *Zeitschrift für Tierpsychologie*, 3, 37–60.

Tinbergen, N. & Tinbergen, E.A. 1972. *Early Childhood Autism: An Ethological Approach.* Berlin: Paul Parey.

Tinbergen, N., Brockhuysen, G.J., Feekes, F., Houghton, J.C.W., Kruuk, H. & Szulc, E. 1962. Egg shell removal by the black headed gull, *Larus ridibundus*: a behaviour component of camouflage. *Behaviour*, 19, 74–117.

Toates, F.M. 1983. Models of motivation. In: T.R. Halliday & P.J.B. Slater (eds.), *Animal Behaviour*, vol. 1, pp. 168–96. Oxford: Blackwell Scientific Publications.

Toates, F.M. 1986. *Motivational Systems.* Cambridge: Cambridge University Press.

Toates, F.M. & Jensen, P. 1991. Ethological and psychological models of motivation: towards a synthesis. In: J.-A. Meyer & S. Wilson (eds.), *From Animals to Animats*, pp. 194–205. Cambridge, MA: MIT Press.

Todt, D. 1975. Social learning of vocal patterns and modes of their applications in Grey Parrots. *Zeitschrift für Tierpsychologie*, 39, 178–88.

Tomasello, M. & Call, J. 1997. *Primate Cognition.* New York: Oxford University Press.

Tooby, J. & Cosmides, L. 1990. On the universality of human nature and the uniqueness of the individual: the role of genetics and adaptation. *Journal of Personality*, 58, 17–67.

Toone, W.D. & Wallace, M.P. 1994. The extinction in the wild and reintroduction of the California condor (*Gymnogyps californianus*). In: P.J.S. Olney, G.M. Mace & A.T.C. Feistner (eds.), *Creative Conservation*, pp. 411–19. London: Chapman & Hall.

Tosini, G. & Menaker, M. 1996. Circadian rhythms in cultured mammalian retina. *Science*, 272, 419–21.

Tramontin, A.D. 1998. Seasonal plasticity and sexual dimorphism in the avian song control system: stereological measurement of neuron density and number. *Journal of Comparative Neurology*, 396, 186–92.

Tramontin, A.D. & Brenowitz, E.A. 1999. A field study of seasonal neuronal incorporation into the song control system of a songbird that lacks adult song learning. *Journal of Neurobiology*, 40, 316–26.

Tramontin, A.D. & Brenowitz, E.A. 2000. Seasonal plasticity in the adult brain. *Trends in Neurosciences*, 23, 251–8.

Tregenza, T. 1995. Building on the ideal free distribution. *Advances in Ecological Research*, 26, 253–307.

Trivers, R.L. 1971. The evolution of reciprocal altruism. *Quarterly Review of Biology*, 46, 35–57.

Trivers, R.L. 1972. Parental investment and sexual selection. In: B. Campbell (ed.), *Sexual Selection and the Descent of Man, 1871–1971*, pp. 136–72. Chicago: Aldine-Atherton.

Trivers, R.L. 1985. *Social Evolution*. Menlo Park, CA: Benjamin/Cummings.

Trivers, R.L. & Hare, H. 1976. Haplodiploidy and the evolution of social insects. *Science*, 191, 249–63.

Trivers, R.L. & Willard, D.E. 1973. Natural selection of parental ability to vary the sex ratio. *Science*, 179, 90–2.

Turke, P.W. & Betzig, L.L. 1985. Those who can, do: wealth, status, and reprdoctive success on Ifaluk. *Ethology and Sociobiology*, 6, 79–87.

Turner, D.C. & Bateson, P.P.G. (eds.) 2000. *The Domestic Cat: The Biology of its Behaviour*, 2nd edn. Cambridge: Cambridge University Press.

Uetz, G.W. 2001. Understanding the evolution of social behavior in colonial web-building spiders. In: L.A. Dugatkin (ed.), *Model Systems in Behavioral Ecology*, pp. 110–30. Princeton, NJ: Princeton University Press.

Uhlenbroeck, C. 2002. *Talking to Animals*. London: Hodder & Stoughton.

Ungerleider, L.G. & Mishkin, M. 1982. Two cortical visual systems. In: D.J. Ingle, M.A. Goodale & R.J.W. Mansfield (eds.), *Analysis of Visual Behavior*, pp. 549–86. Cambridge, MA: MIT Press.

Vahed, K. 1998. The function of nuptial feeding in insects: a review of the empirical evidence. *Biological Reviews*, 73, 43–78.

Valenza, E., Simion, F., Cassia, V.M. & Umilta, C. 1996. Face preference at birth. *Journal of Experimental Psychology: Human Perception and Performance*, 22, 892–903.

Vander Wall, S.B. 1990. *Food Hoarding in Animals*. Chicago: University of Chicago Press.

van Iersel, J.J.A. 1953. An analysis of the parental behaviour of the three-spined stickleback (*Gasterosteus aculeatus* L.). *Behaviour*, Suppl. 3, 1–159.

van Schaik, C.P. & Janson, C.H. (eds.) 2000. *Infanticide by Males and its Implications*. Cambridge: Cambridge University Press.

van Schaik, C.P. & Kappeler, P.M. 1997. Infanticide risk and the evolution of male–female association in primates. *Proceedings of the Royal Society of London Series B*, 264, 1687–94.

van Schaik, C.P. & van Noordwijk, M.A. 1985. Evolutionary effect of the absence of felids on the social organization of the macaques on the island of Simeulue (*Macaca fascicularis fusca*, Miller 1903). *Folia Primatologica*, 44, 138–47.

Vaughan, W. Jr & Greene, S.L. 1984. Pigeon visual memory capacity. *Journal of Experimental Psychology: Animal Behavior Processes*, 10, 256–71.

Verner, J. 1964. The evolution of polygamy in the long-billed marsh wren. *Evolution*, 18, 252–61.

Vestergaard, K.S. 1982. Dust-bathing in the domestic fowl: diurnal rhythm and dust deprivation. *Applied Animal Ethology*, 8, 487–95.

Vestergaard, K.S., Hogan, J.A., & Kruijt, J.P. 1990. The development of a behavior system: dustbathing in the Burmese red junglefowl: I. The influence of the rearing environment on the organization of dustbathing. *Behaviour*, 112, 99–116.

Vestergaard, K.S., Kruijt, J.P. & Hogan, J.A. 1993. Feather pecking and chronic fear in groups of red junglefowl: its relations to dustbathing, rearing environment and social status. *Animal Behaviour*, 45, 1117–26.

Vestergaard, K.S., Damm, D.I., Abbot, U.K. & Bildsøe, M. 1999. Regulation of dustbathing in feathered and featherless domestic chicks: the Lorenzian model revisited. *Animal Behaviour*, 45, 1127–40.

Vining, D.R. 1986. Social versus reproductive success: the central theoretical problem for human sociobiology. *Behavioral and Brain Sciences*, 9, 167–216.

Visalberghi, E. & Limongelli, L. 1994. Lack of comprehension of cause–effect relations in tool-using capuchin monkeys (*Cebus apella*). *Journal of Comparative Psychology*, 108, 15–22.

Vom Saal, F.S. & Bronson, F. 1980. Sexual characteristics of adult females correlates with their blood testosterone levels during development in mice. *Science*, 208, 597–9.

von der Emde, G. & Schwarz, S. 2001. How the electric fish brain controls the production and analysis of electric signals during active electrolocation. *Zoology*, 103, 112–24.

von Frisch, K. 1967. *Dance Language and Orientation of Bees* (translated by L.E. Chadwick). Cambridge, MA: Belknap Press of Harvard University Press.

von Schantz, T., Bensch, S., Grahn, M., Hasselquist, D. & Wittzell, H. 1999. Good genes, oxidative stress and condition-dependent sexual signals. *Proceedings of the Royal Society of London Series B*, 266, 1–12.

von Uexküll, J. 1921. *Umwelt und Innenwelt der Tiere*. Berlin: Springer.

Waddington, C.H. 1966. *Principles of Development and Differentiation*. New York: Macmillan.

Wade, M.S. 1987. Measuring sexual selection. In: J.W. Bradbury & M.B. Andersson (eds.), *Sexual Selection: Testing the Alternatives*, pp. 197–207. New York: John Wiley & Sons.

Wagner, A.R. 1976. Priming in STM: an information-processing mechanism for self-generated or retrieval-generated depression in performance. In: T.J. Tighe & R.N. Leaton (eds.), *Habituation: Perspectives from Child Development, Animal Behavior, and Neurophysiology*, pp. 95–128. Hillsdale, NJ: Lawrence Erlbaum Associates.

Wagner, A.R. 1981. SOP: a model of automatic memory processing in animal behavior. In: N.E. Spear & R.R. Miller (eds.), *Information Processing in Animals: Memory Mechanisms*, pp. 5–47. Hillsdale, NJ: Lawrence Erlbaum Associates.

Wallace, M.P. 2000. Retaining natural behaviour in captivity for re-introduction programmes. In: L.M. Gosling & W.J. Sutherland (eds.), *Behaviour and Conservation*, pp. 300–14. Cambridge: Cambridge University Press.

Wallraff, H.G. 1981. Clock-controlled orientation in space. In: J. Aschoff (ed.), *Biological Rhythms. Handbook of Behavioral Neurobiology*, vol. 4, pp. 275–98. New York: Plenum Press.

Ward, P. & Zahavi, A. 1973. The importance of certain assemblages of birds as "information centres" for food finding. *Ibis*, 115, 517–34.

Ward, P.I. 2000. Cryptic female choice in the yellow dung fly *Scathophaga stercoraria* (L.). *Evolution*, 54, 1680–6.

Waring, G.H. 1983. *Horse Behavior*. Norwich, NY: Noyes Publications.

Waring, G.H. 2003. *Horse Behavior*, 2nd edn. Norwich, NY: Noyes Publications.

Washburn, S.L. 1978. Human behavior and the behavior of other animals. *American Psychologist*, 33, 405–18.

Watson, J.B. 1924. *Behaviorism*. New York: W.W. Norton.

Watson, J.B. 1928. *Psychological Care of Infant and Child*. New York: W.W. Norton.

Watson, P.J. 1986. Transmission of a female sex pheromone thwarted by males in the spider *Linyphia litigiosa* Keyserling (Linyphiidae). *Science*, 233, 219–21.

Watson, P.J., Arnqvist, G. & Stallmann, R.R. 1998. Sexual conflict and the energetic costs of mating and mate choice in water striders. *American Naturalist*, 151, 46–58.

Watt, P.J. & Chapman, R. 1998. Whirligig beetle aggregations: what are the costs and the benefits? *Behavioral Ecology and Sociobiology*, 42, 179–84.

Weary, D.M. & Fraser, D. 1995. Calling by domestic piglets: reliable signals of need? *Animal Behaviour*, 50, 1046–55.

Weaver, D.R. 1998. The suprachiasmatic nucleus: a 25-year retrospective. *Journal of Biological Rhythms*, 13, 100–12.

Webb, W.B. 1998. Sleep. In: G. Greenberg & M.M. Haraway (eds.), *Comparative Psychology: A Handbook*, pp. 327–31. New York: Garland.

Webster, J. 1994. *Animal Welfare: A Cool Eye towards Eden*. Oxford: Blackwell Science.

Wedekind, C. & Füri, S. 1997. Body odour preferences in men and women: do they aim for specific MHC combinations or simply heterozygosity? *Proceedings of the Royal Society of London Series B*, 264, 1471–9.

Wedekind, C., Seebeck, T., Bettens, F. & Paepke, A.J. 1995. MHC-dependent mate preferences in humans. *Proceedings of the Royal Society of London Series B*, 260, 245–9.

Weingardt, K.R., Loftus, E.F. & Lindsay, D.S. 1995. Misinformation revisited: new evidence on the suggestibility of memory. *Memory and Cognition*, 23, 72–82.

Weir, A.A.S., Chappell, J. & Kacelnik, A. 2002. Shaping of hooks in New Caledonian crows. *Science*, 297, 981.

Weiss, E. 2002. Selecting shelter dogs for service dog training. *Journal of Applied Animal Welfare Science*, 5, 43–62.

Welch, A.M., Semlitsch, R.D. & Gerhardt, H.C. 1998. Call duration as an indicator of genetic quality in male gray tree frogs. *Science*, 280, 1928–30.

Welsh, D.K., Logothetis, D.E., Meister, M. & Reppert, S.M. 1995. Individual neurons dissociated from rat suprachiasmatic nucleus express independently phased circadian firing rhythms. *Neuron*, 14, 697–706.

Wemelsfelder, F. 1993. The concept of animal boredom and its relationship to stereotyped behaviour. In: A.B. Lawrence & J. Rushen (eds.), *Stereotypic Animal Behaviour: Fundamentals and Applications to Welfare*, pp. 65–95. Wallingford, UK: CAB International.

West Eberhard, M.J. 1983. Sexual selection, social competition and speciation. *Quarterly Review of Biology*, 58, 155–83.

Wheeler, W.M. 1902. "Natural history," "ecology" or "ethology"? *Science*, 15, 971–6.

Whitehead, H. & Hope, P.L. 1991. Sperm whalers of the Galapagos Islands and in the Western Pacific, 1830–1850: ideal free whalers. *Ethology and Sociobiology*, 12, 146–61.

Whiten, A. & Byrne, R.W. 1988. Tactical deception in primates. *Behavioral and Brain Sciences*, 11, 233–44.

Whiten A., Custance, D.M., Gomez, J.C., Texidor, P. & Bard, K.A. 1996. Imitative learning of artificial fruit processing in children (*Homo sapiens*) and chimpanzees (*Pan troglodytes*). *Journal of Comparative Psychology*, 110, 3–14.

Wiersma, C.A.G. & Ikeda, K. 1964. Interneurons commanding swimmeret movements in the crayfish, *Procambarus clarkii* (Girard). *Comparative Biochemistry and Physiology*, 12, 509–25.

Wilczysnki, W., Rand, A.S. & Ryan, M.J. 2001. Evolution of calls and auditory tuning in the *Physalaemus pustulosus* species group. *Brain, Behavior and Evolution*, 58, 137–51.

Williams, G.C. 1966. *Adaptation and Natural Selection*. Princeton, NJ: Princeton University Press.

Williams, G.C. 1992. *Natural Selection: Domains, Levels and Challenges*. New York: Oxford University Press.

Williams, J.H.G., Whiten, A., Suddendorf, T. & Perrett, D.I. 2001. Imitation, mirror neurons and autism. *Neuroscience and Biobehavioral Reviews*, 25, 287–95.

Wilson, D.S. 1994. Adaptive genetic variation and human evolutionary psychology. *Ethology and Sociobiology*, 15, 219–35.

Wilson, E.O. 1975. *Sociobiology: The New Synthesis*. Cambridge, MA: Belknap Press of Harvard University Press.

Wilson, E.O. 1978. *On Human Nature*. Cambridge, MA: Harvard University Press.

Wilson, E.O. 1992. *The Diversity of Life*. Cambridge, MA: Belknap Press.

Wilson, M. & Daly, M. 1985. Competitiveness, risk taking, and violence: the young male syndrome. *Ethology and Sociobiology*, 6, 59–73.

Wilson, M.I., Daly, M. & Weghorst, S.J. 1980. Household composition and the risk of child abuse and neglect. *Journal of Biosocial Science*, 12, 333–40.

Wilson, M., Daly, M. & Gordon, S. 1998. The evolved psychological apparatus of human decision-making is one source of environmental problems. In: T. Caro (ed.), *Behavioral Ecology and Conservation Biology*, pp. 501–23. Oxford: Oxford University Press.

Wimberger, P.H. & de Queiroz, A. 1996. Comparing behavioral and morphological characters as indicators of phylogeny. In: E. Martins (ed.), *Phylogenies and the Comparative Method in Animal Behavior*, pp. 206–33. Oxford: Oxford University Press.

Wingfield, J.C., Hegner, R.E., Dufty, A.M. & Ball, G.F. 1990. The "challenge hypothesis": theoretical implications for patterns of testosterone secretion, mating systems, breeding strategies. *American Naturalist*, 136, 829–46.

Wingfield, J.C., Hunt, K., Breuner, C. et al. 1997. Environmental stress, field endocrinology, and conservation biology. In: J.R. Clemmons & R. Buchholz (eds.), *Behavioural Approaches to Conservation in the Wild*, pp. 95–131. Cambridge: Cambridge University Press.

Winterhalder, B. & Lu, F. 1997. A forager-resource population ecology model and implications for indigenous conservation. *Conservation Biology*, 11, 1354–64.

Winterhalder, B. & Smith, E.A. 2000. Analyzing adaptive strategies: human behavioral ecology at twenty-five. *Evolutionary Anthropology*, 9, 51–72.

Witherington, B.E. 1997. The problem of photopollution for sea turtles and other nocturnal animals. In: J.R. Clemmons & R. Buchholz (eds.), *Behavioural Approaches to Conservation in the Wild*, pp. 303–28. Cambridge: Cambridge University Press.

Wood-Gush, D.G.M. 1971. *The Behaviour of the Domestic Fowl*. London: Heinemann Educational.

Wood-Gush, D.G.M., Duncan, I.J.H. & Fraser, D. 1975. Social stress and welfare problems in agricultural animals. In: E.S.E. Hafez (ed.), *The Behaviour of Domestic Animals*, 3rd edn, pp. 182–200. London: Baillière Tindall.

Woodroffe, R. 2001. Strategies for carnivore conservation: lessons from contemporary extinctions. In: J.L. Gittleman, S.M. Funk, D. Macdonald & R.K. Wayne (eds.), *Carnivore Conservation*, pp. 61–92. Cambridge: Cambridge University Press.

Woodroffe, R. & Ginsberg, J.R. 2000. Ranging behaviour and vulnerability to extinction in carnivores. In: L.M. Gosling & W.J. Sutherland (eds.), *Behaviour and Conservation*, pp. 125–40. Cambridge: Cambridge University Press.

Woodward, A.A., Fink, A.D. & Thompson, F.R. 2001. Edge effects and ecological traps: effects on shrubland birds in Missouri. *Journal of Wildlife Management*, 65, 668–75.

Wüstenberg, D., Gerber, B. & Menzel, R. 1998. Long- but not medium-term retention of olfactory memories in honeybees is impaired by actinomycin D and anisomycin. *European Journal of Neuroscience*, 10, 2742–5.

Wyatt, T.D. 2003. *Pheromones and Animal Behaviour: Communication by Smell and Taste.* Cambridge: Cambridge University Press.

Wynne, C.D.L. 2001. *Animal Cognition: The Mental Lives of Animals.* Basingstoke, UK: Palgrave Press.

Wynne-Edwards, K.E. 2001. Hormonal changes in mammalian fathers. *Hormones and Behavior*, 40, 139–45.

Wynne-Edwards, V.C. 1962. *Animal Dispersion in Relation to Social Behavior.* New York: Hafner.

Zeh, J.A., Newcomer, S.D. & Zeh, D.W. 1998. Polyandrous females discriminate against previous mates. *Proceedings of the National Academy of Sciences USA*, 95, 13732–6.

Zucker, Z. 2001. Circannual rhythms: mammals. In: J.S. Takahashi, F.W. Turek & R.Y. Moore (eds.), *Circadian Clocks. Handbook of Behavioral Neurobiology*, vol. 12, pp. 519–25. New York: Kluwer Academic/Plenum.

Zuk, M. 1990. Reproductive strategies and sex differences in disease susceptibility: an evolutionary viewpoint. *Parasitology Today*, 6, 231–3.

Zuk, M. & Kolluru, G.R. 1998. Exploitation of sexual signals by predators and parasitoids. *Quarterly Review of Biology*, 73, 415–38.

Zuk, M., Thornhill, R., Ligon, J.D. et al. 1990. The role of male ornaments and courtship behavior in female mate choice of red jungle fowl. *American Naturalist*, 136, 459–73.

# glossary

**absolute number judgment**  Ability that requires the animal to select the correct number of items. The animal must therefore choose on the basis of a fixed number, e.g., five, as opposed to relative differences in quantity.

**acrophase**  The peak of a cosine function fit to a set of data.

**action-specific energy**  In the Lorenz model of **motivation**, internal **causal factors** (energy) that activate only the **behavior mechanism** for the specific action pattern under consideration.

**activating effects**  A term used for the direct effects of hormones on behavior in adult individuals. See also **organizing effects**.

**adaptation**  Trait whose design is the consequence of **natural selection** acting to maximize its contribution to the bearer's **fitness**.

**affective state**  Feeling or emotion experienced as hedonically positive (pleasure, contentment) or negative (pain, fear, hunger) that may help to stimulate behavior.

**algorithm**  Blueprint, procedure, or formula (calculating rule) for solving a recurrent problem. In mathematics and computer science, a problem is solved algorithmically by means of elementary instructions accomplished stepwise in an appropriate language. In neurobiology, an algorithm ("software") is implemented by a **neuronal** network ("hardware"). The word "algorithm" derives from the name of the mathematician Mohammed ibn-Musa al-Khwarizmi (780–850), who was part of the royal court in Baghdad.

**Allee effect**  Decrease in individual survival or breeding output when the population size is low. This may occur across the population or within groups within a population, as when small groups are unable to catch large prey or fight off predation attempts successfully.

**alpha**  Highest-ranking individual in a **dominance hierarchy**.

**alternative strategies**  Two or more mutually exclusive sets of actions leading to the same goal.

**altruism**  See altruistic behavior.

**altruistic behavior**  Behavior by an individual (the altruist) that helps the recipient of the behavior but costs the altruist, in terms of survival or future reproductive success.

**ambivalent behavior**  A behavior pattern containing elements of behavior patterns belonging to two or more **behavior systems**.

**amplitude**  Difference between the **acrophase** and the mean value of cosine function. Also used less formally to describe the range of oscillation of a **rhythm**.

**ampulla**  Part of the **spermatophore** that contains sperm.

**analogous**  Refers to structures that share the same **function** even though the two structures may have very different evolutionary origins.

**animal welfare** (1) Traditionally, a good or satisfactory condition of existence or quality of life of animals; hence, "animal welfare advocates" are those who promote a good quality of life for animals. (2) In science, a scale running from poor to good pertaining to the quality of life of animals.

**antagonistic coevolution** Where a characteristic in one lineage acts as a selection pressure on another lineage favoring a counteradaptation, which then acts as a selection pressure on the original lineage. In sexually antagonistic coevolution, the lineages refer to males and females.

**anthropocentrism** The tendency to study animals from a human perspective, asking questions about whether animals can solve the tasks that humans can solve and if so whether they can do so using the same processes.

**anthropomorphism** The tendency to view animals as humans and thus explain their behavior by imputing human cognitive abilities such as **conscious** thought.

**appetitive conditioning** Conditioning procedure in which the **reinforcer** is a valued event (such as food for a hungry animal).

**approach gradient** Strength of the tendency to approach a goal object (or place) as a function of the distance from that object (or place).

**apyrene sperm** Sperm that lack nuclear material and therefore cannot fertilize eggs (cf. **eupyrene sperm**).

**arms race** A dynamic pattern of evolution that results from interactions among organisms such that the evolution of one character which decreases the **fitness** of individuals without the character favors the evolution of a second character in these individuals that mitigates the effect of the first. An arms race can occur within or between species.

**assessor** Strategy in a competitive game between two individuals in which the individual assesses its competitive ability compared with its assailant and only fights if it is superior in competitive ability (see also **bourgeois**).

**attachment theory** Theory proposed by John Bowlby and developed by Mary Ainsworth that is meant to explain how an infant develops a bond with its mother or other caregiver. This bond produces maintenance of proximity to the caregiver and upset when separated from it.

**autoshaping** Classical conditioning procedure used with pigeons in which the bird comes to peck an illuminated disk (the response key) that has been presented immediately before the delivery of food.

**aversive conditioning** Conditioning procedure in which the **reinforcer** is an unpleasant event (such as electric shock).

**avoidance gradient** Strength of the tendency to avoid an object (or place) as a function of the distance from that object (or place).

**azimuth** Location, or bearing, of a point on the horizon, measured in degrees of angular rotation from a reference point such as north.

**Batesian mimicry** See mimicry.

**behavioral adjustment** Change in allocation to alternative behavioral strategies in response to payoff contingencies.

**behavioral ecology** The study of how both natural and **sexual selection** can account for and predict the behavioral patterns we observe in organisms.

**behavioral enrichment** Environmental manipulations or events that improve the welfare of captive animals by allowing them to perform more natural behavior.

**behavioral flexibility** Measure of the degree to which individuals can alter or adjust their behavior through **learning** or cognition to changing circumstances. Most often used in reference to the degree of flexibility among different members of a population.

**behavioral neuroscience** Study of the brain mechanisms involved in behavior.

**behavioral scan sample** An observational technique in which the observer briefly looks at all subjects (scans) at fixed preestablished time intervals noting some or all behavior occurring during the scan.

**behavioral toxicology** Study of changes in behavior in response to the effects of a toxic substance, often used to detect sublethal effects of a chemical or pollutant on an organism.

**behaviorism** An approach to behavior proposed by John B. Watson that consists of accepting that only measurable behavioral manifestations can be the object of scientific scrutiny, excluding all mental processes that produce behavior. When applied to **learning**, behaviorism maintains that all learning has to do with the formation of associations between stimuli and responses.

**behavior mechanism** Hypothetical structure in the central nervous system that, when activated, produces an event of behavioral interest, such as a particular perception, a specific motor pattern, or an identifiable internal state. Similar to cognitive structure.

**behavior system** Any organization of perceptual, central, and motor units that acts as a larger unit in some situations.

**binaural fusion** Process of combining different sounds received by the two ears to produce the perception of a single external sound source.

**binding of features** Brains of animals and humans can effortlessly bind the attributes of stimuli to form coherent perceptual categories. This requires the activity of **neurons**/neuronal groups, each specialized to respond to certain features, such as shape and motion. "Binding problems" may be solved by (i) concurrent inputs from different feature-analyzing neurons, (ii) binding through selective synchronization of dynamically formed neuronal groups, and (iii) binding through the influence of "higher" attentional processes.

**blocking** The observation that establishing one event as a **conditioned stimulus** will prevent the animal from **learning** about a second event when both are presented together along with the same **unconditioned stimulus**.

**bourgeois strategy** Strategy in a competitive game between two individuals in which an individual fights if it possesses a resource, but withdraws if its opponent possesses a resource.

**brainstem** Part of the brain consisting of the **midbrain, pons,** and medulla oblongata, and which forms the connection between brain and spinal cord.

**Bruce effect** The observation that a pregnant female rodent will abort her fetus if an intruder male takes over the nest and/or kills the male.

**byproduct mutualism** Behavior by an individual that benefits that individual as well as another, if another is present (see also **mutualism**).

**canalization** A term suggested by Conrad Waddington; essentially it means that under certain circumstances a particular **developmental** process will follow a fairly fixed and predictable path.

**cardinality** Sequence of number tags or labels used to count the number of items in the array. The last or cardinal number in the array represents the total number of items.

**categorization** Categorization of objects is a basic cognitive process. It refers to the act of arranging things into classes or categories of the same type. A category can be a class of behaviorally significant objects that share a set of defining features.

**causation** One of the four questions that characterizes **ethology** according to Niko Tinbergen. It refers to the study of the immediate external (stimuli) and internal (states) **causes** of any given behavior pattern.

**cause or causal factor** Agent that activates or brings about change in a **behavior** mechanism.

**cell membrane potential** The electric potential across the membrane of a **neuron**. The inside of the neural membrane is negative compared with the outside; the potential is typically around − 70 mV.

**character mapping** Constructing a hypothesis about the evolution of a character by associating the states or values of the character of extant species on a **phylogenetic tree**, and then using a variety of methods to reconstruct the state or values of the characters at ancestral nodes of the tree.

**chase-away model** Model of **sexual selection** stating that females evolve resistance to male traits that increase male **fitness** at the expense of female fitness.

**chunking** Formation of a group of items that may serve to expand the capacity of **working memory**.

**circadian** Latin "about a day"; a biological **rhythm** in which the average duration of a complete cycle approximates the solar day (24 h).

**circalunar** Biological **rhythm** in which the average duration of a complete cycle approximates the lunar month (~ 30 days).

**circatidal** Biological **rhythm** in which the average duration of a complete cycle approximates the tidal cycle (~ 12.5 h).

**classical conditioning** Procedure devised by Pavlov in which two stimuli are paired (usually the conditioned stimulus is presented slightly before the **unconditioned stimulus**). As a consequence a **conditioned response** develops to the conditioned stimulus.

**clock genes** One or more genes that exhibit **circadian rhythms** of expression and are essential for the generation of circadian rhythms in cellular functions and outputs. The term is meant to imply that the gene has an essential role in the production of cellular circadian rhythms, but boundaries between this set of genes and the sets of genes regulating inputs to and outputs from the core circadian **oscillator** are as yet undefined.

**cochlea** Spiral structure in the inner ear in which sound **signals** are converted to neural signals. Sound pressure waves in the fluid-filled chambers of the cochlea deform the basilar membrane and stimulate auditory receptor **neurons**.

**coefficient of relatedness ($r$)** Probability that an individual shares a gene with another by common descent.

**coevolution** Changes brought about by two groups of organisms exerting a selection pressure on each other, e.g., predators and prey, parasites and hosts.

**cognitive neuroscience** Study of the brain mechanisms involved in cognitive processes. See also cognition.

**cognitive psychology** The scientific study of mental processes, such as thought and **information** processing. Cognitive psychology arose in the 1950s in response to the then prevailing school of **behaviorism**.

**command releasing system (CRS)** Neuronal interface that translates sensory input (perception) into motor output (behavior). A CRS involves groups of **neurons** (command elements) with stimulus-feature-analyzing and stimulus-localizing properties ("**sensorimotor code**"). A CRS is subject to inputs from systems involved in **motivation** and **learning**. CRS is the redefined neurophysiological equivalent of the ethological concept of releasing **mechanism**.

**common environment effects** Similarity in phenotype among relatives as a result of sharing a common environment. For example, siblings may have shared the same nest, or parents and offspring may have grown up in a similar kind of environment.

**communal crèche** When breeding females of the same species form a close association and keep their young together in a group.

**comparative approach** A research program where statistical methods are used to partition the effects of homology, highlighting those characteristsics which have evolved repeatedly and then searching for a common explanation for that repeated evolution.

**comparative psychology** Study of behavioral mechanism in animals, in relation to those in humans, using similar methods as human psychology.

**competence** A term suggested by Conrad Waddington, meaning that certain parts of an embryo can cause **induction** of different other parts at different times.

**competitive exclusion model** Model of **imprinting** proposed by Patrick Bateson that posits experience with the imprinting **stimulus** as the **causal factor** for the end of the **sensitive period**.

**condition-dependent trait** Trait that shows greater expression (or size) or develops to a larger size when an individual is in better body condition.

**conditioned emotional response** A complex of fear-related responses elicited by a **conditioned stimulus** that has been paired with an aversive **unconditioned stimulus**.

**conditioned response (CR)** Response evoked by a **conditioned stimulus** as a result of **classical conditioning**.

**conditioned stimulus (CS)** Stimulus that has acquired the power to evoke a new response as a consequence of **classical conditioning**.

**conditioned taste aversion** Rejection of a taste that has previously been associated with a state of nausea.

**conditioning** Procedure for producing **learning** in the laboratory; of two types, classical and instrumental (or **operant**).

**configural cue** Novel cue generated when separate stimulus elements are presented as a compound.

**configurational stimuli** Configuration (*Gestalt*) refers to the arrangement of parts or elements. The configuration of a stimulus refers to the parts of a stimulus (features, attributes) that are arranged to each other in a certain relationship (e.g., spatially or spatiotemporally). A configurational stimulus is not recognized by the sum of its parts, rather as a whole. The recognition process involves **invariance** when the physical stimuli in question are considerably changed; while their relations are kept constant, the configuration remains the same. The underlying recognition involves a "**binding problem**."

**conflict (motivational)** A state where **causal factors** for more than one **behavior system** are present at the same time.

**confusion effect** Reduction in the efficiency with which a predator is able to capture a prey individual because of the association of prey into a group.

**connectionism** Theoretical approach to the analysis of **learning** (and cognition generally) which attempts explanation solely in terms of changes in the effectiveness of connections among a large number of **neuron**-like units.

**consciousness** A term used (often inconsistently) for a range of mental states, including wakefulness, awareness, attention, reflection, and self-awareness, and whose attribution to animals raises both philosophical and empirical difficulties.

**consolidation** Process of laying down **information** in **reference memory**.

**conspecific attraction** Animals may use the presence of members of their own species to ascertain the suitability of **patches** or to direct their movement among patches.

**contiguity** In general, the co-occurrence of two events; more specifically the proposal that **conditioning** depends on such co-occurrences.

**contralateral** On the opposite side.

**cooperation** See cooperative behavior.

**cooperative behavior** Joint action for mutual benefit

**cooperative hunting** Pursuit of prey by two or more predators that results in a higher success of capture.

**corridor** A linear habitat, embedded in a dissimilar matrix, that connects two or more larger blocks of habitat. Corridors are also sometimes used in a functional sense of whether animals travel between two habitat **patches**.

**cospeciation** Extent to which patterns of **speciation** of one group are congruent with patterns of speciation of another. Speciation in the first group may or may not be directly influencing speciation in the second group. Originally proposed in the context of host–parasite evolution.

**crepuscular** Active primarily at dawn and dusk.

**critical period** A term used previously for what is now called **sensitive period**.

**critical reserve size** Size of a protected area that will allow a population to persist for a given period of time as specified by researchers, such as 100 or 1000 years.

**cross-fostering** When young of a certain species are reared with adults ("foster parents") of another species.

**cryptic female choice** When females influence paternity in favor of particular males through processes that follow copulation; it is cryptic simply because, unlike conventional female choice, the process is not visually obvious.

**cultural adaptation** Behavioral trait that enhances an individual's **fitness** and is acquired non-genetically through some form of **social learning**, **imitation**, or cultural transmission.

**currency of fitness** A hypothesis of how a trait contributes to an individual's **fitness**. The currency is used to compare the **survival value** of alternative courses of action.

**dead reckoning** When animals (including humans) navigate by dead reckoning they use **information** about the direction and distance of each leg of the journey with no reference to landmarks.

**deception** See tactical deception.

**decision** A point at which the individual is confronted with a set of alternative courses of action.

**delayed matching-to-sample (DMTS)** A procedure for studying **working memory** in which a sample stimulus is presented followed by a **retention interval** and then a choice between the previous sample and an alternative. Correct choice of the sample is rewarded.

**depolarization** Decrease in electrical polarization of the neural cell membrane caused by movement of positively charged ions into the cell. The **neuronal** action potential is the propagation of cell membrane depolarization.

**development** One of the four questions that characterizes **ethology** according to Niko Tinbergen. It refers to the process of change and maturation that occurs in an individual from conception to death. Also known as **ontogeny**.

**developmental instability** Inability of individuals to develop a stable phenotype under given environmental conditions.

**differentiation** An embryological term denoting that different parts of the embryo develop into different organs and body parts.

**diffraction** Bending of a **waveform** around an obstacle or edge.

**dilution effect** Decrease in the probability that an individual is selected by a predator because the individual associates with other individuals and the group is not proportionately more likely to be detected by a predator or attract more predators.

**dioecious species** Those species in which the two sexes are in different individuals.

**diploid** The condition whereby the cells of an individual contain two sets of chromosomes (and genes), one from each parent.

**direct benefits** Material benefits that females obtain from their mate choice in the current generation.

**direct fitness** Fitness gained by an individual from its efforts in producing its own offspring.

**direct fitness benefits** Mate choice has evolved to provide females with direct material benefits. Such benefits include males with sperm of high fertilizing ability, males with high courtship feeding rates, males with better territories, males that defend females from harassment by other males, males that provide females with environments with low risk of predation or parasitism, or males that provide the offspring with high-quality paternal care.

**directed-forgetting paradigm**   Used for studying cued recall effects on **working memory**. During the **retention interval** of a **delayed matching-to-sample** paradigm, the animal receives a cue to indicate whether or not they will receive a choice test.

**directionality of signals**   Extent to which a **signal** spreads out from its source. Can be determined by features of the signal (e.g., wavelength) and **signaler** (e.g., size).

**discrimination training**   Procedure in which the animal receives a **reinforcer** in the presence of one stimulus but no reinforcer (or a different reinforcer) in the presence of a different stimulus.

**dishabituation**   Restoration of a habituated response produced by application of a novel and intense stimulus.

**disinhibition theory**   A theory proposed by Sevenster, among others, that when two **behavior systems** are strongly activated, the **inhibition** they exert on each other will result in a release of inhibition on other behavior systems, and a **displacement activity** will occur.

**dispersal**   Permanent change in location from one place or social group to another.

**displacement activity**   Behavior pattern belonging to a **behavior system** different from the behavior systems that are expected to be activated in a **conflict** situation.

**display**   Pattern of **ritualized** behavior that transmits **information** within members of a species.

**diurnal**   Active primarily during the day.

**dominance hierarchy**   A pattern of social ranking within a group that results from the outcome of pairwise competitive interactions such that there is often an individual ranked above all the others (the **alpha**) and others ranked below this individual. Linear dominance hierarchies are those in which individual A ranks over B, C, and D, B ranks over C and D, C ranks over D, and D does not rank over any of them.

**Dove**   See Hawk–Dove game.

**eavesdropper**   A **receiver** using **information** in **signals** that are primarily directed at other receivers. Interceptive eavesdroppers intercept signals intended (in an evolutionary sense) for another individual, usually to the cost of the **signaler** (e.g., bats preying on calling frogs). Social eavesdroppers gather information on other individuals by attending to their signaling interactions with conspecifics. For further details see Peake 2004.

**ecological traps**   Arise when the cues that an animal uses to assess the quality of a habitat become decoupled from the true value of a habitat, often as a result of human perturbation. Animals continue to be attracted to habitat in which their **fitness** is reduced.

**effective population size**   Size of an ideal population that would lose genetic variation via genetic drift at the same rate; in essence, a measure of the number of individuals that are "effectively" contributing genetically to the next generation.

**effective reserve size**   See critical reserve size.

**elevation**   Height of a point above the horizon, measured in degrees of angular rotation from the horizon.

**embryonic induction**   Process by which one part of an embryo influences a neighboring part, thereby making that part develop into an organ which it would not otherwise have done.

**endogenous (or spontaneous) behavior**   Behavior that occurs without any apparent external cause. The **causes** for the behavior lie within the central nervous system.

**entrained**   Synchronized to an external time cue (e.g., a 24-h light–dark cycle) by **phase** and **period** control of an endogenous **oscillator** (e.g., a **circadian** oscillator).

**entrainment**   Process of **oscillator phase** and **period** control by which **endogenous rhythms** are synchronized to external time cues.

**environmental preference research**   Identifies environments or environmental features that an animal chooses ahead of other options.

**environment of evolutionary adaptedness (EEA)**   Hypothetical environment that occurred in the past and within which a contemporary trait acted as an **adaptation**.

**epigenesis** The idea that the adult features of individuals are not already represented in the embryo but develop. This is the opposite of **preformation.**

**epigenetic landscape** A visual metaphor for **developmental** processes, proposed by Conrad Waddington. See Chapter 6 and Fig. 6.1.

**episodic recall** Ability to remember specific past experiences that integrates **information** about what happened where and when.

**ethology** Study of behavior from a biological perspective including **causation, development, survival value** and **evolution.** Known today as biology of behavior.

**eupyrene sperm** Normal, fully functional, fertile sperm (cf. **apyrene sperm**).

**eusociality** "True" sociality, defined as involving the following three characteristics: (i) cooperation by individuals other than parents in caring for the young; (ii) overlap of at least two generations capable of contributing to colony labor; and (iii) reproductive division of labor, with a mostly or wholly sterile worker caste working on behalf of individuals engaged in reproduction.

**evolutionarily stable strategy (ESS)** A strategy or mixture of strategies that, once fixed in a population, cannot be bettered by an alternative.

**evolutionary arms race** See arms race.

**evolutionary psychology** Study of human behavior based on the assumption that contemporary human behavior is the result of selection pressures acting in the evolutionary past. See also **sociobiology.**

**exclusive paternity** When a male fertilizes all of the female's eggs.

**experience projection** Ability to use your own experience to predict another individual's intentions and to understand what they might be thinking ("putting yourself in someone else's shoes").

**extinction** The procedure of discontinuing presentation of the **reinforcer** after initial **conditioning**; also the effects of this procedure (a decline in the vigor or likelihood of the trained response).

**facilitation** A term introduced by Gilbert Gottlieb referring to one of three ways in which experience can affect the development of perceptual preferences. In this case, the development of perceptual preferences is accelerated by a certain experience, which may be unrelated to the preference (nonspecific experience). See also **induction** and **maintenance,** and Fig. 6.5.

**fair raffle** When each competitor has an equal chance of winning the competition.

**feminization** The process of confirmation of the genetic sex of female birds by means of surge of the female sex hormone estrogen around hatching.

**filial imprinting** Process whereby early social preferences become restricted to a particular stimulus, or class of stimuli, as a result of exposure to that stimulus.

**Fisherian character** A purely attractive **secondary sexual character** that does not show evidence of condition dependence.

**Fisherian mating advantage** Mate choice has evolved to increase the attractiveness of sons independent of other aspects of genetic quality. If females prefer males with slightly exaggerated traits, and if males with such traits tend to mate with females with strong mate preferences, then alleles for mate preference and male trait become linked. The mate preference and the male trait will then evolve to ever more extreme values in a "runaway" fashion, either until balanced by oppositely directed **natural selection** or until genetic variation in mate preference or male trait becomes depleted.

**fitness** Measure of an individual's success in passing on copies of its genes to future generations (see also **direct fitness, indirect fitness** and **inclusive fitness**).

**flavor aversion learning** Classical conditioning procedure in which animals come to reject a foodstuff with a given flavor after having previously experienced this flavor followed by a state of nausea.

**fluctuating asymmetry**  Departures from bilateral symmetry in structures that are symmetrical "by design."

**free-run**  The state of a circadian pacemaker, and the rhythms that it drives, in an environment lacking external time cues that would normally synchronize the pacemaker to local time.

**frequency**  Number of cycles per unit time (inverse of **period**).

**frontal cortex**  The cortex of the frontal lobe of the brain.

**function**  Adaptive purpose of a trait.

**game theory**  Mathematical tool developed by economists to model and analyze optimal decisions when the outcome of these **decisions** are dependent on decisions adopted by others.

**gene–culture coevolution**  Process whereby the adoption of a culturally acquired trait creates an opportunity for **natural** or **sexual selection** to operate and hence modify the frequency of genes in a population.

**generalist**  In the context of foraging theory an individual that accepts all prey types as encountered.

**generalization**  Ability of stimuli different from a trained stimulus to evoke a **conditioned response** to some (usually lesser) extent.

**genetic complementarity**  Mating arrangement where partners more often have dissimilar genotypes than predicted by chance. An example is genetic complementarity between partners for the major histocompatibility complex in humans.

**genetic mating system**  The **mating system** when the true parentage of offspring is considered. Brood parasitism and extrapair paternity cause the genetic mating system to differ from the social mating system.

**gene transcription**  Copying of a DNA base sequence into messenger RNA; the first step in gene expression.

***Gestalt* psychology**  The German School of Gestalt-Psychologists, founded by Max Wertheimer (1880–1943), was to some extent a rebellion against the molecularism of Wilhelm Wundt's program for psychology (molecularism means to break **information** down to its smallest parts in order to obtain a thorough understanding of psychological concepts). In fact, the word *Gestalt* means a unified or meaningful whole, which was to be the focus of psychological study instead. The original observation was Wertheimer's, when he noted that we perceive motion where there is nothing more than a rapid sequence of individual sensory light events, the basic principle of visual motion pictures. Wertheimer explained that you are seeing an effect of the whole event, not contained in the sum of the parts. In perception, there are many organizing principles called *Gestalt* laws.

**glial cells**  Nonneuronal cells of the nervous system. Glial cells serve a variety of functions, including insulation, structural support, nutrition, and movement of neurons.

**goal emulation**  Involves observational **learning** of response-reinforcer contingencies. A distinction can be made between true **imitation**, which literally involves the observer copying the actions of the demonstrator in order to achieve the desired goal, and goal emulation, in which the observer attempts to reproduce the results of the demonstrator's action rather than precisely copying the form of his or her action.

**good genes**  Genes that provide choosy individuals with a genetic advantage for their offspring, for example due to parasite or disease resistance.

**grandmother neuron**  Historically, this term stems from a debate on the neuronal basis of feature detection and pattern recognition. One party argued that the different features of an object are analyzed by different types of **neurons** and that object recognition results from convergent inputs of these neurons to a complex recognizer-cell. The other party argued that object recognition results from parallel processing of features in neuronal assemblies, where the activity pattern in this assembly should represent the object. Driving the concept of a recognizer-cell ad absurdum, the idea of a grandmother neuron was created, i.e., a neuron tuned specifically to grandma which, if lost, would mean that grandma would not be recognized again. Today, it is commonly accepted that a complex stimulus situation can be monitored by various types of neurons including highly complex ones. However, a complex stimulus situation cannot be monitored by a highly complex neuron alone.

**group selection**   Change in the frequency of genes and the traits that they influence that results from selection acting on groups of individuals as opposed to single individuals. This process was made explicit by Wynne-Edwards (1962).

**habitat fragmentation**   Degree to which regions of similar habitat type are broken up into smaller patches and are disconnected or isolated from other patches of similar habitat type.

**habitat matching**   Expected outcome of the **ideal free distribution** in which the ratio of the populations in two habitats matches the ratio of the resources available in each habitat.

**habitat selection**   Measure of the active choice or process of selection for specific habitats, often indexed as the use of a given habitat relative to its availability.

**habituation**   Waning of an **unconditioned response** with repeated application of its eliciting stimulus.

**Hamilton's rule**   Equation that expresses the conditions under which **altruistic behavior** will spread in a population: $Br - C > 0$, where $B$ is the benefit of the behavior to the recipient, $r$ the **coefficient of relatedness** between the altruist and the recipient, and $C$ the cost of the behavior to the altruist.

**handicap**   Conspicuous cost of the **signal**, a cost that may ensure honesty.

**handicap hypothesis**   Only individuals in prime condition are able to obtain the benefits from **developing** an exaggerated **secondary sexual character** because of their superior condition. Individuals in poor condition are prevented from cheating because of the differential cost (the handicap) of developing a large secondary sexual character. This provides a mechanism that causes secondary sexual characters (and other **signals**) to provide reliable **information** about the **signaler**.

**handling time**   In foraging theory, time spent manipulating and ingesting a food item.

**hands**   Observable output of a clock; can be used as a measure of the **phase** of the clock.

**haplodiploidy**   Breeding system in which females are **diploid** and males are **haploid**, such that unfertilized eggs **develop** into males and fertilized eggs develop into females.

**haploid**   The condition whereby the cells of an individual contain only one set of chromosomes; gametes (sperm and eggs) of **diploid** individuals are usually haploid.

**Hawk**   See Hawk–Dove game.

**Hawk–Dove game**   A two-strategy, two-person game describing interactions of resource defense. Dove is a nonaggressive strategy that gives up when the opponent escalates fighting to injurious levels. Hawk is a strategy that consists of escalated fighting that only gives up if injured.

**helpers**   Individuals in a social group that help other individuals in their group reproduce (e.g., by **helping** to guard or feed the other individuals' young).

**helping behavior**   Behavior by one individual that contributes to the survival and reproductive success of another individual.

**heritability**   Similarity in phenotype between relatives due to the effects of quantitative genes. Heritability ranges from 0 (no resemblance among relatives) to 1 (complete resemblance). Heritabilities are typically 0.3–0.5 for most characters.

**heterogeneous summation**   Cases where the effects of different (heterogeneous) stimulus features add together (summate) to influence behavior. This algebraic summation of the effects of stimulus features is different from nonalgebraic summation. A **configurational stimulus** (*Gestalt*) is recognized not by the algebraic sum of its components but rather by nonalgebraic summation of the components whose effect is much bigger.

**heterozygosity**   Proportion of genetic loci that are heterozygous within one individual.

**high vocal center (HVC)**   A song control nucleus in the forebrain of songbirds; formerly called the hyperstriatum ventrale pars caudale.

**homeostasis**   Latin "similar standing"; a process by which a variable (typically physiological, such as body temperature) is maintained at some desired value (typically but not exclusively by negative feedback).

**home range**   Area normally used by an individual animal in the course of its activities, usually over a year.

**homologous behaviors**   Behaviors of different species that owe their resemblance to inheritance through a common ancestor.

**homologous structure**   Behavior patterns or other structures that are similar in different species and are presumed to have evolved from a common ancestor.

**homoplasious**   Behaviors of different species that owe their resemblance to parallel or convergent evolution.

**honest signaling**   The signal gives an accurate indication of the **information** of interest, e.g., signaler body size, condition, **motivation**. For an example of dishonest signaling, see Batesian mimicry.

**ideal free distribution (IFD)**   Theoretical distribution of individuals that are ideal in the sense that they know instantaneously the value of alternative habitats or resource **patches** and free in the sense that they can go without cost to any available habitat or resource patch. The ideal free distribution is reached when individuals are distributed in such a way that no individual can gain by moving from one area to another.

**imitation**   True imitation has been defined as the "copying of a novel or otherwise improbable act or utterance, or some act for which there is clearly no instinctive tendency" (Thorpe 1963). So the behavior to be copied should not be part of the observer's prior behavioral repertoire.

**immediate early genes**   Genes transcribed rapidly following extracellular stimulation of a cell.

**immunocompetence handicap hypothesis**   A handicap mechanism based on the observation that secondary sexual characters often develop under the influence of sex hormones, and that such hormones have negative effects on immunity. Therefore, individuals can only develop large secondary sexual characters under the influence of high levels of sex hormones if they are particularly resistant to parasites.

**imprinting**   Process by which early experience promotes the **development** of perceptual mechanisms. See also **filial imprinting** and **sexual imprinting**.

**inclusive fitness**   The sum of **direct fitness** gained by the individual's investment in its own offspring and **indirect fitness** gained by its effects on the reproduction of nondescendant relatives.

**independent contrasts**   Method to control for the statistical and phylogenetic nonindependence of species used in **comparative** studies that assigns character values to nodes of a **phylogeny**.

**indirect benefits**   Genetic benefits such as parasite resistance that females gain from their mate choice through their offspring in the subsequent generation.

**indirect fitness**   Fitness gained by an individual from the effects of its behavior on nondescendant kin (e.g., **helping** an aunt produce nieces that share genes with the **helper**) (see also **fitness, direct fitness** and **inclusive fitness**).

**induction**   A term derived from embryology. When applied to behavioral development it denotes that a certain perceptual preference only appears after some kind of experience, which may be unrelated to the preference (nonspecific experience). See also **embryonic induction**.

**information** The word is used in two senses in the communication literature: (1) knowledge (sometimes referred to as **semantic information**); (2) reduction in a **receiver**'s uncertainty following reception of a **signal** (sometimes referred to as **statistical information**).

**information center** A group of animals that have congregated at least partly because of the advantages that individuals gain from gathering **information** about the location of resources from the behavior of other group members.

**infradian rhythms** Rhythms with an average cycle duration longer than **circadian** (e.g., **circalunar** and circannual rhythms).

**inhibition** The effect that one **behavior mechanism** has in suppressing the expression of other behavior mechanisms.

**innate** An outdated and controversial term to indicate that a behavior is somehow present at birth and not learnt. In fact, the term has at least seven different meanings (see Chapter 6). The term "innate" is not very useful for understanding the mechanisms of behavior and can be very misleading. For this reason, it is placed in quotation marks in this book.

**innate releasing mechanism (IRM)** Historical concept of a sensorimotor interface innately mediating between **sign–stimulus** and corresponding species-specific behavior, in a rigid manner. For example, an IRM should allow an animal to recognize a behaviorally relevant object that the animal had never seen before. The IRM has recognition and localization properties and can be gated or inhibited by **motivational** inputs.

**insight** That Eureka experience of suddenly discovering a solution to a problem. The critical ingredients seem to be (i) the abruptness of the solution and (ii) the complexity of the actions.

**instrumental conditioning** Procedure for generating **learning** in which an event (e.g., delivery of food) is made contingent on the occurrence of some response.

**intensity of sperm competition** Absolute number of males whose sperm compete for the ova of a single female.

**interceptive eavesdropper** See eavesdropper.

**intersexual selection** Sexual selection arising from mate choice by individuals of the choosy sex, usually females.

**interval timer** Device that measures a single interval of time; must be reset to initiate another cycle (e.g., an hourglass clock).

**intrasexual selection** Sexual selection arising from competition among individuals of the chosen sex, usually males.

**invariance** Recognition of a **configurational stimulus** (*Gestalt*) involves invariance when the physical stimuli in question are considerably changed while their relations to each other are kept constant, i.e., the configuration is maintained. For example, a melody is invariant regardless of the instrumentation (e.g., piano, guitar, trumpet, or comb).

**ipsilateral** On the same side.

**irreversibility** A concept used in the context of **imprinting**, suggesting that once a social preference has been formed for a particular stimulus, the animal cannot form a preference for another stimulus. It has been demonstrated that imprinting preferences can in fact be reversed.

**jet lag** Malaise caused by rapid travel across time zones, resulting in a mismatch between internal **circadian** time and local external time. Typically associated with disruptions of sleep and arousal.

**kin selection** Selection for traits that improve the survival of shared genes whether they are in the bodies of offspring or nondescendant kin.

**law of effect** Thorndike's proposal that a response that produces a desired outcome will become linked to the stimulus situation in which it occurs; more generally, the principle that the effect produced by an action will change the likelihood of occurrence of that action.

**learning** Process by which an animal interacts with its environment and becomes changed by the experience so that its subsequent behavior is modified.

**lek** Aggregation of males on small display territories that are visited by mate-searching females.

**loaded raffle** When, for various reasons, certain competitors have an advantage over their rivals and hence are more likely to win the competition.

**local enhancement** Social learning is categorized as local enhancement if exposure to the demonstrator or its products (scent cues, feces) draws the observer's attention to the location of the stimuli with which the demonstrator was interacting. Note that the observer's attention is drawn to a particular locale in the environment because the demonstrator is also located in that specific area, hence the term local enhancement (cf. **stimulus enhancement**).

**long-term potentiation (LTP)** Increased response of a **neuron** to stimulation following repeated stimulation.

**maintenance** A term introduced by Gilbert Gottlieb referring to one of three ways in which experience can affect the development of perceptual preferences. In this case, certain perceptual preferences may disappear unless the individual is provided with a certain experience, which may be unrelated to the preference (nonspecific experience). See also **induction** and **facilitation**, and Fig. 6.5.

**masculinization** In mammals, where female is the default phenotypic sex, the results of a surge of the male hormone testosterone around birth, leading to a genetic male developing into a phenotypic male.

**mate guarding** Where a male prevents rival males from mating with his mate.

**maternal effects** Resemblance in phenotype between parents and offspring due to the direct material effects of the mother (or the father) on the phenotype of the offspring. For example, mothers may provision their eggs with different amounts of yolk or hormones, and such substances can affect the subsequent appearance of the offspring.

**mating plug** Material placed over the female genital opening and which prevents further mating.

**mating success** Number of mates acquired by each individual. Under **monogamy** mating success will be dichotomous with either mated or unmated individuals, whereas under **polygyny** males can have from no mates up to more than a dozen.

**mating system** The social association between males and females during the reproductive season, including the relative roles of males and females in reproductive activities. Common mating systems are **monogamy, polygyny,** and **polyandry**.

**metapopulation** Collection of subpopulations of the same species, each of which occupies a separate **patch** of subdivided habitat.

**metarepresentation** Ability to form more complex representations, including mental representations of other individuals and mental representations of other individuals' mental representations.

**midbrain** Smallest and most anterior part of the **brainstem**, containing nuclei of the auditory and visual systems as well as nuclei controlling eye movements and skeletal muscles.

**mimicry** Imitation or close resemblance, usually applied to appearance or sounds. (1) **Batesian** mimicry: edible prey gain protection by mimicking species that predators avoid (e.g., harmless hoverflies mimic the yellow and black stripes of stinging social wasps). (2) **Mullerian** mimicry: resemblance between different species that are all noxious or dangerous (e.g., warning coloration of poisonous sea snakes).

**mirror neuron** Neuron that fires either when the animal makes a specific movement or when it sees another animal make the same movement.

**monogamy** Reproductive relationship between one male and one female.

**monogynous** Where males mate once only.

**monophyletic** Group that contains the common ancestor and all taxa that have descended from it.

**motivation** Study of the immediate **causes** of behavior.

**motivational isocline** Line connecting points of equal probability that a behavior will occur as a function of the strength of internal and external **causal factors** for that behavior.

**motivation analysis** A technique used to analyze **ambivalent behavior**, in which the form of the behavior, the situation in which it occurs, and other behaviors that occur in association with it are examined.

**Mullerian mimicry** See mimicry.

**multimodal** Signals that require **receivers** to use two or more senses.

**multiple-bearing hypothesis** Kamil and Cheng (2001) suggested that animals might use multiple landmarks to work out their position in space and that they could do this by taking compass bearings to individual landmarks or by using the relative geometric positions of the landmarks.

**multiple mating** Usually refers to females that mate with more than one partner during a reproductive cycle and thus creates the opportunity for her eggs to be fertilized by different males (see also **polyandry**).

**mushroom body** Mushroom-shaped structure in the anterior region of the arthropod brain.

**mutualism** Behavior by two or more individuals that benefits both the individuals performing the behavior.

**natural selection** A process involving differences in **fitness**, the capacity of individuals to survive and reproduce, and hence leading to evolution as a result of change in the genetic representation from generation to generation.

**neuroethology** Research discipline investigating the neurophysiological bases of behavior. Historically the term can be traced to E. von Holst (1939) who laid the foundation of *Verhaltensphysiologie* (comparative behavioral physiology); N. Tinbergen (1951) used the term "ethophysiology," J. Seegar (1961) proposed "ethoanatomy," while J.L. Brown and R.W. Hunsperger (1963) introduced "neuroethology."

**neuron** Cell in the nervous system that carries electrical signals along an extended process called the axon and which communicates chemically with other neurons at points of contact called synapses.

**neurotransmitter** Chemical that carries a signal from one **neuron** to another at a synapse between neurons. Neurotransmitters are released at the synapse when a neuron fires and may stimulate or inhibit firing by other neurons.

**nocturnal** Active primarily at night.

**nuptial gifts** Any form of nutrient transferred from the male to the female during or shortly after courtship and/or copulation.

**observational conditioning** This is a form of Pavlovian **conditioning** in which an **unconditioned response** of the demonstrator acts as an **unconditioned stimulus** that elicits a matching response on the part of the observer.

**ontogenetic adaptations** A term introduced by Robert Oppenheim, denoting that each **developmental** phase may involve unique behavioral **adaptations** to the environment of the developing animal.

**ontogeny** See development.

**operant** Behavior pattern that originally occurs (or is emitted) spontaneously and has some effect (operates) on the environment. As a result of its effects (**reinforcement**), such a behavior pattern comes to be controlled by external factors.

**operant conditioning** Another name for **instrumental conditioning**.

**operational sex ratio** Ratio of fertilizable females to sexually active males at any given time.

**optimal foraging theory** A body of **optimality** models and empirical findings that deal principally with **decisions** pertaining to prey choice and **patch** exploitation time.

**optimality model** Mathematical expression that computes for a specific **decision** the best alternative, expressed as a **currency of fitness** given a set of constraints. Simple optimality models apply when outcomes of behavioral strategies are *not* frequency-dependent.

**optimality theory** An approach that consists of postulating that a trait under scrutiny is optimally designed to accomplish a **function** of importance to the animal's **fitness**, and then predicting the characteristics that this trait ought to possess if it were so designed through natural or **sexual selection** processes (see also **optimal foraging theory**).

**ordinality** Principle that during counting each number tag must occur in a fixed order (e.g., 1, 2, 3, 4, 5, 6, etc.).

**organizing effects** A term used for the indirect effects of hormones on differentiation of an individual's body or behavior during development. See also **activating effects**.

**oscillator** Device that produces a **rhythm**.

**overflow theory** In the context of the Lorenz model of **motivation**, the theory that when **causal factors** for a particular **behavior system** are strong but the behavior is prevented from occurring, the energy from the activated system flows over to another behavior system that is then expressed as a **displacement activity**.

**oviposition** Act of laying eggs, typically used when describing this behavior in invertebrates.

**pacemaker** An **oscillator** that sets the **phase** and **period** of a number of **rhythms**.

**parse** To analyze a **signal** or message in an orderly way by resolving it into its component parts.

**partial preference** In the context of optimal prey models, when the predator sometimes accepts and sometimes rejects the same prey type.

**patch** Spatially localized area containing resources separated from other such areas by space that contains less or no resources.

**Pavlovian conditioning** See classical conditioning.

**peak shift displacement** Displacement of the peak of a generalization gradient in the direction away from a negative stimulus during **discrimination training**.

**perceptual learning** Process by which mere exposure to stimuli can change the way in which they are perceived, making similar stimuli easier to discriminate.

**perceptual sharpening** Process by which the release of a certain behavior toward a stimulus requires refined recognition of the stimulus. This process may involve ontogenetic maturation of the recognition system as well as **learning**.

**period** Duration of one complete cycle of an oscillating process.

**persistence of signals** Duration of **signals**, i.e., their continued existence through time. Acoustic signals persist for a much shorter time than some chemical signals.

**phase** A point on a cycle, e.g., wake-up time.

**phase-locked** Property of a transducer that emits a signal only at a particular **phase** of an oscillating input.

**phase-response curve (PRC)** A plot of the magnitude and direction of a **phase** shift against the **circadian** phase at which a phase-shifting stimulus was applied.

**phase shift** Change in the **phase** of a cycle. A phase-advance shift describes movement to a later phase of a cycle (thereby acutely, and permanently, displacing the cycle forward in its progression). A phase-delay shift describes movement to an earlier phase of a cycle (thereby acutely displacing the cycle backward in its progression).

**phenotype matching** Process of kin recognition in which an individual matches its own characteristics, or characteristics that it has learned from its kin, to characteristics of another individual and biases its behavior toward that individual based on the degree of similarity.

**pheromone** Hormone-like substances (sometimes called ecto-hormones or socio-hormones) that are released outside the organism to transmit **information** between individuals of a species for social communication. Among these are sexual attractants (sex pheromones), marking substances (orientation pheromones), and alarm substances (recruitment pheromones).

**philopatry**   Latin "love of home"; when an individual remains in the place or social group in which it was born.

**photopollution**   Increased levels or altered wavelengths of light introduced into an environment, causing disruption to behaviors that use light as **signal** or cue or that require specific light conditions.

**phylogenetic reconstruction**   Process of constructing a hypothesis of the genealogical relationships among taxa, often presented in the form of a branching diagram.

**phylogenetic tree**   Branching diagram that illustrates a hypothesis about genealogical relationships among taxa.

**phylogeny**   History of descent with modification among species.

**polyandry**   Reproductive relationship between one female and several males.

**polygyny**   Reproductive relationship between one male and more females. Polygyny may be (i) harem polygyny, where each polygynous male defends a group of females, or (ii) resource-defense polygyny, where each polygynous male defends the resources necessary to attract a group of females.

**polygyny threshold model**   Theoretical model explaining why females under certain distributions of resources may benefit from choosing a **polygynous** mating status by mating with an already-mated male having many resources rather than becoming **monogamous** through mating with an unmated male with few resources.

**pons**   Latin "bridge"; part of the **brainstem**, with functions that include relaying **information** between the cerebellum and the cerebral hemispheres, the control of eye movements, and the integration of converging auditory **signals** from the two ears.

**positron emission tomography (PET)**   Technique measuring the concentrations of positron-emitting radioisotopes within the tissue of living subjects by use of tomography. For example, local **neuronal** activity in the brain can be determined by the local density of flow of blood loaded with $^{15}O$. Radionuclide decay, which reduces excess positive charge on the nucleus, can occur in two ways: neutralization of a positive charge with the negative charge of an electron, or the emission of a positron from the nucleus. The positron will then combine with an electron from the surroundings and annihilate. Upon annihilation both positron and electron are converted to electromagnetic radiation in the form of two gamma-quants that can be detected.

**potential**   See cell membrane potential.

**predispositions**   Behavioral tendencies, such as perceptual preferences, that may develop in an individual without any experience with the particular stimuli involved. The term is also used to denote the underlying mechanisms.

**preformation**   The idea that, at the time of fertilization, the egg or the sperm already contains the basic features of the adult individual.

**primacy effect**   Enhanced memory for the initial items in a list, observed as an upward turn at the beginning of a **serial position function**.

**priming**   Change in an animal's internal **motivational** state that is brought about by presentation of a stimulus and that outlasts the presence of that stimulus.

**principle of parsimony**   When there are competing hypotheses put forward to explain the same data, the preferred hypothesis is the one that requires the fewest ad hoc assertions about the data.

**prisoner's dilemma**   A two-person game in which each individual has two possible strategies: cooperate or defect. The payoffs of the prisoner's dilemma game are such that cooperation brings a reward but this is not as high as the payoff to an individual that defects when its companion cooperates. There is thus a temptation to cheat (defect).

**proactive interference**　Disruption in performance in recalling a current item due to the occurrence of a prior event.

**proboscis**　In insects, mouthpart for sucking liquids, consisting of an elongated tube and associated cutting or piercing structures.

**producer–scrounger game**　A two-strategy, $n$-player game in which individuals can obtain resources by using one of two **alternative strategies** looking for resources (playing producer) or looking for individuals that have already found resources (playing scrounger).

**promiscuity**　Mating relationship when neither males nor females form stable associations (pair bonds) with partners, and when males are not **displaying** in aggregations.

**proximate**　Refers to a level of questions about behavior that encompasses mostly **causation** and **development**. These are also known as "how" questions, to the extent that they deal mostly with the machinery of behavior operating within individual organisms.

**punishment**　Instrumental **conditioning** procedure in which an aversive event is contingent on the response.

**pursuit-deterrent signal**　Signal prey directs at a predator to indicate their ability to escape from the predator, e.g., "stotting" by gazelles.

**quantitative genetics**　The discipline of genetics that deals with quantitative characters, i.e., those that differ in size rather than kind. Numerous characters, such as body height and body mass, show quantitative genetic variation.

**radial maze**　Apparatus for studying working and **reference memory** that contains a central platform with several arms radiating from the center. **Reinforcers** may be placed at the end of an arm.

**reactivation**　Exposure to an environment in which **learning** previously occurred in an attempt to aid subsequent recall.

**receiver**　An animal picking up a **signal**, e.g., another bird. Also referred to as detectors or reactors.

**recency effect**　Enhanced memory for the final items in a list, observed as an upward turn at the end of a **serial position function**.

**receptive field**　Region of the total sensory field to which a neuron preferentially responds. In the visual system, the receptive field of a neuron might be a part of the visual field, a direction of motion, or a range of wavelengths. In the auditory system, the receptive field of a neuron might be the location of a sound or a range of auditory frequencies. In the somatosensory system, the receptive field of a neuron might be a region on the body surface.

**reciprocal altruism**　Exchange of **altruistic behavior** by two or more individuals in which the benefits of receiving the behavior are greater than the costs of **altruism**.

**redirected behavior**　Behavior pattern belonging to a **behavior system** that is activated, but which is directed to a stimulus that does not normally activate that behavior system.

**reference memory**　Permanent **information** store that contains experiences of prior events.

**refractory period**　Time following mating when a female is unreceptive to subsequent mating attempts.

**rehearsal**　Process of actively maintaining **information** in **working memory** by practicing the recall of that information in some manner.

**reinforcement**　The procedure (also the effect) of presenting a **reinforcer**.

**reinforcer**　In instrumental (or **operant**) conditioning, an event that, when made contingent on a response, increases the probability of occurrence of that response; in **classical conditioning**, another term for the **unconditioned stimulus**.

**relatedness**　See coefficient of relatedness.

**relative number judgment**　Ability to compare sets of items according to whether they contain more or less.

**relaxed selection** Removal or amelioration of a selection pressure that was formerly believed to affect a population in the past.

**releasing mechanism (RM)** Ethological concept of a sensorimotor interface mediating between **sign-stimulus** and corresponding behavior. An RM assures a linkage between a sign-stimulus and the corresponding behavioral response. The RM has recognition and localization properties and it can be gated or inhibited by **motivational** inputs. Furthermore, an RM can be modified by **learning**. The concept of **command releasing system** suggests a neurophysiological equivalent of RM.

**releasing stimulus** Stimulus that activates a specific perceptual mechanism and that allows a specific behavior pattern to occur.

**remodeling** A brain structure "designed for" or "dedicated to" a certain sensory or motor function can be rearranged morphologically and functionally, for example in order to serve a different function. The underlying processes in the brain may involve activity-gated plasticity and cross-modal plasticity.

**representation** A cognitive or neural mechanism in an individual's mind or brain that is related to a stimulus or event in that individual's internal or external environment.

**reproductive skew** Degree to which reproduction in a group is unevenly divided between group members. If only one adult of a sex breeds and other adults of that sex do not, reproductive skew is complete. If all adults of the same sex are equally likely to breed, there is no skew.

**retention interval** Delay between the presentation and subsequent recall of **information**.

**retinal snapshot** Cartwright and Collett (1983) suggested that when bees are trained with a single landmark they remember the size of its retinal image at the goal by making a "retinal snapshot" of the landmark.

**retrieval** Process of recovering **information** from **reference memory**.

**retroactive interference** Disruption in performance in recalling a current item due to the occurrence of an event during the **retention interval**.

**retrograde amnesia** Condition in which loss of memory for past experiences may occur, usually as a result of head trauma.

**retrogressive process** A term introduced by Robert Oppenheim to denote that certain behavior patterns may disappear during **development**.

**reverse engineering** Procedure that consists in hypothesizing a **function** for a trait and then computing whether its design features correspond to those that maximize the efficiency of that hypothetical function.

**rhythm** Any process that repeats at more or less regular intervals.

**risk of sperm competition** Probability that a female mates with more than one male during a reproductive cycle.

**ritualization** Process of simplification, exaggeration, repetition, and increased **stereotypy** of a behavior that initially contains some **information** (also termed the **signal** precursor) that results in the evolution of a signal.

**runaway selection** See Fisherian mating advantage.

**schema** Type of perceptual mechanism that can be said to recognize particular objects.

**search(ing) image** In the search for an object, an animal (or human) develops a certain image of the goal object. This results in a search image which the searcher selectively pursues. This in turn leads to a change in the searching behavior and to the preference for a certain type of object, which assures greater success.

**seasonal affective disorder (SAD)** Clinically significant depression associated with shortening of daylength in fall and winter, or (more rarely) lengthening of daylength with spring and summer.

**secondary sexual character** A usually exaggerated character that has evolved as a consequence of sexual selection. Examples include antlers of deer and the train of the peacock.

**seismic signals** See vibrational signals.

**selection** See natural selection.

**selfish herd** Group of individuals that results because each is seeking cover from predation by hiding behind others.

**selfish individuals** Individuals that behave in ways that increase their own reproductive success at the expense of that of others.

**semantic information** See information.

**sensitive period** A phase in the **development** of behavior of great susceptibility to certain types of experience, preceded and followed by a period of lower sensitivity to the same experience.

**sensorimotor code** The concept of **command releasing system** considers combinatorial aspects of stimulus perception in a sensorimotor interface. A coded command involves different types of **neurons**, A, B, C, etc., each type monitoring or analyzing a certain stimulus aspect (features, location in space, etc.). In a certain combination {A B C}, the neurons (command elements) **cooperatively** activate a motor pattern generator. It is suggested that certain command elements can be shared in different sensorimotor codes, e.g., {B D E}.

**sensory bias** Mate choice has evolved as a side effect of a preference for particular types of food or environments, subsequently giving rise to evolution of particular male **secondary sexual characters**.

**sensory exploitation** (1) Process of **signal** evolution driven by preexisting **sensory biases** built into **receivers**. (2) Phenomenon where males evolve traits that exploit preexisting biases in females.

**sensory preconditioning** Training procedure in which two neutral stimuli are paired prior to one of them being used as the **conditioned stimulus** in a **classical conditioning** procedure. As a result, the other stimulus acquires the power to elicit the **conditioned response**.

**serial position curve** Another name for **serial position function**.

**serial position function** Relationship between recall accuracy and the position in a list in which an item occurred, usually a U-shaped function.

**sex ratio** Ratio of the number of sons to the number of daughters.

**sexual cannibalism** In which the female kills and cannibalizes a male at some stage during courtship and mating.

**sexual differentiation** The developmental process of becoming a female or a male.

**sexual imprinting** Process by which early social experience determines the object to which later sexual behavior will be shown.

**sexual selection** Difference in **fitness** of individuals due to a nonrandom relationship between phenotype and **mating success**. Larger variation in mating success in one sex rather than the other will give rise to more intense **sexual selection** in the sex with greater variation.

**sexual size dimorphism** Difference in the size of a character or overall body mass in males relative to females.

**signal** Something evolved to transmit **information**, e.g., the song of a bird.

**signal attenuation** Overall loss of energy contained in the **signal** during propagation caused by the signal spreading out and energy being absorbed by the **transmission medium** and habitat.

**signal distortion** Changes in the **signal** during propagation caused by the **transmission medium** and habitat. Also referred to as degradation.

**signaler** An animal producing a **signal**, e.g., a singing bird. Also referred to as senders, generators, or actors.

**signal modality**   The sense used by the **receiver** to detect the **signal**, e.g., hearing. Also referred to as the signal channel.

**sign-stimulus**   Stimulus that is adequate to activate a **releasing mechanism**, which then sets in motion a species-specific action pattern. A sign-stimulus represents a complex object by a few characteristic features. The occasionally used term "key-stimulus" is based on the idea that the releasing cues are analogous to a key which opens a lock. However, this could misleadingly suggest a high specificity of the **releasing stimulus**, which is actually not the case so far as configurational and combinatorial feature components of the stimulus are concerned. A sign-stimulus comprises a category. A redefined concept of key-stimulus regards the "key" as the **algorithm** (calculation rule) by which the sensory system gets access to that category.

**sinks**   Habitats in which population growth rates are negative and there is a net loss of individuals; other individuals may immigrate into these areas but the net population growth remains negative.

**social eavesdropper**   See eavesdroppers.

**social intelligence**   Ability to understand and reason about the minds of other individuals, and thus to deceive, manipulate, and predict the intentions of other members of the social group. Furthermore, the "social function of intellect" hypothesis states that the complexities of social life have led to an increase in general intelligence.

**social learning**   Ability to learn from other individuals.

**social perception**   Ability to form representations of other individuals as separate entities, with individual physical, vocal, and behavioral characteristics.

**sociobiology**   A subset of **behavioral ecology**, it concerns specifically the evolutionary study of social organization. Sociobiology is often associated with the theory of **kin selection** and other devices such as **Hamilton's rule** associated with the evolution of **altruism, cooperation**, and **selfish behavior**.

**sources**   Habitats in which population growth rates are positive (birth rates exceed death rates) and there is a net production of new individuals, some of which disperse and emigrate to other areas or habitats.

**spatial discrimination**   Discrimination training procedure (and its results) in which different places are associated with different **reinforcers**.

**specialist**   An individual whose prey choice consists of attacking only the most profitable prey type, excluding all others.

**speciation**   Irreversible splitting of cohesive historical lineages of interbreeding organisms.

**species recognition**   Mate choice has evolved to ensure mating with the correct species.

**speed of propagation**   Velocity with which a **signal** travels through the **transmission medium**, e.g., sound signals travel at 343 m/s through air at 20 °C and 0% relative humidity.

**spermatophore**   Membranous sac, formed by the secretions of the male accessory glands, which contains sperm.

**spermatophylax**   Part of the **spermatophore** that does not contain sperm and which, in some insects, is consumed by the female.

**sperm competition**   Occurs when the sperm of several males coexist in proximity to the female's unfertilized ova, and thus compete for fertilization success.

**stable equilibrium frequency**   Equivalent to an **evolutionarily stable strategy**, except that it is reached by **behavioral adjustment** instead of **natural selection**.

**statistical information**   See information.

**stereotyped behavior**   Pattern of behavior that is performed repetitively, in a largely invariant way.

**stimulus control** In operant conditioning, the ability of a given stimulus to modulate the rate at which a response occurs.

**stimulus enhancement** Social learning is categorized as stimulus enhancement if exposure to the demonstrator or its products (scent cues, feces) draws the observer's attention to the stimuli with which the demonstrator was interacting. Thus the observer attends to a particular object or part of an object that a demonstrator had been interacting with, irrespective of its location (cf. local enhancement).

**strange situation test** Test standardized by Mary Ainsworth in which a stranger approaches an infant with and without the caregiver being present, and various aspects of the infant's behavior are measured.

**subjective day** That portion of the circadian cycle when the organism behaves as if it were daytime.

**subjective night** That portion of the circadian cycle when the organism behaves as if it were nighttime.

**supernormal stimulus** Artificial stimulus (dummy) that elicits a particular behavior pattern more easily than the appropriate natural sign-stimulus. In such a stimulus (also called a supranormal stimulus), certain characteristic features of the natural sign-stimulus are exaggerated.

**suprachiasmatic nucleus (SCN)** Bilaterally paired nuclei in the ventral anterior hypothalamus responsible for the generation of circadian rhythms and their entrainment by light–dark cycles.

**surrogate species** Species used as a shortcut to solve conservation problems. Surrogate species are used to monitor the health of ecosystems, to identify areas of species richness, to delineate the boundaries of a reserve, or to attract public funding and attention.

**survival value** An expression that denotes a trait's contribution to the animal's fitness by affecting its survival.

**syrinx** Vocal organ of birds consisting of vibrating membranes located at the junction of the bronchi and trachea.

**tactical deception** Behaviors in the normal repertoire which are used at a lower frequency than they are normally expressed honestly, which function to mislead or deceive other individuals, and so advantage the initiator of the behavior.

**tagging** Ability to assign a label (or tag) to each of the items to be counted.

**tarsus (*plural* tarsae or tarsi)** In insects, the terminal part of the leg.

**temporal cortex** Region of cortex in the temporal lobe, so called for its location at the temple in the human brain. Functions of the temporal cortex include auditory, visual, and vestibular processing, memory, and language comprehension.

**temporal isolation** An environment lacking information about time of day; also called "constant conditions."

**theory of mind** Premack and Woodruff (1978) coined this term to refer to the ability to impute mental states to individuals.

**tit-for-tat** Strategy in a two-person game in which the individual cooperates on the first move, and then copies whatever the opponent did in the previous move.

**tonic immobility** Temporary, complete suppression of movement, often after a fear-producing event.

**tonotopic** Arrangement of neurons in the auditory system in which the relative position of frequency-sensitive neurons preserves frequency information in a map-like fashion.

**torpid** Reversible state of reduced metabolism and behavioral responsivity exhibited by some organisms during the usual sleep period or in response to adverse environmental conditions (e.g., the cold and short days of winter).

**transmission medium**  The matter in which the **signal** is propagated, e.g., air is the transmission medium for birdsong.

**ultimate**  Refers to a level of questions about behavior that encompasses mostly **survival value** and **evolution**. These are also known as "why" questions, to the extent that they deal mostly with the population processes such as **natural selection** and **sexual selection** that have altered the behavior of organisms across generations.

**ultradian rhythms**  Rhythms with a **periodicity** shorter than the **circadian** range (e.g., the 90-min REM–NREM sleep stage cycle).

**ultrasonic vocalization**  Vocal energy produced by an animal, the **frequency** of which is higher than a human observer can hear (i.e., > 20 kHz).

***Umwelt***  The concept of *Umwelt*, introduced by J. von Uexküll (1934), suggests that every kind of animal has its own *Umwelt* formed by the kinds of **information** its senses can process. The internal world of an animal interacts with its external world (*Umwelt*) through a perceptual side and an effectual side. The perceptual world according to Uexküll can be summarized as follows: (i) an object from the *Umwelt* has no meaning until (unless) it is incorporated into a functional cycle, into an existential semiotic dialog; (ii) an interaction of meaning-carriers and meaning-**receivers** makes a functional circle; (iii) organisms evolved proclivities to interact with certain aspects of the world and not others; (iv) organisms have existential tolerances beyond which they cease to function.

**unconditional cooperation**  Cooperative behavior in which the benefits of cooperation to the actor are not contingent on strict reciprocation to the actor by the recipients of the actor's behavior.

**unconditioned response (UR)**  Response evoked by a stimulus before the animal has experienced any explicit training involving that stimulus.

**unconditioned stimulus (US)**  Event that elicits an **unconditioned response** (also referred to as an unconditional stimulus).

**vacuum activity**  See endogenous behavior.

**vibrational signals**  Essentially sounds transmitted through solids, e.g., foot stamping by rabbits. Also referred to as **seismic signals**.

**vigilance**  Behavior by an individual (e.g., scanning) that increases its chances of detecting a predator.

**waggle dance**  Used by honeybees to indicate the direction and distance of resources (e.g., food, water) from the hive relative to the sun. Also referred to as dance language.

**waveform**  Shape of an oscillation, as revealed by plotting its values as a function of time.

**within-event learning**  Process by which associations are being formed between the representations of different elements of a stimulus. The phenomenon was first demonstrated in taste–odor **learning** in rats and subsequently demonstrated in **filial imprinting**, when chicks are exposed simultaneously to an auditory and a visual stimulus.

**working memory**  Temporary memory storage buffer in which **information** is maintained while it is being processed.

**Zeitgeber**  German "time giver"; a stimulus capable of entraining an **endogenous** oscillation.

**Zeitgedächtnis**  German "time memory"; the ability to use an **endogenous circadian** clock to recognize time of day.

**zigzag dance**  Special pattern of movements of the courting male three-spined stickleback, addressed to the female. The zigzag dance is the male's first reaction in the stimulus–response chain of mating behavior: female's appearance → male's zigzag dance → female courts → male leads → female follows → male shows nest → female enters nest → male trembles → female spawns → male fertilizes.

# author index

# subject index